CW00553143

East Anglia's History

Studies in honour of
Norman Scarfe

Norman Scarfe leading the 1976 Aldeburgh Festival Walk across Blaxhall Heath (Nigel Luckhurst, photographer)

East Anglia's History

Studies in honour of
Norman Scarfe

edited by
Christopher Harper-Bill, Carole Rawcliffe
and Richard G. Wilson

THE BOYDELL PRESS

THE CENTRE OF EAST ANGLIAN STUDIES
UNIVERSITY OF EAST ANGLIA

First published 2002
Published by The Boydell Press, Woodbridge
in association with
The Centre of East Anglian Studies
University of East Anglia, Norwich

ISBN 0 85115 878 1

The Boydell Press is an imprint of Boydell & Brewer Ltd
PO Box 9, Woodbridge, Suffolk IP12 3DF, UK
and of Boydell & Brewer Inc.
PO Box 41026, Rochester, NY 14604–4126, USA
website: www.boydell.co.uk

A catalogue record for this book is available
from the British Library

Library of Congress Cataloging-in-Publication Data
applied for

This publication is printed on acid-free paper

Printed in Great Britain by
St Edmundsbury Press Ltd, Bury St Edmunds, Suffolk

Contents

Illustrations

A First Stirring of Suffolk Archaeology?

Sir Nicholas Bacon and the Building of Stiffkey Hall

Shrubland before Barry

Garden Canals in Suffolk

Estate Stewards in Woodland High Suffolk

Thomas Gainsborough

Ipswich Museum Moralities

The Caen Controversy

Published in conjunction with the Centre of East
Anglian Studies, University of East Anglia, Norwich
with the aid of a grant from Miss Ann Ashard Webb's
Bequest for the history of Suffolk

Editors' Preface

The essays gathered in this volume are a reflection of the breadth of the historical community that wishes to pay tribute to a scholar whose remarkable chronological range is rivalled only by the wide extent of his generosity, expressed in so many ways, to fellow workers in the field. The contributors include four who have been successively Director of the Centre of East Anglian Studies at the University of East Anglia, who would all wish to thank Norman for his unstinting support over many years. There are essays, too, from those who have collaborated with him in fostering, in his beloved county of Suffolk, an enviable tradition of publication, both of editions through the medium of the Suffolk Record Society and of learned articles in the *Proceedings of the Suffolk Institute of Archaeology and History*. Many of the contributors have benefited personally both from his expertise and from his very practical help. Norman, however, has always been adamant that local and regional history should not be merely parochial or antiquarian, and his determination to set Suffolk, in every age, in the context of a wider world is reflected in contributions from a former Keeper of the Public Records and three professors of the University of Oxford. The essays also reflect Norman's insistence, before it became fashionable, on the equal importance of written records and material remains in the interpretation of the past. The theme of the single paper not East Anglian in inspiration is a reflection of the honorand's own military service and historical account of the crucial campaign in which he fought.

The editors are grateful to all those who have given permission for the reproduction of illustrations; to Mrs Jenni Tanimoto for her work in harmonising the text on word processor; and to the staff of Boydell and Brewer for their customary care and efficiency in the production of the volume.

The Editors July 2001

Abbreviations

AgHR	*Agricultural History Review*
Antiq. Journ.	*Antiquaries Journal*
Arch. Journ.	*Archaeological Journal*
BAR	British Archaeological Reports
BHM	*Bulletin of the History of Medicine*
BIHR	*Bulletin of the Institute of Historical Research*
BL	British Library
Blomefield, *Norfolk*	F. Blomefield and C. Parkin, *An Essay towards a Topographical History of the County of Norfolk*, 11 vols, London 1805–10
BRUC	A.B. Emden, *A Biographical Register of the University of Cambridge to 1500*, Cambridge 1963
Cal. Feudal Aids	*Feudal Aids: Inquisitions and Assessments relating to Feudal Aids, with other Analogous Documents*, 6 vols, HMSO 1899–1921
Cal. Inq. Misc.	*Calendar of Inquisitions Miscellaneous*, 7 vols, HMSO 1904–69
CChR	*Calendar of Charter Rolls preserved in the Public Record Office*, 6 vols, HMSO 1903–27
CCR	*Calendar of Close Rolls*, 67 vols, HMSO 1902–63
CFR	*Calendar of Fine Rolls*, 22 vols, HMSO 1911–63
CIPM	*Calendar of Inquisitions Post Mortem and other Analagous Documents*, proceeding, HMSO 1904–
CPR	*Calendar of Patent Rolls*, 60 vols, HMSO 1901–74
CRR	*Curia Regis Rolls . . . preserved in the Public Record Office*, proceeding, HMSO 1922–
CSPD	*Calendar of State Papers, Domestic*, 104 vols, HMSO 1856–1960
DB	Domesday Book
DNB	*Dictionary of National Biography*
EcHR	*Economic History Review*
EHR	*English Historical Review*
GEC	*Complete Peerage of England . . .*, ed. G.E. Cockayne, new edn by V. Gibbs *et al.*, 13 vols in 14, London 1910–59
HistJ	*Historical Journal*
HMCR	*Historical Manuscripts Commission Reports*
IJ	*The Ipswich Journal*
JBS	*Journal of British Studies*
JEH	*Journal of Ecclesiastical History*
Jocelin of Brakelond	*The Chronicle of Jocelin of Brakelond*, ed. H.E. Butler, London 1949

LPFD	*Letters and Papers, Foreign and Domestic, of the Reign of Henry VIII, 1509–1547*, 22 vols, HMSO 1864–1932
MPME	C.H. Talbot and E.A. Hammond, *The Medical Practitioners in Medieval England*, London 1965
NA	*Norfolk Archaeology*
NCC	Norwich Consistory Court
New DNB	*New Dictionary of National Biography*
NRO	Norfolk Record Office
NRS	Norfolk Record Society
ns	new series
OED	*Oxford English Dictionary*
os	old series
PRO	Public Record Office
PSIA	*Proceedings of the Suffolk Institute of Archaeology and History*
reg.	register
RO	Record Office
RS	Rolls Series
SCH	*Studies in Church History*
SR	*Suffolk Review*
SROB	Suffolk Record Office, Bury St Edmunds
SROI	Suffolk Record Office, Ipswich
SROL	Suffolk Record Office, Lowestoft
SRS	Suffolk Record Society
TRHS	*Transactions of the Royal Historical Society*
UEA	University of East Anglia
VCH	*Victoria County History*
VE	*Valor Ecclesiasticus*, ed. J. Caley and J. Hunter, 6 vols, Record Commission, London 1810–34

Norman Scarfe MBE MA Hon LittD FSA

Vice-President of the Suffolk Institute of Archaeology and History
Founder-Editor and President of the Suffolk Records Society
Vice-President of the Suffolk Preservation Society and
of the Suffolk Historic Churches Trust

THE CAREERS of few academics are crowned with a *Festschrift*; how rarely has one been the recipient of two. In honour of Norman's seventieth birthday in 1993, Jeremy Greenwood commissioned and assembled a delightful garland of tributes from his many friends, mostly in prose, but also in photographs and drawings – there is even a song, the words and music in manuscript facsimile. The book's impeccable design and its well-balanced mixture of reminiscence and sharp personal insight completely capture every age and stage of Norman's then seven fruitful decades. Now that he is approaching the next major milestone, a smaller group of historians and archaeologists has contributed to this more conventional *Festschrift* for their friend and colleague who is rightly referred to, increasingly often, as the doyen of Suffolk historians.

In writing this, I am resisting the temptation to mine that earlier tribute for the apt and telling phrases that there abound, but hope nevertheless to do justice to Norman and his many achievements. Others could bring longer perspectives to this appreciation. Pam and I first met Norman and Paul within weeks of arriving in Ipswich in 1972, and that one meeting was enough to seal friendships which led to many fruitful collaborations. At the time Norman was about halfway through the hundred or so summer excursions he directed for the Suffolk Institute of Archaeology over twenty years. He was looking for a new President and my fate was sealed in minutes, an instance of his talent for spotting, enthusing and recruiting people.

How is it that Norman has so much of Suffolk in his veins? His maternal grandmother, a Lambeth girl, was visiting Brigg Fair, while staying with friends in Yorkshire. There she met, and later married, a young well-engineer, and went to live at Grimsby. Their youngest daughter, Alma, became her father's secretary and book-keeper and, because of this, sometimes travelled with him in the course of his work. He had worked for the Pretyman family at Riby Grove near Grimsby, and it was natural that they should ask him to find water at Orwell Park and their other properties along the southern edges of the Deben peninsula. When he came to do this, he brought his daughter with him. They lodged at Trimley, where she soon became acquainted with the son of the local wind-miller, also Norman. World War One, and injuries received at Gallipoli, interrupted their courtship, but they married after the war, and Norman junior was born on his father's birthday, 1 May 1923.

Norman tasted briefly the education provided for boys at the grammar school in Felixstowe before going off to board at King's School, Canterbury, under the legendary Canon 'Fred' Shirley. In 1942 there was just time for a services short course in PPE at Magdalen, Oxford, Wolsey's *alma mater* (rather than his foundation), and to discover with the help of Bruce McFarlane that he was more historian than philosopher or economist. Reading R.H. Hodgkin's *History of the Anglo-Saxons* at McFarlane's suggestion was the turning point; after the war, Norman read History, and spent a lifetime following up his 'insatiable curiosity about the origins of East Anglia and especially Suffolk'. And the twenty-six letters that McFarlane wrote to Norman between 1944 and 1966, recently published,[1] demonstrate the rapport between teacher and gifted pupil.

After the first brief spell at Oxford it was time for other experiences which contrasted sharply with academic life in cathedral close and college quad. Enlisting in the Royal Artillery, it was as a subaltern that Norman landed on Sword Beach in Normandy on 6 June 1944; he was promoted Captain during the advance into France and Germany. He had his first success as a writer in *Assault Division*, published in 1947, an arresting account of the 3rd Division's role in the great invasion that turned the tide, a history taken up to the surrender of Germany.

Back at Magdalen, reading medieval history, he took Schools in 1949 and became assistant lecturer, then lecturer at Leicester in Jack Simmons' department, with Joan Thirsk and later Geoffrey Martin as entirely congenial colleagues. There, W.G. Hoskins was pioneering the study of local and regional history, and of the English landscape. Inspired by what Pevsner did for the buildings of England and Hoskins for their setting, Norman reinterpreted Suffolk for us in his Shell Guide and *The Suffolk Landscape*. Later on, totally avoiding the charge of one-county parochialism, Norman gave us equally illuminating Shell Guides for Essex and Cambridgeshire which show him prepared to look further afield for contrasts and parallels. For all three guides his artistic collaborators, particularly John and Edward Piper, Angus McBean and Edwin Smith, provided images as memorable as is Norman's prose, albeit severely compressed in the gazetteer entries. Re-read Debach or Eyke, Orford or Parham, and learn or be reminded of enough to enhance your next visit. In Great Waldingfield church, 'fantastic jumble of mosaics round sanctuary result from fossicking holidays of the Misses Baily in Rome and Egypt, 1867–69', explains everything. We take heart that the Trimleys are 'saved by the by-pass, 1973', and set off, away from the main road, to search for Thomas Cavendish's home, but are pulled up short by the warning that, adjoining, there is 'the hideous warehousing of Felixstowe Dock'. Norman is a master of the felicitous phrase; where did we read about his 'punctiliously ailletted knight', I wonder?

It was in 1963 that Norman and Paul decided that Leicester was almost as far from the coast as you can get, particularly the Suffolk coast, and improved their proximity by a move to Shingle Street. Whatever the loss to Leicester, Suffolk and East Anglia gained greatly. In this new phase, Norman developed quite new interests and talents, all closely allied to his writing. By praise and criticism, as appropriate, he

[1] *K.B. McFarlane: Letters to Friends 1940–1966*, ed. Gerald Harriss, with a memoir by Karl Leyser, Oxford 1997.

used (and still uses) his pen as a powerful tool, sometimes as a weapon, in working relentlessly for the conservation and preservation of all that is best in East Anglia. In the days when councillors could be and were independent, and authorities had the humility to realise that co-opted members on planning and leisure services committees could bring invaluable breadth of vision to discussions, Norman served, unelected but invited, valued and effective. Another task helped to lure him back to Suffolk, the first stirrings in 1962 of plans to set up a Museum of East Anglian Rural Life. Norman helped to choose and install everything from whole buildings to small artefacts at Abbots Hall, Stowmarket, and became the founder chairman of the Friends there four years later. He was involved from their beginnings with the Suffolk Preservation Society (in its amateur days, when he was the Society's man in East Suffolk) and the Historic Churches Trust; these and many other bodies have profited from his enthusiasm and committed hard work. One thing makes his environmental campaigning unusual. While he is always ready to attack shoddy and downright ugly intrusions into the East Anglian landscape, he is quick to discern truly creative and imaginative kinds of development, and to praise them warmly, as he did the work of Tayler and Green in the Waveney valley.

There is not space for a thorough appreciation of Norman's impressive list of publications; they all speak for themselves, and show how he often returns to the problems posed by some of his favourite subjects. However many times he has written about Edmund or Jocelin, Sutton Hoo or the Elmhams, we can be sure that we have not heard his last word on them. In further postscripts he refines his theories, argues for his solutions, and enjoys combat with scholars who, against (his) reason, prefer others.

The founding, with Geoffrey Martin as his fellow general editor, of the Suffolk Records Society in 1958 has been one of his most notable and enduring achievements. Eight years into his well-earned retirement from that editorship he has still more than half the present total of forty-three volumes to his credit, including eight volumes of Constable Correspondence. Since the mid-1980s, the La Rochefoucaulds, 'the boys' he has come to call them, and their faithful tutor Lazowski have been his almost constant companions. In 1988, as Suffolk Records Society Volume 30, he replaced the inadequate 1933 publication of the tour in Suffolk, and the new book quickly ran to a second edition. Norman's translation of the original accounts shows him a master of the language of our continental neighbours. Next, after following them around England, he gave their further travels the inspired title *Innocent Espionage*, and the fiery jacket that Richard and Helen Barber at Boydell designed makes it one of the easiest books to find on one's shelves. In April 2000, Norman and Paul made a fortnight's expedition to discover how the boys travelled and what they saw on the West coast of Scotland. I kept their postcards full of vivid description to use as markers in the book which now completes the set, a trilogy which will probably stand as Norman's proudest monument. The first volume alone earned its author the memorable accolade 'historien de classe' from the duchesse Edmée de La Rochefoucauld. One can, however, forgive Norman his readiness for the end of the project; exciting and revealing, it has also been exhausting.

Some of the other pieces that Norman writes regularly surely deserve gathering together: for example his many articles for Aldeburgh Festival Programmes, and those he writes each summer for Music in Country Churches in one or another great Suffolk church. His Framlingham account, splendidly illustrated by Ken Adlard's colour photographs, has become an exemplary church guide.

Norman's decision to leave university life and teaching nearly forty years ago will have been an unconscious loss to the many research students he might have tutored, but he has instead continued to inspire and teach, informally of course, a wide circle of East Anglian historians and archaeologists. Most of the authors of these essays owe him much, perhaps more than they realise. At UEA, particularly as chairman of the committee of the Centre of East Anglian Studies, he gave massive support to its first Directors, and notably generous help to the 1987 appeal. He it was who first encouraged quite full reports of work in progress which never fail to enliven the latter part of the twice-yearly meetings. Generally encouraging and always promptly and courteously helpful, he does not shrink from pointing out the shortcomings of inadequate or ill-conceived work. And the generous assistance goes beyond the scholarly when necessary; practical, tangible, even financial help may be given through the Scarfe Charitable Trust. He and his fellow trustee, Eric Maule, could allocate the fund's resources over and over again, but the Trust has enabled projects and publications in all the main cultural fields. Again, some of our contributors have been benificiaries.

Norman and Paul, however, have far wider interests than history, archaeology and the landscape: art, architecture, music, opera, drama and natural history, at home and abroad, keep them busy and always breathless (even when writing) to share new discoveries. What enviable energy they have, and what a warm welcome awaits guests at the Garden Cottage, their home since 1982. Cottage may be an understatement, but the garden, a joint effort and delight, deserves its part of the name. Their table is advantageously oval, the wine delectable, and conversation always sparkles. The food, for the variety and quality of which Paul must take the credit, is always satisfying and imaginative without ever being filling (the heaviest word in gastronomy).

Norman, few of us are left to salute you as soldier, but we can all do so as scholar, historian, archaeologist, teacher, enthusiast, encourager, East Anglian exponent and defender, benefactor, host and friend, and this we do, unreservedly, whole-heartedly and with much love and admiration.

John Blatchly
November 2001

Domesday Herrings

James Campbell

FOR MANY HUNDREDS of years myriads of herring gathered in the southern North Sea, every autumn, to spawn. Their number was prodigious. The most productive herring-fishing season was that of 1913. Six hundred thousand tons of herring were caught, mainly by vessels fishing out of Yarmouth and Lowestoft.[1] This was some 6,500,000,000 fish, almost half of which were exported, principally to eastern Europe.[2] Large-scale fishing continued after the Second World War. Familiar to someone brought up in Lowestoft was the autumnal sight of drifters crowding into harbour, heavy with herring, of hundreds of Scottish 'fisher girls' gutting herring on the Denes, of so many herring lying in the gutters that the very cats hardly bothered. It seemed that such things were a normal and permanent part of the year. Not so. Before long the North Sea herring stock was almost fished out. There are still some there to be caught, bought and eaten. But the watery protein mine in the North Sea was lost; a mine so rich that the eminently nutritious herring was for many centuries exceedingly important in the diet of the poor, though not scorned by the rich.[3]

It was steam propulsion that made possible the immense catches of the twentieth century; and large, though lesser, catches in the nineteenth.[4] In earlier times herring fishing was confined to coastal waters. Its scale was, nevertheless, notable. In 1336 Philip VI of France was advised to attack the Yarmouth herring industry at the time of the autumn fishing. He was informed that there would be 6,000 small fishing vessels there; over a thousand of these would be English; each might have a crew of fifteen.[5] Spies exaggerate; but the Valois agents were not too wildly off the mark. Dr Saul's research, largely based on the Yarmouth customs accounts, provides our earliest definite information on the scale of the Yarmouth herring fishing.[6] In the second generation of the fourteenth century up to 400 foreign vessels can be shown

1 W.G. Hodgson, *The Herring and its Fishery*, London 1957, 106.
2 A.M. Samuel, *The Herring, its Effect on the History of Great Britain*, London 1918, 171.
3 L. Cutting, *Fish Saving: A History of Fish Processing from Ancient to Modern Times*, London 1955, 31–2. Samuel, *The Herring*, 40. R.E. Hallam, *Rural England 1066–1348*, n.p. 1981, 65–6.
4 L.E. Richards, *Eighty Years of Shipbuilding and Designing*, Lowestoft 1956, 14–17.
5 C. de la Roncière, *Histoire de la marine française*, i, Paris 1899, 434–5.
6 A. [R.] Saul, 'Great Yarmouth in the Fourteenth Century: A Study in Trade, Politics and Society' (unpublished Oxford D.Phil. thesis, 1975) chapters 5 and 6; and A. [R.] Saul, 'The Herring Industry at Yarmouth *c.*1280–*c.*1400', *NA* xxxviii, 1981, 33–43.

to have visited Yarmouth annually. At a conservative estimate some 600 English vessels were involved.[7] The most productive fishing season (so far as these accounts tell) was that of 1336–37 when over 5,000 tons of herring are recorded. In seven other years between 1331 and 1368 the recorded catch exceeded 2,000 tons.[8]

For earlier periods we are dependent on casual references. Most famous, indeed important, is Mathew Paris's, when he says that in 1238 the impact of the Mongols was such that the men of Gothia and Frisia did not come to the Yarmouth fishing and, as a result, herrings were very cheap in England that year.[9] Our first evidence for Yarmouth herring as an important element in London's food supply comes from near the end of the twelfth century in Jocelin of Brakelond's account of the Londoners' rage when tolls were levied at Bury on their carts bringing herring from Yarmouth.[10] An early indication that herring were an item of general consumption is the appearance of *harengarius* ('herring seller') as the occupation of two Winchester tenants at the time of Edward the Confessor.[11] Our earliest evidence for an overseas fleet coming to Yarmouth for the fishing comes from a twelfth-century life of St Osyth, which mentions a fleet of forty German vessels returning from an annual visit to Yarmouth at some time between 1107 and 1127.[12] The first reference to the men of the Cinque Ports having an important role (which long continued) at Yarmouth during the herring season comes from an account of Herbert Losinga as bishop of Norwich (*c.*1094–1119).[13] In short, there is enough evidence (if only just enough) to justify the supposition that, by the twelfth century, important in the English economy were herring in general and the Yarmouth herring fishing in particular.

This gives special interest to the herring renders recorded in Domesday Book.[14]

7 Saul, 'Great Yarmouth in the Fourteenth Century',191–2.

8 These figures derive from the Yarmouth murage accounts, Saul, 'Great Yarmouth in the Fourteenth Century', 192, 325. These accounts record mainly the herring of English and Bayonne merchants leaving the port. So the figures given must understate, considerably, the total catch, Saul, *ibid.*, 192, 338–41. The accounts give quantities in lasts. A last was 12,000 herrings (or maybe 13,200) and a last of 'full herring' is estimated at two and a half tons. R.D. Connor, *The Weights and Measures of England*, London 1987, 173–320; Samuel, *The Herring*, 75.

9 *Matthei Parisiensis Chronica Majora*, ed. H.R. Luard, 7 vols, RS 1872–84, iii, 488–9.

10 *Jocelin of Brakelond*, 75–7.

11 *Winchester in the Early Middle Ages* (Winchester Studies I), ed. M. Biddle, Oxford 1976, 202, 429–30, 432, 459.

12 D. Bethell, 'The Lives of St Osyth of Essex and St Osyth of Aylesbury', *Analecta Bollandiana* lxxxviii, 1970, 94.

13 *The First Register of Norwich Cathedral Priory*, ed. H.W. Saunders, NRS XI, 1939, 32, 33. I assume that the *Portenses* described as resisting by force of arms Losinga's attempt to establish an outpost at Yarmouth were men of the Cinque Ports rather than, as Saunders supposed, men coming from 'neighbouring ports'. In considering the bishop's Yarmouth ambitions it is worthy of note that he had been prior of the monastery at Fécamp, a main centre of the Norman herring fishery. For Yarmouth and the Cinque Ports, Saul, 'Great Yarmouth in the Fourteenth Century', chapter 5.

14 H.C. Darby, *Domesday England*, Cambridge 1977, 285–6 for an overview. All references to Domesday below are to shire sections by folio with the addition of the item number from the Phillimore edition.

Such renders are recorded in five shires: Kent, Surrey, Sussex, Norfolk and Suffolk.[15] The references relating to London and the south-east can be categorised as follows. Two relate to renders of herring from properties in London or Southwark: 2,000 from fifteen *masurae*, 500 from one.[16] Two relate to major herring renders from big ecclesiastical estates. Sandwich provided 40,000 herrings to Canterbury *ad victum monachorum*, Southease (or possibly Lewes) in Sussex provided 38,500 herrings for St Peter's, Winchester.[17] There is a similar reference to a render from a demesne manor of William of Warenne: Ilford, 16,000 herrings.[18] The other references are to smaller quantities: 4,000 herrings 'from rents' at Brighton and the same amount from forty-four 'closes' in Lewes.[19] Lastly there is a little rent of 300 herrings from a fishery on the Thames estuary.[20]

The most remarkable feature of these renders is not the large contributions to major landowners, rather is it the way in which herring are referred to in connection with the payment of rents; in this connection they appear almost as a kind of currency. This is to be seen also in a contemporary survey which mentions thirty *masurae* at Sandwich paying to the monks of St Augustine's 'four thousand herrings or ten shillings'.[21] That Domesday does not mention this herring render from Sandwich is a reminder how incomplete its account of such matters must be. Thus there is no difficulty in entertaining the supposition that there were far more such renders in Norfolk than the sole example in Domesday: 2,000 herrings from Thorpe St Andrew near Norwich.[22] For example, the abbey of Bury may by this time have enjoyed a render of a last of herring from its church of St Laurence at Norwich.[23]

Suffolk is better documented, though all our evidence comes from the north-east corner of the county. The renders can be categorised as follows. Four are large. The king received 60,000 herrings from Dunwich and 3,000 (formerly 10,000) from Blythburgh.[24] The abbey of Bury received 60,000 herrings from Beccles (a render which had doubled since 1066) and 25,000 (formerly 20,000) from Southwold.[25] In addition, though Domesday mentions no herring render to Ely, it is plausible to

15 The relevant entries are surveyed and mapped in *The Domesday Geography of South-East England*, ed. H.C. Darby and E.M.J. Campbell, Cambridge 1962, 129, 393, 455, 474, 538–9, 552, and H.C. Darby, *The Domesday Geography of Eastern England*, 3rd edn, Cambridge 1971, 185–7.

16 *DB Surrey*, fos 54b (no. 15/2), 35a (no. 19/21).

17 *DB Kent*, fo. 3a (no. 2/2).

18 *DB Sussex*, fo. 17b (no. 7/1).

19 *DB Sussex*, fo. 26a (no. 12/3).

20 *DB Kent*, fo. 10c (no. 5/160).

21 *An Eleventh-Century Inquisition of St Augustine's Canterbury*, ed. A. Ballard, London 1920, 20.

22 *DB Norfolk*, fo. 138a (no. 1/216).

23 C.R. Hart, *The Early Charters of Eastern England*, Leicester 1966, 82.

24 *DB Suffolk*, fos 311b–312a (no. 6/84), 282a (no. 1/12). Another lord received a render of 6,000 herrings from a tenant at Dunwich.

25 *DB Suffolk*, fos 369b–370a (no. 14/120), 371b (no. 14/163).

connect Ely's eighty burgesses at Dunwich with a render of 30,000 herrings evidenced not later than 1131.[26]

As elsewhere, the smaller renders are much harder to understand than the larger. Those from Suffolk are not only concentrated in two hundreds, Lothingland and Wangford (with one just over the border of an adjacent hundred) but all came from the lands of one lord, Hugh de Montfort.[27] He owned eighteen properties in fifteen villages (see Table 1, p. 17 below). All but one owed herring by 1086. One was fairly large, reckoned at over one and a half carucates with fifteen freemen and one villein. The others were all small: twelve out of the eighteen were held by one or two freemen. The total of the herring renders was 10,900, the largest of them 3,000, the smallest 100. In seven instances it appears that the herring renders had been introduced since 1066; though one cannot be quite sure of this. In three instances increased renders, including herring, were accompanied by a reduction in the number of ploughs. This could suggest circumstances in which fishing was growing in importance.

What is to be made of all this? Could it be that tenants of Hugh de Montfort were exceptional in having access to herring? This seems highly unlikely. It is more likely that these renders indicate a general availability of herring through participation in the coastal fishing in the autumn. The inhabitants of the villages concerned all lived within walking distance of the sea or, alternatively, would have got there by boat, either via the Waveney[28] or more probably via the Hundred river. The navigability of this river is virtually proved by Domesday's reference to *portus maris* at Frostenden. For Frostenden lies on a today inconsiderable stream parallel at a few miles to the Hundred river and reaching the sea at Easton Broad. If that stream were navigable, so too should the river have been. A dock or quay at Frostenden would have been convenient for fishing craft.[29] De Montfort's tenants would hardly have been in the position of the fisherman in Aelfric's *Colloquy* (*c.*1000), who is made to say that it was only rarely that he fished in the sea because it was too far to row.[30] In any case it is a fair assumption that the peasants of the north-eastern corner of Suffolk, or at least the more prosperous peasants, had supplies of salt herring.

Why should we learn of herring being required from virtually all the de Montfort tenants but not from those of anyone else? Perhaps de Montfort's reeve had better records or a better memory than others, so that his contribution to Domesday was more detailed than that of others. If so, maybe herring renders were normal in this countryside. Why should de Montfort be concerned to gather herring renders? Like all great men he must have had many mouths to feed, in his household or, it may be,

26 *DB Suffolk*, fo. 385b (no. 21/47); E. Miller, *The Abbey and Bishopric of Ely*, Cambridge 1951, 282 cf. 244.

27 *DB Suffolk*, fo. 407ab (nos. 31/21–34). The exception was Stoven in Blything hundred, fo. 406a (no. 31/7).

28 The convenience of this route would have depended on whether Lake Lothing existed at this period and, if it did exist, on the presence and nature of a neck of land dividing it from the sea.

29 *DB Suffolk*, fo. 414b (no. 33/6). For a claim (which I have not yet sought to verify) to have identified such a dock at Frostenden, C. Morley and E.R. Cooper, 'The Sea Port of Frostenden', *PSIA* xviii, 1922–24, 167–70.

30 *Anglo-Saxon Prose*, ed. M. Swanton, London and Totowa 1975, 110.

locally. Perhaps herring renders should be seen as comparable to the ubiquitous renders of hens: as something not difficult to extract and, in sum, rather useful. It is not really likely that de Montfort wanted herring for personal delectation. Herring renders could, however, have a gourmet aspect. A most remarkable render in that regard was that of the herring pies which Norwich rendered annually to the king.[31] This render is attested from the thirteenth century; twenty-four pies each containing five of the first fresh herring to come to the city. At least by the fifteenth century the pies were elaborately spiced. They continued to be sent until 1816. There is some reason to suppose that this render may be as old as Domesday.

The East Anglian herring renders recorded for 1086 total 164,900. To attempt to guess what proportion this may have been of the whole catch is not quite an absurdity, but just worthwhile. We know major renders may have been unrecorded.[32] We can most reasonably guess that the de Montfort tenants are highly unlikely to have been unusual in disposing of lots of herring. It is moderate indeed to suppose that so many as one in twenty of the herring caught swam into Domesday Book. Still, put it at that: so, a total estimated catch of 3,298,000. Herrings are not a meaningful commodity unless conserved. Thus there was an umbilical relationship between catching herring and producing salt. How much salt would it have taken to stop over three million herrings going bad? On a modern expert calculation 1.7 oz. per fish.[33] But once we know about herring conservation, which is not until the fourteenth century, it seems that while some ('white') herring were just salted, others ('red') were partly salted, partly smoked. The methods of preservation used in the eleventh century are unknown; the antiquities of the bloater lie hidden in the smoke of time. We depend on information from even so late as the eighteenth and nineteenth centuries. This varies, and no doubt there were different processes from time to time and place to place. The highest estimates say that a ton of salt was needed per last of herring.[34] The lowest say a quarter of a ton.[35] Taking the low estimate and putting the last at 13,200 this comes out at near enough two thirds of an ounce of salt per fish. Thus, on the lowest assumptions, well over five tons of salt would have been needed to conserve the herring catch. We who see salt as a little pile in the corner of the plate do not always fathom the extent to which earlier societies demanded salt for survival.

Whence came the salt? Here one must notice the remarkable concentration of *salinae*, salt-works, in extreme south-east Norfolk. Domesday indicates that there were at least 118 of these, including forty-five at Caister.[36] It is reasonable to assume

31 *The Records of the City of Norwich*, ed. W. Hudson and J.C. Tingey, 2 vols, Norwich and London 1906–10, ii, pp. xiii, 207–8. *Tenures of Land and Customs of Manors originally collected by Thomas Blount*, ed. W. Carew Hazlitt, 5th edn, Epsom 1999, 49, 429–30.

32 Note the cases of St Augustine's and of Ely, pp. 7–8 above.

33 A.R. Bridbury, *England and the Salt Trade in the Later Middle Ages*, Oxford 1955, 3.

34 E.g., for information on what peat digging could add to manorial income, Smith in J.M. Lambert, J.N. Jennings, C.T. Smith, C. Green and J.M. Hutchinson, *The Making of the Broads* (Royal Geographical Society Research Series, III), London 1960.

35 E.g. A. Young, *General View of the Agriculture of the County of Suffolk*, London 1813, 230.

36 Darby, *Domesday Geography of Eastern England*, 134–7, 369–72.

that locally produced salt preserved the herring catches until its replacement by salt from Bourgneut Bay, beginning in the thirteenth century.[37] Local salt was produced by an elaborate procedure, involving in its final stage boiling heavily salted water to evaporation point; a most fuel-intensive process.[38] Whence came the fuel?

The answer was almost given by the scholars who, remarkably and definitively, proved in 1960 that the Norfolk Broads were humanly produced, that they are peat-mines, flooded in the newly bad climate of the late thirteenth and early fourteenth centuries.[39] Showing that the mining operations were on the largest scale, these scholars calculate that 900 million cubic feet were extracted. Much of this must have gone to keep East Anglians warm. But a great deal must have gone to boil out the salt, which preserved the herring, which fed many people.[40] When did all this start? We know, approximately, when the peat-mines flooded; but when were they opened? It could be that they were worked for up to four centuries but certainty is hard to be had.

Here, in a merely speculative way, one might consider the problem of the Domesday description of two villages in the north-eastern corner of Suffolk: Barnby and Herringfleet. In both vast increases in payment had been exacted by Aluricus (Aelfric) 'the reeve': at Barnby eight freeman who had paid 13s 6d now paid £30;[41] at Herringfleet one freeman, two villeins and a bordar who had once paid 20s now paid £50.[42] How had Aelfric, plainly a useful man, been able to make these important additions to revenues from royal lands? In the case of a third village, Ringsfield, we are told how he did it by 'adding' eighty-three freemen who had once paid nothing, but now £15.[43] The wording of the Barnby and Herringfleet entries minimises such a possibility there. I wonder whether the explanation may not be as follows. Nowadays Barnby Broad, the southernmost and smallest of the broads, is just a very big pond, a hundred yards across and not much more than a foot deep. There was once another broad there, Barnby Old Broad. Both broads were formerly of considerable size.[44] If, as seems possible though questionable, they are the relicts of a single stretch of water then maybe what one would have seen there *c.*1300 is an enormous opencast peat mine, say a mile long, a quarter of a mile wide and eight or nine feet deep. If it were in operation by 1086 might not this account for Barnby's ability to pay so much? Similarly, Herringfleet is near another broad, Fritton Decoy.[45]

37 Bridbury, *England and the Salt Trade*, 44–76.

38 L. Keen, 'Coastal Salt Production in Norman England', *Anglo-Norman Studies* xi, 1988, 133–79.

39 Lambert *et al.*, *Making of the Broads*; T. Williamson, *The Norfolk Broads, a Landscape History*, Manchester and New York 1997, 84–91, makes valuable additions.

40 Smith, in Lambert *et al.*, *Making of the Broads*, 83–4.

41 *DB Suffolk*, fo. 283a (no. 1/30).

42 *DB Suffolk*, fo. 284b (no. 1/60).

43 *DB Suffolk*, fo. 282b (no. 1/16), cf. fo. 287b (no. 1/17).

44 Lambert *et al.*, *Making of the Broads*, 32–5.

45 *Ibid.*, 38–40. The wording of the Domesday item is a little puzzling. 'Omnes isti homines' make the payments. 'Omnes' seems extensive for four men. If the intention was to include the

Let us move from Lothingland to its northern neighbours, the Norfolk hundreds of East and West Flegg. Flegg had at one stage been an island near the mouth of a great estuary which extended over what became the Halvergate marshes and up the later river valleys. Its drying out and draining determined the economic history of the area: Yarmouth developed on what had been a sand-bank and a vast area of grazing marshes became available. The consensus is that these crucial developments took place in the late Anglo-Saxon period.[46]

A most extraordinary thing about Domesday's description of the former island of Flegg is its demonstration of a very dense population. This can be illustrated by comparing the recorded population in 1086 with that set down in the census of 1801 (excluding Yarmouth).[47] As so often in studying Domesday, one cannot but be struck by the fact that lists of named places with over seven hundred years between them coincide closely. The total recorded Domesday population is 454½. The total 1801 population is 2,821. A multiplier of five to turn the recorded Domesday population into the actual population must be well within the range of acceptability, not least in an area where the possibility of unrecorded sub-tenants is considerable.[48] In one instance the *recorded* Domesday population exceeded that in the 1801 census: 1086 Ashby 23, Oby 32; 1801 census: Ashby with Oby 47.[49] There are two other (relatively small) places where the 1086 population must have exceeded that for 1801: Billockby 1086 (recorded) 22, 1801 42;[50] Clippesby 1086 (recorded) 23, 1801 46.[51] Similarly high populations are recorded in adjacent hundreds. Domesday seems to show that south-eastern Norfolk was the most densely populated part of England.[52] Fairly interestingly, the most comparable area was coastal Sussex, where there was also herring business.[53]

Two centuries later Flegg seems to have been yet more densely inhabited. The crucial evidence is an immensely detailed survey of Norwich priory's manor of Martham.[54] This survey was first studied by W.H. Hudson in a number of most important articles.[55] He showed the scale and detail of the circumstances. In 1292

men of the villages described immediately before Herringfleet, then Fritton itself is among them. For extensive peat working here in the fourteenth century, N. Scarfe, *The Suffolk Landscape*, London etc. 1972, 182.

46 Williamson, *Norfolk Broads*, esp. 12, 16–17, 40–2.

47 All the 1801 figures quoted are from *Comparative Account of the Population of Great Britain in the Years 1801, 1811, 1821 and 1831*, London 1831.

48 Darby, *Domesday England*, 73–4.

49 *DB Norfolk*, fos 174b (nos 9/14, 9/22), 216b (nos 17/13, 17/15), 200b (no. 10/84), 216b (no. 17/11), 224b (no. 19/30).

50 *DB Norfolk*, fos 174b, 201a, 272b (nos 9/19, 10/90, 17/14, 64/6).

51 *DB Norfolk*, fos 113a (nos 1/46, 47), 174b (no. 9/16), 201b (no. 10/91), 217a (no. 17/15), 272a (no. 64/4).

52 Darby, *Domesday England*, 91.

53 P. 7 above.

54 BL MS Stowe, 936.

55 'Traces of Primitive Agriculture Organisation as Suggested by a Survey of the Manor of Martham (Norfolk) 1101–1272', *TRHS*, 4th series, i, 1918, 28–58; 'Status of "Villani" and Other Tenants in Danish East Anglia in Pre-Conquest Times', *TRHS*, 4th series, iv, 1921,

over 2,000 plots of land were held and the names of over 900 tenants given. The study of this extraordinary place has been taken further, in particular by Dr Williamson.[56] He puts the total number of tenants there at approaching 370; the average holding was two and a quarter acres, with over two thirds below the average.[57]

How could such populations have been supported in East and West Flegg and in nearby hundreds? These areas have long been recognised as outstandingly fertile. Thus Nathaniel Kent, in 1796, wrote of 'the prime parts of the county, comprising the hundreds of East and West Flegg [and 6 others in east Norfolk] . . . equal in value to the best parts of the Austrian Netherlands to which it is similar'.[58] Kent's mention of the Netherlands anticipates a remarkable article by Dr B.M.S. Campbell.[59] Dr Campbell argues that already by the early fourteenth century in parts of Norfolk, especially eastern Norfolk, and even more particularly in Broadland, an agricultural revolution had taken place. Fallowing had been largely abandoned but yields were nevertheless very high: up to eighteenth-century levels at Martham and the adjacent Norwich priory manor of Hemsby. Many peasant holdings were very small, but nevertheless viable. Important in this economy were marling, the intensive use of labour, the transport of manure and night soil from a distance, and the cultivation of legumes. An associated development was the increased use of horses. In many respects the intensive, almost horticultural, agriculture of east Norfolk resembled that of the Netherlands as identified by Slicher van Bath; Norfolk developments sometimes anticipate Netherlandish. It is a powerfully interesting case.

It is not easy to know when the developments concerned began. Dr Campbell puts their beginning in the later thirteenth century. A difficulty here is that none of the accounts which form his main sources are earlier than 1238 and with the exception of one set of St Benet's accounts none are earlier than *c.*1255.[60] Thus his earliest sources produce his first references to the agricultural use of horses and to marling.[61] One cannot but wonder how far the important developments he charts began in the twelfth century, or even earlier. An associated difficulty is that of knowing how far Domesday may under-record populations by omitting peasant subtenancies, thus distorting our view of population growth between the eleventh century and the fourteenth.

Natural advantages of the easternmost corner of England were, of course, always *in situ*. Very important was the fairly close network of inland waterways which made

21–48; 'The Anglo-Danish Village Community of Martham, Norfolk', *NA* xx, 1921, 273–316.

56 T. Williamson, 'Norfolk: Thirteenth Century', in *The Peasant Land Market in Mediaeval England*, ed. P.D.A. Harvey, Oxford 1984, 30–106, esp. 60–84.

57 *Ibid.*, 69, 74.

58 *General View of the Agriculture of the County of Norfolk*, Norwich and London 1796, 12–13. Cf. A. Young, *General View of the Agriculture of the County of Norfolk*, London 1804, 12–14.

59 'Agricultural Progress in Mediaeval England: Some Evidence from Eastern Norfolk', *EcHR*, 2nd series, xxxvi, 1983, 26–46.

60 *Ibid.*, 44–46.

61 *Ibid.*, 33, 36.

this part of England more like Holland than any other. Two points made about this around 1800 would have been equally valid many centuries before. Kent said that inland navigation ensured that there was more food for people, horses being 'the greatest devourers of the produce of the earth'.[62] If marl was important then so too was the advantage of river transport 'much felt in the conveyance of marle'.[63] One great and economically beneficial change which had come about in our area by the eleventh century was the draining and exploitation of the former great estuary. In this East Anglia belongs to a wider context. Many of the coasts of the North Sea in the tenth and eleventh centuries saw extensive enterprises of draining and new exploitation.[64] Another development perhaps coming at the same time and perhaps of equal importance was that of sea fisheries.[65] Both these things affected easternmost East Anglia by the eleventh century. The draining and exploitation of what had been a great estuary made land, above all grazing land, available on a large scale. The dispersed pattern of parochial boundaries in the marshlands must reflect the division of newly gained land among the villages on the higher surrounding ground. Dr Williamson emphasises the connections between marshland grazing and extensive sheep-keeping.[66] A good instance of this is a grant made by King Stephen to John de Chesney (1135x1146).[67] It includes a *bercaria* for a thousand sheep, lying between Yarmouth and Norwich, and with it went 'dominico marisco meo quod pertinet ad bercariam meam' (my demesne marsh which pertains to my sheep run). Wool had to be a major item in the economy: Domesday England contained, at an absolute minimum, two million men, women and children who needed to be clothed. In addition it could well be that there was already an important wool export, though the most explicit evidence for this does not come until *c.*1130.[68] The importance of the drained marshes in the thirteenth century economy of our area appears in Dr Campbell's admirable analysis. In general terms the wide open spaces of the grazing lands were complementary to the crowded peasants with their little plots in such a place as Martham. It is very likely that conditions of this kind prevailed by the time of Domesday.

It looks as if eastern East Anglia gained not from one major economic development, but from two. The likely importance of the herring business is indicated not

62 *General View*, 18.

63 Young, *General View, Norfolk*, 15. For mediaeval transport costs for turf, Smith in Lambert *et al.*, *Making of the Broads*, 84–5.

64 H. Stoob, 'Landausbau und Gemeindebildung an der Nordseeküste in Mittelalter', *Die Anfänge der Landgemeinde und ihr Wesen*, i, Stuttgart 1964, esp. 389–414; R.H. Bautier, *The Economic Development of Northern Europe*, London 1971, 83; R. Doehaerd, *Le haut moyen âge occidental*, Paris 1971, 107.

65 J.D. Richards, *Viking Age England*, London 1991, 74.

66 *The Broads*, 43–4.

67 *Regesta Regum Anglo-Normannorum 1066–1154*, iii, ed. H.A. Cronne and R.H.C. Davis, Oxford 1968, no. 175.

68 P.H. Sawyer, 'The Wealth of England in the Eleventh Century', *TRHS*, 5th series xv, 1975, 162–3. *Henry Archdeacon of Huntingdon Historia Anglorum*, ed. D. Greenway, Oxford 1996, 10–11.

only by the herring renders of Domesday but also by the Domesday account of Dunwich. Eleventh-century Dunwich was a most important and remarkable place. Only for Lincoln, Norwich, Thetford, York and Bury St Edmunds does Domesday record higher populations for 1086.[69] It is difficult to deduce real populations from Domesday urban data; and these data are not consistent from town to town. All the same these figures do indicate Dunwich as a very important place. It was also a growing place, notwithstanding the encroachment of the sea; it had 120 burgesses in its main holding in 1066, by 1086 236.[70] Dunwich retained its importance into Henry II's reign. In the table of average aids raised from English towns (which unlike Domesday includes London and Winchester) it ranks sixth.[71] Yarmouth appears as a much less populous place in Domesday; and one may wonder whether, at this juncture, Dunwich was not the more important centre for the fishing industry.[72] The most unusual thing about Dunwich is its ownership. Domesday says that Eadric of Laxfield held it in 1066 and that it had passed to Robert Malet. No other English town of remotely comparable importance had a secular lord other than the king (or the king with the earl). Eadric was not only a major local figure, with nearly all his rich lands concentrated in East Anglia; he was also one of the greatest of English landowners, on Domesday valuations the twelfth richest after the earlish families and he was the most important lay landowner in East Anglia.[73] Ecclesiastical landowners were similarly represented in the area of eastern wealth. In 1086 Hemsby, adjacent to Martham, was a recent acquisition of the East Anglian see. It had been acquired by Æthelmaer, bishop from 1047 to 1070.[74] The monks of Bury came to believe that it had acquired Beccles in the reign of Eadwig (955–59); the acquisition may have been later; but in any case by 1086 this *villa abbatis sancti Edmundi* was thriving, making a large herring render and appearing as a place of refuge for former burgesses of Norwich.[75] Ely had acquired a substantial part of Dunwich and property at Southwold by 1086, it is unclear when.[76] Thus three of the four major churches of East Anglia established economic bases in the land of the herring. This could have been simply because they needed fish. It is more likely that they also wished to enjoy profits from a rich area. The fourth major church, the abbey of St Benet at Holme, hardly needed to reach out towards the coast for it was

69 Darby, *Domesday England*, 364–8.

70 *DB Suffolk*, fos 311b–213a (no. 6/84). The reference to the loss of a carucate to the sea is a strong indication that the East Anglian carucate had territorial as well as fiscal significance.

71 C. Stephenson, *Borough and Town: A Study of Urban Origins in England*, Cambridge Mass. 1933, 225. Again one should not invest these figures with too precise a significance.

72 The only evidence which Domesday provides for fishing at Yarmouth is a reference in the Suffolk section to twenty-four fishermen there who belonged to the manor of Gorleston: *DB Suffolk*, fo. 283a (no. 1/32). It is hard to believe that there were no others.

73 P.A. Clarke, *The English Nobility under Edward the Confessor*, Oxford 1994, 2, 5, 32, 36, 41, 59–60, 77, 94–9, 98, 115–26,149, 154, 283–302; C. Morley, 'Eadric of Laxfield, the King's Falconer', *The History Teachers' Miscellany* i, 1923, 113–16.

74 *DB Norfolk*, fo. 195a (no. 10/30).

75 C. Hart, *Early Charters*, 248. *DB Norfolk*, fo. 117b (no. 1/61).

76 Pp. 7–8 above.

itself situated on an island of higher ground in the marshland; but it had acquired a number of holdings in West Flegg.[77]

If the rich gained from promising economic conditions, so too did the poor. It has been argued that by the thirteenth century maybe two out of five English households were not supported by enough land to keep a family.[78] 'By employments' may well have been important much earlier in such crowded villages as those of Flegg. One of these employments was, doubtless, fishing. The herring renders from peasants in Lothingland and Wangford hundreds indicate that many people would in the season go to sea to catch herring, which they would then salt to last the year. One would not have needed a very big boat to catch longshore herring; and they would have been easy to catch. The idea of herring fishing as a promising by-employment comes in the *Haemskringla* of Snorri Sturluson.[79] It says that St Olaf's brother-in-law Erling allowed his slaves to work in such a way that they could buy their freedom in one to three years: 'to some . . . he showed how to work in the herring industry; to others he showed some useful handicrafts; and some cleared his outfields and set up houses. He helped all to prosperity'. The possibly major economic effects of large-scale herring fishing are multiple. Not only could it provide by-employment but also, to the extent that cheap food can cheapen labour, it may have aided developing landlords. A remarkable document, probably of near the end of the tenth century (with some later additions), relates to purchases in connection with the improvement of the estates of Thorney Abbey.[80] The first item on the list is a very cheap one: 40 pence for 2,000 herrings; dinners for the workers?

The organisation of the eastern East Anglian salt industry is poorly documented. In considering its possible relationship to peasant employment it is worth considering detailed information from Dorset *c.*1170.[81] The East Anglian system need not have been the same, but it could well have been. Salt works at Poole harbour represented one hide. Twenty-three people were involved. The majority of them held one *plumbum* (salt was boiled out in lead pans). In all forty-four *plumba* were involved; 2s 11d was a common rent for a *plumbum*, together with a load of salt. This gives some indication of the possible scale of *salinae* and of the possible extent of peasant participation. It is a question as to how much labour would, at any particular period, have been employed in digging peat, perhaps not so very much. It has been calculated, admittedly on a most approximate basis, that if peat extraction went on for three centuries at an even rate, the labour of twenty men from each of twenty-eight

77 *DB Norfolk*, fos 216b–217a (nos 17/9–15).

78 C. Dyer, 'Were Peasants Self-sufficient? English Villages and the Market 1050–1350', in *Campagnes médiévales: l'homme et son espace. Études offertes à Robert Fossier*, ed. E. Mornet, Paris 1995, 653–66.

79 *The Haemskringla or Chronicle of the Kings of Norway*, trans. S. Laing, 3 vols, London 1844, ii, 19. This is *inter alia* a reminder that the Scandinavian element in East Anglia (notably strong in Flegg) may have had some particular part to play in economic development. Snorri died in 1241.

80 *Anglo-Saxon Charters*, ed. A.J. Robertson, Cambridge 1939, 252–3.

81 *The Dorset Domesday*, ed. L. Keen, London 1991, 23.

villages working for three weeks annually could have sufficed.[82] In this, as in other regards, one can only speculate on how far conditions which are documented at a later date also prevailed at an earlier. A good example is this. It is known that Norwich cathedral priory consumed up to 410,000 peats in the early fourteenth century.[83] This must have been simply for heating and cooking. How much more might the city as a whole have consumed, particularly in an earlier period, if peat was used for heating the kilns of what was, until the twelfth century, a major pottery industry?[84]

It is not possible to be categorical on such a question as: 'Was Norwich peat-heated by 1066?' Nevertheless, it is certain that no account of the east East Anglian economy in the eleventh century can possibly be complete without reckoning very seriously with Norwich. By 1066 its population cannot have been less than five thousand and it is anything but absurd to think of ten thousand.[85] It was a major centre of government and of manufacture, quite likely also of foreign trade. In the early middle ages it probably was a major port, having access to the sea via the Yare. It is probably this that accounts for there having been herring renders from Norwich. Later in the middle ages Yarmouth was the main port. Notwithstanding the rivalries between the two places they were closely linked economically. Nowhere else in England were two such important places so close together, and joined by so easy a water link. (York and Hull are the nearest parallel but Hull is of much later growth than Yarmouth.) In 1334 the fourth most heavily taxed provincial town in England (Yarmouth) was joined to the sixth most heavily taxed (Norwich) by twenty-five miles of navigable river.[86] The area with which this paper is concerned had among its major advantages the herring trade, the great grazing marshes and a close network of river communication unparalleled elsewhere in England. This was the Holland of England. East Anglia as a whole was an area of economic development in the eleventh century. The great increase in Domesday *valets* between 1066 and 1086 may well not be attributable to Norman extortion alone: those for Norfolk (omitting *terra regis*) rose 38 per cent, a higher rise than that for any other shire; Suffolk had the fifth highest rise, 20.5 per cent.[87] In such growth the area and factors discussed above would have played a major part. And in this, as in so much else, we have to wonder how far what we can see fairly clearly in the thirteenth century was already there in the eleventh. As usual it is Domesday, Domesday alone, which establishes the seriousness of the speculation.

[82] Lambert *et al.*, *Making of the Broads*, 104.

[83] *Making of the Broads*, 84.

[84] B. Ayers, *Norwich*, London 1994, 39. B. Ayers, *Waterfront Excavations and Thetford Ware Production, Norwich*, East Anglian Archaeological Reports XVII, Gressenhall 1983.

[85] J. Campbell, 'Norwich', in *The Atlas of Historic Towns*, ed. M.D. Lobel and W.H. Johns, London 1975, 3.

[86] *The Lay Subsidy of 1334*, ed. R.E. Glasscock, London 1975, 198; W.G. Hoskins, *Local History in England*, London 1959, 176.

[87] H. Welldon Finn, *The Norman Conquest and its Effects on the Economy*, London 1971, 35.

Table 1. Lands in the fee of Hugh de Montfort in the hundreds of Lothingland, Wangford and Blything
DB Suffolk, fo. 406b (no. 31/7), fo. 407b (nos 31/21–34)

'h' = herrings; 'm' = of meadow. Unidentified places are italicised.

	Place	Acreage	Render 'then'	Render 'now'	Ploughs 'then'	Ploughs 'now'	Contributors
	Lothingland Hundred						
1.	*Beketuna*	60	45	21s.4d. + 1500 h.	1	½	6 freemen
2.	Carlton Colville (a)	30	not stated	3s. + 400 h.	1	1	2 freemen
3.	Carlton Colville (b)	30 + ½ m.	5s. + 300 h.	5s. + 300 h.	1	0	1 freeman
4.	Gisleham (a)	1½	not stated	2s.6d. + 200 h.	not stated	½	2 freemen
5.	Gisleham (b)	16	not stated	5s. + 300 h.	not stated	½	1 freeman
6.	*Hornes*	5	not stated	3s. + 100 h.	not stated	not stated	1 freeman
7.	Kessingland (a)	30 + 1m.	5s.	8d.	1	1	1 freeman
8.	Kessingland (b)	90 + 1m.	10s.	22s. + 1000 h.	2	2	4 freemen 2 bordars
9.	Kirkley	12	2s.	3s. + 200 h.	½	0	1 freeman
10.	*Rodenhalla*	40 + 1½ m.	5s.	9s. + 600 h.	1½	1½	1 freeman 4 bordars
11.	Rushmere	16	not stated	5s. + 300 h.	1	½	1 freeman
12.	*Wimundahalla*	12	2s.	3s. + 500 h.	½	½	2 freemen
	Wangford Hundred						
13.	*Hathelburgfelda*	60	10s.	11s.8d. + 900 h.	2	1½	6 freemen
14.	Weston	16	not stated	5s. + 400 h.	not stated	½	1 freeman
15.	Willingham (a)	3	not stated	18d. + 100 h.	not stated	not stated	1 freeman
16.	Willingham (b)	18 + 1½ carucates	60s.	30s.30d. + 3,000 h.	7	6	15 freemen 2 villeins
17.	Worlingham	60 + 2 m.	10s.6d. + 1,000 h.	10s.6d. + 1,000 h.	2	2	5½ freemen 1 bordar
	Blything Hundred						
18.	Stoven	60 + ½ m.	7½s. + 100 h.	7½s. + 100 h.	1	1	3 freemen (formerly 4)

Searching for Salvation in Anglo-Norman East Anglia

Christopher Harper-Bill*

IN 1992 Dr Eamon Duffy, in a remarkable book, described and analysed the vibrant traditional religious culture of England at the close of the middle ages, and very much of his evidence was drawn from East Anglia.[1] This paper is an attempt, on an infinitely smaller scale, at a reconstruction of the religious climate of the region in the century and a half after the Norman Conquest. The task is hampered by the complete lack of various categories of evidence which provide valuable information on the period prior to the Reformation. There are no churchwardens' accounts, no devotional texts aimed at the laity, and above all no wills, which in their thousands have been so valuable in reconstructing the religious sentiments of late medieval English men and women. The pious investment which resulted in the great rebuilding of East Anglian churches in the perpendicular style between the 1370s and the 1520s brought about the destruction of by far the greater part of the region's twelfth-century romanesque heritage – it is symbolic that at Blythburgh there stands one of the finest of fifteenth-century parish churches, while almost nothing remains of the small Augustinian Priory which in an earlier age had attracted so many donations from the neighbourhood.[2] What survive in profusion, however, are charters: grants and confirmations, usually of land or rent, sometimes of rights and privileges, in effect title deeds. In the earliest years of the twelfth century these are rare and precious, written in the name only of those at the apex of society. By the mid-thirteenth century they are relatively common, recording the gifts even of peasants and shopkeepers. Charters can to some extent act as a source analagous to late medieval wills as a window on lay piety, especially before the 1180s when the devotional phrases of earlier deeds of gift were giving way to legalistic common form. By using these, supplemented by chronicles and miracle collections, it may be possible to appreciate

* This paper was originally delivered as an Inaugural Lecture as Professor of English History at the University of East Anglia, Norwich, on 27 April 1999. It is offered now to Norman Scarfe, not only in recognition of his scholarship and of much personal kindness, but also as an acknowledgement of his devotion, over so many years and in so many practical ways, to the Centre of East Anglian Studies at UEA.

1 E. Duffy, *The Stripping of the Altars: Traditional Religion in England, 1400–1580*, New Haven and London 1992.

2 *The Cartulary of Blythburgh Priory*, ed. C. Harper-Bill, 2 vols, Suffolk Charters II–III, SRS 1980–81.

something of this earlier world just as, to employ an architectural analogy, one passes from the perpendicular exterior of Wymondham abbey to the glories of the priory's romanesque nave.

East Anglia in the twelfth century was no rural backwater, but an extremely prosperous region. 'Whoever once enters Norfolk', wrote a monk of Peterborough, 'will not wish to leave it as long as he lives, for once he has seen so good a land, he will declare it a little Paradise.'[3] The chronicler of the great rebellion of 1173–74, not himself an East Anglian, believed that no clerk 'could tell me of or name me any land between here and Montpellier as good as the county of Norfolk, of which you hear me talk, or more honourable knights or a more fruitful soil or more gracious ladies adept at open-handed generosity', and a few stanzas later added that 'there is no more prosperous region on earth than Bury St Edmunds'.[4] Contemporaries therefore appreciated that East Anglia was flourishing particularly at the time of economic take-off in western Europe. It was not only wool and cloth but, as Professor James Campbell explained in a notable Creighton Lecture, herring fishing and peat digging to provide for smoking the fish (which created the modern Broads), and salt production along the coast to preserve them in another way, which created the paradigm of a burgeoning economy with intensive contact with the Continent.[5] Trade brought with it, however indirectly, the exchange of ideas, which was facilitated by ecclesiastical contacts. Herbert de Losinga, the first bishop of Norwich, and John of Oxford, the fourth, were regular travellers to mainland Europe.[6] Baldwin, abbot of Bury St Edmunds, whose career spanned the Norman conquest, came from Chartres via St Denis at Paris, and his successor in the early twelfth century was the Italian Anselm of St Saba.[7] The ideas which were first propounded, in an age of intellectual revolution, at the papal court or the great legal centre of Bologna or the leading theological schools of northern France were almost certainly discussed at Norwich and Bury. Certainly the great abbot Samson of Bury had studied at Paris at a time when radical theology was the common currency of the lecture halls, and later in the 1180s and 1190s he preached to the populace; and although the Bury chronicler implies that the people of Suffolk had grave difficulty in understanding his Norfolk accent, it is surely likely that something was transmitted in conversation to the higher levels of East Anglian lay society.[8]

If new ideas were in the air, one theme remained constant. The medieval church was as persistent as charities in the 1990s in bombarding its members with appeals.

3 John of St Omer *Norfolchiae descriptionis impugnatio*, in *Early Mysteries and other Latin Poems of the Twelfth and Thirteenth Centuries*, ed. T. Wright, London 1838, 106. I owe this reference to D. Crouch, *The Image of Aristocracy in Britain, 1000–1300*, London 1992.

4 *Jordan Fantosme's Chronicle*, ed. R.C. Johnston, Oxford 1981, 97 (unfortunately he adds 'leaving aside the city of London, whose equal nobody knows'); 99 for Bury.

5 For a synopsis, see 'Domesday Herrings', above, pp. 5–18.

6 *English Episcopal Acta* VI: *Norwich, 1070–1215*, ed. C. Harper-Bill, British Academy 1990 (hereafter *EEA* VI), Itineraries, 368–70, 373–5.

7 D. Knowles, C.N.L. Brooke and V. London, *The Heads of Religious Houses, England and Wales, 940–1216*, Cambridge 1972, 32.

8 *Jocelin of Brakelond*, 40, 44.

In post-Conquest East Anglia the agenda was set by a sermon of Bishop Herbert: 'Abound in the works of mercy; find opportunities for almsgiving, because alms extinguish sin as water does fire.'[9] It was perhaps in direct response to this that Alan son of Flaald, when granting his manor of Eaton to Norwich cathedral priory, allowed the monastic scribe to expand on the generosity of God to mankind and man's obligation to return some of these gifts to divine service.[10] Indeed, the pressure did not only come from the church, but from great lords eager to increase the endowment of their own foundations. When in 1090 Gilbert Fitz Richard of Clare established his priory there, he exhorted the barons of his honour that, while avoiding the disinheritance of their heirs, they should make gifts to the monks from their churches and tithes, an invitation which they eagerly accepted. Two generations later his grandson Roger of Clare, when the monks, now transferred to Stoke by Clare, took their relics on a fundraising tour, issued them with letters enjoining his friends and neighbours and ordering his men to receive them generously, expressing the conviction that for whatever they gave God would reward them an hundredfold in the next world.[11]

One remarkable charter, indeed, implies that there was a fixed tariff for donations to the church by magnates and knights. Around 1140 Roger de Valognes, son of the founder of Binham priory, confirmed to the monks the land of Barney, given by Walter de Valognes, probably his uncle.[12] This confirmation was made 'by the exhortation, request and counsel of the lord Theobald, archbishop of Canterbury and primate of all England, who showed me by most reasonable and unanswerable arguments that a noble and liberal man who has the fee of six knights should give not only the third part of a knight's land to God and holy church, but the whole of a knight's land, or more'. The obligation upon the heir was, furthermore, clearly spelled out: 'if this man's heir should try to take away the alms which is placed as a bridge between his father and paradise, by which his father may be able to pass over, the heir is . . . disinheriting his father from the kingdom of heaven, and therefore ought not to obtain the inheritance which remains, since he who has killed his father has proved himself no son'. The thousands of charters granting lands, churches and tithes to East Anglian monasteries testify to the effectiveness of the message, but just occasionally there is a note of exasperation, as in the charter of Henry of Essex, issued in the 1150s: 'I am urged every day that it is required that from my abundance I should with proper benevolence fulfil the demands of the poor.' He gave a

9 E.M. Goulburn and H. Symonds, *The Life, Letters and Sermons of Bishop Herbert de Losinga*, 2 vols, Oxford and London 1878, ii, 27–9.

10 *The Charters of Norwich Cathedral Priory*, ed. B. Dodwell, 2 vols, Pipe Roll Society XL, XLVI, 1974–85, ii, no. 304.

11 *Stoke by Clare Cartulary*, ed. C. Harper-Bill and R. Mortimer, 3 vols, Suffolk Charters IV–VI, SRS 1982–84, i, nos 35, 37.

12 F.M. Stenton, *The First Century of English Feudalism*, Oxford 1932, 260–1, and discussed *ibid.*, 38–41; translated in *English Historical Documents*, II, *1042–1189*, ed. D.C. Douglas and G.W. Greenway, London 1953, 934–5; see also Crouch, *Image of Aristocracy*, 110.

mark (13s 4d) of silver a year to the Hospitallers from a sheepfold at Eastwood, Essex, 'so that they may demand no more than this'.[13]

Henry of Essex was noted by Jocelin of Brakelond as being mean, and of course he came to a bad end, accused of cowardice on the Welsh campaign of 1157, defeated in a judicial duel and forfeiting his estates – perhaps just retribution for his parsimony.[14] To balance his apparent reluctance, there are many examples of quite spontaneous generosity to the church, most notably by his own mother, Gunnora, who in the early twelfth century had, with the consent of her husband Robert of Essex, granted to the Cluniac priory of Thetford four East Anglian churches on the day of their son's birth, because of their delight at his safe delivery;[15] understandably so, as when a few years before Gunnora's kinswoman Matilda Bigod had died in childbirth, William d'Albini her husband, weeping and wailing, had given to his newly founded priory of Wymondham, where she was buried, the manor of Happisburgh, and also an exquisite silver casket containing fragments of Christ's manger, the True Cross and the Blessed Virgin's sepulchre.[16] In joy as in desolation, then, twelfth-century lords made donations to the church but, not surprisingly, devotional charity was most strongly expressed as death approached, as illustrated by a touching letter of Warin Fitz Gerald, the royal chamberlain, to Henry II in 1160–61, begging him to listen to what were, he was sure, his last words, and to love and honour St Edmund and, if he had any feeling for Warin, to safeguard his grants to Bury.[17]

What was the motivation for this lavish almsgiving to the church? We must start, surely, from a presupposition of deep and abiding guilt, the overwhelming fear of damnation and the pains of hell which was the negative, but perhaps more compelling, side of the hope of salvation and eternal beatitude. In the second decade of the twelfth century Ralph Fitz Brien, in daily terror of death, contemplated the foundation of a monastery at Great Bricett, realising that while he still lived he should make amends for his sins.[18] Almost a century later, Robert of Ashbocking restored Hemingstone church to Colchester abbey, because he wished neither to go against the advice of his friends nor to be in a state of sin.[19] The psychological impact of the terror of damnation can be illustrated by two vignettes from the *Life and Miracles of St William*, the story of the after-life of the boy allegedly ritually murdered by the Jews of Norwich in 1144. One very sick man was transported, no doubt delirious, by an angel to a region where 'he saw countless multitudes being tortured with dif-

13 *The Cartulary of the Knights of St John of Jerusalem in England: Secunda Camera, Essex*, ed. M. Gervers, Records of Social and Economic History ns VI, British Academy 1982, no. 264.

14 *Jocelin of Brakelond*, 69–71.

15 T. Martin, *History of Thetford*, London 1779, 126.

16 W. Dugdale, *Monasticon Anglicanum*, ed. J. Caley, H. Ellis and B. Bandinel, 6 vols in 8, London 1817–30 (hereafter *Monasticon*), iii, 330–1.

17 *Feudal Documents from the Abbey of Bury St Edmunds*, ed. D.C. Douglas, Oxford 1932, no. 189.

18 *Monasticon* vi, 174.

19 *Cartularium monasterii sancti Johannis Baptiste de Colecestria*, ed. S.A. Moore, 2 vols, Roxburghe Club 1897, 208, 260.

ferent punishments, and among them he recognised many whom he had known when alive', who entreated him to go to their kindred to urge them that 'the same torments were prepared for them, unless they should repent and desist from those crimes known to them'.[20] A very holy Norfolk maiden also experienced a vision of 'the realms of punishment, all full of mourning and horror everywhere. There was an unbearable stench and horrible impenetrable darkness, and a burning unquenchable heat, and cold that gave no relief', and there she saw 'an innumerable concourse of souls subjected to various torments, hurried from one to another by various changes of suffering'.[21] The path to heaven was narrow, and according to the minute analysis of Jacques Le Goff, Purgatory was not 'invented' until the 1170s, in the schools of Paris, and so there was not even until then the prospect for sinners of an ascent, however gradual and painful, towards salvation, but rather a single stark alternative.[22]

It was the mighty of this world, the *potentiores*, who were most surely consigned to damnation, unless they made considerable reparation for the violence and injustice which habitually accompanied their acquisitiveness. The legislation of the church and the homilies of preachers emphasised that it was particularly difficult for the military aristocracy to pass the scrutiny of St Peter, the key-bearer.[23] The Norman conquest, of course, had given peculiar opportunities for violent seizure – Little Domesday records allegations of sixty-three instances of unjust disseisin in Norfolk alone.[24] The monks of Ely were quite convinced of the damnation to hell of William de Warenne because he had seized manors from them, and certainly did not consider that his own lavish monastic foundations had saved him.[25] The breakdown of order in Stephen's reign, however partial, gave further opportunities for wrongful dispossession, for which subsequent atonement was only prudent, to avoid the wrath not only of God but of King Henry II. Before that king's accession, however, in 1150, William de Chesney founded Sibton abbey 'because of the many ills which he had committed in the region' – in fact while he was sheriff – and around the same time Gilbert de Gant, earl of Lincoln, made a grant to Norwich cathedral priory in recompense for 'his excesses committed against the church of Norwich at Lynn'.[26]

Occasionally it is possible to draw a more detailed picture of the process of restitution, to God and man, for an act of violence. Sometime in King Stephen's reign Stephen de Danmartin, steward of the honour of Clare, abused his position to seize the estate of Pitley (Great Bardfield, Essex), and sanctioned the murder of the right-

20 *The Life and Miracles of St William of Norwich*, ed. A. Jessopp and M.R. James, Cambridge 1896, 68–9.

21 *Life of St William*, 75.

22 J. Le Goff, *The Birth of Purgatory*, trans. A. Goldhammer, Chicago and London 1984.

23 C. Harper-Bill, 'The Piety of the Anglo-Norman Knightly Class', *Anglo-Norman Studies* ii, 1980, 63–77, 173–6 (notes).

24 R. Liddiard, ' "Landscapes of Lordship": Norman Castles and the Countryside in Medieval Norfolk, 1066–1500', UEA Ph.D. thesis, 2000, 75–6.

25 *Liber Eliensis*, ed. E.O. Blake, Camden Society, 3rd series, XCII, 1962, 202.

26 *Sibton Abbey Cartularies and Charters*, ed. P. Brown, 4 vols, Suffolk Charters VII–X, SRS 1985–88, iii, no. 470; Stenton, *First Century*, 244.

ful heir, the son of William of Bardfield.[27] In 1170 the new Clare earl of Hertford ordered certain of his men that they should not swear before the king's justices that Stephen had ever been the rightful tenant. By then, however, Gilbert de Danmartin, the culprit's son, had in an impressive ceremony granted the disputed estate to Stoke by Clare priory, for the salvation of himself, his father and the late earl and on condition that the community would accept him as a monk when he so wished and would celebrate his anniversary in perpetuity. Land violently misappropriated was surrendered to the servants of God in the hope of redemption. The monks, however, could hardly rest assured of possession when there was such an obvious rival claim; and so, probably after the investigation by the royal justices and certainly after protracted negotiation, there was another great ceremony. Hugh of Bardfield, brother of the murdered man, appeared in the priory church with all his sons and heirs. They stood before the high altar, with the Host set upon it, and solemnly renounced to the monks all right in Pitley. Hugh, now a fairly old man, was received into confraternity, with all its spiritual benefits and with food and clothing, as long as he held to his oath, and on his deathbed he might be received as a monk, in return for half his chattels. Thus he, as well as the monks, profited from the transaction. A claim which would have been difficult to enforce was abandoned in return for security in old age and the greater hope of eternal beatitude.

A second story comes from the records of the *curia regis*. In 1208 John the chamberlain accused of Hugh of Pattesley of killing his brother Drogo by first shooting him with an arrow and then stabbing him in the heart – certainly not an accidental homicide.[28] Ultimately an agreement was reached before the royal justices that Herbert should go to Jerusalem and stay there for seven years; if he returned beforehand he would face judicial punishment. Herbert's accomplice was to pay 40s compensation to the kin of the murdered man, but was also to arrange for one of them to be received as a monk or canon in a Norfolk monastery. This reveals that, occasionally, at least, even the king's judges regarded the redemptive effects of the Jerusalem pilgrimage and prayer in a convent as more important than the legalistic execution of the common law. The two cases together indicate that atonement for violence was a matter both of salvation and of reconciliation within earthly society, effected through monastic benefaction.

The other great occasion of sin, and cause of guilt, must surely have been sexual activity. This is far more difficult to document, as no charter specifically states that a grant is being made in reparation for an illicit sexual act. In the wake of the papal reform movement, however, and even more after the compilation of Gratian's *Decretum* in 1140, the canon law of the universal church was increasingly discussed and practised in England, and judges and lawyers were much exercised by sexual and matrimonial matters.[29] Ecclesiastical intervention may be illustrated by two papal decretals addressed to East Anglian prelates. In a letter which can be dated

27 The story can be reconstructed in *Stoke by Clare Cartulary* i, no. 50; ii, nos 538–40; cf. *ibid.* iii, 14, and Stenton, *First Century*, 81–3.

28 *CRR* v, 182, 244–5.

29 J.A. Brundage, *Law, Sex and Christian Society in Medieval Europe*, Chicago 1987, chs 5–8.

1176x1181, Pope Alexander III informed Bishop John of Norwich that a certain William had gone to the pope (probably in fact sent by the bishop) and confessed that he had taken a woman into his house, had a child by her and promised before many witnesses to marry her.[30] In the meantime he had stayed a night with a neighbour, slept with his daughter and been caught out by the father, who had forced him to marry her. With which woman, he rather pathetically asked the pope, should he stay? The pope instructed the bishop that if he found that the man had had intercourse with the first woman after his promise to her, he should remain with her; otherwise, he was indeed married to the girl, with whom he should stay, unless he had wed her through fear of such coercion as would break a constant man. Another decretal of Pope Alexander, addressed to the abbots of Bury St Edmunds and Ramsey, explicitly tied salvation to marital fidelity.[31] Emma, the appellant, and Andrew had sworn marriage oaths in the presence of clergy and laity, and thereafter had lived together and had children; but then Andrew deserted his family. The judges were instructed to compel him to look to his salvation, put away the other woman, return to his wife and expiate his guilt by penance; should he refuse, both culprits must be excommunicated and shunned by all, until satisfaction should be made. Female sexuality, and guilt, is revealed in a very different source, the *Life and Miracles of St William*, whose author had been told by the bishop's confessor of the young daughter of a wealthy Dunwich family who was constantly visited and tempted by an incubus in the form of a handsome young man; she was only liberated from these fascinating visions when she was persuaded to pray at St William's tomb.[32]

From the mid-twelfth century the church increasingly intruded on sexual conduct, albeit often with beneficial effects, especially for women.[33] The degrees of consanguinity within which marriage might be contracted were more restrictively regulated; fornication and especially adultery was more widely condemned; and even the occasions on and manner in which married couples might have intercourse were increasingly limited. Of course, the great majority of the laity did not observe these rules, or indeed even know of many of them – there were none of the pastoral and confessional manuals which were the eventual aftermath of the Fourth Lateran Council of 1215. The aristocracy and higher ranks of the knightly class, however, came from the same social milieu as bishops, legal scholars and those clerks who had attended the cathedral schools of northern France where a succession of teachers from Peter Abelard onwards were placing a novel emphasis on individual intention

30 'Decretales' (hereafter *X*) in E. Friedberg, ed., *Corpus Iuris Canonici*, 2 vols, Leipzig 1879–81, IV. i, 15; P. Jaffé and S. Löwenfeld, *Regesta Pontificum Romanorum . . . ad annum 1198*, 2 vols, Leipzig 1885–88 (hereafter JL), 13902, 14159; identified as Bishop John in BL MS Royal 10 B iv, fo. 45v.

31 *X*, IV. i. 9; JL 13872.

32 *Life of St William*, 79–85.

33 C. Duggan, 'Equity and Compassion in Papal Marriage Decretals to England', in his *Decretals and the Creation of the 'New Law' in the Twelfth Century*, Aldershot 1998, IX.

and conscience, and were evolving the science of moral and pastoral theology.[34] It would be unwise to underestimate the intellectual powers of the secular aristocracy and their households. The chronicler Orderic Vitalis speaks approvingly of those knights who visited the Norman priory of Maule to discourse with the monks, and the same may have happened in East Anglian cloisters.[35] We know, from a chance reference in a charter, of one great lady of the region, Euphemia, countess de Vere, who had her own confessor long before such a practice was the norm, and that he was called 'confessor' rather than the normal 'chaplain' must mean that she frequently revealed her sins to him.[36] In the later middle ages, the consciences of many of the captains of the Hundred Years War were prompted by new trends in confessional technique, and they became leaders of a movement of affective lay piety.[37] Although there simply is not the evidence, it is very possible that from the mid-twelfth century a deep-seated sense of sexual guilt was added to remorse for the violence necessary to carve out a position in the world as motivation for almsgiving designed to avoid the pains of hell.

Neither guilt nor exhortations to charity, however, explain why it was the monastic order which was perceived to be the channel of salvation, the surest road to heaven. The Norman Conquest, after all, occurred in the middle of the period which saw a great programme of establishment of those local churches which were to become parochial, and nowhere were they more prolific than in East Anglia.[38] There is evidence in Little Domesday Book of the existence by 1086 of a very large number of village churches – at least 217 in Norfolk, 345 in Suffolk, and this is not counting boroughs, which each contained several or many.[39] The process, moreover, was far from complete, as the *Taxatio Ecclesiastica* of 1291 records 1165 parish churches in the diocese of Norwich, the vast majority of which were almost certainly in existence before 1215.[40] Those surviving pre-Conquest wills which contain

[34] C. Morris, *The Discovery of the Individual, 1050–1200*, London 1972, 64–79; M.T. Clanchy, *Peter Abelard: A Medieval Life*, Oxford 1997, ch. 12.

[35] Orderic Vitalis, *Historia Ecclesiastica*, ed. M. Chibnall, 6 vols, Oxford 1969–80, iii, 206.

[36] *Cartularium Prioratus de Colne*, Essex Archaeological Society, Occasional Publications I, 1946, no. 56.

[37] J.L. Catto, 'Religion and the English Nobility in the Later Fourteenth Century', in *History and Imagination: Essays in honour of H.R. Trevor Roper*, ed. H. Lloyd Jones *et al.*, London 1981, 43–55.

[38] R. Morris, *Churches in the Landscape*, London 1981, chs 4–5; *Minsters and Parish Churches: The Local Church in Transition, 950–1200*, ed. J. Blair, Oxford University Committee for Archaeology, monograph no. 17, 1988, ch. 1, 12–13.

[39] These figures are from H.C. Darby, *The Domesday Geography of Eastern England*, Cambridge 1952, 138, 190–2. Other estimates are higher: 286 in Norfolk, excluding Norwich, Thetford and Yarmouth, in D. Dymond, *The Norfolk Landscape*, Bury St Edmunds 1990, 81; 417 in Suffolk, in N. Scarfe, *The Suffolk Landscape*, Bury St Edmunds 1972, 139.

[40] *Taxatio Ecclesiastica Angliae et Walliae auctoritate Papae Nicholai IV, circa 1291*, ed. S. Ayscough and J. Caley, Record Commission 1802, 78–90; that this list has numerous omissions and that the true total is 1,349 is argued by W. Hudson, 'The Norwich Taxation and the *Taxatio Nicholai*', *NA* xvii, 1910, 69–70. N. Batcock has counted 818 Norfolk parish churches recorded in the Valuation of Norwich of 1254 (*An Architectural Atlas of Norfolk*, ed. P. Wade Martins, Norwich 1994, 60).

bequests in East Anglia, and which provide such a welcome contrast to the lack of early charter material for the region, record lavish gifts to such recently founded churches.[41] Obviously such endowment did not cease after 1066, since so many more local churches were established. Charters in the Castle Acre cartulary suggest that some gifts made nominally to the monks were in reality directed towards the churches of Haverhill and Westbriggs, now in their hands;[42] and for the majority of parish churches which were not granted to a religious community we have no written evidence at all. It is, nevertheless, obvious that there was after the Conquest a large-scale shift in patronage in favour of the newly founded monastic houses. Just as Eamon Duffy wrote his account of late medieval religious sentiment with hardly any reference to monasteries, so it would be possible to present a picture of twelfth-century lay piety with little reference to parish churches, which appear in the sources merely as revenue-yielding appendages of religious houses.

The expansion of regulated monasticism in East Anglia after 1066 was dramatic. The region was not quite the monastic desert which the land north of the Humber had become, but at the Conquest there were precious few monks, and no nuns at all, in the East Anglian diocese. Tiny communities of priests there certainly were, relics of the ancient minsters, but 'Benedictinisation' had not proceeded far; there was only St Benet of Holme and Bury St Edmunds, both associated with King Cnut, with small cells respectively at Rumburgh and Thetford.[43] While first Wessex and then Mercia had been transformed by the establishment of numerous Benedictine houses in the late tenth century, regular monasticism had only recently penetrated East Anglia.[44] The situation was rapidly changed in the generation after the Conquest, and far less attention has been paid to this transformation than to the monastic plantation in northern England.[45] The existing communities had divergent fortunes. St Benet's was allegedly harassed and plundered by Roger Bigod, for whom the Conquest brought a rise from relative obscurity to great riches; but he had some justification since the abbot, a trusted adherent of King Harold, had taken to piracy to retaliate against the new rulers.[46] Bury, on the other hand, had prospered mightily under the French abbot Baldwin, physician to both the Confessor and the

41 D. Whitelock, *Anglo-Saxon Wills*, Cambridge 1930, *passim*, see Index; for translations of some immediate pre-Conquest East Anglian wills, see *English Historical Documents*, II, *1042–1189*, 836–42.

42 BL MS Harley 2110 (Castle Acre Cartulary) fos 81v, 102r–103v.

43 For an important study, see T.J. Pestell, 'An Analysis of Monastic Foundation in East Anglia, c. 650–1200', UEA Ph.D. thesis, 1999, which it is hoped will soon be published. Pestell argues convincingly that many 'new' twelfth-century foundations were on sites formerly occupied by small groups of priests.

44 For lists, see M.D. Knowles and R.N. Hadcock, *Medieval Religious Houses, England and Wales*, 2nd edn, London 1971 (hereafter *MRH*), 52–82; also M.D. Knowles, *The Monastic Order in England*, Cambridge 1940, chs 3–4; C.J. Godfrey, *The Church in Anglo-Saxon England*, Cambridge 1962, ch. 18.

45 Most recently, J. Burton, *The Monastic Order in Yorkshire, 1069–1215*, Cambridge 1999.

46 F.M. Stenton, 'St Benet of Holme and the Norman Conquest', *EHR* xxxvii, 1922, 225–35, at p. 233.

Conqueror, who was adept at identifying the interests of his community with those of the new regime.[47]

St Edmund at Bury, as a warrior saint, held an obvious appeal for the Norman military aristocracy. The Benedictine liturgy, too, was admirably suited to their mental world, which has been characterised as 'a theology of armed action'.[48] The monastic choir was the scene of a ritual battle against the forces of evil led by Satan, in which the prize of victory was the souls of mankind, but most particularly of founders and benefactors.[49] The monks were regularly described as 'knights of Christ' and their houses as 'fortresses of prayer'.[50] This ethos held great attraction for those whose worldly fortunes were shaped by war. A particularly good example is provided by William de Warenne, one of the few Norman lords who can be proved to have fought at Hastings. According to later tradition, probably reliable, William and his wife, returning from pilgrimage to Rome, stayed at the great Burgundian monastery of Cluny, judged by contemporaries to be the yardstick of religious observance.[51] So impressed were they by the incessant round of masses offered to God for the salvation of benefactors that they begged St Hugh, the abbot, to let them have a contingent of Cluniac monks to settle in the shadow of their castle at Lewes in Sussex, from which a few years later Castle Acre priory was colonised.

Nor were other tenants-in-chief prepared merely to enrich further existing pre-Conquest houses. In their homeland, the new aristocracy which had emerged in the 1040s and 1050s had signalled their arrival at the apex of society by founding a monastery, thereby making a social as much as a religious statement. This process of lavish endowment was repeated in East Anglia. One by one, between 1080 and 1107, the Conqueror's baronage established monasteries designed to secure their salvation and to assert their dominance over the land (as much as did the castles by which they so often stood). Military and religious colonisation marched hand in hand.[52] Around 1080 Robert Malet established at Eye a daughter house of the Norman monastery of Bernay, and Gilbert Fitz Richard followed soon thereafter with a priory dependent on Bec at Clare. Binham and Wymondham were founded by Peter de Valognes and William d'Albini as daughters of St Albans, itself now thoroughly Normanised. Roger Bigod emulated William de Warenne in looking to

[47] A. Gransden, 'Baldwin, Abbot of Bury St Edmunds', *Anglo-Norman Studies* iv, 1982, 65–76 (notes) 187–95.

[48] D.C. Douglas, *The Norman Achievement*, London 1969, 101.

[49] B.H. Rosenwein, 'Feudal War and Monastic Peace: Cluniac Liturgy as Ritual Aggression', *Viator* ii, 1971, 129–57.

[50] For examples of sustained military imagery by St Anselm, see R.W. Southern, *St Anselm and his Biographer*, Cambridge 1963, 109–10; by St Bernard, *The Letters of St Bernard of Clairvaux*, trans. B.S. James, London 1953, no. 95.

[51] *Monasticon* v, 12–13, discussed in *Early Yorkshire Charters*, ed. W. Farrer and C.T. Clay, 12 vols, Yorkshire Archaeological Society Record Series, extra series, 1935–65, viii, *Honour of Warenne*, 59–62; see also B. Golding, 'The Coming of the Cluniacs', *Anglo-Norman Studies* iii, 1981, 65–77 (notes) 208–12.

[52] For these foundations, see *MRH*, 59, 65, 68, 81, 92, 103. For Eye, *Eye Priory Cartulary and Charters*, ed. V. Brown, 2 vols, Suffolk Charters XII–XIII, SRS 1992–94; for Horsham, *Monasticon* iii, 635.

Cluny for his foundation at Thetford; and it was the intervention of St Foi in saving Robert Fitz Walter from a robber ambush while returning from her shrine at Conques which induced him in 1105 to found a house dedicated to her at Horsham St Faith. All this was in addition to the new monastic cathedral, established in 1096 by Herbert Losinga in accordance with the Norman policy of moving episcopal sees to major regional centres, and also with the peculiar English habit of having cathedrals staffed by monks – about the only feature of the Anglo-Saxon church of which the Normans had approved.[53] By 1107, forty years after the Conquest, there were in East Anglia ten major Benedictine foundations, eight of them established after the Conquest.

The process of foundation continued unabated through the twelfth century, and one reason for this, and for the benefactions of those not sufficiently wealthy to establish their own house, was probably the insistence of the reformed papacy, and of the bishops who followed its lead, on clerical celibacy.[54] Although there is no evidence of papal appeals to the English to boycott the masses of 'incontinent' priests,[55] it is inconceivable that the upper echelons of Anglo-Norman society should not have known of the new insistence on sexual abstinence amongst those who ministered at the altar. The battle for chastity among the higher clergy had been won around the middle of the century. Bishop Everard (1121–45) had children, and was surrounded at Norwich by a remarkable number of nephews – and as Pope Alexander III later allegedly remarked, when the Lord deprived bishops of sons, the Devil gave them nephews.[56] Everard, however, was the last of his kind, as so too at a slightly less exalted level was the engagingly scandalous archdeacon Walkelin, the last of a generation of ecclesiastical dignitaries who could openly live with a wife (probably a fairer description than mistress), although even he was forced to abandon her long before his death in the late 1180s.[57] With the parochial clergy, however, the situation was very different. Bishop Herbert obviously felt that the canon of the Council of Westminster of 1102 prohibiting priests who cohabited from celebrating mass would destroy the pastoral ministry within his diocese, but he was sharply instructed by Archbishop Anselm that if things were that bad, he must get monks into the parishes as a short-term solution.[58] All the Norwich priests men-

53 B. Dodwell, 'Herbert de Losinga and the Foundation', in *Norwich Cathedral: Church, City and Diocese, 1096–1996*, ed. I. Atherton *et al.*, London 1996, 36–43.

54 For two references among a potential multitude: C. Morris, *The Papal Monarchy: The Western Church from 1050 to 1250*, Oxford 1989, 101–8; C.N.L. Brooke, 'Gregorian Reform in Action: Clerical Marriage in England, 1050–1200', in his *Medieval Church and Society*, London 1971, 69–99.

55 As Pope Gregory VII urged the people of Milan and Cambrai; R.I. Moore, *The Origins of European Dissent*, London 1977, 54–5, 60–2.

56 *EEA* VI, p. xxxii, nos 36–7, 41, 43, 49–50; *Monasticon* iii, 330. Gerald attributed this dictum to the pope: *Giraldi Cambrensis Opera* ii, *Gemma Ecclesiastica*, ed. J.F. Brewer, RS XXI, 1862, 304.

57 *The Letters of John of Salisbury*, I, *The Early Letters*, ed. W.J. Millor, H.E. Butler and C.N.L. Brooke, London 1955, nos 14–15.

58 *The Letters of St Anselm of Canterbury*, ed. W. Fröhlich, 3 vols, Cistercian Studies XCVI–XCVII, CXLII, Kalamazoo 1990–94, ii, no. 254.

tioned in the *Life and Miracles of St William*, written around 1169, seem to have been married men, and one episcopal actum (1155x1163) records the admission of a clerk to a city church by hereditary right, 'as is the custom of the city of Norwich'.[59] Successive bishops of Norwich might seek papal support for the deprivation of married clergy and the exclusion of their sons from the fathers' living,[60] but in fact it is possible to trace three generations of hereditary priesthood at Thornham, where the advowson pertained to the church of Norwich, and the abbots of Battle and St Benet of Holme happily tolerated hereditary succession to churches in their gift, either for financial gain or family advantage.[61] The reality of the situation in many parishes is most tellingly revealed by a case in 1194, when the royal justices were enquiring into the right of patronage of the church of Dunston, where the parson had just died.[62] The oldest inhabitants, summoned to testify, swore that they had never seen any incumbent presented or installed by anybody, but always the parsons held it, son succeeding father, until the recent death of the last, who had left only a daughter. That the judges decided that she must, in default of sons, be the patron shows how engrained was the notion of the hereditary church. Yet the insouciance of these Norfolk villagers may not have been shared by their social superiors, more aware of the orthodox line on priestly celibacy, and the chastity of those living under a rule within a monastery may have been an additional incentive to direct benefactions to monasteries where the Mass would certainly be celebrated with greater ceremony, dignity and ritual than in the parish church.[63]

It was the canons regular, following the Rule of St Augustine, who made the greatest impact on East Anglia in the twelfth century.[64] Ranulf de Glanvil, King Henry II's justiciar, founded an Augustinian house at Butley in 1171 and a community of the white canons of Prémontré at Leiston in 1183. That acerbic contemporary observer Gerald of Wales purports to reveal his motivations: Glanvil wrote off the Benedictines as too luxurious and the Cistercians who, attracted to wide open spaces, made little impact in East Anglia, as too avaricious, despite their apparent austerity; the canons he thought to be both more moderate and more useful.[65] The

59 *EEA* VI, no. 153.

60 Such attempts were made by Bishop William Turbe, 1158x74 (*EEA* VI, 365, no. 81); and William Raleigh (*Entries in the Papal Registers relating to Great Britain and Ireland*, I, *Papal Letters, 1198–1304*, HMSO 1894, 190).

61 For Thornham, *CRR* xvi, no. 1659; *The Chronicle of Battle Abbey*, ed. E. Searle, Oxford 1980, 240; *St Benet of Holme, 1020–1210*, ed. J.R. West, 2 vols, NRS II–III, 1932, i, no. 70.

62 *Rotuli Curiae Regis*, ed. F. Palgrave, 2 vols, Record Commission 1835, i, 37–8.

63 For two excellent short accounts of what patrons and benefactors expected, see C.J. Holdsworth, *The Piper and the Tune: Medieval Patrons and Monks*, The Stenton Lecture 1990, Reading 1991; D. Postles, *Lay Piety in Transition: Local Society and New Religious Houses in England, 1100–1280*, Friends of the Department of English Local History, Leicester 1998.

64 For the canons, see especially J.C. Dickinson, *The Origins of the Austin Canons and their Introduction into England*, London 1950; R.W. Southern, *Western Society and the Church in the Middle Ages*, Harmondsworth 1970, 240–50.

65 *Speculum Ecclesiae*, in *Giraldi Cambrensis Opera* iv, ed. J.S. Brewer, RS XXI, 1873, 244–5; see R. Mortimer, 'Religious and Secular Motivation for some English Monastic Foundations', *SCH* xv, 1978, 77–85.

first house of canons in Norwich diocese was probably West Acre (1102x1126) on the estate of Ralph de Tosny, and the recently rediscovered foundation charter provides a fine example of the motivation which prompted such an initiative.[66] It reveals that the original impetus came from a married priest and his son, eager to lead a new celibate life with a few others, at first funded on a very small scale by their lord. It cites early Christianity at Jerusalem, as described in the *Act of the Apostles*, as their exemplar – they were a 'textual community',[67] who looked beyond Augustine's rule for their legitimisation. The canons saw their role as apostolic rather than eschatological;[68] they were not as the monks, in theory at least, dead to the world, but actively sought involvement in it, taking on the care of parish churches and often supervising hospitals. They were attracted to an urban environment, where they could fulfil their mission, and so were well suited to this region, with its multitude of small market towns. Their appeal is obvious. Hugh Bigod and William III de Warenne established Augustinian communities at Pentney (*c.*1130) and Thetford (*c.*1140), whereas their ancestors had invested their spiritual capital in the Cluniacs.[69] Yet because their demands were normally fewer than those of the monks, and their liturgical life, although complete and dignified, less elaborate than that of the Benedictines, those lesser families who may be described as the 'gentry' of the age could often afford to found a small house of canons. For example, Dodnash priory was established in 1188 by Wimer the chaplain, who acquired land from various vendors with which to endow it in the year that he resigned as sheriff of Norfolk and Suffolk, offering the king a large fine that he might be acquitted of any process against him for maladministration – that is, lining his own pocket.[70] Just as the Benedictines offered salvation to those who had made their way in the world by the sword, so did the canons to those who had achieved this goal by graft and peculation.

In all, there were in Norfolk and Suffolk by 1215 thirty-four communities of monks and canons large enough to maintain a full liturgical round, six nunneries and thirty-three small male houses with less than a dozen inmates.[71] In addition there were already at least thirty hospitals, some attached to monasteries, others independent but with brothers or sisters living under a rule. Excluding hospitals, in 1066 3.3 per cent of English religious houses were located in the East Anglian

66 N. Vincent, 'The Foundation of Westacre Priory (1102 x 1126)', *NA* xli, 1994, 490–4.

67 A term used for various dissident groups by B. Stock, *The Implications of Literacy: Written Language and Models of Interpretation in the Eleventh and Twelfth Centuries*, Princeton 1983, ch. 2.

68 For an excellent discussion of distinctive canonical spirituality, see C.W. Bynum, *Jesus as Mother: Studies in the Spirituality of the High Middle Ages*, Berkeley and Los Angeles 1982, 22–58; also C.N.L. Brooke, 'Monk and Canon: Some Patterns in the Religious Life of the Twelfth Century', *SCH* xxii, 1985, 109–29.

69 *MRH*, 170, 175–6. For a case study of shifts in religious allegiance, see J.C. Ward, 'Fashions in Monastic Endowment: The Foundations of the Clare Family, 1066–1314', *JEH* xxxii, 1981, 427–51.

70 *Dodnash Priory Charters*, ed. C. Harper-Bill, Suffolk Charters XVI, SRS 1998, 1–2.

71 These figures are based on the tables in *MRH*. The figures of Pestell (see n. 43) from 1066 to 1200 are 71 institutions (38 in Norfolk, 31 in Suffolk, 2 in Cambridgeshire), excluding hospitals and preceptories of the military orders.

diocese; by 1215 the figure had risen to 10 per cent of the national total. The landscape and the religious geography of the region had in the intervening years been totally transformed, and hardly anyone with surplus wealth, from the king and the higher aristocracy to the free peasantry and the shop-keepers of Bury and Sudbury, had failed to make some contribution.

Closely associated with monasteries was the cult of saints and relics. There was particularly a great need for saints with local roots. East Anglia, like England as a whole, acknowledged the whole community of saints recognised by the universal catholic church, but churches dedicated to St Peter, St Paul or St Andrew were not 'theirs' in the way that Italian churches actually founded by the apostles were.[72] The dedication of Ely was to St Peter and St Etheldreda, but everyone thought of the abbey as St Etheldreda's, the seventh-century foundress of the community. East Anglia had an even more eminent native saint in Edmund, martyred by the Danes in 869. Probably no saint, save only Cuthbert at Durham, exercised greater influence over his region, and his potency is revealed by the urgency with which the Normans appropriated him to themselves – he was far too dangerous to be ignored.[73] The endowments received from the king and the regional aristocracy by Bury St Edmunds in the first post-Conquest generation were quite exceptional for a pre-existing monastery.[74]

The cult was assiduously fostered by the monks by ceremonial and by preaching. A collection of the saint's miracles was compiled in the late eleventh century and updated in the late twelfth.[75] Many of them were thaumaturgic, the healing of contrite pilgrims who journeyed to the shrine, but Edmund does also seem to have been particularly vindictive in the safeguarding of his own rights. His most famous act of retribution was the blinding, by branches when riding, of the Norman bishop Herfast, who was seeking to annex the abbey to the bishopric.[76] According to Bury tradition relayed by John of Salisbury, Eustace, King Stephen's son, was struck dead by St Edmund in 1153 after violating the abbey's liberty – thus opening the succession to Henry II, who might be expected to be suitably grateful.[77] In the late eleventh century the men of Robert de Curcon who attempted to occupy St Edmund's manor of Southwold went mad, but some families never learn – his successor William de Curcon many years later (1154x1175) revived the claim to Southwold and obtained a favourable judgement in the royal court. On the way

72 R. Brentano, *Two Churches: England and Italy in the Thirteenth Century*, Berkeley and Los Angeles 1988, 228–9.

73 S.J. Ridyard, *The Royal Saints of Anglo-Saxon England*, Cambridge 1988, 228–33.

74 E. Cownie, *Religious Patronage in Anglo-Norman England*, London 1998, 66–79.

75 *Memorials of St Edmund's Abbey*, ed. T. Arnold, 3 vols, RS XCVI, 1890 (hereafter *Memorials*), i, 26–92 (Hermann's *De miraculis sancti Edmundi*); 107–208 (rewriting and revision attributed to Abbot Samson).

76 *Memorials* i, 62–4; and below p. 43.

77 *Memorials* i, 357–8; C.J. Nederman, trans., *John of Salisbury: Policraticus*, Cambridge 1990, 213, a section on tyrants who came to a miserable end, from the Old Testament to his own times. In an earlier age St Edmund had wrought his revenge on another tyrant, Swein (*Memorials* i, 114–19).

back from London he was taken ill at Chelmsford and was raving mad by Colchester, only recovering his senses when, at the insistence of the prior, he repented and abandoned his claim.[78] Nor was it only the great who suffered from Edmund's ire: a poacher who made off with a peacock belonging to one of the saint's tenants was drowned – the peacock escaped and returned home.[79]

St Edmund could, however, provide a secure refuge for those who resorted to him – even for the hated Flemish mercenaries fleeing from the battle of Fornham in 1173.[80] There was a confraternity, confirmed by Abbot Ording around 1150, rather different to the individual fraternity agreements entered into with various monasteries by substantial donors.[81] Membership was secured by payment of a penny a year, and it was expected that as members felt the approach of death they should give what they could; in return for this they would be sharers in all the spiritual benefits of the church by day and by night and the abbey bells would be rung for them at their death. The members of this gild must have been largely the merchants of the borough and the abbey's tenants in nearby vills, and it is remarkable that in the twelfth century they saw themselves as auxiliaries of the monks in the quest for salvation through St Edmund's intercession, whereas by the fourteenth century the saint was seem primarily as a landlord, whose monastic agents were the victims of violent attack in 1327 and 1381.

Of the two Norfolk saints, one is totally obscure and the other distressingly problematic. For Walstan of Bawburgh we have only late medieval accounts of a pre-Conquest personage who surely existed, but whose dates and career are shrouded in mystery.[82] A prince who abandoned his inheritance in a quest for apostolic poverty, he took service with a farmer and died in a field while praying for the sick and for cattle – a very comfortable saint, rather akin to the well-attested Norfolk man Godric, who finished a long life at Finchale near Durham and was a great protector of animals.[83] In 1309 the offerings to Walstan at Bawburgh, a church belonging to the cathedral priory, were enough to maintain six chantry priests in addition to the vicar and to finance the rebuilding of the chancel, and it is attested that farmers came to the church to obtain a blessing on themselves and their animals. This does not sound like a novel practice in the early fourteenth century.

The cult of little St William of Norwich was eagerly taken up by a group of monks of the cathedral priory, keenly aware that they lacked a saint to rival St Edmund at Bury. When in 1144 the body of a boy, murdered in a most horrific way, was discovered in Thorpe Wood, it was widely alleged that this was a ritual killing performed by the Jews in mockery of Christ's Passion. This is the first instance of

78 *Memorials* i, 79–80, 148–9.

79 *Memorials* i, 365–6.

80 *Memorials* i, 364–5.

81 *Feudal Documents from Bury St Edmunds*, no. 137 (1148x1156).

82 M.R. James, 'Lives of Walstan', *Norfolk Archaeological Society Papers* xix, 1917, 238–67; D.H. Farmer, *The Oxford Dictionary of Saints*, Oxford 1982, 397–8. For an account of the survival of the cult to modern times, see C. Twinch, *In Search of St Walstan*, Norwich 1995.

83 *Oxford Dictionary of Saints*, 174–6.

this libel in England, and perhaps in western Europe, although it was to have a dark future.[84] In the immediate context, during the twenty-five years of miracles recorded around 1169 by the monk Thomas of Monmouth, St William provided all that could be required by every level of East Anglian society. The lady Mabel de Bech was a particular patron after her children were cured of mortal disease by scrapings of stone from his tomb; the son of Ranulf, a knight of Haughley, was healed of epilepsy; two terrifying madmen suddenly recovered at the shrine. Animals benefited too: a candle lit to St William cured Sir Goscelin de Gros's oxen of murrain, and the falcon of Albert de Gresley was saved.[85] Best of all for the monks, a murderer from Lincolnshire on a penitential pilgrimage had his iron fetter miraculously fall away at William's tomb, having achieved no result at the shrine of St Edmund.[86]

East Anglian pilgrims did not restrict themselves to their native region, nor even to England. The miracle collections of St Edmund and St William both refer to pilgrims returning from continental shrines, and it was particularly satisfying that, having visited some of the greatest repositories of relics in the West, they were only saved from shipwreck or some other disaster by resorting to the intercession of the local saint.[87] Occasionally a charter provides evidence of overseas pilgrimage. In the early years of Henry II's reign Robert Popi sold land in Flegg to finance his journey to St James of Compostella and Maurice of Barsham quitclaimed land and goods to Castle Acre priory for the safety of his soul should he not return from his pilgrimage to St Gilles in Provence.[88] Nor was it only the relatively prosperous who went – the wife of the cook of the Norwich monks had been to both these shrines.[89]

The martyrdom of Thomas Becket in 1170 transformed the geography of intercession and thaumaturgy. Canterbury was elevated almost immediately to the status of a major European shrine. Among the early miracles are two from East Anglia, from very different social levels. The infant James of Clare, son of Earl Roger, was first cured of a hernia through St Thomas's intercession, and a few weeks later was revived from apparent cot-death.[90] The daughter of Jordan of Plumstead, who many years before had served the young Becket as a groom, was miraculously cured of lesions which had brought her near to death, called a 'cancer'.[91] Perhaps the most telling indication of the perceived power of St Thomas is that the Bury miracle cycle,

84 For discussion, see G.I. Langmuir, 'Thomas of Monmouth, Detector of Ritual Murder', *Speculum* lix, 1984, 820–46; J.M. McCulloch, 'Jewish Ritual Murder: William of Norwich, Thomas of Monmouth, and the Early Dissemination of the Myth', *Speculum* lxxii, 1997, 698–740, arguing for continental antecedents.

85 *Life of St William*, 135, 154, 174, 223–7, 258–60.

86 *Life of St William*, 236–9.

87 *Memorials* i, 80–1, 92.

88 *HMCR Various Collections* VII (Arundel), 242–3; BL MS Harley 2110, fo. 44r.

89 *Life of St William*, 178.

90 *Materials for the History of Thomas Becket*, ed. J.C. Robertson, 7 vols, RS LXVII, 1875–85, ii, 234–6.

91 *Becket Materials* ii, 255–7. Another East Anglian miracle of Becket involved the cure of a monk of Norwich, for whom presumably the intercession of St William had been inefficacious (*Becket Materials* ii, 104).

which usually lost no opportunity to score points off other saints and shrines, twice associated Becket with Edmund in performing joint miracles, perhaps through fear that the martyr-king would otherwise be eclipsed.[92]

The late twelfth century is the period of the prehistory of another pilgrimage centre which was eventually to outstrip even Canterbury. Some time before 1152 Richelde de Favarches had a vision of the Blessed Virgin Mary instructing her to build a chapel modelled on the Holy House at Nazareth where she had received the Annunciation.[93] Richelde and her son Geoffrey established at Little Walsingham a house of Augustinian canons to act as its guardians. The foundation did not take place in a vacuum. The collection of miracle stories relating to the Virgin was one of the distinctive contributions of England to the twelfth-century renaissance, and although they originated as a defence mechanism for Old-English monasteries dedicated to St Mary against the aggression of new Norman lords, they were also a reflection of a new preoccupation with the human Jesus, His family and the places associated with Him which manifested itself in monastic cloisters and cathedral schools.[94] One of these collections, perhaps the earliest, was produced by Anselm of St Saba, the Italian abbot of Bury (1121–48), who was also one of the foremost advocates of the feast of the Immaculate Conception. Twelfth-century devotion to the Blessed Virgin was not an insular phenomenon, and Marian shrines rose to prominence in north-western France, where they were deemed to be particularly effective against frequent outbreaks of ergotism. It is not at all remarkable that a Marian shrine should be established in East Anglia, although it is unusual for not being located in an existing cathedral or monastery; and although there is no evidence of pilgrimage until 1226, when King Henry III first visited, it is inconceivable that he would have gone there had not at least a regional tradition already developed. In that year too the king went to Bromholm priory to venerate a portion of the True Cross brought from Constantinople after the crusaders' sack of the city by an East Anglian priest who had temporarily served in the entourage of the first Latin emperor; by 1223 miracles were reported at Bromholm.[95] However suspect the origins of the Holy Rood, however, it too is symptomatic of a gradual shift towards a more Christocentric piety which is characteristic of the later middle ages.

The greatest of all pilgrimages, of course, and the ultimate destination for searchers after salvation, was the Holy Land. It has been demonstrated, in a remarkable

92 *Memorials* i, 364, 368.

93 J.C. Dickinson, *The Shrine of Our Lady of Walsingham*, Cambridge 1956. For the wider setting of Walsingham, see C. Rawcliffe, 'Pilgrimage and the Sick in Medieval East Anglia' and C. Harper-Bill, 'The Foundation and History of the Medieval Shrine', in *Walsingham: Pilgrimage and History*, R.C. National Shrine, Walsingham 1999, 39–80.

94 R.W. Southern, 'The Place of England in the Twelfth-Century Renaissance', in his *Medieval Humanism and Other Studies*, Oxford 1970, 172–4; *idem*, 'The English Origins of the Miracles of the Virgin', *Medieval and Renaissance Studies* iv, 1958, 176–216; B. Ward, *Miracles and the Medieval Mind*, Aldershot 1982, ch. 8.

95 F. Wormald, 'The Rood of Bromholm', *Journal of the Warburg and Courtauld Institutes* i, 1937–8, 31–45; *Chronica Rogeri de Wendover*, ed. H.G. Hewlett, 3 vols, RS LXXXIV, 1886–89, ii, 274–6.

study of the Limousin and Gascony, based mainly on charter evidence, that crusading enthusiasm originated in the continual contact between the military classes and the religious at the altars and in the chapterhouses of monastic communities.[96] The same urgent desire which prompted donation, pilgrimage and conversion, even on deathbeds, to the religious life led naturally to widespread compliance with the appeal of Urban II, and subsequent popes, for volunteers for the East. The crusade and the Jerusalem pilgrimage supplemented rather than supplanted other expressions of profound lay piety, and was yet another manifestation of a deeply engrained value system; and the monks were eager to fund, albeit at a price, those seeking the Holy Sepulchre. East Anglian evidence confirms this view.

Knowledge of participants in the first crusade is limited to Ralph de Gael, the Breton earl of Norfolk exiled after his rebellion in 1075, and Edith, sister of William de Warenne, who may herself have never come to Castle Acre.[97] Rather more significant as an indication of currents of religious sentiment is the notice in an early twelfth-century charter that the totally obscure Peter, son of Cunigar, obtained an additional five shillings from the monks of Stoke by Clare when his father sold them land, in order to subsidise his journey to Jerusalem.[98] When the second crusade was preached in 1146, Philip Basset of Postwick granted to St Benet of Holme a marsh, in return for 15 marks [£10] and remission of rent for seven years from the departure of the expedition.[99] Around the same time Hugh Tirel, a Clare tenant, sold his manor of Langham (Essex) to Gervase of Cornhill for 100 marks for his journey to Jerusalem.[100] At the highest social level, William III de Warenne, just before his departure on the expedition during which he was to die in action, founded an Augustinian priory of the Holy Sepulchre at Thetford and also obtained the dedication of the new priory church at Castle Acre.[101] The main contingent from East Anglia took a circuitous route to the Holy Land, by sea, landing on the west coast of the Iberian peninsula. Their leader, Harvey de Glanvil, delivered an inspirational speech before the walls of Lisbon; during the onslaught seven young men of Ipswich valiantly defended a siege engine against the defenders' attempts to burn it; and after the taking of the city, Gilbert of Hastings, a member of a prominent East Anglian family, became the first bishop.[102]

The Lisbon campaign was the one success of the second crusade, however far removed from its goal, and the situation declined thereafter. When news reached the West late in 1187 of the loss of the Holy City and the True Cross, Abbot Samson of

96 M. Bull, *Knightly Piety and the Lay Response to the First Crusade: The Limousin and Gascony, c.970–c.1130*, Oxford 1993.

97 C. Tyerman, *England and the Crusades, 1095–1588*, Chicago 1988, 15.

98 *Stoke by Clare Cartulary* ii, no. 264.

99 *St Benet of Holme* i, no. 155.

100 *Sir Christopher Hatton's Book of Seals*, ed. L.C. Loyd and D.M. Stenton, Oxford 1950, nos 84, 105.

101 *MRH*, 175–6; BL MS Harley 2110, fos 3v–4r.

102 *De Expugnatione Lyxboniensi*, ed. C.W. David, New York 1936, 104–11, 160–1, 178–81.

Bury began to wear haircloth drawers and shirt and to abstain from meat.[103] Encouraged by the example of Richard, heir to the throne, many great men in the Anglo-Norman realm now took the cross. Richard of Clare, earl of Hertford, granted a wood to the monks of Stoke by Clare – in fact a concealed sale, as they gave him 30 marks [£20] towards his journey to Jerusalem, before reaching which he died in Palestine in October 1190.[104] The Pipe Rolls reveal that tenants of his honour went with him, and also knights of St Edmund's abbey.[105] On the fifth crusade in 1211, after the fall of Damietta, two mosques were converted to churches dedicated to St Thomas Becket and St Edmund, and in the latter wall-paintings showing his martyrdom were commissioned by Richard of Argentan, a lesser member of the East Anglian aristocracy.[106]

As late as 1240, almost certainly associated with the crusade of King Henry III's brother Richard of Cornwall, a certain William of Cley next the Sea leased land to another layman for three years, as he had it in mind to visit the Holy Land and stay there as long as possible, with God's help; he received 6 marks [£4] to help with his journey.[107] By this time, and probably during the twelfth century, two preceptories of the Hospitallers and four of the Templars had been established in East Anglia, local bases through which the less adventurous might channel their contributions to the holy war.[108] Certainly it was advisable that some should never set out. A papal decretal directed to the bishop of Norwich, probably in 1166–67, concerned an infirm clerk who had, as a boy, pledged with a friend to make a pilgrimage to the Holy Land, but now he was too ill to be of any use, and in any case it was illicit for a clerk in holy orders to bear arms or shed blood. Pope Alexander III absolved him from his oath, made in tender years out of enthusiasm rather than deliberation, and ruled that he should fulfil his obligation through almsgiving.[109] This ruling found its way into the universal legal code of the Roman church, but the young priest's enthusiasm, combined with the other East Anglian evidence, serves to corroborate Sir Maurice Powicke's judgement that 'the preaching of the crusade was the temporary culmination of an ever-present appeal, a high tide in the perpetual ebb and flow of the religious life'.[110]

To conclude this survey with pilgrimage to the Holy Land is to reiterate the cos-

103 *Jocelin of Brakelond*, 39–40.

104 *Stoke by Clare Cartulary* i, no. 40; *Chronica Rogeri de Houedene*, ed. W. Stubbs, 4 vols, RS LI, 1868–71, iii, 89.

105 Tyerman, *England and the Crusades*, 70–1.

106 Tyerman, 98, citing *Memoriale Walteri de Coventria*, ed. W. Stubbs, 2 vols, RS LVIII, 1872–73, ii, 242–3; *Matthei Parisiensis Chronica Majora*, ed. H.R. Luard, 7 vols, RS LVII, 1872–84, iii, 164. See also *Memorials* i, 376–7, for retribution visited on a man who had insulted St Edmund in his church at Damietta.

107 *Norwich Cathedral Charters* ii, no. 140.

108 Cavenham, Dunwich, Gislingham and Haddiscoe for the Templars; Battisford and Carbrooke for the Hospitallers.

109 *X*, III. xxxiv. 2; JL 11339. For the wider context, see J.A. Brundage, *Medieval Canon Law and the Crusader*, Milwaukee 1969, 68.

110 F.M. Powicke, *The Thirteenth Century*, Oxford 1962, 81. A rather different view is taken by C. Tyerman, 'Were there any Crusades in the Twelfth Century?', *EHR* cx, 1995, 553–77.

mopolitan, western European context of religious experience within the region during the 'long twelfth century'. Ideas, institutions and personnel were imported from the continent, and the main channel of transmission was the network of religious houses established in the wake of the Norman Conquest by patrons who looked to mother houses in the duchy, or as far away as Cluny in Burgundy and Conques in Rouergue. As the Papacy expanded its jurisdictional competence, these monasteries increasingly resorted to Rome for protection and for the resolution of disputes, as did bishops for guidance on a wide range of problems requiring clarification through papal interpretation of the rapidly evolving canon law, itself considered a branch of theology.

How different was this world from that of the century before the Reformation, so well illuminated by Eamon Duffy? There are remarkable strands of continuity: in the desperate desire for salvation and commemoration, in the confidence in the merits of saints, the reality of miracles and the efficacy of pilgrimage, and in the recourse to Rome for privileges and exemptions. The *ecclesia Anglicana* was in 1500 still most definitely a member of the universal church of Latin Christendom, although more distinct in its own identity, and the evidence of architecture and of wills demonstrates that East Anglia was unsurpassed in the enthusiasm of its inhabitants for the orthodox faith. Whereas, however, in the twelfth century initiatives and exemplars had been largely French, by the late fourteenth century there had developed an innate sense of the superiority of religious belief and practice in England to that of other national churches. God, increasingly seen as an Englishman,[111] was constantly invoked to sow confusion among England's enemies, particularly of course France.

The end of the Angevin empire in the early thirteenth century and the commencement of a near-permanent state of hostility with France in the mid-fourteenth inevitably weakened, and ultimately destroyed, the links of many monasteries with their cross-Channel mother houses. Yet this alone does not explain the decline of monasticism as the yardstick of religious experience. Soon after 1200 new foundations became a rarity and the stream of benefactions to existing houses began to dry up, to be replaced by sales and exchanges which reveal the monks and canons to be participants on an equal footing in an active land market. It is possible that the religious, and the monks in particular, were, or were perceived to be, doing less for the communities among which they existed. As C.N.L. Brooke has observed, the size of naves of twelfth-century monastic churches implies that the people flocked to them, but by 1250 there are indications that the monks were becoming 'either too holy, or too superior, or too idle' to do much for the laity in return for the tithes and other revenues with which they had been handsomely endowed in perpetuity.[112] By the mid-thirteenth century the new orders of mendicant friars had arrived in East Anglia to fill the gap. Two events may be seen as symptomatic – the bitter and

111 J.W. McKenna, 'How God Became an Englishman', in *Tudor Rule and Revolution: Essays for G.R. Elton*, ed. D.J. Guth and J.W. McKenna, Cambridge 1985, 25–43.

112 C.N.L. Brooke, 'The Churches of Medieval Cambridge', in *History, Society and the Churches: Essays in Honour of Owen Chadwick*, Cambridge 1985, 49–76, at p. 57.

prolonged resistance of the monks of St Edmund, from 1233 to 1262, to the attempts of the Franciscans to settle in their borough, partially at least for fear that the friars would diminish their own spiritual influence and revenues;[113] and the attack on Norwich cathedral priory in 1272 by townspeople resentful of the monks' jurisdictional claims.[114] The monks were by now showing themselves resistant rather than responsive to lay needs, and in consequence there are signs of lay indifference to the cloistered religious, and even occasionally of active hostility, which was to become more common in the fourteenth century. By then, the parish churches, created in the late Anglo-Saxon and Anglo-Norman age, had come into their own as the focus of religious devotion for the vast majority of East Anglians.

113 *MRH*, 224; *The Chronicle of Bury St Edmunds, 1212–1301*, ed. A. Gransden, London 1964, 22–4, 27–8.

114 N. Tanner, 'The Cathedral and the City', in *Norwich Cathedral: Church, City and Diocese* (as n. 53), 255–80, at pp. 259–62.

'On the Threshold of Eternity': Care for the Sick in East Anglian Monasteries

Carole Rawcliffe[1]

> Before all things and above all things care must be taken of the sick, so that they may be served in the very deed as Christ Himself; for He has said: 'I was sick and ye visited me' and 'As long as ye did it to one of these, my least brethren, ye did it to me.' But let the sick themselves consider that they are served for the honour of God, and not grieve their brethren who serve them by their importunity. Yet must they be patiently borne with, because from such as these is gained more abundant reward. Therefore the Abbot shall take the greatest care that they suffer no neglect.
>
> *The Rule of St Benedict*[2]

EARLY FATHERS of the Christian Church and many subsequent theologians recognised that the inherent conflict between physical and spiritual medicine would pose particular problems for professed religious. The widespread belief that human ills followed ineluctably from Original Sin, and that individual acts of wrongdoing might additionally be punished with disease or disability made it seem impious to question the will of God by seeking earthly remedies. Moreover, since fortitude in the face of suffering helped to cleanse the soul of impurities and thus prepare it for a speedy ascent to heaven, pain was, in theory, to be embraced as a divine gift or mark of election.[3] Such an austere approach to the discomforts of medieval life was neither expected of nor, one assumes, much practised by ordinary laymen and women, but appeared desirable in those who had abandoned the world for the cloister. As Bernard of Clairvaux (d.1153) warned one house of Italian Cistercians whose community, like many in East Anglia, was riddled with malaria:

> I have the very greatest sympathy for bodily sickness, but I consider that sickness of the soul is far much more to be feared and avoided. It is not at all in keeping with your profession to seek for bodily medicines, and they are not really condu-

1 I am indebted to Miss Barbara Harvey and Professor Joan Greatrex for reading and commenting on an early draft of this paper. They and Dr Philippa Maddern have generously supplied me with references. My particular thanks go to Norman Scarfe for a decade of kindness and encouragement, extended, with his customary warmth, since my arrival in East Anglia.

2 *The Rule of St Benedict*, ed. J. McCann, London 1921 (hereafter *Rule of St Benedict*), 258.

3 For the complex relationship between the medieval Church and medical practice, see D.W. Amundsen, *Medicine, Society and Faith in the Ancient and Medieval Worlds*, Baltimore 1996 (hereafter *Medicine, Society and Faith*), 175–221.

> cive to health. The use of common herbs, such as are used by the poor, can sometimes be tolerated, and such is our custom. But to buy special kinds of medicines, to seek out doctors and swallow their nostrums, this does not become religious . . .[4]

Implicit in Bernard's remarks is a characteristic jibe at the Benedictines, among whose ranks were to be found some of the leading medical practitioners of his day. For these monk-physicians the healing arts were part of God's handiwork, to be deployed, along with every imaginable component of the rapidly expanding medieval pharmacopoeia, for the benefit of mankind. With *Christus medicus* as their model and a long tradition of humanist writing in the Stoic vein upon which to draw, they could legitimately claim both biblical and classical authority for their endeavours. The Rule of St Benedict (d.550) twice required the abbot to act as a *wise physician*, and makes forceful use of medical metaphors, enlisting, for instance, the imagery of poultices, unguents, medicaments, cauteries and amputation in the section dealing with delinquent monks. It also displays a compassion for the physical frailties of the old, the young and the sick which accorded well with the emphasis placed by Roman authors upon such matters.[5]

The inevitable tension, whereby medicine was simultaneously regarded 'as both a gift of the creator and as a potential lure away from submission to him',[6] surfaces quite clearly in accounts of healing miracles, such as those composed at Norwich to establish the cult of William, the boy martyr, and at Bury to bolster that of St Edmund. Two of William's miracles, recorded shortly before 1170, are especially striking in this respect, since they both concern monks who had retired to the infirmary because of ill health. The first tells of brother Richard, who was suffering from a fever (perhaps malaria) and left his bed to spend the night by the martyr's tomb in the hope of a cure. Far from bringing the customary relief vouchsafed by the young saint to innocent layfolk, his dreams were shattered by a vision of the devil, disguised as a black pig. This the saint deemed a salutary warning to one who had not only removed candles from his shrine, but had initially placed his faith in earthly rather than celestial therapeutics.[7] A far worse fate lay in store for the sacrist, some of whose debilitating symptoms William had already helped to alleviate. After a second bout of illness, the monk was permitted to drink holy water in which two of the martyr's teeth had been immersed, but only on condition that he would henceforward refuse 'any medicine except this of mine'. The threat of certain death should he break this oath did not, however, prevent him from accepting medical help during a relapse,

4 *The Letters of St Bernard of Clairvaux*, ed. B. Scott James, Stroud 1998, no. 388.

5 E. Molland, '*Ut Sapiens Medicus*: Medical Vocabulary in St Benedict's *Regula Monachorum*', *Studia Monastica* vi, 1964, 273–97, at pp. 274, 283–6, 293–5; J. Kroll and B. Bachrach, 'Sin and the Etiology of Disease in Pre-Crusade Europe', *Journal of the History of Medicine and Allied Sciences* xli, 1986, 395–414. For the humanist tradition in medical writing, see F.M. Getz, *Medicine in the English Middle Ages*, Princeton 1998 (hereafter *Medicine*), 46.

6 Amundsen, *Medicine, Society and Faith*, 206.

7 Thomas of Monmouth, *The Life and Miracles of St William of Norwich*, ed. A. Jessopp and M.R. James, Cambridge 1896 (hereafter *William of Norwich*), 136–45.

and he paid the ultimate price. As William's hagiographer smugly remarked: 'He yielded to the advice of physicians and sought refuge in the deceits of medicine (*fallacis medicine asylo se contulit*).'[8] The clear impression, conveyed by this and other twelfth-century *vitae*, that professional treatment was freely available to, and indeed urged upon, sick monks is, however, worth noting, since it shows just how hard conservatives such as St Bernard were having to swim against the tide.[9]

The demands of ecclesiastical propaganda sometimes required a more subtle approach, in which saint and physician worked together, albeit in an unequal partnership akin to that of consultant and houseman. A monarch as well as a martyr, St Edmund far outdid the petulant Norwich apprentice in acts of vengeance, most notably against those who attempted to undermine the authority of his spiritual sons, the monks of Bury. The near-blinding of their enemy, Bishop Herfast, as he rode heedlessly through a forest provided the monastic chroniclers with a story of great dramatic power. A series of vivid tableaux describes the severity of his injuries, which not even the two great classical healers, Hippocrates and Galen, could have cured. We learn of his abject and penitent arrival at Bury St Edmunds in search of treatment; of Abbot Baldwin's virtuoso skill with fomentations and cauteries; and of the ultimate triumph of St Edmund, the source of Baldwin's healing grace.[10] Baldwin was, in fact, a man of rare ability, having acquired his medical training in France, quite possibly at the famous cathedral school at Chartres, before being summoned as a physician to the court of Edward the Confessor. Although he failed to cure the ailing Abbot Leofstan of Bury, whom he attended in 1065, he so impressed the monks that they chose him as their next abbot shortly afterwards. This proved a wise decision, as Baldwin was retained by William the Conqueror, Archbishop Lanfranc and other members of the Norman aristocracy who valued his medical expertise. It was perhaps under his aegis that the Bury scriptorium produced the magnificent herbal, now in the Bodleian Library, Oxford, which testifies to the interest in natural sciences apparent in so many monastic houses (Plate 1).[11] Like other monk-physicians who combined high ecclesiastical office with a lucrative practice, he ploughed back much of his wealth into building schemes, thus earning for himself a lasting memorial:

> Baldewynus, a monk off Seynt Denys,
> Gretly expert in crafft off medycyne,
> Ful prouydent off counseyl and ryht wys,

8 *Ibid.*, 145–6, 174–7.

9 See, for example, *Materials for the History of Thomas Becket*, ed. J.C. Robertson, 7 vols, RS 1875–88 (hereafter *Materials*), i, 416–17; ii, 242, for the case of Elias, the leprous monk of Reading, whose abbot put his faith in baths and medication.

10 *Memorials of St Edmund's Abbey*, ed. T. Arnold, 3 vols, RS 1890–96, i, 62–5.

11 C.H. Talbot and E.A. Hammond, *The Medical Practitioners in Medieval England*, London 1965 (hereafter *MPME*), 19–21. A survey of monastic practitioners may be found in E.A. Hammond, 'Physicians in Medieval English Religious Houses', *Bulletin of the History of Medicine* xxxii, 1958, 105–20. Effusive descriptions of the naturalism of the Bury herbal (as, for example, E.J. Kealey, *Medieval Medicus*, Baltimore 1981, 6–9) are corrected by M. Collins, *Medieval Herbals: The Illustrative Traditions*, London 2000, 196–9.

Plate 1. The entry describing the properties of the blackberry from the late eleventh-century Bury St Edmunds herbal. Recent research suggests that the manuscript itself was executed at some speed from an exemplar, and the illustrations repainted with greater subtlety at a later date. *Bodleian Library, Oxford, MS Bodley 130, fo. 26r.*

Sad off his port, fructuous off doctryne,
After by grace and influence deuyne
Chose off Bury Abbot, as I reede,
The thrydde in ordre which dide ther succede,
To seynt Edward he was phesecien;
To many siknesse he did remedye.[12]

Did Baldwin, the quintessentially 'wise physician', treat any of his own monks? Or was he too busy cultivating distinguished patients? Fear that members of religious orders would be tempted to 'promise health in return for detestable money and thus make themselves physicians of human bodies' prompted a series of conciliar rulings in the 1130s, prohibiting monks and canons regular from the study of medicine for crude material gain.[13] Often misunderstood by medical historians, these regulations did not curtail the activities of men such as Master Walter the physician, a senior monk at Bury St Edmunds in the late twelfth century, who gave 'a large donation of money that he had made from his medical practice' towards the construction of a new stone almonry and thus avoided allegations of personal acquisitiveness.[14] His generosity may, none the less, have been prompted by an uneasy conscience, as monk-physicians found themselves increasingly liable to censure. Far more restrictive and sweeping in its consequences, a further decree of 1163 had forbidden professed religious to leave the cloister 'for the study of law and for pondering medical concoctions under the pretext of aiding the bodies of their sick brothers'.[15] It did not, even so, condemn the art of medicine *per se*, and during the next century we encounter a number of monastic practitioners who presumably either trained in the schools before taking their vows or were taught by skilled fellow monks in the cloister. Both Master John (*fl.*1200), *monachus medicus* of the Benedictine house of St Benet Holme, and Master Stephen (d.1257), *medicus infirmarius* of Bury St Edmunds, fall into this category. Although the convent made generous provision for the celebration of Stephen's obit, the revenues assigned for this purpose had been generated by his prudent management of resources rather than through the largesse of patients. It was, indeed, his zeal as infirmarer, notably during an outbreak of sweating sickness, which merited especial commendation.[16]

12 BL MS Harley 2278 (verses by John Lydgate, monk of Bury), fo. 116r.

13 Amundsen, *Medicine, Society and Faith*, 206.

14 Jocelin of Brakelond, *Chronicle of the Abbey of Bury St Edmunds*, ed. D. Greenway and J. Sayers, Oxford 1989 (hereafter *Chronicle of Bury St Edmunds*), 16, 85.

15 Amundsen, *Medicine, Society and Faith*, 230–1. The position of religious who practised medicine in the community remained highly ambivalent. See, for instance, the case of the Yorkshire monk who had an affair with his female patient and then killed their go-between: *Rolls of the Justices in Eyre for Yorkshire, 1218–1219*, ed. D.M. Stenton, Selden Society LVI, 1937, 377–8.

16 *St Benet of Holme 1020–1210*, ed. J.R. West, NRS II, 1932, nos 287, 291; BL MS Lansdowne 416 (Register of Thomas Ickworth, infirmarer of Bury St Edmunds, 1425), fos 4r, 21v. Monastic medical libraries of the period containing Latin translations of Arab authors new to the West suggest that knowledge was widely diffused: *A Descriptive Catalogue of the Medieval Manuscripts in Worcester Cathedral Library*, ed. R.M. Thomson, Woodbridge 2001, pp. xxiv, 25–6, 44, 99–100, 120, 142–3, 149, 151–2, 157, 182–3.

We have already seen that Abbot Baldwin, like many monks of his generation, had a fine grasp of surgery as well as physic, a combination which came increasingly to invite official disapproval. The risk of accidental homicide, ever present in an age before antisepsis, blood transfusion and reliable anaesthesia, jeopardised a monk's ability to perform his priestly duties.[17] Nor, in any event, did it seem fitting that hands polluted with the bodily fluids of a patient – and especially a female patient – should celebrate the Eucharist. As early as 1109 Abbot Faritius of Abingdon had been deemed an unsuitable occupant of the archbishopric of Canterbury because, as a court physician, he so often inspected women's urine.[18] The Fourth Lateran Council of 1215 duly ordered *all* clergy in higher orders, whether secular or religious, to abandon any procedures involving bloodshed or cauteries, although medicine, a more theoretical and academically respectable subject, remained permissible within the boundaries noted above.[19] Henceforward, monasteries were obliged to employ laymen or clerks to perform any surgical operation, however routine. In 1272 the monks of Ely leased one of their messuages in the town for life to Master Adam, a surgeon from St Albans. The rent of 5s a year was offset by the simultaneous award to him of a corrody of two loaves, two gallons of ale and two dishes from the prior's larder every day while he continued in residence. In return, he undertook 'in accordance with [a] corporal oath . . . taken in full chapter with his hand upon the Holy Gospels' that he would 'diligently and faithfully tend the diseases of our brethren in all that belongs to the art of surgery'. It is worth noting that any member of the community, 'greater or lesser, one or more', might call upon his services.[20]

Master Adam was clearly a practitioner of distinction, with other patients and commitments. The advantages of employing less eminent but permanently available surgical staff for mundane operations such as bloodletting soon became apparent. From at least 1284 onwards, and probably far earlier, the establishment at Bury St Edmunds included a resident phlebotomist (*minutorius*), who ranked alongside other lay employees, such as the granger, beadle and miller, and was entitled to a similar allocation of food and drink.[21] At Norwich cathedral priory the communar had by this date assumed responsibility for paying the convent's barbers, who let blood as well as cutting hair and subsequently formed their own craft guild in the city. The infirmarer initially retained a barber of his own, but at some point between 1314 and 1344 a full-time servant took charge of monks who were undergoing venesection. This post was regularised during the late fourteenth century under the

[17] P. Ziegler, *Medicine and Religion c.1300: The Case of Arnau de Vilanova*, Oxford 1998 (hereafter *Medicine and Religion*), 8–9.

[18] *Chronicon Monasterii de Abingdon*, ed. J. Stevenson, 2 vols, RS 1858, ii, 287.

[19] Amundsen, *Medicine, Society and Faith*, 235–9.

[20] T.D. Atkinson, *An Architectural History of the Benedictine Monastery of St Etheldreda at Ely*, 2 vols, Cambridge 1933 (hereafter *Monastery of St Etheldreda*), i, 103–4. Such arrangements did not always work well in practice, as the legal records testify: J.B. Post, 'Doctor versus Patient: Two Fourteenth-Century Law Suits', *Medical History* xvi, 1972, 298–300.

[21] BL MS Harley 3977 (Customal of Bury St Edmunds abbey, 1284), fos 30r, 104v.

title of *clericus minutorum* and accorded a slightly higher fee, perhaps in recognition of the occupant's status as a member of the lower clergy.[22] Local surgeons were occasionally employed on an *ad hoc* basis to treat specific patients whose cure lay beyond the skill of a phlebotomist. During the course of a long illness, which dragged on from 1428 until his death a decade later, William Manyngton, former prior of the dependent cell at Aldeby, needed such expert attention. The infirmarer's outlay in *cirurgia et mediciniis* for him came to 5s 4d in 1430–31 alone: in comparative terms, this represented sixteen days' wages for a Norwich carpenter and his labourer, and was thus a far from inconsiderable sum.[23]

The dissemination throughout Europe of classical medical and scientific texts in new translations from Greek, Arabic and Hebrew gave a dramatic impetus to the study of medicine in the thirteenth and fourteenth centuries. Rustic Cistercian empirics who knew nothing of Galen or Hippocrates and were ignorant of recent developments in pharmacy now invited ridicule rather than praise. As eager to take lucrative employment in the monasteries of medieval England as they were to enter noble or episcopal households, newly qualified physicians from Oxford and Cambridge offered the most advanced treatment then available.[24] Men such as Master Roger de Paston (1285–86) and Master Geoffrey de Suffield (1344–50) were engaged, respectively, at the abbey of St Benet Holme and Norwich cathedral priory to diagnose and prescribe in accordance with the principles of Galenic medicine.[25] Being for the most part secular clergy, or more occasionally Dominican or Franciscan friars, this new breed of practitioner fitted easily into the life of a religious house.

Encouraged by the success of their new surgeon, the Ely Benedictines arranged for the physician, Master John de Walford, to lodge in considerable comfort within their walls, eating at the prior's table whenever he wished to do so. The lengthy contract of 1278, by which he agreed to treat the monks and 'their friends and sick acquaintances . . . in the science of medicine, tending [them] with all heedfulness, giving diligence, help and aid with faithful zeal', stipulated that he would find 'another discreet and careful physician' to practise during his absence. The chapter thus

22 *The Early Communar and Pittancer Rolls of Norwich Cathedral Priory*, ed. E.C. Fernie and A.B. Whittingham, NRS XLI, 1972, 56, 60, 63, 66, 68, 72, 74, 87, 89, 94, 98, 102, 113; NRO, DCN 1/3–38. Save for the years between about 1460 and 1496 and 1511 and 1530 the infirmarer's staff invariably included either a barber, a servant or a clerk responsible for phlebotomised monks.

23 NRO, DCN 1/10/19. In 1347–48 Master Geoffrey, 'ceroger', received 2s for his services (DCN 1/10/6), but no other surgeon is actually named in these records. For examples of contemporary East Anglian wage rates, see NRO, Norwich City Records, 24A, Great Hospital Archive, box of Norwich accounts, 1415–60, account for 1430–31.

24 Giraldus Cambrensis, *Opera, IV, Speculum Ecclesiae*, ed. J.S. Brewer, RS 1873, 173–4; C. Rawcliffe, *Medicine and Society in Later Medieval England*, Stroud 1995 (hereafter *Medicine and Society*), chapter V. Not surprisingly, given its wealth, Westminster abbey boasted a high level of medical provision: B. Harvey, 'Before and after the Black Death: A Monastic Infirmary in Fourteenth-Century England', in *Death, Sickness and Health in Medieval Society*, ed. S.J. Ridyard, Sewanee Medieval Studies X, 2000, 5–31.

25 NRO, DCN 1/10/3–8; DN/EST 1/3; *MPME*, 54. Each was paid 20s a year as a retainer.

Plate 2. This mid-fifteenth-century roof boss from the north transept of Norwich cathedral depicts a consultation between the deranged King Herod and his physician, who wears the robes of a university graduate. The scene is taken from a mystery play, although it is tempting to speculate that the mason may be satirising one of the distinguished Cambridge *medici* he encountered in the precinct. *Reproduced by kind permission of Julia Hedgecoe.*

ensured that expert care would be constantly available, and, indeed, appears to have retained a series of resident specialists until the Dissolution.[26] This was by no means unusual. Master Conrad, a Cambridge physician who examined the urine of sick monks at Norwich, was permitted in 1471 to rent a chamber and garden in the almonry complex for use during extended visits (Plate 2).[27] Whereas recourse to professional help had once seemed beset with spiritual dangers, any infirmarer who now failed to provide fully qualified medical support ('unum medicum in arte medicinali peritum') whenever it might be needed risked censure or even removal from office.[28] Individual obedientiaries, meanwhile, sometimes preferred to make

26 Atkinson, *Monastery of St Etheldreda*, i, 104–5; *MPME*, 194–5.

27 NRO, DCN 1/6/85, 1/10/29; *MPME*, 30.

28 *The Customary of the Cathedral Priory Church of Norwich*, ed. J.B.L. Tolhurst, London 1948 (hereafter *Customary of Norwich*), 244; *The Observances in Use at the Augustinian Priory of S. Giles and S. Andrew at Barnwell, Cambridgeshire*, ed. J. Willis Clark, Cambridge 1897 (hereafter *Observances*), 207; D.J. Stewart, *On the Architectural History of Ely Cathedral*, London 1868 (hereafter *Architectural History of Ely*), 274. See also complaints made at Butley

their own arrangements. In 1360–61, for example, the master of the cellar paid William de Rougham, *medicus* and distinguished fellow of Gonville Hall, Cambridge, 20s for his services, quite possibly as the prior of Norwich's personal physician. But it is clear from the accounts of his successor, Alexander de Totyngton, that holders of this office might charge their own medical expenses to the prior's annual budget too.[29]

Despite this trend towards the privatisation of treatment, the principal locus of care for sick and elderly monks remained the infirmary. Its importance is reflected in the scale of the buildings themselves, which were often large, richly decorated and imposing. As was the case in the medieval hospital, the sick initially lay together in an open ward or aisled hall, situated, where possible, in the quieter east or south-east quarter of the monastic complex. No East Anglian infirmary could rival the massive hall constructed by Abbot Kent (d.1247) of Fountains in Yorkshire, whose expenditure on what was effectively 'a separate monastery for the old and infirm' would have appalled his fellow-Cistercian, Bernard of Clairvaux. Surviving architectural evidence suggests, even so, that the twelfth-century infirmary hall at Ely must have been a remarkable building. Nine bays long, with elaborately carved arcading, it gave on to an ornate chapel, and measured in all no less than 58 metres in length.[30] Only three substantial pillars, known to have been 'highly enriched' with elaborately carved and painted capitals, now testify to the splendour and size of the infirmary constructed by Prior Hoxne and Bishop Turbe at Norwich shortly after a fire of 1171 had destroyed the original hall. Despite the damage inflicted on the fabric during the riots of 1272 and even more extensively after the Dissolution, this 'glorious pile' continued to impress observers until its demolition in 1804 (Plate 3).[31]

Such spacious accommodation was needed not simply for monks with acute or chronic diseases, injuries or other incapacitating disabilities, but also for day patients, who had been prescribed rest and a special diet but did not require nursing round the clock. At Bury St Edmunds, and quite probably most other large monasteries, part of the infirmary (to the west) was reserved for long-stay patients. Having already been hospitalised for a year without evident improvement, each had secured a special licence from the abbot to remain.[32] Most of them would have been elderly members of the community (*stagiarii*), towards whom monastic rules showed con-

priory that the canons lacked expert help when they were sick: *Visitations of the Diocese of Norwich, 1492–1532*, ed. A. Jessopp, Camden Society, ns XLIII, 1888 (hereafter, *Visitations*), 286.

29 NRO, DCN 1/1/47, 55. Rougham's work at Norwich cathedral priory is not mentioned in *MPME*.

30 G. Coppack, *Fountains Abbey*, London 1993, 28, 59–61; A. Holton-Krayenbuhl, 'The Infirmary Complex at Ely', *Arch. Journ.* cliv, 1997 (hereafter 'Infirmary at Ely'), 118–72, at pp. 127–37.

31 W. Buston, 'The Monastic Infirmary, Norwich', *NA* xxviii, 1945, 124–32.

32 *The Customary of the Benedictine Abbey of Bury St Edmunds in Suffolk*, ed. A. Gransden, London 1973 (hereafter *Customary of Bury St Edmunds*), 15. For infirmaries in general, see S. Rubin, *Medieval English Medicine*, London 1974, chapter VII, and Lord Amulree, 'Monastic Infirmaries', in *The Evolution of Hospitals in Britain*, ed. F.N.L. Poynter, London 1964, 11–26.

Plate 3. The last days of the infirmary of Norwich cathedral priory, conveyed somewhat fancifully in a watercolour of about 1804 by John Crome. *Reproduced by kind permission of Norfolk Museums Service.*

siderable solicitude. One of the more benign miracles ascribed to William of Norwich concerned brother Thomas, the priory's oldest monk, who lay sleepless and 'inflicted by long debility' in the infirmary. Later generations of *stagiarii* were allowed treats and 'recreations': in 1453–54, for example, the infirmarer spent 4s 2d on special meals for them and their friends. The proximity of young boys, perhaps from the almonry, must also have enlivened their days. At various points in the fifteenth century, mattresses (*dongges et flockis*) were bought for youngsters who shared the same quarters as the sick, possibly helping to look after them in return for board and lodging. As was certainly the case at Bury St Edmunds and elsewhere, the Norwich monks seem to have brought their own bedding with them when they entered the infirmary, but a laundress was available to keep it clean.[33]

The elaborate and sophisticated system of water supply and waste disposal serving the infirmary of Fountains abbey belies many long-held assumptions about

33 Thomas of Monmouth, *William of Norwich*, 134–5; NRO, DCN 1/10/11–13, 23; *Customary of Bury St Edmunds*, 80.

the squalor of medieval life. It is harder to determine how effective sanitation may have been in East Anglian monasteries, although there is enough evidence to suggest that steps were taken to provide infirmaries with clean water and the means of eliminating sewage. Situated on the banks of the river Linnet, the infirmary complex at Bury St Edmunds boasted a well, garderobe chute and cesspit.[34] The Norwich infirmarer's accounts likewise reveal the presence of a well and latrines, although these were not always adequately maintained. It was after a sojourn in the infirmary, in 1454–55, that John de Elingham, sometime chamberlain of the cathedral priory, gave 15s towards work on the adjacent *domus necessariorum*, which clearly needed serious attention. The cost of cleansing and repairing the masonry of the latrines, great gutter and pavement came to over 52s in labour and materials; new seats were constructed by a local carpenter; iron latches, keys and window frames provided greater security; and the four windows were reglazed. The loss of infirmarer's accounts for the next five years makes it impossible to tell if this marked the start of major improvements to the adjacent waste disposal system, but the master mason, John Everard, was still busy on a new 'gotyer' near the infirmary in 1460.[35]

Concern about the elimination of sewage and avoidance of noisome smells assumed particular urgency during epidemics, which took a formidable toll on urban monasteries.[36] The first outbreak of plague, in 1349–50, had a devastating impact in both town and country throughout East Anglia, searing itself into the collective memory of religious communities across the region. In July 1349 alone Bishop Bateman of Norwich was obliged to confirm no fewer than eleven new superiors in houses devastated by pestilence. Elections could not then be held at either Mountjoy or Hickling, or subsequently at Pentney, Alnesbourn, Letheringham and

[34] A.B. Whittingham, 'Bury St Edmunds Abbey: The Plan, Design and Development of the Church and Monastic Buildings', *Arch. Journ.* cviii, 1951 (hereafter 'Bury St Edmunds Abbey'), 168–87, at p. 181. For monastic sanitation in general, see G. Coppack, *Abbeys and Priories*, London 1990, chapter IV.

[35] NRO, DCN 1/10/22, 24, 25. In 1464–65 Everard mended the door and aqueduct in the latrines and cleaned them out: DCN 1/10/26. For Elingham see J. Greatrex, *Biographical Register of the English Cathedral Priories of the Province of Canterbury c. 1066–1540*, Oxford 1997 (hereafter *Biographical Register*), 504.

[36] See B. Harvey, *Living and Dying in England 1100–1540: The Monastic Experience*, Oxford 1993 (hereafter *Living and Dying*), chapter IV, for the impact of disease at Westminster abbey and Christ Church, Canterbury; and J.A. Gribbin, 'Health and Disease in the English Charterhouses: A Preliminary Study', in *Die Kartäuser und die Künste ihrer Zeit*, ed. J. Hogg, A. Girard and D. Le Blévec, Analecta Cartusiana CLVII, 2001, 197–209, for Carthusian attitudes to hygiene. Awareness of the dangers to health of smells and dirt was not, however, a phenomenon new to the fourteenth century. The cartulary of Wherwell abbey, Hampshire, contains a striking account of the sanitary reforms of the Abbess Euphemia (d.1257). She built a large infirmary at some distance from the main complex, along with a 'dorter and other necessary offices'. A culverted watercourse ran beneath the infirmary, 'through which a stream flowed with sufficient force to carry off all refuse that might corrupt the air'. Recreational space, adorned with vines and trees, was provided for the nuns 'to enjoy the pure air': *VCH Hampshire II*, 133.

Chipley because no-one had survived to cast a vote.[37] Indeed, at Hickling three priors died in quick succession, the last actually expiring at the moment news of his election was brought to his sickbed in the infirmary.[38] The complement of monks at Bury St Edmunds fell from eighty in 1260 to forty-seven in 1381, while the Premonstratensian canons at Langley lost about a third of their community over roughly the same period.[39] Other epidemics, such as the sweating sickness, could be just as terrible. In about 1506, for example, all the remaining Augustinian canons at Creake abbey, Norfolk, were carried off by an 'infectious or epidemical disease', leaving only the old prior who died shortly afterwards without anyone left to succeed him.[40] Not surprisingly, the chronicler of Butley priory, constantly alive to the 'periodic shadow of pestilence, famine and flood', gave heartfelt thanks in his entry for 1528 that God had spared his community the 'sudor pestilentia' then sweeping England.[41] Having, meanwhile, buried approximately half their number in the 1349–50 plague epidemic, and seen the nearby Dominicans 'wiped out almost to a man', the Norwich Benedictines clearly took to heart the account in the Book of Revelation of plague-bearing angels with their 'seven golden vials full of the wrath of God'. The celebrated Apocalypse cycle of bosses in the cathedral cloister contains several on this theme: the terror portrayed on the faces of the victims – most striking among whom is a tonsured monk prostrate in a sea of blood – reflects in graphic detail the 'noisome and grievous sore' inflicted upon the priory.[42]

More eloquent still is the incomplete annual account compiled by the infirmarer, Ralph de Swanton, which terminates abruptly in an ominous blank space shortly before 11 July 1349, when he evidently died. A young monk lacking any administrative background stepped in to fill the breach for a short but difficult time. His more experienced successor, John de Hederset, noted that some receipts had been tendered in 'false money', further evidence of dislocation being apparent in the theft of 52s from his coffers and the unusually heavy balance of over £27 in unspent receipts carried over from one year to the next. Hederset, who had moved from the almonry at short notice, relinquished office suddenly on 24 December 1350, to concentrate upon the second post (as pittancer) he had been obliged to assume in September.[43] A sense of hopelessness in the face of overwhelming disaster, together with an understandable reluctance to question the judgement of God upon sinners,

37 *The Register of William Bateman, I*, ed. P.E. Pobst, Canterbury and York Society LXXXIV, 1996, pp. xxxi–xxxii.

38 *Chronica Johannis de Oxenedes*, ed. H. Ellis, RS 1859, 437.

39 D. Knowles and R.N. Hadcock, *Medieval Religious Houses, England and Wales*, 2nd edn, London 1971, 61, 190.

40 J. Nichols, *History and Antiquities of the County of Leicester*, 3 vols, London 1795–1804, ii, 551.

41 *The Register or Chronicle of Butley Priory, Suffolk, 1510–1535*, ed. A.G. Dickens, Winchester 1951, 22, 54.

42 C. Harper-Bill, 'The English Church and English Religion after the Black Death', in *The Black Death in England*, ed. W.M. Ormrod and P.G. Lindley, Stamford 1996, 97; M. Rose, *The Norwich Apocalypse*, Norwich 1999, 122–46.

43 NRO, DCN 1/10/7, 8. For Hederset and his predecessor, Alexander de Castre, see Greatrex, *Biographical Register*, 491, 518–19.

probably explains his apparent failure to augment the convent's medical supplies. He did, however, purchase half a pound of saffron on assuming office, this being considered a valuable prophylactic against infections such as plague. A comparatively expensive commodity, it was cultivated from at least 1460 onwards by the infirmarer, who must sometimes have been tempted to corner the supply for his own use. Denis Hyndolveston, who held office in 1492, was criticised on this score, although his general neglect of the sick aroused far greater resentment.[44]

Just as in the medieval hospital, the high altar or chapel where Mass was celebrated at least once a day offered a promise of spiritual health to sick monks, and was thus the focal point of any infirmary complex.[45] The layout of the Cluniac houses at Thetford and Castle Acre and of the Benedictine monasteries at Ely, Norwich and Bury St Edmunds reveals that such chapels were often spacious and impressive.[46] The celebration of the liturgy, a vital element in the quotidian life of all religious, required a decent provision of lights, plate, vestments and service books, for which the infirmarer or his clerk remained responsible. Might an organ or other musical instruments be provided as a further adjunct to medical treatment? Medieval therapeutics placed great importance on the value of music in raising the spirits, and it is interesting to note that the customal of St Augustine's abbey, Canterbury, allowed sick monks who wished to enjoy the uplifting sounds and harmony of sacred melodies to do so in the seclusion of the infirmary chapel.[47] Professed religious were not, however, the only beneficiaries of such rituals. The dedication of the new infirmary chapel at the priory of Stoke by Clare, Suffolk, in 1225, was a notable occasion marked not only by the presence of Bishop Goldcliffe of Llandaff but also of numerous donors attracted by the promise of a fifteen days' indulgence in return for financial support. A grant of land made to the infirmary at about this time by Robert Sorel of Stoke was undoubtedly prompted by the hope that he might secure even greater benefits in the life to come. Right up to the Dissolution, anniversary masses were sung by the Thetford Cluniacs in their early thirteenth-century infirmary chapel, which lay to the north of a discrete cloister or 'monastery in miniature' reserved for the sick and elderly. Ordinations were conducted there by the suffragan

44 NRO, DCN 1/10/25 (in 1464–65 surplus supplies were sold by the infirmarer on the open market: DCN 1/10/26); *Visitations*, 4, 6.

45 See C. Rawcliffe, *Medicine for the Soul: The Life, Death and Resurrection of an English Medieval Hospital*, Stroud 1999 (hereafter *Medicine for the Soul*), chapter IV, for a discussion of the impact of the liturgy upon hospital design, and *Observances*, 204–5, for the centrality of the Mass.

46 M. Thompson, *The Medieval Hall*, Aldershot 1995, 64–5, 67; Holton-Krayenbuhl, 'Infirmary at Ely', 127, 130, 132–3; Whittingham, 'Bury St Edmunds Abbey', 181. Buston's puzzlement as to what lay to the east of 'the great arch' in the Norwich infirmary ('Monastic Infirmary, Norwich', 131) is easily solved: it had opened into a large chapel.

47 *Customary of the Benedictine Monasteries of Saint Augustine, Canterbury, and Saint Peter Westminster, I*, ed. E. Maunde-Thompson, London 1902 (hereafter *Customary of the Benedictine Monasteries*), 329. See also C. Page, 'Music as Medicine in the Thirteenth Century', in *Music as Medicine: The History of Music Therapy since Antiquity*, ed. P. Horden, Aldershot 2000, 110–11.

bishop of Ely in 1518–19, against a background which appears from the surviving remains to have been both decorative and imposing.[48]

For monastic patrons such as William the Sheriff, whose endowment of the infirmary of Sibton abbey in the previous century was undertaken specifically *pro salute anime mee*, the equation between the physical care of monks and the *salus* (both health and salvation) of their own immortal souls was clear cut and incontrovertible.[49] Indeed, during a fund-raising campaign of 1310–11, the infirmarer of Bury St Edmunds promised benefactors that their names would be entered in the *martyrologium* of the abbey as well as the infirmary's own missal, thus offering a secure guarantee of perpetual commemoration. Usually modest in size, these gifts of land or annual rents helped to supplement more substantial revenues from appropriated livings and were sometimes earmarked for specific purposes. On this occasion, it was hoped to generate enough money to provide candles for the common table used by ambulant monks in the infirmary, presumably when they were being phlebotomised or otherwise allowed to withdraw from the refectory.[50] If the surviving deeds are any guide, the residents of Norwich and its environs were considerably less forthcoming in their support for the infirmary than they were for the almonry of the cathedral priory, which helped the sick poor and thus seemed to perform a more immediately practical – and visible – work of charity. Its few benefactors, such as William de Stoke, a cleric who conveyed property in Bracondale to the infirmarer in 1319, may perhaps have served him in some secular capacity. Oliver Wyth of Great Yarmouth, who left rents of 13s 4d a year or a cash sum of £6 13s 4d in lieu to the infirmarer of Carrow priory, to the south-east of Norwich, in 1291 'for the solace of feeble ladies and the infirm' was certainly familiar with the house, since two of his own daughters were nuns there.[51]

Even in comparatively wealthy houses, such as Norwich cathedral priory or Bury St Edmunds abbey, extra support of this kind could make an appreciable difference. The monastic infirmarers of East Anglia customarily worked within tight financial margins, and in monetary terms, at least, ranked among the lesser obedientiaries. At the abbey of St Benet Holme, during the mid-fourteenth century, for example, the infirmarer's annual receipts never rose above £18 and were usually less than half this amount, while the cellarer's fluctuated between £225 and £167.[52] At just under £38

[48] *Stoke-by-Clare Cartulary*, ed. C. Harper-Bill and R. Mortimer, 3 vols, Suffolk Charters IV–VI, Suffolk Records Society 1982–84, i, no. 103; ii, no. 645; *The Register of Thetford Priory*, ed. D. Dymond, 2 vols, NRS LIX and LX, 1994–96 (hereafter *Register Thetford*), i, 22, 28, 97; ii, 357, 371; F.J.E. Raby and P.K. Baillie Reynolds, *Thetford Priory*, London 1979, 6.

[49] *Sibton Abbey Cartularies and Charters*, ed. P. Brown, 4 vols, Suffolk Charters VII–X, Suffolk Records Society 1985–88, iii, no. 473.

[50] BL MS Lansdowne 416, fos 17r–17v.

[51] NRO, DCN 44/16/9–10 (see C. Rawcliffe, *The Hospitals of Medieval Norwich*, Norwich 1995, 26–7, for an analysis of charitable giving to and by the cathedral priory); P. Rutledge, 'The Will of Oliver Wyth', in *Norfolk Record Society Miscellany*, ed. *idem* and others, NRS LVI, 1991, 20. The infirmary at Carrow lay to the east of the precinct: R. Gilchrist and M. Oliva, *Religious Women in Medieval East Anglia*, Norwich 1993, 41.

[52] NRO, DN/EST 13/4.

in 1312–13 and a relatively healthy £35 a century later, the Norwich infirmarer's income held up quite well under the strains of the late fourteenth-century economic crisis. Yet although he spent a mere fraction of the priory's annual receipts of around £2,200 a year, he was vulnerable to draconian cuts once recession really began to bite. His own stipend was halved to 10s a year in 1467–68, 'propter exilitatem officii', the rapidly declining revenues at his disposal (a mere £13 in 1482–83) necessitating the stringent economies which caused so much irritation when the priory was inspected by its episcopal visitors.[53] In keeping with their modest budgets, monastic infirmarers retained a small staff of employees, which contrasts sharply with the large establishments run by the wealthier obedientiaries. During the late thirteenth century, the infirmarer at Bury St Edmunds was allowed his own servant, a cook (who prepared special dishes for the sick), a *minutorius*, a keeper or warden, a dish-washer, a hearth-keeper, a door-keeper and a *claviger*, who was responsible for general security. His department was approximately one tenth the strength of that run by the cellarer.[54]

The complement at Norwich comprised four or five attendants (including a keeper, laundress, boy and clerk of the chapel), but provision was not made for a cook. Since, in accordance with general monastic practice, the infirmary boasted its own kitchen (situated in 1467–68 next to the parlour), we may assume that culinary staff were supplied from elsewhere. Of all the East Anglian houses, evidence about personnel is by far the best for the cathedral priory, where the names of no fewer than twenty-eight infirmarers serving between 1309 and 1532 are known.[55] Because of gaps in the surviving accounts we cannot tell when six of their number actually held office, let alone for how long, although it looks very much as if four others did so for less than a year. The rapid turnover is striking. Only Richard Marsham (1474–84), who died in office, and William de Thetford (1394–1408) apparently occupied the post for a decade or more, albeit in the latter case with occasional breaks to allow for other duties. Continuity and expertise may have been provided by the keeper, who probably undertook most of the routine care of patients and *stagiarii*. It is, however, significant that fourteen infirmarers (exactly half of the

53 NRO, DCN 1/10/1–38. *Status obedientiariorum*, or statements of the priory's finances, of which six survive (DCN 1/13/1–6), were compiled every year, showing the income and expenditure of each office.

54 BL MS Harley 3977, fos 29v–30r, 32r, 104v, 107r–107v.

55 Geoffrey de Totyngton* (1309–13), Ralph de Betele (1316–17), John de Clipesby* (bef. 1345), Peter de Donewich (1345), Ralph de Swanton* (1345–49), Alexander de Castre (1349), John de Hederset (1349–50), John de Kirkeby (1387–94), William de Thetford (1394–1408), Thomas de Hyndringham (1422), Thomas de Corpusty (bef. 1433), Thomas Cawmbrygge (1427–35), Robert de Jernmuth* (1440–41), Nicholas Burgate (1453–54), John de Fornesete* (1454–55), John Palgrave (1460–61), William Fode (bef. 1464), John de Lenn (1464–65), Richard Salthouse (1467–68), Richard Marsham (1474–84), William de Lenn (1484), Denis Hyndolveston* (1492), Simon de Lenn (1496–97), Thomas Swafham (1497–98), Robert Mutford* (bef. 1511), Nicholas Bedyngham (1511–18), Henry Manuell (1526–29), Thomas Sall (1532). Names derived from NRO, DCN 1/10/1–38 and Greatrex, *Biographical Register, sub nomine*. Monks who studied at Oxford or Cambridge universities are starred.

entire group) were appointed towards the very end of busy and hitherto demanding monastic careers. Nicholas Bedyngham (1511–18) was actually described as 'senex et surdus' shortly after being replaced, and may not have been unusual in serving at a relatively advanced age.[56] Few infirmarers were young: the appointment of the untried Alexander de Castre in 1349 occurred during a period of crisis occasioned by the plague, and reflects the extremity of the situation then facing the community. The demands of office were quite clearly different from those made in departments with high revenues and heavy administrative responsibilities, where financial acumen and energy stood at a premium. Often barely distinguishable from one of his elderly patients, the ideal infirmarer personified calm reassurance, not least because he himself had survived for so long. As we shall see, possession of the qualities of patience, solicitude and piety expected of those who tended the sick and dying presupposed a lengthy sojourn in the vale of tears. Indeed, at Ely, in 1300, Bishop Walpole ruled that this work was to be carried out humbly and diligently 'per ministros fideles et maturos'.[57]

Such concerns went hand in hand with other developments. A reduction in the size of monastic communities, coupled with the desire for greater privacy and comfort, led to the creation in the fourteenth and fifteenth centuries of individual chambers or even suites of rooms in what had previously been shared communal space. Reflecting, if not actually anticipating, a trend apparent in many long-established English hospitals, where open wards and dormitories were being partitioned into cubicles for elderly corrodians, this move towards an 'almshouse' model is evident in several late medieval monastic infirmaries. At Ely, for example, it is possible to reconstruct in remarkable detail the creation of private dwellings with fireplaces in what had been the north and south aisles of the infirmary hall and chapel. Some occupied two storeys and one even had its own garderobe, suggesting that the residents may well have been royal placemen or elderly obedientiaries accustomed to a more pampered existence.[58] Although archaeological evidence remains wanting for Norwich, the documentary sources reveal that similar building works were begun just before the first outbreak of plague. Between 1346 and 1348 the infirmarer purchased two fothers of lead, 500 corner-stones, forty-eight wooden posts, 500 pounds of Spanish iron, sixty-one ells of canvas and 600 pieces of wainscot, while also recording a modest outlay on the construction of at least one small chamber. We know that a brother named Henry Prior occupied a room of his own in the infirmary in 1479–80; and that, during his inspection of 1514, Bishop Nykke was

56 *Visitations*, 193.

57 *Ely Chapter Ordinances and Visitation Records 1241–1515*, ed. J.A. Evans, Camden Society Miscellany, 3rd series XVII, 1940 (hereafter *Ely Chapter Ordinances*), 17; D. Nebbiai-Dalla Guarda, 'Les livres de l'infirmerie dans les monastères médiévaux', *Revue Mabillon*, ns V, lxvi, 1994, 66–7.

58 Holton-Krayenbuhl, 'Infirmary at Ely', 149–54. The infirmary cloister range at Thetford priory had likewise been converted into comfortable private rooms with fireplaces by the end of the fifteenth century: *Register Thetford*, i, 97; Raby and Baillie Reynolds, *Thetford Priory*, 6. See also Coppack, *Fountains Abbey*, 71–2.

disturbed by the frequency with which outsiders strayed from the prescribed confines of the infirmary parlour to pay personal calls on monks in their quarters.[59]

Notwithstanding the trend towards greater seclusion, certain 'intolerable' diseases which appeared contagious or unusually repugnant demanded the isolation or even removal of patients to extra-mural hospitals. Most, if not all, of the numerous leper houses run under the auspices of English monasteries received infected monks, nuns or priests, whose continued presence was regarded with alarm by their communities. Places at St Michael's hospital, Whitby, St Laurence's, Canterbury, and St Margaret's, Taunton, for example, were set aside for neighbouring religious afflicted with leprosy, while Abbot Geoffrey of St Albans (d.1146) endowed a *leprosarium* where monks and servants of his monastery might follow a religious rule. A second hospital for nuns was established by one of his successors at the end of the twelfth century.[60] Priests celebrating in the charnel at Bury St Edmunds who succumbed to any contagious disease were admitted, from 1301 onwards, into the monastic leper house of St Peter's, just outside the town gates. According to an entry in the abbey's *Liber Albus*, Benedictine brothers with leprosy either went there too or entered another extra mural refuge, founded by Abbot Northwold in 1215 for the sick poor. Whatever their destination, they continued to receive all the customary privileges accorded to sick monks until they died. Although, contrary to general practice regarding the interment of lepers, they were then allowed burial in the monastic cemetery, the funeral itself was to be a modest and speedy affair, celebrated by only six monks at the hospital, in order to minimise the presumed dangers of infection.[61] Senior religious, such as Abbot Wallingford of St Albans (d.1336), ended their days more comfortably in special accommodation, but the need for proper diagnosis to determine whether or not an individual was, indeed, leprous remained paramount.[62] Before permitting Richard Walsham, a hitherto assiduous obedientary, to live apart as a hermit at the cell of St Leonard's on Mousehold Heath, Prior Molet of Norwich insisted that he undergo exhaustive medical tests to resolve any doubts occasioned by certain suspicious 'infirmities'. To this end, he summoned a number of learned and experienced physicians and surgeons, who analysed Walsham's urine and examined him carefully on several occasions for all the recognised signs and symptoms associated with leprosy. He was pronounced entirely free of the disease shortly before January 1456. Clinical diagnoses of this kind, undertaken according to precise and detailed guidelines, were already quite common in continental Europe, but are rarely documented in England.[63] That the favourable outcome of

59 NRO, DCN 1/10/5, 6, 29; *Visitations*, 77, 79.

60 *VCH Yorkshire III*, 334; W. Somer, *Antiquities of Canterbury*, London 1703, 38; *Materials*, i, 428–31; BL MS Cotton, Nero D I, fos 188r–192v; Thomas Walsingham, *Gesta Abbatum Monasterii Sancti Albani*, ed. H.T. Riley, 3 vols, RS 1867–69 (hereafter *Gesta*), i, 200–5; ii, 503–10.

61 *VCH Suffolk II*, 135; *Customary of Bury St Edmunds*, appendix VIII.

62 *Gesta*, ii, 193, 199, 207–8, 284–96.

63 NRO, DCN 35/7; L. Demaitre, 'The Description and Diagnosis of Leprosy by Fourteenth-Century Physicians', *Bulletin of the History of Medicine* lix, 1985, 327–44. Walsham's case may be compared with that of Joan Nightingale of Brentwood, Essex: *CCR, 1468–76*, 30–1.

these consultations was formally recorded by the prior, and certified in writing by his team of medical experts, shows how far the fear of leprosy and other noisome diseases had been intensified by an even greater terror of plague. For his own protection, Walsham needed to explain exactly why he had elected to withdraw from the communal life.

Unlike their leprous brethren, the majority of monks who qualified for admittance to an infirmary were deemed responsive to medical attention. What could they expect in the way of treatment? In a world before 'scientific' medicine as it is understood today, when knowledge of human physiology was inevitably circumscribed, a holistic approach to sickness and health dominated practice as well as theory. In this respect the Classical Greek emphasis upon moderation and self-control accorded well with Christian teachings and ensured that medical texts on the proper management of the body, the *Regimen Sanitatis*, would find an avid readership in religious as well as secular society. Many *regimina* derived from the *Secreta Secretorum*, a treatise of Arab origin, which offered accessible advice about avoiding illness, and of which the Norwich Benedictines possessed at least one copy. Their library also included a book on diet and the *Questiones Physicorum*, another practical guide to man's place in the cosmos and its effects upon his health.[64] The fundamental principle from which all forms of therapy derived was the need to keep the four bodily humours (choler, phlegm, black bile and blood) in a state of equilibrium. In order to tread the tightrope between deficiency and excess, six external factors, known as non-naturals, had to be carefully regulated. Since it was believed that the humours were generated from food and drink through a cooking process in the stomach, diet remained the most important of the non-naturals, being universally recognised as 'the first instrument of medicine'. This was why St Benedict permitted the eating of meat 'to the sick and the very weak, that they may recover their strength', and thus sanctioned the breach of what in theory, if decreasingly in practice, constituted a strict vegetarian rule.[65] One reason, besides convenience, for having a kitchen and cook in the infirmary was so that otherwise prohibited dishes could be prepared separately for invalids according to the recommendations of an attendant physician or some other person with medical knowledge. But such concessions were bought at a price. As the Bury St Edmunds customary reveals, however legitimate the reason, monks who temporarily abandoned the dietary and liturgical rules of their order could only be readmitted after abasing themselves as penitents and seeking absolution. Nor was permission to enter the infirmary, especially as an in-patient, accorded lightly.[66]

Diagnosis was principally achieved through uroscopy, or the examination of urine, an extremely sophisticated procedure which enabled the specialist to establish

64 N.R. Ker, *Monastic Libraries of Great Britain*, 2nd edn, London 1964 (hereafter *Monastic Libraries*), 137; H.C. Beeching and M.R. James, 'The Library of the Cathedral Church of Norwich', *NA* xix, 1917, 109–10. For the *Secreta* see Getz, *Medicine*, 53–64, and for the *Questiones* L. García-Ballester's 'Introduction' to *Practical Medicine from Salerno to the Black Death*, ed. *idem*, Cambridge 1994 (hereafter *Practical Medicine*), 17–21.

65 *Rule of St Benedict*, 260.

66 *Customary of Bury St Edmunds*, 14–15.

exactly what food, medication or manual operation would best serve to restore the humours to a more balanced state. At Norwich between 1421 and 1455, for instance, Master Mark, a physician, was paid 13s 4d a year 'pro inspeccione urinarum' in the infirmary, earning quite substantial sums in addition for prescribing clysters and laxatives to remove potentially life-threatening impurities.[67] Under normal circumstances the infirmarer would have used purgatives made of herbs and other domestic ingredients for routine prophylactic as well as curative purposes. The medieval fear of constipation, intensified no doubt in monasteries where food was often high in protein and low in fibre, sprang from concern over the effective elimination of corrupt humours. Prominent among the other non-naturals, 'evacuation and repletion' also included bathing, a staple of the *Regimen Sanitatis* and one of only two specific recommendations made by St Benedict for the treatment of sick monks. His advice was, however, regarded with some ambivalence by early English monastic communities, whose members were concerned about the underlying moral dangers of such a decadent practice. Even the Saint, who grew up in a society where public baths played a major part in daily life, took care to restrict this indulgence to the elderly, ailing and infirm. The ever watchful Archbishop Lanfranc (d.1098) had permitted healthy monks and boys at Christ Church, Canterbury, no more than three carefully supervised ablutions a year. These preceded the major Christian festivals of Christmas, Easter and the Annunciation (25 March), the ritual aspect of cleansing being far more important than considerations of hygiene or comfort.[68]

Sin as well as dirt was to be washed away, making it especially important that the warmth and conviviality of the bath-house should not engender the vices of sloth or *luxuria*, and thus poison the soul with 'secret foulness'.[69] Herbert de Losinga (d.1119), first bishop of Norwich and founder of the cathedral priory, exercised great vigilance on this score, writing to admonish one of his more sybaritic monks:

> I have been given to understand . . . that you are repeating your violation of discipline, and have returned again to your old habit of indolence: you are . . . seldom seen in the cloister, often in the parlours; slow in resorting to the church, swift in resorting to the grange, and the public roads which skirt it; *you are constantly getting leave to have your blood let, constantly getting leave to have a bath*. You are indulging your body, you are ruining your soul, and not only yours, but perchance also some of those souls which I had entrusted to your care . . .[70]

Even though the sick might immerse themselves with a clear conscience, sweating out humoral impurities or simply gaining a few moments of blissful relief from pain in a world without effective analgesics, scrupulous brethren were still disposed to

67 NRO, DCN 1/10/14–24.

68 *The Monastic Constitutions of Lanfranc*, ed. D. Knowles, London 1951, 9–10, 26, 62.

69 The customal of St Augustine's Canterbury, composed in about 1334, stipulated that the convent might bathe twice a year at Christmas and Whitsuntide. Permission was otherwise granted only in cases of infirmity or debility, 'et non pro affectu voluptatis, sed pro remedio et cura salutis': *Customary of the Benedictine Monasteries*, i, 200.

70 *The Life Letters and Sermons of Herbert de Losinga*, ed. E.M. Goulburn and H. Symonds, 2 vols, Oxford 1878 (hereafter *Letters of Herbert de Losinga*), i, 105–10.

question the propriety of obeying medical advice which might endanger their spiritual health. The Augustinian canons at Barnwell, Cambridgeshire, were ordered to bathe 'without grumbling when instructed to do so by a physician' and obediently to follow expert advice.[71] At Norwich cathedral priory, on the other hand, attitudes to bodily comfort relaxed considerably over the years. 'Murmurings' about the lack of tubs and other facilities for bathing and shaving led the prior and senior monks to rule in 1379 that the brethren might wash whenever they wished. Here the cellarer recorded modest expenses in *balneatione fratrum*, whereas at Ely the chamberlain met the bill.[72] Situated on the south side of the infirmary garden, the bath-house at Ely boasted a piped water supply by 1288 and had been fitted with glass windows before the 1380s. It lay conveniently close to a fresh supply of the sweet smelling herbs and flowers which were customarily added to medieval baths as both a therapeutic and a prophylactic measure.[73]

Medieval responses to scent were infinitely more subtle and complex than our own, largely because smells were regarded as material substances, existing in a vaporous state somewhere between water and air. Once inhaled, they immediately began to affect the vital and animal spirits, which were seated, respectively, in the heart and in the brain, and they could thus be administered to strengthen, nourish and restore the entire body. Just as all medical and culinary preparations were graded according to their relative heat, coldness, moisture or aridity, so smells also appeared to possess similar qualities.[74] 'Cool' aromas, such as rose or violet, were prescribed to rectify complaints occasioned by too much blood or choler, while an excess of phlegmatic or melancholic humours could be addressed through the use of mint, aloes and other 'hotter' scents.[75] On the assumption that 'good' scents drove away corrupt, disease-bearing air, perfumed candles and fumigants were widely deployed in medieval society, especially after plague became endemic in the mid-fourteenth century.[76] It is worth noting at this point that one of the reasons for building such lofty infirmary halls on the scale apparent at Ely, Norwich and Bury St Edmunds was to allow the free circulation of air, and thus prevent the accumulation of potentially lethal miasmas.

Scented oils, essences and waters could either be purchased ready-made from an

71 *Observances*, 15. Walter Daniel, biographer of the saintly Cistercian abbot, Ailred of Rievaulx (d.1167), felt moved to justify the regimen of baths necessitated by his various ailments: *The Life of Ailred of Rievaulx*, ed. F.M. Powicke, London 1950, 34, 55.

72 *Customary of Norwich*, 243; *Letters of Herbert de Losinga*, i, 109. Harvey, *Living and Dying*, 133–4.

73 Holton-Krayenbuhl, 'Infirmary at Ely', 165, 168 and map on p. 161; Stewart, *Architectural History of Ely*, 273–4, notes that one of the priory gates was called the 'ostium versus balnearium'.

74 R. Palmer, 'In Bad Odour: Smell and its Significance in Medicine from Antiquity to the Seventeenth Century', in *Medicine and the Five Senses*, ed. W.F. Bynum and R. Porter, Cambridge 1993, 61–8.

75 For example, in Bodleian Library, Oxford, MS Ashmole 1438, the rose is described as 'cold and drye in two degrees' (p. 83), the violet as 'colde and moiste in two degrees' (p. 85), and calamint as 'hoot and drye in two degrees and so seythe Gaylen . . .' (p. 86).

76 C. Classen, D. Howes and A. Synott, *The Cultural History of Smell*, London 1994, 61–6, 71.

apothecary or produced *in situ*, using herbs and flowers grown by the infirmarer in his own garden or cultivated in other parts of the precinct.[77] Archaeological finds from monastic sites at Kirkstall, Pontefract and Selborne suggest that each of these houses possessed the equipment necessary for sublimation and distillation, which were widely practised in late medieval England.[78] That the Norwich infirmarers were able to keep the priory supplied with fortified waters, oils and tinctures is evident not only from their regular expenditure on glass phials (also used for uroscopy), flasks, pots and other storage vessels,[79] but additionally from the numerous references to distillation equipment which appear in the fifteenth-century accounts. The acquisition of a new alembic weighing 25 pounds, in 1420–21, was marked by the construction of a clay-built furnace, fuelled, as later sources reveal, by Broadland peat. Protective clothing of sorts may have been worn by the monk or servant who actually worked the equipment, as in 1464–65 a special tunic (*tabardum*) was bought for the *domus stillatoriorum*. Nothing more is heard of this workshop or its contents after 1484, when the alembics were repaired and a supply of 1,500 turves was bought to heat them.[80] Complaints about declining standards of care, discussed below, seem to be substantiated in the late fifteenth- and early sixteenth-century accounts, which suggest that the infirmarer had abandoned some of his earlier responsibilities.

Since so many foodstuffs, ranging from garlic and onions to honey and almonds, were deemed to possess important therapeutic qualities, any distinction between *medicina cibalis* and *medicina medicinalis* (food and medication) broke down in practice. This is notably the case with regard to the use of electuaries, which were thick, syrupy concoctions taken after or during meals both as digestives and correctives for disordered humours. Sugar had been added to the classical pharmacopoeia by the Arabs, who thus made palatable a variety of animal, mineral and vegetable products which, in their natural state, were disagreeable to the human palate.[81]

77 For the infirmary garden at Norwich see C. Noble, 'Norwich Cathedral Priory Gardeners' Accounts', in *Farming and Gardening in Late Medieval Norfolk*, ed. *eadem*, C. Moreton and P. Rutledge, NRS LXI, 1997, 6–9; and for that at Westminster abbey, J.H. Harvey, 'Westminster Abbey: The Infirmarer's Garden', *Garden History* x, 1992, 75–115 (although he mistakenly regards the surgeon, John of Ardern, as a monastic employee).

78 S. Moorhouse, 'Pottery and Glass in the Late Medieval Monastery', in *Advances in Monastic Archaeology*, ed. R. Gilchrist and H. Mytum, British Archaeological Reports, British Series CCXXVII, 1993, 127–48, at pp. 140–2; P. Murray Jones, *Medieval Medicine in Illuminated Manuscripts*, London and Milan 1998, 73–5.

79 References to such purchases occur in 21 of the 38 surviving account rolls: NRO, DCN 1/10/1–7, 11–16, 20–2, 24, 26, 29–31. In certain cases, as in 1344–45, 1432–33, 1434–35 and 1482–83, specific mention is made of vessels for storing waters (DCN 1/10/3, 20, 21, 30); in 1479–80 and 1482–84 these are 'per conservacionem aquarum stillatorum' (DCN 1/10/29, 30, 31). A fine example of a mortar made especially for the infirmary of St Mary's abbey, York, in 1308, appears in *Age of Chivalry: Art in Plantagenet England 1200–1400*, ed. J. Alexander and P. Binski, London 1987, no. 130.

80 NRO, DCN 1/10/14, 24, 26, 31. Another furnace was made in 1474–75, at a cost of 2s 6d (DCN 1/10/28).

81 Rawcliffe, *Medicine and Society*, 149–52. Norwich monks were individually well informed about diet, especially after the Black Death. One brother, possibly William Silton, copied a

Electuaries purchased ready-made by the infirmarer of St Benet Holme in 1285–86 contained, among other things, sandalwood (for bronchitis), cumin (for flatulence), gum arabic (for coughs), trifa sarazencia (a purgative), saffron and calamint (for chest complaints), none of which could have been consumed without sweetening.[82] The monks were attempting to redress the malign effects of their phlegmatic environment, made worse by a diet so reliant upon fish, through judicious humoral therapy. Being warm and moist, and therefore of a sanguine complexion, sugar was itself deemed perfect food for invalids, especially those with respiratory problems. But it was as a base for sweet, often highly scented quasi-medicinal preparations that most monastic supplies were used.[83] The infirmarers and masters of the cellar of Norwich cathedral priory and the sacristan at Ely, who generally bought all their own ingredients in bulk, laid in regular supplies of honey and sugar (sometimes scented with roses and violets) for this purpose.[84] Special purchases were frequently made for individual obedientiaries and senior monks: in 1308 alone, for example, the master of the cellar spent a not inconsiderable sum of 6s 2d on *triasandali* and other electuaries for Henry de Lakenham, the moribund prior of Norwich; and in 1366–67 Nicholas de Hoo, who had clearly been living too high on the hog while absent on official business, cost his successor almost 9s in remedies for an apparently serious digestive disorder.[85] In so far that they relieved a monotonous diet, and catered for the sweet medieval tooth, electuaries may well have promoted a real sense of wellbeing.

As the spice trade expanded to more distant and exotic markets, so the ingredients available to the monks of East Anglia grew infinitely more varied:

> Gynger, galingale,
> Cubibes, saffran,

tract of 1383–84 'pro sanitate corporis conservanda contra morbum pestilencialem' into a collection of devotional treatises: J. Greatrex, 'Horoscopes and Healing at Norwich Cathedral Priory in the Later Middle Ages', *The Church and Learning in Later Medieval Society: Essays in Honour of Barrie Dobson*, ed. C.M. Barron and J. Stratford, Stamford 2002 (hereafter 'Horoscopes'), forthcoming.

82 NRO, DN/EST 1/3. For a beginner's guide to electuaries, such as *diacalamentum* (prescribed for diseases of the chest caused by phlegmatic humours), see Bodleian Library, Oxford, MS Ashmole 346, fos 44v–48v.

83 A classic remedy for the cough, for example, comprised an ounce of rose-flavoured sugar, a quarter of clarified honey, a pound of liquorice, crushed in a mortar, a quarter of a pound of powdered ginger and a gallon of water, boiled together and strained through a cloth. To be drunk twice daily: Wellcome Institute Library, London, Western MS 408, fo. 62r.

84 Thus, for example, the master of the cellar of Norwich cathedral priory bought 60 pounds of sugar in 1309–10, 104 pounds in 1313–14, 109 pounds in 1314–15 and 264 pounds in 1320–21. The last of these purchases cost over £7 (NRO, DCN 1/1/21, 23, 24, 28). The infirmarer's purchases, including boxes for storing electuaries, are itemised in DCN 1/10/1–38. Those made by the sacristan at Ely are recorded in *Sacrist Rolls of Ely*, ed. F.R. Chapman, 2 vols, Cambridge 1907 (hereafter *Sacrist Rolls of Ely*), ii, 4, 17, 40, 53, 78; and at Thetford in *Register Thetford*, ii, index *sub* groceries.

85 NRO, DCN 1/1/19, 50; Greatrex, *Biographical Register*, 525, 531. Prior Lakenham had evidently been sick for some time as his medicine cost the master of the cellar 9s 3d in 1303–4 (DCN 1/1/17).

Pepre, comyne,
Sugre white and broun,
Flour of cammelle [cinnamon],
Anyse, graynes of paradys:
Of thise thinges be made confections
And good poudres
Whereof is made
Good suasses
And electuaries for medicines.[86]

Cost was apparently not an issue, at least in the case of leading members of a monastic community, such as John Fornesete, who ran up a personal bill of £3 on medication while he was prior of Lynn in 1440–41.[87] But in theory, at least, even the humblest choir monk could expect to benefit from the burgeoning pharmacopoeia. The regularity of illness in the lives of these men, whose communal existence made them especially vulnerable to infectious diseases, has been recognised by demographers. At Norwich up to thirty per cent of a community fluctuating in size between sixty-five (1348) and fifty (1504) resident monks might pass through the infirmary in any one year.[88] For some, such as Robert Cawston, who cost the infirmarer 21s 8d in medicines between 1427 and his death in 1430, this sad record of human suffering is all that remains to illuminate a short monastic career.[89] 'It should rarely or never happen', warned the Augustinian Observances at Barnwell, 'that [the infirmarer] has not ginger, cinnamon, peony and the like ready in his cupboard, so as to be able to render prompt assistance to the sick.'[90] All these commodities and the others listed above were readily available at Ely and Norwich, along with liquorice, fennel, rice, cloves, mace, cassia, aniseed, zedoary, poppy seeds, prunes, turbit, agaric, nutmeg, stomaticon (for sore mouths), frankincense, dragon's blood and other spices which we today associate with cookery rather than healing.[91] One

86 William Caxton, *Dialogues in French and English*, ed. H. Bradley, Early English Text Society, extra series LXXIX, 1900, 19–20.

87 NRO, DCN 2/1/36. He recovered and became infirmarer in 1454–55 (DCN 1/10/24).

88 Names and numbers of individual monks treated by the infirmarer are recorded in 20 of the 38 surviving accounts: 3 in 1312–13; 11 in 1344–45; 24 in 1345–46; 20 in 1346–47; 23 in 1347–48; 5 in the plague year 1349–50; 8 in 1421–22; 9 in 1427–28; 11 in 1428–29; 10 in 1429–30; 7 in 1430–31; 6 in 1431–32; 9 in 1432–33; 11 in 1434–35; 17 in 1440–41; 16 in 1453–54; 10 in 1454–55; 5 in 1464–65; 2 in 1467–68: NRO, DCN 1/10/1, 2, 4–7, 14–24, 26–7. Obedientiaries and other senior monks usually made separate provision for themselves.

89 NRO, DCN 1/10/15–17; Greatrex, *Biographical Register*, 494. For a detailed discussion of morbidity in a monastic community, see B. Harvey and J. Oeppen, 'Patterns of Morbidity in Late Medieval England: A Sample from Westminster Abbey', *EcHR* liv, 2001, pp. 215–39.

90 *Observances*, 203. At St Mary's abbey, York, the infirmarer was required to keep cumin, pepper, almonds, saffron and 'various spices and unguents necessary for the sick': *Chronicle of St Mary's Abbey, York*, ed. H.H.E. Craster and M.E. Thornton, Surtees Society CXLVIII, 1934, 98.

91 See above, note 84. A far wider range of medicaments was available at Westminster abbey, a richer house, with easy access to international markets: E.A. Hammond, 'The Westminster Abbey Infirmarers' Rolls as a Source of Medical History', *Bulletin of the History of Medicine* xxxix, 1965, 261–76.

remedy from the *Compendium Medicinae*, made by the celebrated English physician, Gilbertus Anglicus, in about 1240 and widely circulated in both Latin and English thereafter, will suffice as an example of the way in which the infirmarer used this *materia medica*. Recommended as 'a thing that purgeth alle humours of a mannes hede, and is gode for akyng of ioyntis, and for the potagre [arthritis], and for the dropsey', this compound would have been popular among communities of rheumatic East Anglian monks, whose lives had been spent in draughty stone buildings:[92]

> Take of salt armoniac [ammonium chloride] of cost 12 ounces; of black pepper 5 ounces; of cumin, ginger, white pepper, fennel, cinnamon, of each the same, 3 drachms; of cloves, zedoary, galingale, cubebes, cardamum, of each the same, 3 drachms; of hyssop, thyme, marjoram, caraway, aniseed, wild celery, parsley, lovage, of each one and a half ounces. Make a powder of all this and use it instead of salt with food. And if you wish to make it into a laxative as well, add to it 2 drachms of scammony and drink it with mead.[93]

But diet and drugs alone could not always be relied upon to discipline the wayward humours. Deployed as both a curative and prophylactic measure for centuries before Christ had been phlebotomised on the Cross to purge the sins of the world, bloodletting offered the most immediate means of restoring a healthy balance and ridding the body of corruption.[94] Although the theoretical literature on the subject grew increasingly scholarly and technical, the practice itself remained an *operatio manualis*, which required empirical rather than academic training.[95] A basic knowledge of astrology was, however, deemed essential. The importance of observing the heavens, and thus avoiding potentially inauspicious days for bleeding, was recognised in Anglo-Saxon England, where venesection was widely performed in communities of religious.[96] A fifteenth-century folding vellum calendar, which measures over seven feet in length when extended, but could easily have been carried in a purse or wallet by the *minutorius*, survives from the diocese of Norwich and incorporates much of this traditional lore.[97] It is typical of the kind of *vademecum* which the infirmarer's lay assistant would have used. On one side it presents in diagram-

[92] In 1532 the Augustinians at Butley priory complained that the refectory was so cold in winter that they were succumbing to this complaint and other conditions brought on in freezing temperatures. Bishop Nykke duly ordered improvements. The effect of cold on the health of elderly monks must have been pernicious: *Visitations*, 286.

[93] *Healing and Society in Medieval England: A Middle English Translation of the Pharmaceutical Writings of Gilbertus Anglicus*, ed. F.M. Getz, Wisconsin 1991, 9.

[94] For the theological resonances of phlebotomy, see Ziegler, *Medicine and Religion*, 105, 182–3; *The Ancrene Riwle*, ed. M.B. Salu, Exeter Medieval English Texts and Studies 1990, 50–2; and note 105 below.

[95] P. Gil-Sotres, 'Derivation and Revulsion: The Theory and Practice of Medieval Phlebotomy', in García-Ballester, *Practical Medicine*, 110–55, provides a comprehensive overview of theory and practice.

[96] W. Bonser, *The Medical Background of Anglo Saxon England: A Study in History, Psychology and Folklore*, London 1963, 294–9; *Bede's Ecclesiastical History*, ed. B. Colgrave and R.A.B. Mynors, Oxford 1969, 460–3.

[97] BL MS Egerton 2714.

matic form the type of basic information about planetary and astral influences, prognostications and 'perilous days' then deemed essential for the practice of minor surgery, while the other offers advice of a popular nature to be found in scores of contemporary vernacular remedy books. 'In the monyth of Ianuarie', for example, the reader is urged to avoid venesection near the heart as well as the use of laxatives, bolstering his humoral resources at a debilitating time of year with a medicinal glass of wine. The entry for September, by contrast, recommends bathing ('be stuwyd thrys') and phlebotomy to purge any autumnal impurities.

The Norwich Benedictine, William Buckenham, who spent some time in the infirmary during the late 1420s, produced two short English tracts on uroscopy which still survive.[98] The translation and simplification of medical texts likely to assist surgeons and phlebotomists whose Latin may, at best, have been rudimentary, was a recognised work of pastoral charity undertaken by many religious in the later middle ages, often for named practitioners.[99] Buckenham may possibly have wished to provide the convent's *minutorius* with an accessible guide to diagnostic procedure, which would have helped him determine how heavily to bleed individual patients when a physician was not available to give expert advice. 'Urine rede as blode in ye glas signifieth feuer of to mekil [much] blode', runs the terse but functional commentary, adding 'thanne lete him blede, but [not] ghif the mone be in the medyl of the signe of Geminorum'.[100] If, like Chaucer's clerk in *The Miller's Tale* ('wel koude he laten blood and clippe and shave, and maken a chartre of land or acquitance'), the Norwich *minutorius* was literate, he would himself have been able to consult the more intellectually demanding chapter on phlebotomy in Avicenna's *Canon*. A copy of this influential medical textbook was available in the cathedral library, along with the Pseudo-Galenic *De Passionibus Puerorum* and several astrological manuscripts, designed for practical use.[101] It is worth noting that Doctor John Stukeley, a fourteenth-century Norwich Benedictine and Oxford theologian, was the reputed (but unlikely) author of one set of astrological tables which were still being deployed in 1501.[102]

98 Wellcome Institute Library, Western MS 408, fos 4r–13r (*Colores urinarum per Willelmum Bokynhamum, ecclesie catholice Sancte Trinitatis Norwici monachum*); NRO, DCN 1/10/16–17. See Greatrex, *Biographical Register*, 485, for Buckenham's career.

99 F.M. Getz, 'Charity, Translation and the Language of Medical Learning in Medieval England', *Bulletin of the History of Medicine* lxiv, 1990, 1–17; L.E. Voigts and M.R. McVaugh, 'A Latin Technical Phlebotomy and its Middle English Translation', *Transactions of the American Philosophical Society* lxxiv, 1984, 11–25.

100 Wellcome Institute Library, Western MS 408, fo. 4r.

101 Greatrex, 'Horoscopes', forthcoming; Ker, *Monastic Libraries*, 137. Bury St Edmunds abbey also owned a copy of the *Canon*, along with two other works on medicine and its celebrated herbal: *ibid.*, 17, 20.

102 Bodleian Library, Oxford, MS Ashmole 340, fo. 81v; Greatrex, *Biographical Register*, 560–1. The survival of a compilation of receipts and charms in Latin, Anglo-Norman and Middle English made by brother John de Grenburgh, the infirmarer of an unspecified religious house (identified by Greatrex, *Biographical Register*, 356, as the cathedral priory of Coventry) between 1375 and 1408, suggests that such works were by no means unusual. Grenburgh's avowed aim was to collect proven cures by 'English, Irish, Jewish, Lombard and Salernitian

From the late eleventh century onwards, the elaborate ritual surrounding phlebotomy was carefully ordered in English monastic customals, along with the diet, dress and conduct of brethren who submitted to this routine surgical procedure on an average of every six or seven weeks. Because prophylactic venesection ('the seyney') was usually accompanied by three days' relaxation of the rules concerning diet and liturgy, it was forbidden at major feasts and restricted during Lent. The care taken at houses such as Bury St Edmunds to impose strict regulations further reflects the moral ambiguity surrounding a practice so closely associated with human fallibility.[103] A universal resort of all but the very young, elderly or weak, blood letting assumed even greater importance in religious communities, where sexual activity of any kind was strictly forbidden. Although medical authorities, including the omniscient Galen, regarded excessive coitus as potentially debilitating, most believed that celibacy, too, could undermine the health, most notably in those of a studious or contemplative (essentially melancholic) disposition. In theory, the spare vegetarian diet and bodily privations of the religious life served to curb the libido and keep the blood free of impurities. Regular venesection offered a further means of avoiding moral and physical pollution, and was prescribed as such by physicians. Episcopal visitors were understandably just as anxious that all aspects of the procedure should be efficiently managed: it has, indeed, been suggested that the blood-letting hall built to the south of the infirmary chapel at Ely in 1416 constituted a response to Bishop Fordham's demand for additional phlebotomy sessions, which he presumably considered necessary on moral as much as medical grounds. At Barnwell priory special arrangements were made for canons who could not follow the usual rota 'without danger', but had to be bled more than once a month.[104]

That newly phlebotomised monks, flushed with wine and replete with the delicacies of a well stocked table, might be especially vulnerable to the stirrings of the flesh seems to have escaped those who supervised their welfare. The stark contrast between the comfortable environment of the monastic 'seyney' and Christ's public phlebotomy was a common *topos* in the medieval preacher's handbook:

> Noblemen and religious are bled in pleasant and secret surroundings and receive better food and drink. But Christ was openly put to show before all men on Mount Calvary and was given gall and vinegar to drink, so that we should let our blood spiritually in the same way for his love and our own salvation: that is we should abstain from sinful deeds for which we are moved by the fleshly nature of our blood.[105]

Despite the powerful freight of spiritual imagery which they carried, sessions with the *minutorius* seem to have offered monks a genuine, if brief, opportunity 'to lead a

physicians', although he remained sceptical about such 'experts': *Popular Medicine in Thirteenth-Century England*, ed. T. Hunt, Woodbridge 1990, 33–4, 86–7.

103 *Customary of Bury St Edmunds*, 50–1, 76–8.

104 Ziegler, *Medicine and Religion*, 117–18, 262–6; Holton-Krayenbuhl, 'Infirmary at Ely', 161, 163, 168–9; Stewart, *Architectural History of Ely*, 274; *Observances*, 200–1.

105 *Fasciculus Morum: A Fourteenth-Century Preacher's Handbook*, ed. S. Wenzel, Pennsylvania 1989, 207.

life of joy and freedom from care in comfort and happiness'.[106] Such ideas reflected classical medical theory, which insisted upon a proper period of tranquillity and recuperation as well as a nourishing diet after venesection. The sacrist's rolls of Ely cathedral priory suggest that during the early fourteenth century, at least, practice followed precept. Monks were then bled on an average of between seven and nine times a year, sometimes in the rural surroundings of the home farm at Turbutsey, and liberally supplied with additional delicacies such as beef and poultry. In 1403, and again almost a century later, complaints were voiced about the poor quality of catering on these occasions, which may suggest rising expectations as much as falling standards.[107]

Great emphasis was placed in the Barnwell Observances upon the provision of heating, lighting, towels, utensils and clean table linen for phlebotomised monks, and this, too, was a priority at Norwich, where the infirmarer made regular purchases of turves, faggots, candles, covers for the 'great table', vessels, spoons, fresh rushes and matting for the floor and other creature comforts.[108] His stock, which included some valuable silver plate, was supplemented by tasteful gifts from individual monks. From Nicholas Gys came a silver *pecia* with a glass cover and a ewer for the *camera minutorum*, while Ralph de Marsham, the prior of Lynn, gave another covered cup and four dishes. The purchase of quantities of 'pewtyrvesshell' and a 'banker de tapeserwerk . . . cum bordur de nubibus' for the principal bench in the infirmary, in 1440–41, coincided with the promotion of the infirmarer's servant to the office of butler, at a fee of 20s a year and gratuity of 3s 4d for his labour.[109] By this date, the once illicit practice of meat-eating in monastic communities had become firmly entrenched, although, in deference to their rule, most religious set aside a special room, or misericord, for this purpose. Since it was already equipped with kitchens and dining facilities where meat dishes were consumed on a regular basis, the infirmary often seemed the obvious place to cater for what, in some houses, proved an almost insatiable demand for carnivorous fare. Clearly, by the mid-fifteenth century, the infirmary at Norwich had taken on aspects of a gentlemen's club.[110] The availability of separate 'seyney' halls or chambers in houses across the region to allow monks the comfort and privacy so demonstrably denied the phlebotomised Christ further encouraged this trend.

Whatever welcome relief it brought from the regimentation of the cloister or the

106 *Observances*, 201.

107 *Sacrist Rolls of Ely*, ii, 5, 7, 8, 26, 39, 53, 65, 77, 88, 103, 105–6, 114, 129, 141, 152, 163, 175, 187; Greatrex, *Biographical Register*, 429, 432; Atkinson, *Monastery of St Etheldreda*, i, 121; *Ely Chapter Ordinances*, pp. xiv–v, 43, 54. See also Harvey, *Living and Dying*, 96–7.

108 *Observances*, 201; NRO, DCN 1/10/1–38. Expenditure on linen for cloths and towels was high at Norwich: in both 1312–13 and 1421–22 it cost almost 50s. Regulations of 1379 had insisted upon the proper supply of fuel by the prior (*Customary of Norwich*, 243–4), and in addition the infirmarer purchased large quantities of peat and kindling.

109 NRO, DCN 1/10/22. An inventory of 1393–94 lists 30 silver spoons, 14 pieces of plate and 9 wooden mazers in the infirmary (DCN 1/8/48).

110 D. Knowles, *The Religious Orders in England*, 3 vols, Cambridge 1948–59, ii, 245; Harvey, *Living and Dying*, 31–42.

burdens of office, life in the monastic infirmaries of medieval East Anglia none the less posed particular hazards. Phlebotomy was certainly a risk, as accounts of miracle cures frequently attest.[111] Alongside the obvious fact that many monks would have been weakened rather than fortified by their sessions with the *minutorius* must be set the immediate perils of infection, incompetence, ignorance and excessive zeal. As Robert Reynes of Acle in Norfolk observed, 'of onwys blood-lath comyth many sekenesse', among which he identified 'perlyows feuers, palseys, sores, mychell bledyng at the nose, pestelens' and, most ominously of all, 'sotheyn deth'.[112] John Kirkby, bishop of Ely, apparently went mad in 1290 after having been bled too often by his barber, and would have died but for the intervention of St Etheldreda, whose shrine in the cathedral was the focus of a healing cult.[113] None of the region's many nunneries could claim a figure as notorious as the prioress of Kirklees in Yorkshire, who kept her phlebotomy-irons wrapped in silk, and was said to have treacherously murdered Robin Hood by bleeding him to death after he had gone to her for treatment.[114] The need to appoint a skilled infirmarer with an understanding of medicine was, however, especially important in female houses because it was essential to avoid intimate contact with the type of rude mechanical who practised minor surgery.[115] Given the parlous state of their finances, which slumped considerably as a result of the economic and demographic upheavals of the later middle ages, nunneries such as Redlingfield in Suffolk were unable to provide adequate care for the sick, possessing neither an infirmarer nor even special quarters for them during the early sixteenth century. The sisters at Flixton made similar complaints, adding, for good measure, that the prioress withheld special privileges from those who were ill, even forcing them to rise early for matins.[116]

It should not, however, be assumed that such failings were confined to female houses. The chronic shortage of beds, bedding and food for patients in the infirmary proved a running grievance at Westacre priory during the decades before the Dissolution, while brethren at Bromehill, Buckenham, Butley, Coxford, Eye, Norwich, and Wymondham bemoaned the general lack of proper facilities, including professional medical and surgical support and servants to tend the sick. Care was then available at Hickling, but only at a price, which the brethren resented paying.[117] Even worse, at the abbey of St Benet Holme one monk had died untended, a shock-

111 R.C. Finucane, *Miracles and Pilgrims*, New York 1995, 60–1, 63.

112 C.W. Louis, *The Commonplace Book of Robert Reynes of Acle: An Edition of Tanner MS 407*, New York 1980, 156, 169; Gil-Sotres, 'Derivation and Revulsion', 141.

113 Bartholomew Cotton, *Historia Anglicana*, ed. H.R. Luard, RS 1859, 174.

114 *The English and Scottish Popular Ballads*, ed. F.J. Child, 5 vols, New York 1957, iii, 104–5.

115 It is interesting to contrast the 'progressive' views of Peter Abelard (d.1142) on medical treatment in nunneries with those of his arch-rival Bernard of Clairvaux, quoted above: *The Letters of Peter Abelard*, ed. B. Radice, London 1974, 215–16.

116 *Visitations*, 139–40, 185. At the nunnery of Campsey Ash it was alleged in 1532 that sisters had to pay for their own necessities when they were ill, although the house at least possessed an infirmarer: *ibid.*, 290–1.

117 *Visitations*, 4, 6, 22, 24, 28, 54, 74, 87, 102, 106, 111–12, 166–7, 178, 242, 264, 266–7, 277–8, 286–7, 295–6, 313–14. Poor dietary provision for the sick, and often for the healthy, too, was a widespread feature of English monastic life: C. Harper-Bill, 'The Labourer is

ing indictment of a house whose Order placed so much importance upon the rituals of death and the consolation of the dying. The indulgence previously shown there to brother William Bynham, a notorious and slothful malingerer who had feigned illness to avoid rising for matins, also aroused criticism.[118] Just as wrath was believed to upset the humoral balance by generating excessive choler, so idleness, another of the Seven Deadly Sins, produced too much phlegm. But concern about the spiritual health of sick brethren went far beyond the nice calculations of Galenic Medicine. It had, predictably, exercised monastic chapters and visitors throughout the middle ages. To them the miasmas of sin carried far worse contagion than any earthly sickness and were to be avoided by stringent prophylactic measures.

The freedom with which women gained entry to the infirmary and other parts of the precinct disturbed Bishop Walpole on his visitation of Ely in 1300. Concern that sick monks should, in any event, be spared the noise and distractions of secular life led him to prohibit salacious and noisy gossip outside the infirmary door, and to insist upon an atmosphere of calm and solicitude in which those near to death could make a good end. Matters seem hardly to have improved over the next fourteen years, as the prior and chapter once again felt it necessary to remind brethren about the interconnected issues of security and morality. The main infirmary door was henceforward to be bolted and only those unlikely to excite scandal were to be admitted.[119] These rules were reiterated in 1466 by Bishop William Grey, whose warnings about indifference or negligence on the part of the infirmarer suggest that standards may once again have slipped. That he specifically drew the attention of senior staff to Christ's injunctions about visiting the sick (incorporated, as the quotation at the start of this essay shows, in the Benedictine Rule) is in itself revealing.[120] At Norwich the gender and intrusiveness of visitors constituted a similar threat. As we have seen, the relatives and friends of monks strayed beyond the confines of the parlour set aside for their use in the infirmary complex; and it was alleged in 1514 that women were gaining access to the infirmary itself.[121] Female guests posed less of a problem at the isolated Broadland abbey of St Benet Hulme, but the reading of scripture to monks during their carnivorous 'recreations' in the infirmary hall there had evidently been abandoned to the detriment of good discipline and spiritual welfare.[122] On the other hand, the prior's refusal to wear sandals, which infringed the monastic dress code, was accepted on the ground that he suffered from 'aliquo morbo in tibiis', quite probably the ulcerated varicose veins so

Worthy of his Hire? – Complaints about Diet in Late Medieval English Monasteries', in *The Church in Pre-Reformation Society*, ed. *idem* and C.M. Barron, Woodbridge 1985, 95–108.

118 *Visitations*, 214–15, 281.

119 *Ely Chapter Ordinances*, 11, 13, 17, 42. A hall to the north of the infirmary, begun in the 1330s, was assigned for the entertainment of female visitors, and was under the infirmarer's authority: Holton-Krayenbuhl, 'Infirmary at Ely', 149, 169. For similar ideas about the need to preserve the spiritual environment of hospitals, see Rawcliffe, *Medicine for the Soul*, 38–45.

120 *Ely Chapter Ordinances*, 60.

121 *Visitations*, 76, 77, 79.

122 *Visitations*, 62. Meals in monastic infirmaries were customarily accompanied by the reading of holy scripture.

common among medieval religious. We do not know if the monks of St Benet's followed the example of the Westminster Benedictines in employing a female empiric, skilled in the use of herbal remedies for chronic ailments of this kind, but one suspects that such experts were often admitted into what was otherwise supposed to be a strictly segregated space. The payment of one shilling to a woman named Alice Baldry 'pro custodia infirmorum' at Thetford priory in 1501, and of a similar sum to the Cambridge MD, Robert Harydance, for then treating the prior, would suggest that all but the most cloistered communities exploited the rich diversity of contemporary medical practice, regardless of gender.[123]

That the sick might well prove demanding and difficult, testing the Christian forbearance of their carers was understood by those who regulated for their support. The Observances at Barnwell, for example, required the infirmarer to be 'gentle, good-tempered, kind, compassionate to the sick, and willing to gratify their needs with affectionate sympathy', while his servant was warned against any kind of behaviour which might promote quarrels, loose talk or backbiting. Fears about the incidence of 'sarcastic or abusive language . . . jeers and evil speaking . . . strife and contention' among their charges, and particularly those who had time to kill while recuperating from phlebotomy, were evidently borne of experience.[124] Such a relaxed atmosphere led monks to abandon their customary reticence, as Jocelin of Brakelond noted when describing life at Bury St Edmunds in the late twelfth century:

> I once saw Samson the subsacrist sitting in the kind of little groups that used to form at blood-letting time, when cloister monks would tell one another their private thoughts and discuss things together. I saw him sitting silently, smiling and noting what everyone else said, able to recall twenty years later some of the comments I have recorded . . .[125]

The loss of vital spirits carried in the blood made it medically as well as morally essential to foster concord and amity at a time of such vulnerability. But professional advice often fell on stony ground. It was in the infirmary, in 1532, quite probably after having his blood let, that Edward Woode, a monk at the Benedictine abbey of Horsham St Faith, smashed a 'croke', or earthenware pot, over the head of one of his brothers in Christ, allegedly fracturing his skull. A man whose excessive choler posed a threat to others as much as to himself, he had also abused the sub-prior with unseemly language, calling him a 'churle'.[126] As the above-mentioned case of brother

123 *Visitations*, 280; *Register Thetford*, i, 131–32. At Westminster a surgeoness undertook such a cure in 1374–75, and in 1386–87 a *medica*, or female physician, attended ten monks: Harvey, *Living and Dying*, 83, 85–6, 109–10. That women may quite often have treated the religious is apparent from the *practica* of the eminent Cambridge physician, John Argentine, who records a case in 1475 of a woman at Ware curing a Franciscan of *podagra*: Bodleian Library, Oxford, MS Ashmole 1437, fo. 10r.

124 *Observances*, 200–5; Gil-Sotres, 'Derivation and Revulsion', 154; Rawcliffe, *Medicine and Society*, 212–13.

125 Jocelin of Brakelond, *Chronicle of Bury St Edmunds*, 14.

126 *Visitations*, 316.

Richard Walsham of Norwich so clearly reveals, the stresses of office could exact a remorseless toll on both physical and mental health. His own longing for the eremitical life, doubtless intensified by the embarrassment of a disfiguring disease, was one response to such pressure. Three decades of labour in the demanding posts of master of the cellar, sacristan and prior of St Leonard's, during which he had also played an active part in diocesan affairs and served as monastic penitentiary, had clearly pushed his constitution to its very limits.[127] William of Lynn, for whom electuaries, poultices, medicaments and a new bed were purchased by the infirmarer between 1345 and 1350, had previously been relieved of his post as prior of the dependent cell at Hoxne because 'the heavy burden of office' had clouded his mind as well as punishing his body.[128] At the other extreme, the erratic behaviour of Prior William Bury of Wymondham, who was alleged in 1514 to have threatened two monks with a drawn sword, thrown stones at others and destroyed a musical instrument, supports the view that he was 'aliquando lunaticus'. Bishop Nykke did, indeed, remove him from office, although the problems of running such an ill-disciplined community would surely have goaded all but the most phlegmatic of individuals beyond endurance.[129]

Recognising that 'the irksome life in the cloister' might prove inimical to health, the Augustinians at Barnwell made provision for brethren who needed 'repose and comfort' rather than a course of medication in the infirmary. In accordance with the *Regimen Sanitatis*, their rule prescribed moderate exercise in the pleasant surroundings of garden, vineyard, riverbank or woodland, a nourishing diet and freedom from the daily liturgical round.[130] Such recommendations were a natural extension of the idea that a patient's environment and, above all, the accidents of his soul played a fundamental part in the preservation or recovery of health. For this reason during the later middle ages 'seynes' were frequently transmuted into periods of recreation, during which monks might, quite literally, take a holiday from their customary duties in the countryside.[131] Convalescent and elderly Benedictines at Norwich cathedral priory were permitted to recuperate by the sea, in the bracing air of Yarmouth and Lynn, where the house maintained dependent cells. The accounts of the prior of Lynn record regular annual payments, often in excess of £4, 'in carragio monachorum' and ancillary costs sustained in transporting invalids and others to and from the mother house for their 'recreations'.[132] Nearer home, monks

127 NRO, DCN 35/7; Greatrex, *Biographical Register*, 568–9.

128 Greatrex, *Biographical Register*, 535.

129 *Visitations*, 95–101.

130 *Observances*, 204–7. A similar regimen was prescribed for those who had been bled (*ibid.*, 200–1). Recognising their need for a healthier lifestyle, the Durham Benedictines complained in 1455 that in the period before Lent they not only ate 'pancakes and sausages for the most part made of flesh, very hurtful to the body', but were also suffering the effects of lack of exercise in a crowded precinct. Food poisoning may have added to their woes, for 'in consequence of the said unwholesome food they were affected with diverse sicknesses, rendering them so ill that they were kept from divine offices . . .': *Calendar of Papal Letters, 1455–1464*, 5–6.

131 *Bishop Geoffrey Blythe's Visitations c.1515–1525*, ed. P. Heath, Collections for a History of Staffordshire, series 4, VII, 1973, pp. xxxviii–xxxix.

132 See, for example, NRO, DCN 2/1/21 (accounts of the prior of Lynn, 1397–1408).

who were too sick to travel far might spend a few days on the hillside priory of St Leonard's overlooking Norwich. When the precentor fell ill, in 1356–57, the expenses charged to his office included 29s 10d on medicines, 2s 8d for phlebotomy, 7s 3d on the wages of clerks tending him day and night in the infirmary and almost 2s in costs sustained at St Leonard's.[133] The treatment accorded to him was not simply the best East Anglia then had to offer, but also a paradigm of the holistic care for body and mind which the larger monasteries were especially well suited to deliver. Sick monks at Bury St Edmunds, who could not explore the monastic gardens, were allowed to lie on the side of the infirmary which looked across the rivers Linnet and Larke to the rolling meadows beyond. Quite possibly intended as a reminder of man's fall into sin and disease in the garden of Eden, the prospect also offered a more reassuring image of natural beauty in the best traditions of the classical world.[134]

133 NRO, DCN 1/9/8. See also the case of William de Penteney, another precentor, who underwent a similar cure 'in infirmaria, camera minutorum et apud Leonardum', in 1394–95 (DCN 1/9/24).

134 *Customary of Bury St Edmunds*, 15; Whittingham, 'Bury St Edmunds Abbey', 181.

The Parson's Glebe: Stable, Expanding or Shrinking?

David Dymond[1]

> Cursed be the man that taketh away or hindereth the Lord's portion; blessed be the free presenter
>
> *quoted from unknown source in Robert Shelford's Rectory Book of Ringsfield, Suffolk, c.1603*

HISTORIANS STEADILY ACCUMULATE detailed evidence to show how the medieval church acquired its landed wealth. Generally this was a process whereby lay people, ranging from royalty to commoners, gave land in varying quantities to religious houses, other major churches and holders of high ecclesiastical office.[2] Also well studied is 'the plunder of the church' in the sixteenth century when much of that landed property found its way back into lay hands.[3] Curiously, however, one major aspect of the church's territorial possessions has attracted much less attention: the way land was acquired, and to an extent retained, by parish churches and their clergy. By looking principally at Suffolk, it is the purpose of this essay to look more closely at the history of 'glebe' – the landholding or tenement, including a dwelling, which was provided in the great majority of parishes for the support of a resident cleric.[4] Over a thousand years or so, the glebe has given successive priests and

1 By his writing and his teaching and encouragement of others, Norman Scarfe has contributed more to Suffolk's history than any other living person. What follows is offered to him with much gratitude and affection.

NOTE: quotations from original sources are reproduced with modern spelling and punctuation (except for personal names and minor place-names). In writing this paper I have received valuable help from Dr J.H. Bettey, Prof. Claire Cross, Edward Martin and Peter Northeast. Phillip Judge drew the two maps.

2 For example, S. Wood, *English Monasteries and their Patrons in the Thirteenth Century*, Oxford 1955; E. Cownie, *Religious Patronage in Anglo-Norman England, 1066–1135*, Royal Historical Society 1998; J. Burton, *The Monastic Order in Yorkshire, 1069–1215*, Cambridge 1999; and volumes produced by the Suffolk Records Society in its expanding Charter Series.

3 J. Youings, *Devon Monastic Lands: Calendar of Particulars for Grants, 1536–58*, Devon and Cornwall Record Society ns 1, 1955; T.H. Swayles, 'The Redistribution of the Monastic Lands in Norfolk at the Dissolution', *NA* xxxiv, 1969, 14–44; J. Thirsk, ed., *The Agrarian History of England and Wales*, iv, Cambridge 1967, 306–55.

4 Latin *gleba* = soil, earth.

ministers a place to live, land to farm directly or to rent to others and, since the mid-nineteenth century, land which could be sold to provide an alternative income from investments.[5]

The Origins of Glebe

Recent archaeological and documentary research has thrown valuable light on the origins of parish churches. Many were founded in the later Anglo-Saxon and Norman period (broadly ninth to twelfth centuries) by lay landowners, and sometimes by groups of freemen.[6] The cumulative effect was to fill the gaps between older 'minsters', which had formed the looser and more collegiate system of Middle Saxon times (seventh to ninth centuries).[7] These new and more localised places of worship, known to historians as *eigenkirchen* or proprietorial churches, were primarily for the benefit of the founder's family and household. Thus, in her will of *c.*990–1066 Siflaed of Marlingford in Norfolk referred unambiguously to 'my' church and 'my' priest.[8] By 1086, however, Domesday Book was displaying the beginnings of a new terminology. It referred to some local churches as 'church of this vill (*ecclesia huius ville*)', and occasionally used the words 'parish' and 'parishioners' in their modern senses. Yet it was probably not until the thirteenth century that local people, including the patron or founder's successor, fully acknowledged the communal value of these churches and created a more complex system giving responsibilities to the laity and their elected officers.

From an early date too, founders and other benefactors gave further endowments of land to local churches, that is, other than the sites on which they stood. For example, in his will of *c.*1040–1057 a Norfolk man called Edwin gave ten acres to each of six churches, eight acres to another, four acres to another, and two acres each to two more: a total of seventy-six acres to ten churches.[9] In 1086 a church at Stonham in Suffolk had twenty acres 'which nine freemen gave thereto for their souls'.[10] Gifts of this kind were surely intended to help maintain a resident priest in each church and, with other sources of income such as tithes and offerings, were the first discernible attempts to build up a permanent 'living' or benefice for him and his

5 Ecclesiastical Leasing Act, 1858, and Glebe Lands Act, 1888 (*Statutes Revised*, vi, 1950, 764–9; xi 1953, 353–9). In 1887 the glebes of England and Wales were estimated at 659,548 acres, and valued at £908,282 (*British Parliamentary Papers*, 1887, LXIV).

6 They often provided sites for churches close to their own 'halls'. The institutional cluster of church, manor-house, parsonage, gildhall, etc. is a common topographical feature, regardless of the fluctuating pattern of local settlement.

7 J. Blair, ed., *Minsters and Parish Churches: The Local Church in Transition, 950–1200*, Oxford 1988.

8 D. Whitelock, ed., *Anglo-Saxon Wills*, Cambridge 1930, 93.

9 C.R. Hart, *The Early Charters of Eastern England*, Leicester 1966, 83.

10 A. Rumble, ed., *Domesday Book: Suffolk*, Chichester 1986, ii, 64.2.

successors. Indeed later documentary evidence suggests that gifts to more than one church, though on a lesser scale than Edwin's, were probably quite common.[11]

Norman Scarfe, more than anyone else, has emphasised the significance of Little Domesday Book and its references to early churches, their confusing sub-divisions and their endowments. He shows that in Suffolk some 418 churches were listed in 1086, more than are mentioned for any other English county, and four-fifths of the total number recorded in 1291.[12] He further calculates that those churches had lands averaging about 24½ acres each.[13] In most cases a single total figure is given, though sometimes meadowland, being particularly valuable, is measured separately. These endowments, said to be held freely (*libera terra*) or in alms (*in elemosina*), varied from very small to so large that they were already organised as manors with their own tenants. For example, while Brightwell had no land, Hinderclay had one acre, Hargrave had twelve acres, Lackford had twenty acres, Barking had eighty-three acres plus fifty-two acres of meadow, Eye had a manor of 243 acres, and Ipswich St Peter had more than 720 acres. The higher acreages probably indicate former minsters, but the great majority of Suffolk's churches had modest holdings of between ten and thirty acres.[14] It cannot be doubted that all these lands recorded in Little Domesday are, wholly or in part, the glebe of later centuries.

The Medieval Glebe

For several centuries after 1086, it is difficult to track the history of individual glebes. The best snap-shot is provided by the Inquisition of the Ninths of 1340–41, when the crown decided to take from the clergy a ninth of the value of corn, wool and lambs, equivalent to the great tithes of each parish.[15] Although the inquiry is primarily concerned with incumbents' tithes, it often mentions their lands as well. In Suffolk the normal entry makes it clear that these lands belonged to the benefice and were held by the rector or vicar 'of the demesnes of the aforesaid church (*de*

11 After the Reformation glebe terriers frequently describe pieces of glebe lying adjacent but belonging to two or more parishes; these seem best explained as gifts from the same benefactor, divided among two or more churches. A good example is 'Three Parsons Bush' in Bacton, Suffolk, where three small pieces totalling only seven roods belonged to Bacton, Cotton and Finningham (SROB, E14/4/1).

12 Record Commissioners, *Taxatio Ecclesiastica*, London 1802, 115–33.

13 This may, or may not, have included the churchyard. See Norman Scarfe, unpublished notes entitled 'Suffolk Churches recorded in Domesday Book', and 'Domesday Churches' in D. Dymond and E. Martin, eds, *An Historical Atlas of Suffolk*, Ipswich 1999, 52–3; Rumble, ed., *Domesday Book: Suffolk*, 2 vols, Chichester 1986; H.C. Darby, *Domesday Geography of Eastern England*, 3rd edn, Cambridge 1971, 190–2.

14 Scarfe, 'Domesday Churches', 52–3.

15 Record Commissioners, *Inquisitiones Nonarum*, London 1807, 63–105. Historians seem to have studied tithe more intensively than glebe; see E.J. Evans, 'Tithing Customs and Disputes . . .', *AgHR* xviii, 1970, 17–35, and *The Contentious Tithe*, London 1976; E.J. Evans and A.G. Crosby, *Tithes: Maps, Apportionments and the 1836 Act: A Guide for Local Historians*, British Association for Local History 1997.

dominicis predicte ecclesie)', or 'of the endowment of the church (*ad dotem ecclesie*)', or simply 'of the glebe of the church (*de gleba ecclesie*)'. A house is usually taken for granted, but sometimes is actually mentioned. For example, each of eleven benefices in Lothingland Deanery had a messuage 'of the endowment of the church', while Shimpling's rector held a messuage and dovecot 'belonging to his church' and worth 12 shillings.[16]

Arable land, which formed the bulk of Suffolk's glebeland in 1341, was generally worth from 4d to 8d an acre (though as high as 18d in Great Barton, and as low as 1d in Elveden). Frequently the glebe also included smaller but more valuable amounts of pasture (worth from 1s to 2s an acre) and mowing meadow (2s to 4s an acre). Sometimes other economically valuable forms of land-use are mentioned such as woodland (about 1s an acre), heath, sheepwalks and marsh. In general the glebe can be regarded, within its own farming region, as a fairly typical medieval tenement, similar to those of the incumbent's more prosperous neighbours, villein or free, and usually intermixed with their's.

In 1341, too, the glebes of individual parishes varied greatly in size. Usually the acreage was higher than in 1086. Indeed it is often the highest recorded at any period, before or since (see Figs 2 and 3, pp. 88, 90). Presumably medieval benefactors had continued the practice begun in Anglo-Saxon times of giving or bequeathing land to augment benefices. No doubt charters once existed for these gifts, similar to those carefully preserved by religious houses, but they do not, it seems, survive in parochial or diocesan records. Nevertheless, compensatory glimpses do appear occasionally in wills. In 1479, for instance, Thomas Wynnyff of Brettenham bequeathed to his church a piece of land called 'Kynges Croft', containing four acres. This was not town or charity land, nor was it to provide masses or to endow a chantry. The croft was clearly left to the benefice in perpetuity, to add to the glebe: 'to every parson of the said Brettenham, one after another'.[17]

The next major source of information is the *Valor Ecclesiasticus* of 1535.[18] This survey of ecclesiastical incomes on the eve of the Reformation frequently mentions the glebe of individual parishes and usually gives an annual valuation. It also reveals that this land could be entirely rented out: in the Norfolk deanery of Rockland, for example, twenty out of about thirty-five parishes managed their glebes in this way (*firma terr' gleb'*).[19] Regrettably the East Anglian entries never match the detail of, say, the parish of Little Chart in Kent. There the incumbent had a house and garden worth 6s 8d, thirteen acres of meadow worth 30s 4d, ten acres of arable worth 17s

16 See A. Hamilton Thompson, *The English Clergy and their Organization in the Later Middle Ages*, Oxford 1947, ch. 4.

17 SROB, Hervye, 163. Unfortunately, 'Kynges Croft' cannot be recognised with certainty in later terriers. It reappears as King's Close in 1844, when it was again in private hands (SROB, T23/1). I am grateful to Peter Northeast and Edward Martin for these references.

18 *VE* iii, 403–88 for Suffolk in Norwich diocese.

19 For the economic options facing glebe-farmers, see R.N. Swanson, *Church and Society in Late Medieval England*, Oxford 1989, 206–8, 229–30, 239–42.

8d, a 'rushy meadow' worth 16d, and 2½ acres of 'barren pasture ground' worth 20d.[20]

The monetary values which are normally the only details given for Suffolk glebes cannot, unfortunately, be satisfactorily converted into acreages.[21] In fact, only for eight Suffolk parishes is an actual acreage stated in 1535. In six of them the figure is lower than for 1341, and the average is only 19.3 acres per glebe (Fig. 1). In addition, about twenty Suffolk parishes had no income from land in 1535, either by direct farming or from rents, yet most of them had possessed glebes in 1341.[22] In some cases land had been appropriated by religious houses when they became legal rectors, for example at Acton where the prior of Hatfield Peverel (Essex) had absorbed 36¾ acres, and at Haughley where a large glebe of over 100 acres fell to the abbot of Hailes (Gloucestershire). Elsewhere glebe may have been annexed by lay neighbours: this threat can be appreciated more clearly a generation or two later.

Fig. 1. Valor Ecclesiasticus, 1535: Suffolk parishes with glebe acreages[23]

rect. = rectory house; vic. = vicarage house; con. = consolidated with another parish; [ ] = no separate data

Parish	Acreage	Value	Acreage in 1086	Acreage in 1341	Acreage in 1887
Ashbocking	17 + vic.	20s.	19.00	3.50	21.75
Eyke	23 + rect.	44s. 6d.	?16.00	43.00	31.50
Kenton	16 + vic.	20s.	30.00	?67.00	29.00
Monewden	36 + rect.	40s.	31.50	40.00	51.50
Sibton	5 + house	18s. + 2s. for rented glebe	21.00	7.00	60.00
South Elmham St Michael	16	nil: 'in hands of duke of Norfolk'	[ ]	8.00	con.
Thornham Magna	30	30s.	[ ]	62.00	con.
Wenham Combust	11.5 + rect.	15s.	[ ]	30.00	15.75

20 *VE* i, 64.

21 A crude estimate is possible using the valuation of 6½d per acre, an average revealed by detailed information given for Heacham Deanery in north-west Norfolk (*VE* vi, 1834, i–v). The same source gives the acreage of glebe for thirteen parishes, and lists great and little tithes (e.g. for cheese, hemp, saffron, mallards and fish).

22 They are (with glebe acreages of 1341): Acton (36.75), Coddenham (unknown), Culpho (23), Dunwich St John (none), Endgate (none), Felixstowe (unknown), Framlingham with Saxtead (100), Hacheston (20), Haughley (108+), Ipswich St Stephen (unknown), Knodishall (24), Reydon with Southwold (12), South Elmham St Michael (8), Stoke by Nayland (102+), Stowmarket SS Mary and Peter (60), Sudbury All Saints (12), Walton (16.5) and Weston (2 roods). Most of these were vicarages.

23 These data give an annual average valuation of 9.82d per acre (*cf.* note 21).

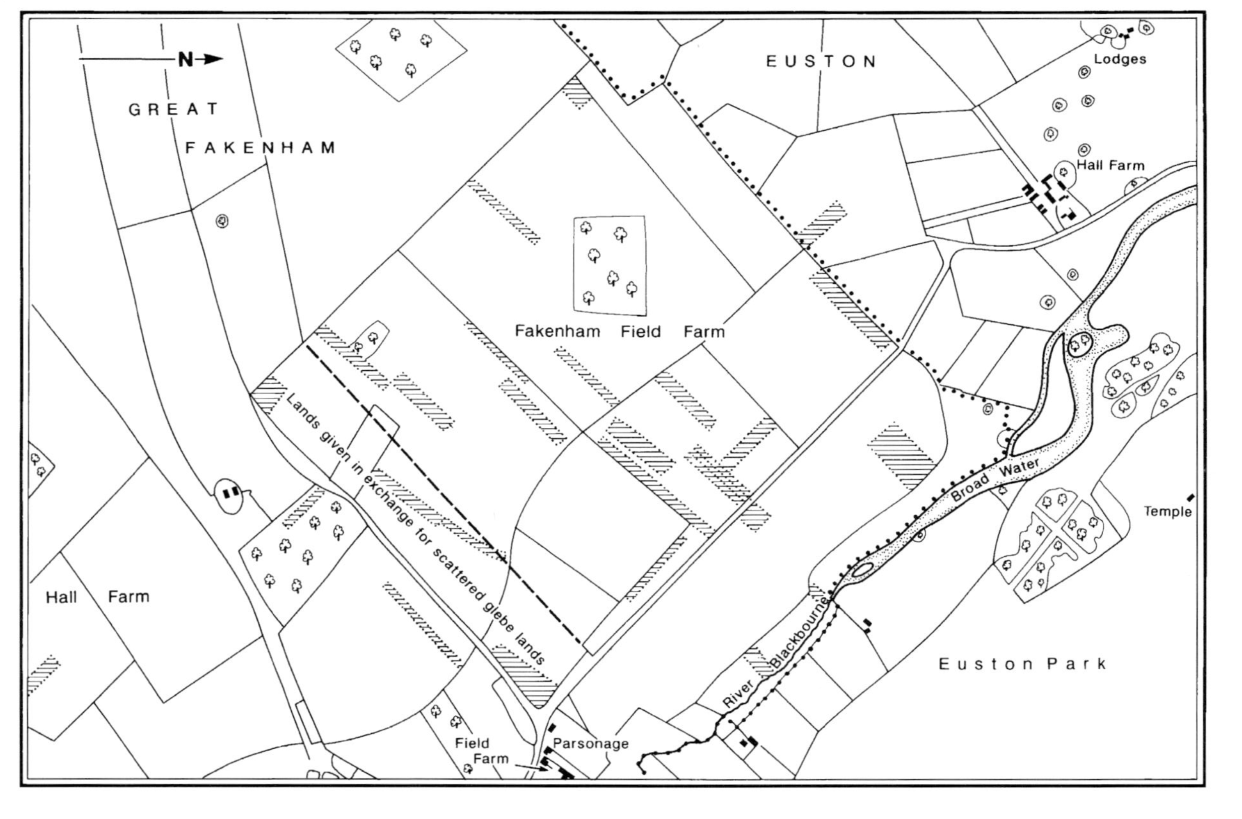

Map 1. Part of Great Fakenham, Suffolk, redrawn from J.G. Lenny's map of 1828 (Euston Estate Office). This area was privately enclosed *c.*1803 by the third Duke of Grafton, to create large and generally rectilinear fields, but small parcels of glebe are still shown in their original, scattered and mainly strip-like form. This legal, if not agricultural, persistence of the medieval glebe, is seen on many nineteenth-century maps. In 1830, in place of thirty-three small parcels amounting to 42¼ acres, a single block of 33½ acres was agreed as a new glebe, and crudely overdrawn on Lenny's map (see also SROB, FE500/3/Great Fakenham/1).

The Glebe after the Reformation

The establishment of a new, protestant Church of England did not of itself affect parochial endowments, and from the late sixteenth century onwards the history of the glebe can be studied in far greater detail because of the organised writing of glebe terriers.[24] These surveys of the possessions of individual benefices were made obligatory, as a 'perpetual memory thereof', by canons of 1571 and 1604. They were taken at regular intervals, and frequently survive among parochial and diocesan records.[25] The following account is largely based on a good, though not complete, series of early seventeenth-century terriers for Sudbury Archdeaconry (effectively the western half of Suffolk), in particular on two sets prepared for metropolitan visitations in 1613–14 and 1635, and on one set for the primary visitation of a bishop of Norwich in 1638.[26]

A glebe terrier was meant to be a 'just inventory' of parochial property, based on a 'view' or survey by 'honest' local men.[27] In the titles of Suffolk terriers, these participants were variously described as 'sworn men', 'chief inhabitants' and 'the most ancient men of the parish', and included the incumbent, churchwardens and sidesmen.[28] The clergy might be relative newcomers, unsure of their true possessions and rights, but respected lay parishioners were expected to know how the benefice was composed. Although standards varied greatly, some terriers were surprisingly detailed and written with great care. Thus, at Thorpe Morieux (1635), where the patron also joined in, one tiny piece of glebe was measured as five by forty-two perches and described as 'doled on the north side with a broad rising green meer, in the midst whereof groweth an ancient thorn; at the upper end an oak, and at the nether end a very old ash as a landmark'.

Yet the work was beset by many practical problems. The glebe was usually a complicated scatter of 'parcels' or pieces of land, frequently 'disposed in roods and half-acres'[29] and often difficult to measure precisely or to describe by 'abuttals' (Map 1). This applied both to Breckland parishes with their extensive open-fields,

24 Medieval terriers survive occasionally, e.g. Pakenham (1432, said to be 'renewed') and Little Livermere (1401, entitled 'rental of church lands'). Based on earlier writings, some seventeenth-century terriers mention defunct religious houses as landowners (Stradishall and Yaxley, both 1613).

25 For the administrative system behind glebe terriers, see D.M. Barratt, ed., *Ecclesiastical Terriers of Warwickshire Parishes*, Publications of the Dugdale Society XXII, 1955, i; Ian Mortimer, ed., *Berkshire Glebe Terriers*, Berkshire Record Society II, 1995; Richard Potts, ed., *A Calendar of Cornish Glebe Terriers, 1673–1735*, Devon and Cornwall Record Society ns 19, 1974.

26 SROB, E14/4/1–4. Within these classes, individual terriers are not numbered. In this section they are therefore mentioned by place-name and date, the latter usually in brackets (n.d. = no date). On its western edge Sudbury archdeaconry also included several Cambridgeshire parishes.

27 E. Cardwell, *Synodalia* i, Oxford 1842, 130, 214, 296; see also ii, 734–40 for later modifications.

28 Sidesmen (or sidemen) were also known as 'questmen' or 'assistants'.

29 Thrandeston (n.d.).

where the glebe contained scores of small scattered strips, and to much more enclosed parishes where a piece of glebe could turn out to be in the middle of another man's hedged field. The difficulties were compounded when land was rented or leased to others: then the parson[30] retained only a financial interest and was no longer concerned with day-to-day farming.[31]

Not surprisingly, the surveyors often displayed doubt and uncertainty. When recording the sizes of parcels, they often used phrases like 'estimated more or less at . . .', 'in common estimation' and 'so far as we certainly know'. Very often they were forced to rely on opinion or hearsay. This uncertainty could develop into real anxiety, as at Burgate in 1613:

> Not meaning to prejudice any man's right, if we happen to name any piece of land for glebe which by better evidence may prove another man's land, nor willing to hinder the parsonage, though perhaps for want of knowledge we leave unmentioned any piece of glebe land lying within other men's lands . . .[32]

At this period the glebe was certainly changing physically. Many individual pieces were described as 'divided' into two or more parts (Bildeston, 1613; Shimpling, 1614), or as 'enclosed' (Thelnetham, Mellis, both 1613).[33] Quite often these changes were qualified by adverbs such as 'lately', 'newly' or 'now'. Occasionally, by looking at successive terriers, one can deduce more accurately when changes had happened. At Barningham three roods in 'Churchcrofte', 'now a pightle lately enclosed', were hedged between 1613 and 1635. Other enclosures took different forms. At Thorpe Morieux (1613) a field of six acres had been lately absorbed 'within the New Park', and at Flempton (1613) one rood of arable was enclosed for 'a sheep pin' or sheepfold. Sometimes the actual means of enclosure or division was specified. A large field of eighteen acres at Whatfield (1613) was said to have been 'lately ditched in', and at Thwaite (n.d.) a seven-acre close was subdivided by planting a green hedge (*cepes*).

Some glebes, particularly in the south-east of the archdeaconry, were concentrated around the parsonage house and contained large blocks of land (Map 2). This suggests either that they had always been more concentrated or had, at some stage, been re-organised. For example the glebe at Lavenham (1613) consisted of large parcels, including Parsonage Field of forty acres, 'now divided into two', while Mendlesham (1635) had twenty acres in only two pieces. By 1613, the glebe of

30 The words 'rector' (Latin *rector*) and 'parson' (*persona*) were synonymous in medieval times. By the seventeenth century, 'parson' was used to signify all kinds of incumbent (rector proper, vicar or perpetual curate).

31 Occasionally a terrier describes a consolidated glebe with all land concentrated around the parsonage (see pp. 80–1). A few places like Hunston and Ixworth Thorpe (both 1638) had no glebe; Little Bradley (1638) had neither glebe nor parsonage. Yet in 1341 Hunston had possessed 60 acres of glebe, Ixworth Thorpe 27 acres, and Little Bradley 24 acres.

32 SROB, E14/4/1, Burgate (1613).

33 Many parcels were described simply as 'closes' or 'several' fields.

about forty acres at Aldham was in a single consolidated block of six fields around the parsonage house. At Shimpling too (1614), some sixty-seven acres were arranged in ten parcels and 'lie one within another adjoining to the rectory houses, and therefore need no other abuttalling'.[34]

Also mentioned were changes of land-use. Several woodland areas of glebe were 'lately stubbed' (Thorpe Morieux, 1635), and converted to arable (Hitcham, 1613) or more frequently to meadow (Thelnetham, 1613; Hessett, 1635). Similarly, open-field strips on the edge of the Breckland were said to be 'now ley', that is, put down to grass (Barrow, n.d.). At Great Bradley (1613), half a meadow had been made into a 'hop ground', while at Aldham (1686) an earlier hempland was replaced by a 'Teasle Yard'.[35]

Terriers frequently reveal the existence of open- or common-fields (Map 2). Parishes on the Breckland employed the complete open-field terminology: fields, furlongs, *quarentinae*, wongs, wents, unwents, shifts, outshifts, headlands, *forerae*, meers and intercommons. Brandon (1638) was typical and divided its glebe among four 'infields' and six 'outfields'. Similar large-scale open-field farming was practised in the western chalk belt, for instance at Dalham (1613) and Ousden (1638). In other parts of Suffolk, terriers refer specifically to 'common fields', though they were probably never as extensive or as regulated as those on the Breckland. They occur, for example, in the Stour valley at Great Thurlow (1613) and Cornard Parva (1638), and on the heavy clays of High Suffolk at Hundon (1613), Hawkedon (1638) and Chelsworth (1613). Others are implied by the use of terms such as wong, went, furlong and headland, as at Wortham (1614), Thrandeston (n.d.) and Westhorpe (1638), or when several small arable parcels lay in larger, named 'fields', as at Gislingham (1613) which had glebeland 'in divers fields not inclosed'. Other relevant features mentioned occasionally are ridges or 'riggs', 'up and downs' and stetches. At Wattisfield (1638), a strip of glebe was said to contain 'eight stetches, four furrows to a stetch', while at Barrow (n.d.) two strips butting end-to-end in Risby Field were 'now ploughed together as but one piece in length'.

Some terriers go further and throw light on the overall balance of land-use. For example, at Eriswell (1614) on the Breck–Fen edge, the glebe comprised 102½ acres of arable strips scattered around its open-fields, and only 16 acres of enclosed pastures and orchards surrounding the parsonage house. On the heavier clayland, Burgate (1613) presented a very different picture: on a large glebe of 85½ acres, grassland accounted for 51 acres and arable for 31¼. Put another way, 60 per cent of the farmed glebe was pasture. Here, in High Suffolk, the emphasis had been on mixed farming, and particularly on dairying, since at least the fifteenth century. In relative terms the surviving arable common-fields of this district were of declining

[34] A separate study of the seventeenth-century parsonage house will appear in *Historic Buildings of Suffolk* (Suffolk Historic Buildings Group), ii.

[35] One frequent ambiguity is the mention of 'land *and* pasture' and 'land *or* pasture'. This may mean arable and grass side-by-side, or the rotation of arable and grass leys.

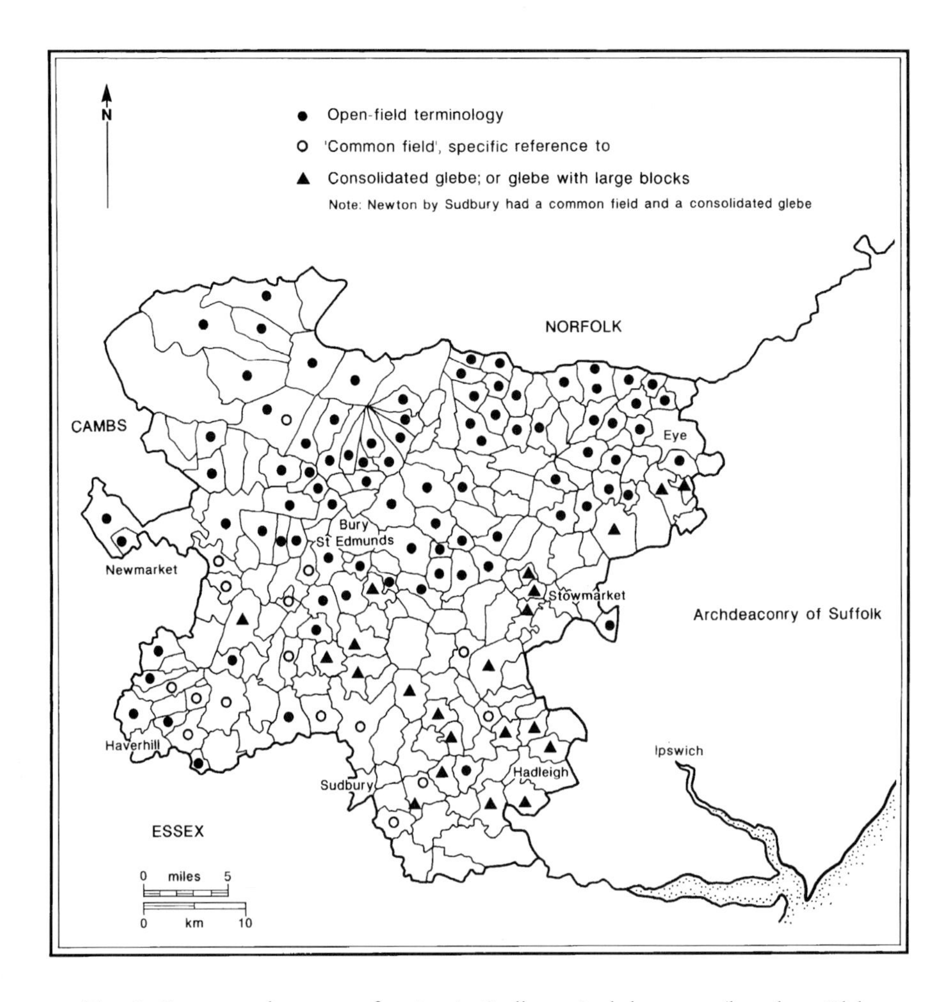

Map 2. Seventeenth-century farming in Sudbury Archdeaconry (based on Glebe Terriers). The north-west, consisting of the Breckland and adjacent parts of High Suffolk, appears to have been much more dominated by open-field farming than the south-east with its occasional 'common fields' and more consolidated glebes. The symbols within each parish do not show precise sites; two symbols indicate where two parishes once existed (e.g. Icklingham, All Saints and St James). Note that terriers do not exist for all parishes, and that the Cambridgeshire part of the archdeaconry is omitted.

significance:[36] at Brettenham (n.d.) five pieces of glebe lay in 'Ditchfeild', which was described as 'being once a common field'.[37]

Glebes were normally mixed up with the lands of lay people who ranged from gentry and major leaseholders, through substantial yeomen, to small freeholders and copyholders. It may be that open-field parishes, where the number of small arable strips could be very large, lost proportionally less glebe than those in other areas – presumably because everyone had an interest in maintaining a 'communal' system, which often survived until parliamentary enclosure in the early nineteenth century. The threat was much greater when parcels of glebe, in the course of time and agricultural change, became embedded in the lands of *one* relatively prosperous individual. It was worse still if that individual's land was enclosed, and the glebe was therefore a small island in a private property of increasing value, prosperity and enterprise. Such situations were frequent in the early seventeenth century. Half an acre of land in Wetherden (1635) was 'compassed about with the grounds of . . . Henry Hinchly'; at Naughton (1614) two acres of glebe in a field called 'Dunsetters' were 'within the lands of Nedging Hall' which lay north, south, east and west. One acre at Thurston (1613) was 'encompassed with Sir Robert Druryes grounds on every side'; at Whelnetham Parva (1623) one half-acre in a field called 'Chappell Hill' abutted 'every way upon the land of the lord of the manor'.

Parsons reacted to changing circumstances in various ways. Occasionally they enclosed pieces of glebe to separate them more effectively from their surroundings: at Mellis (1613) an arable piece of three acres lying in a field of Richard Smith was itself 'newly enclosed'. A far more tempting option was simply to rent the land to the enveloping owner. At Eye (1613) Robert Mason 'giveth yearly consideration as the vicar and he can agree' for pieces which were 'intermixed' with his. Nine pieces at Thorpe Morieux (1613) were let 'unto sundry men for whose use they do lie most conveniently'. Sometimes the agreement to rent was obviously of long standing. At Wetherden (1635) a survey was made of three small parcels 'reputed as rectory lands': they had not been in the possession of several successive incumbents, who had nevertheless 'received rents for the same' and 'have continual claims to the same in the right of the church'. Some glebes, for example at Thelnetham (1613) and Bures (1638), were entirely farmed by tenants.

Once rented out, 'surrounded' pieces of glebe could slide away from the parson's control and even melt from local knowledge – especially when tenants deliberately destroyed boundary markers. In Thorpe Morieux (1635) a piece of glebe occupied by Stephen Humphry lay within his close called 'Homefield', but 'all the meers and doles which did formerly distinguish the said glebe from other lands of the said Humphry's are digged or plowed up, all the trees growing thereon felled down, and

36 F. Hervey, ed., *Suffolk in the Seventeenth Century: The Breviary of Suffolk by Robert Reyce*, London 1902, 14, 26, 29, 37–42; D. MacCulloch, ed., *The Chorography of Suffolk*, SRS XIX, 1976, 19–20.

37 In 1577 Walsham le Willows contained a 'common or open field' called West Street Field which was described as 'now divided into sundry parts with hedges and dykes' (K.M. Dodd, ed., *The Field Book of Walsham-le-Willows, 1577*, SRS XVII, 1974, 88).

the said glebe . . . so confounded and mixed with the said Humphry's own freehold lands that no apparent mention of the ancient green meers doth now appear'. Similarly, at Cavendish (1638) a croft of four acres had been reported as glebe 'by several of the ancient inhabitants who are now deceased' but it had 'neither hedge nor ditch nor any stanty[38] to distinguish [it]'. Problems of access could also arise, whereby the parson's right of way was questioned, disputed and finally denied. Without a clear, legal right of way, often across the land of other people, he could not farm his glebe efficiently or ensure an accurate record of it.

The complications of access are well illustrated at Felsham (1638), where the way to a piece of glebe was

> through the narrow lane going from the south end of Gedding Green, and so directly along through the ground now in the occupation of John Bridges, until we come to a field called High Field, and so directly along in High Field till we come to a balk which leadeth to a lodge, which lodge standeth upon the way leading to the said glebe.[39]

Sometimes, when challenged, a parson could call on local support, as at Newton by Sudbury (1613) where the route to one acre was attested by three inhabitants, one of whom had 'reaped corn growing in the said piece and saw it carried through the way aforesaid'. At Thorpe Morieux (1635) the parson's routes were defined in great detail, distinguishing stile-ways, footways, cartways and driftways, and noting responsibilities for maintenance. While tenants of one farm were denied any right of way over one piece of glebe, another farmer was allowed to 'drive over' the same piece 'upon sufferance and leave'. Access to a large close of glebe had previously been the subject of an order from the court of King's Bench. In other parishes rights of way were totally lost. At Milden (1613) a grove belonging to the glebe had 'no known way to it', while Barningham (1635) had five pieces of glebe for which 'we do not know of any way the parsons of Barningham had to the said piece'.

Another stage in the absorption of church land was a refusal to pay rent. Thus a piece of land in Thornham Magna, but belonging to the glebe of Thornham Parva (1613), lay in a field belonging to Mr Ling, but no rent was paid and 'the townsmen cannot say upon their knowledge' that it ever was.[40] At Milden (1613) a pasture, previously a wood, was enclosed in Mr Cutler's ground with no known access; at a later date it was occupied by Thomas Kinge who paid 16d a year to the parson but 'now' defaulted.

To avoid the potential loss of land, incumbents had one other choice: they might negotiate an *exchange*. An eight-acre piece called 'Hilles' at Rishangles (1613) had been exchanged 'time out of mind' for land elsewhere. At Little Thurlow (1613) the resident squire, Sir Stephen Soames, and Sir George le Hunte, of neighbouring

38 'Stanty' = stake or post (*OED*).

39 SROB, E14/4/3, Felsham (1638).

40 When the glebe of one parish lay in another, doubts could all the more easily arise. For example, Hepworth had glebe in neighbouring Weston and Barningham, while Onehouse had land in three other parishes, Harleston, Shelland and Haughley.

Little Bradley, had made at least five exchanges with the rector. A piece of seven acres at Wattisfield (1634) was added to the rectory in 1608 in exchange for twelve small pieces of land: the necessary indenture was signed by the bishop of Norwich, the local patron and the incumbent. This process went on for generations. In 1712 the rector of Hopton wrote that 'finding the glebe land chiefly to consist in small pieces, I made it my business for the good of the church to exchange as many of them as I could'. In fact, he exchanged nineteen pieces with ten local owners.[41] Similar agreements could be negotiated which gave an incumbent an *increase* of land. At Aldham (1613) the glebe contained a grove of one and a half acres, given at some unspecified date to compensate the rector for the loss of wood previously paid to him as tithe. By 1686 it was claimed that six acres of woodland 'were laid to the rectory in lieu of tithe wood'.[42]

As has been said, compilers of terriers had frequent doubts about parcels of glebe: their precise positions, shapes and sizes, and even their legal status. Barningham (1635) was much troubled in this way and its surveyors twice bemoaned, 'we know not certainly where it lieth, for that it hath not been used by the parson within the memory of man'. However in one case 'as we have heard', a man called Reve had paid 16d rent for forty years, and was succeeded by John Reve who paid 8d for about five years. A half-acre at Gislingham (1613) drew a similar remark: 'where it lieth we know not as yet'. A piece of land at Milden (1635) produced a rent but 'whether glebe or not glebe [is] yet in question'. Polstead (1638) referred to 'a flying report' that a block of sixteen acres 'hath formerly been rectory land'.

One of the most telling disagreements occurred at Preston (1613) over an arable piece in a field called 'Potkyns'. The vicar 'sometimes affirmeth five acres and sometimes but one acre', but the patron Robert Reyce, who 'never denied' that he paid 4d a year rent for the land, had it re-measured and found it to be only 'ten perches or poles'. The churchwardens and sidesmen were perplexed, not knowing whether to side with their rector or squire. They took refuge in humility:

> Of both which affirmations, which should be the truth we are unable to set down, considering we are poor, ignorant and unlearned persons, no ways understanding to write or read and newly come into the town, having no means to help us or authority to direct us, and therefore speaking here only from hearsay and report.[43]

These obsequious and disingenuous words hint strongly at the open conflicts and hidden tensions within the early modern parish, and the way in which economic, social, cultural and religious affairs were inextricably mixed.

Such uncertainties could undoubtedly lead to the complete loss of glebeland. A half-acre at Wattisfield (1638) was debated thus: 'we find by some ancient books that it was belonging to the church, but cannot find when it was in the possession of

41 The exchange of glebe land and houses was facilitated by an Act of 1815 (55 Geo. II, c. 147). Further Acts followed in 1816–26.

42 For later exchanges of glebe (seventeenth to nineteenth centuries), see NRO, GLE/1 and SROB, 806/3/1–9.

43 SROB, E14/4/1, Preston (1613).

the church, neither do we know how to find [it]'. A small piece of glebe at Brettenham (1636) lay within a close belonging to Mr Reyce, but 'we cannot lay out the said ground . . . for we do not know which is the piece in all the field'. Sheer bloody-mindedness could also come into play. At Cavendish (1686) one local man acknowledged that he had formerly tenanted three pieces of glebe 'but he would not discover them', and another 'never paid anything or acknowledgeth any glebe'.

Sometimes determined parsons, and their lay supporters, could stem the tide and even turn it.[44] In December 1603 Mr Robert Cooke carried away soil from the head of an arable strip at Langham (1613) but 'divers men [were] ready to testify that they have ploughed and carried corn to the use of the rector'. At Brent Eleigh (1613), Vicarage Field measuring about eight acres was 'now recovered to the vicarage'. Three pieces at Horringer (1638) were for thirty years 'wrongfully detained from the church by the ancestors . . . of William Lucas', but two were exchanged for a New Parsonage Close in 1626 and the third 'was restored to the church the 21st of March 1627'. The battle continued into the next century. In 1784 the rector of Cavendish made a plan of the glebe, because several pieces were 'very near being lost for want of the boundaries being properly kept up by posts and doles'. He then fixed on every piece 'small oak posts, painted white at the top and marked with a G'.

To sum up, the modern historian soon discovers that early terriers have irritating defects, of which imprecision and unevenness are the worst. In consecutive terriers the glebes of individual parishes tend not to be described consistently by name, acreage or abuttals.[45] Often one is not sure that one is dealing with the same piece of land. Nor is it unusual for parcels to be mentioned but not measured.[46] When, on the other hand, surveyors merely copied earlier terriers and manorial extents,[47] as many were prone to do, they risked losing touch with reality on the ground. Nevertheless, when studied in large numbers over sizeable areas, terriers do have considerable historical value, perhaps more in qualitative terms than quantitative. At their most informative, they expose the vulnerability of glebeland in a period of major agricultural change, and the widely differing responses of the clergy.[48]

44 Two Suffolk clerics who in the seventeenth century defended their benefices ferociously were Nathaniel Bisby of Long Melford (SROB, FL509/3/15–16) and Robert Shelford of Ringsfield (see below, pp. 87, 89).

45 Some parcels were measured *with* boundary features: 'with the meers' (Long Melford, n.d.) and 'with the greens' (Stansfield, 1613).

46 Pieces of common meadow were often measured by breadth and not by area: at Cornard Parva (1638) a meadow was described as 'five foot breadth in each end'.

47 Some glebe was copyhold, as at Nedging (1613), and may represent relatively late gifts to the benefice.

48 Commonwealth Surveys of 1650 are available for about twenty benefices in east Suffolk; they mention the values of glebes (not acreage), and show that they were normally worth less than tithes (Cambridge University Library, Microfilm 6617).

Ringsfield: A Case Study

The dangers threatening glebes were best described by parsons who fought to defend their rights. A good example is provided in the Rectory Book of Robert Shelford, Laudian rector of Ringsfield cum Redisham Parva in north-east Suffolk.[49] Over many years this feisty individual argued with his neighbours, and penned strong advice and detailed evidence for the benefit of his successors. When he took over the living in 1603, it was certainly at a low ebb. His predecessor, Thomas Sawin, had been rector for about thirty years but suffered 'much suit and trouble in law amongst his neighbours'. As a consequence he had fallen 'into distraction of his wits [and] despair of his salvation', pretending 'that the adversary had entered him'; he hired curates to do his parochial work and remained housebound for about twelve years. By gathering verbal and documentary evidence Shelford showed that several local landowners had taken advantage of Sawin's incapacity and illness.

For instance, Mr Nicholas Garneis of Redisham Parva had carried out a classic piece of encroachment. At the end of a glebe field he obliterated a hedge ('fence') and row of trees, throwing the soil 'to him selfward', and made a new hedge of layered whitethorn on the glebe. The stumps of the earlier hedge showed quite clearly where 'the fence by right ought to go'. Ten acres of glebe also lay in Garneis's lands, but 'before my time the divisions and meers were so ploughed up to obscure the ground that I could never learn certainly where they lay'.

Another foe was Mr Thomas Fletcher. In Sawin's time he hired two pieces of glebe, but retained one of them 'as his own and would acknowledge no more for glebe'. On his arrival Shelford won an arbitration from two magistrates 'who gave me the whole by their award but he [Fletcher] would not yield me the possession'. Fletcher also ploughed up part of a glebe close, destroyed an old meer and planted a new hedge elsewhere. 'Let men of goodwill judge', said Shelford, 'whether he did not this to bring the close out of knowledge, to defeat the church of her glebes.' Furthermore, in trying to diminish rents payable to the rector Fletcher doctored an old survey book by changing 's' to 'd', that is shillings to pence! In spite of this 'notable corruption', as Shelford called it, Fletcher did the rector a good turn by showing him the book. Without it, 'I should never have had any knowledge of the glebes lying among other men's lands, for the owners of those lands concealed what they could, by ploughing up the meers and detaining of rents by fair means or foul (*per fas et nefas*).'[50]

[49] SROL, FC2/C1/1A; microfilm copy at SROI, JC1/18/1. Shelford also wrote about the parsonage, church, churchyard, tithes and mortuaries. For his life, see T. Copsey, *Suffolk Writers from the Beginning until 1800*, Ipswich 2000, 432. Shelford's will is dated 1638 (PRO, 70 Harvey).

[50] The glebe terrier of Ringsfield (1613) tells the same story: '. . . there are other glebes belonging to the rectory, of which for the most part we have no perfect knowledge for the laying of them out, because they lie among the severals of other men, and have been occupied among such severals by other men time out of mind. We therefore have thought good to set these down as we find them recorded in an ancient drag book [survey] made by Sir Thomas Garnet, sometime parson of Ringsfield in *anno domini* 1543' (SROI, 01/19/56).

Fig. 2. Cosford Deanery, Suffolk: glebe acreages 1086–1887

R/V/C = Rectory/Vicarage/Perpetual Curacy

R/V/C	Parish	1086	1341	17th c.	*c.*1840	1887	Notes
R	Aldham	?7.00	15.50	38.50	44.25	42.00	two churches in 1086; glebe consolidated by 1613; map of glebe 1716; glebe sold with consent of Board of Agriculture & Fisheries 1920.
R	Bildeston	41.00	45.00	51.50	50.75	47.25	
R	Brettenham	24.00	32.00	29.25	24.25	24.25	
R	Chelsworth	30.00	28.00	28.25+	49.00	30.50	by 1834, 12 acres sold to redeem Land Tax
R	Elmsett	15.00	49.00	42.50	29.00	52.00	
R	Hadleigh	?120.00	12.00	no terrier	0.00	nil	in 1086 church had 1 carucate and a mill; ?an early minster
R	Hitcham	2.00	33.00	26.50	32.50	30.75	
C	Kersey	3.00	61.00	no terrier	?	1.25	appropriated to Kersey Priory
R	Kettlebaston		40.00	13.25	14.50	15.25	no mention of church in 1086
R	Layham	41.00	83.00	25.00+	69.75	68.50	pole of 16 feet
C	Lindsey	10.00	67.00	no terrier	?	2.50	appropriated to Kersey Priory; 20 acrres of wood in 1341
R	Naughton		74.00	54.50	55.50	52.00	no mention of Naughton in 1086
R	Nedging	7.00	22.00	12.75	29.75	30.00	
R	Semer	31.00	76.00	61.00	65.25	65.00	
R	Thorpe Morieux	52.00	30.00+	22.25+	21.50	23.00	
C	Wattisham		53.00	24.25+	27.00	nil	no mention of Wattisham in 1086; appropriated to Gt Bricett Priory
R	Whatfield	?2.00	116.00	67.75+	75.50	70.50	?the second church under Aldham in 1086

In 'Advice to my successor' Shelford wrote, 'I beseech thee in the Lord that thou have as great a care how you exchange or let to farm from the glebes . . . lest in tract of time they be either denied . . . or else an ancient custom of under rent prevail upon them, as in the rest of the glebes which are occupied from the parsonage.' Yet in 1663 one of his successors, William Caly, found that Sir Edwin Rich refused to pay a long established rent for ten acres of glebe. The rent had been discontinued during the Civil Wars and Commonwealth, when Rich was a prominent parliamentarian and the rector of the day, Gosling, 'was obnoxious to the power then in being'. Rich fobbed Caly off with 'fair promises', and only when threatened with a bill in Chancery did he agree to start paying the rent again, and with only two years' backlog.

Conclusions

Figures 2 and 3, based on forty parishes in mid Suffolk,[51] attempt to show the sizes of individual glebes across eight hundred years. The following sources were used: Little Domesday Book (1086), the Inquisition of the Ninths (1341), *Valor Ecclesiasticus* (1535), selected glebe terriers (mainly seventeenth-century), tithe apportionments (*c.*1840)[52] and the parliamentary Return of Glebe Lands in England and Wales (1887).[53]

Not surprisingly, the columns show considerable variations and competing trends. Where differences appear within a parish, it is not certain how far these represent genuine changes of acreage, or how far they reflect different methods and standards of survey. Other problems are more technical. First, in appropriated parishes the pre-Reformation sources sometimes identify the rector's portion of glebe, but do not specify what was left (if anything) to the vicar. Secondly, the acre obviously varied in size according to the local perch or pole. In 1341 Debenham used a perch of twenty-one feet; Blaxhall in *c.*1600 a perch of eighteen feet;[54] Thorpe Morieux (1635) a pole of sixteen feet; while Mellis (1613) recorded three pieces of glebe as 'great acres'.[55] Thirdly, one cannot always tell whether the parsonage house, its outbuildings and its immediately surrounding land (gardens, yards and orchards) were included in the total glebe acreage. Fourthly, on a similar point, it is often

51 Thedwastre was a deanery and hundred (Fig. 2), whereas Cosford was a half-hundred and only part of the deanery of Sudbury (Fig. 3). See J. Martin, 'Ecclesiastical Jurisdictions' and E. Martin, 'Hundreds and Liberties', in Dymond and Martin, *Historical Atlas of Suffolk*, 24–7. In Figs 2 and 3, the symbol + indicates a minimum figure, because some terriers do not give acreages for all parcels.

52 R.J.P. Kain and H.C. Prince, *Tithe Surveys for Historians*, Chichester 2000.

53 *British Parliamentary Papers*, 1887, LXIV, gives acreages of glebes in England and Wales, parish by parish, with estimated values.

54 *Inquisitiones Nonarum*, 83; MacCulloch, ed., *Chorography of Suffolk*, 30. The latter also gives the acreage of some glebes, and records that clergy had been deprived of glebe and rents at Cookley (p. 37) and Brent Eleigh (p. 50).

55 The standard perch or pole was 16½ feet, as used at Hitcham (1635).

Fig. 3. Thedwastre Deanery, Suffolk: glebe acreages 1086–1887

R/V = Rectory/Vicarage

R/V	Parish	1086	1341	17th c.	*c.*1840	1887	Notes
R	Ampton	8.00	27.00	18.00	14.75	14.25	
V	Barton, Great	30.00	120.00	88.00		357.00	appropriated to Bury Abbey; 349 acres given to vicar for tithes, glebe and common rights at enclosure, 1805
R	Beyton		12.00	3.25+	9.50	8.75	
R	Bradfield Combust		9.00	4.50	4.75	nil	
R	Bradfield St Clare	10.50	41.00	no terrier	31.75	29.00	
R	Bradfield St George		7.00	7.00	11.25		with Rushbrooke in 1887
R	Drinkstone	12.00	60.00	39.25+	81.00	86.75	
R	Felsham	10.00	13.00	6.50	3.75	4.00	
R	Fornham St Genevieve	14.00	27.00	no terrier		6.50	
R	Gedding	6.00	18.00	8.00	1.50	6.75	
R	Hessett	12.00	24.00	14.00	17.25	19.50	
R	Livermere, Great	12.00	80.00	60.25+	72.00		67 parcels in 1639; with Lt Livermere in 1887
V	Pakenham	30.00	?230.00	79.25+	66.75	68.25	appropriated to Bury Abbey; terrier of 1432
R	Rattlesden	24.00	42.00	37.25	41.00	42.25	39.75 acres in 1678
R	Rougham	40.00	44.00	21.00+		15.00	
R	Rushbrooke		30.00	no terrier			with Bradfield St Geo. in 1887
R	Stanningfield	16.00	54.00	34.25	42.00	43.75	
V	Thurston	30.00	40.00	52.00+	62.75	82.75	appropriated to Bury Abbey
R	Timworth	30.00	36.00	31.50	27.00		with Ingham in 1887
R	Tostock	12.00	18.00	17.75+	12.00	11.50	
R	Whelnetham, Great	40.00	47.00	41.00	54.00	56.00	
R	Whelnetham, Little		40.00	13.50	16.75	23.00	
R	Woolpit	15.00	40.00	34.25	30.50	30.50	

unclear whether the churchyard was included. For example, God's Acre was normally *ex*cluded from seventeenth-century glebe terriers, but *in*cluded in tithe apportionments of *c.*1840. As these two classes of document are the only ones which survey glebeland in detail, the acreages of the churchyard and of the parsonage house and its immediate surroundings have been deliberately excluded from Figs 2 and 3. All other sources merely give a single acreage for each parish, and do not explain how it was calculated.

We can, therefore, only take the figures at face value and look at very broad and crude trends. First, at all dates it is obvious that glebes differed greatly in size. This emphasises the highly variable values of benefices in general – even within tight localities. Secondly, acreages for individual parishes (Figs 2 and 3) give the impression, and no more, that glebes accumulated from late Anglo-Saxon times, probably reaching their maxima in the fourteenth century. Thereafter, some remained stable, others rose, but most seemed to fall. The evidence in terriers certainly suggests why and how glebes may have shrunk in the later medieval and early modern periods. On the other hand, certain parishes appeared to *gain* glebeland after the seventeenth century: the reasons may lie in in the recovery of some land,[56] in new gifts and re-endowments,[57] in allotments in lieu of tithe,[58] and in the effects of parliamentary enclosure.[59] Much more work is needed to dissect and measure the history of glebe. For example, how far were glebelands directly farmed by clergy, and how far rented out? (It is certainly true that probate inventories of post-Reformation incumbents often list crops, animals and farming equipment.) Similarly, how primitive or how advanced was clerical farming across the centuries?[60] Until such questions are more systematically probed, preliminary surveys of this kind can at least demonstrate how vigilant the church had to be in defending its parochial land.

The parson's glebe, in a sense, was the last surviving medieval tenement in the modern landscape. As such its history is contradictory. On the one hand it was a bastion of tradition, a holding which normally retained its fragmented distribution across the centuries (until exchanges or sales took place). On the other hand it was peculiarly vulnerable to the self-interested devices of lay tenants and neighbours; as a result it strongly reflected the agriculture and concerns of whole communities, and even of entire regions.

56 For example, Brent Eleigh (1613) and Horringer (1638).

57 White Kennett, *Impropriations and Vicarages*, London 1704.

58 As at Aldham; see above, p. 85.

59 As at Great Barton; SROB, Q/RI 47, p. 314.

60 See R. O'Day, *The English Clergy: The Emergence and Consolidation of a Profession, 1558–1642*, Leicester 1979, 172–89; M.L. Zell, 'Economic Problems of the Parochial Clergy in the Sixteenth Century', in R. O'Day and F. Heal, eds, *Princes and Paupers in the English Church, 1500–1800*, Leicester 1981, 36–7.

Suffolk Churches in the Later Middle Ages: The Evidence of Wills

Peter Northeast

NEARLY THIRTY YEARS AGO Norman Scarfe reported to the world that I was 'going methodically through all the surviving late-medieval wills to see what bequests relate to work on church fabrics'.[1] While it was true that I was collecting references to church-building from Suffolk wills,[2] 'going methodically through all' was a generous exaggeration of what I was actually doing. Because of other pressures, such as 'teaching school' full-time and involvement in adult education part-time, the coverage of my searches was akin to those early archaeological distribution maps purporting to show the spread of artefacts, whereas what they actually showed was where archaeologists had been most active. In my case, though, it was the areas in which there were centres of the old Cambridge Extra-Mural Board; the wills to be examined were determined by the location of the centre(s) at which I was teaching, or about to teach, at any one time. Similarly, 'all' needed qualification, for a rough count showed that well over 23,000 wills written before 1550, and relating to Suffolk, had survived:[3] life was just not going to be long enough.

Fortunately, both Norman and I have survived this long; now seems to be an appropriate occasion on which to present something of a progress report. While reading the wills in the early years of my searches it soon became apparent that many of them contained a wealth of interest, in addition to the church-building they might mention. I therefore abandoned my original practice of simply noting references to church fabric and, instead, made a 'full abstract' of each will that I dealt with. This inevitably slowed down progress but has been more satisfactory in the long run, throwing light on many other facets of parish life; for instance, it was

1 N. Scarfe, *The Suffolk Landscape*, London 1972, 202.

2 Adrian Allan, an archivist in the old West Suffolk Record Office in the 1960s, had been combing the Sudbury archdeaconry wills in preparation for the forthcoming revision of Pevsner's *Suffolk*, and convinced me of the value of this source.

3 These are made up of wills in the following collections (totals very approximate): records of the archdeaconry of Sudbury, including those proved in both the sacrist's and the archdeacon's courts ('Bury wills'), 8,000; records of the archdeaconry of Suffolk ('Ipswich wills'), 8,500; records of the consistory court of Norwich ('NCC wills'), 5,500; records of the Prerogative Court of Canterbury, now held by the Public Record Office ('PCC wills'), 1,200; others, chiefly the registers of the Archbishops of Canterbury ('Lambeth wills'), 130.

largely references in wills that made possible the identification of over five hundred religious gilds and about 150 medieval chapels in the county.[4] At the time of writing I have completed abstracts of something over 13,000 wills,[5] which means that a large number remain unexamined, and some patches of the county have hardly been looked at. Consequently, any conclusions arrived at for the county as a whole must be provisional, although it does not seem unreasonable to regard 13,000 as a substantial and reliable sample. The dates (of writing) of these wills run from 1353 to 1550, the latter, in view of the enormous changes then taking place in the English church, seeming to be a suitable cut-off date.[6] Fortuitously this period of time largely coincides with that during which the Perpendicular style of architecture was prevalent. The large number of our churches exhibiting examples of 'Perp.' is an indication of just how much building activity there was in those years, and we would expect this to be reflected in the wills.

The great majority of pre-Reformation testators left money to their parish churches, almost as an obligatory custom, like the payment for forgotten tithes. In the main they used general terms, like 'to the use/work/reparation' etc. of the parish church, but it is when they left bequests to specific aspects that our interest is especially aroused. One of the difficulties, though, is that the medieval will-maker used the term 'reparation' (both in Latin and English) for any type of building-work, not only for repairing, as is made clear in expressions such as 'to the reparation of the new tower'. When the word 'new' is not actually stated, the reader has to use his or her judgement to assess the character of the work being aided. A look at the surviving building often solves the problem: 'reparation' of a Saxo-Norman tower in the fifteenth century was obviously repair; 'reparation' of a Perpendicular porch is likely to have been building. One area, though, where care has to be taken, is that of some towers, for example Felsham, which Pevsner categorised as Decorated, i.e. early fourteenth-century, although wills show them being built in the fifteenth century; he seems to have been misled by the continued use of ogee tracery in windows, usually regarded as being distinctive of the Decorated period.

While I remain mindful of the number of wills yet to be examined, the totals of building projects so far discovered, and their dates, can be summarised in the following table:

4 See *An Historical Atlas of Suffolk*, ed. D. Dymond and E. Martin, 3rd edn, Ipswich 1999, 56, 74.

5 But over six hundred of these, among the earlier Bury wills, consist of 'probates only', that is, containing no actual wills, only probate sentences.

6 The earliest (Suffolk) will known in each of the collections is as follows: Bury, 1353 (sacrist's) and 1434 (archdeacon's); Ipswich, 1436; NCC, 1370; PCC, 1361; Lambeth, 1368.

	pre-1400	1401–25	1426–50	1451–75	1476–1500	1501–25	1526–50
Aisle/chapel	3	5	16	23	26	18	17
Clerestory	nil	nil	nil	3	3	5	3
Roof	2	3	3	16	11	32	14
Tower	18	20	53	63	33	26	22
Porch	3	nil	14	26	15	8	4
Window	7	5	8	27	20	15	5

NOTE: the above figures represent 'projects', not bequests; when a project continues from one period into another it has been entered in *both* periods and would therefore be duplicated in any totals derived from the figures.

These figures, however incomplete, impressively emphasise the amount of church-building going on in the county in the fifteenth century and continuing into the sixteenth. It has to be borne in mind that the figures for the first two date-periods are not strictly comparable with the remainder, since no archdeaconry wills have survived from before the 1430s; those two sets of numbers have, therefore, been generated from a far smaller body of wills than the later ones. Aisles have been combined with chapels since it is difficult to differentiate them; for instance, Walter Fulburn's chantry chapel at Wickham Market is now regarded as the south aisle; sometimes the contemporaries were not sure, as indicated by building at St Matthew's, Ipswich, which was described as 'a le ele or a le peugh'.[7] 'Roof' indicates money given to some kind of work on a roof, not necessarily the erecting of one of Suffolk's marvellous timber roofs. Similarly it is frequently impossible to tell whether it was the stone or the glass that was meant by 'window'. Towers, clerestories and porches are more unequivocal, and the figures indicate that more than twelve per cent of Suffolk churches were building their towers in the third quarter of the fifteenth century. Donations were sometimes made to chancels, but as they were the responsibility of rectors, and not laity, they are not included here. An exception worthy of notice is that of Blythburgh, to the chancel of which many bequests were made over the period 1443–75, although the priory there, as rector, should have been responsible for any work done on it.

Bequests, it has to be remembered, were statements of intent, not evidence of accomplished action. This is well illustrated by the wills of William Cady of Rushmere St Andrew and his wife.[8] Early in 1497 William stated in his will that his executors should pay all the mason's costs of building a 'steeple' if the parishioners agreed to build one. Twenty years later, when the widow came to write her will, nothing had been done and she reiterated her husband's promise to pay the mason's costs. This time, presumably, the parish availed themselves of the offer, for Rushmere has a Perpendicular tower. The case of Debenham's vestry was similar; after two abortive bequests in the 1460s Robert Cheke left a substantial gift for its

7 Will of Richard Rendelsham, 1448: SROI, IC/AA2/1/71.

8 NRO, NCC 44 Multon; SROI, IC/AA2/8/201.

building in 1476, and agreed to more than double it if the parishioners actually began the vestry within the next three years.[9]

The bare figures of the table are, of course, derived from very diverse and varied bequests and relate to diverse and varied building activities. The inclusion of any element of church-building in a will is something of a lottery, depending on the coincidence of several factors – the desire on the part of the will-maker to give to such a cause in the first place, the existence of a need, the sympathy of the testator (and the 'pushiness' of the clergy) for the project, the available wealth of the individual and perhaps the demands and opinions of his or her family. Consequently, we have to count our good fortune, and make use of it, when we do discover useful building references, but not make any assumptions when we do not; deductions from negative evidence are not valid in this context. For instance, the virtual rebuilding of both Lavenham and Long Melford churches is well reflected in many bequests,[10] whereas the erection of Beccles church from scratch went largely unnoticed by testators, after an initial donation in 1369,[11] until an avalanche of contributions to the tower over a period of thirty years in the sixteenth century. Similarly, on the other side of the county, the extensive fifteenth-century work in the impressive church of Mildenhall received no mention in wills, but the building of a lady chapel over the north porch elicited many donations. One wonders just what determined testators to give or not to give; it must have been to do with the way each individual campaign was organised and funded. This reminds us that, though here we are looking at will-giving, many donations were also being made by people during their lives, and much rebuilding, as at Mildenhall and Long Melford, must have been financed in this way. Denston church is another fine fifteenth-century building not referred to by testators; presumably that was paid for by the founders of the associated college.

Towers and porches seem to have been projects given most support by will-makers, perhaps because the building of each continued for some years, and so would have been very much in evidence. Of the towers, Beccles (1515–47), Bungay St Mary (1441–72), Eye (1453–79), Framlingham (1483–1521), Kersey (1430–72), Laxfield (1444–76), Rougham (1458–88), Stoke by Nayland (1439–62) and Woodbridge (1444–63) are some of the fine examples dated by bequests. At Helmingham, for which a contract of 1488 survives and to which gifts were made in the 1480s and 90s, things were obviously desperate by 1538 when John Wythe donated £5 to the 'battlement of the steeple' on condition that 'Mr Talmach or eny man els begin to make it within iiij^{or} yeres after my departing owt of this worlde or els none to be paied',[12] while at Lavenham, despite several huge injections of money

9 Will: SROI, IC/AA2/2/329.

10 See 'Bequests to Lavenham Church (1374–1540)', in A. Betterton and D. Dymond, *Lavenham, Industrial Town*, Lavenham 1989, Appendix 2, and C. Paine, 'The Building of Long Melford Church', in *A Sermon in Stone*, ed. C. Sansbury, Lavenham 1983, 9–18.

11 Robert Botild, chaplain, of Mutford, left 3s 4d 'to the fabric of the new church of Bekles': NRO, NCC 17 Heydon; there were also two gifts to the porch in the 1450s.

12 Will: NRO, NCC 356 Attmere.

from local clothiers, they never did quite finish their grand tower and it is still without its pinnacles. The epitome of lost causes, though, was the attempt to build a tower at East Bergholt, where, after an initial gift early in 1527 and a further £20 ten years later, 'when the parish do build the said steeple', clothier Thomas Grythe chanced his last throw in the form of a hundred marks in 1542;[13] but it was too late, the Reformation was upon them, and Bergholt was left with a stump, illustrating, according to local folklore, the fall of Wolsey (in 1529!).[14]

The building of several of the best porches in the county can, similarly, be dated through bequests. These include Boxford (1441–80), Stratford St Mary (1523–26), Ufford (1466–75), Woodbridge (1455–63) and Woolpit (1430–73). In Woolpit's case, the last contribution to the actual building of the porch was in 1451, but in 1473 a dying rector left money to provide five statues to fill the niches that had stood empty for over twenty years. Again, there are notable omissions, one being that of Lavenham where it is assumed that the earl of Oxford funded the porch since his arms were included in the stonework (and which perhaps discouraged other contributions).

As has been said above, it is not safe to rely on negative evidence in the matter of church-building. The absence of bequests is by no means proof that no work had been carried out. One clue to otherwise unrecorded building activity is a reference to 'hallowing'. It was ecclesiastical law that when substantial alterations to the fabric of the building had taken place, the church should be 'hallowed' or 'reconciled' using salt and water, the standard means of purification. At Earl Stonham there is no record of the making of that church's remarkable carved roof, but in his will of 1534 Thomas Wissoncroft left 40s 'to the church of Stonham for to have the church and churchyard reconciled and new hallowed . . . the money to remain in my executors' hands until the township have the church hallowed'.[15]

It can be seen from the table on p. 95 that the number of projects supported by testators in the last period is far smaller than those in the preceding ones. Examination of the bequests year by year shows that the numbers of those given to church-building had been decreasing throughout the 1530s and by the early 1540s had dropped to a little more than a handful in any one year. A few on-going projects continued to receive support, like Beccles tower (until 1547), the roofs of Chattisham (1545) and Helmingham (1540) and Halesworth north aisle (1543). New proposals were the building of an aisle at Bruisyard (1544) and making a new chancel at Aldeburgh (1545), though whether either was pursued we are unable to tell, due to later, post-Reformation, work at both. A large extension, including five new windows, to the south aisle of St Mary le Tower, Ipswich, was ordered in 1540,

13 Will: PCC 3 Spert.

14 For the part played by the gentry in tower-building, see C. Carpenter, 'The Religion of the Gentry of Fifteenth-Century England', in *England in the Fifteenth Century*, ed. D. Williams (Woodbridge 1987), 53–74, esp. 65–6, and C. Richmond, 'The English Gentry and Religion, *c.*1500', in *Religious Belief and Ecclesiastical Careers in Late Medieval England*, ed. C. Harper-Bill (Woodbridge 1991), 121–50, esp. 132–3.

15 NRO, NCC 237 Attmere.

but that was to accommodate portman Thomas Manser's grandiose ideas for his tomb.[16] It is clear from this that, as they approached the mid-sixteenth century, testators were giving less frequently to church fabric, which, presumably, implies that less work on it was being undertaken, although, bearing in mind the dangers of using negative evidence, we cannot be too categorical about this. Superficially, at least, the approaching Reformation would seem to have been affecting the attitude of either builders or givers, or both.

Evidence of the great majority of building projects indicated by bequests can still be found in the fabric of our churches, apart from the few instances where it has been obliterated by over-enthusiastic nineteenth-century restorers. When we turn to church interiors, however, it is a different matter. As we can see only too well today, clergy and congregations continually adapt ('re-order' seems to be the favourite word) arrangements, decoration and equipment to changing ideas of worship, and thus it has always been. Even before the Reformation, changes had occurred in the long evolution of Christian worship and new practices had been adopted in this development,[17] so that, although to modern eyes medieval churches had a uniform internal arrangement, there were bound to be local variations, and even the norm is difficult to assess because of the many subsequent changes. The numerous incidental references to internal arrangements in churches that occur in wills are therefore of considerable interest and of great value.

The marked contrast between any Anglican church today and a medieval church, although the building is virtually the same, is in the relationship between its two major components, nave and chancel. Before the Reformation the two were regarded almost as separate buildings, looked after and used by two different sets of people – the clergy and their assistants in the chancel and the laity in the nave. The two were physically divided by the rood-screen, surmounted by loft and rood, which presented a major visual impression to all worshippers entering the building. The term 'rood-screen' was not used by the medieval will-maker; to him or her it was always the 'rood-loft' or the 'candlebeam', the two terms being synonymous and implying the whole structure of screen, loft and rood. Occasionally, 'perch' (sometimes 'perk') was also used, with the same meaning, apparently likening the rood-beam to a perch within a hen-house.

Bequests to roods and rood-lofts in the county were numerous through most of the fifteenth century and continued until almost the eve of the Reformation, when all roods, viewed by the reformers as the epitome of idolatry, were hauled down. The earliest gift found to a rood-loft was in 1439, when William Baron left 66s 8d, a considerable amount, to the making of the rood-loft in All Saints, Newmarket, then only a chapel, and technically in Cambridgeshire.[18] It is known that rood-screens had existed in our churches long before that,[19] so the fifteenth-century work must

16 Will: NRO, NCC 152 Cooke.

17 See, for instance, R.W. Pfaff, *New Liturgical Feasts in Later Medieval England*, Oxford 1970.

18 SROB, Baldwyne 4.

19 See, for example, M.H. Bloxam, 'On Rood Screens, Rood Lofts and Rood Altars', in *Reports and Papers of Associated Achitectural Societies* xii, 1874, 176–85.

have been mainly in the addition, or development, of lofts. This supposition is supported by the bequest, only a few months after that of Baron, to the fabric of 'la vyce of la rodeloft' in Haverhill church.[20] Over the county as a whole substantial sums of money were given to the constructing, painting and gilding of lofts and the figures of the Virgin Mary, Christ on the cross and St John the Evangelist above them. At Haughley they were accompanied by two angels[21] and at Blythburgh by two archangels[22] – a form of one-upmanship? And behind the figures in some churches was painted boarding, as still to be seen at Wenhaston, though no longer *in situ* there: in 1457 John Jenowr of Old Newton left instructions for 'board, to make a reredos at the back of the crucifix in an honest and good manner, to be provided for the carpenter and the parishioners of the same town'.[23]

The amount of money that could be involved in the erection of rood-lofts is illustrated by Agnes Sexten's bequest of a hundred pounds to a Lavenham candlebeam in 1520, which, even for cloth-rich Lavenham, was a lot of money.[24] Just occasionally we learn the identity of the craftsmen involved in this work, as in the case of John Horold of Clare, 'clothman', who referred in his will of 1478 to an indenture made between the churchwardens there and Thomas Goche of Sudbury, carver, for the making of the new roodloft.[25] At Huntingfield, in 1510, we learn of bargains made with a certain John Wade for painting the candlebeam, two tabernacles and three other images.[26] The painting of rood-screen panels seems never to have been mentioned specifically, though it was, no doubt, included in the more general description of painting the candlebeam. Donors to screens were certainly recognised by their contemporaries, for individuals' names have survived on the woodwork of some, as at Bedfield and Westhall. One would like to think that the term 'pane' (variously spelt) sometimes referred to a panel, but it seems always to have meant a section of the rood-loft itself. No mention of an organ on a rood-loft has been found (although Roger Martin's wonderful description of Long Melford church refers to one),[27] but an altar on the Assington loft was implied by the request in 1470 for the vicar there to celebrate masses 'on the rodeloft'.[28] Bequests to rood-lofts and candlebeams became less frequent in the 1530s, as in the case of general church-building, although as late as 1545 Richard Fryer left a bequest to the 'ceiling of the candlebeam' in the church of Statford St Andrew – either a canopy of honour or vaulting beneath the loft.[29]

20 Will of William Claydon: SROB, Baldwyne 8.
21 Will of Robert Cooke, vicar, dated 1537: SROB, Poope 24.
22 Will of John Wulsy, dated 1506: SROI, IC/AA2/4/226.
23 SROB, Baldwyne 187.
24 Will: PCC 31 Ayloffe.
25 PCC 35 Wattys.
26 Will of Robert Barker, parson: NRO, NCC 303 Spyltymber.
27 D. Dymond and C. Paine, *The Spoil of Melford Church*, Ipswich 1992, 2.
28 Will of John Framelyngham, clerk: NRO, NCC 41 Betyns.
29 Will: SROI, IC/AA2/15/235. Norfolk, of course, is particularly rich in rood-screens: see S. Cotton, 'Mediaeval Roodscreens in Norfolk – their Construction and Painting Dates', *NA* xl, 1987, 44–54.

While the rood-loft and rood were together the visual centre of the medieval church, the spiritual centre was the high altar at the east end of the chancel, which members of the laity normally saw only from afar, through the rood-screen. Virtually every testator left a sum of money, however small, to the high altar, in lieu of forgotten tithes or other dues. This payment often gives an indication of the wealth and status of the testator, although it is a yardstick that must be used with care; payments of over a pound indicate wealth and under a shilling (usually) limited means, but one must beware the miserly rich man.

The tithe-payment was made to the high altar as representative of the incumbent of the church, but numerous bequests were made to the actual, physical, altar. These varied enormously, from small kerchiefs for use on the altar during mass to huge retables standing at the back. Table-cloths (some remarkably long) and sheets were given as altar-cloths, often accompanied by towels, while ornate bed-covers were given to spread on the floor before the altar for major festivals. Money was given for the purchase of the equipment used during services – chalices, cruets, thuribles, censers, ships, pyxes, paxes, chrismatories, even a 'monster' (monstrance). Most of these were made of silver, towards which silver table-ware or ornaments were sometimes given, but good quality brass was also specified. Contributions towards service books were frequent, or volumes were donated, especially by the clergy or the wealthy out of their private chapels. Cloths were given for canopies, varying from small ones for the pyx (as can still be seen at Dennington) to more elaborate arrangements covering the whole altar, later giving way to the device known as a trimmer.

The prize for ingenuity, though, goes to John Almyngham's brain-child at Walberswick: 'a canopy over the high altar, well done, with Our Lady and four angels and the Holy Ghost going up and down, with a "chyine" (or "chyme") (?chain or chime)'.[30] Almyngham obviously realised that this was a little over the top and proposed a tabernacle for the church's patron saint as an alternative. The problem with any canopy must always have been the means of suspension. One solution was to panel the section of roof above the altar and paint it as a canopy of honour, or simply paint that piece of roof.[31] Presumably it was such a canopy of honour that Master Thomas Moryell of Chelsworth intended when he instructed his executors to 'cover over the high altar in that church with planed wood',[32] and what was meant by the 'selyng over the sacrament' to which Rose Lightsterk bequeathed £5 at Nayland.[33] Similar canopies of honour were made over the

30 Will dated 1500: SROI, IC/AA2/4/67.

31 Perhaps the finest canopy surviving in the county is that of John Baret in St Mary's church, Bury St Edmunds. In his remarkably detailed will he requested burial by Our Lady's altar, and specified 'iij merours of glas to be sette in the myddys of the iij woytes [vaults] above my grave'. The mirrors can still be seen in the ceiling, together with Baret's 'reson' [motto]. His long will of 1463 (SROB, Hawlee 95) was printed by Tymms in his *Bury Wills* (Camden Society, 1850).

32 Will dated 1495: NRO, NCC 229 Wolman.

33 Will dated 1504: PCC 17 Holgrave.

rood-loft, as seen in John Coole's bequest to the 'celyng over the candlebeam' at Falkenham.[34]

At each end of the high altar in a late-medieval church was a tabernacle housing the image of a saint, the one the patron saint of the church and the other the Virgin Mary.[35] If the patron saint of a particular church was the Virgin Mary, the second tabernacle would house another saint with whom the church felt an affinity. Numerous bequests were made to the making, painting and gilding of these tabernacles, and their enclosed images, together with others in the church, throughout the fifteenth century and up to the Reformation. 'Tabernacle' is a confusing word: the tabernacles housing saints were ornately decorated niches, whereas the tabernacle in a Roman Catholic church today is a box-like receptacle holding the sacrament. This second meaning was also used in the medieval church contemporaneously with the first, as seen in the gift of £5 made by John Prentyzys of Kersey 'for a tabernacle to be made of gold and silver, for carrying the chalice containing the body of Christ on holy Corpus Christi day'.[36]

The skill of the carver and painter was also in great demand for the production of panels, retables or reredoses (Latin *tabula*) for the altars in the church, not just the high altar. Each altar in the church probably had some form of *tabula* standing on it, though those at the high altar would have been the grandest. They were often of alabaster, like the panel depicting the Adoration of the Magi now preserved in the wall at Long Melford, but many were of wood and could be large, as we learn from Martin's description of the reredos behind the high altar at Melford, 'made of one great tree'.[37] Bequests to the making of such retables were extremely common, though few give us much idea of what was to be depicted on them. Typical are the donations of a cleric of Stowmarket, who gave the church of St Mary 'a retable to stand behind the altar',[38] and the vicar of Southwold who left 'a retable of alabaster' to the town.[39] More specific, however, was the gift of the rector of Kedington who bequeathed 'a panel depicting the passion of Christ and superaltars for the high altar, *viz.* one of the passion of Christ, one of the resurrection and one of the Trinity'.[40]

All churches had side, or low, altars, in addition to the high altar. Many had side aisles or chapels which housed these other altars, but failing that, they would have been placed on the nave side of the screen, either side of the entrance to the chancel. The instructions of Margaret Bedyngfeld (sister and heir to the powerful Sir Thomas Tuddenham, knight, of Oxburgh) for her burial at Eriswell describe the situation there: she wished 'to be buried before the image of the holy cross [i.e. the

34 Will dated 1526: NRO, NCC 175 Groundesburgh.

35 Care is needed when referring to patron saints of medieval churches; they were largely 'forgotten' during the Reformation and when re-introduced in the eighteenth century were sometimes changed. The dedication of more than thirty Suffolk churches was changed in this way.

36 Will dated 1445: SROB, Baldwyne 122.

37 *Spoil of Melford*, 1.

38 Will of John Freschese, clerk, dated 1423: NRO, NCC 119 Hyrnyng.

39 Will of Robert Scolys, vicar of Reydon *cum* Southwold, dated 1470: NRO, NCC 83 Betyns.

40 Will of John Lenne, clerk, dated 1375: NRO, NCC 138 Heydon.

rood], next to the altar of the Blessed Virgin Mary in the nave of the parish church of St Peter, Eriswell'. From this we can see that the Lady altar was beside the central aisle, in the nave, against the screen. Unfortunately, she did not say which side of the aisle it was; evidence from some wills makes it seem likely that Lady chapels were formerly on the north side of the church, but were sometimes switched to the south later in the fifteenth century.

Burial directions in wills often give glimpses of the internal arrangements of churches at the time. Obviously, only a minority of those dying in a parish would be buried in the church. Incumbents and patrons were allowed to be buried in the chancel, and burial in the nave for the laity depended on wealth and status – as seen by contemporaries of the deceased, not by the deceased him or herself. So William Style of Ipswich St Nicholas had to add 'if it please the parishioners of the said parish' to his request for burial before the image of St Saviour there,[41] but, even though his burial had been agreed to, his widow was still unsure that she would be allowed to be buried by him, when making her will.[42] Nearly twenty years later John Fynne of the neighbouring parish of St Stephen showed in his will how the vicissitudes of life could affect a person's position after death, when he wrote that he wished 'to be buried in the church or in the churchyard of St Stephen's; if God fortune me of the value at that time of my departing, that then to lie in the said church; if I be not of power and value, then to lie in the churchyard'.[43] In another Ipswich parish, that of St Clement, space in the church was obviously becoming restricted, for the gravestone of John Forgon, a wealthy tanner, was to be laid 'as the rome will serve'.[44] Across the county, at Lavenham, there were so many 'of power and value' that it is surprising that room continued to be found in the church for all those qualifying.

John Forgon the tanner had requested burial 'before the pew where my wife doth use to sit, in the cross aley of the said church'. The 'cross aley' was presumably that between the north and south doors, and the term 'pew' implies that some form of special seat or box pew had been erected, because the open seats of the medieval church were usually referred to as stools or benches. Nave interiors were much more open than those to which we are accustomed, as can be seen from the words of John Barker of Long Melford, although space was evidently becoming scarcer there, too; he wanted to be buried in the church 'especially in the place thereas I go walking if any space at that time there may be had'.[45] Immediately before the rood was the prime place for the burial of those who did not qualify to be in the chancel. In a building in which parishioners rarely went beyond the rood-screen, that spot before the rood was of great significance in the life, and death, of the inhabitants. It was where the major part of the marriage ceremony took place and, as we learn from Gerard Sothyll of Euston, it was where the bier stood during the funeral service,

41 Will dated 1463: SROI, IC/AA2/2/291.
42 Will of Isabel Style, dated 1487: PCC 40 Milles.
43 Will dated 1525: PCC 40 Porch.
44 Will dated 1525: PCC 39 Bodfelde.
45 Will dated 1495: PCC 5 Horne.

'where the bere is wont to stand' in his words.[46] Although a member of the gentry, Sothyll was not the patron and so could not claim burial in the chancel. The patron, on the other hand, could sit in the chancel during service-time and be buried there. Thus, Robert Reydon of Creeting St Peter could request burial in the chancel 'afore the desks where I was wont to say my prayers and before St Peter', showing that his seat was to one side of the high altar, close to the image of the patronal saint.[47]

The third element to attract popular devotion and substantial gifts in the medieval church, after the rood and high altar, was the sepulchre, otherwise known as the sepulchre of Our Lord or the Easter sepulchre. Despite being in use on only three days in the year it received donations from the great majority of testators. In essence it was a kind of cupboard, or receptacle, but took many forms. It could be built as part of the fabric or set up annually, always on the north wall of the chancel. It represented the tomb of Christ in which his body was laid after the crucifixion. The consecrated Host was placed in it on Good Friday, together with a cross, and taken out with great ceremony on Easter Sunday, in commemoration of the resurrection. Martin described the Melford form of the ceremony, but was not very explicit about the sepulchre itself.[48] A tomb, usually purpose-built or specially adapted, was often used and burial under the sepulchre was one of the prime positions in the church, for the great Easter ceremonies would be conducted about you for evermore. Sir Thomas Barnardiston, of Kedington, was one who specified burial under the 'sepulker'.[49]

From Good Friday till Easter morning the sepulchre would be decorated with rich cloths and surrounded by many lights, and ceremonially 'watched' day and night – one of the rare occasions when members of the laity would enter the chancel. At Long Melford it was John Clopton, lord and benefactor of that place, who provided the rich cloths, 'cloths of velvet with all manner of branches, flowers and all other stuff', which he wanted put over his grave at his funeral and then to be kept for use on the sepulchre for ever.[50] All churches seem to have been continually refurbishing their sepulchres, and many bequests were made to their gilding and painting and occasionally their renewal (at Little Bealings a new sepulchre was to be made 'after the best fashion of any hereabout').[51] But it was primarily to the lights about the sepulchre that most gifts were made. Numerous tapers and candles of various sizes feature in the bequests, and different groups, such as 'singlemen', 'maidens' and 'husbandmen' added their lights to those of individuals and to 'the common light' which was provided by the parish as a whole. At Bramford part of the sepulchre was what sounds like a miniature candle-beam, in its original meaning: 'the beam in the chancel that the tapers stand on at Easter'.[52]

46 Will dated 1528: PCC 4 Thower.
47 Will dated 1505: NCC 243 Ryxe.
48 *Spoil of Melford*, 3–4.
49 Will dated 1542: PCC 11 Spert.
50 Will dated 1494: PCC 17 Horne.
51 Will of Robert Cole, dated 1504: NRO, NCC 23 Garnon.
52 Will of John Sekilmere, dated 1524: SROI, IC/AA2/8/430.

Lights, in their great variety, were the aspect of church maintenance most consistently supported by testators. Torches provided the illumination of the church, tapers were used for votive purposes, that is, in honour of particular images or supporting specific petitions; all were at times referred to as candles. There were also lamps, usually using oil rather than wax. Torches were used to illuminate funerals; the executors of the wealthy provided what they needed (often giving the unburnt portions to local churches), while others used the parish torches, paying for what they had used during the funeral (called the 'waste'). Every church had a number of images, all of which had votive lights burning before them, provided by parishioners. Lights also burnt before the high altar and before the rood. Some of these would have been provided by the parish, the 'common light', the remainder by individuals. There were many lights on the candle-beam (as the name suggests), and often a rowel or chandelier hanging before it. All received contributions from testators and other parishioners, who often gave personal lights also. Any chapel would have its own set of lights, supported by its own devotees. Testators left money to support specific lights, the most popular being those of the Virgin Mary, of whom there might be three statues in the church, one at the high altar, one in the Lady chapel and Our Lady of Pity (the *pietà*), the last of these apparently becoming popular during the fifteenth century.

Virtually all this giving to different aspects of the church was, explicitly or implicitly, for the good of the testator's soul. The doctrine of purgatory dictated that the soul of each individual (except the holy or the damned) had to go through a purging process before being able to progress to heaven, and the associated belief was that its passage could be aided both by deeds of charity and by the prayers of third parties. In this discussion of varying bequests we have so far seen much of what to the medieval mind would have been deeds of charity but little of third-party prayer, whereas the truth is that testators throughout the fifteenth century and well into the sixteenth spent practically as much money and effort in procuring the saying of prayers as they did on the maintenance and improvement of churches. The great majority of testators set aside money for the hiring of priests to celebrate mass for their souls. The wealthy set up chantries (of varying numbers of years) for the purpose, whereas the less well-off had to be satisfied with a year, or a fraction of a year, of a priest's service. Many gifts were made to houses of friars, in the hope that they would add their multiple prayers. The four main orders of friars were Augustinian (Austin), Dominican (Preachers or Black), Franciscan (Grey) and Carmelite (White), and some testators aimed to give to all four (in case one order should have the edge over the others?), although not everyone could afford this. The friars, in their wanderings among communities, in contrast to cloistered monks, had obviously made themselves very popular. They seem to have been trusted more than the parish clergy, for instance, in the celebration of St Gregory's trentals (sets of thirty masses said on certain specified feasts). They were even used by the parish clergy themselves, although the two were traditionally reputed to be at loggerheads.

Among several devices for getting as many people praying for your soul as possible, the practice called a 'sangred' (an East Anglian word) or 'certain' was adopted. This consisted of having one's name added to the parish bede-roll so that the priest read it out each Sunday from the pulpit, during mass, bidding his hearers to pray for that soul. For this the priest was paid 4s 4d for the year (1d per Sunday).

The choice of burial place was influenced by this wish for people's prayers. Inside the church, somewhere in an 'alley' was a desired spot, for large numbers of folk attending church would walk over the grave, read the inscription on the stone and (it was hoped) say prayers for the deceased. For example, John Bakon of Hessett instructed his executors to have engraved on his stone, 'Wee praye yowe for to praye for the soules of John Bakon and Agnes and Margery his wyffes, on whoes soules Jesu have mercye'.[53] Out in the churchyard, paths, especially near doors, were for the same reason favoured burial spots. Since it was believed that prayers were particularly valuable at anniversaries of the date of death and/or burial the accurate recording of the date on the gravestone was of vital importance.

The porch was particularly sought after as a place of burial. Not only would all the worshippers coming to church read the tombstone (or have it read to them) but the wall could also be used for a commemorative plaque. One of the rectors of Hitcham saw this potential: after specifying burial in the porch he asked for a stone to be placed in the wall and in it 'to be set a piece of latten and thereon written in letters my name and the day of my sepulture, so as my good friends may have remembrance to pray for my soul, and the letters therein to be gilt'.[54]

Names displayed on donated items in the church were another common means of encouraging prayers for the deceased. Inscriptions on the rood-loft (as at Woodbridge and Westhall), on the font (Blythburgh and Hessett) and on the outside of the church (Long Melford) all gave names to be prayed for. These have all (to a varied extent) survived the centuries, but names were also recorded on more ephemeral objects such as vestments. John Thurston, a wealthy goldsmith and embroiderer of London, who was, apparently, originally of Earl Soham, left vestments to five London churches, and to two churches in Norfolk and to three in Suffolk, on all of which were to be woven requests (in Latin) for prayers to be said for Thurston and his wives. At Earl Soham similar exhortation to prayer (this time in English) specified the souls of Thurston's parents as well as those of himself and his wives – these to be recorded on each item making up the vestments.[55]

Gathering numbers of people together to make use of their prayers was also the purpose of generous funerals; food and drink encouraged good attendance and giving 1d each to the poor (in hope of their prayers) got them to come. The medieval practice of seven-day, thirty-day and anniversary commemorations, with the incentive of further doles, ensured the continuing attendance of prayer-sayers.

As the sixteenth century progressed, the practice of hiring priests and paying friars to say masses for souls became less regular, although testators varied from one area to another. This trend seems to have begun in the early 1530s, but some places would appear not to have been affected until the 1540s. If the popularity of the

53 Will dated 1536: PCC 10 Crumwell.

54 Will of Thomas Fyssher, dated 1505: PCC 30 Holgrave.

55 Will dated 1520: PCC 23 Maynwaryng.

friars was waning, it might explain why Henry VIII and Thomas Cromwell were able to close down the friaries without any substantial opposition; had they tried to do so fifty years previously they might well have been met with a popular outcry. Although professional praying for souls appears to have been going out of favour, there was no sign of moving away from traditional ceremonies – thirty-day and anniversary commemorations were still going ahead, together with their concomitant prayers. It is particularly surprising that a lady such as Margaret Clerke, a widow from Stoke by Nayland, whose will opens with a strongly protestant preamble, should follow it up with 'my body to be buried within the church of the said Stoke with such honest ceremonies as laudably be accustomed to be observed in the said church, no rights nor duties to be abridged or withholden'.[56] This reminds us of the danger of viewing people's attitudes in the past with modern preconceptions.

The Reformation swept away most of the fittings and decoration of the medieval church. Few illustrations of English church interiors of that time have survived, and none of Suffolk. We have, therefore, to be thankful that so much detail was given by testators well into the sixteenth century. Never again was this to be so, and consequently we are in the fortunate position of knowing more about the internal arrangements of late medieval churches than we do of those of the next two centuries.

[56] Will dated 1539: SROB, Poope 230.

Sir John Fastolf and the Land Market: An Enquiry of the Early 1430s Regarding Purchasable Property

Colin Richmond

BRITISH LIBRARY Additional Manuscript 39220, which is printed below in its entirety, is to be found in the Woodhouse family collection. Why what is so evidently a document relating to Sir John Fastolf's pursuit of property should have ended up in another East Anglian family's archive is unclear to me. I have not pursued the matter; perhaps others will do so. A single property and a group of properties are the subject of the enquiry. The single property comprised two manors, Walcotes and Boules in Little Snoring, Norfolk, once in possession of the Cockerel family; the material on Walcotes and Boules occupies only the first of eleven written folios and is no more than a series of notes on the recent history of the two manors. The group of properties consisted of the Norfolk estates of the Paveley family; they had been the subject of a thorough investigation by the agents of Sir John Fastolf, the results being set out on folios 3–8 of the document. The hand of the Paveley investigation is not that of the notes on Walcotes and Boules. It seems to me recognisable as that of one of Fastolf's employees. I am unable to identify it with certainty, but have the idea (possibly fanciful) that it is the same hand as that of a Fastolf pedigree in the Bodleian Library and of Lovel Paper 8 at Magdalen College, Oxford.[1] The latter is one of a number of documents relating to a not dissimilar enquiry concerning Titchwell, Norfolk, a manor which Fastolf bought from John Roys in 1431.[2] Moreover, William Norwich, who appears both as an important informant and as in possession of relevant evidence in the Paveley investigation, was a lawyer retained by Sir John Fastolf. Immediately prior to the time that our document is to be dated, William was involved in the sale to Fastolf of two estates, Mundham in Norfolk and Cockfield Hall in Yoxford, Suffolk, which had belonged to a relative,

1 Bodleian Library, Oxford, Norfolk Charters a.8, no. 722; for the Lovel Papers at Magdalen, see P.S. Lewis, 'Sir John Fastolf's Lawsuit over Titchwell 1448–55', repr. in P.S. Lewis, *Essays in Later Medieval French History*, London 1985, 225–9. A. Smith, 'Litigation and Politics: Sir John Fastolf's Defence of his English Property', in *Property and Politics: Essays in Later Medieval English History*, ed. A.J. Pollard, Gloucester 1984, 59–75, is also of the utmost importance.

2 A. Smith, 'The Acquisition of Sir John Fastolf's Estates', in *Rulers and Ruled in Late Medieval England: Essays presented to Gerald Harriss*, ed. R.E. Archer and S. Walker, London 1995, at p. 145.

John Norwich.[3] British Library, Additional MS 39220 is to be dated between November 1431, when an escheator's inquisition concerning Walcotes and Boules was held and which is recorded in the document, and 1434, when Fastolf bought Hainford, one of the ex-Paveley properties, from Ela Shardlow, widow of Sir Robert Shardlow (d.1399), their son, Sir John Shardlow, who had acquired it from John Paveley in 1420–21, having died in 1433.[4]

First, the manors of Walcotes and Boules in Little Snoring: a property that Sir John Fastolf did not buy. It was probably just as well that he did not. The estate's history as recorded in our document, the violent deaths of two John Cockerels excepted, is to some degree borne out by the record evidence. Katherine, wife of John Cockerel, died in 1427, and in 1428 William Phelip, lord Bardolf, was given custody of the Cockerel lands in Norfolk and Suffolk during the minority of Katherine, daughter of the younger John Cockerel.[5] Robert, lord Willoughby's intervention has, however, left no trace.[6] Although the inquisition jury of November 1431 apparently had been unable to name an heir on the death of Katherine Cockerel while still a minor, in December 1431 the escheator was required to deliver the Cockerel lands to George Heath, son of Agnes, sister of Katherine Cockerel, grandmother of the under-age Katherine who had died in October 1431.[7] George Heath of Mildenhall, Suffolk, is not mentioned in BL Add. MS 39220, but William de la Pole, earl of Suffolk, is. William de la Pole, to whom sharp practice appears to have been second nature, was the man behind the inquisition which had found George Heath to be Katherine Cockerel's heir, or so George declared some years after William de la Pole's death:[8]

> when the inquisicion was take he knewe right not therof and was at London, [where] William Dalling, Maister Clement Charlez and Crane a lernyd man

3 Smith, 'The Acquisition of Sir John Fastolf's Estates', 145.

4 Smith, 'The Acquisition of Sir John Fastolf's Estates', 145; C. Richmond, *John Hopton: A Fifteenth-Century Suffolk Gentleman*, Cambridge 1981, 27, 80–1.

5 *CFR 1422–30*, 187, 194, 208–9. For Sir Robert Wingfield of Letheringham, Suffolk, see J.C. Wedgwood, *History of Parliament: Biographies of the Members of the Commons House 1439–1509*, London 1936, 956; R.L. Storey, *The End of the House of Lancaster*, London 1966, 226–7.

6 The 'Walcot in Norfolk' that Robert, Lord Willoughby, owned and John Paston wrote about in the early 1460s was Walcott in the Hundred of Happing to the south of Bacton and Bromholm: *The Paston Letters and Papers of the Fifteenth Century*, ed. N. Davis, 2 vols, Oxford 1971–76, i, no. 67.

7 *CFR 1430–37*, 56.

8 *CCR 1454–61*, 77–8. The declaration was made on 20 July 1455. William Dalling, often vice-sheriff, deputy escheator, or coroner, and de la Pole stooge, was a thorn in the side of both Judge William Paston and Sir John Fastolf: Davis, *Paston Letters*, ii, no. 869; Lewis, 'Sir John Fastolf's Lawsuit over Titchwell 1448–55, *passim*. Robert Crane was a lawyer (d.1445); he built himself a grand house at Chilton near Sudbury in Suffolk: N. Scarfe, *Suffolk: A Shell Guide*, London 1966, 67. Like William Galion, the accommodating escheator of November 1431, Robert Crane, was in William de la Pole's pocket. For William Galion's widow and the earl of Suffolk founding a chantry for her husband and his family at Thetford in 1442–43, see *CPR 1441–46*, 135, 178.

> comme to him and saide that the duk of Suffolk shulde sende fer him, and badde him to be ware for he shulde be straitly examined, and he askyde theym wherfore, and Dallynge seide that he was founde next heir to yonge Katerine Cokerell, that the abbot of Bury and the priour of Walsyngham shulde have part of the land by eschete and the duc wolde see an other meane therefore, and he saide agayne he durst not for he is tenaunt to the abbot, and Clement Charlez archedekene of Sudbury seide that the abbot shulde be reuled as the duc wolde malgre his hede, and doo therin as the duc wyll commaunde, that when he came to the duc he saide unto the said George that he shulde be reulyd aftyr him, for he was founde next heir by his advis, where as in dede he was not . . . to the which he prayed the duc to holde him excused . . . and the duc seide that if he wolde not be reuled by hym he shulde be so hevy lord unto him that he shulde not be able to bere it, and went unto his chambyr in the Olde Vyntyre, and dede feche forth a messebooke and had him ley his hand on the booke and swere to make noon estate nyver relese withoute his advise, and he wolde see that shulde be savyde harmless . . . and undyrstandyng that his hevy lordship shulde be importable, for fere therof he ded swere to fulfille his desire, and whan he had sworne the duc layde his hande upon the book, and seide as he was true knught and by the book he shulde saave him harmless, and he shulde have 40 li. for his labour, but he shulde goo by thadvyse of his counsell into the chauncerie and aske lyvere of the lande, and than the duc sente him forthe, and Crane with othirmore of his counsel with him, and he asked lyvere of the lande . . . and thanne he went home.

George went on to say that Sir Thomas Tuddenham had the Cockerel estate of Wangford, Suffolk, while Richard Dogget took Walcotes and Boules. Both men were members of the de la Pole mafia. He also said that after Richard, duke of York, had been on pilgrimage to Walsingham in October 1450, 'the seide George waytinge upon hym as his duete was',[9]

> at his comynge home Richard Doket of Copdock and Roger Bukwode [recte: Rookwood] of Euston come to him unto Mildenhale there he dwelles, and praiede Maister Thomas Ryngstede vycary of the toune to entrete him to make a relees to Richard Doket and his feffees of the seide manoirs [Walcotes and Boules] in Norffolk, yevynge to him a certain somme for the relees and amendys of the grete lossys which he had by them, and they war bounde to him in severall obligacions

9 The Duke of York went on pilgrimage to Walsingham in the second week of October 1450: P.A. Johnson, *Duke Richard of York 1411–1460*, Oxford 1988, 85. Richard Dogget of Copdock near Ipswich was another de la Pole hanger-on (Richmond, *John Hopton*, 108–9). Richard died in 1458 desiring burial in the porch of Copdock church; he died childless, and after the death of his widow Joan his estates were to descend to Roger, son of Roger Rookwood of Euston, Suffolk, in tail male; Joan and Roger were his executors: see Roger Virgoe's unpublished notes on the will, PRO, PCC 18 Stockton. The late Dr Roger Virgoe's extensive notes on East Anglian gentry families are temporarily in my possession; I am grateful to his widow Norma for agreeing to my having them on extended loan. Did Richard Dogget know the 'great diapered red-brick barn' in the field beside Copdock church (Scarfe, *Suffolk: A Shell Guide*, 69)? Roger Rookwood the elder did not die until sometime in 1479–82; he wished to be buried in the chancel of Euston church, for which church his executors were to make a new roof; his wife Alice is likely to have been Richard Dogget's daughter: Roger Virgoe's unpublished notes on his will (SRO, Ipswich, Arch. Suff., Reg. Hervye, fo. 263, dated 30 April 1479, proved 8 May 1482). Thomas Ryngstede, B.Cn.L., was vicar of Mildenhall 1423–53: *BRUC*, 499–500.

> . . . that aftir the day of payement the said Richard and Roger of malice came ageyn to him, and thret for suche services done to my lorde of Yorke he shuld be hanged, drawe and quartered without that he wolde delyvere to them the obligacion and make unto them a generall acquitaunce . . . [and] by cause of these dredes which reyned in that partie in thoo dayes he delyvered to them the obligacion and made unto them a generall acquietance.

Sure enough: enrolled on the Close Roll and dated 25 November 1450 is a quitclaim by George Heath of Mildenhall, esquire, to Humphrey, duke of Buckingham, Sir Henry Inglose, Thomas Dennis, William Wethered, and Richard Dogget, of the manors of Walcotes and Boules, Little Snoring, Norfolk.[10] Richard Dogget, it seems, had replaced one patron by another. If George Heath's circumstantial narrative were only partially true it would nevertheless display an historical truth: how the bland official record can hide rather than reveal what actually has happened. George's story is as valuable an insight into the underhand dealings of William de la Pole as the Watergate tapes were into those of Richard Nixon. Both escaped impeachment, yet, whereas President Nixon escaped retribution William de la Pole did not: he was a politician who got what he deserved, an occurrence, it has to be said, commoner in the fifteenth than in the twentieth century.[11]

There was, nonetheless, a mightier in the land than even Humphrey, duke of Buckingham, at any rate for a few months after the battle of St Albans in 1455, and Richard Neville, earl of Warwick, duly alighted (vulture-like) on Walcotes and Boules. He informed John Paston that he had bought them from the prior of Walsingham and asked John for his good will and favour 'so that I may by your frendship the more peasably reioy [*sic*] my forsaid purchase'. Perhaps there were difficulties, because Richard, duke of York, had also to write to John Paston requesting him to see that the earl of Warwick's officers were enabled to take possession of the two manors.[12] It is evident that Warwick obtained possession, as Walcotes and Boules appear in the accounts for 1485–86 of John Walsh, supervisor and receiver-general of the lands once those of Isabel, daughter of Richard Neville, earl of Warwick, and wife of George, duke of Clarence, in royal custody during the minority of Edward, the son and heir. Walcotes and Boules were not, however, in royal custody: John Walsh accounted for nothing from them for they were in the

10 *CCR 1447–54*, 244.

11 R. Virgoe, 'The Death of William de la Pole, Duke of Suffolk', *Bulletin of the John Rylands Library* 47, 1965, 489–502. The C.W. Richmond of p. 492, n. 6, ought to have been C.F. Richmond.

12 Davis, *Paston Letters*, ii, nos 504 and 505. Warwick's letter (no. 505) is dated from Middleham on 23 August; the duke of York's (no. 504) is dated from Sandal on 19 August. Davis put both in 1454. George Heath's declaration is, however, dated 20 July 1455; it makes no mention of the earl of Warwick. It seems to me, either that both letters are of 1455, or, more likely, because York surely wrote *after* Warwick had done so, that Warwick's letter is of 1455 (he was at Calais in 1456), and York's letter is of 1456, when he spent the summer at Sandal: Johnson, *Duke Richard of York* , 175. Johnson himself follows Davis in dating the letters to 1454: *ibid.*, 145.

hands of Sir Henry Heydon.[13] They remained Heydon property for a further hundred years.[14]

Secondly, the Paveley lands. The Paveleys were originally of Paulerspury, Northants, named after them, but Paveleys were in possession of Little Ryburgh, and probably of their other Norfolk manors, from the early fourteenth century.[15] John Paveley made his will at Hainford on 20 April 1379 and was killed at Hainford on 11 July 1379.[16] His son, also John Paveley, made his will at Little Ryburgh on 10 May 1421 and died either later that year or early in 1422.[17] A John Paveley junior, king's knight to Richard II, who had died nearly thirty years previously in 1393, looks like a red herring, but as he seems to have been the last of the Northampton-

13 Staffordshire RO, D1798/4, *sub* Norfolk, Snoring Parva. I owe my knowledge of this document to the kindness of Dr Philip Morgan. The Kingmaker's possession is also demonstrated by his presenting to the rectory of Little Snoring in 1460 and 1466: Blomefield, *Norfolk*, iii, 856.

14 Blomefield, *Norfolk*, iii, 855–6.

15 *CCR 1413–19*, 138–9; *Cal. Feudal Aids*, iii, 406, 518.

16 The will is NRO, NCC, Reg. Heydon, fo. 163; it was proved on 23 July 1379. I have inferred that it was composed at Hainford from the fact that the rector of Hainford was one of John's two executors. The will is brief: he desired burial in All Saints church, Little Ryburgh, left 2s to the high altar of that church, and the same sum to the high altar at Hainford, gave a quarter of barley each to unspecified orders of friars in Norwich, and a bushel apiece to the poor of Hainford, and that was that. There is no mention of a wife, let alone of Emma, who, according to one witness in our document, was pregnant at the time of her husband's murder with Margaret (later the wife of John Palgrave of Gunton, Norfolk), and who after his death, said the same witness, had two children by the priest John Rudwell. However, Katherine, one of those children and therefore (one might suppose) a more reliable witness, said that it was a William Paveley of Little Ryburgh who was her father, and that it was William who was the bastard. According to Katherine, she had two sisters and a brother, John Paveley a priest, and they were William Paveley's children by Emma, daughter of Thomas Fisher of Fakenham. The clerical John Paveley was undoubtedly 'prest of the charnel in yermoth', as our document says, and probably the clerk who was about to go abroad in 1390: *CCR 1389–92*, 573. For John Paveley's murder, see *CPR 1377–81*, 437; *CPR 1381–85*, 220; *CPR 1388–93*, 503: his killers, including the robber and rapist, John Godfrey of Kirby Cane, were pardoned.

17 His will (NRO, NCC, Reg. Hyrnyng, fo. 95v) is even briefer than his father's: he also wished to be buried in All Saints, Little Ryburgh, and he left everything to his three executors, Walter Noon, rector of Stibbard, John Ling of Little Walsingham, and James Arnold, tailor. The will was proved on 15 March 1422. It almost seems as if John did not care, which being the last of his line he may not have done; he had, after all, recently sold Hainford to Sir John Shardlow: Blomefield, *Norfolk*, v, 1348. Walter Noon and James Arnold make their appearance in our document, where as John Paveley's executors they are said to have sold the manor of Stibbard Paveleys to William Lexham, who in turn sold it to Sir William Oldhall. Sir William Oldhall is also said there to be holding Little Ryburgh; he was certainly doing so in 1428: *Cal. Feudal Aids*, iii, 578. William Lexham was the brother-in-law of Sir William Oldhall, having married his sister Margaret; Margaret died in 1473 and in her will desired burial in the chancel of the parish church of Houghton, Norfolk: Roger Virgoe's unpublished notes on her will, PRO, PCC 8 Wattys. In his will of 1460 Sir William Oldhall had left William Lexham both money and property, naming him one of his executors: Roger Virgoe's notes on PRO, PCC 21 Stockton; cf. J.S. Roskell, 'Sir William Oldhall', repr. in J.S. Roskell, *Parliament and Politics in Late Medieval England*, II, 1981, 175–200.

shire Paveleys he requires more than a footnote.[18] Sir John Paveley was a young man who died before his promising career had barely begun. In 1387 when he had married at the command of the king, Sir John and his wife Isabel were granted an annuity of a hundred marks during the lifetime of Sir John's father.[19] If Sir John's father was Sir John Paveley, three times sheriff of Northampstonshire between 1379 and 1390, and it seems virtually certain that he was, then that lifetime ended only a few months before his son's, Sir John Paveley the elder (as he was known) dying between June and October 1393.[20] John Paveley of Little Ryburgh, who died in 1421 or 1422, as witnesses in BL Add. MS 39220 agreed, never had any children; indeed, he may never have had a wife. They also agree that he was the last of his line and that he said that he was. He was indeed the last of all the Paveleys.[21] To judge from his strikingly brief will John Paveley of Little Ryburgh died a lonely man. Perhaps he was also a dispirited one, for he had begun disposing of his lands before his death, Hainford to Sir John Shardlow sometime in 1420–21. The manors of Stibbard Paveleys and Little Ryburgh went shortly after he had died to Sir William Oldhall, as possibly John knew they would.[22] His heir, according to our document,

18 He made his will (PRO, PCC 7 Rous) at Dover on Thursday in the feast of St Andrew 13 [*blank*]; it was proved at St Paul's cathedral on 7 January 1393, viz. 1394. He was to be buried where God willed. He left most of his goods, including 'uno magno Nowche quod est in custodia Ricardi Stury', to his wife, but a gold cup given him by the earl of Nottingham he left to his father and another given him by Richard II he left to his mother, along with a set of red worsted bed-hangings. His armour went to John Warwick, presumably his squire. His wife Isabel, John Warwick, and his 'dear friend' Richard Stury were to be his executors. Administration of the will was granted on 7 January 1394 to John Warwick. He was probably John Warwick I of Great Houghton, Northants, who in 1394 was at the outset of a successful career in royal service: *The History of Parliament: The House of Commons 1386–1421*, ed. J.S. Roskell, L. Clark and C. Rawcliffe, 4 vols, Stroud 1993, iv, 776–7. Sir John Paveley had been a feoffee of Richard Stury's in 1386: *CCR 1385–89*, 263.

19 *CPR 1385–89*, 352. Anne of Bohemia, Richard's queen, gave them an additional annuity of £20; Anne confirmed the annuity to Isabel in 1394 after Sir John's death: *CPR 1391–6*, 477. The £20 continued to be paid to Isabel and, when she remarried Sir John St John, to her and her second husband until December 1422: *CPR 1399–1401*, 7; *CCR 1401–1408*, 194; *CPR 1413–16*, 74; *CCR 1413–19*, 142; *CPR 1422–29*, 19; *Cal. Inq. Misc.*, vii, 167.

20 *CFR 1377–83*, 170; *CFR 1383–91*, 151, 306; *CPR 1391–96*, 90, 165, 287, 292, 293, 320.

21 The Wiltshire Paveleys had come to an end on the death of Sir Paveley of Brooke in 1361 (*CFR 1356–68*, 197); he left only daughters: *The History of Parliament: The House of Commons 1386–1421*, ii, 554–5. Sir Walter Paveley, a man of Kent, died childless in 1379: *CIPM 1–7 Richard II*, 166–7.

22 See note 17. Sir William Oldhall was in possession of Little Ryburgh in 1428: *Cal. Feudal Aids*, iii, 578. John Marchall esquire and Katherine, *née* Reppes, as well as their son William, feature in our document, fos 7v–8, as the owners of the other manor in Stibbard, namely Stibbard Reppes. Blomefield, *Norfolk*, iii, 857, it should be noted, does not distinguish two manors in Stibbard. Little Ryburgh and Stibbard were Townshend estates by the end of the century: Blomefield, *Norfolk*, iii, 844, 857; C.E. Moreton, *The Townshends and their World: Gentry, Law, and Land in Norfolk c. 1450–1551*, Oxford 1992, *sub* index. Thomas Shouldham of Watlington, Norfolk, to whom, reported the rector of Colkirk, William Marchall gave Stibbard Reppes, died sometime in 1467–68: Roger Virgoe's unpublished notes on his will, NRO, NCC, Reg. Betyns, fo. 137, dated 30 August 1467, proved 30 April 1468. Between 1425 and 1461 the rector of Colkirk, Norfolk, was Walter Baker: Blomefield, *Norfolk*, v, 987.

was Richard Bozun, although quite why I am at a loss to understand.[23] The Bozuns were lords of Whissonsett, Norfolk, from the early fourteenth century (if not from long before that) until 1657.[24] Richard Bozun was known to Sir John Fastolf, or ought to have been, as in 1425 (or 1428) they exchanged manors: Bozuns in Caister for Peak Hall in Tittleshall.[25] Richard died in 1451. His will offers no clue as to his kinship with the defunct Paveleys.[26] In such circumstances it is no wonder that Sir John Fastolf instigated an investigation, nor that it was a Paveley property sold before the last John Paveley's death which he ultimately purchased: it was an ex-Paveley estate with a secure title.

British Library Additional Manuscript 39220 demonstrates what we already know about Sir John Fastolf's preoccupation with acquiring property whose title was as clear as might be had in the murky conditions of the land market of fifteenth-century England: fraudulent feoffees, defaulting executors, lawyers not above chicanery and worse, and landowners (himself included) careless of how they settled their

Robert Pynchmore, rector of Hainford, was much less informative than the rector of Colkirk, even though he had been rector at Hainford for forty years; it is hard to believe that he was over eighty years old, as he did not die until sometime in 1458–59, when, had he been eighty in the early 1430s, he would have been well over a hundred. Eighty in BL Add. MS 39220 appears to be longhand for old, over-eighty for very old. Robert Pynchmore (according to Blomefield, *Norfolk*, v, 1349) had been appointed to Hainford rectory in 1403 by someone who appears in the testimony of Walter Baker, that is John Barton, rector of Downham Market, said by Walter Baker to have sold Stibbard Paveleys to John Paveley esquire. Robert Pynchmore, priest, made his will on 29 March 1458; it was proved on 26 April 1459: NRO, NCC, Reg. Brosyerd, fo. I04v. He desired to be buried in the chancel at Hainford, left to the guild of All Saints there twenty pence, the same sum to the guild of St Thomas at nearby Spixworth, and to the poor of Hainford a paltry sixpence, to go to those whom his executors reckoned most needy. He left everything else to the discretion of his sole executor, John Baker the rector of Hainford. Robert must therefore have been retired. He also appears to have been poor. Can one discern here an exemplary parish priest, after Chaucer's model in *The Canterbury Tales*?

23 The wife of John Bozun, Richard's father, was Jane, daughter of Richard Spinke of Norwich, in the pedigree of the family in Roger Virgoe's unpublished notes; no Agnes Reppes features, anymore than does a John Bozun son of John Bozun. Nor does a Richard Reppes make an appearance in Roger Virgoe's notes on the Reppes family. Robert Reppes is a different matter; for him see especially Davis, ii, no. 439. The Robert Ashfield esquire to whom the second John Bozun is said to have sold the manor of Stibbard Reppes is presumably Robert Ashfield of Stowlangtoft, Suffolk, who died in 1401: *CIPM 1399–1405*, 185–6. It was Robert Ashfield esquire, *alias* Robert Davey, who rebuilt Stowlangtoft church: Scarfe, *Suffolk: A Shell Guide*, 161. His wife Margaret died before him; she wished to be buried in the chancel at Stowlangtoft; her husband was her only executor: Roger Virgoe's unpublished note of her will, NRO, NCC, Reg. Harsyk, fo. 246, dated 3 November 1397, proved 10 May 1398.

24 Blomefield, *Norfolk*, v, 1088–9.

25 Tittleshall was next door to Whissonsett. *The Paston Letters 1422–1509*, ed. James Gairdner, Library edn, London 1904, ii, no. 9, suggests 1425; Blomefield, *Norfolk*, v, 1076, has 1428, as does Anthony Smith, 'The Acquisition of Sir John Fastolf's Estates', 143. Richard Bozun died seised of Tittleshall: Blomefield, *Norfolk*, v, 1076.

26 NRO, NCC, Reg. Aleyn, fos 68v–69, dated 4 January 1451, proved 5 March 1451. One of the greater rather than smaller mysteries encountered during the course of my enquiries concerning BL Add. MS 39220 is that among Roger Virgoe's extensive files on Norfolk gentry families there is nothing whatsoever on the Paveleys or the Cockerels.

estates.[27] It also witnesses to one contribution, and probably by far the most significant contribution, to the beginnings of English history-making. 'Fear of defective title was, I believe', wrote K.B. McFarlane, 'the source of that interest in manorial descents that English antiquaries showed from the first. The complications of the land law were a powerful incitement to historical research.'[28] It also, I think, reinforces the view of Anthony Smith that there was no shortage of property for purchase in the fifteenth century.[29] A principal reason for that was what we might bluntly call a failure of families to breed, at any rate within wedlock.[30] Paveleys and Cockerells, as well as Shardlows, are but three examples of many, even if Paveleys and Cockerells escaped William Worcester's notice, as they do not figure in his lists of East Anglian gentry families who in recent times had failed to produce a male heir.[31] These are familiar themes. Less so, or less so in the last forty years, has been the theme of late medieval England beset by mayhem and murder. The idea of a fairly widespread tendency to violence on the part of the fifteenth-century gentry is, one detects, about ready for revival. Our document tells of three murders, of two Cockerells and a Paveley. It might be a jarring note on which to close a piece written to honour one of nature's gentlemen, Norman Scarfe undoubtedly being such a phenomenon, yet there is no getting away from the fact that his East Anglian forerunners of the later middle ages were, naturally or unnaturally as one wishes to think of them, a murderous bunch.

I have transcribed the document without any attempt at modernisation. It is not a tidy piece of writing. Dr Philip Morgan has been patient in helping me bring an acceptable version into being; the editors, Carole Rawcliffe and Christopher Harper-Bill, made further refinements; I am humbly grateful to them all. I am no palaeographer, and, the facsimile apart, there is no satisfactory way of representing the thing itself. My diplomatic skills are as limited as my palaeographic ones are unrefined: the two great men who attempted to teach me those arcane arts would, if asked, have said as much. It is high time, nonetheless, that I acknowledge what I did learn from them: that an historical document deserves to be examined with an open-minded humility. Pierre Chaplais and Neil Ker, I salute you.

27 K.B. McFarlane, *England in the Fifteenth Century*, London 1981, 193–4.

28 *Ibid.*, 194.

29 Smith, 'The Acquisition of Sir John Fastolf's Estates', 150. Sir William Oldhall, as our document testifies, was as busy in the land market as was Sir John Fastolf. Both Norfolk men, they might be regarded as competitors, for example for the Paveley inheritance, were it not for the fact that Oldhall sold Loundhall in Saxthorpe to Fastolf in 1428 (*ibid.*, 146), so there is the beguiling possibility that they might also have been partners.

30 K.B. McFarlane, *The Nobility of Later Medieval England*, Oxford 1973, 143–9.

31 Their names do not appear in NRO, MS 7197, for which see McFarlane, *England in the Fifteenth Century*, 219–20.

British Library Additional Manuscript 39220
(published by permission of the Trustees of the British Library)

[folio 1] Johannes Kokerell et pekerell [inquisitionis . . . pro snoryng]

[folio 1v *blank*]

[folio 2]

Quidam Johannes Cokrel de Orford tenuit maneria de Boules et Walcotes in parva Snoryng de priore de Walsyngham per servicium militare

Idem Johannes mutilatus et occisus per quondam inimicum obiit circa annum ultimum R[egni] R[egis] h[enrici] iiij

Idem Johannes reliquit post se Johanem filium suum et heredem existentem infra etatem

Katerina uxor Johannis Cokrel mater iam dicti Johannis Cokrel junioris racione minoris etatis eiusdem Hugoni tunc priori de Walsyngham pro [*erased* relevio] warda et maritagio xxx li.

Idem Johannes postea circa annos xxiiij etatis sue a quondam latente inimico fuit intoxicatus unde media nocte sequente subito interiit

[*erased* Idem Johannes reliquit post se Katerinam filiam et heredem suam existentem infra etatem Katerina que fuit uxor Johannis Cokrel senioris tenuit die quo obiit [. . .] [*erased* feoda] predicta maneria de Bowles et Walcott in parva Snoryng. Et dicta Katerina obiit primo die octobris anno R[egni] R[egis] h[enrici] sexti vj]

Dominus Rex qui nunc est racione minoris etatis predicte Katerine filie et heredis predicti Johannis Cokrel junioris concessit domino Willelmo Philipp militi custodiam omnium terrarum et tenementorum que per mortem Katerine uxoris Johannis Cokrel senior capti fuerunt in manus eiusdem domini Regis

Idem Willelmus Philipp miles dedit predictam custodiam predictorum terrarum et tenementorum Roberto Wen[geford] militi durante minorum etate predicte Katerine filie Johannis Cokrel minoris que Katerina existens in custodia dicti Roberti racione minoris etatis sue obijt die martis proximo ante festum sancti luce evangeliste anno decimo R[egni] R[egis] qui nunc est

Post mortem iam dicte Katerine dominus Robertus de Wilby intravit omnis terras et tenementa in Orford que nuper fuerunt Johannis Cokrel senioris pro defectu heredum quia predicta terra et tenementorum tenebat de eo ut de castello suo in Orford

Abbas de Buria modo consimili et eadem causa intravit maneria de Ikwurth et Wangford set idem abbas minas Comitis tunc Suffoch non sustinens remisit jus suum ad totum tempus vite sue pro ducentis marcas. Et abbas ibidem qui nunc est firmiter proponit intrare predicta maneria tanquam eschaetas suas racione predicta Inquisitio fuit capta apud Wetyng sexto die novembris anno R[egni] R[egis] h[enrici] sexti post conquestum decimo coram Willelmo Galion Eschaetori domini Regis in comitatu Norfolchie virtute cuiusdem brevis eiusdem domini Regis eidem escaetori deliberati et huic inquisitioni consuti per sacrum et cetera. Qui dicunt super sacrum suum quod manerium de parva Snoryng cum advocacione ecclesie ville cum suis pertinentiis in Comitatu predicto per mortem Katerine nuper uxoris Johannis Cokrel in breve huic inquisitioni consuto nominata et racione minoris etatis Katerine filie Johannis Cokrel similiter in eodem breve nominate ad manus domini Regis nunc deveneret et eadem in manu dicti Regis ad huc existunt. Et dicunt quod predictum manerium de snoryng cum predicta advocatione cum suis pertinentiis teneretur de priore de Walsyngham per servicium militare. Et dicunt ulterius quod predictum manerium cum suis pertinentiis valet per annum in omnibus exitibus iuxta verum valorem eiusdem ultra reprisam x libras. Et dicunt quod predicta Katerina Cokrel filia obiit die martis proxima ante festum sancti luce evangeliste proximum ante datum presentis huius inquisitionis et qui est heres eius propinquor juratores predicti ignorant ad presens. Et dicunt quod nulla alia neque plura terra seu tenementa tenuit de dicto domino Rege in capito alio in dominico neque in servicio dicto die quo obiit

[folio 2v *blank*]

[folio 3] fastolf

heynfforth
qweteacre
ytryngham
qweyt
northhelmham
testerton
lytelryboro
stybyrd paveles reppes

[*in left margin*] pavele lord of
mertofte
goche
thomas furwel

[*added in right margin*] Aske these questions that folowyth and alle othyr that come to your mend of the purchasours of alle these manneres. And telle hem that they schal be intrykyd but if they be war and kan shew for hem for he that cleymyth litel ryboro cleymyth alle the [*erased* to the] tothere del be f[o]rce of a tayle

qwat hygth the seyd pavele
qwat isswe hadde he and qwat hygth they. qwer dwellyd they. qwer deyd they.
qwer arne they byeryd
to qwom were they maryed
qwich of the seyd lordshepes were taylid
qwether was the tayl made to the eyres general or to the eyres male
qwan was it made and be qwom and qwo hath the tayl and qwe[ther] was it tayld be dede or be fine
hugh were the seyd maneres alyend. and be qwom. and to qwom

qwat evidences hath the ownerys of the seyd godes to entitle hem therin
qwo were inffeffed in ryburgh and styberd or in alle the goodes and be qwom wer thei inffeoffed and qwanne [*erased* and qwey]
and to qwom hath thei made astate all. or ony of hem

qwere deyid the last pevele sesyd or not
qwether made he ony testament or wylle [*erased* and qwer arne they]. and qwo hath hem
qwych were his executours. And qwat astate hadde thei in the godes to make ony sale therof
qwich were executours to hys executours
ho many wyffys hadde he. and qwat hygth they. qwat hadde he with them in maryage and qwat issw of hem and qwat higth here fader

[folio 3v]

qwo was fader and moder to syr john pavele prest of the charnel in yermoth and parson of [*blank*]
qwat bretheryn and systeryn hadde he be fader and moder
qwether were they bore in wedlok
qwat hyth here fader qwat hygth here moder qwat hygth here grawnsyres and grawndames

In qwat toun dwellyd here fader and moder and in qwat place of the toun and ho longe is it sone they deyid

Reymeston Jonet the wyf of rychard blake
Kateryne late the wyf of thomas peper

[*added in right margin*] qwether be they sisters be fader and moder to syr john and qwat isswe hath they [*erased* and] in matrymonye

John blake sone of the seyd Jonet math [*maketh*] clayme in the godes be force of a tayl and be gyfte of syr john pavele prest and mayster Hwe Acton mayster of the hoppital is his brother in lawe and he claymyth blake of the kynges hows esqwyr and blake his brother balyf of swofham to his cosynes qwich were bore in sotherey and the seyd John hath a sone in lawe callyd wylliam blake in sentpulcers paryche late cownt roller of london as he seyth

the seyd John [*erased* seyth] told me that syr john pavele prest and katerine peper were begotyn in bast[ardy] of Emme pavele be one syr john Rudwelle parson of hengham bergh qwich emme late beforn that was wyf to pavele qwich was sleyn at heynfforthe and he seyth that his moder Jonet was but half syster to the sayd syr john pavele and katerine

[folio 4]

Johannes pavele [*erased* dominus] dominus de heynforth qweteacre Itryngham tweyt elmham testerton parve ryburgh and [*erased* repp] stybyrd fuit occisus apud heynforth predictum [*erased* cuius filius et heres] qui habuit filium et heredem Johannem pavele ultimum qui post decessum patris sui fuit dominus omnium predictorum

[folio 4v] [*blank*]

[folio 5]

Informacio domini roberti Pynchemore Rectoris de heynforth per xlv annos et e[tiam] etatis iiij xx [*score*] annorum et amplius

seyth that John pavele that last dyed in lytel ryburgh sone to John pavele that was slayn in heynforth seyd [th]at he stode so in [*erased* his] alle his lyfflond that he might gyfyt or sellyth or make hys eyre ther of qwan that he wuld

Informacio Johannis garyte de heynforth etatis lxxv annorum

seyth that his fader and his moder were servawntes with John pavele that was slayn in henyforth and he seyd that they herd men sey that ever he hadde never more chyler in wedlok but John pavele that last dyed in ryburgh and margiarete that was weddyd to pallegrave of gunthon and he herd also John pavele that last dyed seyn that he might gyf and selle alle his lyflod to qwom that he wuld and so he dede of divers partys of his lyflod. and never man seyd that he dede wrong

Informacio Johannis Waxham de heynforth etatis iiij xx [*score*] annorum

he was servawnt to the seyd John pavele that last dyed and with hym rode and yede with hym be the terme of xxx winters and as his neygthburghe sey he trustyd hym and told hym more of alle his cowncel than he dede alle the werd [*world*] after. and he seyth that the seyd John pavele that last dyed seyd at oftyn tymes that he hadde never brothyr ner syster but one margarete Pallegrave. ner none eyr but he was last of the stok

[folio 5v]

Willelmus Otyn de heynforth etatis lx yers et .v. sayth that John pavele that last dyied was myche conversawnt with his fader and the seyd William seyth that he herd the seyd John pavele oftyn tymes say that he mygth make [*erased* the] hym eyre of alle the good that he hadde [*erased* and] or sellyd to qwom he wuld

Agnes qwytnesse de heynforth etatis iiij xx [*score*] annorum She was servaunt in her chyldhode to John pavele that was slayn and sche says that the wyf of hym qwan sche sey hym so hurt a child steryd in her wumbe qwech child was after a woman callyd margarete and sche was weddyd to pallegrave and sche dyed withowtyn isswe. And sche seyth that John pavele that last dyed hadde never more brotheryn ne systeryn [*erased* but] in wedlok but the seyd margarete. and the seyd agnes seyth that sche knew the last John pavele rygth wel qwan he was a yonge child and qwan he fled into asaxishale qwan John his fader was slayn. and sche herd the last John pavele seyn an hundred tymes that he had none eyre b[u]t he mygth gyf or selle alle the land that he hadde to qwom he wuld

[folio 6]

Informacio Hugonis stone de styberd qui fuit serviens Johannis pavele in parva ryburgh Johannes pavele that was slayn in heynforth hadde a son John pavele that last dyed and a dawghter callyd margarete qwiche margarete was weddyd to one palgrave of gunton [*erased* no] and [*erased* neither] the seyd John pavele ner his sister margarete hadde nevyr isswe in wedlok. and [*erased* heres] the moder of hem was biered at langelle abby. and the seyd John pavele was byryed at lytel ryburgh. and the seyd John seyd oftyn tymes er he dyed that busson of Wyssyngset schuld be his eyr if any owyth to ben

Informacio Ricardi gybb de ryborough magna etatis iiij xx [*score*]et ult[ima] seyth that john pavele the fader of the last John pavele and margarete was slayn at heynforth and his wyff sorowruyd at langelel [*sic*] and ther is sche byried

Katerine rowet de parva ryborough etatis iiij xx [*score*] annorum sche herd oftyntyme the seyd last john pavele sey that oldhalle or bosun schuld be his eyr If ony shuld he have

Alicia myll de parva ryborough sche asked the seyd last john pavele hoo shuld be his eyr and he seyd he himself was last oft the stokke and he knewe none that shuld have tytlle ther to but if [it] wer buzon or oldhalle

[folio 6v]

Informacio katerine peper de reymeston sororis [*erased* matris] Johanne matris Johannis blake glacewryth et dicta katerina e[tatis] iiij xx [*score*]

Sche seyth that one Wylliam pavele dwelling in ryborough the lesse [*erased* was fader] and emmot his wyff dowgter to Thomas Fysher of Fakenham [*erased* were] hadde iiij chylder in wedlok Johanna wyf of rychard blak of reymeston and syr John pavele prest and katerine peper of reymeston and one roberd qwiche robert dyed qwan he was iiij yeres old and the seyd katerine seyth pleynly that the the seyd William here fader was a bastard of one of the paveles and fer of the kynne. and sche seyth that the seyd William here fader was byried at greston and emmot here moder at hynghsbergh. and the seyd Katerine seyth that emmot here moder told here ofte tymes that here fader William pavele was a bastard. and the seyd Katerine seyth that sche herd here moder emmot seyn oftyn tymes that John pavele that last dyed seyd that and Wylliam here fader hadde be no bastard he schuld a ben his eyre and yet he seyd to the seyd William you are fer of my kynne. and sche herd here moder sey to syr John pavele here brother that he schuld have be eyre to the seyd John pavele if his fader William hadde be no bastard. and sche seyd that William pavele here fader seyde that he shuld a bene eyre of [*erased* the pavele] the seyd John pavele but that he was a bastard and that repentyth hym rycth evyl. and sche seyth here fader was pasyd lx yeres er he dyed sothenly at greston in his bedde and there is byryed

[folio 7]

this copy delivered William of Norwich and he hath many other and alle they record fe simple of alle the sayd goodes and londes with clauses of warerntes and with evidences according to the same

Sciant presentes et futuri quod ego Robertus filius Johannis Pavele de Parva Ryborough dedi concessi et hac presenti carta mea confirmavi domino Fulcony persone ecclesie de Falsham et domino Willelmo at Grene de Styberd capellano maneria mea et omnes terras et tenementa mea et servicia et consuetudines liberorum tenentium meorum et omnes nativos et eorum villenagia, simul cum reversione omnium terrarum et tenementorum, cum servicio et consuetudine liberum tenentium, nativis et eorum villenagiis, que Margeria que fuit uxor Johannis Pavele patris mei detinet in dotem, et omnibus aliis pro firmo et in perpetuum, in Parva Ryborough, Heinford et Styberd, habenda et tenenda predicte Margerie terras et tenementa predictis Fulconi et Willelmo, heredibus et assignatis eorum, cum clausa warantizationis predicti Roberti etc. Anno xxiii Edwardi tercii cum sigillo armorum

Informacio Willelmi Norwich

seyth he herd menne sey that the seyd blame hath no rygth. but he seyth that john the son of john pavele that was sleyn set to mortgage to a s[q]wyre of Suffolkke ryburgh styberd and heynforthe for an hundred mark to swe apele for the deth of his fader and he delivered state and his evidence to the seyd esqwyre and he in defawt of payment to rejoyte and ineryte the seyd lyflode. and the seid s[q]wre was never payid of the seyd mony ne he never relesyd to no man. and the seyd Willelmus seyth that ther is a parson in the frawnches of byry and he hath grawnt hym to delyver hym alle the dedys of the maneres and a relese of the last eyres of the ffeffes of the seyd es[q]wre and [*erased* that was] for the valwe of x mark with a reward over for himself the seyd

[folio 7v] warante as suffisawnt evydens and lawful astate of the seyd lyflode

Informacio Rectoris de Kotkyrk

qui dicit quod Ricardus Reppys habuit duas filias Agnetem et Katerinam quas reliquit heredes. Et agnes nupta domino Johanni Buze militi habuit maneria de stybyrd vocata Reppys et hylington et congham. Katerina nupta Johanni marchal armigero habuit manerium de Reppes et manerium de Hobes et advocacionem ecclesie de stybyrd. Agnes uxor Johannis Buze habuit filium vocatur Johannem qui vendidit manerium de stybyrd vocatum Reppes Roberto Aschfeld armigero. Et Johannes Barton Rector de Downham in suffolchia ffeoffatus in dicto manerio de stybyrd vendidit dictum manerium Johanni paveley armigero post cuius mortem dominus Walterus Noon et Jacobus Taillour de Norwiche vendiderunt dictum manerium Willelmo lexham qui quidem Willelmus vendidit dictum manerium Willelmo Oldhalle militi. Et sciatis pro certo quod dominus Johannes hacon [*Barton*] nunquam relaxavit jus suum in dicto manerio. Katerina habuit filium vocatur Willelmum marchal qui dixit se esse heredem dictorum maneriorum de stybyrd hylyngton et congham scilicet ut dicitur dictus Willelmus recuperavit dicta maneria de hylyngton et congham et ante mortem suam dedit dicta maneria cum manerio de stybyrd vocato reppis Thome

[folio 8] Scholdham sed dictus Willelmus et Thomas nunquam habuerunt possessionem in manerio de stybyrd vocato Reppes. Willelmus Oldhalle miles post mortem Johannis pavele intravit maneria de parva ryborough et stybyrd vocat paveles ut heres. Tunc ut dictum fuit Ricardus bozun fuit verus heres et idem Ricardus relaxavit jus suum dicto domino Willelmo Oldhalle. Et utrum Johannes pavele habuit sororem vel non, ego nescio, sed de hoc est unus in stybyrd vocatus hugo at stane que fuit famulus dicti Johannis Pavely qui scit de hoc informare de veritate

Sir Philip Bothe of Shrubland: The Last of a Distinguished Line Builds in Commemoration

John Blatchly and Judith Middleton-Stewart

BETWEEN 1525 and 1535, a group of craftsmen in terracotta, perhaps from the continent, travelled through Essex, Suffolk and Norfolk working mainly for Marney, Bothe and Bedingfield patrons, themselves connected by marriage. Their work for Sir Philip Bothe at Shrubland Old Hall and churches nearby repays particularly detailed study. Realising that he would be the last male in a line of distinguished clerics and scholars, Sir Philip planned and built to sustain their souls in heaven and commemorate their names on earth for ever.

I

The Terracotta Trail

John Blatchly

Norman Scarfe has always been intrigued by the Renaissance work of high quality of the 1520s and 1530s at Layer Marney, Shrubland and Oxborough, all in the latest Italian fashion of the time, and discernibly by the same craftsmen. After the Suffolk Institute excursion he led to Shrubland in May 1982, he suggested 'a brief article . . . including illustrations of the whole local group of terracotta windows . . . and the Higham drawing'. What appeared was certainly brief, with only one drawing, and something fuller is now overdue.[1] We therefore invite him to take with us a longer journey from north Essex to west Norfolk following a hypothetical sequence of execution of this most decorative work, noting the links between families using and recommending the terracotta artists, and the inspiration behind some oft-repeated details. That Bedingfields of the same generation were involved in inviting the craftsmen into their own counties in succession was merely noted *en passant* by

The authors are most grateful to Dr Phillip Lindley for his advice and critical comment on earlier drafts of parts of the article, and to Professor Robert Swanson for his help with the Bothes of Barton.

1 The first of 'Excursions 1982', in *PSIA* xxxv, 239 and pl. XIII.

Evelyn Wood;[2] and decorated windows in three Suffolk churches nearby have often and wrongly been alleged to have been rescued and resited from the Old Hall at Shrubland after its partial demolition in the nineteenth century.[3] New work at Barham, Henley and Barking churches was in fact ordered by Sir Philip Bothe of Shrubland, probably after the craftsmen had finished making windows for the chapel at his mansion there in about 1525.[4] It should be stated at the outset that contemporary work in terracotta in Suffolk at Westhorpe Hall, Wolsey's College in Ipswich, and in Norfolk at East Barsham Hall and Great Snoring Rectory is in quite different styles, probably the work of other schools of craftsmen. As long ago as 1968, A.P. Baggs listed seven places in East Anglia where there were terracotta tombs, but he did not know of the Shrubland group of windows, and drew a complete distinction between the terracotta on tombs and on houses. If he had seen the fine mouldings used to frame windows at Shrubland Old Hall and churches nearby, he could hardly have concluded that 'the quality of the workmanship of the tombs is higher and the decoration more sophisticated than that on the architectural details of buildings like Layer Marney . . .'. The Old Hall craftsmen had made similar units on a larger scale for the far grander Layer Marney Towers. However, many of Baggs's helpful suggestions are gratefully acknowledged in what follows.[5]

Essex: Layer Marney Tower

The earliest and grandest work here was commissioned by Sir Henry Marney K.G., Captain of the Bodyguard to Henry VII and Henry VIII, who was engaged in building a house fit for a Privy Councillor and Lord Privy Seal to entertain his sovereign. Created first Baron Marney on 9 April 1523, the new lord enjoyed his enoblement for only six weeks before his death (see Family Tree 1). He married twice: his first wife gave him his son and heir John, and the second a daughter, Grace, who married Sir Edmund Bedingfield of Oxborough. Edmund's sister Alice married Sir Philip Bothe of Shrubland, and thus the terracotta workers' route northwards is already sketched in. The second Lord Marney died only two years after his father, leaving two daughters and no male heir, so the barony was shortlived. It was Sir Henry who had seen terracotta work at Hampton Court, old Whitehall Palace and on royal monuments and could afford to embellish his house in the same way. To impress the

2 E. Wood, 'Notes on the History of Shrubland', *PSIA* xvii, 123–6.

3 H.M. Cautley, *Suffolk Churches and their Treasures*, Ipswich 1937, 271, and most guides to those churches, but D.E. Davy on his church visits of the 1820s found them all *in situ* and accepted them as new work for Bothe. On a scrap of manuscript in Davy's hand and dated 8 July 1827, he writes: 'The window in the Dormitory or Chapel on the North side of Barham church bears a great resemblance to one in the Nave of Henley church, and they were both, no doubt, built by members of the same family; probably by the same person . . . Sir Philip Bothe of Shrubland, Kt.'

4 During the nineteenth century the Middletons divided that chapel horizontally into large rooms on two floors.

5 A.P. Baggs, 'Sixteenth-Century Terracotta Tombs in East Anglia', *Arch. Journ.* cxxv, 1968, 296–301.

Family Tree 1

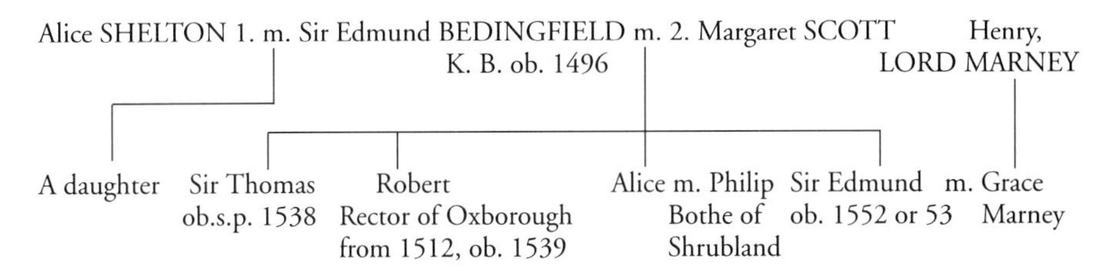

king on a visit, Marney ordered large windows for the grandest chambers in the colossal tower, one each on first and second floors; each was to have eight lights to north and south decorated inside and out with terracotta. Winged putto heads are the motif over each vertical mullion in these windows (Plate 1). The windows of the first floor rooms of the west wing (the east wing is a rebuild) were given similar treatment to north and south, but urns take the place of putti in otherwise similar lintels (Plate 2). The tower parapet decorations, semi-circular shell gables each surmounted by pairs of dolphins, have small square cartouches bearing the Roman letters M and a reversed C. It has been suggested that this was the work of John, second Lord Marney, the letters standing for him and his first wife Christine, daughter of Sir Roger Newburgh. As she died in 1517, when John's father Sir Henry was only planning the building, this cannot be the explanation. It is far more likely that the initials stand for Marney and *Capitanus*, referring to his command of the King's Bodyguard.

A collection of spare moulded terracotta units are exhibited in the tower: dolphins, shell gables and mullion facing bricks. All have flat rear surfaces, like those *in situ* to be seen from the leads of the tower, where parts of the decoration rise above the brick courses to which they are mortared.

As soon as they had completed magnificent tombs for the two Lords Marney in the north-east chapel of the church nearby, itself all built *c.*1517–25, the terracotta craftsmen moved into Suffolk where Philip Bothe had plenty for them to do, and we are fortunate that so much that he adorned has survived.

Suffolk: The Old Hall at Shrubland

Philip Bothe (Booth or Bouthe), son of William Bothe, was knighted 17 November 1501 as part of the celebrations on the marriage of Prince Arthur. He was made a JP in 1501, 1509 and 1515, and was Sheriff in 1506. At his death in 1539 he left only a daughter Audrey (born about 1460), by his first marriage to Margaret, daughter of Sir William Hopton (died 1484) and Margaret Wentworth his wife. His second wife, Alice Bedingfield, died without issue. Through Audrey Bothe's marriage to William Lytton, the estate passed successively by daughter's and grand-daughter's marriages through the Little family to the Bacons. It came to the Bothes in a similar way through the Shrublands (who were probably originally Codmanstons who changed their name to that of their property) and the Okes. The fifteenth-century marriage of Richard Bothe with Katherine, daughter of Philip Oke or Oake (she died 1446), was important, as the quality of the canopied tomb in the chancel of Barham church decorated with boars' heads (from the Bothe coat) on oak leaves (from the Oke arms), testifies (Plate 3). This is likely to be where William Hervy during his Visitation of the county in 1561 read the inscription: 'Katharine Bothe quondam uxoris Rich. Bouth of Suff: armiger qui obijt xiij day of July A^{o} m^{o}iiij^{c} xlvj^{o}'.[6] Bloyse notes 'a raised stone for Richard Booth Esq defac'd'; this fits the date of the brass matrix of an armoured figure on the later tomb chest jammed into the canopy opening.[7] Richard survived his wife until the seventeenth year of Edward IV's reign: 1477/8, just right for the style of armour shown. Hervy also took notes 'In Sir Philip Bouthes house called the man^{r} of Shryblande', although by then the property had passed to Sir Thomas Little of Bray in Berkshire by his marriage with Elizabeth Lytton. The arms he found to draw in the house, presumably in glass, illustrate the descent of the property:

Bothe impaling Oke
Oke impaling Shrubland
Bothe impaling Newport

In Barham church, in the parish of which Shrubland is partly situated, as well as the canopied tomb, he saw the arms of Bothe, Bothe impaling Oke, Oke impaling Shrubland, Bothe impaling Newport, and, of greatest interest, Bothe quarterly: 1 and 4 Bothe, 2 Weyland, 3 Oke impaling Bedingfield of three: 1 Bedingfield, 2 Tuddenham, in base [3 and 4] Scott. The crest is a Katherine wheel, a device which occurs in all of Sir Philip's terracotta commissions. Katherine Oke was not a saint, but she brought Shrubland to the Bothes. Later, the case will be argued for the Bothe family adopting Katherine of Alexandria as their patron saint many generations before Philip. This impaled coat represents his second marriage to Alice Bedingfield; her mother was a Scott and her grandmother a Tuddenham.

Humphrey Repton made a watercolour drawing of the Hall on 23 July 1789 in the Red Book he was preparing for William Middleton, Esq., MP of Crowfield, when the house presented a long frontage facing north-east with the chapel at the north-west end. He was concerned that there were already plans to demolish the Hall, 'this motley pile' as he called it, and pleaded that at least the chapel and the chequer-board flushwork porch might be retained; he would devise a walk on which they would become objects to be admired.[8] His diplomatically worded suggestions

6 William Hervy: BL Add. MS 4969, fos 52v–54r.

7 William Bloyse: SROI GC 17:755 vol. III, 201. It seems probable that Richard Bothe's tomb originally occupied the space in the Bothe chapel now filled by the larger tomb for Edward Bacon (d.1618), and his wife Helen. The move would account for the loss of Katherine's inscription, even an effigy or brass. It would be of the greatest interest to know what lies beneath the present chest.

8 A photographic copy of the 1789 Red Book in SROI: P 617/2. In it, Repton wrote: 'I cou'd wish for the reverence due to antiquity, that some part might be preserved, particularly the Chapel and the chequered porch.'

Plate 1. Layer Marney Towers, Essex: five-light south window of the first-floor state room. Winged putti above each vertical mullion.

Plate 2. Layer Marney Towers: two- and four-light south windows of a ground-floor room west of the tower. Urns above each vertical mullion.

Plate 3. Barham St Mary: detail of Katherine Oke's tomb canopy showing boars' heads lying on oak leaves in the spandrels, the equivalent of impaling the arms of Bothe and Oke for her marriage to Richard Bothe.

Plate 4. The Chapel, Shrubland Old Hall: pen-and-ink drawing by Thomas Higham, 27 May 1825, given to D.E. Davy by the artist. BL Add. MS 19177, fo. 34 (ii). *By permission of The British Library.*

Plate 5. The Chapel, Shrubland Old Hall: three-light north-east window as drawn by Thomas Higham. Three sets of impaled arms of Philip Bothe's first marriage below the window (but the other marriage on the sill inside).

Plate 6a. Terracotta tile unit used at Shrubland Old Hall and at Barham and Barking churches. Drawing by Birkin Haward, May 1997.

Plate 6b. The same drawing repeated and arranged to show how the tile could be used to make a parallel-sided lintel (above, as at Barham north chapel), or, cut away (below, as at the Old Hall chapel) to give a decorative top to each light.

Plate 7. Detail of south-west window of the Chapel, Shrubland Old Hall. Terracotta tile unit used vertically here and at Barking church. Dogs chase hares and small shields bear three acorns slipped as an abbreviated form of the Oke arms.

Plate 8. The Chapel, Shrubland Old Hall: head of north-east window inside showing four Katherine wheels, two dolphins and three urns (as outside at Henley St Peter church).

Plate 9. Barham St Mary: north window of north chapel, formerly the Bothe chantry, with terracotta decorated vertical mullions. Lintel parallel-sided with uncut tiles, cut into the rubble wall to left and right to leave a complete Katherine wheel above each vertical mullion.

Plate 10. Henley St Peter: three-light south nave window embellished with terracotta mouldings to vertical mullions, above (dolphins and urns) and below (impaled arms of Philip Bothe and his two wives).

Plate 11. Barking St Mary: westernmost north aisle Katherine window from outside. The vertical mullions of a Perpendicular window clad with terracotta units for decoration.

a

b

Plate 12. Barking St Mary. Inside: (1) Two details of decoration of chamfered window jambs: (a) Katherine wheel units (uncut) and (b) a vine trail unit not found elsewhere.

(2) Fragments and Katherine wheels in stained glass left in upper tracery lights.

in the Red Book did not save the porch, but William Middleton decided to clean and fit up the chapel 'with the intention of making it the Burial place of his family'. That plan did not get far, but Davy noted winged garbs, the Middleton crest, on a frieze running around the building at half its height. When Thomas Higham junior drew just the chapel from the same side as Repton in 1818 (Plate 4), it appears as though demolition of the wing of the hall to which it was joined had already taken place, yet some accounts state that it was the second baronet (who succeeded only in 1829), who ordered that work.[9] Higham wrote this to accompany Repton's view and his own of the chapel which Davy added to his collections:[10]

> The old Hall was pulled down by Sir Wm. Middleton [i.e. the first baronet] who at the same time had begun to demolish the chapel and had proceeded so far as to unroof it, when further proceedings were stopped by the Bishop; Sir William placed a new roof on it which he covered with thatch, as it at present appears. The drawings on the annexed leaf were made by Mr Thos Higham junior,[11] the upper one from a drawing by Mr Repton in the possession of Sir William, the other [the chapel only] taken by himself from nature.

9 Wood, *op.cit.*

10 D.E. Davy's MS Collections for the Hundred of Bosmere and Claydon, s.v. Coddenham, BL Add. MS 19,084.

11 Higham's dates were 1795–1844, see *DNB*. He drew most of the plates for Grieg to engrave for his *Excursions in the County of Suffolk*, 2 vols, 1818 and 1819.

The chapel in Higham's drawing does look thatched, if thinly, and it shows that the east end (really north-east), had a large three-light (now six-light) terracotta mullioned window (Plate 5), with a small two-light window in the gable, decorated to match. Katherine wheels can be seen along both lintels in the drawing, and on the lower window today. The drawing suggests that the north side fenestration was orthodox gothic, perhaps fifteenth-century, but that has all been filled in. The window heads here and at Layer Marney derive their similar and unusual forms by cutting out unmoulded parts of the surface of the rectangular terracotta units (Plate 6), but where Lord Marney chose winged putto heads or urns to fill the remaining triangles, Sir Philip had Katherine wheels.

Below the sill of the window there is a broad decorative band made up of three large terracotta tiles each showing Bothe quartering Oke impaling Bedingfield quartering Tuddenham, representing Sir Philip's second marriage. Looking like supporters are the heraldic badges of Bothe, a boar rampant, and Bedingfield, a unicorn rampant. Inside, the equivalent tiles show the first marriage: Bothe quartering Oke impaling Hopton quarterly, with the boar badge for Bothe facing the Hopton griffin segreant. At the 'west' end of the building today the lower part of the window has been reconstructed to replace a former west door into the chapel. At the middle level of the present six-light window the heraldic band outside has, three times, the heraldry of the first, Hopton, marriage. On smaller shields found regularly spaced on vertical elements on which dogs chase hares, three acorns slipped must be an abbreviated form of the Oke arms (Plate 7). At the top of both east and west windows, inside (Plate 8), the lintels are decorated with pairs of dolphins with urns between and beyond each.

Barham St Mary

Reference has already been made above to a Bothe-Oke tomb in the chancel here, and there is also a north-east chapel, its only window decorated with terracotta tiles. Further discussion of these features will follow in the second part of this article: 'St Katherine and the Bothes'.

Henley St Peter

Over the west door a decorative stone frieze includes a prayer for the souls of Thomas and Margaret Seckford; he died in 1505. Sir Philip Bothe put his mark on this, the church of another parish where he owned land, by decorating the three-light south nave window to the east of the porch with terracotta mouldings (Plate 10). Rather than change the fifteenth-century cusped trefoil gables to the three lights, the mullions were replaced inside and out to the point where the inward curvature begins. Inside, that is the extent of the change. Outside, extra panels of terracotta tiles are set into the flint wall. Above the window are the same three urns and two dolphins as are to be seen at the heads of the windows inside the former chapel at Shrubland. Below, there are three shields with Bothe impaling, from left to right, Hopton, Hopton, Bedingfield, and the usual animal badge 'supporters'.

Barking St Mary

The three-light windows of the north aisle at Barking church, seen from a distance outside and at first glance, are uniformly fifteenth-century in style. Closer inspection reveals that the vertical mullions of the westernmost window have been replaced by terracotta units, and the same has been done inside. In 1644, William Dowsing the iconoclast recorded something here in his Journal which gives him a slender claim to antiquarian status:

> BARKING, Aug. the 21st. There was St. Catherine with her Wheel.

The two central top lights of the terracotta window retain Katherine wheels which have survived his visits and the implicit order to destroy what was in the main lights lower down – no doubt a figure of the saint. Running up each chamfered window jamb from the sill there are vine trails of a type not seen elsewhere in the three counties, surmounted by two and rather more than another half of the units used as lintels at Shrubland and Barham, here set vertically and untrimmed (Plates 11 and 12). Three Katherine wheels decorate each side of the three-light window therefore, but no Bothe heraldry occurs. It seems very likely that Sir Philip endowed the stipend of another chantry priest to sing Masses at the Katherine altar which would have stood below that saint's window here until the Reformation, but nothing was recorded at the chantry survey of 1548.

Barsham Holy Trinity near Beccles

In the chancel a tomb of four bays stands out from the north wall into which the remainder of the chest was built in 1869. When it was taken to pieces to stow it in this way so that it would not project too far, fragments of early glass and pieces of the inscription from the monument were found inside. Just 'Hic jacet d'n's Ed' was legible, as recorded by Florence Horatia Suckling. The will of Sir Edward Echyngham, who died in 1527, mentioned a chapel of St Katherine on the north side of the chancel, and he wished to be buried under the foundations of the wall (presumably between chancel and chapel), so that, as at Barham, his tomb chest under an arch allowed communication between side and high altars. What remains is only part of the monument, for not only is the upper work gone, but the four-foot-high carved statues of his advower saints (including Katherine) have disappeared. He left a widow, Anne (who had to commission the tomb), and two young daughters, Anne and Mary, who became his coheiresses. Mary married a Blennerhassett, but Anne (1525–1600) eventually married Sir Owen Hopton of Yoxford, great nephew of Margaret, first wife of Sir Philip Bothe, and sister of his grandfather Sir George

Hopton. This admittedly later event nevertheless shows what is likely in any case, that Echynghams and Hoptons were all members of the county set with Bothes and Bedingfields.[12]

In NORFOLK, the terracotta artists seem to have tackled one major and three minor works. They arrived too late to decorate the entirely fifteenth-century Oxburgh Hall, but were given a marvellous opportunity in the church. The idea of large state rooms on first and second floors of the entrance tower may have come to Layer Marney from Oxburgh. As there are excellent photographs of Norfolk terracotta work in A.P. Baggs's article, the reader is referred to that.

The magnificent tomb-screens in the west and north walls of the south-east Bedingfield chapel in OXBOROUGH CHURCH make little or no heraldic reference to the family. They have no effigies, and no brass indents, though there is a matrix at the east end of the chapel floor. The will of Margaret Bedingfield (d.1514) makes provision for the chapel, but her son Edmund lived almost forty years longer than her. The tombs could be for both generations, but all record is lost. There is, however, plenty of carved heraldry on shields in the roof of the chapel. Many of the terracotta moulded units here occur also at Wymondham and at Bracon Ash: tilting shields which probably never had painted coats, and urns 'supported' by what might just be Bedingfield eagles displayed, but, if they bear this meaning here, they bear none at the other two churches. A few fragments of the work, rescued when the church tower fell, are now to be seen in a small guard room in the Oxburgh entrance tower.

At BRACON ASH, the eighteenth-century Berney mausoleum, entirely classical when seen from the north churchyard, has its entrance in the north wall of the chancel framed with slender terracotta work, many units in common with Wymondham and Oxborough. Coincidentally, the monument over the entrance is to an eighteenth-century Bedingfield. Baggs nevertheless describes this as a three-bayed canopied tomb, only one side of which is visible. His photograph shows no more than is there today, so that 'canopy of a tomb' would be a better description. He draws parallels with the tomb of the first Lord Marney at Layer Marney. One can only conclude that the Berneys broke through a monument of the 1530s to give the entrance doorway to their mausoleum a dramatic flourish. Baggs goes on to suggest that as the Appleyards, merchants of Norwich, were the chief family in the parish, and, since their head Roger Appleyard died in 1529, the tomb may have been his. Roger left bequests to the church but wished to be buried in the Norwich Greyfriars, whence his monument may have been moved at the Dissolution.[13]

At WYMONDHAM abbey the decorative screen filling a romanesque arch south of the high altar and now used as sedilia has long been thought, without documentary evidence, to be the monument of Elisha Ferrers, last abbot here from 1532 to the Dissolution in 1539, after which he served as archdeacon of Suffolk and a

[12] PRO, PCC wills of Sir Edward Echyngham, 28 Porch 1527, and Dame Anne Echyngham (nuncupative), 15 Crunwell 1539.

[13] Will of Roger Appleyard: PRO, PCC 15 Jankyn 1529.

prebendary of Norwich until his death in 1548. Pevsner, comparing it with the work at Oxborough, suggests the date 1525, which does not fit the attribution to Ferrers. Baggs points out signs of rebuilding using a mixture of complete units and broken fragments, and suggests that in 1539, when the eastern part end of the abbey was stripped and left open to the elements, a terracotta tomb there was dismantled and eventually rebuilt as sedilia and monument to Ferrers.

In the north aisle of the church of ST GEORGE COLEGATE in Norwich, there is a table monument of three bays which in Blomefield's time retained part of a memorial inscription to Robert Jannys whose will was proved in 1530. Baggs tells us that the tomb was formerly beneath the north arcade. Jannys was sheriff of Norwich in 1509 and the founder of the free school at Aylsham. The pulpit provided for at St George Colegate in his will is now at Catton and dated 1537. Alternate side panels contain the arms of the Grocers' Company of London (granted 1532), impaling Jannys's merchant's mark, and medallions with a seated long-hooded figure with a rosary. A date for this tomb in the mid-1530s is likely, because Jannys's bequest to the Guildhall only took effect in 1534.[14]

A.P. Baggs also reports terracotta elements from the same moulds at ARMINGHALL OLD HALL, demolished shortly after 1900, including pilasters of the Layer Marney type and figure panels like those at St George Colegate. They were the least spectacular features at the Old Hall arranged at random around two highly decorative medieval doorways. Some were rescued and built into a vinery at Russell Colman's house in Trowse Newton, along with an inscription for William Gladwyn, whose will of 1487 requested burial at Norwich Whitefriars, dissolved in 1538. Baggs again suggests that a terracotta tomb may have been moved to decorate a manor house after the Dissolution.[15]

To summarise, no close parallels to the works described have been found in England or on the near continent. The resited work at Wymondham and Arminghall cannot be dated, and the tomb-screens at Oxborough church could have been made at any time between the death of Margaret Bedingfield and that of her son Edmund. All the remainder fits neatly into just five years from 1525 to just after 1530, and a progress by the craftsmen from south to north of the region.

14 Will of Robert Jannys: PRO, PCC 1 Thrower 1530. J.K. Floyer, 'The Tomb of Robert Jannys', *NA* xxi, 1926, 243–5. Dr Floyer assumes Italian craftsmanship and goes on to speculate about work for Sir Thomas Lovell in London and at his East Harling mansion before 1524 which, had it survived, might have paralleled the terracottas of our tour.

15 P.G. Lindley, ' "The Arminghall Arch" and Contemporary Sculpture in Norfolk', *NA* xl, 1987, 19–43.

II
St Katherine and the Bothes

Judith Middleton-Stewart

On 13 November 1488 Philip Bothe, accompanied by Sir Ralph Shelton, arrived at the chapel of the hospital of St Thomas of Acon to meet the wardens of the Mercers' Company of London. His intention was to found a chantry at Barham in memory of his father, William, and his grandfather, Richard Bothe. Philip owned tenements in London, lying in the parish of St Margaret Bridge Street, in the parish of St Michael the Archangel in Crooked Lane, and in St Antonin's parish in Budge Row.[16] Land and tenements in the capital were always popular as a means of endowment because London property was exempt from mortmain, and Philip was anxious to reach an agreement with this most prestigious of livery companies. He attempted to persuade it to accept his London property as an endowment for a chantry foundation for the support of two priests, on which he would need a return of £14 a year.[17] One of the Mercers' wardens was Richard Feldyng, of whom more later, but among the assembled liverymen was Nicholas Shelton. Nicholas was, perhaps, a relative of Bothe's companion, Sir Ralph, and may have been a possible link through whom Bothe hoped to do business with the Mercers' Company or, at the least, to gain an introduction.

The Mercers had already viewed the properties, 'whereof part of them be very old and chargeable for to keep . . .'. They also commented that one priest was as much as the endowment could maintain. Fearing their refusal, Bothe then undertook to pay a pension of £4 *per annum* for twenty-five years, leaving the Company to bear the remaining £10, 'rather than anything of the will of his foresaid ancestors should be broken or minished'. The Mercers, however, still rejected his offer and his property, and in the following month it was reported, 'they heve geven hym his thanke for his good will and prosure and so departed'. In July 1490 the prior and convent of Ely granted Bothe a plot of ground at the west end of Barham church, possibly to erect a free-standing chantry chapel or, more likely, on which to build a house for a chantry priest sometime in the future.

Philip Bothe's role as a chantry founder is not evident again for some twenty-five years, when his name appears in the archives of Pembroke College (formerly Hall),

[16] Cambridge, Pembroke College Archives A5, the conveyance of the property by the bishop of Hereford to Richard Feldyng, 11 December, 10 Henry VIII; Pembroke College Archives B5, an exemplification acquitting the college of the annuity of £6 to the chantry of Barham, 9 October, 8 Elizabeth: here, the properties are named. The Black Ball, Bell or Bull (depending on which part of the archive is read) was in Bridge Street, Powle Hede (perhaps Paul's Head) was in Crooked Lane, and The Wrestlers in 'Bridge' Row.

[17] F. Watney and L. Lyell, *The Acts of Court of the Mercers' Company 1453–1527*, Cambridge 1936, 185–6; K.L. Wood-Legh, *Perpetual Chantries in Britain*, Cambridge 1965, 43.

Cambridge. This was in 1516, but whether he had repaired his London property in the interim is uncertain. He now enfeoffed his close relative, Charles Bothe, bishop of Hereford, a graduate of Pembroke Hall.[18] The bishop, with a group of trusted friends, conveyed the properties to Richard Feldyng, formerly the Mercers' warden, and within two months Feldyng had drawn up an agreement with Pembroke Hall.

> Richard ffeldyng for certeyn causes and consideracyons him movyng hath graunted bitaken and to ferme letten unto the said Master and felowes alle and syngular his lands and ten[emen]ts rents rev[er]cyons and servyces w[i]t[h] shoppes cellers solers and all theyr appurtena[u]nces whatsoev[er] they be set lying and beyng in the p[ar]isshes of saynt Margaret in Bryggestrete St Michael and St Anthony . . . the master to hold for fifty yeres paying one pepp[er]corn at the ffeast of pentecost.[19]

Feldyng's will, dated 25 February 1518, required the master and fellows of Pembroke to order a priest of good conversation after the decease of Sir Philip Bothe to sing for the soul of Philip, William Bothe, Richard Bothe, their heirs and ancestors, and to sing for Feldyng's soul, too. Feldyng also founded two fellowships and a foundation for one bible clerk, with the provision that if '. . . there be any scoler of the same kyndred and name of the foresaid S[ir] Philp Bothe w[i]t[h]ynne the univ[er]sitie of Cambridge havyng good learning [he] to be elected'.[20]

In Barham church, the north-east chapel, now the vestry and lumber room, is almost twice as long as it is wide (6.4 m by 3.53 m), and the lower rood stair entrance lies just outside the chapel's south-west door. The 'low pillar' for an image, which Davy saw in the south-east corner of what he called the dormitory, may still exist behind pine panelling. In the middle of the chapel stands the later tomb-chest of Edward Bacon and his wife, Helen Little, which nearly fills the chapel. Beyond it, on the east wall, there is no evidence of an earlier altar or an east window as might be expected; and neither is there any trace of a piscina in the south-east corner. The room is lit by a single window on the north, and it is the decoration of this window that indicates that this humble extension to Barham church has an interesting pedigree.

The window is tall (see Plate 9). It is of four lights with vertical mullions and the lintel is made of rectangular Katherine wheel terracotta tiles which extend beyond the width of the frame below. The tiles are uncut so that the lights are square-headed. From the outside the decoration is there, but from a distance the window looks plain and domestic and it is in a state of disrepair. Inside, many layers of whitewash have obscured much of the detail. The Katharine wheels are clear enough; the band of Bothe/Oke-Bedingfield/Tuddenham impalements with animal badge 'supporters' below the sill are thickly coated with whitewash, but the unicorns can just be discerned. Outside, the Bothe/Oke-Hopton shields which Davy saw on the sill are no longer visible; either the terracotta tiles have been mortared over or replaced

18 *BRUC*, 77.

19 Pembroke College Archives A9.

20 Pembroke College Archives A11.

in plain stone. Surely this is a sixteenth-century chapel, intended as the Bothe chantry and mortuary, with an altar where the priest could sing Masses for the souls of Richard, William and Philip Bothe, who were also commemorated in the terracotta mouldings on the widow frame?

The chapel is now in poor condition and has undergone several changes. In the seventeenth century, Candler mentioned a second window, but whether it lit the chapel or was positioned to the west thereof in the area of the later Middleton family pew is difficult to say: 'In two severall windowes on the North side over the Isle beelonging to Shribland hall – the Armes of Booth as before under one of them is written John Booth'.[21] William Bloyse referred to 'a raysd stone for Ric. Booth Esq defac'd', which may have been situated in the chapel where the Bothe chantry was to be celebrated.[22] If so, it is likely that it was moved after the Reformation so that the Bacon-Little tomb could be accommodated in what had, by that time, become their family mortuary chapel. Richard's 'raysd stone' was later jammed in under Katherine Oke's canopy 'carved with oaken leaves and boares heads' on the north chancel wall, where the brass matrix of the armoured figure on the tomb fits the date of Richard's death *c.*1477.

Without citing his source, however, Bloyse gave the chapel an even greater antiquity: 'Oke built a Chappel nigh the church. Sr Phil. Booth repayrd a part of it on the outside . . .'. This reference complicates matters because it means that the chapel was built perhaps some eighty or one hundred years beforehand as a chapel for a member of the Oke family other than Katherine. It was built perhaps for Katherine's father, but was 'personalised' by Philip Bothe who added the terracotta decoration after he had established the chantry for the Bothe family in the already ancient chapel.

In the chancel, the position of the Oke/Bothe tomb, which backs on to the south wall of the chapel, suggests that in the original arrangement there would have been an opening above the tomb but below the arched canopy. Through this, a priest would be able to see the elevation of the Host at the high altar in the chancel while he celebrated at the chapel's side altar. Katherine Oke's tomb was placed in this most sacrosanct site to which, as the Lady of Shrubland, she would have been entitled, and here her tomb would have housed the Easter Sepulchre in the Lenten liturgy. John Hopton, the grandfather of Philip's first wife, Margaret Hopton, had just such a tomb and chapel at Blythburgh, his table-tomb undoubtedly serving the same purpose, and a similar arrangement may still be seen in the Clopton chantry chapel in Holy Trinity church, Long Melford. The greatly altered chancel at Barham, however, longer than originally planned and now with a raised floor, makes Katherine's chantry-chancel arrangement difficult to visualise. The dedication of the chapel at Barham is unknown, and there is no indication of the dedicatee of the later chantry either. It would be natural and rather endearing to think that the Bothes, grandfather, father and son, dedicated chapel and chantry to St Katherine in

21 BL Add. MS 15520, fo. 20.
22 SROI, GC 17: 755, III, 201.

memory of Katherine Oke, who had brought them the sumptuous prize of Shrubland. It is here, however, that the story takes a new turn.

The Bothes were not of East Anglian stock. They had originally come from a branch of the extensive family of Bothe of Barton-upon-Irwell, their home territory being on the Lancashire-Cheshire border.[23] The family had acquired the manor of Barton through marriage in the late thirteenth century and, after another advantageous union in the late fourteenth century, this time with the Worsleys, they found themselves related to several important Lancashire families. Twenty-one Bothes became clerics in the fifteenth and sixteenth centuries, including two bishops and two archbishops of York, which earned them the title of 'The Clerical Bothes of Barton';[24] and, between 1368 and 1460, various members of the family established the three chantry foundations in the parish church of Eccles, a few miles from Manchester.

Thomas Bothe (d.1368), was Philip Bothe's great-great-grandfather (see Family Tree 2). He founded the first of the three Eccles chantries and dedicated it to St Katherine, but why it is impossible to say. His wife's name was Ellen (Worsley), and Thomas's affection for St Katherine, therefore, may have had no familial connotations at all, but could have been a purely personal choice. The chantry was established in Eccles parish church, but little standing structure survives from the fourteenth century. The responds to the arch of the south transept may belong to the building of 1368, but these are all that remain from that period – and there are no saintly attributes left to identify which St Katherine Thomas Bothe was honouring. It is most unlikely, however, that his dedication would have been to the 'other' Katherine, the saint of Sienna (1347–80). She had barely got into her stride by 1368, becoming a tertiary sister of the Dominican order only a few years previously, and it was not until 1375 that she became politically involved with Pope Gregory XI in exile at Avignon.[25] It is not she who is associated with the Katherine wheel, and this Siennese saint was not canonised until 1461. It is St Katherine of Alexandria who is remembered by the spiked wheel, the cause of her prolonged and agonising torture.[26] She was a well-proven saint of great antiquity, of high estate and deep learning, and was therefore the patron of students, especially philosophers. In her turn, she was often favoured by royal, aristocratic or gentle patrons. Thomas Bothe's providential marriage possibly had more than a little to do with his choice of saint, as he experienced elevation in both rank and fortune through his marriage to Ellen Worsley.

In his will of 1368, he requested to be buried within St Mary's church, Eccles, before the altar of St Katherine the Virgin, which suggests that the chantry was

[23] E. Axon, 'The Family of Bothe (Booth), and the Church in the 15th and 16th Centuries', *Transactions of the Lancashire and Cheshire Antiquarian Society* liii, 1938, 32–82.

[24] R.N. Swanson, *Church and Society in Late Medieval England*, Oxford 1989, 79–80.

[25] P. and L. Murray, *The Oxford Companion to Christian Art and Architecture*, Oxford 1996, 95.

[26] E Duffy, 'Holy Maydens, Holy Wyfes: The Cult of Women Saints in Fifteenth- and Sixteenth-Century England', *SCH* xxvii, 1990, 175–96, at 184–5.

Family Tree 2. The Relationship between the Bothes of Shrubland and selected Bothes of Barton-upon-Irwell, Lancashire

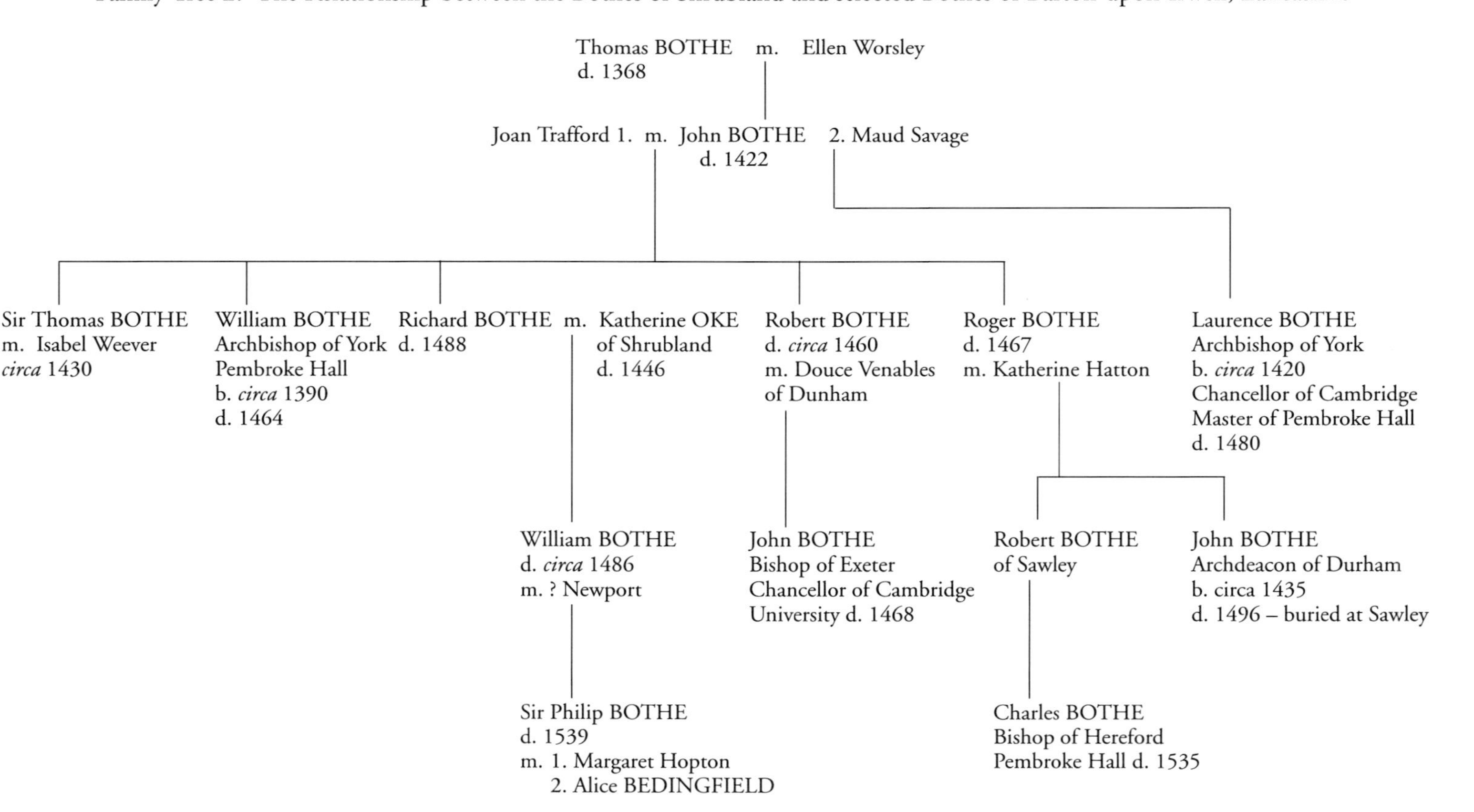

already in existence and had been set up during his lifetime.[27] He also bequeathed £30 towards the building of Salford bridge, on which he is thought to have founded a chapel. Leland described it: 'Ther be divers stone bridgis in the toune, but the best of iii. arches is over Irwel, cawllid Salford bridge. This bridge devidith Manchestre from Salford, the wich is as a large suburbe to Manchestre. On this bridge is a praty litle chapel.'[28] The chapel, eventually reduced to being the local lock-up, was destroyed in 1802.

Thomas was succeeded by his elder son, John, who was elected knight of the shire in 1411 and 1420. John had an extensive family of at least six or seven sons, and as many daughters, by two women. Through his marriage to Joan Trafford, he was the father of William, the bishop of Lichfield and Coventry and later, from 1452 to 1464, the first Archbishop Bothe of York; and John was also the father of the shadowy Richard Bothe of Shrubland, about whom so little is known. By Maud Savage, whom he probably did not marry, John fathered Laurence, the bishop of Durham, who became the second Archbishop Bothe of York in 1476. The episcopal seal of Laurence bore the Bothe arms within an engrailed border, 'one of the recognized marks of illegitimacy', according to Axon; but the two archbishops, Laurence and William, were extremely close and shared 'a family affection so strong that it might be thought to be nepotism', from which the family's clerical network greatly benefited.[29]

Laurence was at Pembroke Hall, becoming Master in 1450, and was Chancellor of Cambridge University from 1456 to 1458, as well as chancellor to Queen Margaret of Anjou and tutor and guardian to the Prince of Wales.[30] In 1450 he was co-founder of the second Bothe chantry dedicated to St Katherine in St Mary's parish church, Eccles, which was a foundation for two priests. The licence was granted to William Bothe, bishop of Coventry and Lichfield, Sir John Byron (William's brother-in-law), Richard Bothe (William's brother and Philip's grandfather), Seth Worsley (William's cousin), and Laurence Bothe, 'clerk', the half-brother, but the provisions of the chantry were written very much with William in mind.[31] It was, truly, a family foundation, and the mesh of Bothe relations was manifest in a list of names painted on 'a descent board or table'. This was hung above the altar of St Katherine 'that the chaplains may see it, and may daily pray for those whose names are thereon inscribed'.[32] Those mentioned were the immediate descendants of John Bothe and Joan, his wife, but Maud Savage, Laurence's mother, was point-

27 F.R. Raines, *A History of the Chantries within the County Palatine of Lancaster, being the Reports of the Royal Commissioners of Henry VIII, Edward VI and Queen Mary*, pt 1, Chetham Society 1862, 131.

28 J. Leland, *The Itinerary of John Leland in or about the years 1535–1543*, IV, pts vii and viii, ed. L. Toulmin-Smith, London 1964, 43.

29 Axon, 'The Family of Bothe', 36; Swanson, *Church and Society*, 79. Biographies of John Bothe (Booth) and his brother, Henry, may be found in J.S. Roskell, L. Clark and C. Rawcliffe, eds, *The History of Parliament: The House of Commons 1386–1421*, 4 vols, Stroud 1993, ii, 288–93.

30 *BRUC*, 78.

31 *CPR 1446–1452*, 322.

32 Raines, *Lancashire Chantries*, 134.

edly not mentioned. Laurence was buried in Southwell Minster in the chantry chapel which he had founded for two chaplains. It was not dedicated to St Katherine, and was destroyed in 1847.

William, the first Archbishop Bothe of York, was at Gray's Inn and perhaps at Pembroke Hall, too, although here there is some disagreement as to whether he was or not.[33] He became bishop of Lichfield and Coventry in 1447 and archbishop of York in 1452. His second chantry, the third Bothe chantry to be founded in Eccles church, was a college chantry dedicated to the College of Jesus and the Blessed Virgin Mary, and was founded by licence dated 1 December, 1459, to be celebrated in St Mary's church for the good estate of the king (Henry VI), and the archbishop and for their souls after death, and the souls of certain others who were to be named by the founders. Richard Bothe, esquire, and Seth Worsley were again co-founders, this time with Nicholas Byron and Robert Clyfton, the archbishop's brothers-in-law.[34] The mortmain licence granted by Henry VI mentions the building of a manse which would serve as a residence for the chaplains of the chantry of St Katherine and the College of Jesus and Mary, that they 'shall have a common hall and shall table together'.[35] In 1464, Archbishop William wrote his will. Richard Bothe was an executor and, with other patrons, he presented to the chantry in 1466 and 1468. By 1487, Richard must have died, for his name was no longer on the list and the patron was another William Bothe, perhaps the son of Richard and father of Philip.

John Bothe, Chancellor of Cambridge University and bishop of Exeter from 1464 to 1478, was the nephew of Richard Bothe. His arms can be seen in Exeter cathedral and so can his Katherine wheels. His brass, in East Horsley church, Surrey, shows him with the Bothe arms, three boars' heads, with a label of three points. As a first cousin once removed, his relationship to Sir Philip Bothe of Shrubland and Charles Bothe, bishop of Hereford from 1516 to 1535, was similar, and it was to Charles, another graduate from Pembroke Hall, that Sir Philip turned for help in establishing his chantry. Charles had obtained the degree of doctor of Law from Bologna university and, from 1495, steadily rose in the Church, although by now there were no clerical members in the family who were sufficiently senior to aid his promotion. He had been one of the Prince's Council, the body of ten men which had accompanied Arthur, prince of Wales, into the Principality on Arthur's marriage, and later he was in attendance on Queen Katherine at the Field of the Cloth of Gold. In 1516, he was made bishop of Hereford. Here, on a little doorway adjoining the north porch which he had built, his arms were displayed and here he was buried.[36] There is no record of Katherine wheels at Hereford.

The foundation of Sir Philip Bothe's chantry was accomplished in gradual stages between 1518 and 1522. On 18 July1522, the master and fellows of Pembroke Hall granted to Sir Philip £12 per annum, £6 for a chaplain in Barham church and £6 for

33 *DNB*, 288.

34 *CPR 1452–1461*, 526.

35 Raines, *Lancashire Chantries*, 135.

36 A.T. Bannister, ed., *Registrum Caroli Bothe, Episcopi Herefordensis, AD MDXVI–MDXXXV*, London 1921, i–ix.

a preaching priest, less than he had originally hoped.[37] Sir Philip's foundation is included in the Chantry certificates of 1548, where it is described as being endowed with 'certain lands and tenements granted to Pembroke Hall, Cambridge' which provided the stipend for a priest 'to sing for ever in the parish church'.[38] The master and fellows of Pembroke engaged William Mason, citizen and draper of London, to be their bailiff, to oversee all repairs and keep a good account of rents and expenses at Christmas, Lady Day, John the Baptist's day and Michaelmas, or within five weeks of each feast.[39] Mason was to be paid 13s 4d each Michaelmas for his services.

Sir Philip Bothe did not die until 1539, by which time the chantry was running successfully, Mason collecting the rents, the college paying Sir Philip the stipends for the two priests. Nevertheless, an unsigned letter written to the Master of Pembroke Hall by one of Bothe's servants a few years before Bothe's death sheds light on the old man's anxiety for his endowment.

> Ryght wourshypfull Mast[er] Rob[er]t Whynborne yf plese you to under stands and al y[e] cu[m]peyne what answere I have had of Syr Phylipp Bothe. Thys yt is. The cause of hys dysplesure is he sent worde to ye tennants of Lond[on] to paye no more rents untyll suche tyme as hys lernyd counsell and yow[rs] had convynde to gyther for a more surety of ye lands. Was thys ye last Ester [he sayd] he apoyntyd hys counsell to [c]ome frome Londone and left wourd w[i]t[h] Mason to sende wourd unto ye coll[ege] yf yow and one or ii of y[our] college shulde a[ttend] --- to Syr Phylyppe Bothys and a resonde to gyther f[or] suerty of y[e] lands And hys cownsell came and taryd hym iii or iiii days at hys grete cost and [ch]arge and n[one] of ye college came and w[i]t[h] yt he toke a grette dysplesur and thought y[e] college dyd mouke w[i]t[h] him And he sent hys serva[n]t to London and asked of Mason howe yt chansed that none of college came to mete hys masters counsell at his masters howse and he said that he had sent worde to y[e] college of yt and thus Mason put all ye faute on y[e] college. Howbeyt he is nowe co[n]tente y[f] y[e] nexte yow a poynt a daye at Lond[on] to mete w[i]t[h] his counsell for hys counsell shalbe there all ye nexte terme and brynge wyth you suche wryghtyngs as you have for y[e] suerty of y[e] lands and so to co[n]clude and make yt as suer as can be and you shall fynde hym as you have before tyme . . .'[40]

Sir Philip's chantry was suppressed in 1548. The chantry priest at the time was Thomas Ryding, aged fifty.[41] He was receiving a stipend of £6 and was described as 'of very small learning', which may have been true, but which probably meant, too, that he was not of the new persuasion.

So the Katherine wheels with which Philip Bothe had decorated his terracotta windows were not there to commemorate Katherine Oke after all. They were there as a personal reminder to Philip Bothe of the saint to whom his family had shown honour and devo-

37 Pembroke College Archives A14.

38 V.B. Redstone, 'Chapels, Chantries and Gilds in Suffolk: II Chantry Certificates No. 45', *PSIA* xii, 1906, 30–69, at 30–1.

39 Pembroke College Archives A16.

40 Pembroke College Archives B2.

41 Redstone, 'Chantry Certificates', 30–1.

tion in a different 'country' and in previous centuries. And it is fortunate for Suffolk that, some seventy years before Katherine's death and a further seventy before Philip's foundation, the choice of Thomas Bothe of Barton in distant Lancashire had fallen on Katherine of Alexandria to be his patron and 'advoye', a saint with such a distinctive attribute. Without the Katherine wheels, Richard Bothe, the husband of Katherine Oke, would have remained in the shadows.

A First Stirring of Suffolk Archaeology?

Diarmaid MacCulloch

NORMAN SCARFE, as one of the most distinguished promoters of Suffolk's archaeology, may feel some affinity for a Tudor and Jacobean parson who, as far as I am aware, is the first person recorded as having taken a scholarly spade to Suffolk soil. No doubt the clergyman's motives were far from the disinterested enquiry of modern times, but archaeology has undergone many transformations in its history. It is a particular pleasure for me to record this tiny archaeological footnote, since the protagonist was the Rev. Robert Westley, rector of the small central Suffolk parish of Wetherden, and so a predecessor of my late father, the last resident rector, who was himself no mean local historian. Westley was rector from 1571 to 1600.[1] Sometime before the death of Queen Elizabeth I, he conducted the Tudor equivalent of an archaeological dig in his own churchyard, resulting in a significant discovery which awaits further investigation in the future.

In 1604 Westley's successor as rector of Wetherden, Miles Syll, found himself defending a suit in the Court of Exchequer from John Paucke or Pancke, the guardian of a boy called Richard Parincheife the younger, who was certainly not a local, and was probably the son of a London tradesman.[2] The dispute was about tithe, parochial revenues and the use of the rectory house, and it was founded on much older disagreements: a tussle for possession of the parish revenues between two rival religious houses apparently ill-matched in power and wealth, in which the lesser contestant had won. In the twelfth century the powerful Benedictine abbey of St Edmund at Bury had been foiled in its designs on the living of Wetherden by the determination of the East Anglian magnate family of de Scales, who owned the main manor of Wetherden Hall, to provide an endowment for their own family

1 He may have been the Robert Weslye who matriculated as pensioner from Clare, Easter 1566: *Alumni Cantabrigienses Part I: From the Earliest Times to 1751*, ed. J. and J.A. Venn, 4 vols, Cambridge 1924, iv, 372.

2 PRO, E134(Exchequer Depositions)/3 James I/Trinity 7. Neither Paucke nor Parincheife appear to have a local connection, although all four deponents (Westley, Rosyer, Devoryce and Brooke) said that they knew Parincheife as well as Syll. Paucke is described as a gentleman. Parinchief must be related to the later ultra-Royalist writer Richard Perrinchief, b.1621. The *Dictionary of National Biography* suggests that this later Richard may have been born in Hampshire; more specifically, *Alumni Cantabrigienses to 1751*, ed. Venn, iii, 349, makes him the son of Gabriel Perrinchief, joiner of St Botolph Aldersgate, London, who would probably be of the same generation as the litigant.

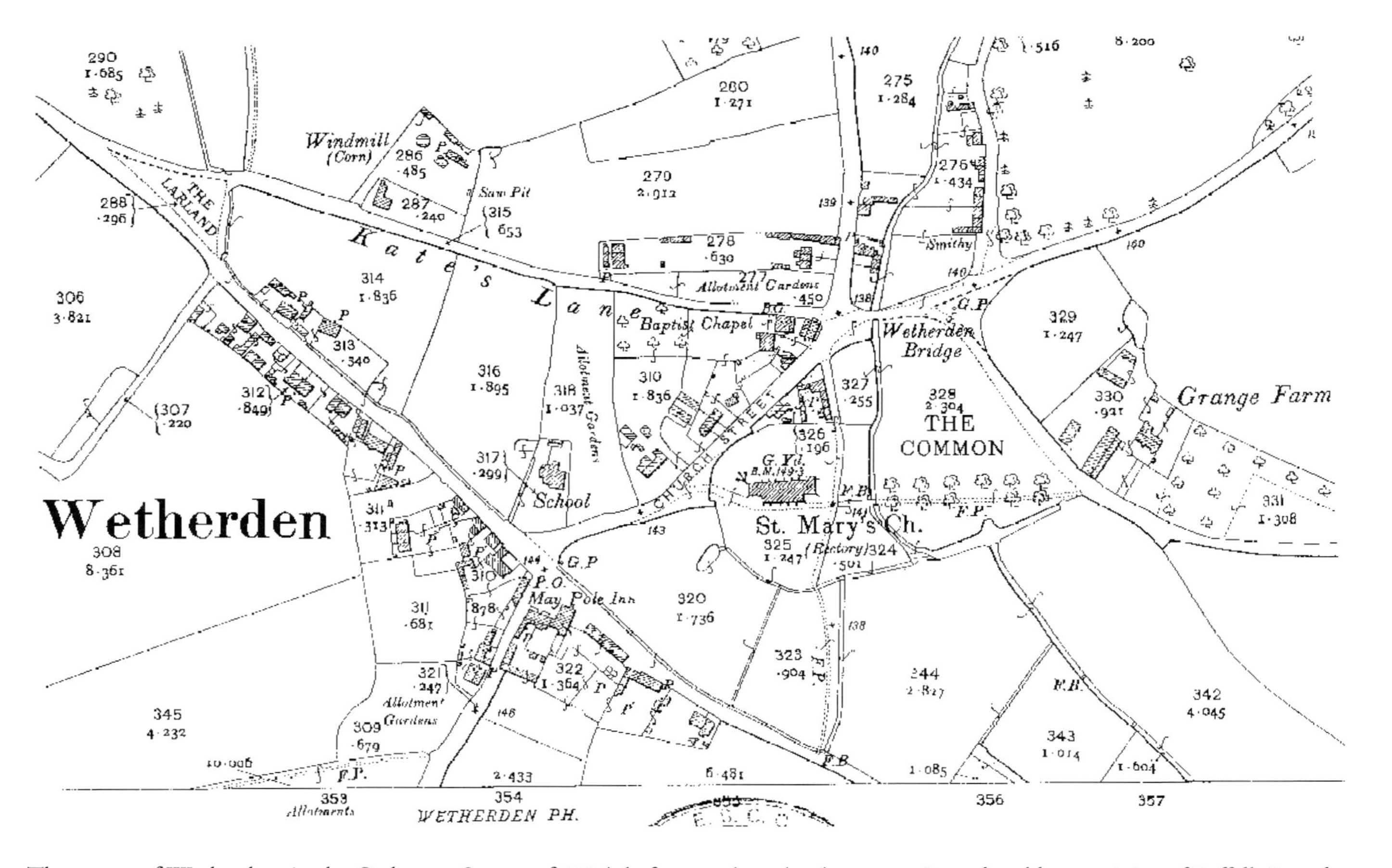

The centre of Wetherden, in the Ordnance Survey of 1904, before modern development. *Reproduced by permission of Suffolk Record Office, Ipswich.* Note the oval shape of the churchyard and buttsyards taken together, and the roads and paths converging within the oval. The parsonage house is the last house opposite the west end of the church before the nineteenth-century school building.

Benedictine foundation at Blackborough in the parish of Middleton in Norfolk. This small and not especially well-endowed priory settled down fairly quickly from its original twin community of monks and nuns to become exclusively a nunnery. So perhaps it was out of a wish to avoid upsetting the nuns that Bury abbey refrained from exploiting its formidable political and economic power to secure sole control of Wetherden; more cynically, one might hazard that the de Scales were just too powerful an adversary for Bury to take on.[3]

The arrangement which the nuns of Blackborough came to enjoy, according to the 1604 Exchequer lawsuit, was the possession of a mediety of the rectory (in fact in practice, rather less than half): the prioress took one tithe sheaf of corn for every two of the rector's, with equal shares of the glebeland between both. Blackborough lands, listed in detail in the priory's cartulary and partly summarised in the depositions of the 1604 lawsuit, included glebe nearest to the church itself; the field to the south, which (although built over in very recent years) separates the churchyard from the main Stowmarket–Elmswell road; and a close behind the parsonage (now the substantial Tudor cottage known as the White House) which lies across the road from the west end of the church.[4] The *Valor Ecclesiasticus* entry for Blackborough recorded in 1535 a pension of 23s 4d from Wetherden rectory and rents of lands amounting to 24s 7d; further lands in Wetherden seem to have been sold in the fifteenth century.[5] Wetherden represented the nuns' only property holding in Suffolk, yet for a long time they seem to have been punctilious about maintaining their rights there, having originally been charged with maintaining a vicar for their mediety of the rectory. When in 1349 Thomas de Totyngton the rector of Wetherden died (presumably in the Black Death), the Blackborough community carefully listed which of Wetherden parish church's vestments, plate, ornaments and liturgical books belonged to the priory, including a separate chest to keep them in, and Blackborough still had a clerk called John Hutton as 'procurator' for its interests in Wetherden.[6] By contrast, the monks of Bury ended up from the twelfth century settling for the right of presentation to the rectory and a contribution towards the salary of their grammar school master. Bury's original aim had almost certainly been to annex the rectory of what was a rather well-endowed church, and replace it with a

3 *Jocelin of Brakelond*, 64, 95; *Medieval Religious Houses: England and Wales*, ed. D. Knowles and R.N. Hadcock, London 1953, 59, 210.

4 PRO, E134/3 James I/Trinity 7, depositions of Robert Westley and Thomas Rosyer. See the detailed list made in 9 Henry VIII, in BL MS Egerton 3137, fo. 202rv, and a briefer rental of 24 June 20 Henry VI, *ibid.*, fo. 219v.

5 *VE* iii, 395; confirmed in BL MS Egerton 3137, fo. 202rv (the cartulary of Blackborough priory, formerly owned by Sir Henry Spelman and the Gurney family). By contrast, there is nothing recorded about the rectory at Wetherden under the entry for Bury St Edmunds abbey: *ibid.*, 459–65. For Blackborough's sale of Wetherden lands in 1477–78 to the Sulyards, see PRO, C3(Chancery Proceedings)/128/141, answer of Sir John Sulyard; and for a grant to the Rosier family, temp. Henry VI, PRO, E134/3 James I/Trinity 7, deposition of Thomas Rosyer.

6 BL Egerton 3137, fo. 105v, pr. W. Dugdale, ed. J. Caley, H. Ellis and B. Bandinel, *Monasticon Anglicanum*, 6 vols, London 1846, iv, 204, note g. See also the note of the pension recorded in the Ministers' Account pr. in Dugdale, *Monasticon*, iv, 210. Charters mentioning the maintenance of a vicar for the mediety are at BL Egerton 3137, fo. 103v.

vicarage, thus complementing the abbey's secular possession of the lesser manor of Wetherden, Pulham's Hall. However, thanks to the dispute with the de Scales family and with Blackborough, this never happened; the living of Wetherden remains a rectory to the present day.[7]

A state of affairs which was the result of compromise, and which was a cause of discreetly discontented comment on Bury's loss of revenue by the celebrated abbey chronicler Jocelin of Brakelond, was very likely to cause trouble after the dissolution of the monasteries; so it proved. Robert Westley was the first person recorded as having to face the problem. He clashed with one of his parishioners, Henry Muskett of Wetherden and Harleston, a rich and litigious local yeoman. Westley was trying to regain the close behind Wetherden parsonage which was part of the Blackborough lands, and which had been leased to Muskett by the Crown in 1567. At some subsequent date in the reign of Elizabeth I, before Muskett's death in 1595, the two men became entangled in a lawsuit in the Court of Requests.[8] After this came the turn of Miles Syll, the defendant in the Exchequer lawsuit brought by Paucke in 1604 over the former Blackborough priory lands and rights. Syll was rector from 1600 to 1604, and a clergyman of some scholarly attainments, a Cambridge graduate from St John's College, later B.D. and a Fellow of St Catharine's Hall, Cambridge.[9] The details of the property under dispute can be reconstructed by working outwards from the clues provided by a set of Exchequer depositions in the suit. These were taken on 11 October 1604 by Sir Robert Jermyn, Sir George Waldegrave, Thomas Rivet and Edward Bacon: a rather high-powered *dedimus potestatem* commission of local gentlemen drawn from a wide area of the county, whose status indicated that this was considered a case of some significance.[10]

The interrogatories for the depositions (constructed, one ought to note, on behalf of the plaintiff) discussed a portion of tithes and land and a barn at the parsonage in Wetherden which had belonged to Blackborough priory; these had been leased first by Westley and then by Syll from the Crown, and the lands included one half of the parsonage house, originally leased by the rectors from the prioress of

7 See Abbot Samson of Bury's quitclaim of the advowson of the mediety of the church to Robert de Scales, BL Egerton 3137, fo. 101v. Further entries of charters for Wetherden are gathered *ibid.*, fos 101v–104v. See also *English Episcopal Acta* vi: *Norwich 1070–1214*, ed. C. Harper-Bill, Oxford 1990, nos 171, 177.

8 PRO, REQ2(Proceedings in the Court of Requests)/42/89, undated. For some of Muskett's other lawsuits, see PRO, C3/61/4 (concerning alleged oppressive behaviour and overstocking at Harleston) and PRO, C1(Early Chancery Proceedings)/1471/41. Muskett's 1567 lease from the Crown, described in the deposition of Thomas Rosyer, PRO, E134/3 James I/Trinity 7, is also recorded in PRO, E401(Exchequer Docquet Books)/1810 s.v. 20 November [1567]. For Muskett's inquisition *post mortem* and pedigrees, see *Suffolk Manorial Families*, ed. J.J. Muskett and F.O. Johnson, 2 vols and 3 parts, Exeter 1900–14, ii, 370–81.

9 *Alumni Cantabrigienses to 1751*, ed. Venn, iv, 75.

10 PRO, E134/3 James I/Trinity 7 (I have not been able to locate any other proceedings in this case). Jermyn and Waldegrave were the only commissioners to take the depositions and return the writ. The depositions were evidently lost after they were sent from Suffolk, so there is a fresh writ dated 23 April 1605, and its return by Jermyn and Waldegrave with a new copy of the depositions is dated 28 May 1605.

Blackborough. The interrogatories went on to enquire about a murky transaction which amounted to a simoniacal deal between Westley and Syll; they asked whether Miles Syll had contracted with Westley for his resignation, and for how much money. Westley was the first to reply to the interrogatories; by now he was an old man described as around eighty years old, still living in Wetherden despite having left his cure. In his answers he frankly admitted the plaintiff's accusations of simony between himself and Syll; it was a sad story. Westley had been imprisoned for debt in the King's Bench prison in London; perhaps the debt had accumulated during the course of his earlier Requests suit against Henry Muskett. While lying in King's Bench, the aged rector was approached by Mr Syll and Richard Ridding, one of the esquire bedells of Cambridge University (Syll and Riding were both Yorkshiremen, had been undergraduate contemporaries at St John's Cambridge, and had probably therefore also been schoolfriends).[11] They offered Westley £70 to resign his benefice, and he accepted. Once the deal had gone through, and Syll's money had been lodged with a kinsman of his who was a vintner near Holborn bridge, Westley's son-in-law Simon Humphrey (a resident in Wetherden, and a lessee of some of the rectory lands) received the simoniacal bribe on the old man's behalf.[12] Westley nevertheless complained that Syll continued to withhold five pounds of the agreed sum; evidently he was now no friend of his successor, and perfectly prepared both to testify in detail for Syll's opponent and to reveal what had triggered the resignation of his cure.

The deposition of another Wetherden yeoman, a tailor called George Brooke, may supply a reason for the disagreement between Westley and Syll; he testified that the former rector had before his resignation reserved out of the rectory a house for Brooke and his wife for their lifetimes. It is likely that Brooke's wife was another of Westley's children, and it is also likely that Westley was lodging with them or with his other son-in-law Simon Humphrey; he is still described as resident in Wetherden in his deposition.[13] Westley's was no easy retirement, since he was continuing to act as parochial chaplain of the little neighbouring parish of Harleston. Harleston church lies just over a mile from Wetherden, and it would be an uncomfortable uphill walk for a man who was nearly eighty; nor was Harleston without its troubles, once more thanks to Westley's old adversaries the Musketts. When Westley made a return for Harleston to the archdeacon of Sudbury's enquiry in 1603, he was not sparing in his complaints: 'Harleston is holden for an Impropriation, and a

11 Ridding is called 'Mr Reading' in the depositions, but the identification is easy as he is also described as a university bedell. On his career, including his matriculation at St John's in 1587, a year after Syll, see *Alumni Cantabrigienses to 1751*, ed. Venn, iii, 457. His will of 28 November 1626, Cambridge University Library, University Archives Wills 3, fos 163v–164r, does not reveal anything relevant to this case.

12 Humphrey married Martha Westley at Wetherden on 2 January 1598 (apparently calculated New Style, since the entry is sandwiched between a wedding of November 1597 and one of June 1598): SROI, FB222/D1/1. I am very grateful to John Blatchly for searching the registers of Wetherden and Harleston for me on this and other matters.

13 Dr Blatchly's search of the Wetherden and Harleston registers has not revealed any marriage for George Brooke.

Donatyve, theare is no Vicaredge indued [endowed], his stipende is but v li a yeare for his service. The sayed personage impropriate (if it be such a one) is valued in the King's Book at v li; one Richarde Muskett, gent., taketh all the fruites.'[14] Muskett was the son and heir of Henry Muskett, Westley's former legal opponent; one wonders who had appointed Westley to a confrontational and unrewarding cure. Perhaps he was still doing his best to serve Harleston when he died in 1612, by then in his late eighties.[15] Syll did not take prolonged enjoyment from his dubiously acquired parish at Wetherden. If he was not forced out for his grave breach of canon law, he may at least have been embarrassed by the publicity about his dealings, or demoralised by the litigation in which he was becoming embroiled. In late 1604 he resigned Wetherden to another Fellow of St Catharine's Hall, William Kilbourne, and took a living suitably far away in Bedfordshire. Kilbourne's arrival has all the signs of haste, which may suggest a hurried replacement for Syll from among his colleagues at St Catharine's. The bishop of Norwich (who had previously been Master of Corpus Christi College, just across the street from St Catharine's) ordained Kilbourne deacon and priest at Norwich on the same day, 23 December 1604, and by 17 January 1605 he was rector of Wetherden. Nevertheless, once Kilbourne was there, he stayed: in contrast to Syll, he lasted as rector until his death in 1644.[16]

We cannot tell what effect such sadly commercial manoeuvrings had on pastoral provision for the parishioners of Wetherden, although the Catholic squire, Edward Sulyard, and his staunchly recusant household at Wetherden Hall, must have regarded the sordid affair as proving everything that they had ever believed about Protestant clergy.[17] Neither is it clear whether there was any religious dimension to the quarrels, although there are one or two straws in the wind. The Muskett family were closely related to the ultra-godly network of Suffolk and London Puritan families which included the Winthrops of Groton (Henry Muskett's second wife Joan Sharpe was a relative and close friend of Adam Winthrop, the father of the pioneer of Massachusetts). By contrast, St Catharine's Hall was becoming a hotbed of 'Arminian' sympathisers at the end of the sixteenth century; Syll and Kilbourne may have been numbered among such critics of Puritans and thus adversaries of Suffolk's

14 'The Condition of the Archdeaconries of Suffolk and Sudbury in the Year 1603', *PSIA* xi, 1901, 1–46, at p. 28.

15 *Suffolk Manorial Families*, ed. Muskett and Johnson, ii, 381. For Muskett's will of 1626, *ibid.*, 373; he wished to be buried in Harleston church. Alice Westley was buried at Wetherden on 29 December 1611, and Robert on 5 March 1612 (Wetherden parish registers, SROI, FB222/D1/1). The Harleston registers were recopied by the parson there from 1617 to 1642, and so do not reveal any clue about Westley's activities there: SROI, FB213/D1/1.

16 NRO, REG (Episcopal Registers)16/22, fo. 6v; *Alumni Cantabrigienses to 1751*, ed. Venn, iii 15. I am indebted to Matthew Reynolds for supplying me with further details about Kilbourne.

17 On the prominent Roman Catholic recusant family of Sulyard, see N. MacCulloch, *Brief Notes on the History of Wetherden*, Wetherden 1996, 'The People'; and index references *sub nomine* in D. MacCulloch, *Suffolk and the Tudors: Politics and Religion in an English County 1500–1600*, Oxford 1986. In 1603 Syll reported the unusually high total of seventeen individuals in Wetherden, a village of 146 communicants, as refusing to come to communion: 'Condition of the Archdeaconries of Suffolk and Sudbury in 1603', 29.

godly elite.[18] What is important for our present purposes was that naturally the ongoing disputes about the legacy of the Blackborough mediety preoccupied Robert Westley during his incumbency; in every sense, his living was in peril. That sent him literally to delve into the past, as he recounted in his deposition in the Syll case. 'Alsoe he sayth that in the Churchyard of Wetherden as he hath herd, ther did stand a severall chappell belonging to the Pryoress of Blackbarow, and this he doth believe to be true because he did digg in the same Churchyard, and ther found the seate, and foundation of such a Chappell.'

That is all we know of Westley's proto-archaeology. Yet his anxious investigations into the tangled history of his rectory's revenues have preserved what seems to be the only definite relic of this lost chapel of medieval Suffolk, and they have added a hitherto unknown example of that phenomenon which in England is at its commonest in East Anglia, the churchyard containing more than one church. There is no subsequent record of a rediscovery of these chapel foundations at Wetherden, and one cannot be certain as to whether the chapel lay to the north or the south of the parish church, although there is much more space on the south side of the church to accommodate it. Only one other documentary reference may reveal something of the chapel. On 1 April 1505 Margaret Parker, a prosperous widow of neighbouring Haughley, made her will: in it she left 'to the chapel of St Ronwod in Wetherden, 6s 8d'.[19] It is remarkable that none of the surviving medieval wills from Wetherden itself mention the chapel amid their various bequests to the parish church. Unless one can associate the chapel with a number of references to the village's two gilds of Jesus and of St John the Baptist (and there is no direct reason to do so), it does not seem to have been a cult centre of any description, and the silence in the wills suggests that it was not particularly esteemed locally.[20] Nor, one should notice, did the nuns of Blackborough achieve any mention in the wills of Wetherden folk.

Was Margaret Parker's reference indeed to the lost churchyard chapel? To confuse matters, the wealthy Sulyard family around 1500 had financed the building of an expensive south aisle and south chancel chapel to the parish church itself, with a dedication now unknown. However, Margaret also left a separate half-mark sum to the repair of Wetherden church, which is a fair indication that the two buildings were distinct in her mind, and there would have been no reason for her to make a contribution to the Sulyard family aisle. If we can associate her benefaction with Westley's foundations of a chapel, the dedication which she mentions raises intriguing questions about the antiquity of the vanished building. St 'Ronwod' is St

[18] For Muskett's second wife Joan Sharpe, see *Suffolk Manorial Families*, ed. Muskett and Johnson, ii, 379, 381. For general discussion of St Catharine's, see *St Catharine's College, Cambridge 1473–1973: A Volume of Essays to Commemorate the Quincentenary of the Foundation of the College*, ed. E.E. Rich, Cambridge 1973.

[19] PRO, Prerogative Court of Canterbury wills (hereafter PCC) 30 Adeane. I am very grateful to Peter Northeast for reminding me of the existence of this will.

[20] References to gild of Jesus: Margery Roding, SROB, Sudbury Archidiaconal Probate Wills (hereafter SAPW), 453 Baldwyne (1470); Walter Betts, SAPW 175 Hervye (1477); Sir Nicholas Bateman, PCC 29 Bennett (1509). To gild of St John Baptist: Margery Roding, SAPW 453 Baldwyne (1470); John Baker, SAPW 494 Baldwyne (1471).

Rumwold, an obscure Anglo-Saxon royal child saint from Buckinghamshire, who was otherwise only commemorated in East Anglia by the dedication of a now-demolished town centre parish church in Colchester. His cult in monastic centres seems to have lapsed after the Norman Conquest, but he seems to have retained a popular following.[21] A Saxon dedication to a little-known saint suggests an early origin for the chapel. Perhaps, therefore, we should seek its position in the church in the more extensive southern half of the churchyard, flanking the existing parish church, itself a building retaining a massive north nave wall which (below some fourteenth or fifteenth century heightening) is probably of twelfth-century date.

If the chapel was indeed early and of pre-Conquest date, Westley's surmise about his discovery associates it with the twelfth-century Bury/Blackborough compromise. There seems no reason why the nuns of Blackborough should have had any particular devotion to St Rumwold, and so they may have taken over an existing building with an Anglo-Saxon dedication; perhaps the grouping of lands which they were given was the survivor of some older accumulation of property and rights. Nor is there any direct mention of the chapel itself in the cartulary of Blackborough priory (BL Egerton MS 3137), but the chapel's existence would provide a very plausible explanation for the cartulary's fourteenth-century inventory of Blackborough liturgical items at Wetherden (mentioned above); the collection could have been intended for the celebration of masses in the chapel, separate from those in the parish church. We cannot be sure when this building was demolished, but it may have been some time before the closure of Blackborough priory; it is significant that Westley, instituted as rector only three decades after the dissolution of the monasteries, clearly did not know the chapel's exact whereabouts, and had to dig to find its foundations. Perhaps the previously-mentioned sales of Wetherden lands by Blackborough priory to the Rosyer family in the reign of Henry VI and to the Sulyard family in the time of Edward IV together mark the era when the nuns decided to reduce their direct interest in their remote Suffolk property, and the time when their chapel in the churchyard began to fall into disuse. Yet Margery Parker could still make her gesture of support to St Rumwold's chapel in Wetherden in 1505. Perhaps a widow sadly remembering a lost child would look with tenderness on the image of a little boy who was a saint and securely in heaven.

Westley's observation is a marker for any subsequent investigation of what is potentially an exceptionally interesting site. Wetherden churchyard is a classic example of an undisturbed burial-place; it was preserved (partly through my father's concern) from the mania of the 1960s and 1970s for uprooting and sweeping aside gravestones in order to create meaningless lawns around medieval churches, and so it remains a richly varied memorial to a continuing community, built up over centuries of individual lives. The most cursory stroll round it will reveal the signs of its very early date, if one observes its roughly circular boundary. This becomes all the

21 G. Buckler, *Twenty-Two of the Churches of Essex*, London 1856, 220–3; *The Oxford Dictionary of Saints*, ed. D.H. Farmer, Oxford 1978, 404–405.

more clear when looking at a map (illustrated is the Ordnance Survey map of 1904). Taken together with the small plots of land to the east of the churchyard (which were still known at the time of the 1841 tithe map as the buttsyards, in commemoration of their use for parish archery), the combined boundary forms an oval, the shape only interrupted on the eastern side by the stream, whose straight course seems to have been deliberately diverted westwards at this point in order to cut into the oval.

The oval enclosure is thus a primary site: it is centrally placed in the rectangular parish of Wetherden, lying at right angles to the course of the gentle river valley which gives the parish its name, and with the churchyard, the elevated western half of the oval, dominating the common land on the other side of the stream. The map makes clear how parish roads and footpaths aligned north–south and east–west converge in a cross-roads at the mathematical centre of the oval (immediately to the east of the church). On its south side, there remains a formidably deep water-filled ditch. This is no ordinary churchyard; it is either a sacred site or an occupation site of great antiquity. Around the church clusters what in Scotland would be known as a 'kirktoun', a church-centred settlement which, until the housing developments of the last quarter century, was geographically separate (admittedly by no more than around a hundred yards) from the second and secondary medieval village settlement strung along the king's highway, the Stowmarket–Elmswell road. The twin village centres are most unlikely to have any association with the two 'medieties' of the parish which the twelfth century compromise between Bury abbey and the de Scales family had created; nevertheless, in a pleasing continuity over eight centuries, the small fields which formed the void between 'kirktoun' and street village were the heartland of Blackborough priory's possessions in Wetherden, over which Robert Westley and Henry Muskett contested four centuries ago. When, at some subsequent date, the opportunity arises to undertake some investigation of this area, the Rev. Robert Westley will have made his small and unwitting, yet possibly originating, contribution to Suffolk's archaeological record.

Concept and Compromise: Sir Nicholas Bacon and the Building of Stiffkey Hall

Hassell Smith[1]

I

WHERE THERE IS no evidence there can be no history. That much is evident. But where there is evidence its interpretation is often controversial; therein lies the fascination of history – especially for Norman who has squared up with verve to some of the most controversial and ambiguous sources. It would therefore seem appropriate that an essay in his honour should attempt to explain, even to reconcile, some of the ambiguities presented by the fabric of a great house. And how felicitous that, in an essay dedicated to one of Suffolk's foremost antiquaries, this house should have been built by Suffolk's greatest Elizabethan son – Sir Nicholas Bacon, Lord Keeper of the Great Seal to Elizabeth I.

The story of how he came to build at Stiffkey, a small coastal village situated on the north Norfolk coast midway between Wells and Blakeney, is easily told. By 1568 he was anxious to find a bride for his second son, Nathaniel, then aged twenty-two. After unsuccessful overtures to two parties in Suffolk,[2] he seems to have accepted that his son had fallen in love with Anne, the base daughter of Sir Thomas Gresham (brother-in-law of Sir Nicholas) by the Netherlandish wife of one of his household servants.[3] By late July Anne had been naturalised, a certificate granted for their mar-

1 In studying this house over many years I owe much to many people: first and foremost to the Feilden Condominium (Randle and Anne, Sir Bernard and Tina and his late wife Ruth, and Margaret) for its friendship, hospitality and advice without which this essay could not have been written; to Tony Baggs, Peter Cornell, Nesta Evans, Hugh Feilden, Alayne and George Fenner, Douglas Jordan, Philip Judge, Adam Longcroft, Diarmaid MacCulloch, Vic Nierop-Reading, Paul Rutledge (who discovered the plan on which this article is based), the late Philip Schwabe and Jozia, the late Elizabeth Stern, Mavis Wesley and Susie West for their advice and generous assistance; to the Viscount Townshend of Raynham for his hospitality and to Scilla Landale for enabling my access to the Raynham manuscripts; to a cohort of students who annually studied this house with me on bleak February days. Finally I owe most to Fergie who helped so much and waited so patiently for this essay to appear.

2 University of Chicago, Joseph Regenstein Library, Redgrave Collection (hereafter Chicago, Bacon MSS), MSS 4089 and 4094.

3 Thomas Dutton. He was one of Gresham's factors at Antwerp and Hamburg. He had a house at Isleworth, on or near Gresham's estate at Osterley. See *The Papers of Nathaniel Bacon of*

riage without banns, and the event solemnised.[4] What role Sir Nicholas and Sir Thomas played in this match we do not know, but they contrived to bestow on the couple a miscellaneous group of manors stretching from Combs in mid-Suffolk to Langham-*cum*-Morston in north Norfolk.[5] These manors had at least one thing in common: their demesnes had been let, which meant that there was no suitable residence for the couple.[6] When, therefore, the principal manor in Stiffkey, a parish adjacent to Morston and Langham, came up for sale with its demesne in hand, Sir Nicholas purchased it.[7] This was a shrewd move since it provided a manor-house which could be rebuilt, began the consolidation of a fragmented estate and, in terms of East Anglian politics, expanded the Bacon influence into north Norfolk.[8]

Of the house which he and his son began to build in 1576 only half has survived. What remains hides itself demurely behind the churchyard, only to be discovered by the persistent enquirer. So far it has been viewed as a sad monument to the demise after a single generation of the north Norfolk Bacon line, rather than as a piece of Elizabethan architecture.[9] When Nathaniel died in 1622 without a male heir, the property passed, *via* his eldest daughter Anne (who had predeceased him), to the Townshends of Raynham. Her son, Sir Roger Townshend, and his family dwelt there while he built Raynham Hall – a masterpiece which remained unfinished when he died in 1637.[10] Thereafter the Stiffkey property became an outlier, if not a backwater, of the great Raynham estate; in consequence the status of the Hall slowly declined. At first it was let, together with its demesne lands, to Sir John Tracey,[11] and then to the Earl of Westmorland;[12] next, the house with its gardens and surrounding meadow/parkland was let separately as a residence; then, by the mid-eighteenth century, it was occupied by tenant farmers;[13] by 1780, no doubt badly dilapidated, it

Stiffkey, ed. A. Hassell Smith, G.M. Baker and R.W. Kenny, 3 vols, Norwich 1979–90 (hereafter *Bacon Papers*), i. 291 n. 40.

4 *CPR, 1566–69*, 349. G. Leveson-Gower, *Genealogical Memoranda Relating to the Family of Gresham*, London 1883, 20.

5 Sir Nicholas gave them Eccles and Stanford in south-west Norfolk; Sir Thomas gave them Combs in central Suffolk and Langham-*cum*-Morston in north Norfolk (*Bacon Papers*, i. 33, 40, 146).

6 *Bacon Papers*, i. 34–6, 40–1. University of Reading Library, Farm Records, Norfolk, 20, pp. 15–21.

7 *Bacon Papers*, i. 14–20.

8 For the latter point see A. Simpson, *The Wealth of the Gentry 1546–1660*, Cambridge 1961, 96 (hereafter Simpson, *Gentry*).

9 See the articles on Stiffkey by Mrs Herbert Jones and H.L. Bradfer-Lawrence (*NA* viii, 1879, 143–68 and xxiii, 1929, 308–40).

10 L. Campbell, 'Sir Roger Townshend and his Family: A Study of Gentry Life in Early Seventeenth-Century Norfolk', University of East Anglia Ph.D. thesis, 1990, 1–112.

11 Sir John Tracey of Stanhoe. He died 1664 (PRO, PCC Bruce 60).

12 Mildmay Fane, second Earl of Westmorland (d.1666). He married secondly Mary, Lady Townshend, who was widowed when Sir Roger died in 1637 (*DNB*).

13 The documentation for the tenants of the Hall post 1660 is elusive. The principal sources used here are: Raynham Hall Attic, Boxfile labelled 'seventeenth-century misc. accounts, 1606–86'; 2 boxes labelled 'Norfolk estate accounts fifteenth to eighteenth century'; box labelled 'from cellar March 1988 estate accounts 1664–77 & 1688–91'. Also Raynham Hall Library, boxes 65, 69, 74 and 89.

had been partially ruinated. A sketch by Humphry Repton, engraved in that year, shows it substantially as it appears today, with half the main range and the entire east wing in ruins.[14] Its final degradation occurred in the nineteenth century when a farm-steading was built cheek by jowl with its west wing. Better times began in 1911 when Colonel Robin Gray acquired the property from the Townshend estate and had it sensitively restored.[15] Now, after several vicissitudes, it is in the sympathetic hands of the Feilden family.

At first glance what remains of its fabric suggests that it was a fairly typical Elizabethan 'E'-plan house with a main range and two unusually long wings (see Fig. 1). Internally, a screens passage in the main range divides the ground floor between the family side and the servants' side; between great hall, great parlour and chamber to the east and buttery, pantry, steward's room, kitchen and backhouse to the west. On the first floor (see Fig. 2) a similar division pertained between the great chamber and other principal chambers to the east and the nurseries and lesser family chambers to the west.

Perhaps not surprisingly, given its sad history, architectural historians have largely dealt with this house by ignoring it. Those, however, who have spared it a glance have tended to comment on its unusual features: on the great length of its wings,[16] on the Renaissance mathematical ratios in its layout[17] and, more speculatively, on the fact that its two turreted staircases may have been prototypes for similar features in Sir Francis Bacon's essay 'Of Building'.[18] Closer examination merely multiplies the number of unusual features to the point where the building becomes an enigma. This essay will first follow this trail and then attempt to resolve the enigma. In so doing it may also contribute one more thread to the rich tapestry of Elizabethan architectural history.

II

First, then, the unusual features. The most distinctive feature of Stiffkey Hall is its six turrets which articulate its four outer and two inner corners (see Figs 1–4). These are not reminiscent of the tall, slender octagonal towers which soared above the roof-tops of early and mid-Tudor palaces and mansions; instead they are relatively squat, almost drum-like, harking back to Bodiam Castle. They create an ethos which contrasts sharply with that of the next unusual feature: a set of renaissance axial terraced

[14] The question as to when this ruination occurred, and under whose direction, would repay investigation.

[15] *Country Life*, 9 Feb. 1916, 243.

[16] N. Pevsner and B. Wilson, *The Buildings of England, Norfolk I: Norwich and North-East*, London 1997, 676.

[17] M. Airs, 'The Designing of Five East Anglian Country Houses, 1505–1637', *Architectural History* (hereafter *Architect. Hist.*) xxi, 1978, 63.

[18] H. Jones, 'Stiffkey: A Sketch', *NA* viii, 1879, 149–50.

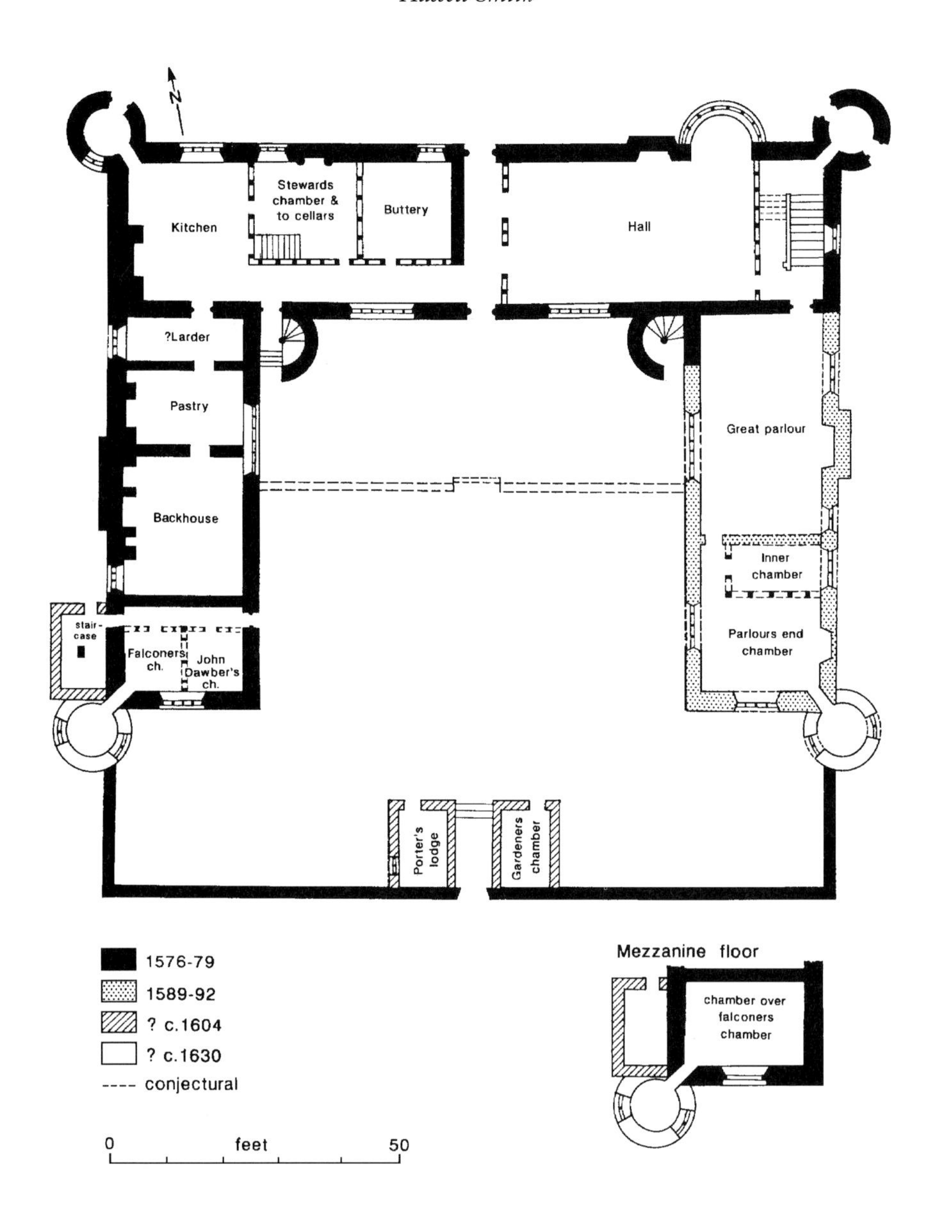

Fig. 1. Stiffkey Hall: plan of ground floor 1576–*c.*1700, based on a measured survey, a manuscript plan of *c.*1573 (see Fig. 7) and documentary sources. Room names have been extracted from inventories made in 1622/3 (Folger Shakespeare Library, Washington DC, MS V.b.161) and in 1637 (*NA* xxiii, 1929, 321–34).

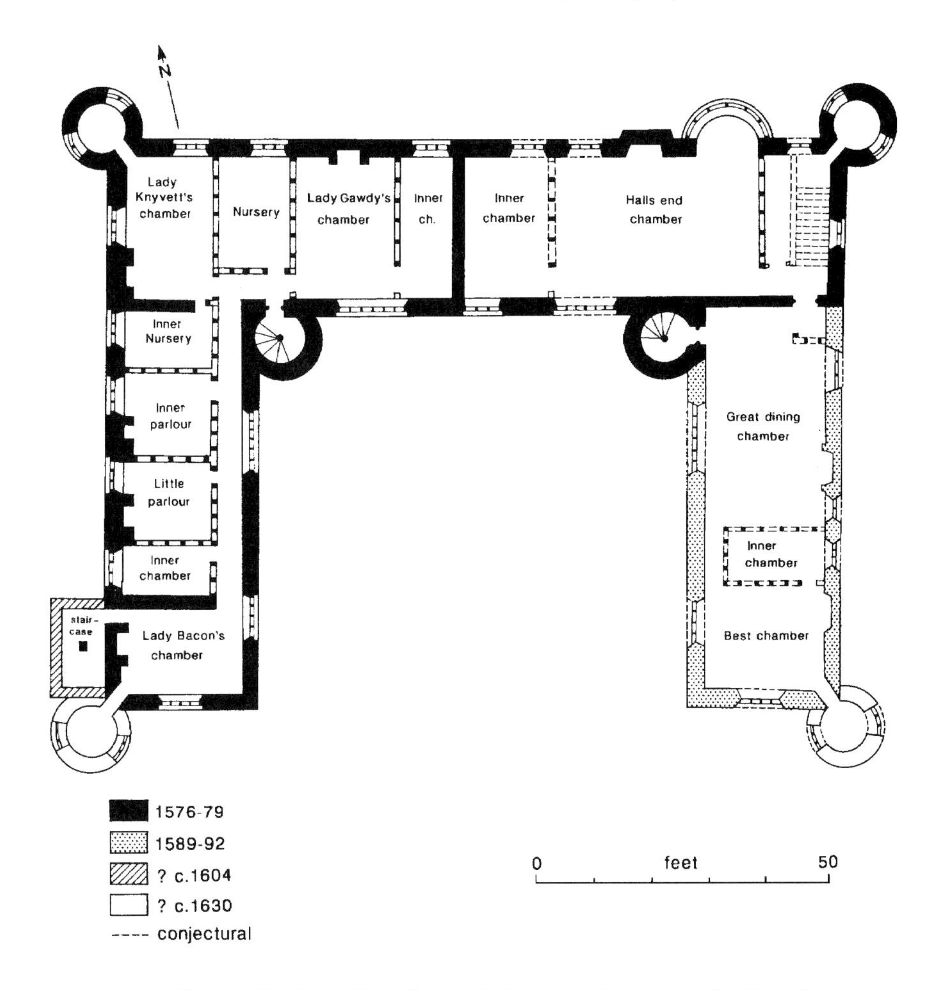

Fig. 2. Stiffkey Hall: plan of first floor 1576–*c.*1700 (sources as for Fig. 1).

gardens to the north and east of the house (see Figs 4 and 9) which must be one of the earliest examples in England of this type of Italianate garden design.

Next, too, this house lacks the quintessential Elizabethan entrance porch or articulated doorway to the main range, a surprising omission since Sir Nicholas had made a particular feature of this when he built Redgrave[19] Hall and Gorhambury House.[20] As if by way of compensation, a gatehouse[21] has been built opposite the

19 E.R. Sandeen, 'The Building of Redgrave Hall 1545–54' (hereafter Sandeen, 'Redgrave'), *PSIA* xxix, 1961, 13.

20 J. Summerson, *Architecture in Britain 1530–1830* (hereafter Summerson, *Architecture*), Harmondsworth 1977, 47.

21 For the gatehouse see below, pp. 184–6.

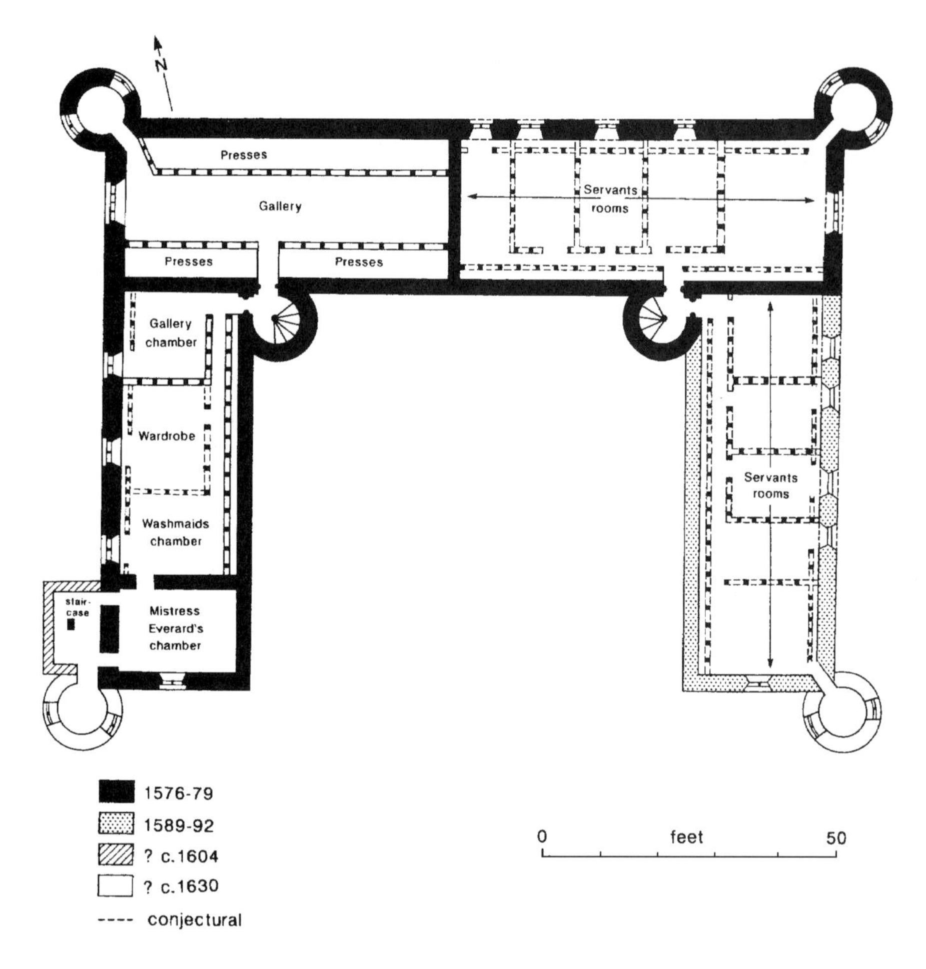

Fig. 3. Stiffkey Hall: plan of attic floor 1576–*c.*1700 (sources as for Fig. 1).

unarticulated doorway (see Fig. 1).[22] Such an arrangement was common in courtyard houses, but it was an unusual feature in an Elizabethan 'E'- or 'H'-type house where the gatehouse, if built at all, would normally have fronted a walled entrance court rather than the domestic court, as for instance at Montacute House, Doddington Hall, or indeed Melford Hall. The unusual location of this gatehouse is compounded by its being perched on top of what must have been a low terrace (see Fig. 9).

Then there are ambiguities within the fabric of this building. For instance its courtyard fenestration is at variance with that on its external façades. The former

[22] The present carved stone doorway is almost certainly a later insertion. Stylistically it matches the inner face of the gatehouse which was built in 1604. The original doorway was probably in moulded brick with a simple hollow chamfer, as is the doorway in the north-east turret which leads to the banqueting house.

Fig. 4. Stiffkey Hall: aerial photograph (looking north-west) showing the ruinated great hall and east wing, the churchyard and the flight of terraced gardens to its south. *Photograph by Dereck A. Edwards, courtesy the Norfolk Museums and Archaeology Service.*

consists of large wide windows each comprising six double lights after the style of Thorpeland Hall (*c.*1500); the latter, of well-proportioned ones comprising three double lights with an occasional one of four double lights at the gable ends (see especially Fig. 2). There is also ambiguity between the building's status and the materials in which it is built. Doorways and fireplaces are executed in plain brick, finished with a chamfer (see Fig. 5); the principal ones, not surprisingly, having been re-modelled in stone either by Nathaniel in 1604 or by Sir Roger Townshend in the 1620s. Similarly the mullioned and transomed windows are in moulded brick rather than dressed stone, with the exception of those in the south-facing gable ends where stone has been used. The masonry work is a mixture of rubble and unknapped flint with brick dressings (see Fig. 6). This is a combination common enough in smaller houses in north Norfolk, but rare in high status buildings which were usually built of brick with stone dressings[23] as at Felbrigg, Barningham, Heydon and Irmingland Halls.

23 But not quite always. At Oxnead Clement Paston had used moulded brick (*Bacon Papers*, i. 179).

Fig. 5. Doorway leading to upper terrace and banqueting house. It shows the concave chamfer applied to doorways and fireplaces. *Photograph by Carole Rawcliffe.*

Internally there are some idiosyncratic features which may reflect the mind-set of the designer. Most interesting is the pair of stone walls which were built to serve as fire-breaks, one located at the outer extremity of the backhouse, the other at the kitchen side of the screens passage. These walls rose from the foundations to the ridge-piece and were only pierced where absolutely necessary (see Figs 1, 2, 3). Consequently they more or less divided the house internally into three almost separate parts. These walls apart, all internal partitions were in studwork which facilitated alterations to the internal layout. Finally the use of corridors, especially on the first floor of the west wing, is more pronounced than in most Elizabethan buildings. If these features are on the credit side, what are we to make of a substantial Elizabethan mansion, built by a leading statesman of his day, which has only a narrow, virtually unlit, attic gallery (Fig. 3); or of the mezzanine floor which is botched into the west wing, south of the backhouse wall (see Fig. 1) in such a crude manner that a single four double-light window does duty to illuminate the two floors; or, indeed, of a house which is so badly laid out internally that a separate extruded staircase had to be added in the seventeenth century to provide reasonable access to the southern part of the west wing (see Figs. 1–3)?

It has become a truism that the golden age of Elizabethan building had its roots in the eclecticism of its builders; in their ability to blend features from many traditions, new and old, foreign and vernacular. But the wrong blend could produce a hotchpotch rather than a masterpiece, as may possibly have happened at Stiffkey Hall. If this be so it would not be difficult to imagine Sir Nicholas, the builder of this house, disdainfully expostulating in his sententious oratorical style that 'a building which is everything is nothing'. But it is difficult to believe that this wise, learned, judicious and practical man who had already built two substantial mansions and who, through the high office he held, had occasion to visit every palace and prodigy house throughout south-eastern England, could have commissioned this unfathomable building. Therefore, before dismissing it, and with it Sir Nicholas's architectural aspirations, we must surely attempt to unravel the story of how this house came to be as it is.

III

As Norman would undoubtedly advise: 'first survey the building'; an exercise which leaves little doubt that it has never been completed. The principal evidence for this appears at the south-east corner of the west wing where the wall is toothed (courses of brickwork alternately left projecting and indented) in order, presumably, to provide bonding for a subsequent extension (see Fig. 6). Other evidence that this wing is incomplete appears in its roof-framing where the southernmost truss is mortised in preparation to take the tennoned purlins of the next bay. If this be so, one wonders what this building's layout and appearance would have been had it been completed. Or, to start at the beginning: what sort of house did Nathaniel and his father set out to build?

By good fortune an early version of their plan is extant among the Bacon papers at Raynham Hall (Fig. 7).[24] It shows the first floor layout and room-use of a single-courtyard house which is defined by eight turrets standing respectively at each of its outer and inner corners. The outer turrets provide small closets to each corner room, while the four inner ones house staircases providing access to all parts of the building; only one stairway, that leading to the great chamber, is located within the carcass of the building. The main range has an open hall to the east and suites of chambers westward, these also extending throughout the west wing. The east wing, the 'side of state', comprises a sequence of interconnecting rooms (great chamber, withdrawing chamber, bedchamber and inner chamber), a layout developed in France and adopted in English palace and prodigy house building. To the south

24 Raynham Hall MSS, Box 81. On loan to the Norfolk Record Office as NRO, Raynham MS 6/50 (A217C).

Fig. 6. Toothing at south-east corner of west wing.
Photograph by Carole Rawcliffe.

both wings open into a long gallery with a central bay window, the latter undoubtedly serving to articulate an entrance gateway beneath. Although this plan is not endorsed, its provenance, together with its distinctive turrets and the coincidence between its room-layout in the west wing and that in the extant west wing, leaves no doubt that it must be a version of the plan to which Sir Nicholas built.

One of its most striking aspects is the sheer scale of the house it portrays. With a ground floor area of approximately 11,500 square feet it would have been larger than the principal courts of several mid-Tudor courtier houses, including those of Sir Thomas Smith, Sir William Petre, Sir Anthony Cooke and Sir Nicholas himself.[25] Its long gallery (118 feet), albeit not in the same league as those at Montacute or Worksop, would have come a close second to that at Blickling.[26] This,

[25] For comparative sizes see *Religion, Culture and Society in Early Modern Britain*, ed. A. Fletcher and P. Roberts, Cambridge 1994, 147.

[26] Montacute, 170 feet; Worksop, 212 feet (M. Girouard, *Life in the English Country House*, London 1980, 102). Blickling, 123 feet (*Blickling Hall*, National Trust 1987, 87).

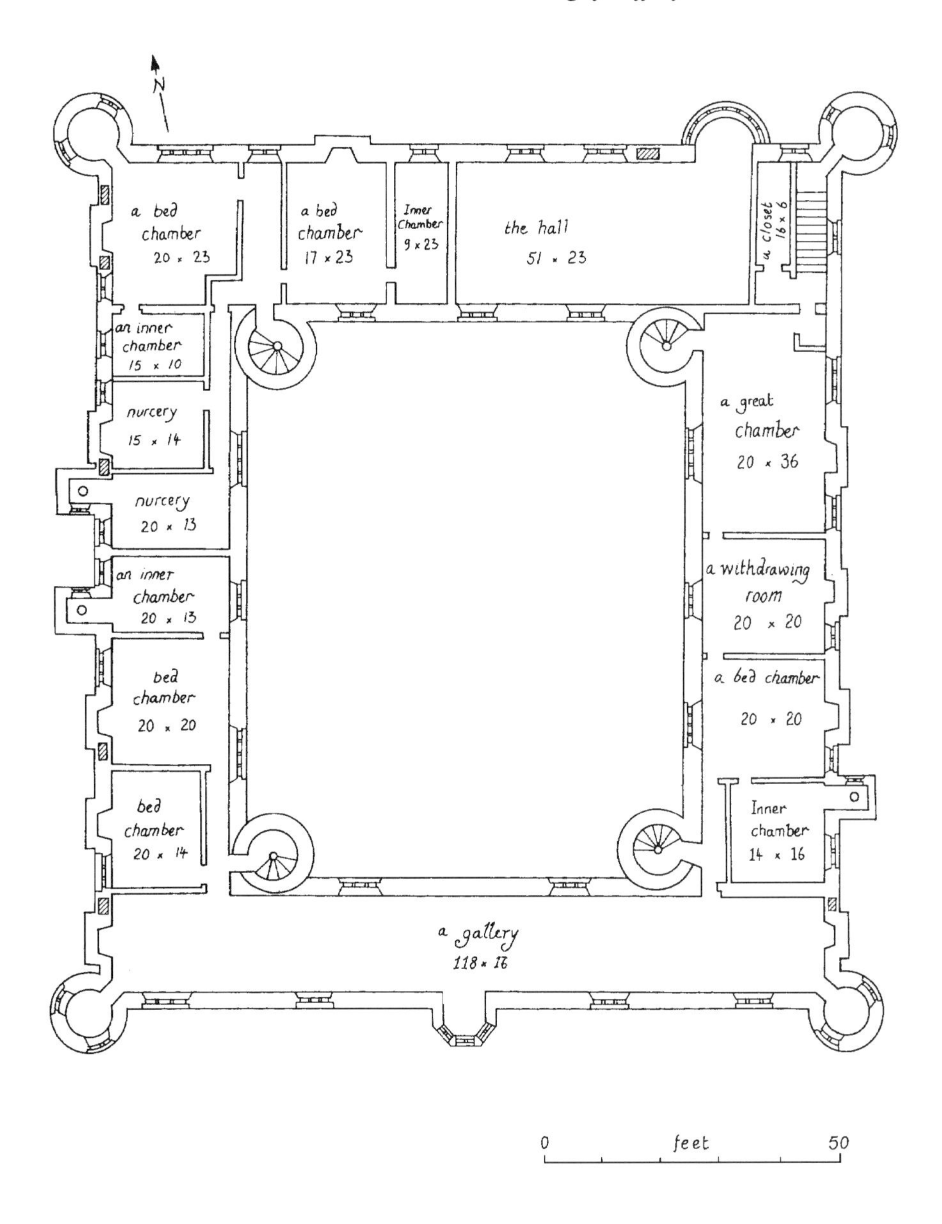

Fig. 7. Stiffkey Hall: a 'plat' for the first floor, *c.*1573. *Redrawn from the original manuscript, courtesy of the Norfolk Record Office, MS Raynham 6/50.*

together with its suite of state rooms, would have provided accommodation fit for the Queen and her court. All of which seems a bit over the top for a younger son of mean estate (see below p. 179) who had barely made his mark in county affairs and who showed no inclination to cut a figure either at court or in central administration. A possible explanation for the scale of this proposed building will be advanced later (see below p. 179).

A further striking feature of this plan is the manner in which it defines the house with eight corner turrets – an arrangement which seems without precedent in either late medieval or sixteenth-century English domestic architecture. There were houses, such as Charlecote (*c.*1559), Mount Edgcumbe (1546), Thorpe Slavin (1570s) and Rycote (mid-sixteenth century) which had four outer corner turrets, but no inner ones.[27] There were houses with two, and plans by Robert Smythson of some with four inner corner turrets, but these had no outer ones.[28] For a similar plan embodying eight corner turrets we may have to look to French domestic architecture.

We should not, however, be too concerned about the genesis of individual features, since the dominant characteristic of this plan is its coherence rather than its eclecticism. Essentially it embodies elements of most of the underlying principles of renaissance planning as expounded by Alberti and his successors – notably Palladio – down to the mid-sixteenth century. These were: symmetry, the application of harmonic ratios, the architectural integration of house and gardens, and the use of classical ornamental features.

Symmetry in this plan requires little elaboration. Turret answers to turret about each axis as does window to window within the courtyard. Externally, the south façade is well balanced; but on the others symmetry has yielded to internal convenience. Even on these façades, however, by the time building commenced, a great deal of tidying up had taken place by the removal of garderobes and most of the extruded stacks (cf. Figs 2, 7). And of course the normal clutter of service buildings had been removed by relegating them to a site 200 yards across the river (see Fig. 9).

The case for the embodiment of harmonic ratios[29] in this plan must be approached with caution since it is possible to posit them where, in fact, none exist, especially if one is tolerant (as surely one must be) of the hit and miss measurements of sixteenth-century craftsmen. It has, for instance, been claimed on the basis of a measured survey that Stiffkey Hall embodies the simple ratio of 1:2; that, for instance, the width of a turret is half the width of its wing and that the width of a

[27] M. Girouard, *Robert Smythson and the Elizabethan Country House*, New Haven 1983 (hereafter Girouard, *Smythson*), 99, 119–20; M. Howard, *The Early Tudor Country House: Architecture and Politics 1490–1550*, London 1987, 71; G. Tyack, *The Making of Warwickshire Country Houses 1500–1650*, Warwickshire Local History Society IV, 1982, 33–6.

[28] T. Garner and A. Stratton, *The Domestic Architecture of England during the Tudor Period*, London 1911, ii. 139; 'The Smythson Collection', ed. M. Girouard, *Architect. Hist.* v, 1962, 23–183.

[29] For ratios see: R. Wittkower, *Architectural Principles in the Age of Humanism*, London 1973, particularly parts III and IV.

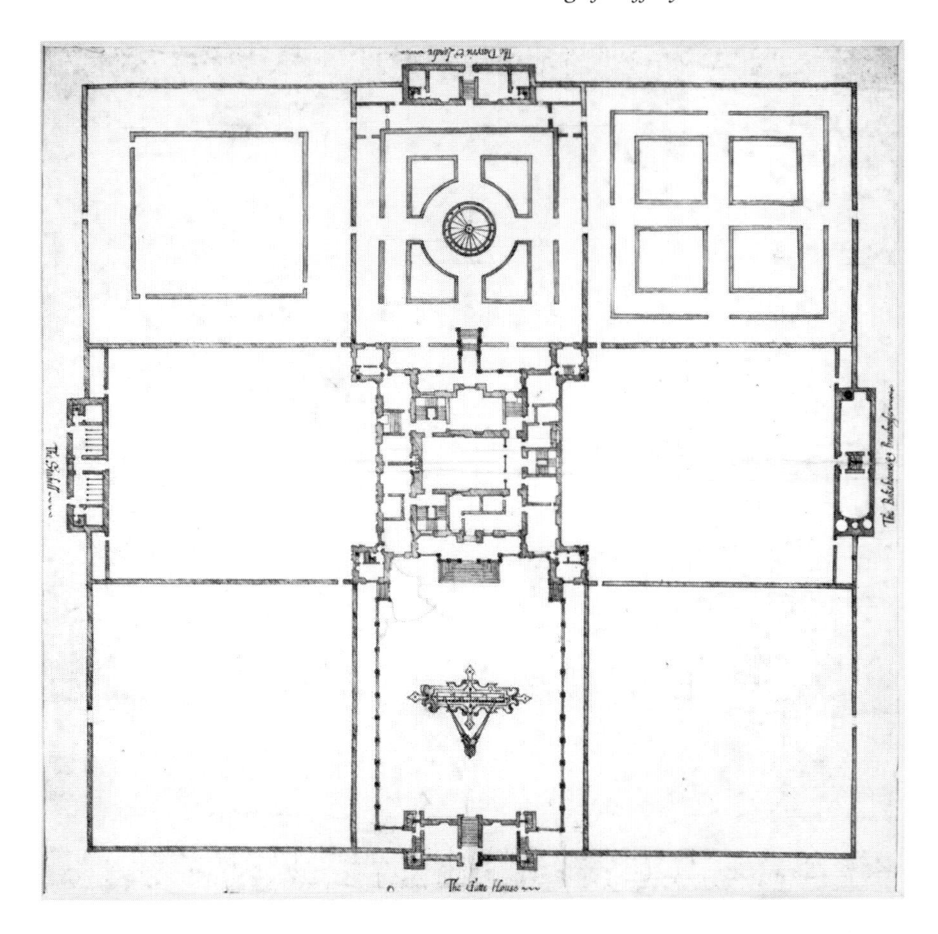

Fig. 8. A plan by Robert Smythson for Wollaton Hall. *By courtesy of the British Architectural Library, RIBA, London: Wollaton Hall, Plan I/25.i.*

turret together with its wing is half the width of the courtyard.[30] Such claims are, in fact, substantially confirmed by this plan, but this confirmation depends upon the accuracy of the draughtsman who was working to a very small scale. For most measurements, however, we need not depend on the diligence of either draughtsman or surveyor since our contemporary plan supplies the dimensions of each room. Those for the great hall are 51 x 23 feet which, without getting into inches, provides a ratio 1:1½ x 2 – the ratio recommended by Palladio for important rooms and which, incidentally, was also embodied in the chapel which Sir Nicholas had designed for his college, Corpus Christi, Cambridge. Nor can it be by chance that three other chambers in this plan, including two in the grand suite of rooms, are square (20 x 20 feet) which is also a figure recommended by Palladio for high status rooms.

30 See note 16 above.

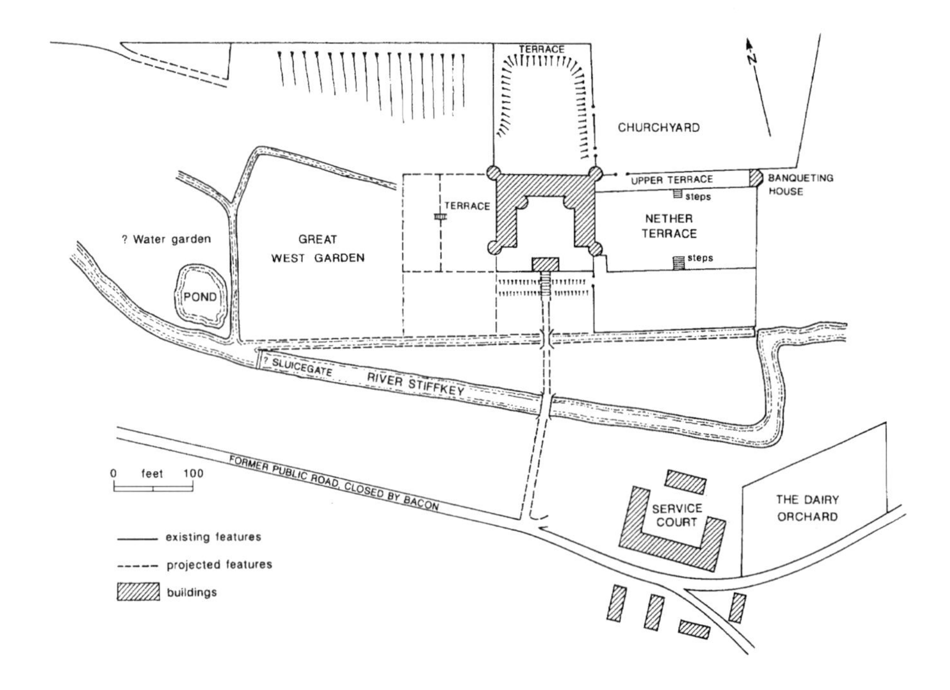

Fig. 9. Plan of Stiffkey Hall gardens and service complex *c.*1620, based on a measured survey, the Ordnance Survey 1:2500 map (1906 edition), an estate map of Stiffkey *c.*1628 (NRO, HMN 7/227/1, 2) and archaeological observations.

The integration of house and garden within one coherent architectural scheme had been stressed by Alberti in his *De re aedificatoria* (1452). In this treatise 'the garden is seen in architectural terms as an extension of the house, both being conceived in terms of Renaissance harmony and proportion expressed by means of geometry'.[31] His message had proved popular among late-fifteenth- and sixteenth-century Italian villa and French chateau builders, but had little impact in England before the seventeenth century. Nonetheless here and there a probing mind stirred. For instance, Robert Smythson, in the course of building Wollaton Hall for Sir Francis Willoughby in the 1580s, produced a chequer-board plan in which each façade of the house was matched by an axial garden court whose area more or less reflected that of the house (see Fig. 8). Gatehouse entrances to each of these courts concealed the necessary service buildings and the geometry of the scheme was completed by four corner garden courts. Smythson's plan may never have been fully implemented at Wollaton;[32] meanwhile a decade earlier the designer of Stiffkey Hall proposed something very similar. On each side of the house he planned a complementary garden court which matched the façade in width and probably the house in

31 R. Strong, *The Renaissance Garden in England*, London 1979, 15.
32 *Ibid.*, 56–9.

area. The evidence for this scheme comes, not from the plan under analysis (since it is a drawing of the first floor), but from the archaeology of the site where several of the garden courts are extant (see Fig. 9).

As to classical ornamental features, the situation is less clear. Since our plan is not fleshed out with any drawings of particular features, we must rely on evidence from the extant fabric. This reveals an austere building devoid of the entire classical repertoire: no columns, pilasters, entablatures, pediments or balustrades; only a simple string-course at first floor level relieves the severity of the courtyard façades. Undoubtedly the use of vernacular building material (flint and brick) diminished the scope for ornamental features, but one cannot escape the conclusion that those who devised this plan, while endeavouring to apply most of the fundamental principles of renaissance design, deliberately eschewed the most striking elements of this architectural style. Thus, in conception, this building differs from that sequence of great mid-Tudor buildings – Longleat, Kirby Hall, Hill Hall and Holdenby – which are distinguished by the manner in which they integrate either borrowed or pure classical detail into the English Gothic tradition.

What this plan does have in common with these famous contemporary buildings is the extent to which its particular classical elements are likewise integrated into a basically Gothic structure. It is a courtyard house, replete with open hall, screens passage and oriel window. Its turrets, almost certainly battlemented, are resonant of the fourteenth century and the unarticulated entrance to the main range in association with a gatehouse is a typical late medieval feature. So, too, is the bay window above the entrance porch and the concave chamfer applied to the moulded brick mullions and transoms.

It is however important to note that this plan eschews vernacular and antique decorative features with as much thoroughness as it does the pure classical ones. There is none of the effusive moulded brick or terracotta work which distinguishes nearby East Barsham manor house (*c.*1530). Even the chimney tops appear to have been plain until Nathaniel had them rebuilt in moulded brick in 1580. There is no porch, as already stressed, and the oriel window has been relegated to the rear façade of the Hall. Even dormer windows which serve to relieve the roofline and provide scope for ornamentation are sparingly used (there being none, for instance, to light the long gallery) and apparently confined to the outer façades of the house. In short, as an architectural statement this house is cool to the point of bleakness. In turning their backs upon the decorative features of both vernacular and classical architectural traditions Stiffkey's designers appear to presage that 'restraint and plainness' which is evident in so many late Elizabethan houses and which is so well exemplified in Wimbledon House, Surrey (1588).[33]

So much for the house that never was; or at least was never built. Certainly it *was* in so far as it had been conceived and planned and Sir Nicholas intended to build it. It is the contention of this essay that in order to understand, and so to appreciate,

33 Girouard, *Smythson*, 36. For the chimney tops see *Bacon Papers*, ii. 180.

the extant building it is necessary to unravel the sequence of events by which this original plan became compromised and through which the present building has been fashioned.

IV

The story can best begin by attempting to clarify who was responsible for this plan which, in the early 1570s, was unusual if not unique in England. Architectural historians are generally agreed that prior to Inigo Jones there were no professional architects in England. Instead, the Elizabethan nobility and substantial gentry designed and built their houses through some sort of corporate process which enabled the interplay of ideas and information between the client (informed by architectural treatises and pattern books from the European presses), the craftsman-designer (who might both plan and supervise the building work), and particular craftsmen (who might contract to provide special features such as chimney tops, fire-places and stone dressings). The input from each of these design-sources depended on a client's personality, interests and circumstances; he might be very much 'hands on' or he might be quite detached and heavily dependent upon his craftsman-designer.[34]

The client in this case was Sir Nicholas Bacon. His was one of the most outstanding Elizabethan minds; and one which, unusually, embraced both the liberal and mechanical arts. An acute lawyer, a devoted classicist steeped in dialectic, rhetoric, and philosophy, and a patron of mathematicians, he was also practical and able to empathise with craftsmen and labourers.[35] In fact he was so 'hands on', so self-reliant and so integrated into the artisan world that in a strange way he felt little need of its planning assistance. All the evidence certainly suggests that his hand alone is apparent at every stage of a very protracted planning process.

As early as October 1573 Nathaniel's brother, Edward, had reported that 'my Lord hath drawne a plat for a house, I assure yow both faire and fynely conveyed'.[36] This had probably been drafted by Sir Nicholas's secretary, John Osborne, who was certainly responsible for drawing and annotating the plan we have just analysed.[37] It is more than competently drawn, the wording and style of notation suggesting that Osborne was familiar with the idiom of current architectural plans and treatises and that he may even have been copying or adapting from a manuscript drawing or printed plan. He also drew a plat for the chapel which Sir Nicholas built for the

[34] Girouard, *Smythson*, 4–18; A.T. Friedman, *House and Household in Elizabethan England: Wollaton Hall and the Willoughby Family*, Chicago 1989, 27–37, 71–108.

[35] For his mindset see P. Collinson, 'Sir Nicholas Bacon and the Elizabethan *Via Media*', *HistJ* xxiii, 1980, 255–73. For his mathematical interests see Hassell Smith, 'The Gardens of Sir Nicholas and Sir Francis Bacon: An Enigma Resolved and a Mind Explored', in *Religion, Culture and Society in Early Modern Britain*, ed. A. Fletcher and P. Roberts, Cambridge 1994, 152–4.

[36] *Bacon Papers*, i. 90.

[37] This statement is based upon his unmistakable handwriting.

Master and Fellows of Corpus Christi College, Cambridge.[38] Since it was not unknown for skilled craftsmen-designers to enter the service of aristocratic families,[39] was Osborne one of these? His career-line suggests not. A minor gentleman from Harkstead (Suffolk),[40] in 1569 (aged twenty-four) he joined Sir Nicholas's household as secretary,[41] became his household steward and headed the list of gentlemen-officers in his funeral procession.[42] Undoubtedly well educated and practised in limning, he may well have contributed more to his master's planning and building activities than would have been normal for a secretary but his was not the hand of an experienced artificer. Nor is there any other evidence of such a person's involvement. A perusal of the Stiffkey Hall estate-yard wages books[43] reveals no reference to any craftsmen-designers in the mould of John Gybbon at Redgrave,[44] Robert Smythson at Wollaton or Robert Lyminge at Hatfield and Blickling.[45] Oversight at Stiffkey rested with Nathaniel, albeit in close consultation with his father who appears to have been in total control of all stages in the planning process. Osborne does become involved on one further occasion, but only in his role as draughtsman when Nathaniel loses the plan and calls for a duplicate.[46]

The most convincing evidence that Sir Nicholas was responsible for this plan, and that he treated the planning process as a dilettante exercise in which he occasionally relaxed from the cares of high office, derives from the procedures by which he fitted his plan, conceived in London, to the limitations of a difficult site. This process continued for over two years, in the course of which his grand concept was seriously compromised before the first sod had been cut.

It is not known whether Sir Nicholas ever visited Stiffkey, but it is reasonable to surmise that he did and that the gently rising ground to the south and west of the churchyard inspired him to undertake his third major building project. He would also have been mindful that the old manor house stood there and that to build on its site, albeit not on its foundations,[47] would provide an aura of continuity for a family which had no roots in the neighbourhood. That said, the site imposed immense constraints. First and foremost, while it may have inspired his ambitious plans, it was in fact too small to accommodate them; a situation which was only resolved

38 E.R. Sandeen, 'The Building of the Sixteenth-Century Corpus Christi College Chapel', *Proceedings of the Cambridge Antiquarian Society* lv, 1962, 23–35.

39 Girouard, *Smythson*, 10–11.

40 He had been granted arms in 1578 (J. Corder, *A Dictionary of Suffolk Arms*, SRS VII, 1965, 406).

41 He seems to have remained in the service of Sir Nicholas Bacon and his son Nicholas until at least 1589 (Chicago, Bacon MSS 4095–4158). He may have left family service in 1592 when he bought Wattisfield Hall (W.A. Copinger, *The Manors of Suffolk*, London 1905, i. 396), where he died in 1619 (SROB, IC 500/1/132/47).

42 *Bacon Papers*, ii. 51.

43 University of Reading Library, Farm Records, Norfolk, 20. Chicago, Bacon MS 991–A. NRO MS 1600 (box 1 C 9).

44 Sandeen, 'Redgrave', 5–6.

45 Summerson, 67–8, 86–9.

46 *Bacon Papers*, i. 261–3.

47 The old manor house was occupied in autumn 1577 (*Bacon Papers*, i. 245).

after two years of negotiations to purchase property to the west of the church.[48] Certain physical constraints, however, were non-negotiable. First the river Stiffkey and its flood plain bounded the entire site to the south. Secondly, the churchyard effectively butted into its north-east corner. Thirdly, much of the ground to the south-west was liable to flooding and therefore unsuitable for building (see Fig. 9).

In these circumstances it might be expected that Sir Nicholas would seek professional assistance. Instead, over a period of two years, he endeavoured to reconcile his plan with the site by a series of piecemeal surveys undertaken by remote control. These consisted of questionnaires, despatched from York House in London to Nathaniel in the country, which were carefully crafted to provide him with data relating to particular parts of the site. Two sets of questions and one of answers are extant,[49] but, as is the way with historical records, the counterpart to each is missing. Even so they suggest that initially he planned to build the house and gardens in the more spacious area west of the churchyard. Unfortunately, Nathaniel's responses about levels and suitable building ground were discouraging. Then our documents are silent for a year, by which time Sir Nicholas is exploring the possibility of moving his entire scheme eastwards and incorporating the churchyard into his pattern of garden courts. Hence Nathaniel received a new series of questions:

> 1575, August. Sonne, I send you herewith the plat that I drewe for Styfkey to the end that you showld set out theise thinges followyng, which I cannot do by the informacions I have alredy receyved. . . .
>
> Item advertyse me howe many fote it is by a strayght lyne from the sowth west corner of the church yard to the ryver's side.
>
> Item howe many fot the church yard doth stretch from the est to the west on the sowth side.
>
> Item how many fote it is from the sowth east corner of the church yard to the ryver by a straight lyne.
>
> Item a straight lyne beyng drawen from the sowth west corner of the church yard to the ryver, howe many fote it is from that lyne's end by the ryver unto the place where the ryver turneth, measuring by the ryver's side, . . .[50]

This glimpse of Sir Nicholas's survey methods reveals him in process of deciding to wrap the north and east axial garden courts round the south and west sides of the churchyard, thereby *de facto* privatising the latter by making it one of his corner garden courts (see Fig. 9). Hence the location of the Hall with one quarter of its north-east turret standing in the churchyard, and hence the three garden gates which give access to that yard from the north and east garden courts.

It was an inspired solution, which enabled Sir Nicholas to fit his integrated building scheme into this constricted site; but not without his making compromises which seriously impaired his integrated plan to the point where it almost loses credi-

48 A barn owned by Thomas Barker of Blakeney. For its purchase see *Bacon Papers* i. *infra.*

49 *Bacon Papers*, i. 110, 163, 172–3.

50 *Ibid.*, 173.

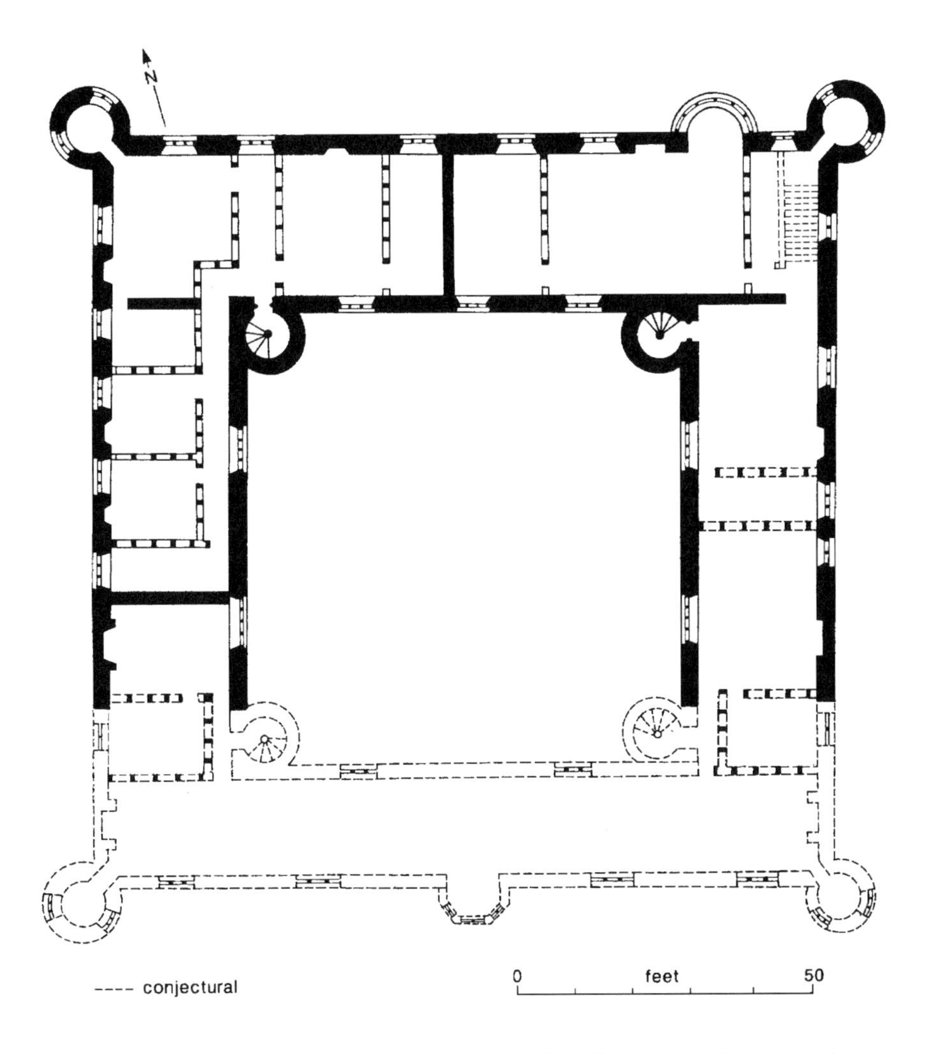

Fig. 10. Stiffkey Hall: a conjectural plan for the first floor *c.*1576 (conjectural plan A), based on a 'plat' of *c.*1573 (see Fig. 7).

bility. These arose because there was insufficient space between house and river to provide an axial entrance court whose area would reflect that of the house; indeed there was scarcely room for any entrance court at all! This led to two compromises. One was to reduce the depth of the house either by relocating the galleried south front so that it lay between rather than across the wings (see Fig 10) or by scrapping it altogether and relegating the gallery to an attic (see Fig. 11). As we shall see, the former appears to have been Sir Nicholas's preferred option (see below p. 181). Either way the house became less commodious since it lost all or a substantial part of its south range. Even when this had been done the area of the court still fell short of that of the house. But all was not lost in Sir Nicholas's efforts to achieve an harmonic

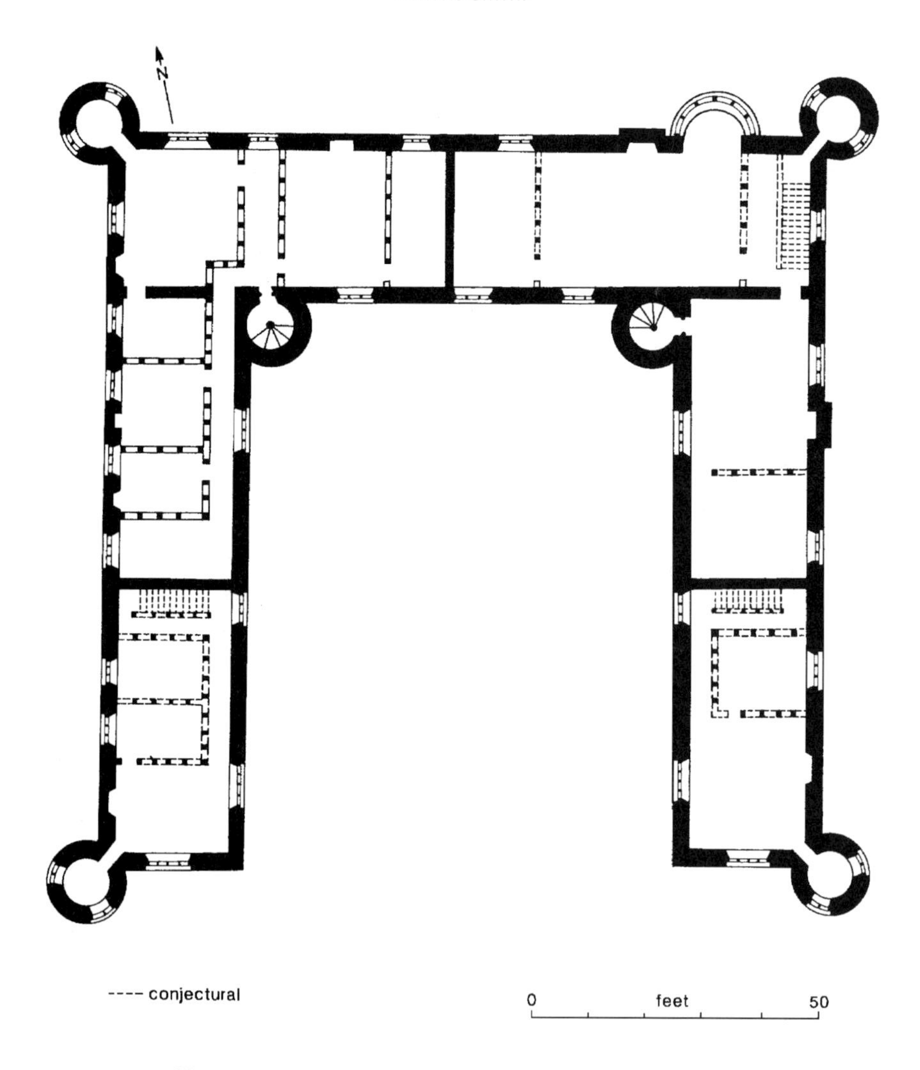

Fig. 11. Stiffkey Hall: a conjectural plan for the first floor *c.*1576 (conjectural plan B), based on a 'plat' of *c.*1573 (see Fig. 7).

balance between house and garden courts – at least apparently not in his mind – since his second compromise was to increase the area of the north court by as much as that to the south fell short (see Fig. 9).

What governed the length of the axial court to the east remains an enigma, since it appears to stop at a point which leaves it mathematically unrelated to both the house and other courts (see Fig. 9). One must assume that, since the length of the south churchyard wall (254 feet) is exactly double that of the north façade of the house (127 feet), Sir Nicholas planned this court to extend to the end of the wall so that its area was twice that of the house (2:1 ratio). It can be surmised, almost with relief, that this court stops short at a spot determined, not by any mathematical considerations, but by the sheer quantity of infill required to complete the scheme! The reader may well feel, as sometimes does the writer, that we have here entered the realm of metaphysics; but one further point is worth pondering. It was suggested earlier that this building was conceived on a scale disproportionate to the status of its occupier. Could it be that its dimensions (a courtyard house of 127 feet square) were dictated by the length of the churchyard wall? (see Fig. 9); that the mathematics of Sir Nicholas's scheme, the quest for harmony and balance between house and garden courts, for once overrode his sense of mediocrity, of well-balanced judgement, enshrined in his motto *mediocria firma*?

V

If this series of compromises was not sufficient to jeopardise Sir Nicholas's grand scheme, worse was to follow. When in 1574 Edward Bacon had informed his brother that their father had designed a house for him which was 'both faire and fynely conveyed', he had added the warning note 'but I feare he meaneth not to be at any charge in the buylding', thereby underlining one element in a disastrous equation. The other was, of course, Nathaniel's own financial state which was, in a word, dire. Both his father and father-in-law had been mean in their marriage provisions. Although Gresham had settled the manors of Langham-*cum*-Morston and Combs on Nathaniel and Anne, they yielded a mere £100 annually since he had granted 99 year beneficial leases to most of his demesne tenants, thereby ensuring that much of the income remained in his estate.[51] Sir Nicholas was scarcely more generous. He bestowed on the couple the Breckland manors of Eccles and Stanford. These were let to two of his servants and jointly yielded £158 17s 8d per annum,[52] but when he bought the principal manor in Stiffkey in 1571 (and further property there subsequently) he settled it on himself with remainder to Nathaniel and Anne, and took the profits down to his death, allowing them annually £95 in lieu.[53] Such modest sums as accrued from these tight-fisted settlements, together with the profits from the foldcourses of these manors,[54] from a joint farming venture with his father's bailiff at Stiffkey[55] and from some minor trading activities,[56] yielded a meagre annual income of £500 to £600;[57] a sum which left little, if anything, in hand for building.

51 *Ibid.*, i. 33, 35. Raynham Hall Library MS, Box 34, Petition in a case between Bacon and Robert Grickes, 1618. For beneficial leases see V. Morgan, 'Country, Court, and Cambridge University, 1558–1640: A Study in the Evolution of a Political Culture', University of East Anglia Ph.D. thesis, 1983, 323–32.

52 University of Reading Library, Farm Records, Norfolk, 20, pp. 15–21, *sub* Hawes and Boldero, Henry.

53 *Bacon Papers*, i. xxxvii–xli.

54 University of Reading Library, Farm Records, Norfolk, 20, pp. 15–21, various entries for sale of wool, lambs and sheep. *Bacon Papers*, i. 192.

55 *Bacon Papers*, i. 118, 164, 172, 272–3.

56 *Ibid.*, i. 139, 156, 192; ii. 15, 132, 292.

57 University of Reading Library, Farm Records, Norfolk, 20, pp. 15–21.

By 1575 Nathaniel had broached with his father the possibility of selling either the manor of Eccles or the manor-house in Stanford in order to start building.[58] In the event neither proposal materialised and Sir Nicholas seemed content to pursue his occasional interest in designing with no immediate inclination to build.

This was a grim scenario for Nathaniel and his young bride, by now married for six years. Four of them had been spent as sojourners, first in his father's household at Gorhambury, under the rigorous eye of his brilliant but not much loved stepmother, then in Norwich with his neurotic sister Elizabeth Wyndham and finally with another sister and his ne'er-do-well brother-in-law Henry Woodhouse at Waxham.[59] Throughout these years Anne waited patiently for a house of her own, but her letters testify to her boredom and craving to be mistress in her own establishment. Occasionally she voiced her frustrations. 'I cannot sojorne in a better place as I thinke', she wrote from the Wyndham household in Norwich, 'yet I colde very well be content to be in a house of myne owne. For though my care shold then be greater than it nowe is, yet it beinge bestowed about busines of myne owne wolde very litle troble me.'[60] To her natural mother she complained in words which have rung down the ages: 'My husbande hetherto hath provided nothinge towardes our goinge to house. I thinke the let be because he is not able. It were a hard matter by our one yeare's savinge to spare so mutch as wolde serve to provide us stuff for our house but in the meanest sort.' By autumn 1573 Nathaniel had rented a small manor house at Cockthorpe, a parish adjacent to Stiffkey. Anne considered it no more than a step in the right direction. 'Though the house be meane,' she informed Lady Anne Bacon, 'yet I am very well content withall.'[61]

By the spring of 1576 Nathaniel, no doubt goaded by Anne and frustrated by his father, had decided to bounce the latter into action by willy-nilly starting to build; and to do so at a precipitate rate. By the end of June workmen had cut a new channel to divert the river from close proximity to the garden site (see Fig. 9); others were excavating the huge cellar which lies beneath the north range and digging foundations for the west wing; at Mileham Wood teams were felling, hewing and carting oak timber. The outlay for the wages of forty or more craftsmen and labourers[62] had already exhausted Nathaniel's meagre resources. 'Onlesse your Lordship be good unto me', he informed his father, 'I am well nere at the furdest I can go.'[63] Nonetheless work continued apace. By mid August rough-masons had begun to lay the foundations; Nathaniel was frantically borrowing to pay their wages,[64] while from afar Sir Nicholas tut-tutted. 'I knowe', Nathaniel wrote apologetically, 'your Lordship

58 *Bacon Papers*, i. 163, 172.

59 *Ibid.*, i. 12, 22–3, 23–4, 25–6, 60–1, 64, 74, 75, 78, 85.

60 *Ibid.*, i. 26.

61 *Ibid.*, i. 25, 87.

62 This figure has been calculated from the total outlay of the bailiff for building for the period April–Oct. 1576. It is likely to be an under-estimate of the total workforce (University of Reading Library, Farm Records, Norfolk, 20, pp. 1–14).

63 *Bacon Papers*, i. 196.

64 University of Reading Library, Farm Accounts, Norfolk, 20, pp. 15–21. This borrowing was short-term, mainly from his neighbours and for sums of £40 or under.

seeth the charg of these thinges is to heavie for me to beare. Yf your Lordship thinke I go to hastely forward with them, I crave pardon & that I maie be excused but for this yeare. I consider, yf I shold nowe in this beginning quaile, I might worthely be condemned for having begone, & therfore I stick not to borowe to serve this present torne.'[65] Sir Nicholas responded with a gift of £200 and gave his blessing to the sale of Eccles in order to fund further building work. This was, of course, to mortgage the future; in any event it did not happen, since potential purchasers baulked at the asking price of £1,700.[66] Consequently, when the second building campaign started in spring 1577, Nathaniel was again heading into debt.

By then, however, as a temporary measure in the interest of economy, he and his father had decided to shorten the wings. As early as June 1576 Nathaniel had broached this matter with his father:

> I desier to knowe . . . yf it be your Lordship's pleasure that I shall this sommer fetch the fundacion of the whole west side of the house untill it be brought unto the south west gable end, or that it shall go but u[nto] the backhouse, which is but about the midell part of the wes[t] side of the house. The masons tell me that building with calion [flint], to bring up one pece after an other it w[ould] hardly be joyned without some daunger of cracck[ing ther]after, and therfor thei wish that a whole side be [?brought] up to gether.[67]

In the event the wing was not truncated at the 'backhouse' wall, but at what today seems a rather indeterminate point 16 feet to the south (Fig. 1). In fact this point is precisely determined. It is exactly where, according to Sir Nicholas's revised plan A, the south-west staircase turret, when built, would have been bonded into the wing (see Fig. 10). Presumably Sir Nicholas, heeding the masons' advice, thought that the turret would both buttress and conceal the masonry joints.

This apparently small point is important for the argument of this essay since it indicates that in 1577 Sir Nicholas was still intent on building his distinctive eight turreted courtyard house, and to do so according to revised plan A. Realistically this was the point at which he could have settled for a medium sized E-type house. But he didn't. Consequently Stiffkey Hall must be seen as an incomplete courtyard house which was fitted out on a temporary basis so that life could continue until funds became available to complete it. Of course this was never done, as we know with hindsight. Hence the absence of an entrance porch into the great hall, hence the absence of anything which could be graced with the name of a long gallery, and hence the somewhat chaotic internal layout which, since it was all done in stud-work, could have been refashioned easily when the wings were completed and the galleried southern entrance range built. Meanwhile Nathaniel and his family would have to manage without upwards of 30 per cent of the planned floor space. In an effort to shoe-horn as much as possible of the original planned accommodation into a smaller area, Sir Nicholas inserted a floor in the open hall to provide a great

65 *Bacon Papers*, i. 201.
66 *Ibid.*, i. xi, 219, 231, 242.
67 *Ibid.*, i, 196.

chamber above. Similarly at the end of the west wing, he created the mezzanine floor and may well have done the same in the east wing. How he contrived internal staircases for access to chambers at the wing ends remains a mystery to us and presented a problem to him which, in the west wing at least, was only resolved later by adding the rectangular external staircase (see Figs 1–3).

Thus, when building work recommenced in the spring of 1577, Sir Nicholas Bacon's plans had been further compromised as regards both their internal layout and external appearance. But at least the financial economies thereby achieved ensured that work could continue apace on the north range and shortened west wing. By September Nathaniel could report to his father that: 'the building goeth forward, & that wellnere finished which I appointed to do this yeare, which was to laie the first flowre of the whole north rang & 43 fote of the west, & this floure for the west part is already laid'.[68] The bad news – that yet more borrowing had left him with a debt of over £300 – he withheld, presumably for a subsequent letter which has not survived. Once more his father bailed him out, but this time only by advancing the £200 which in his will he had bequeathed to Nathaniel 'towardes the building of his house in Stiffkey'.[69]

Nathaniel's haste and hurry undoubtedly explains why Sir Nicholas's intentions to build in ashlar, or at the very least to provide stone dressings, was abandoned in favour of rendered flint and moulded brick masonry. In late 1575 both Nathaniel and his father had tried, unsuccessfully, to procure stone from Binham priory, then in the possession of Edward Paston. Next, they had sought supplies from the earl of Lincoln and Sir Christopher Wray, both of whom seemed willing to oblige them. However, as late as September 1576 not a single load had been delivered, presumably because the hard-bargaining Sir Nicholas had insisted that the stone be examined for quality and that price and transport costs should be 'not very chargeable'.[70] Meanwhile, on site at Stiffkey, as soon as the masons began work on the foundations, Nathaniel must have taken steps to ensure that a shortage of stone should not delay his building programme since he had ordered moulds to be made for casting the dressings in brick.[71] As far as he was concerned the best was not to be the enemy of the good. Thereafter, since we hear no more about freestone, the vernacular idiom of this building appears to have been sealed, and construction continued apace.

By 1578 the main range and west wing must have been nearing completion,[72] since late that year or early in 1579 Nathaniel and family moved in.[73] Pending the building of the east wing and galleried south front, Sir Nicholas seems to have enclosed the eastern and southern sides of his courtyard with a rendered flint wall

68 *Ibid.*, i. 266.

69 University of Reading Library, Farm Records, Norfolk, 20, p. 21; *Bacon Papers*, ii. 28.

70 *Bacon Papers*, i. 170–2, 175, 179, 224, 226–7.

71 *Ibid.*, i. 196.

72 But as late as the autumn of 1579 carpenters were at work fitting out the attic gallery (*Bacon Papers*, ii. 150–1).

73 As early as June 1578 Sir Nicholas addressed a letter to Nathaniel 'at Styffkey'. In July one was addressed to him 'at Cockthorpe or Stukye'. No document refers to his place of residence again until May 1579. Thereafter Stiffkey is consistently mentioned. *Bacon Papers*, ii. 14, 16, 75.

and a modest classical gateway executed in dressed stone and displaying the Bacon crest (a boar passant) (see Fig. 12). Guests at any house-warming party approached from the south, over the new cut of the river, and dismounted in the forecourt where the gently ascending ground led them, *via* a series of shallow terraces, through this gateway into the courtyard. Here they progressed *via* a further shallow terrace to the great portal door (see Fig. 9).

VI

One hopes that Sir Nicholas joined such a party since he died early in 1579, leaving his impecunious son to build the west wing, the galleried-entrance range and the terraced east gardens. For a decade nothing further was done. Such building work as Nathaniel undertook (stables, barns and sea-bank repairs)[74] represented investment in his estate, where at last he was master. This policy soon bore fruit, since by the early 1590s his annual income had just about doubled, but probably never reached £1,500.[75]

In 1589, with increased means, three daughters approaching marriageable age,[76] an expanding household, and his position established in county government and society,[77] Nathaniel turned his attention to building the east wing. This he completed in 1592,[78] just in time for his daughter Elizabeth's marriage to Thomas Knyvett, and barely two years before Anne, his long-suffering wife, died.[79] Next, in 1594 and 1595, he built the great flight of terraces stretching from the churchyard wall to the waterside. Their construction, together with the garden lay-out of the axial 'nether' terrace (see Fig. 9), is recorded in considerable detail[80] and leaves little doubt that Sir Nicholas would have been well pleased.

Even so, one senses that Nathaniel was not really on his father's wavelength. Although he inherited the latter's diligence, his was a lesser mind; certainly a nar-

74 Chicago, Bacon MS 991–A. NRO, MS 1600 (I C 9).

75 It is not possible to arrive at a precise figure. This estimate is based upon the household steward's accounts for income and expenditure for the decade 1587–97. It is clear that this official handled most of the income and expenditure, but there must have been a privy purse. This I have estimated at £200 per annum, a sum which is probably too high in view of Nathaniel's unostentatious lifestyle. For the household steward's account book see: Raynham Hall MSS, Box 33; NRO, MSS Sotheby 4/6/76 (S. 187A), and Emmet & Tacon 29/7/75.

76 Anne, aged fifteen (bapt. 7/8/1573), Elizabeth aged thirteen (b.1575), Winifred aged ten (bapt. May 1578).

77 A. Hassell Smith, *County and Court: Government and Politics in Norfolk 1558–1603*, Oxford 1974, especially parts iii and iv.

78 This second phase of building (*c.*1589–92) can be deduced from the estate-yard weekly wages book (Folger, MS E.b.2) which lists weekly everyone employed, and frequently indicates their trade or task.

79 Elizabeth was married at Stiffkey in October 1592. Anne died *c.* June 1594.

80 Raynham Hall Library MSS, Box 33, household steward's account book 1587–97, various references to the purchase of materials for the 'nether terrace'. Folger, MS E.b.2, estate-yard wages book. Work undertaken is sometimes specified.

rower one. He cared little about the aesthetic quality of his environment,[81] and, although well read in law, theology and history (to judge by his library and his life-long pursuits), he did not share his father's interest in classical literature, mathematics or building and garden design.[82] Or so it would seem, since he never completed the wings at Stiffkey, let alone the galleried entrance front. Indeed, he may not even have bothered to respect the integrity of his father's plans by building the two southern outer corner turrets (see Fig. 1). Documentary evidence suggests that these had to await the more aesthetic eye of Sir Roger Townshend in 1630.[83]

As well as these failures of omission he perpetrated acts of commission which further compromised his father's scheme. He must surely have been responsible for substituting the large six-double-light windows which dominate the courtyard façades in place of the three and four double light ones which his father had planned (cf. Figs 2, 7). Fenestration was clearly under discussion between them as early as June 1576, when Nathaniel agreed with his father that 'the forme of the square windowe is both rare and good and I judg cheapest'.[84] A year later, however, in a letter which is badly faded, he appears to be defending the insertion of the larger six-double-light ones.[85]

Unquestionably he was responsible for the gatehouse which stands where the galleried entrance range would have been (see Fig. 1). He started it in 1604, once more in a great haste and hurry. 'Your buyldynge goethe forward as ffast as tyme and wether hytherto wolde permytt', wrote his servant Henry Armiger in April, 'Brett and his companye beinge 8 in number besyds 2 morter men began the worke the mondaye next before Easter day.' The lime kiln was 'at woork withoute intermyssyon' and a team of free masons from Norwich had 'begun to sett up the gate and the dores of both lodges'.[86] Possibly he intended this little building to celebrate his knighthood (July 1604), but such a gesture was not in keeping with his undemonstrative character. More likely he built it at the behest of his second wife Dorothy, whom he had married in 1597. She was a wilful woman who came of a distinguished Suffolk family (the Hoptons of Cockfield and Blythburgh) and who dis-

81 For instance the 'best chamber' was not fitted out and decorated until his marriage to Dorothy Smith in 1597. Consequently when his daughters were married in 1592 and 1594 tapestries were borrowed from family members, trundled across Norfolk and tacked up to make them fit (Raynham Hall Library MSS, Box 33, household steward's account book 1587–97, esp. fos 215, 221, 272, 398, 405, 408).

82 For his mindset and principal interests see his entry in the forthcoming *New Dictionary of National Biography.*

83 The evidence as to when these two turrets were built is inconclusive. They cannot have been built during the first building phase which ended *c.*1579, since the intention at that time was unequivocally to extend the wings. That they had not been built when Nathaniel died in 1622 is suggested by their non-appearance in an inventory of household stuff made at that time. This could have been because they contained nothing worth listing, but since they provided an inner chamber to at least four high-status chambers they must surely have merited a mention had they been there.

84 *Bacon Papers*, i. 196.

85 *Ibid.*, 266.

86 NRO, MS RAY 255.

Fig. 12. Gatehouse from the south-west. The roof and building beyond are later, as is the infill of the gateway. *Photograph Crown copyright, National Monuments Record.*

played the very characteristics which Nathaniel lacked: social and cultural sophistication.[87] She was indeed an epicurean who disliked the Baconian stoicism and the architecture which went with it.

The result was disastrous for Sir Nicholas's scheme, since this gatehouse is pure pastiche. To the south it incorporates his classical gateway but this has been flanked by two crude half-octagonal brick pilasters of indeterminate design (see Fig. 12). On the north façade the gateway, now lost, must have been executed in the English gothic style of the two surviving lodge doorways which flanked it, while above it blazed the Bacon and Hopton coats of arms together with the crests of both families. Stylistically this façade represents a step backwards from Sir Nicholas's work on the south side, while symbolically it declares that the household is under new management. This was certainly true, but that is another story. Such unity as this building has is provided by a stone cornice which continues on all four sides, but is much more elaborate on the north façade. The upper part of this building has been greatly altered so that we do not know how the roof was finished, but in aspect it may have been similar to the gatehouse at Irmingland Hall, a house which Nathaniel began to build in 1604 as a residence for Lady Dorothy's eldest son. How Sir Nicholas would

[87] 'The Letters and Will of Lady Dorothy Bacon, 1597–1629', ed. Jane Key, *NRS* LVI, 1991, 77–112.

have shuddered. Not only is this building a botch, but the entire project was misconceived. If a gatehouse was to be built at all it should have been at the entrance to the southern axial court.

Whether Nathaniel was responsible for the rectangular staircase turret which uneasily abuts the west façade of the west wing remains an open question (see Figs 1–3). Throughout his and Sir Roger Townshend's lifetime the first floor of this wing was occupied by the ladies of the house, the southernmost room serving as Lady Bacon's and then Lady Townshend's chamber. Initially, access to this room must have been either along the corridor and through the backhouse stone wall or via an internal staircase from the mezzanine floor. Neither provided appropriate access to this high-status room, so it is reasonable to assume that this final and unfortunate modification of Sir Nicholas's plan was undertaken sooner rather than later. The finger thus points at Nathaniel.

VII

This essay has traced the processes, largely ones of subtraction, through which Sir Nicholas Bacon's grand concept became transmuted into the present inscrutable but romantic pile. Undoubtedly it is a story of an architectural disaster; but it also provides a window into aspects of Elizabethan life which can only be listed here. At an intellectual level the gulf between Sir Nicholas's concept and the reality – a gulf which Sir Nicholas clearly found acceptable – tells us something about the impact of Neoplatonism on the Elizabethan mind. For Sir Nicholas it was the ideal which mattered; hence his dilettante planning and his conception of a house and its gardens which was clearly unrelated to any site, let alone the difficult one he chose. Since in his view reality must always be a pale reflection of an ideal type, he is able to accept compromise so long as a shadow of the ideal remained; hence his mind-boggling compromises over the mathematics of the garden courts.

For the architectural historian there may be sufficient evidence here to rank Sir Nicholas with that exclusive band of magnate-builders who came as near as was possible in Tudor England to being their own architects.[88] For surely he was a polymath who straddled both the intellectual and mechanical arts. It may also turn out that this enterprise in north Norfolk is one of the earliest (if not the earliest) attempts to build a house and its gardens as an integrated entity. At a more prosaic level there is much to ponder here for those interested in the building process and even more to buttress the claim that the glory of Elizabethan architecture rests in its individualism and particularist design features.

This story, however, raises more questions than it answers. Why, for instance, did Sir Nicholas plan a house on this scale for a second son? A possible explanation, in terms of the mathematics and geometry of his integrated building scheme, has already been suggested, but there are others which need exploring. For instance, at a

88 Girouard, *Smythson*, 9.

political level he may have aspired to provide his sons with appropriate accommodation for a bid to fill the power vacuum in East Anglia created by the execution of Thomas Howard, duke of Norfolk, in 1572,[89] his eldest son Nicholas being ensconced in an adequate mansion at Redgrave and Nathaniel in a magnatial structure at Stiffkey. That they lacked the vision, will, and ability for this role may not have been apparent in 1572 when neither of them had reached their thirtieth year. On another tack, why, in designing and building this house, did be eschew almost all decorative features from both the vernacular and renaissance vocabularies? Could this reflect his stoic philosophy as displayed by the fifty-nine *sententia* which he selected mainly from the works of Seneca and Cicero and had inscribed on the walls of his long gallery at Gorhambury?[90] Undoubtedly he would have agreed with his greatest son, Francis, when he wrote: 'Houses are built to live in and not to be looked at . . . Leave the goodly fabrics of houses, for beauty only, to the enchanted palaces of the poets; who build them with small cost.'[91]

89 D. MacCulloch, *Suffolk and the Tudors: Politics and Religion in an English County 1500–1600*, Oxford 1986, 102–3.

90 *Sir Nicholas Bacon's Great House Sententia*, ed. E. McCutcheon, English Literary Renaissance Supplements III, Amherst 1977, 66–91.

91 *Francis Bacon's Essays*, Everyman's Library 1962, 133 (his essay 'of Building').

Shrubland before Barry: A House and its Landscape 1660–1880

Tom Williamson

SHRUBLAND PARK is one of the most imposing of Suffolk's country houses – a great nineteenth-century Italianate pile, with a soaring south tower, perched on the edge of a steep chalk escarpment overlooking the Gipping valley. Its vast park, graced by ancient sweet chestnuts and oaks, adds to the splendour of the setting. But more impressive still are the extensive gardens, terraced and balustraded, laid out on two levels above and below the dramatic slope (Fig. 1).[1]

The credit for this imposing *ensemble* is usually given to Charles Barry, the celebrated architect of the Houses of Parliament and designer of numerous English country houses, who in the 1840s and 50s modified Shrubland Hall and made alterations to the grounds.[2] As early as 1895 he was being recognised as the hall's principal architect. Particulars printed in that year, when the estate was to be let, describe how the building had been 'greatly enlarged and practically rebuilt in 1851, by the late Sir Charles Barry'.[3] But it is the gardens, in particular, which are usually seen as largely or entirely his work. Typical is the entry for Shrubland in *The Oxford Companion to Gardens*, which states baldly that 'the present garden dates from 1851–4, when Sir Charles Barry was called in to make alterations to the house'.[4] This, too, is a long-established view, the 1895 particulars simply describing how the forty acres of gardens and pleasure grounds 'were laid out by the late Sir Charles Barry'.[5] In reality, plans, illustrations, and correspondence in the Shrubland archives, together with material published in the nineteenth-century gardening press and documents in the Suffolk Record Office, reveal a more complicated story, and show that much that has traditionally been ascribed to Barry has, in reality, rather earlier origins.

1 My thanks to Eric and Susie (Lord and Lady de Saumarez) for all their help and enthusiastic support for my researches at Shrubland. Thanks also to Doug Atfield and Alastair Tuffill for the photographs; and to Philip Judge for the line drawings.

2 See, for example, the description by Nicholas Pevsner in *The Buildings of England: Suffolk*, London 1961, 387: while acknowledging the contribution of previous architects, James Paine and J.P. Gandy-Deering, the author suggests that 'it is Barry who dominates the house and its splendid surroundings'.

3 Printed particulars, 1895, Shrubland Hall archive, no catalogue number.

4 G. Jellicoe, S. Jellicoe, P. Goode and M. Lancaster, eds, *The Oxford Companion to Gardens*, Oxford 1986, 516.

5 Printed particulars, 1895, Shrubland Hall archive, no catalogue number.

Fig. 1. The Descent, Shrubland Park.

The Old Hall

The building which forms the core of the present Shrubland Hall was erected in the 1770s, on a virgin site. The house it replaced survives, in much-altered and truncated form, as the 'Old Hall'. This building now serves as the residence of Lord de Saumarez, the owner of the estate: Shrubland Hall itself is used as a health clinic. Before examining the history of this latter building, and its grounds, we must first note briefly one of two things about its predecessor.

The Old Hall as it survives is essentially a nineteenth-century structure, although incorporating much fabric from the original building: most notably, the sixteenth-century terracotta surrounds to the windows of the south range, similar to those in nearby Barham church, which are of some considerable art-historical importance.[6] The hall was acquired, together with the rest of the Shrubland estate, by the Bacon family at the start of the seventeenth century – the prize of a judicious marriage. An illustration of the south elevation of the hall made by Humphry Repton in his Red Book of 1789 (Fig. 2) shows a long, rambling building, evidently incorporating ranges of many different ages, some apparently of medieval, some of sixteenth- and some of seventeenth-century date.[7]

6 E. Wood, 'Notes on the History of Shrubland Park', *PSIA* 17, 1919/21, 123–6.

7 Humphry Repton, 'Plans and Sketches with Observations for the Improvement of Shrubland in the County of Suffolk a Seat of William Middleton Esq, MP, 1789'. Shrubland Hall archive.

Fig. 2. Shrubland Old Hall, as illustrated by Humphry Repton in 1789.

Little can be said about the building's plan, layout or history from the available evidence, but the illustration suggests that it was entered through a porch – flint-built, of fifteenth-century date – which originally gave access to a screens passage. A hall range lay to the south, floored by the late eighteenth century, and services to the north, in a long jettied and gabled range. Beyond the hall another jettied range extended to the south as far as the chapel, the structure which forms the core of the present 'Old Hall'. The earliest map of Shrubland is a survey of 1668 by Edward Clarke.[8] This shows the hall in elevation and suggests that on its northern side there was an enclosed courtyard, bounded to the north by a range of outbuildings. A later and more detailed map, of 1785 (Fig. 3), suggests that the hall itself was ranged around a central courtyard, a feature obscured in the 1688 elevational representation: the range depicted by Repton, that is, probably lay within, and formed the north range of, a courtyard.[9]

Both maps show that immediately to the south of the hall lay a walled garden of unusual, irregular plan. Fish ponds, and a dovecote, lay in close proximity, and the wider landscape to the south and west of the hall was divided into two areas of, we may assume, quasi-ornamental status. On the level ground above the escarpment, south of the hall, the map shows a well timbered area labelled 'Parke'; to the west, on and below the escarpment, a more densely-treed area described as 'Warren'. It is doubtful whether rabbits were still being kept within the latter area by this time, in spite of its name: rabbits and forestry do not mix well. The trees planted here must have been sweet chestnuts, for a number of ancient examples still grow in this precise area. The largest, picturesque with age, are one of the glories of Shrubland, upon which visitors have long waxed lyrical. As the *Gardener's Chronicle* put it in 1888:

8 SROI, HA 93/12/82.
9 SROI, 1467/2.

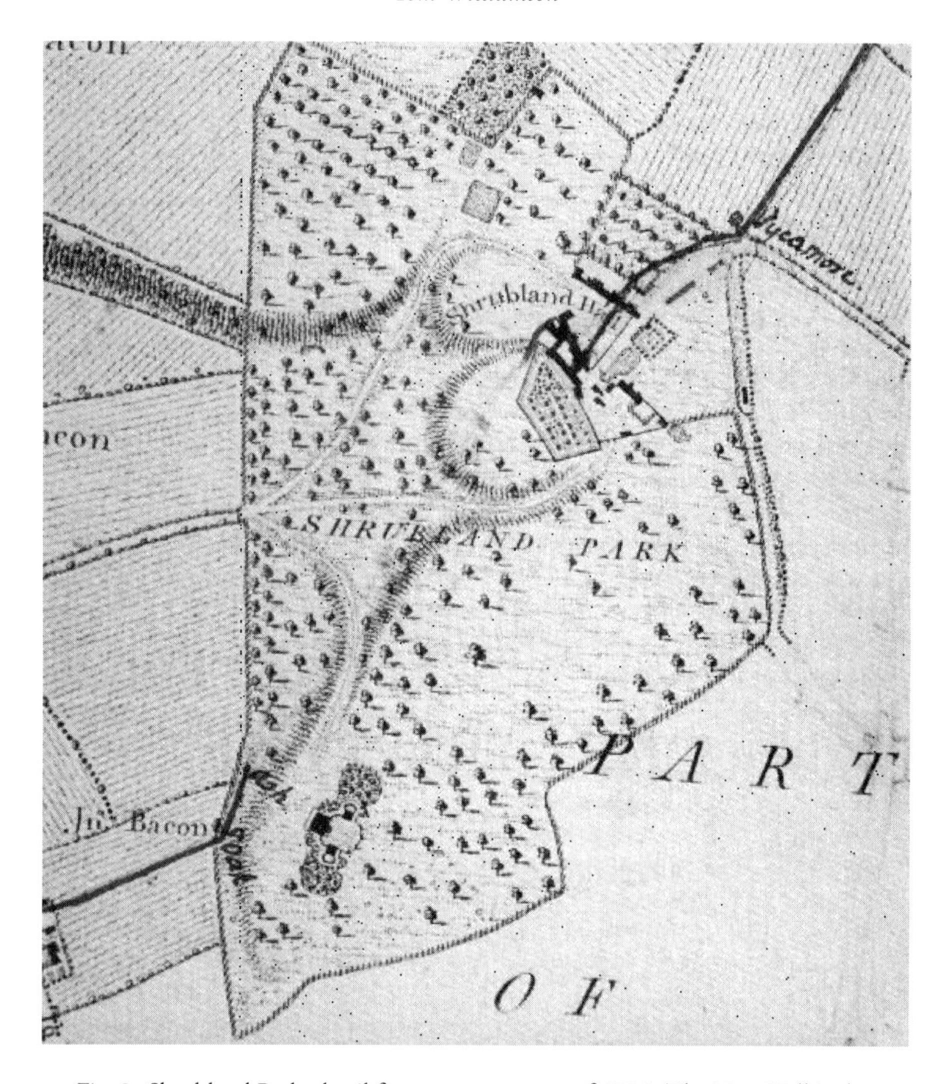

Fig. 3. Shrubland Park: detail from an estate map of 1785. The New Hall is shown, unlabelled, in the south-eastern corner of the park.

'Such boles! such a world of knots and cracks! such spiral furrows ploughed in their bark.'[10]

Some of the largest and finest specimens, some probably more than five hundred years old, flank the gravel path – the Brownlow Terrace – which leads northwards from the 'new' hall, along the crest of the escarpment. At first sight these trees appear to represent the remains of an avenue, perhaps associated with the Old Hall to the north. But on closer inspection it is clear that this cannot be the case, for the lines of

10 *Gardeners' Chronicle*, 22 Sept. 1888, 329.

trees (and the terrace itself) are not quite straight, and do not focus on the site of the hall at all, but on a point slightly to the east. No such avenue is shown on the 1668 map, nor on any later map. The lines of trees do, however, appear to correspond with a straight section of the eastern boundary of The Warren. Evidently, this line was simply utilised as a convenient feature in the landscape when the terrace walk was laid out in the later eighteenth century.

The Building of the New Hall

The Rev. John Bacon inherited the Shrubland estate in 1767 and two years later commissioned the architect James Paine to design a new house, in a new position some 500 metres to the south-west of the old hall.[11] The new site was closer to the edge of the escarpment, and was clearly selected for the magnificent views it afforded across the Gipping valley and southwards towards Ipswich. James Paine (1716–89) was, with Sir Robert Taylor, the most important of the 'second generation' of Palladian architects in England.[12] The two men together dominated English architecture in the middle decades of the eighteenth century: it was said a little later that they 'nearly divided the practice of the profession between them, for they had few competitors till Mr Adam entered the lists'.[13] Both men, although heavily imbued with the ethos of the 'pure' Palladianism propagated by Lord Burlington, Colen Campbell and William Kent in the 1720s and 30s, were less obsessed with the 'correct' use of proportions and orders. They felt able to use Palladio's designs (and those derived from them by Inigo Jones, Kent or Campbell) in flexible ways.[14] Paine believed that many features of the Palladian style, such as free-standing porticoes, were 'very ill-adapted to our climate, still worse to our present mode of living' and were 'consequently . . . not proper models for our imitation'.[15] But other elements of the style were eagerly embraced, and Paine was especially keen to use the Palladian idea of building a country seat as a central block, flanked by lower pavilions, either two or four in number, which were connected to it by quadrant passages. The largest house he designed in this manner was Kedleston Hall in Derbyshire (for Lord Scarsdale, 1757–9) which had four flanking pavilions (Kedleston was actually completed under the direction of Robert Adam, and its final form owes more to him than to Paine).

Paine designed country houses throughout the whole of his career, from the mid 1740s to the 1770s, and was responsible both for great, imposing seats like Wardour Castle in Wiltshire, Kedleston in Derbyshire or Thorndon in Essex, and for smaller

11 P. Leach, *James Paine*, London 1988, 210–11.

12 J. Summerson, *Architecture in Britain 1530–1830*, 6th edn, Newhaven 1993, 342–5.

13 Summerson, *Architecture in Britain*, 344.

14 Leach, *Paine*, 39–48.

15 James Paine, *Plans, Elevations, and Sections of Noblemen and Gentlemen's Houses*, 2 vols, 2nd edn, London 1783, i, p. ii.

Fig. 4. Shrubland Hall: development of the west front, in descending order: (a) as originally built *c.*1772; (b) as altered *c.*1808; (c) after Gandy-Deering's alterations *c.*1830; (d) after Barry's work of 1848–50.

'villa' residences, such as Baldersby Park or Ormesby Hall in Lincolnshire.[16] Shrubland falls into the latter category, a building similar to Hare Hall in Romford, which he completed a few years earlier, although somewhat plainer. It was probably Paine's last major commission. Although this house is now much obscured by later alterations and additions, much is known about its original appearance. Paine

16 Leach, *Paine, passim.*

himself published a plan and elevation in Volume II of his *Works*, the details of which can be corroborated by a number of late eighteenth and early nineteenth-century engravings, and by plans drawn up in connection with various alterations and projected alterations early in the following century.[17]

The hall, which was built of yellowish-grey brick, comprised a central block flanked by two low pavilions, linked to it by curving corridors (Fig. 4a). The main block was of five bays on the principal front. It had a *piano nobile* raised above a rusticated basement, and a central pediment supported by giant Ionic pilasters, rising through two storeys and embracing the central three bays. It was a comparatively small building: the central block measured 55 by 60 feet (16.5 by 18 metres), and contained only four main rooms on the principal floor; the rather simple pavilions measured 30 foot (9 metres) square. Unlike the modern hall, Paine's building had its principal entrance on the west, with a drive approaching from the north-west, climbing the escarpment obliquely. In spite of the scale of later alterations, some of Paine's original decoration still survives in the principal rooms of the hall, notably a number of classical plaster ceilings. What was especially novel about the building was its internal organisation. The entrances opened into a transverse corridor, spanning the width of the building, in the centre of which was a circular area described by Paine as a 'tribune'. The main stairs led off from this, at right angles to the corridor, giving access to the principal rooms at *piano nobile* level.

No building accounts survive for the hall, and it is not clear how long it took to erect nor precisely when it was completed. Later tradition suggests the main structure, at least, was completed by 1773 but dates of 1770 and 1772 appear on rainwater heads. It is noteworthy that on the 1785 estate map already referred to the new house is not actually labelled and that the name 'Shrubland Hall' is still attached to the *old* building. Possibly the new house was only finally completed some time after 1773. Either way, the map suggests that the landscape in which the house was set had not been radically changed since the previous map had been surveyed, in 1668.[18] The 'Park' and the 'Warren' had now been thrown together to form a single area of parkland, but had only been expanded slightly, to the north-west. As a result the new hall stood in a somewhat marginal position towards the south-eastern periphery of the park. Comparison with the earlier map suggests that the trees within the Warren had been somewhat thinned, in order to approximate more closely to the fashionable ideal of the landscape park popularised by Capability Brown and his 'imitators' (Fig. 3). Moreover, in keeping with the fashion of the times, the new hall stood 'free from walls'. There were small areas of shrubbery to north and south, and an area of fenced pleasure ground/garden to the east, but no walled gardens. Food for the household continued to be grown in the enclosed garden beside the Old Hall, which continued to exist, although now apparently downgraded to the status of a home farm.

The 1785 map reveals that another important feature of the Shrubland landscape

17 Paine, *Elevations and Sections*, ii, 20–1, plates 64–7. See, in particular, Shrubland Hall archives, drawings, 4, 11, 12, 13, 14 and 15.

18 SROI, HA 93/12/82; SROI, 1467/2.

had by now come into existence. On the crest of the escarpment, some 550 metres to the north-west of the new hall, the map shows a building – the prospect tower which still survives, although much altered in the nineteenth century. It is undated, but details of internal decoration, notably the restrained 'gothick' interior of the second-floor rooms, suggest that it is probably coeval with the hall itself.

Repton at Shrubland

The Bacons did not remain long at Shrubland after the completion of the new hall. The estate was purchased by Sir William Middleton,[19] of nearby Crowfield, in 1787.[20] Like most new owners, he immediately set about making changes to the property. In 1789 Humphry Repton was asked to advise on the grounds, and prepared a 'Red Book' – one of eight known to have been made for Suffolk clients.[21] Repton was then at the very start of his career: his first paid commission, for Catton near Norwich, had only been made in the previous year,[22] and it is possible that Shrubland was only the third or fourth design prepared in his professional career. Quite how Sir William came to employ this unknown designer remains unclear.

The Red Book (something of a misnomer in this particular case, since the proposals are bound in a *green* paper cover!) typically begins with complimentary comments about the appearance of the park, which Repton describes as 'beautifully varied by inequality of ground, and richly ornamented with timber of prodigious size'. He was, however, more circumspect about the site of the Hall. While acknowledging that this provided panoramic views from the west front he complained that these lacked any well defined foreground, something 'which is essential in a good composition'. The phrase is noteworthy: Repton here betrays that he is thinking along broadly 'picturesque' lines, suggesting that the principal view from the hall should be organised like a picture, following the established rules of painterly composition – that is, with a foreground, a middle ground, and a distant backdrop. Accordingly, Repton's proposals for the immediate surroundings of the hall involved the creation of a new pleasure ground on this side of the building – a 'dressed ground' of grass, gravel paths and shrubs – and careful planting where the ground sloped away steeply to the west. Here there should be 'shrubs towards the summit, and high growing trees at the base', in order to give a feeling of 'safety to the esplanade before the door and make the house appear to stand firmly and proudly embossom'd in wood instead of tottering on the brink of a precipice' (Fig. 5).

19 After 1822, Sir William Fowle Middleton.

20 Shrubland Hall archives, SA 16/2.

21 Humphry Repton, 'Plans and Sketches with Observations for the Improvement of Shrubland in the County of Suffolk a Seat of William Middleton Esq MP, 1789', Shrubland Hall archive.

22 S. Daniels, *Humphry Repton: Landscape Gardening and the Geography of Georgian England*, New Haven and London 1999, 79–90; T. Williamson, *The Archaeology of the Landscape Park: Garden Design in Norfolk, England, c.1680–1840*, BAR British Series 268, Oxford 1998, 195–6.

Fig. 5. Illustration from Repton's Red Book of 1789, showing proposed changes to the view from the west front.

Repton suggested that the woods growing along the escarpment to the north of the hall should be augmented in various ways, and that the prospect tower here should have pinnacles added in order to give it a 'more light and pleasing' appearance. More striking are his suggestions concerning the Old Hall. He opposed Sir William's desire to completely demolish this, arguing that parts should be retained as an interesting incident in the landscape:

> In taking down the old mansion, I cou'd wish for the reverence due to antiquity, that some part might be preserved, particularly the chapel and the chequered porch.

Walks were to be made, leading from the new pleasure grounds laid out around the hall to 'seats in, or near these remnants of ancient Piety and hospitality'. The walled kitchen garden adjacent to the old house should be extended, and planted up with shrubberies, in order to form a small detached area of pleasure ground. Again, these proposals are of considerable interest. Not only do they show (once again) that the designer was, at the start of his career, thinking along broadly 'picturesque' lines – in spite of the acrimonious dispute which was shortly to erupt with the chief proponents of picturesque landscape design, Richard Payne Knight and Uvedale Price.[23]

23 P. Goode, 'The Picturesque Controversy', in G. Carter, P. Goode and K. Laurie, eds, *Humphry Repton, Landscape Gardener*, Norwich 1982, 33–9.

They are also early evidence for that enthusiasm for 'gothic' architecture which was to become so marked a feature of Repton's later work.[24]

Repton's other proposals for Shrubland are less obviously 'picturesque' in character, but are likewise interesting in that they show how already, at the very start of his career, many of his most characteristic ideas had taken shape. Particular attention was thus paid to entrances and approaches.[25] As already noted, the main drive to the hall approached from the north-west: it led off the turnpike road to Norwich, curving southwards on entering the park, gradually climbing the escarpment and terminating on the west side of the house. Repton suggested that this line should be altered, so that it ascended the escarpment further to the north and led to a new entrance on the *eastern* side of the hall. He also urged that changes should be made to the landforms here, noting that the drive would 'ascend the hill without difficulty when part of the ridge is thrown down'. In addition, he urged the creation of an entirely new drive, which would approach the Hall from the south. This would leave the turnpike road in a gentle curve (a typical Repton touch) at a new lodge flanked by plantations, and then run in a grand sweep through the landscape. This, Repton suggested, would provide a more fitting approach to the hall.

Many other proposals are contained in the Red Book. Repton suggested various minor alterations to the architecture of the hall, in order to improve the views from the rooms within; he urged that new plantations should be established beside the proposed south drive, and more widely within the park; and suggested that a new gamekeeper's cottage should be built on the eastern edge of the park, 'a delightful object in the approach with the smoke curling in fleecy folds against the dark grove of trees which terminates the landscape'. This, again, is a typical Repton touch, one of many which serve to distinguish his style from that of 'Capability' Brown. The latter's designs were, for the most part, characterised by a kind of monumental exclusivity: the grand landscape of gentility was to be quite divorced from the everyday world. Repton in contrast was keen to introduce signs of life into the landscape of the park. Nevertheless, the park at Shrubland was to be made larger, through expansion both to the west and to the south, Repton proposing that:

> The whole of the grounds through which the approaches pass, be thrown into open lawn, removing the hedges & leaving occasional single trees, or Groups, and foresting the plains with thorns and maples.

The Tithe Award maps for the parishes of Coddenham and Barham, surveyed in 1839 and 1840 respectively, and a number of early nineteenth-century drawings and paintings, show that some of Repton's proposals were implemented by Sir William.[26] The suggested pinnacles were added to the prospect tower and the planting in the park appears to have been augmented, more or less in the ways that

24 See H. Repton, *Fragments on the Theory and Practice of Landscape Gardening*, London 1816.

25 See Williamson, *Archaeology of the Landscape Park*, 195–9.

26 SROI, P461/66 and P461/11. Drawings in Shrubland Hall archive; see in particular number 4, which shows the pinnacles on the prospect tower, later removed when this was heightened in the nineteenth century.

Repton had suggested. The main entrance of the house was moved to the east and the southern drive was put in place, although the lodge does not appear to have been built. Nevertheless, much of his advice appears to have been ignored. The proposed gamekeeper's cottage in the east of the park was not erected, and the park did not expand southwards until after 1808, or westwards until after 1820. Intriguingly, an undated early nineteenth-century painting of the hall in the Shrubland collection suggests that not even the shrubbery proposed for the immediate vicinity of the house was created.

It is noteworthy that one of the finest features of Shrubland's landscape appears to have been created through the *partial* implementation of one of Repton's proposals. Although his suggestion for making a path all the way from the hall, to the site of the Old Hall and its gardens, was not adopted by Sir William, Repton's description of the first part of its route – 'along the natural Terrace under the spreading branches of the venerable Chestnut Trees' – is so reminiscent of the present Brownlow Terrace, the gravel walk which runs northwards from the house, that it is hard to believe that this feature was not created following his advice. It was certainly in place by 1840, when it was depicted, rather schematically, on the Barham Tithe Award map.[27]

The Early Nineteenth Century

Published discussions of the architecture of Shrubland Hall invariably leap directly from the 1770s house designed by James Paine, to the alterations carried out by J.P. Gandy-Deering in the 1830s.[28] In fact, there is no doubt that the hall was extensively altered in the intervening period. Paine's house was, as already noted, a fairly small building, even allowing for the fact that service areas (and possibly some sleeping accommodation) were hived off into the peripheral pavilions. Sir William evidently considered extending the house, to create a more commodious mansion, soon after he purchased the estate. Two drawings in the Shrubland archive – unsigned and undated, but almost certainly drawn up between 1787 and 1808 – show the house extended in the same Palladian mould as Paine's original core, in order to create an imposing, thirteen-bay, three-storey building.[29] In the event, such an expensive expansion was never undertaken and instead more modest wings, two storeys high, two bays wide and double pile – i.e., two rooms deep – were added to north and south, a choice which was to determine much of the subsequent development, and indeed present appearance, of the house (Fig. 4b). These additions, executed in the same grey brick as Paine's original house, are shown in a number of published engravings and unpublished drawings, and also on plans drawn up in

27 SROI, P461/11.

28 See, for example, N. Pevsner, *The Buildings of England: Suffolk*, London 1961, 386–7; C. Brown, B. Haywood and R. Kindred, *A Dictionary of Architects of Suffolk Buildings 1800–1914*, Ipswich 1991, 111.

29 Shrubland Hall archives, drawings, 21.

connection with the extensions and proposed extensions later in the nineteenth century.[30] They lacked a rusticated basement, which made them sit rather uncomfortably with Paine's original Palladian block. The western rooms in each terminated in canted bays or apses, facing north and south respectively, an unusual arrangement. They were almost certainly built around 1808, for the landscape designer William Wood – whose work at Shrubland we will consider in a moment – noted with approval in that year the 'more pleasing form imparted to the house by the wings now building'.[31] Sir William Middleton's brother, Henry Middleton of Crowfield, won £20,000 in the national lottery of 1801[32] and, according to a strong family tradition, gave part of this substantial sum to his brother, to spend on improving the house, he himself having no children. This tradition receives some support from the painting of Henry which hangs in the Old Hall today, showing him holding a parchment, with an elevation of Shrubland, in his hands.

These alterations to the architecture of the hall were mirrored by changes in the wider landscape. Today we think of Humphry Repton as one of the greatest of English landscape designers. But contemporary landowners did not necessarily revere his work in quite the same way, and it is noteworthy that by 1808 Sir William was asking one William Wood to suggest modifications to the grounds of Shrubland Hall. Wood was a painter by profession, a miniaturist who exhibited in London regularly between 1788 and 1808: he is said to have produced more than 1,200 miniatures in the course of his career, which was terminated by premature death at the age of forty-one in 1810.[33] He also painted landscapes, however, and towards the end of his life developed a keen interest in landscape gardening.[34]

Wood spent most of his working life in London, interspersed with short sojourns in Bristol and Gloucester. But he was born in, or around, Ipswich,[35] and it is likely that his landscaping activities at Shrubland came after a long acquaintance with the Middletons. Certainly, a number of drawings and paintings by Wood survive in the collections at the hall, and his proposals do not seem to have been drawn up for clients who were previously unknown to him. Not only does an uncompleted final draft survive in the Shrubland archives but also a very rough draft and a collection of notes.[36]

Because the accompanying sketches, plans and maps have not survived, Wood's text is sometimes hard to follow, but its essential suggestions are clear enough. He proposed extending the park southwards, much in the way that Repton had advised twenty years earlier. He also suggested altering the line of Repton's southern drive, so

30 See, in particular, Shrubland Hall archives, drawings, 6, 10, 14 and 15.

31 Shrubland Hall archives, uncatalogued.

32 Shrubland Hall archives, SA 1/1/4/3.

33 A. Groves, *A Dictionary of Artists who have Exhibited Works in the Principal London Exhibitions, from 1760 to 1893*, 3rd edn, London 1901, 309; J. Murdoch, J. Murrell, P. Noon and R. Strong, *The English Miniature*, Newhaven and London 1981, 193; D. Foskett, *British Portrait Miniatures*, London 1963, 128–9.

34 Foskett, *Miniatures*, 129.

35 *Ibid.*

36 Shrubland Hall archives, uncatalogued.

that it left the turnpike road rather further to the south, at a more dignified entrance – provided with a lodge, and ornamented with decorative planting. Of particular note, however, are his proposals for a number of extended walks running through the parkland, which would be ornamented with varied planting and embellished with seats. These would be taken past points of interest or beauty – natural or man-made – which would themselves be decorated with additional planting. Thus an old chalk pit would 'contribute a beautiful feature . . . if enriched by a few more trees'. The most important walk was to run from the Hall to the prospect tower, which was to be suitably embellished with ivy in order to appear more picturesque.

Wood also wanted to add to the existing north and south approaches, creating a number of new drives leading through the park to entrance lodges positioned on the public roads (none seem to have existed at this time). Others, it seems, would meander through the neighbouring estate land. Above all, he wanted to establish much new planting in the park, including numerous small clumps. As well as indigenous species like oak and beech, Wood wanted to plant larch, spruce, Weymouth pine and Scots pine, and he had a particular liking for the Lombardy poplar. This was a tree which, he believed, had 'suffer'd from its familiarity; because ill-judging people have seen it improperly plac'd', and because it was widely planted beside the homes of 'the vulgar inhabitants'.

An emphasis on walks and drives running through the estate, an evident enthusiasm for varied planting, involving exotic and coniferous trees and numerous clumps, together with such touches as the planting of ivy on the walls of the prospect tower, all mark Wood out clearly as a designer working in the developed 'Picturesque' mode of the early nineteenth century. His design sounds like something which might have been created by John Claudius Loudon at the start of his career or, a decade or so later, by William Sawrey Gilpin.[37] Once again, it is unclear precisely how many of these suggestions were taken on board by Sir William, but some certainly were. In particular, the line of the south drive was altered much as he suggested, although not for several years, and the park was now (at last) extended southwards. This area – known today as the Dentlings – is still characterised by more varied planting than the other, older areas of parkland, featuring Scots pines, cedars, limes, and beeches (including some copper beeches), as well as oaks.[38]

[37] T. Williamson, *Polite Landscapes: Gardens and Society in Eighteenth-Century England*, Stroud 1995, 160–5; J.C. Loudon, *Observations on the Formation of Useful and Ornamental Plantations*, Edinburgh 1804; S. Piebenga, 'William Sawrey Gilpin (c.1762–1843): Picturesque Improver', *Garden History* 22, 1994, i, 175–96.

[38] Although some of the planting here was added later in the nineteenth century. The draft Ordnance Survey 2-inch survey of 1820 shows the new extension to the park but not, apparently, the new line of the drive, which first appears on the Tithe Award map for Barham, 1840: SROI, P461/11.

Gandy-Deering and the Transformation of Shrubland

Sir William Fowle Middleton died in 1830 and the Shrubland estate passed to his son, William Fowle Fowle Middleton, who had married Anne Cust, the daughter of Earl Brownlow. The Middletons were avid travellers who undertook a number of lengthy Continental tours in the 1810s and 20s, which included an extended residence in Italy.[39] They appear to have shared a particular love for all things Italian, as well as a keen interest in horticulture.

Immediately after he inherited Sir William asked the architect J.P. Gandy-Deering to modernise the hall, which must by now have appeared a rather old-fashioned building. John Gandy – he assumed the suffix Deering in 1828, when he inherited an estate in Buckinghamshire from his friend Henry Deering – is today a rather neglected architect, but was an individual of some skill and originality.[40] He was the youngest of three architect brothers, a pupil of James Wyatt, and attended the Royal Academy school. He was a student of classical architecture and archaeology as well as being a practising architect, and he accompanied Sir William Gell on an expedition, sponsored by the Society of Dilettantes, to Greece and Asia Minor in 1811–13, and collaborated with Gell in a number of scholarly works, most notably their *Pompeiana* of 1818.[41] Not surprisingly, most of his architectural works were in an 'elegant and sophisticated Neo-classical style'.[42]

Gandy-Deering was, by 1830, living the life of a country gentleman rather than working as a professional architect, and his work at Shrubland was apparently done on a friendly, rather than primarily commercial, basis. A number of plans and elevations in the Shrubland archives, apparently in the architect's hand, indicate a variety of approaches to the hall's improvement.[43] The most ambitious designs are striking Neo-classical compositions which feature a substantial free-standing Grecian portico on the west front. The plan eventually executed, however, was more restrained in character, and Fig. 4c shows the principal changes made to the west front of the house. The terminal canted bays of the north and south wings were removed, and replaced by a blank half-bay framed by pilasters, while a balustrade was added at roof level. Both the rusticated basement of Paine's original range and the un-rusticated ground floor of the *c.*1808 wings were obscured by the substantial terrace and steps which today form so distinctive a feature of the west elevation. But the massive

39 Their travels are documented in a series of fascinating journals from the late 1810s/early 1820s: Shrubland Hall archives, SA 1/3/8–13.

40 There is some confusion about the architect's name. Although books on architectural history usually render it 'Gandy-Deering' after 1828, most of the plans etc. at Shrubland are in fact signed 'John Deering'.

41 *The Builder*, 16 March 1850, 134; H. Colvin, *A Bibliographic Dictionary of British Artists, 1600–1840*, 3rd edn, New Haven and London 1995, 387–8; Brown, Haywood and Kindred, *A Dictionary of Architects of Suffolk Buildings*, 111.

42 Colvin, *Dictionary*, 387.

43 Shrubland Hall archives, drawings, 11, 12, 13, 14, 15, 16, 17, 20 and 22.

free-standing portico was never built, the Middletons preferring to retain the existing arrangement, of a central pediment supported by attached Ionic pilasters.[44]

Published accounts often suggest that Gandy-Deering's activities at Shrubland were largely restricted to this remodelling of the west front; and that these alterations to Paine's house 'form the centre of Barry's enlarged mansion of 1848–52'.[45] But this, again, is a misunderstanding of Shrubland's history, for the expansion of Paine's house (itself already extended, as we have seen, in *c.*1808) was actually carried out by Gandy-Deering rather than by Barry. The principal additions were on the eastern side, where Paine's detached pavilions were now united with the main range by substantial two-storey ranges. At the same time an imposing new entrance was created in the centre of a screen running between the two pavilions, replacing the existing entrance on the west front. It took the form of a broad, free-standing corridor which contained an imposing flight of stairs, giving access to the first floor, where the principal apartments continued to be located. The space left between the new corridor, the old pavilions, the new additions and the screen formed two enclosed courtyards.[46] In addition to all this, a number of new rooms were added to the north of the house, and a substantial conservatory – a most imposing feature, which still survives in fine condition – to the south. The result was a rather asymmetrical elevation, although the sheer scale of the new building tends to rather conceal this fact (Fig. 4c). The principal rooms were all on the west front, and formed a sequence (from north to south) of dining room, ante room, drawing room, and library. The south-eastern portion of the original Paine's block was now fitted out as a billiard room, but the rest of the house was occupied by bedrooms, dressing rooms, service rooms and servants' accommodation.[47] Gandy-Deering's work provided the Middletons not only with a much larger house (containing a more extended range of entertaining rooms appropriate to their status as major landowners): but also with a more fashionable one, in a restrained Italianate mode. This choice presumably owed much to the Middleton's own taste. Gandy-Deering's initial Neo-classical designs appear more striking to the modern eye, but to contemporaries probably seemed rather old-fashioned.

The Middletons' Garden 1830–1850

Equally important changes were taking place in the grounds of the house. The return of structured gardens to the main facades of country seats, and the increasing elaboration and proliferation of gardens and pleasure grounds – fashions pioneered by Repton at the start of the nineteenth century – continued through the

44 The appearance of the house after Gandy-Deering's alterations is indicated by elevations made immediately before the further alterations carried out by Barry in the late 1840s; see Shrubland Hall archives, drawings, 23–8. These form the basic source for Fig. 4c.

45 Brown, Haywood and Kindred, *A Dictionary of Architects of Suffolk Buildings*, 111.

46 See in particular Shrubland Hall archives, drawings, 11.

47 Shrubland Hall archives, drawings, 11.

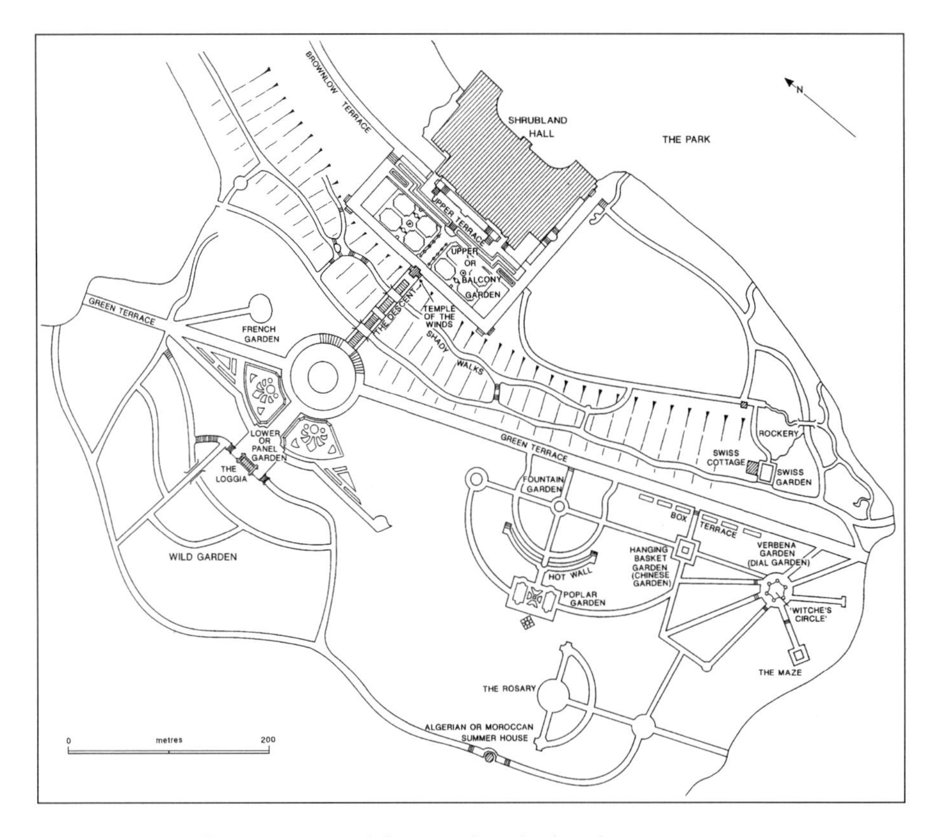

Fig. 6. Map showing principal features described in the text.

1830s and 40s.[48] The Middletons were at the forefront of these developments, and the gardens at Shrubland Hall were among the most celebrated in England. Their principal features still survive, maintained in fine condition. Conventional garden history, as we have seen, ascribes most if not all of this to Barry. But once again, closer inspection reveals a more complex history.

The layout of the nineteenth-century gardens, after Barry's work had been completed, is difficult to describe in words and the reader is advised to examine the plan (Fig. 6). The upper garden or *Balcony Garden* forms a wide level area immediately below the hall and its terrace (i.e. it occupies level ground immediately above the escarpment). It is surrounded by stone balustrading and originally contained a number of elaborate parterres. In the centre of its western side, facing the hall, is a small stone building, variously called the *Temple of the Winds* or the *Pavilion*. This gives direct access to the *Descent*, an immensely impressive flight of balustraded stone steps, ornamented with urns and interrupted by a number of landings, which is flanked by box hedging and a variety of evergreen shrubs and trees (Fig. 1). Passing

48 B. Elliott, *Victorian Gardens*, London 1986.

beneath the steps through a wide tunnel is a broad path, the 'shady walk', which meanders along the densely wooded slope of the escarpment.

The steps divide at the bottom, where they give access to the Lower Garden or *Panel Garden*, again balustraded, and with a central fountain. To north and south of the fountain basin are scrolls of yew which originally defined low-growing parterres, also featuring bedding plants; while to the west was, and is, a double sunken parterre ranged either side of an axial walk. This terminates at an imposing *Loggia* on the western side of the garden. From here, steps lead down to an area of wild garden, containing a rustic bridge, dells, pools, paths and other features.

Crossing the main line of the vista from the Descent to the Loggia is the *Green Terrace*, a ruler-straight grassed path which runs along the base of the escarpment for *c.*250 metres to the north of the fountain, and for *c.*500 to the south. To the north, its line is continued beyond the garden, out into the parkland, as an avenue, and as a vista cut through the woods on the hill beyond. The Terrace was, and is, flanked on its eastern side by areas of woodland and shrubbery running up the steep slope towards the house and upper garden; and on the west by areas of ordered and architectural gardens. Indeed, strung along the Terrace are a number of separate gardens: there were formerly several more. One – the *French Garden* – lay immediately to the north of the Panel Garden. This was a scrollwork parterre surrounded by an elaborate sculpted hedge, which has entirely disappeared.[49] The others lay to the south of the Panel Garden. First, on the western side of the path, came the *Fountain Garden*, a circular parterre of bedding plants, which still survives in simplified form, as does the curving heated *Conservative Wall* which forms its western side. Downhill, to the west, lay the *Poplar Garden*, which has now entirely disappeared; a fate which has also befallen the elaborate *Rosary* which lay a little further to the west.

To the south of the Fountain Garden, and linked directly to it by a straight path, was the *Hanging Basket Garden*, later called the *Chinese Garden*, a complex iron frame supporting a large planked flower basket: and to the east of this, running parallel to and beside the Green Terrace, was the *Box Terrace*, a long thin platform of scrollwork, of box and silver sand, with some 'tiny flower beds' (Fig. 7). This ran all the way from the Fountain Garden southwards as far as the *Dial Garden* (originally known as the Verbena Garden) which again lay immediately below, and to the west of, the Green Terrace. Opposite, on the eastern side of the terrace, was (and is) the *Swiss Garden*, complete with Swiss Cottage, rustic bridge and rockwork. To the west lay a feature, now a raised bed and known as the *Witches' Circle*, originally an arrangement of planting around a large yew; to the south-west of this was the *Maze*, planted with box and recently restored by Lord de Saumarez.

[49] This description of the gardens is based on a number of accounts made in the 1850s and 60s. See, in particular, *Gardeners' Chronicle*, Oct. and Nov. 1867, 1099–1100, 1123; 1170; *Gardeners' Chronicle*, Jan. 1868, 9, 31, 55; *Cottage Gardener*, 29 Sept. 1853, 495–7; *Cottage Gardener*, 6 Oct. 1854, 5–7; *Cottage Gardener*, 23 Sept. 1856, 452–4, 469–71; *Cottage Gardener*, 21 Oct. 1856, 39–41; *Cottage Gardener*,13 Oct. 1857, 18; *The Florist*, May 1856, 151–5. E. Adveno Brooke, *The Gardens of England*, London 1858, unpaginated.

Fig. 7. The Box Terrace, as shown on a photograph of *c.*1860.

All these various gardens and features were separated by areas of lawn scattered with trees and shrubs, some in dense masses; isolated beds; and sculptures. They were connected by a network of straight and curving gravel and grass paths. One, skirting the western boundary of the gardens, ran past the Moss Summer House, also known as the 'Rustic', 'Moroccan' or 'Algerian' summer house, which originally stood in the area occupied by the Lower or Panel Garden.[50]

Charles Barry certainly did play an important part in the making of these astounding gardens. But his prominence was less evident to contemporaries than it is to some modern scholars. As an article in the *Gardeners' Chronicle* put it in 1867, 'Shrubland may be described as the embodiment of the artistic life of the late Sir William and Lady Middleton.'[51] In Adveno Brooke's *Gardens of England* (1858) Barry is *only* referred to in the context of the design of the house: he is not mentioned at all in relation to the gardens, the description noting that

> The designs for the gardens and parterres, and the main features of the mansion have been laid down by Sir William and Lady Middleton – a residence for a considerable time in Italy having imbued them with the spirit of the great masters there . . .[52]

50 It now stands in yet another position, some 200 metres to the north-east.

51 *Gardeners' Chronicle*, 26 Oct. 1867, 1099.

52 Adveno Brooke, *The Gardens of England*, unpaginated.

Sir William was certainly a keen horticulturalist, as well as being a well travelled Europhile. Letters written to him in the 1840s contains various references to the purchase of plants, and to miscellaneous horticultural matters.[53] One is from a plant collector, sponsored by Middleton, working in the forests of Brazil. But there is little doubt that it was *Lady* Middleton, working in close association with their head gardener, Donald Beaton, who was mainly responsible for the development of the gardens. Indeed, Shrubland played a key role in the development of horticulture and garden design in the two decades before the arrival of Barry.

The practice of 'bedding out' – the arrangement of exotic, half-hardy flowers in colourful geometric displays – was growing in popularity through the 1830s and 40s. Initially, a wide variety of plants was employed in designs, including many Mexican and Californian species. By the 1840s, however, a more limited range had become the standard palette of the gardener: Pelargoniums (called geraniums, somewhat confusingly, before the 1860s); Lobelia; Petunia; Verbena; Calceolaria; and Salvia splendens. Through hybridisation and careful selection the colour range of these flowers was extended, by the mid-1840s covering six main groups: yellow, purple, scarlet, blue, pink and white. There was considerable debate in the burgeoning gardening press about the ways in which these colours should be combined in displays. To begin with, under the under the influence of John Caie, head gardener to the Duke of Bedford, the main organising principle of such arrangements was that colours should be 'clean, simple and intelligible': that is, presented in solid masses, not mixed together.[54] But in the 1830s and 40s new forms of bedding were developed, particularly at Trentham by John Fleming, and at Shrubland, by Donald Beaton, who took up the post of head gardener in 1838. Two important innovations were tried here: the ribbon border, a long narrow bed arranged in rows; and the practice of *shading*. This was a revolutionary way of organising colour in a bed, invented (according to Beaton) by Lady Middleton herself. Rows or groups of plants with similar colour were planted next to each other, to 'blend so perfectly that you cannot tell where one ends or the other begins', thus creating seamless spreads of colour. The two developments were intimately connected, as Beaton explained in 1856.

> It is now over twenty years since ribbon planting was originated by Lady Middleton on a twelve-feet wide border, which is almost seventy yards long. This style, unless it is rigidly carried out on the system of contrasts, as the scarlet and yellow is at the Crystal Palace, cannot fail, sooner or later, to suggest that other system called shading . . .[55]

The latter practice was first attempted in the early 1840s in the Fountain Garden, 'and in a year or two after that three tolerable shades of pink, purple, blue and yellow were obtained, and are kept up to the present day'.

By the time that Beaton left Shrubland in 1850, to pursue a career as editor of the journal *Cottage Gardener* (and adviser on bedding at Kew), the gardens here were

53 Shrubland Hall archives, SA 1/1/5.
54 Elliott, *Victorian Gardens*, 87–90, 123–8.
55 *Cottage Gardener*, Sept. 1856, 470.

not only large and complex but also famous. So too was Beaton himself: in the words of the *Gardeners' Chronicle*, looking back from 1867 to the 1840s, Donald Beaton 'made the place and himself honoured names throughout the kingdom'.[56] By 1848 the annual bill for maintaining the Shrubland gardens was already in excess of £1,195.[57] Unfortunately, while the period of Barry's alterations in the 1850s is extremely well documented in the Shrubland archives, there is much less information concerning the development of the gardens in the 1830s and 40s. In a similar way, the rapid growth in the gardening press in the 1850s and 60s ensures detailed descriptions of the garden which are lacking for the 1830s and 40s. These descriptions, however – especially those penned by Beaton himself – do provide some retrospective information about earlier developments and these, together with various stray references in the estate and public archives, allow the principal features of the gardens, as they were at the time of Barry's arrival in 1848, to be reconstructed.

Immediately below the west front of Gandy-Deering's mansion – roughly in the area now occupied by the Balcony Garden – was a small Italianate terrace bounded by a low wall set at intervals with urns – a kind of diminutive version of the later garden. Below, on gently sloping ground above the more precipitous escarpment, was a wide lawn set with islands of shrubs, and interspersed with cypresses and other trees. Both are illustrated in a number of drawings in the Shrubland archive. Beaton described this area in 1853, after it had been destroyed by Barry's improvements: 'in my busy days, the west front opened on two terraces, one above the other, with flights of steps at either end, and a middle flight on the second terrace. From the bottom of the second terrace to the brow of the hill the ground sloped considerably, and on this slope the Italian garden stood where *Punch* first made his appearance . . .' (this was one of the celebrated Shrubland Pelargoniums developed by Beaton).[58] It was called the Italian garden, and consisted – according to Beaton in 1854 – 'chiefly of nine large beds, four on each side, and one in the centre; in each of the eight side beds an Italian cypress (*Cupressuss sempervirens*) was planted in the middle'.[59]

A number of garden areas lay at the foot of the escarpment, quite separate from, and not visually linked to, the 'Italian Garden' and the mansion above. As one visitor put it in 1850, when Barry's alterations were getting under way, 'seeing the House from the Grounds appears hitherto to have been avoided'.[60] Moving from north to south, the first of these gardens was a Rosary, which lay in the area now occupied by the Panel garden, and which was destroyed by its construction.[61] Next came the Fountain Garden, which Beaton (as noted above) implies was in existence by the early 1840s. A design for the frieze which surmounts the Conservative Wall on its

56 *Gardeners' Chronicle*, 26 Oct. 1867, 1099.
57 Shrubland Hall archives, SA 1/2/30.
58 *Cottage Gardener*, 29 Sept. 1853, 493.
59 *Cottage Gardener*, 6 Oct. 1854, 5.
60 Shrubland Hall archives, SA 10/1/5.
61 Shrubland Hall archives, correspondence, Davidson to Middleton, SA 1/1/8, 24 Jan. 1852 and 1 Feb. 1852.

western side exists in the Shrubland archives, folded and sent as a letter and postmarked 1841.[62] A number of undated designs for this area also exist.[63]

To the west of the Conservative Wall lay an area of raised beds, where Beaton experimented with a particular form of shading, in the form of shot silk, in the 1840s.[64] This was later, during the 1850s, incorporated within (or simply renamed as?) the Poplar Garden. Further south lay the maze, which was created by Beaton as one of his final works before his departure from Shrubland. The Swiss Garden to the east was in existence by this time – the Swiss Cottage is clearly shown on the Tithe Award map for Barham, surveyed in 1840.[65] The Moss/Rustic/ Moroccan/Algerian summer house was also in existence before 1850. It originally stood in, or beside, the Rosary, and letters describe how it had to be moved to a new site when the Descent was constructed.[66] The Hanging Basket garden originated as early as 1838, or so Beaton suggested in 1856.[67]

Barry at Shrubland

Careful examination of estate archives and contemporary published accounts thus suggests that Shrubland Hall had attained much of its present form and layout before the arrival of Charles Barry in 1848. Of equal importance, the gardens laid out at the foot of the escarpment were already extensive, elaborate, and famous. Indeed, most of the principal garden areas described in the 1850s, and surviving to this day, had already been established under the direction of Donald Beaton and Lady Middleton.

What, then of Charles Barry? His contribution to Shrubland may have been exaggerated by later writers, but he was nevertheless responsible for a number of important changes and additions, to both house and grounds. The character of his alterations to the west front of the house, executed in the years 1848–50, are indicated in Fig. 4d. As well as making various minor changes of detailing, he removed the central pediments to the east and west fronts and erected additional balustrades to obscure the roof line; added rustication to the ground floor of the north wing; and, most strikingly, built the tall tower to the south of the building, a structure which dominates the surrounding landscape, and which affords magnificent views out across the grounds. Barry originally played with the idea of having a much taller, central tower, and with adding a balancing tower at the northern end of the building, options apparently rejected by the Middletons in favour of the present, dramatically asymmetrical, arrangement.[68] On the east front, he added two vestibules,

62 Shrubland Hall archives, uncatalogued.
63 Shrubland Hall archives, drawings, 1 and 2; the former is by the architect A. Roos.
64 SROI, P461/11.
65 Shrubland Hall archive, drawings, 1 and 2.
66 Shrubland Hall archives, correspondence, Davidson to Middleton, SA 1/1/8, 1 Feb. 1852.
67 *Cottage Gardener*, 23 Sept. 1856, 471.
68 Shrubland Hall archives, drawings currently being catalogued.

intended for the display of sculpture, flanking the entrance to Gandy-Deering's long entrance corridor: well proportioned rooms with niches at their furthest ends. These changes certainly amounted to a significant modification to the building, but they were less far-reaching, perhaps, than has sometimes been supposed.[69]

Barry's key contribution to the grounds was, of course, the creation of the Balcony Garden, the Panel Garden, and the Descent linking them. This ensemble is, indeed, *the* great feature of Shrubland, and seems to follow naturally from his earlier endeavours at Trentham in Staffordshire between 1834 and 1842.[70] But it is worth noting that this whole arrangement appears to have developed piecemeal, rather than having been conceived as a single scheme from the start; and that as we might expect the Middletons, and especially Lady Middleton, were as involved as Barry in the evolution of the design.

The Balcony Garden was planned in the summer of 1850. The first explicit reference to the project in the Shrubland archive comes in August of that year, when Barry wrote to Sir William: 'I approve of Lady Middleton's plan for the Lower Grand Terrace [i.e. the Balcony garden[71]] and the proposed termination of it with the seat.'[72] The contract for the garden was awarded in December 1850 and construction work continued until the end of the year.[73] Attention then turned to the design of the planting, and in December 1851 Barry was apologising to the Middletons that he had been so busy that he had 'only time to *think* about your modifications of my plan for the Parterres at Shrubland'.[74]

So far as the evidence goes, the original idea was to link the gardens in the immediate vicinity of the house, with those at the foot of the escarpment, by an elaborate flight of steps located some way to the south of the Descent, terminating near the Fountain Garden.[75] The Descent in its present form, and location, was apparently the idea of the Middletons, for on 31 December 1851 Barry wrote to Sir William:

> I have no objection to your present proposal of a Villa d'Este descent from the Pavilion opposite to the centre of House to the Gardens below; on the contrary I believe that many advantages and great effect would result from it: but it will I think entail upon you the necessity of making considerable alteration to the laying

69 Shrubland was not the only country house where Barry's contribution amounted, in effect, to an Italianate makeover. His treatment of Harewood in Yorkshire a decade before Shrubland was in many ways similar. Here too he removed the pediment and added a continuous roofline balustrade, and made other alterations to the garden front, but made comparatively few changes to the house in terms of size or internal layout: see M. Mauchline, *Harewood House*, Newton Abbot 1974, 126–8.

70 Elliott, *Victorian Gardens*, 74–8.

71 'Lower' in relation to the narrow terrace beside the hall erected by Gandy-Deering.

72 Shrubland Hall archives, correspondence, Barry to Middleton, SA 1/1/7, 31 Aug. 1850.

73 Shrubland Hall archives, SA 10/1.

74 Shrubland Hall archives, correspondence, Barry to Middleton, SA 1/1/7, 22 Dec. 1851.

75 There are two different plans for this: one labelled 'Mr Roos' design, unexecuted'; the other by Charles Barry, featuring an elaborate belvedere at the top of the hill. Shrubland Hall archives, drawings, 3 and 33.

> out of the Lower garden in order to create a feature of sufficient importance and effect to be worthy of such a descent.[76]

And thus the idea of the Lower or Panel garden was born, and the existing Rosary which occupied its site was swept away. The correspondence in the Shrubland archive leaves little doubt that the Middletons were actively involved in the development of the design of this area, too. On April 22 1852, for example, Barry's son wrote that his father could not give an opinion on the Middleton's proposal for the fountain in the Lower Garden until 'he receives the plan you mention in your letter as not quite finished'.[77]

We should also note that other changes were going on in the gardens in the early 1850s, in which Barry does not seem to have had any part. New garden areas, including a new Rosary (to replace the old one, swept away to make room for the Panel Garden), were created, and the Green Terrace was laid out – or at least, attained its present form – in 1851. These works, together with the construction of the Balcony Garden, Descent, and Panel Garden, were completed by 1854, and Barry fades from view. Yet the gardens at Shrubland continued to develop after this date with the creation – probably in 1855 – of the Wild Garden, below the Panel Garden, again under the direction of Lady Middleton. The *Gardeners' Chronicle* in 1867, describing this area, noted how 'In one of those rapid transitions for which the late Lady Middleton was famous, undressed Nature, in the form of rough wooded scene, creeps right up to the base of this highly artistic wall.'[78]

Conclusion

The completed grounds and house at Shrubland were described in glowing terms by E. Adveno Brooke in 1858:

> The fine mansion with its temples and terraces, the glittering fountains, the exquisite Italian and Moorish gardens, bedecked with innumerable flowers and ornamented with sculpture, and the far-spreading landscape beyond, altogether form a scene such as none can either properly describe or easily forget.[79]

Sir Charles Barry certainly did play a very important part in the creation of this Victorian extravaganza. Yet, as I hope I have shown, he did not have the central, pivotal role that is sometimes implied, or assumed. Indeed, it is noteworthy that in the biography written by his son in 1867 little more is claimed for Barry than has been suggested here. The original hall, he writes, 'had been considerably altered in 1830 from the design of Mr Gandy Deering'. Barry worked with this existing structure:

76 Shrubland Hall archives, correspondence, Barry to Middleton, SA 1/1/7, 31 Dec. 1851.
77 Shrubland Hall archives, correspondence, Barry to Middleton, SA 1/1/7, 22 April 1852.
78 *Gardeners' Chronicle*, 1867, 1123.
79 Adveno Brooke, *The Gardens of England*, unpaginated.

> He added a new entrance, with a sculpture gallery on each side. At the same time he raised a portion of the house, so as to form a beautiful specimen of his favourite Italian towers, and substituted balustrades for the large pediments surmounting the various fronts . . .[80]

His activities in the grounds were similarly limited, restricted to the design of a new lodge[81] and the construction of the Balcony Garden, Descent, and Lower Garden. These latter features were necessary, we learn, because the existing gardens while 'beautiful in themselves . . . seemed to agree too little with the house, which had now assumed some architectural pretensions'.[82] We get here the sense of a talented architect 'tweaking', as it were, what was already a well developed piece of architecture and landscape design: 'Few works produced so much effect, considering their scale . . . as those at Shrubland Park.'

As so often happens, the history of a country house and its grounds have been considerably over-simplified by later generations. In the case of Shrubland, we are fortunate in having a particularly rich archive which allows something of the true, and rather complicated, story to be reconstructed. Elsewhere we are usually less fortunate. Illustrations, plans, proposals and letters make it clear that the nineteenth-century mansion and its grounds were the work of a number of gifted individuals – Gandy-Deering and Donald Beaton as much as Charles Barry – and that the whole great enterprise was closely orchestrated and directed by Sir William and Lady Middleton. Yet all their works rested, very firmly, upon much earlier foundations.

80 A. Barry, *The Life of Sir Charles Barry*, London 1867, 18.

81 Lack of space precludes any discussion of the changes made to the wider parkland in the 1840s and 50s; suffice it to say that the Middletons were very active here, too, carrying out much planting and extending the park to the east. A number of new lodges were erected in this period: one, the Needham Lodge, was designed by Barry (possibly altering an existing building, for a lodge is shown here on the Barham Tithe Award map: SROI, P461/11). The south lodge was the work of the architect A. Roos and probably built in 1841; the Coddenham Lodge was erected after the new road was laid out on the eastern edge of the park in 1848–9.

82 Barry, *Life of Sir Charles Barry*, 119.

Garden Canals in Suffolk

Edward Martin

IN 1724 the architect John James (*c.*1672–1746) of Greenwich built himself a country house – Warbrooks House at Eversley in Hampshire. In front of the house he placed a long, formal, piece of water that he would have described as a 'canal'. James was a keen gardener, a member of the Society of Gardeners, and the translator of an influential treatise on gardening. Published in 1712, James's *The Theory and Practice of Gardening* was a translation of a work by Antoine-Joseph Dezallier D'Argenville that had first appeared in Paris in 1709. In the book he comments on the various water features to be found in gardens:

> For the Form and Figure of Basons, they are most commonly round; however we have some octangular, oblong, oval, square &c. When these Bason exceed a certain size; they are called Pieces of Water, Canals, Mirrours, Fish-Ponds, Pools, and Reservoirs.

These canals were not the waterways used by commercial barges, but were long and thin ponds that were decorative features in formal gardens – to make the distinction clearer I have called them 'garden canals'. Their popularity in the early eighteenth century can be gauged from the high percentage of gardens with canals that are illustrated in Johannes Kip and Leonard Knyff's *Britannia Illustrata* of 1707. However, when formal gardens went out of fashion later in the eighteenth century, many canals were infilled. The loss was so high that when the National Trust restored the canal at Westbury Court in Gloucestershire, they were able to claim it as 'one of the rarest types of garden to have survived in this country'.[1] The work at Westbury has led to renewed interest in some of the other surviving canals, of which those at Hampton Court Palace, Wrest Park in Bedfordshire, and Shotover Park in Oxfordshire are notable examples.

P.F. Springett first brought the existence of the canals at Campsey Ash in Suffolk to the attention of garden historians in an article published in 1974, in which he

Acknowledgements. I am indebted to John Blatchly, Cynthia Brown, David Dymond, Timothy Easton, Rachel Lawrence, Joanna Martin, John Newman, Valerie Norrington, Joan Peck, Monica Place, Jenny Robinson and Anthea Taigel for information about canals. I am also very grateful to all the owners who, at various times, have let me look at their ponds and canals.

1 G. Jackson Stops, *Westbury Court Garden*, National Trust guide, 1988.

compared them to those at Westbury Court.[2] Yet they remained isolated curiosities for a decade and a half. In October 1990 I was invited to investigate a possible fragment of a moat that was being desilted at Boundary Farm, Framsden. The visit rapidly disclosed that this was not a moat, but a long, straight, pond, with a terrace on one side. The only sensible parallels were, once again, the canals at Westbury Court. The fieldwork carried out on this site was probably the first instance of intentional 'garden archaeology' in the county.[3] This discovery led to the identification of further canals that had been previously misidentified as moat fragments or dismissed as mere ponds. Now, after a decade of discovery, a list of fifty-six certain and possible canals can be compiled (see the Gazetteer). Amazingly, in view of the received wisdom about the scarcity of surviving canals nationally, a high proportion of these are still recognisable and water-filled.

The Idea of a Canal

The origin of canals is complex. Some garden historians have looked to Holland for the source of the fashion, citing the drainage canals which surrounded and flowed through many of the gardens in that country.[4] Some have even gone as far as to describe them as 'Dutch' gardens.[5] Others stressed the French prototypes at Fleury-en-Bière (sixteenth-century) and Fontainebleau (1609).[6] Canal-like features can be seen in a number of mid-sixteenth-century engravings of French gardens by J.A. du Cerceau (e.g. Gaillon, Dampierre and Vallery).[7] There was also a long tradition of water features in English gardens stretching back to the moats, fishponds and decorative meres of the middle ages.[8] Although a canal-like feature appeared as early as 1609–29 in the design of the formal garden laid out for Baptist Hicks, first vis-

2 P.F. Springett, ' "Westbury in Suffolk"? or the Lost Garden of Ashe High House', *Journ. of Garden History* 2 pt 3, 1974, 77–89; and ' "Detective Story": Further Enquiries into the Lost Garden at Campsea Ashe, Suffolk', *ibid.* 3 pt 3, 1975, 62–75.

3 E. Martin, T. Easton and I. McKechnie, 'Conspicuous Display: The Extraordinary Garden and Buildings of a Minor Gentry Family in Mid Suffolk', *PSIA* xxxviii pt 1, 1993, 56–74.

4 D. Jacques and A. van der Horst, *The Gardens of William and Mary,* London 1988, 142; J. Dixon Hunt and E. de Jonge, 'The Anglo-Dutch Garden in the Age of William and Mary', *Journ. of Garden History* 8, no. 2/3, 1988, 43–4.

5 I. Triggs, *Formal Gardens in England and Scotland,* London 1902, vol. I, 32; G. Mott, *Follies and Pleasure Pavilions,* London 1989, 112.

6 G. and S. Jellicoe, P. Goode and M. Lancaster, eds, *The Oxford Companion to Gardens,* Oxford 1986, 91 and 188.

7 W.H. Adams, *The French Garden 1500–1800,* London 1979, 26, 28–9.

8 P. Everson, ' "Delightfully Surrounded with Woods and Ponds": Field Evidence for Medieval Gardens in England', in P. Pattison, ed., *There by Design: Field Archaeology in Parks and Gardens,* BAR British Series 267, 1998, 32–8. A striking depiction of a Continental decorative mere can be seen in the background of an anonymous Rhenish painting of *c.*1480, which shows a rectangular mere within which there is a pleasure pavilion – illustrated in F. Gardini, *Europe 1492,* New York and Oxford 1989, 113.

count Campden, at Chipping Camden in Gloucestershire,[9] there can be no doubt that the fashion was really started by King Charles II. On his return from exile, when he would have had opportunities to see both Dutch and French gardens, he commissioned two very dramatic canals of great length, one measuring 853m long x 30m wide at St James's Palace, 1660–61, and another at Hampton Court in 1662. The work was probably overseen by the king's French gardeners, André and Gabriel Mollet, although it is just possible that Louis XIV's own gardener, André le Nôtre, may also have helped with work at Hampton Court.[10] Le Nôtre certainly created a magnificent canal, 1585m long x 122m wide, for Louis at Versailles, *c.*1662–8. King Charles's garden inspired the poet Edmund Waller to write 'A Poem on St James's Park as lately improved by his Majesty', published in 1661.

Although introduced in 1660, it was not until about the 1690s that the fashion for canals took a firm hold. The influence of King William III was probably crucial in this. In 1724 Daniel Defoe commented 'on the strange passion for fine gardens, which has so commendably possess'd the English gentleman of late years, for 'tis evident it is but of late years'. Defoe went on state that this had happened since the accession of William III, who had introduced 'the love of gardening'. For their part, the gentlemen 'follow'd every where, with such a gust that the alteration is indeed wonderful thro' the whole kingdom'. He noted 'that fine gardens, and fine houses began to grow up in every corner'.[11] Kip and Knyff's *Britannia Illustrata* (1707) can be seen as a celebration of these recent achievements, their pictures doubtless inspiring yet more gardens.

The end of the fashion was a gradual affair, caused by the increasing popularity of informal styles of gardening from the 1730s, championed by Alexander Pope (1688–1744), Stephen Switzer (1682–1745) and William Kent (1685–1748). In 1771 that barometer of fashion, Horace Walpole, could refer to the garden at Wrest Park as 'very ugly in the old fashioned manner with high hedges and canals'.[12] By the end of the century they were so out of fashion that in 1791 Humphry Repton, in his Red Book for Garnons at Mansell Gamage, Herefordshire, could assert with confidence that 'As an object of beauty, there can be no room to hesitate about destroying the pond [actually a canal] in front of the present house'.[13] A reaction to this attitude, led by John Claudius Loudon (1783–1843), resulted in a revival of interest in formal gardens in the Victorian period, and the creation of some late canals.

9 P. Everson, 'The Gardens of Campden House, Chipping Camden, Gloucestershire', *Garden History* 17 pt 2, 1989, 109–21.

10 G. Gollwitzer, 'The Influence of Le Nostre on the Euopean Gardens of the Eighteenth Century', in E.B. Macdougall and F.H. Hazlehurst, eds, *The French Formal Garden*, Washington 1974, 79.

11 P.N. Furbank, W.R. Owen and A.J. Coulson, eds, *Daniel Defoe, A Tour through the Whole Island of Great Britain*, New Haven and London 1991, 65.

12 L.C. Halpern, 'The Duke of Kent's Garden at Wrest Park', *Journ. of Garden History* 15 no. 3, 1995, 150.

13 L. Fleming and A. Gore, *The English Garden*, London 1979, 152 and pl. 93.

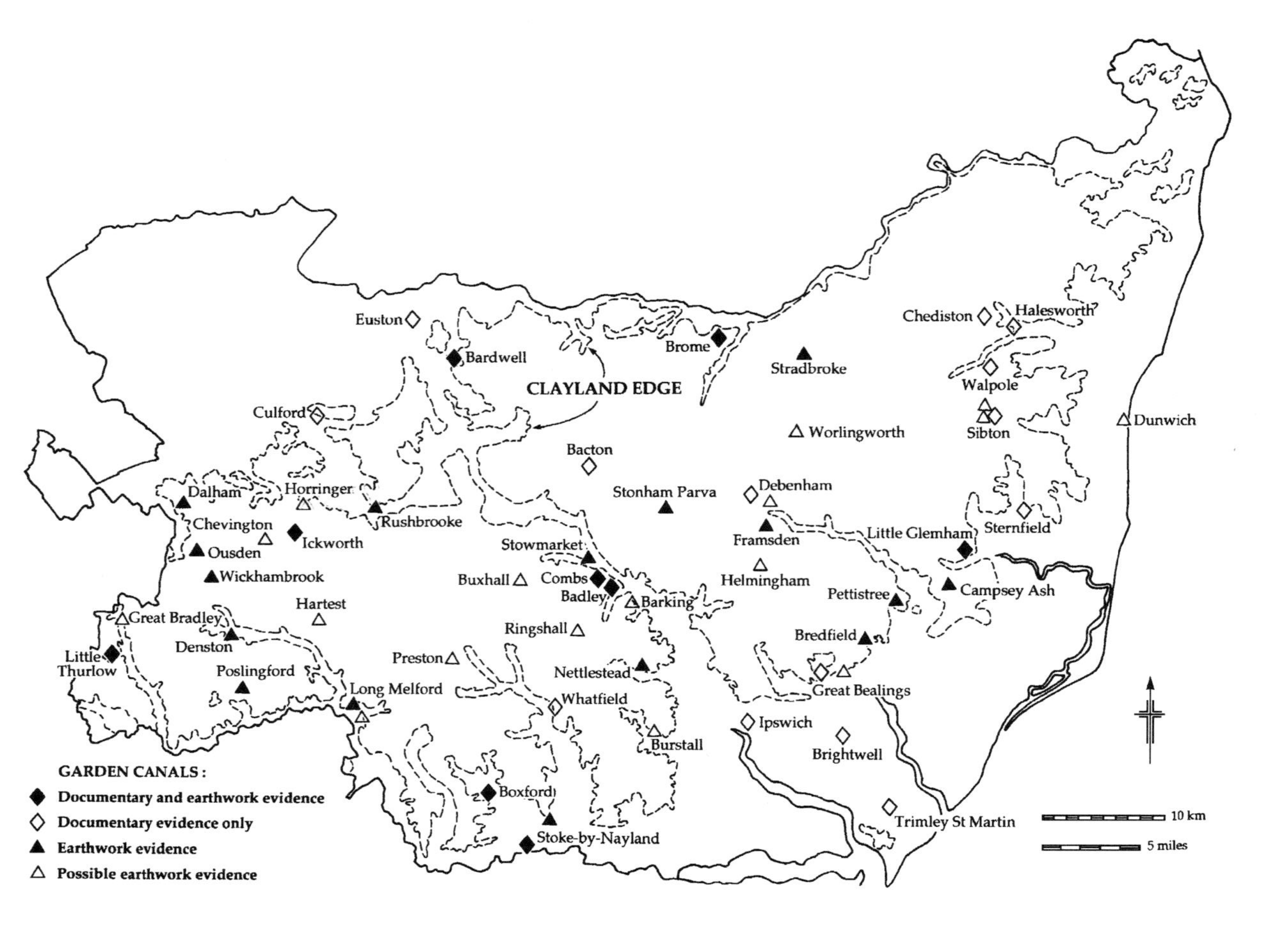

Fig. 1. Garden canals in Suffolk.

The Suffolk Evidence

Details of the canals mentioned here can be found in the Gazetteer (pp. 228–41) below.

The earliest recorded canal in Suffolk was that at Euston, which appears to have been built by 1669. It builder was Henry Bennet, earl of Arlington. The very early appearance of a canal here must be due to Arlington's close links with Charles II – not only was he Secretary of State to the king, but his daughter and eventual heiress was married, in 1672, to Charles's illegitimate son, Henry Fitz-Roy, duke of Grafton. Arlington did, however, also have Dutch connections, in that his wife was Isabella de Nassau.

Soon afterwards another canal was created at Christchurch Mansion in Ipswich. This is shown on a map surveyed in 1674 and was built by Leicester Devereux, viscount Hereford. He too had close links with Charles II, being one of the six peers who were deputed to invite Charles to return to England in 1660. There is then a gap until 1707, when the canals at Brightwell Hall and Brome Hall were depicted in engravings published in *Britannia Illustrata*.[14] The next certain canal is that at Ickworth, where John Hervey, first earl of Bristol, referred to his 'new Canall' in 1717. Thereafter there is documented evidence for a number of canals: at Little Glemham Hall by 1720; Boxford rectory by 1723; Tendring Hall, Stoke-by-Nayland, by 1723; 'Bardwell Hall Manor' (Moat Farm) by 1730; Little Thurlow Hall by 1735; Combs Hall by 1741 (but must have been made pre-1731); Badley Hall by 1741; Culford Hall by 1742; Walpole by 1759; Sternfield rectory *c.*1767; Whatfield rectory *c.*1735–73; Denston Hall by 1778; Bacton by 1783; Debenham rectory by 1790. The canals at Great Bealings Hall and Halesworth are recorded on mid-eighteenth-century maps. Those at Bredfield House and Abbot's Hall, Stowmarket are both associated with summerhouses of *c.*1710. The canal at Pettistree must be contemporary with the adjacent mount, which was in existence by 1741. For the remainder of the canals, the documentation is later, but this does not rule out earlier origins.

There are, however, enough dated examples to see that there was a period of great activity in the first forty years of the eighteenth century. However the fashion had peaked in aristocratic circles by about 1730. The canal at Euston, the first to appear, was also probably the first to disappear. When the gentleman-architect Sir Thomas Robinson of Rokeby Park in Yorkshire visited in 1731, a sinuous lake had appeared instead, and Robinson commented that 'the Duke [Charles Fitz-Roy, second duke of Grafton] has hitherto done very little to it [the park], but is now, entering into a taste'.[15] In the next two decades, Grafton's 'taste' would lead him to transform his park, with the help of William Kent.

In view of this early change in fashion, the estimate for a new canal at Sternfield

[14] It is, however, worth noting that these were the only Suffolk gardens illustrated in that work.

[15] Letter from Robinson to Lord Carlisle, quoted in W.G. Clarke, *In Breckland Wilds*, London 1925, 151–2.

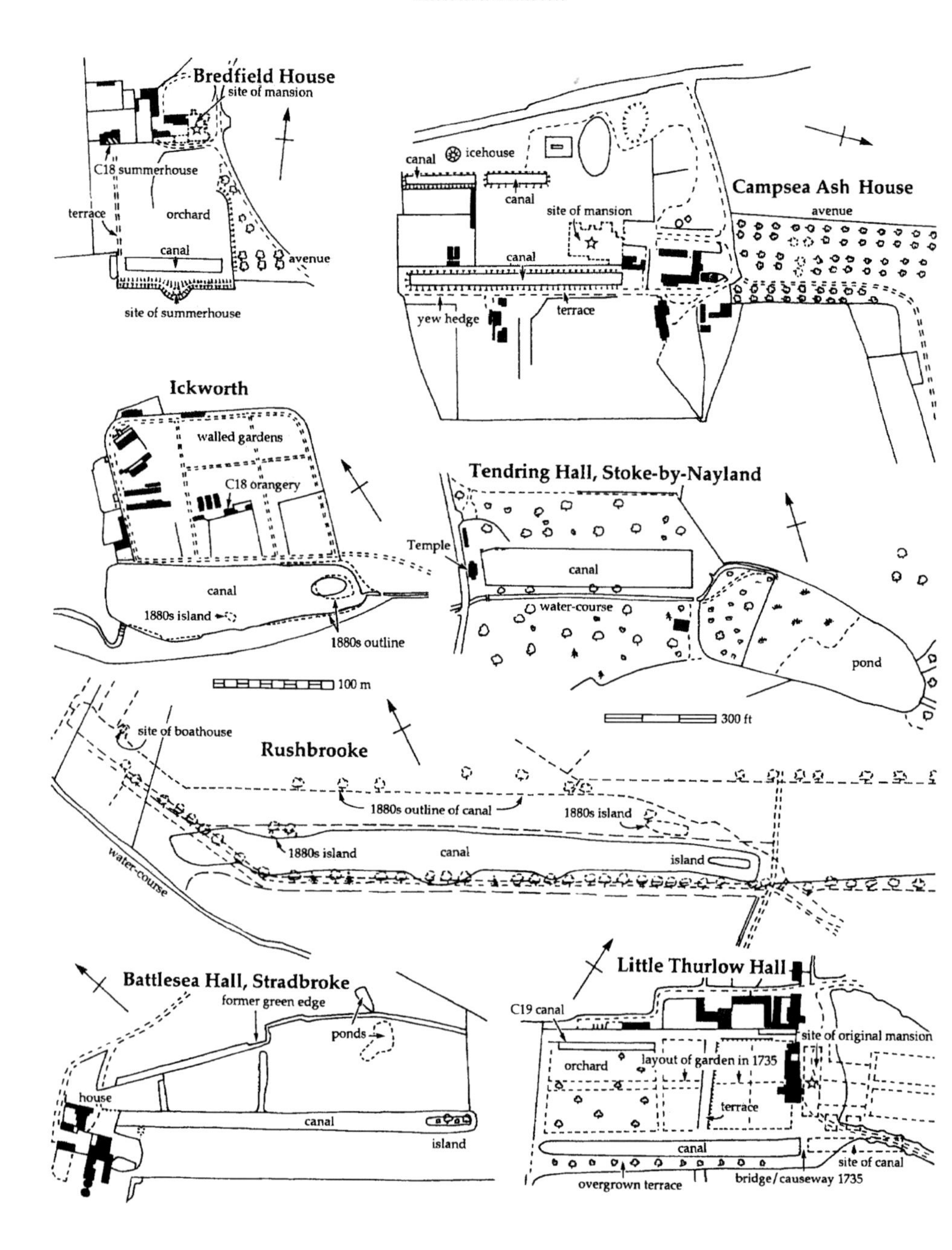

Fig. 2. Plans of selected canals in Suffolk.

rectory, *c.*1767, comes as a surprise. It is a warning not to see the interest in canals at a regional level as necessarily following national trends. The Sternfield canal is all the more surprising in that it was commissioned by an academic cleric whose father was a writer on architectural matters and might therefore have been expected to have been more influenced by contemporary fashions. Some of the canals are, moreover, likely to be the result of the Victorian revival of the fashion – notably those at Burstall, Chediston, Chevington, Dunwich, Hartest and Worlingworth.

Structure, Size and Associated Features

Some canals were created by damming, diverting or straightening streams, as at Combs, Euston, Ickworth and Sibton, but most of the Suffolk canals are, in effect, large ponds. As such, they needed an impervious lining to retain the water. In most cases, this lining was made of clay. The map (Fig. 1) shows that the majority of the surviving canals are in the areas of Suffolk with a clay subsoil, where a waterproof lining was easily and cheaply achieved. It is probably significant that most of the documented canals outside the clayland have failed to survive, largely one suspects because their linings proved less than durable. The canal at Tendring Hall, Stoke-by-Nayland, is off the clayland, but is fed by a strong spring and is still in excellent condition. Brick revetting of the sides is present at Badley, Campsey Ash and Stonham Parva, but the overgrown state of many canals may obscure other examples.

Not unnaturally, there is clear evidence that canal builders took advantage of pre-existing water features in their constructions. Streams were adapted at Combs and Sibton. Earlier ponds seem to have been utilised at Bredfield, Denston, Ickworth and Sibton. Medieval moats were converted into canals at Boxford, Great Bradley, Buxhall, Horringer, Long Melford (both Kentwell and Melford Halls) and Ousden. Normally the unwanted arms of the moat were infilled, but unusually, at Badmondisfield Hall, Wickhambrook, the other arms were screened off, but otherwise left intact. A former green-edge ditch was utilised at Worlingworth and a boundary ditch at Chevington.

The clearest evidence for the conversion of an earlier feature (a moat) comes from Boxford, where a glebe terrier of 1723 records:

> a Green Walk bounded by a Canal of a great Length [actually 68m long], & well stocked with Fish, and made by the late Incumbent in a place, where before was nothing but a foul stinking Ditch.[16]

The maker was John Warren, rector of Boxford 1683–1721, and the proud achievement was recorded by his son Thomas, rector 1721–35.

There are records of only a few garden designers in connection with Suffolk canals. At Ickworth the earl of Bristol, in 1714, purchased 'several evergreen and

16 SROB 806/1/17. I am grateful to Miss Jenny Robinson for this reference.

other plants' (to the value of £16 3s 6d) from 'Smith, Mr Wisa's partner'.[17] 'Wisa' was presumably Henry Wise (1653–1738), Master Gardener to Queen Anne and co-owner of the celebrated Brompton Park Nurseries in Kensington. Whether he offered any advice on the design of the canal is unknown. In 1734 the earl paid William Bridgeman for 'new making & planting my garden'.[18] William shares a surname with Charles Bridgeman (*c.*1685–1738), one of the leading garden designers of the time, but is otherwise unknown. The reference suggests that Bridgeman revamped the existing garden, but was not its original designer. At Little Glemham, a Mr Robinson was employed in the gardens by Dudley North in 1720, but appears to have been guilty of drinking too much ale with other 'Gentlemans Gardeners' who came to visit.[19] At Sternfield rectory, plans for a garden with a canal were prepared, with estimates of costs, by a Henry Ellison, *c.*1767. He is otherwise unknown as a garden designer, though a man of that name was a land agent in co. Durham in the 1720s.[20]

Canals vary considerably in size, though their dimensions are usually proportional, i.e. the width increases in proportion to the length, in keeping with the advice of contemporary writers like Dezallier D'Argenville. The proportions vary from about 1:3 at the wide canal at Ickworth, to 1:23 at the narrow example at Chevington, with most lying between 1:5 and 1:10 (Table 1).

Table 1. Lengths of Garden Canals in Suffolk

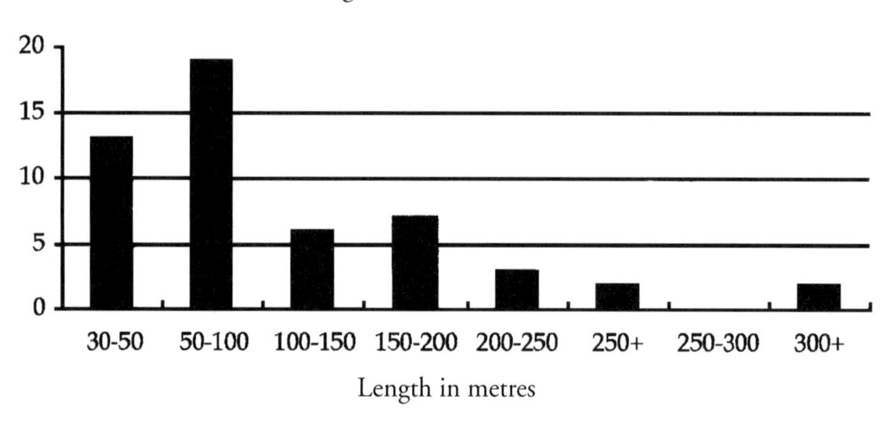

[17] *The Diary of John Hervey First Earl of Bristol*, ed. S.H.A Hervey, Wells 1894, 130. The earl also acquired plants in 1717 and 1718 from William Oram 'nursery man'.

[18] *Ibid.*, 130–1. In 1730 the earl paid Bridgeman 'for a year keeping up my garden'.

[19] SROI HA49/C2/5/2, letter from Daniel Wayth, estate agent, to Dudley North, Mar. 1719–20.

[20] *Dictionary of Land Surveyors and Local Cartographers of Great Britain and Ireland, Supplement*, ed. P. Eden, Folkestone 1979, 408.

As can be seen from Table 2, most canals fall between 50 and 100m in length. The longest canals are those at Stradbroke (300m) and Rushbrooke (460m).

Table 2. Proportions of Garden Canals in Suffolk

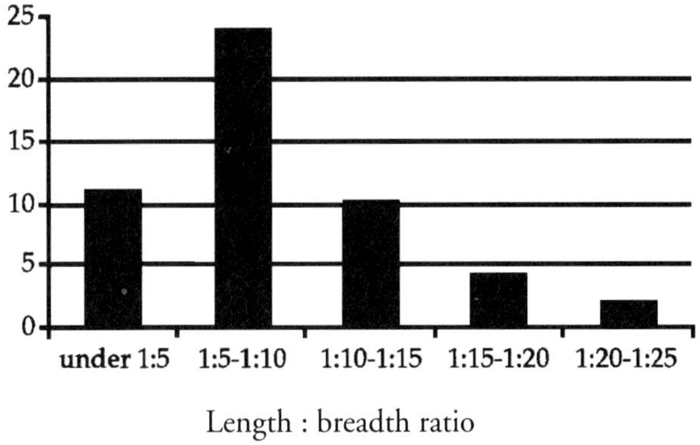

25
20
15
10
5
0
under 1:5 1:5-1:10 1:10-1:15 1:15-1:20 1:20-1:25

Length : breadth ratio

The canals at Preston, Stowmarket and Stradbroke all taper, but only at Stowmarket is the narrow end furthest from the expected main view point, thus adding an illusion of greater length. At Stradbroke, the taper would only work if the main viewpoint was the island at the south-east end. The probably late canal at Barking is waisted.

The canal at Framsden has a brick stair at one end, possibly the remains of a cascade. A cascade is also mentioned at the end of the canal at Euston in the 1670s – this powered a mill that both ground corn and pumped water for the fountains in the gardens. Islands within canals can be found at Barking, Rushbrooke (two), Stowmarket and Stradbroke. Nineteenth-century sources also indicate islands at various spots in the canal at Ickworth, but only one survives. The island at Stowmarket has a small eighteenth-century summerhouse on it and there was a round structure on the Barking island. Summerhouses or orangeries associated with canals occur at Bredfield, Brightwell, Ickworth, Melford Hall, Gifford's and Tendring Halls in Stoke-by-Nayland, and Wickhambrook. Earthen mounts are associated with canals at Buxhall, Pettistree and Ringshall. Nearly all the canals have walkways beside or around them, often on a raised terrace.

The planting of trees and shrubs beside canals is mentioned in a few places. At Euston, Edmund Prideaux's drawing of *c.*1716 shows a line of evenly spaced trees along one side of the canal, which recall those shown flanking the king's canal at Hampton Court Palace in an anonymous painting of *c.*1663–70.[21] Similar lines of trees are depicted as lining the walks beside the canals at Brightwell on Kip's engraving of 1707. Prideaux's view of Euston also shows a tall hedge bounding one side of the walk beside the canal. A substantial yew hedge still bounds one side of the walk

21 S. Thurley, *The Royal Palaces of Tudor England*, New Haven and London 1993, fig. 172.

adjacent to the canal at Campsey Ash. At Ickworth, in 1748, the earl of Bristol wrote to his 27-year-old grandson and heir that:

> I have been several times to see the alterations in the garden which as they seem to please you, need no other recommendation to have the same effect on me, altho' methinks I want my old acquaintances the yews about the Canal, which I used to think had a very good effect.[22]

The yews were presumably amongst the 'evergreen and other plants' that he purchased in 1714 'for my new Spring Garden', from 'Smith, Mr Wisa's partner' (as noted above).

The Hampton Court painting also shows that the canal was a projection of the formal garden into more naturalistic parkland, with deer grazing on the canal edge. Similar parkland settings occur at Dalham, Ickworth, Poslingford and Tendring Hall.

The Positioning of Canals

Analysis of the positions of canals relative to their associated houses indicates that a number of variants can be recognised:

1. Canal at right-angles to the front of the house and aligned on its central axis. This position gave most emphasis to the canal and the axis was frequently extended by having an avenue on the same alignment. Nationally, this category includes the important examples at Hampton Court Palace and Wrest Park. Suffolk examples include those at Culford, Dalham, Horringer (an arm of a pre-existing moat) and Stradbroke.

2. Canal at right-angles to a frontage of the house, but to one side of the central axis. Examples at Badley, Bardwell, Campsey Ash, Great Glemham, and Little Thurlow. The canal at Christchurch Mansion in Ipswich approximates to this position, but it is not at right-angles. A sub-group can be recognised where the canal was clearly made from an arm of a moat, as at Great Bradley, Buxhall, Long Melford and Ousden.

3. Canal parallel to a frontage of the house. The canal at Westbury Court in Gloucestershire is of this type. Suffolk examples are: Boxford (at the rear, adapted from an earlier moat), Brightwell, Brome, Bredfield (to the side or garden front), Chediston, Chevington, Combs, Euston, Framsden, Great Bealings, Hartest, Helmingham, Poslingford (parallel but to the side of the house), Preston, Ringshall (but only approximately parallel), Sibton Abbey, Sternfield, Gifford's Hall in Stoke-by-Nayland (side or garden front), Stonham Parva (but to one side) and Stowmarket. In several cases, the canal forms a 'break' feature between the garden and the park or surrounding landscape, as at Brightwell, Brome, Bredfield, Framsden, Gifford's Hall and Stowmarket.

[22] *Letter-Books of John Hervey, First Earl of Bristol*, ed. S.H.A. Hervey, 3 vols, Wells 1894, iii, 361, no. 1292.

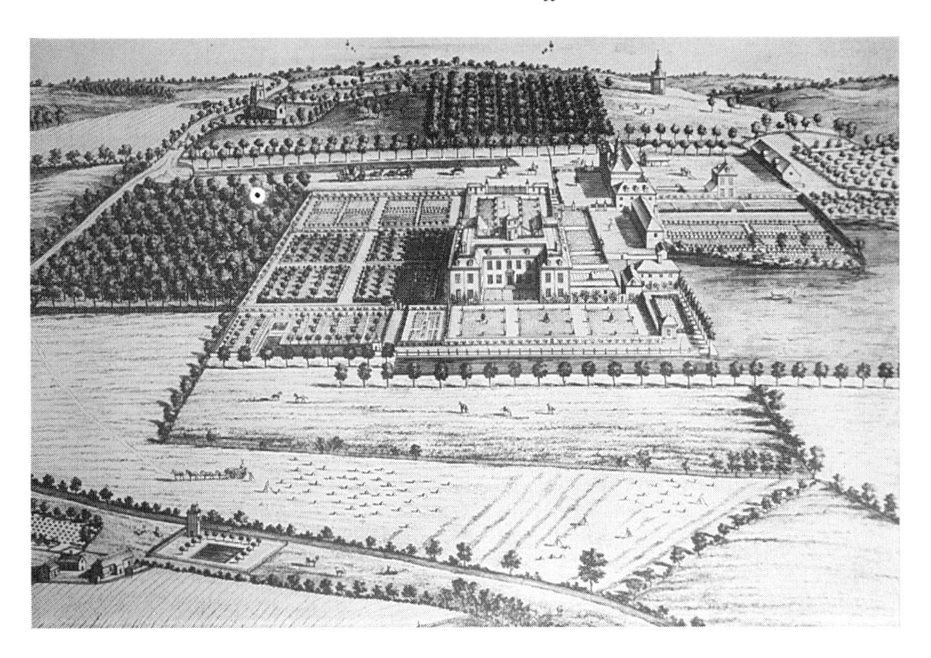

Plate 1. Brightwell Hall and its gardens: engraving by J. Kip 1707

Plate 2. Campsey Ash: view along the then-dry canal from the south

Plate 3. Ickworth: view northwards across the canal, towards the orangery

Plate 4. Tendring Hall, Stoke-by-Nayland: view along the canal towards the Temple at the west end

Plate 5. Battlesea Hall, Stradbroke: view along the recently desilted canal from the north

Plate 6. Little Thurlow Hall: view along the canal from the east

4. Canal in a detached setting. Examples are at Barking, Burstall, Crow's Hall in Debenham, Denston, Dunwich, Ickworth, Pettistree, Rushbrooke and Tendring Hall in Stoke-by-Nayland. In some cases, as at Ickworth, Rushbrooke and Tendring Hall, the canal's position was probably largely determined by practical considerations.

In several places there are multiple canals. Two each at Great Bealings Hall (at right-angles), Brightwell (on the same axis), Campsey Ash (parallel), Ringshall (parallel), Sibton Park (irregular arrangement), Stonham Parva (parallel). At Denston, three canals partially surround a lozenge-shaped garden.

The Status and Use of Canals

The building of a canal was a considerable expense; even a modest example like that at Sternfield (62 x 12m) was estimated to cost £13 5s 6d in about 1767, roughly equivalent to a year's wages for a labourer.[23] The canal was also frequently just one component of a large garden, usually with a formal layout. Even the small rectory garden at Boxford, in addition to its canal, could boast, in 1723, of a 'Parlour Garden' and 'a Large Square Courtyard, with a Gravel Walk in the Middle and Lime Trees on each side leading to the Road'. In the smaller gardens, however, a canal was clearly the dominant feature, as at Framsden. The creation of an ornamental garden was thus a visible display of wealth and leisure. As such, these gardens were clearly seen as indicators of gentry status. Virtually all of the early eighteenth-century examples can be shown to have belonged to members of the aristocracy or gentry. Even the small example at Framsden belonged to a man who claimed gentry status. Edward Mann's family had only recently risen above the level of yeomen. He was connected by marriage to two other recently risen families, the Sheppards of Campsey Ash and the Gibsons of Stonham Parva, both of whom also possessed canals. The clergy were also on the lowest rung of the gentry and it is noticeworthy that small canals feature in several parsonage gardens. By the nineteenth century, the social prestige of a garden had lessened and small canals feature in some farmhouse gardens, as at Worlingworth.

Canals were associated with a number of leisure pursuits. The terrace walks around many canals were linked with a desire to provide healthy exercise, particularly for ladies. The positioning of the canal often enabled the walker to admire not only the water of the canal, but also to look out into the adjoining park or landscape. The provision of summerhouses and orangeries near canals provided places for rest and refreshment while on a walk. The orangery at Euston was a particularly elaborate example, forming part of a whole wing of the house, but other structures were simpler, like the orangery at Ickworth and the summerhouses at Bredfield and Stowmarket. Associated buildings are also recorded at Barking, Brightwell, Stoke-by-Nayland and Wickhambrook.

23 L. Munby, *How much is that worth?* Chichester 1989, 31.

Boating was possible on the larger canals. Boat-houses are recorded, admittedly in late sources, at Barking, Great Bealings, and Rushbrooke (which has two islands that could only have been reached by boat). Kip's engraving of Brightwell, 1707, shows a rowing-boat on the lake that formed an extension of one of the canals. At Ickworth, the earl of Bristol recorded that in October 1717 'I narrowly escaped being drowned in my new Canall at Spring Garden in ye Parke'.[24] In 1724 he recalled the incident in more detail:

> 1717 I was yet in more imminent danger from being some time under water in my new-made canal here, with the boate (out of which I fell topsy turvy) driven by the wind over my head.[25]

The earl may have been fishing from his boat, as canals were frequently stocked with fish. Fish are specifically mentioned at Euston in 1677 (carp), at Bacton in 1782, and in an eighteenth-century survey of Little Thurlow. The canal at Walpole is referred to as a 'canal or fishpond' in 1759. The likely canals at Barking, Burstall, Helmingham and Stowmarket are in fact labelled as 'fishponds' on Ordnance Survey (OS) maps. The pavilion at the end of the canal at Tendring Hall, Stoke-by-Nayland, is sometimes called 'The Fishing Temple'.[26] Fishing with rods became a popular gentry pursuit in the eighteenth century, for both men and women, as can be seen in contemporary paintings.[27]

Conclusion

The number of canals makes it clear that they played an important part in the design of gardens in Suffolk in the first half of the eighteenth century. Their popularity may well be due to the fact that the Suffolk gentry were already accustomed to water features in their gardens, particularly the moats that their ancestors had dug to enhance and ennoble their houses in the middle ages.[28] Canals can be seen as an evolution of the fashion for moats. It is therefore not surprising that several canals were clearly adapted from earlier moats. There is also a link with the fishponds or 'stews' that were to be found in medieval manorial complexes. These appear to have become more common (and complex) in the fifteenth and sixteenth centuries. A linear arrangement of three rectangular ponds, enhanced with decorative structures, shown on a map of 1613 as flanking Melford Hall, is only a short step away from being a canal. In its modern manifestation, with one of the divisions between the ponds removed, part of it could now be termed a canal, though it is rather prosai-

24 *The Diary of John Hervey*, 66.

25 *Letter-Books of John Hervey*, ii, 364, no. 815.

26 G. Mott, *Follies and Pleasure Pavilions*, London 1989, 109.

27 R. Strong, *The Artist and the Garden*, New Haven and London 2000, pl. 87 (painting of 1744–46); D. Souden, *Wimpole Hall*, London 1991, 47 (painting of 1773).

28 E. Martin, 'Medieval Moats', in D. Dymond and E. Martin, eds, *An Historical Atlas of Suffolk*, revised edn, Ipswich 1999, 60–1.

cally called 'the Horse Pond'.[29] With this history of water features around their houses, it is not surprising that the gentlemen of Suffolk took to the new fashion for canals with such enthusiasm. Their efforts, for so long forgotten, are once more being recognised and admired. Undoubtedly, more canals remain as yet unrecognised, both in Suffolk and in neighbouring counties.[30]

GAZETTEER

1. BACTON: Advertisement for a farm to let 1782, mentions 'a genteel brick mansion-house thereon, modern built, with a bowling green, canal and fish ponds, well stocked with fish, and a dove-house, well stocked with pigeons'.[31]

2. BADLEY, BADLEY HALL: Very overgrown pond, 30m x 8m, brick-lined and now virtually dry. Flanks S side of W court of house – gate piers and walls of court are early eighteenth-century in date. Canal shown on 1741 estate map by William Collier.[32] Badley belonged to Poley family from late fifteenth century to 1714. Elizabeth, sister and heir of Edmund Poley, married Sir Richard Gipps of Horringer; their son Richard inherited Badley, but sold it 1735 to Ambrose Crowley of Barking Hall and London. Crowley family had no use for the mansion and it was severely reduced in 1759 to make a farmhouse.

3. BARDWELL, MOAT FARM (formerly BARDWELL HALL MANOR): Long pond shown flanking garden on map of 1730 by William Warren.[33] Five-bay house on map replaced by modern house, but pond, 65m x 10m, still remains. Map bears arms of Sir William Lee (1688–1754) – younger brother of Sir Thomas Lee, third bt. of Hartwell, Bucks. Rose to be Lord Chief Justice of England 1737. First wife was a Goodwin from Bury St Edmunds, which may explain his presence in Suffolk. From size and location of property, it may have been a 'shooting-box' to take advantage of hunting in Breckland. In 1748 he purchased Totteridge Park, Hertfordshire. His brother created striking canal in garden at Hartwell – figures in paintings by Balthasar Nebot 1738.[34]

4. BARKING: Pond 150m long x 33 to 48m wide (slightly waisted), with rounded island at S end. Situated on W edge of Needham Market and formed by damming of a small valley. OS map *c.*1900 shows a bridge linking island to mainland and a small round structure on the island – both now gone. Now tree-covered, there are

29 E. Martin, 'The Discovery of Early Gardens in Suffolk', in *Pastimes of Pleasure*, exhibition catalogue, Bury St Edmunds 2000, 21–2.

30 A number have already been identified in Norfolk: see A. Taigel and T. Williamson, 'Some Early Geometric Gardens in Norfolk', *Journ. of Garden History* 11, nos 1 and 2, Jan.–June 1991.

31 *Bury and Norwich Post*, 14 Aug. 1782, p. 3.

32 SROI P638.

33 SROB M550/1.

34 J. Harris, *The Artist and the Country House*, London rev. ed. 1985, pl. xxa.

yet some flowers and evergreen shrubs surviving from a garden. Boathouse marked at the N end has also gone. Named as *Fish Pond &c* on tithe map of Creeting St Mary 1840, then owned by Rebecca, widow of Samuel Alexander of Goldrood, Belstead, but occupied by her brother-in-law Thomas Maw of Needham Market.[35] Both Alexanders and Maws were Quakers and bankers.

5. GREAT BEALINGS, GREAT BEALINGS HALL: Two canals, at right angles, on a mid-eighteenth-century map.[36] Canals flanked S and E sides of a square area to S of house, with a 'Wilderness' to S. Description published in *Journ. Ipswich Field Club* 1908, mentions 'a fine shubbery that extended to an extensive canal at the further end of which was a boat and boating house'. House demolished in late eighteenth century; nothing remains of it or canals. Estate purchased 1710 by John Pitt, MP (*c.*1673–1731), High Sheriff of Suffolk 1721. He was the son of George Pitt of Stratfieldsaye, Hampshire, and a cousin of William Pitt the elder, politician.

6. GREAT BEALINGS, SECKFORD HALL: Large pond, now 45 x 30m, to S of house, in 'Canal Piece' on Martlesham tithe map.

7. BOXFORD, PARSONAGE FARM (formerly THE RECTORY): Pond 68m x 10m to E of house, made from arm of medieval moat. Mentioned in glebe terrier of 1723, from which it can be inferred that it was made by Rev. John Warren, rector of Boxford 1683–1721 (see main text).[37] Shown on tithe map of 1840.[38]

8. GREAT BRADLEY, GREAT BRADLEY HALL: Pond 120m x 10m adjacent to river and to E of remains of medieval moat that enclosed original Hall. Shown on OS map of 1880s, where it can be seen to be E arm of an extension to the house moat, enclosing an orchard; S arm shown as dry depression. Tithe map of 1842 only shows house moat, whole area named as 'Farm House Home Pasture'.[39] The pond has been taken to be a modern feature, but it is more likely that its omission in 1842 was through the cartographer's indifference.[40] Ownership in early eighteenth century uncertain; was owned by non-resident Brand family by 1764.

9. BREDFIELD, BREDFIELD HOUSE: Canal 80m x 10m, with alignment continued by a short avenue. Walkway on S side, flanked by a bank which rises to a flat-topped 'mount' at its centre. A structure is shown on mount on 1834 map and field to S is named as 'Summerhouse Pasture'.[41] Interestingly, there is a reference to a 'summerhouse and ponds' in this area in 1663.[42] Orchard lies to N of canal and there are signs of a terrace at right-angles to W end of canal, linking it to an early

[35] SROI FDA74/A1/1a.
[36] SROI S1/2/300.2.
[37] SROB 806/1/7.
[38] SROB T116/1,2.
[39] SROB T28/1,2.
[40] B. Charge, 'A Survey of Moated Sites within the Area of Interest of the Haverhill and District Archaeological Group', *Journal of the Haverhill and District Archaeological Group* 3, 1984, 140.
[41] SROI HD11/475/2106.
[42] D.E. Davy Manuscript, vol. 37, SROI microfilm J400/15.

eighteenth-century summerhouse (now extended and converted into 'Bredfield House'). Probably made by Arthur Jenney (d.1729), who succeeded to estate 1695. Account in *PSIA* xxxviii pt 4, 1996, 495–8.

10. BRIGHTWELL, BRIGHTWELL HALL: Engraving by Johannes Kip, 1707, shows large formal garden surrounding H-shaped house. On W side an L-shaped canal with a summerhouse at one end. Parallel to front of house a longer canal, linked to a large lake on E. House now demolished and no sign of canals or lake. In view of sandy soil of the area, there must be some doubt as to whether water features were ever as extensive as engraving indicates. Built for Sir Samuel Barnardiston, first bt. (1620–1707), a London merchant and prominent Puritan.

11. BROME, BROME HALL: Canal, 90m x 13m, to S of house and parallel to its frontage. Engraving by Johannes Kip, 1707, shows canal lying across long axis of avenue that stretched out into the park to S, and separated from it by iron railings. Causeway on this axis divided canal into two sections and connected with a broad path that led to centre of house, via a round basin. Large and elaborate formal garden lay to E of house. Estate map of 1726, however, shows canal without causeway.[43] Another canal (no longer existing) is shown adjoining W side of house. Garden built for Charles, third Lord Cornwallis (1655–98), who is said to have been 'in the especial favour of King William', or his son Charles, the fourth lord (1675–1722).[44] Tudor house demolished in 1963.

12. BURSTALL, BURSTALL COTTAGE. Pond 43m x 10m in 'Fishpond Yard' on OS map of 1950s. Area marked as 'Ozier Ground' on tithe map 1846.[45] Cottage belonged to Robert Ashford in 1864.

13. BUXHALL, FASBOURN HALL: Two linear ponds, roughly parallel to each other, to NE of house; probably remains of medieval moat. Northern pond, 74m (possibly originally longer) x 6m, has small mount close to its N end (rather implausibly, the mound is said to have yielded Viking 'treasures' when it was explored in 1883).[46] S pond, 80m x 6m, is divided by a causeway and balloons out into a circular pond at its N end. Property belonged to Copinger family, local squires, from fifteenth century to 1692. Sold to Sir Edward Ward (d.1714) of London and Stoke Doyle, Northants., Chief Baron of the Exchequer, but occupiers in early eighteenth century unknown.[47]

14. CAMPSEY ASH, CAMPSEA ASHE HOUSE (formerly THE HIGH HOUSE or ASHE HIGH HOUSE): Canal, 178m x10m, continuing alignment of long avenue to N. Has a parallel terrace walk on E, bounded on one side by a yew hedge. Also shorter canal, 118m x 8m, in two lengths, parallel to it, 735m to W. Both

43 SROI HA68/484/753.
44 GEC, iii, 454, n.(a).
45 SROI FDA52/A1/1a.
46 W.A. Copinger, *History of the Parish of Buxhall*, London 1902, 190.
47 *Ibid.*, 190–4.

shown on OS first edition map of 1805 and on tithe map of 1837. Possibly made for John Sheppard (1675–1747), who succeeded to estate on father's death 1708. High Sheriff of Suffolk 1709 and 1714. Married Anne, dowager countess of Leicester. He 'made great additions to the seat at Ash and considerably improved it'.[48] Seventeenth-century house house burnt down 1865; replacement house by Anthony Salvin pulled down in 1953. Gardens further developed by Hon. William Lowther after he purchased estate 1883, and by his son, Viscount Ullswater.[49] The canal is brick lined, but this, and flanking hedge of yews, could be improvements carried out by Lowther in 1880s – *Country Life* article 1905 mentions 'the water and the yew fence have been much improved in late years'. However in 1928 Viscount Ullswater stated that yew hedges were 'planted about the time of William and Mary'.

15. CHEDISTON, CHEDISTON HALL: Pond, 68m x 20m, to N of house, parallel to N front, shown on OS maps, now infilled. Tudor house rebuilt in 1830s for George W. Parkyns, who purchased estate 1833. House demolished 1955. Former seat of Pettus, Fleetwood and Plumer families.

16. CHEVINGTON, CHEVINGTON LODGE FARM: Narrow canal 94m x 4m, crossed near its centre by a bridge. Now in rear garden of Chevington Lodge Farm (built 1875), but is shown, less regular, on 1839 tithe map in front of old Lodge Farm (early/mid-sixteenth century hunting lodge).[50] Less distinctly marked as garden boundary on maps of 1815 and 1822.[51] Belonged to Kytson and Gage families of Hengrave Hall; sold 1716 to John Hervey, earl of Bristol. Seems to be earlier feature that was 'tidied-up' in Victorian period.

17. COMBS, COMBS HALL: Earthwork remains of large rectangular pool 120m x 65m, with substantial earthen dam at NE end. Pool now largely a bog, with an irregular pond dug into its NW end and a recently dug channel on its S side. Terrace walk all around pool. Pool is shown on estate map 1741.[52] Shows that pool formed part of large formal garden. Also shows that stream on N side of pool was dammed and straightened to form a canal 165m x 12m. Stream has now eroded almost sheer-sided channel and little survives of canal. Garden constructed by Orlando Bridgeman (1680–1731) 1710–1731. House that he built 1724, demolished 1756. Full account in E. Martin and A. Oswald, 'The House and Gardens of Combs Hall near Stowmarket: A Survey by the Royal Commission on the Historical Monuments of England', *PSIA* xxxviii pt 4, 1996, 409–27.

18. CULFORD, CULFORD HALL: Canal with rounded ends, *c.*150m x 8m, on estate map by T. Wright, 1742 – possibly Thomas Wright (1711–86), the landscape

48 *Gentleman's Magazine*, 1830, 398 and 513.

49 'Campsea Ash, Suffolk', *Country Life*, 15 July 1905, 54–62; Viscount Ullswater, 'The Gardens at Campsea Ashe', *Journal of the Royal Horticultural Society* liii pt 1, Jan. 1928.

50 SROB T112/1,2.

51 SROB 2323 and FL550/1/9.

52 SROI P638.

gardener and architect. Lay at right-angles to S front of house. Joined to water course at its S end. Shown on Humphry Repton's map of 1791, but infilled as a result of landscaping works that he recommended. Hall remodelled 1790–96 by Samuel Wyatt for first Marquess Cornwallis.

19. DALHAM, DALHAM HALL: Pond 62x20m in park to N of house, at right-angles to its N front and on axis of avenue to S. Axis continued to N by straight ride through woodland (to W of broad cruciform rides through woodland, called 'The Lawns', but now ploughed). Pond has one straight end (nearest house) and one rounded. Traces of a terrace on W side and perhaps on E. Park shown on E. Bowen's *Map of Suffolk* 1755; J. Hodskinson's *Map of Suffolk* 1783 shows axial ride and cruciform ones. Pond not shown on map of park 1808, but perhaps through cartographer's indifference (church also omitted).[53] Marked on draft enclosure map of *c.*1818 – among corrections in red ink.[54] Could have been constructed *c.*1818 for Lt-General Sir James Affleck, third bt. (1759–1833), who succeeded to estate in 1808, but would have been unfashionable at that time. Would be more understandable if contemporary with the avenue and axial ride. Estate formerly of Stuteville family purchased in 1702 by Dr Simon Patrick, bishop of Ely (d.1707). House built 1705. His son Simon sold estate 1714 to John Affleck (*c.*1651–1718). Affleck married Neeltie Schape, daughter of an Amsterdam merchant. Succeeded by son Gilbert Affleck, MP (d.1764).

20. DEBENHAM, CROW'S HALL: Pond 130m x 6m on N side of moated former orchard, which lies on N side of court to W of main house moat. Shown within a wooded compartment and named as 'The Stews' on map of 1818.[55] Position argues against it being an ornamental canal, but shape is suggestive, though thin. Moats probably the work of Framlingham family, owners in fifteenth and sixteenth centuries. Estate inherited by Gawdys in seventeenth century and sold by them to John Pitt, MP in 1697. He subsequently purchased estate in Great Bealings (see above) and moved there, Crow's Hall becoming a farmhouse. Plan and account in *PSIA* xxxviii pt 1, 1993, 109–11.

21. DEBENHAM, VICARAGE: Letter written by Rev. William Hurn in 1790 mentions that behind 'the compact little house . . . is a garden, large and convenient; a handsome long canal at the upper end and pleasing walks around it'. Canal was apparently partly filled up by his successor, Rev. George Smalley (vicar 1823–40).[56] No sign of it on modern maps. Rev. John Clubbe (see Whatfield) was also vicar here from 1730.

22. DENSTON, DENSTON HALL: Three canals outside, and parallel to, sides of lozenge-shaped walled garden: E canal 110m x 8m; S canal 78m x 8m; and N canal 40m (originally 80m) x 10m. W one is shown on map of 1676 redrawn in 1888, but

53 SROB 279/2.
54 SROB 279/5.
55 SROI S1/2/300.14.
56 L. Knowland, ed., *Samuel Dove's Debenham*, Debenham 1986, 77.

rest of garden area is not shown.[57] All ponds and walled garden shown on estate map 1778.[58] Shows that S canal was aligned on a small square structure, probably a dovecote ('Dovehouse Paddock' adjoins), 30m from its W end. Another small square structure lay at midpoint of N canal and may have been a summerhouse. N canal is slightly less formally shaped than other two and could have been made out of an earlier fishpond. Existing Hall built *c.*1690–1700 by Sir John Robinson (*c.*1655–1704), who inherited a Tudor house here on death of his grandfather 1673. Garden possibly the work of his son, Col. John Robinson (*c.*1679–1734), who served under duke of Marlborough in Flanders. Account, with plan, in *PSIA* xxxviii, pt 3, 1995, 376–9.

23. DUNWICH, CLIFF HOUSE: Pond with rounded ends, 44m x 14m , in Cliff Wood ('Canal Wood' on 1950s OS map), with walkway leading to it, aligned on long axis. Shown on OS map 1837. Possibly built for John Robinson, owner in 1844 and 1855.[59] House is early nineteenth-century, possibly with earlier origins.

24. EUSTON, EUSTON HALL: Earthwork traces of canal in grassed area between house and river. Estate acquired in *c.*1665 by Henry Bennet, earl of Arlington, Secretary of State to Charles II, who rebuilt house on a grand scale. Visited in 1669 by Sir Philip Skippon:

> we saw Euston House that the Lord Arlington is repairing and adorning; he hath made faire terrase walks in his garden and brought the river neare it by a new Cutt.[60]

'New Cutt' must be the canal. Seen in 1671 by John Evelyn the diarist:

> My Lord Chamberlains house is a very noble pile consisting of 4 greate pavilions after the french, beside a body of a large house . . . built . . . with a vast expence . . . the Garden handsome, the Canale beautifull . . . The Water furnishing the fountaines is raised by a pretty Engine or very slight plaine Wheele, which likewise serves to grinde his Corne, from a small cascade of the Canale, the invention of Sir Sam: Moreland.[61]

Described again by Evelyn in 1677:

> The Canale running under my Ladys dressing chamber window, is full of Carps, & fowle, which come & are fed there with greate diversion: The Cascade at end of the Canale turnes a Corne-mill which finds the family, & raises water for the fountaines and offices.[62]

Seen by Celia Fiennes on her travels 1698:

57 F. Haslewood, 'Denston', *PSIA* vi, 1888, 433–6.

58 SROB 279/6.

59 *White's Directory of Suffolk for 1844*, 370; and *for 1855*, 306.

60 C.M. Hood, 'An East Anglian Contemporary of Pepys: Philip Skippon of Foulsham 1641–1692', *NA* xii, 1926, 147–89.

61 *Diary of John Evelyn*, ed. E.S. de Beer, 6 vols, Oxford 1955, iii, 591. Arlington only became Lord Chamberlain in 1674, so Evelyn's record must have been rewritten at a later date, perhaps on his second visit in 1677.

62 Evelyn, *Diary*, iv, 117.

> there are good gardens with fountaines and some stone statues, a Cannall by the side.[63]

View of canal drawn by Edmund Prideaux *c.*1716.[64] Shows two-storey wing, described by him as 'orangerie', jutting out into the N end of the canal; canal flanked on W side by a row of evenly spaced trees, and on E by a walkway or terrace. Walkway partly bordered on E by a tall hedge, which separated canal area from S front garden. Prideaux's view and description makes it clear that wing that jutted into end of canal was one described thus by Evelyn in 1677:

> The Orange-Garden [presumably before the S front] is very fine, & leads into a Greene-house, at the end whereoff is a sall to eate in, & the Conservatory very long (some hundred feete) adorn'd with Mapps, as the other side is with the heads of Caesars ill cut in alabaster [on the exterior, in niches along the top of the wall – visible in Prideaux's drawing]: over head are severall appartments for my Lord, Lady, & Dutchesse, with Kitchins & other offices below in a lesser volume, with lodgings for servants.[65]

Arlington died 1685; succeeded by son-in-law, Henry Fitz-Roy, first duke of Grafton (1663–90). Canal probably infilled by 1731, as part of new landscaping carried out for Charles, second duke (1683–1757).[66]

25. FRAMSDEN, BOUNDARY FARM: Canal 54m x 6m with terrace walk on its S side, overlooking a valley. Remains of a brick stair and a culvert containing a wooden pipe at W end. Canal is at rear of house, flanking an orchard. Possibly done for Edward Mann, gent. (b.1680, living 1727). Full account in E. Martin, T. Easton and I. McKechnie, 'Conspicuous display: the extraordinary garden and buildings of a minor gentry family in Mid Suffolk', *PSIA* xxxviii pt 1, 1993, 56–74.

26. LITTLE GLEMHAM, GLEMHAM HALL: Depression 94m x 10m with a small modern pond (10 x 4m) at its centre. Bounded on E by a brick wall (behind which is main garden) and on W by a terrace walk with old yews, with views westward into park. Shown as a water feature on estate map of 1720 by J. Halsey for Dudley North.[67] As now, it was bounded on E by a wall and had a walkway on W. Feature flanked W side of large formal garden divided into rectangular beds and with its long axis aligned on centre of S front of house. House built by Glemham family *c.*1600; they sold estate to Dudley North (d.1729) in 1708. North was the nephew of fifth Lord North and of Roger North, the writer on architecture (see Sternfield). He remodelled house *c.*1717–22 and carried out work on the garden as well – in February 1720 there are references to works on various 'ponds', apparently under the direction of a Mr Robinson.[68]

63 *The Journeys of Celia Fiennes*, ed. C. Morris, 1949, 150–1.

64 J. Harris, 'The Prideaux Collection of Topographical Drawings', *Architectural History* 7, 1964, nos 31 and 32.

65 Evelyn, *Diary*, iv, 117.

66 D. Dymond, *History and Evolution of Euston Park*, Historic Landscape Management Plan report 1995, vol. 3.

67 SROI HD1000/1.

68 SROI HA49/C2/5/1, letters of John Bould to Dudley North, Feb. 1719/20.

27. HALESWORTH, TO THE E OF THE THOROUGHFARE: Mid-eighteenth-century map of 'the House of Mr Peter Jermyn with its Gardens' shows a serpentine pond labelled '*Canal*', separating gardens from a meadow. Map bears border decoration somewhat in style of Thomas Robins the elder of Bath. Jermyn (1737–1810) was a Halesworth attorney and his house is now the offices of Cross Ram, solicitors. Sale catalogue 1810 mentions a 'capital garden . . . judiciously and elegantly laid out with vinery and greenhouse, capital meadow adjoining separated from garden by a canal'.[69]

28. HARTEST, STOWEHILL: Pond 45m x 12m to S of, and parallel to front of house. Marked as 'Fish Pond' on the 1880s OS map. House named as 'Folley' on Hodskinson's *Map of Suffolk* 1783. Later occupied by Rev. Henry Mears, vicar of Hartley Wintney, Hampshire and curate of Rede; described as 'late of Stowe Hill', when he died 1855.

29. HELMINGHAM, HELMINGHAM HALL: 'Fishpond', 75m x 14m, short distance to NE of moated Tudor house and parallel to its side. Moated Tudor garden is on opposite side of the house. Possibly work of Lionel Tollemache, third earl of Dysart (1649–1727).

30. HORRINGER, LITTLE HORRINGER HALL: L-shaped piece of water, partly enclosing an orchard, that is probably remains of a moat. However longer arm (124m x 12m) is very regular and its axis is at right-angles to front of house, suggesting that it was converted into a canal. Shown on 1839 tithe map.[70] Original house said to have been in area of orchard, within moat, but was pulled down by earl of Bristol, who used the materials to build an agent's house.[71] Sale of materials from Hall recorded 1759.[72]

31. ICKWORTH, ICKWORTH HOUSE: Broad canal, 212m x 60m (max.), fed by river Linnet, with an oval island, 32mx20m, at its SE end. By 1950s, SE end had silted up, but has now been re-excavated close to, but not exactly on 1880s outline. Canal appears slightly more regular on OS map of 1880s; this also a second small island, 10mx6m, in middle, but close to S shore. The 1850 tithe map shows only one island in centre, with a tree.[73] On N side is a large walled garden, with an early eighteenth-century orangery on its S side, at the head of a recessed square facing the mid-point of canal. Built for John Hervey, first earl of Bristol (1665–1751), who refers to 'my new Canall at Spring Garden in the parke' in 1717 and to his 'new-made canal' in 1724.[74] Hervey refers to his 'intended kitchin garden to be laid out at Ickworth' in 1713.[75] Canal was constructed in an area that was referred to as

69 Information kindly supplied by Mrs Rachel Lawrence.
70 SROB T106/2.
71 M.W. Hervey, *Annals of a Suffolk Village*, 1930, 123.
72 W. Copinger, *Manors of Suffolk*, Manchester 1909, VII, 68.
73 SROB T12/2.
74 *Diary of John Hervey*, 66; *Letter-Books of John Hervey*, ii, 364, no. 815.
75 *Letter-Books of John Hervey*, i, 356, no. 410.

'Pond Close' on a survey of 1664, so it is likely that Hervey adapted an existing pond to make his canal. Hervey consulted the architect William Talman *c.*1703 and he could have been responsible for design of orangery.[76]

32. IPSWICH, CHRISTCHURCH MANSION: Canal shown flanking W side of elaborate formal garden to W of house, on John Ogilby's *Map of Ipswich*, surveyed 1674 and engraved 1698. Beside 'Great Garden' on map of 1735 by John Kirby – also another wedge-shaped pond in park to N, named as 'Dovehouse Pond'. Canal still shown on OS map of 1880s, when was 90m x 12m, but it has now gone; other pond still exists but was clearly much altered by 1880s. Tudor house of Withipoles passed by marriage, 1642, of Elizabeth Withipole to Leicester Devereux, sixth viscount Hereford (1617–76). Estate sold by Pryce Devereux, ninth viscount, to Thomas Fonnereau in 1735, but latter had been leasing it since at least 1733.

33. LONG MELFORD, KENTWELL HALL: W arm of Tudor garden moat at rear of house was converted into a formal, straight, canal, 70m x 10m, by 1880s. Estate sold 1706 by spendthrift Sir Thomas Robinson, third bt. (1681–1743) to Moore family, London merchants. Moores sold 1828 to Robert Hart Logan, MP. On his death sold 1838 to Edward Starkie Bence.

34. LONG MELFORD, MELFORD HALL: Now dry moat, 150m x 16m, running alongside raised terrace extending E from Tudor summerhouse, may have been intended as a canal. Eighteenth- or nineteenth-century brick wall now runs within depression. Possibly done by Firebrace family, who inherited estate from Cordells in 1704.

35. NETTLESTEAD, NETTLESTEAD CHASE (formerly NETTLESTEAD HALL): Broad canal *c.*90m x 30m, bounding N side of a former outer court. Boathouse shown in middle of N side on 1902 OS map, but not on modern maps. Named as 'The Canal' in late eighteenth-century survey.[77] House is, in part, Tudor mansion of Wentworth family. Wentworths sold estate in 1645 and by 1704 it had passed to John Fuller of Ipswich, and then to his son-in-law William Bradley.

36. OUSDEN, OUSDEN HALL: Linear depression, partly wet, 62m x 12m, running along W side of churchyard. Bounded on W side by flat-topped embankment, which has a line of tall yews on its W side. Yews clearly originated as a hedge bounding one side of a walkway along top of embankment. Undated map shows that depression was originally E arm of rectangular moat around Hall.[78] By early nineteenth century other arms of moat had been infilled and this one is shown as a linear pond.[79] Hall belonged to Moseley family 1614 until 1804, when it was sold to Rev. James Thomas Hand (d.1835). Hand left it to his nephew Thomas James Ireland

[76] J.L. Phibbs and C. Gallagher, *Ickworth: A Survey of the Landscape*, National Trust report 1990, 24.

[77] SROI HB2/1/141.

[78] SROB 1429/11.

[79] SROB 1429/10.

(d.1863). House rebuilt 1835–6 by Thomas Rickman for Ireland; demolished 1955.

37. PETTISTREE, PETTISTREE LODGE: 160m N of house is linear pond 150m x12m, flanked on W side by large mount, 55m in diameter at base and 7.9m high. Scatter of bricks and mortared flints on top of mount suggest that there may have been a structure there. Built by Hunn Wyard gent. (*c.*1680–1746), who in 1745 willed that:

> the Mount now or late erected . . . shall be by all such possessors thereof . . . for ever preserved in as good order or condition as the same now is and no ways defaced or demolished But with free liberty nevertheless to Add unto and Increase the said Mount in such manner as they shall think proper.[80]

Pond named as 'Canal' on tithe map of 1841.

38. POSLINGFORD, NEW HOUSE FARM: Pond 47m x 6m to SE of house. Shown on map of 1806 as set within a small park.[81] Long walkway on the same axis, linked N end of pond to a trapeze-shaped garden, containing a cruciform arrangement of paths. Property belonged to Golding family and their newly built dwelling called '*the Newhowse*' is mentioned in 1572.[82] Most likely builder of canal is George Golding (*c.*1687–1739), who succeeded to estate 1702.

39. PRESTON, SHELFORD HOUSE (formerly THE RECTORY): Pond 48m long, tapering from 8m wide at E end to 4m at W. Roughly parallel to S side of house. Shown on 1839 tithe map as half in rectory garden and half in a pasture field of the glebe; Rev. William Heard Shelford was then rector. Canal builder could be Rev. John Hill, rector 1719–42.

40. RINGSHALL, RINGSHALL GRANGE (formerly THE RECTORY): Two linear ponds (52m x 5m and 24m x 5m) at either end of, and at right-angles to, long terrace walk. Moated house lies between the two ponds, on S side of terrace. Smaller canal has a small mount beside it. From mount there are views across valley N to Ringshall Hall and church. Adjoining field to N called 'Belvedere field' in glebe terrier 1827.[83] Possibly made for Rev. William Peppen (*c.*1684–1747), rector of Ringshall 1707–44. Short account in *PSIA* xxxviii, pt 2, 1994, 234.

41. RUSHBROOKE, NEAR BRIDGE FARM: Overgrown and partly dry pond, reduced in width from its 1880s dimensions of *c.*460m x 70m. Largely silted up by 1926, current reduced size may be result of re-excavation. Appears to be shown on Hodskinson's *Map of Suffolk* 1783. Named as 'Canal' in 1839 tithe apportionment and shown as linear pond with angled ends and containing a small island at each end.[84] Alignment of canal was extended eastward by a long parallel-sided enclosure called 'The Glade', with a plantation of trees at its E end. Then as now, formed part

80 SROI IC/AA1/175/3ii. I am grateful to Miss Joan Peck for this reference.
81 SROB HA537.
82 SROB 537.
83 SROI FB4/C4/5.
84 SROB T59/1,2.

of Rushbrooke Hall estate. Boathouse shown at NW end, near Bridge Farm, in 1880s. Possibly done for Sir Jermyn Davers, fourth bt (*c.*1686–1743), who succeeded his brother 1723. His irregular marital affairs may have made a detached pleasure ground desirable!

42. SIBTON, SIBTON ABBEY: Pond, 240m x 18m (maximum), in Abbey Wood, to N of ruins of Cistercian abbey. Abbey had been converted into house by Scrivener family, but this was demolished, leaving only ancient parts of structure as ruin, by John Freston Scrivener (d.1791) who succeeded to estate 1751. *White's Directory* 1855 states:

> remains of this once splendid abbey may be seen in the walls of Abbey House. A long terrace and the pool which supplied the abbey with water still remain.

Pond is shown on J. Hodksinson's *Map of Suffolk* 1783. Possibly done by John Scrivener (*c.*1650–1720), his brother, Rev. Charles Scrivener (1660–1737), rector of Wilby, or his nephew, Charles Scrivener (1694–1751).

43. SIBTON, SIBTON PARK: Two canals marked and named on 'rough draft' map of 1798. small one formed out of a length of the Minsmere brook and larger one flanking N side of '*The Lawn*' in front of house. Both slightly sinous in outline. House belonged to '. . . Barker esq.' on E. Bowen's *Map of Suffolk* 1755, and to Thomas Staunton on J. Hodskinson's *Map of Suffolk* 1783. House rebuilt on new site 1827 for Robert Sayer. Larger canal shown on tithe map 1840, but had been enlarged into an irregular lake by 1884.

44. SIBTON, HILL FARM: Pond 40m x 8m, adjacent to the S side of the house.

45. STERNFIELD, STERNFIELD HOUSE (formerly THE RECTORY): Map entitled 'A Ground Plan and View of the Intended Gardens and Water-works and Building of the Revd. Doct. Montague North of Sternfeld . . .With an Estimate of the Charges by Henry Ellison', undated.[85] Appears to be two alternative layouts for the grounds, both with a canal 62m x 12m, adjacent to a rectangular kitchen garden. Cost of 'Long Canal and the Walks round the same' was estimated to be £13 5s 6d. The cost of the kitchen garden was £12 10s 6d. Dr Montague North (1712–1779) was son of Roger North (*c.*1653–1734) of Rougham Hall in Norfolk, the writer on architecture. Dr Montague North became rector of Sternfield in 1767 and map is probably of about this date. He became prebendary of Windsor in 1775, but died at Sternfield in 1779. Canal, if created, had gone by 1880s.

46. STOKE-BY-NAYLAND, GIFFORD'S HALL: Canal, *c.*50m x 10m, shown on 1817 enclosure map and on 1840 tithe map at E end of large rectangular walled garden on E side of house. E front of Tudor house was Georgianised and there is a small eighteenth-century orangery against N wall of garden, near house. Garden descends slope to a depression where canal was located. Depression is clearly site of canal and there is a small round pond at its N end. Terrace walk on E side of canal, with views

[85] BL 23005/16.

out into park. Garden and its structures possibly work of Sir Francis Mannock, fourth bt. (1676–1758), who succeeded his father 1714.

47. STOKE-BY-NAYLAND, TENDRING HALL: Regular canal, 174m x 28m, with a pavilion called 'The Temple' or 'The Fishing Temple' at its W end, beside road. Canal shown on estate map of 1723 by Jos. Kendall for Sir John Williams.[86] Sir John (167?–1743) was a London merchant, 'at the head of the Turkey trade' and 'one of the greatest exporters of cloth in England'.[87] Canal probably built for him; Temple added later, perhaps after estate was acquired by Rowley family in 1764.

48. STONHAM PARVA, WESTWOOD HALL: Two parallel canals, 24m apart. One 48m x 11m, with a brick lining; other 46m x 8m. Larger one is adjacent to E side of a cottage, which is small fragment of original hall. Bears inscription 'B.G. 1650', for Barnaby Gibson gent. (1625–1706). Canals shown within 'garden and orchard' on tithe map 1839.[88] Canals possibly work of his son Barnaby Gibson, gent. (1659–1719) or his grandson, Barnaby Gibson (1685–1758).

49. STOWMARKET, ABBOT'S HALL: Large pond, 100m long, tapering from 40m wide at W end, to 28m at E. Rectangular island, 22m x 15m, at broad end bears early eighteenth-century summerhouse and is attached to mainland by a wooden bridge. Terrace walk all around canal. Causeway separates canal from a smaller rectangular moat which surrounded a wooded platform. House dates from *c.*1710 and both it and the canal are likely to be work undertaken for Charles Blosse (*c.*1648–1724). He married, 1681, Alice, daughter and heiress of John Howe of Abbot's Hall (d.1694). Canal is named as 'Fish Pond' in 1840 tithe apportionment, containing 'Summer-House and Garden'; moated site is described as 'Stackyard'.

50. STRADBROKE, THE ROOKERY (also called BATTLESEA HALL): Canal 300m long, tapering slightly from 17m wide at SE end, to 14m at NW, near house. Approximately 5ft deep. At broader end there is a small wooded island. Long axis of canal is at right-angles to S front of house. Marked as 'Moat' on OS maps, but E side of 'moat' is in fact old W edge of former Battlesea Green. Builder was possibly Joseph Fox (died 1747), a Roman Catholic who succeeded his father 1697.

51. LITTLE THURLOW, THURLOW HALL: Canal 223m x 14m, flanking S side of lawn and orchard. There appears to be an overgrown terrace walk on S side of canal. Second smaller pond, 80m long x 6m wide, lies on N side of orchard. Terrace at right-angles to canals separates lawn from vegetable garden and orchard. Larger canal shown on map of 1735 by John Coulter for Stephen Soame.[89] Shows that canal was originally longer and had a bridge or causeway about a quarter of the length from E end. Named as 'Garden Canal' on tithe map 1846, which also shows

86 SROI HA108/10/1.

87 R. Sedgwick, ed., *History of Parliament: House of Commons 1715–54*, 2 vols., London 1970, ii 541–2.

88 SROI FDA237/A1/1a.

89 SROB HA540/7/1.

it as longer.[90] Lawn area is shown in 1735 as a quartered garden in front of house, and an orchard is indicated where it still survives. Smaller pond is not marked on these maps. Eighteenth-century survey states that there were:

> behind the house large gardens & orchard inclosed with a Brick Wall with a delightful Cannell running all alonge on the S side of the house & Gardens stored with fish.[91]

Canal probably made for Stephen Soame (1709–64). Original Elizabethan house destroyed by fire 1809, new house built on slightly different site 1847.

52. TRIMLEY ST MARTIN, CAPEL HALL: Advertisement, 1811, for a shooting box to let, which had a 'lawn . . . kitchen garden, two walled gardens, canal, fish-ponds and stews'.[92] Several ponds are shown on OS map, including one 120m x 14m, subdivided into three sections and attached to a round pond at its NE end. Also a partially water-filled depression 110m x 20m.

53. WALPOLE: Sale advertisement 1759 mentions 'a commodious and convenient dwelling-house with a sashed front . . . a good kitchen garden, and orchard well planted, a handsome canal or fish pond'. Enquiries were to go to Mr Thomas Knight, common-brewer, or Miss Knights in Halesworth.[93]

54. WHATFIELD, THE OLD RECTORY: Note at back of Whatfield parish register, against name of Rev. John Clubbe, rector 1735–73, states 'who made the Gardens and Canals in the Pleasure Garden'. Appears to be in Clubbe's own writing. Clubbe (*c.*1703–1773) was author of satirical *History and Antiquities of the Ancient Villa of Wheatfield* (1758). D.E. Davy visited in 1826 and noted 'in the garden near the House, is a terrace walk, on the edge of a steep descent, from whence there is a very extensive prospect of the valley of the Bret, almost to the Town of Hadleigh' and 'In the garden still remains the Summer House built by the Rev. John Plampin . . . & dedicated to. . . the memory of Mr Clubbe his predcessor' (still exists, bearing a date 1797).[94] 1838 tithe map shows moated rectory, with a rectangular area to its W called 'The Lawn'. Set with trees and had a terrace at its W end, overlooking 'Arbour Field'. Linear pond flanking S edge of The Lawn is also shown – still exists and is 38m x 4m. Another pond, 32m x 4m, at right-angles to N side of 'The Lawn' is only shown as a ditch line.

55. WICKHAMBROOK, BADMONDISFIELD HALL: NW arm of sub-rectangular moat around Hall appears to have been straightened to give it appearance of a canal. It is also screened off from rest of house site by a parallel partition. At N end of this narrow compartment there is a Georgian summerhouse, shown on

90 SROB T103/1,2.

91 BL Add. MS 51357 A.

92 *Bury and Norwich Post*, 4 Nov. 1811.

93 *Ipswich Journ.*, 3 Mar. 1759.

94 J. Blatchly, ed., *David Elisha Davy: A Journal of Excursions through the County of Suffolk 1823–1844*, SRS XXIV, 1982, 85.

tithe map 1841.[95] Hall acquired from North family by Francis Warner in late seventeenth century. Work possibly done for Nathaniel Warner, who succeeded his brother Poulett 1721 and died 1753.

56. WORLINGWORTH, PARADISE FARM: Small canal, 30m x 4m, made out of a former length of ditch surrounding former Great Green, enclosed in nineteenth century. In existence by 1880s. Short account in *PSIA* xxxviii, pt 2, 1994, 230.

95 SROB F652/3/4(2)a.

Estate Stewards in Woodland High Suffolk 1690–1820

Jonathan Theobald

IT IS NOW well established that the absentee landowner was a widespread phenomenon in the seventeenth and eighteenth centuries.[1] The period saw the landed classes increasingly involved with political and business interests in the capital, while also, as road travel improved, enjoying the pleasures of the new spa towns, Tunbridge Wells, Bath, Scarborough and their like. Increased speculation in the land market, and inheritance from geographically ever-widening marriage alliances, also made it likely that proprietors would be absent from at least some of their property. Hands on management of their estates was rare for absentees if their duties and interests in London were time consuming, and their properties far from the metropolis. Though farm rentals were one of their chief sources of income, many absentee landowners possessed only a basic knowledge of agrarian issues and practices. Consequently, it was commonplace for landowners to employ agents, known usually as stewards, to manage their estates in their absence, and to keep in contact with them through correspondence. Some owners seldom wrote to their steward except when problems arose. These principally included choosing new tenants, negotiating the terms of a lease, purchasing or selling land, or most frequently collecting rent arrears. Other proprietors wrote on a more regular basis. The importance of these letters to the agrarian historian of the early-modern period is obvious; they make up the bulk of the primary sources used in this chapter, the main objective of which is to examine and evaluate the management skills displayed by stewards on differing types of property in Woodland High Suffolk (Map).

1 J.V. Beckett, 'Absentee Landownership in the Later Seventeenth and Early Eighteenth Centuries: The Case of Cumbria', *Northern History*, 1983, 87–107; D.R. Hainsworth, *Stewards, Lords and People*, Cambridge 1992; C. Clay, 'Landlords and Estate Management in England', in J. Thirsk, ed., *The Agrarian History of England and Wales*, V (ii), Cambridge 1985, 119–251; P. Roebuck, 'Absentee Landownership in the Late Seventeenth and Early Eighteenth Centuries: A Neglected Factor in English Agrarian History', *AgHR* xxi, 1973, 1–17; B. English, 'Patterns of Estate Management in East Yorkshire c.1840–c.1880', *AgHR* xxxii, 1984, 29–48.

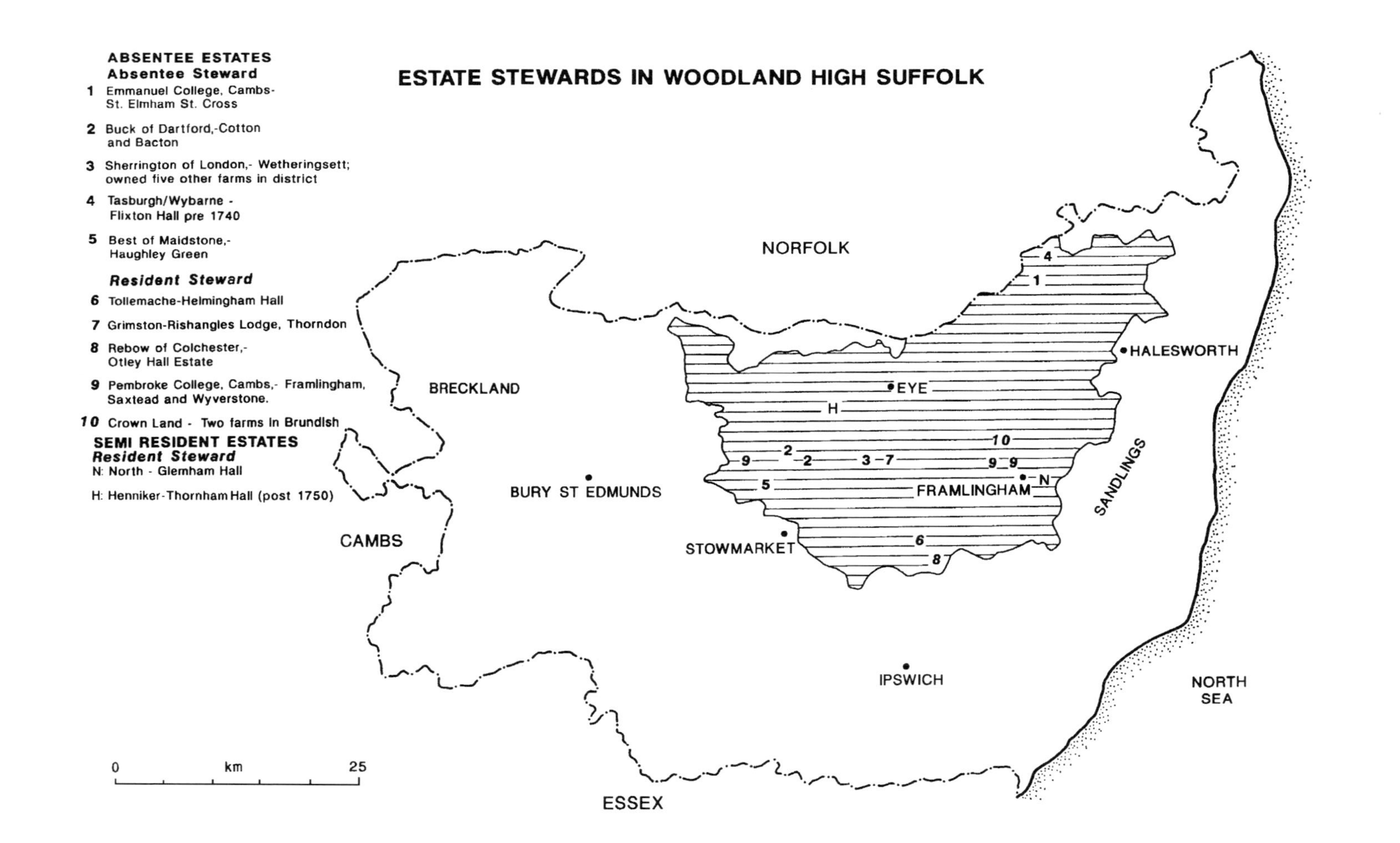
ESTATE STEWARDS IN WOODLAND HIGH SUFFOLK
ABSENTEE ESTATES
Absentee Steward
1 Emmanuel College, Cambs- St. Elmham St. Cross
2 Buck of Dartford,-Cotton and Bacton
3 Sherrington of London,- Wetheringsett; owned five other farms in district
4 Tasburgh/Wybarne - Flixton Hall pre 1740
5 Best of Maidstone,- Haughley Green
Resident Steward
6 Tollemache-Helmingham Hall
7 Grimston-Rishangles Lodge, Thorndon
8 Rebow of Colchester,- Otley Hall Estate
9 Pembroke College, Cambs,- Framlingham, Saxtead and Wyverstone.
10 Crown Land - Two farms in Brundish
SEMI RESIDENT ESTATES
Resident Steward
N: North - Glemham Hall
H: Henniker-Thornham Hall (post 1750)
NORFOLK
BRECKLAND
CAMBS
BURY ST EDMUNDS
STOWMARKET
EYE
H
FRAMLINGHAM
N
HALESWORTH
SANDLINGS
IPSWICH
NORTH SEA
ESSEX
0
km
25

A Comparative Introduction to Woodland High Suffolk

At the outset it is necessary to describe the main characteristics of landownership in Woodland High Suffolk. The national data discussed here were originally verified in the late 1870s by John Bateman from *The Return of Owners of Land 1872–73* (England and Wales), commonly known as The New Domesday. His figures for the proportion of land owned by large landowners and the density of resident seats are almost certainly higher than they would have been 150 years earlier.[2] Nationally, the larger estates were generally to be found in the north of England or on the poorest soils. Land prices were relatively low in these areas, enabling proprietors to accumulate more extensive tracts. Also, as a rule, the counties with the highest proportion of land held by large landowners also had the highest density of resident seats, or 'home' estates. Only south-eastern England significantly bucked this trend, due primarily to its close proximity to London. The pull of the capital also ensured that the majority of the northern 'home' estates had owners who were at least partial absentees. The Cumbrian case studies researched by Beckett certainly confirm this point.[3]

In the 1870s two-fifths of the land in Suffolk was in the hands of large landowners (those owning more than 3,000 acres); a figure slightly below the national mean of 43 per cent. Suffolk was also rather below the national average concerning the density of 'home' seats. The eastern side of the county, however (and in particular Woodland High Suffolk), differed markedly in character with much smaller estates than those found in the west. In his book *Suffolk in the Nineteenth Century* (1854), John Glyde listed forty-three parishes in the county owned by one proprietor; only seven of these were in Woodland High Suffolk. Glyde also examined the deaneries of Bosmere and Claydon, which amounted to 57,899 acres of land which constituted much of the southern boundary of the district studied here. Out of 339 proprietors in the area only six owned more than 1,000 acres, and only two of these possessed over 3,000 acres. There were no fewer than 151 landowners who owned fewer than 50 acres.[4] 'Home' estates were also thinner on the ground in the east. When Defoe travelled through East Suffolk in the 1720s, he noted that 'there are not so many families of gentry or nobility placed here as in the other side of the county' and that 'the pleasure of West Suffolk is much supported' by the rents from the eastern half of the county.[5] Furthermore, as the Map suggests, those 'home' estates which did exist, such as Glemham Hall, Thornham Hall and Redgrave Hall, were the residences of semi-resident owners in the period in question. Two of the resident landlords shown on the above map, namely the Middletons at Crowfield Hall and the Adairs at Flixton Hall, did not move to their respective properties until after 1752. The heavy, sticky clay lands, particularly unpleasant in winter, and the lack of leisure amenities in the neighbourhood, made the area an unfashionable one

2 H.A. Clemenson, *English Country Houses and Landed Estates*, London 1982, 20–6.

3 Beckett, 'Absentee Landownership', 90–1.

4 J. Glyde, *Suffolk in the Nineteenth Century*, London 1854, 325–30.

5 D. Defoe, *A Tour through the Whole Island of Great Britain*, i, London 1962, 124.

in which to live. Therefore, unlike the 'closed' parishes of north and west Norfolk, where whole villages were often huddled around one imposing stately house, many of the tenant farmers in Woodland High Suffolk had minimal contact with the owners and agents of the land they cultivated.

The characteristics of the various estates examined in this chapter correspond to the above pattern. For example, the most substantial property of an absentee studied here is the Tollemache estate in Helmingham and Framsden, which in the early eighteenth century covered an area of approximately 3,000 acres. The Tasburgh/ Wybarne estate at Flixton Hall, roughly 2,000 acres in 1750, was considerably augmented after 1760. All the other examples were below 1,500 acres. The Tollemache estate, along with the Rebow and Grimston properties, were all 'off' properties distanced from the owner's principal estates, respectively in Surrey, Essex and Hertfordshire. The Tollemache family had several estates scattered across the country, and though their original sixteenth-century seat was in Suffolk, their principal residence after 1660s was in Surrey. Pembroke College, Cambridge, also owned land in several counties, though the Framlingham and Saxtead property formed only one of its more sizeable estates. The remainder of the properties owned by absentees comprised just a few scattered farms. Both the Buck and Sherrington estates were owned by merchants or lesser gentry living in or near London. There survive in the archives numerous examples of similar small estates, consisting of a few holdings, and, though locally based gentlemen, large farmers and the clergy owned some of these properties, many were in the hands of owners (particularly merchants) who lived in London or more distant market towns. The absentee small estate was therefore one of the most distinctive landholding features found in Woodland High Suffolk in the early modern period. Conversely, the two semi-resident examples studied here were 'home' estates and ranged between 2,000 and 5,000 acres, the owners of which, North of Glemham and Henniker of Thornham, appear to have spent much of their year in or around London.

Lastly, a brief outline of the agrarian economy of the region is needed to complete this introduction. Up to 1750, at least, Woodland High Suffolk was a pastoral dairying district where farmers rarely had more than one-third of their land in tilth. There was little incentive to farm otherwise through periods of depressed grain prices, especially in the three decades between 1720 and 1750. Sharp upturns in the price of corn, such as those experienced in the 1690s, were transitory and infrequent. Landowners were content to maintain this pastoral economy, safe in the knowledge that their land's store of fertility would be protected. After 1750, however, and particularly between 1790 and 1820, the majority of tenants managed to persuade their landlords to permit the ploughing up of significant areas of pasture and meadow.[6] This was a period of increased farm profits, principally from grain prices responding to sustained population growth, poor harvests and the trade

6 J.A. Theobald, 'Changing Landscapes, Changing Economies: Holdings in Woodland High Suffolk', unpublished Ph.D. thesis UEA, 2000; H. and W. Raynbird, *On the Agriculture of Suffolk*, London 1849, 92–4; A. Young, *A General View of the Agriculture of the County of Suffolk*, London 1813, 160.

restrictions of the French Wars. Though extending the use of the plough meant an increase in labour costs, wage levels still lagged significantly behind inflationary grain prices.[7]

The Role of the Steward

According to Hainsworth, the duties of the English estate steward included collecting payments for rent, fines and dues, ensuring that estate repairs were completed, and drawing up the farm leases of tenants. It was the steward's task to explain the gist of the contract to the tenant, especially if the latter was illiterate. His position also regularly saw him negotiating between lessor and lessee, usually over the contentious issues of rent payment, timber allowances and ploughing restrictions. As Hainsworth states, due to the divergent interests of tenant and landlord the mediative role of the steward was frequently a difficult one.[8] Nevertheless, perhaps the most important role of the steward was to enlist new tenants for unoccupied farms, especially since good tenants possessing the requisite capital resources were always at a premium.

Probably the most commonplace of these various duties involved the collection and setting of rent payments from tenants. It was often a fraught process. This is clearly seen in a series of letters between Emmanuel College, Cambridge, and Daniel Sayer, the steward for the college's estate at South Elmham, St Cross. For example, though Sayer advised the college in 1742 to abate five pounds of their tenant's rent, because 'he gives more than he can afford', he also promised not to weaken the college's hand by telling the tenant that his rent was too high.[9] He admitted to the fellows of the college that even if they did agree to this rebate the tenant, however hardworking, would only 'scrape a mean, poor living'. Relations between the tenant (William Smith) and Sayer inevitably deteriorated. In 1745, the latter warned Emmanuel College that the rent would always be in arrears.[10]

It is maintained that tenants across the whole of England were pleading for rebates in their rent in the middle decades of the eighteenth century.[11] Certainly, examples drawn from High Suffolk, including Mr Richer at Cotton Hill in 1734, and two tenants on the Otley Hall estate in the mid-1720s, support this conclusion. William Armiger, the steward of the latter property in 1725, informed the owner, Sir Issac Rebow, that Mr Bloomfield, the tenant at Spaldings Barn Farm, was having to borrow money to pay his rent and several other debts, including his Poor Rates for the parishes of Framsden and Otley. He also complained that Bloomfield and his family were consuming too much of the wheat grown on the farm. Its sale was essen-

7 M. Overton, *Agricultural Revolution in England: The Transformation of the Agrarian Economy, 1500–1850*, Cambridge 1996, 68, 87.
8 Hainsworth, *Stewards, Lords and People*, 43, 48–51.
9 Emmanuel College Archives, Cambridge (hereafter ECAC), Box 20/N11.
10 ECAC, Box 20/N12.
11 Clay, 'Landlords and Estate Management', 230–2.

tial to make it more likely that Rebow's rent would be paid in full. By the end of the following year, a new tenant, Charles Spalding, had taken over the farm. In addition, Mr Brook, the neighbour of this holding, was hiring three farms, which included part of Otley Hall, Poplar Farm, and a small holding known as White Horse. Together this land totalled over 180 acres. It would seem that Brook did not have the capital to support this size of tenancy because in 1724 he was pleading poverty to Armiger. As the latter reported in near-illiterate style to Rebow, if he 'hould the farm two years he shall not be worth on grot if thar be a nef to pay you'.[12] Ultimately, it proved counter-productive for landlords to ignore these pleadings from stewards and burden their tenants with rent levels they could not afford. Joshua Nelson, steward of Brames Hall, Wetheringsett, admitted to his master while trying to fix lease terms with a new tenant for the farm, 'I was in hopes to have got a greater raise [in rent], but I can't see that twill doe; you having in a few years raised £5 per annum [with the late tenant], which I perceive is known to every body I meet with.'[13] In this period there were 'more farms to let than there were desirable tenants to occupy them'. Frequently this left the steward and landlord in a weakened position. The landlord therefore had to accept a reduction in rent, or run the risk of having farms left unoccupied.[14]

Besides negotiating rent levels, stewards had to draw up leasing agreements with tenants. This could also prove extremely difficult because of the divergent interests between owner and occupier: 'the tenant's interest was in winning the maximum amount of produce from the soil during the duration of his tenancy; the landlord's main concern was the long-term value of his property'.[15] Some of the most contentious issues negotiated between lessor and lessee in this respect included timber felling agreements and ploughing restrictions. It was the steward's duty to warn his master against defective lease covenants already in place or being suggested for new contracts. Again the Otley Hall estate provides a good example. Armiger wrote to Sir Isaac Rebow in 1725 that Mr Brook's arable lands were 'all stried by cropin so ofin', a direct consequence he believed of Rebow giving 'leave to Brook to crop all'.[16] He advised Rebow that even though the three farms Brook hired 'ware all rich land . . . croping thus wand (want) sumerland'. It is more likely that Brook's lease omitted restraints on continual cropping, rather than positively instructing him to do so.

Once the lease contract had been finalised the steward had to convey its stipulations to the tenant. Often the first obligation the steward had to discharge after leases were signed was the repairing of farm buildings, gates and fences, and the cleaning of ditches. Of course, the steward would also have to ensure that lease covenants were properly observed in the following months and years, and that tenant

12 PRO, C112/181, steward's memorandum book; SROI, HB11/1/140, W. Armiger to Sir Issac Rebow, 30 Sept. 1724.

13 PRO, C109/153, J. Nelson to Mr Sherrington, 22 June 1709.

14 Hainsworth, *Stewards, Lords and People*, 54.

15 T. Williamson and S. Wade-Martins, *Roots of Change: Farming and Landscape in East Anglia, c.1700–1870*, British Agricultural History Society 1999, 181.

16 SROI, HB11/1/140. 'Stried' means wasted or destructed.

misdemeanours were not allowed to go unchecked. Certainly, the steward for Flixton Hall estate in 1750 reprimanded Matthew Towers of Wood Farm, Flixton, for neglecting his farming duties and indulging in sporting activities in Flixton Park instead. The tenant was told 'imediately [to] dispose of his doggs and guns, leave sporting, and become the farmer'.[17]

The most critical judgement the steward had to make when enlisting new tenants for unoccupied farms was whether the potential candidate had enough capital to run the holding properly, and if his character was sufficiently honest and industrious. For instance, in 1709 Joshua Nelson wrote to his master, Mr Sherrington, recommending a new tenant (Sutton), for Brames Hall Farm, Wetheringsett. He commented that, 'the young man bears as good a caracter as ever I mett with and seems to be an industrous soberman and for certaine is a man of substance and I believe will use the farm well'.[18] Conversely, before interviewing Sutton, the steward had advised against letting Mrs Benham stay on for a year as tenant on the farm, while a successor was found to replace her late husband. He wrote to Sherrington 'it will impoverish the farm to carry off the stover (straw fodder), besides some other inconveniences and hazards . . . if she stays one more year then she will do considerable damage, making all the advantage they can another year . . . and this I cannot see how we can prevent she being only tenant at will'.[19] Likewise, Lord Henniker's steward in 1820 warned his master that if Samuel Fruer, tenant of Bedfield Hall, was fit to farm then 'any labourer may be thought' to be capable as well. Fruer had broken most of the covenants in his lease, sub-let his grass land to neighbouring farmers, and regularly defaulted on his rent. The steward told Henniker that the farm needed a tenant with at least £1,000 to run and stock it properly. Unfortunately, Fruer, who had never signed a lease, but had taken the farm over at the death of his father, never possessed this amount of money.[20] As the misdemeanours perpetrated by Mr Ward at Cotton and Mr Hempson at Haughley Green will show below, it was imperative that the steward made the right choice. Unfortunately, the problems encountered when selecting a suitable tenant could be substantial. As the steward noted of Mr Hempson, he appeared to be a 'plain, honest countryman, with the outward appearance of a frugal disposition', but he turned out to be a 'hypocrite and a rogue'. With the benefit of hindsight the steward concluded that it was never completely possible to 'tell these people until they are in the estate'.[21]

17 SROL, 741/A4/2/25.
18 PRO, C109/153, J. Nelson to Mr Sherrington, 20 May 1709.
19 PRO, C109/153.
20 SROI, S1/2/200 Bundle 5, two letters inside 1807 lease for Bedfield Hall.
21 Rochester-upon-Medway Study Centre (hereafter RMSC), U480/C18 (Bundle 4).

The Effectiveness of the Steward

(a) Absentee Stewards

It is clear that the steward's role was an important one, and landowners ignored it at their peril. Unfortunately, it would seem that some of the region's landlords did show such disregard; their greatest mistake was failing to ensure that the steward was resident. As Map 1 shows, five of the ten absentee properties examined in this paper had a non-resident steward. It is likely that on these properties regular contact would have been rare for the tenant. The steward for Cotton Hill Farm, for instance, visited the holding only once between 1746 and 1748. He admitted to the owner of the farm, Samuel Buck, that he had no knowledge whether the tenant had changed his foreman in this period because, 'I was not upon the spot.'[22] Similarly, Daniel Sayer, the agent for the Emmanuel College farm at St Cross, only seemed to visit the holding to collect the rent. In July 1745, when the tenant was significantly in arrears, Sayer visited the farm several times in an attempt to settle the college's account. His excursions were in vain and he admitted that the tenant would have to 'be a little threatned by somebody of more authority than myself for my words have almost lost their usual influence on him'.[23]

The crisis that John Wybarne encountered when he came into ownership of the Flixton Hall property in the late 1730s was caused primarily by the non-attendance of Mr Pullyn, the estate steward. The latter was absent from the estate for much of the time, preferring instead to fulfil the role of manorial steward elsewhere. The previous owner, George Tasburgh, had himself been an absentee landlord and was described in the 1730s as an 'indolent man'. When visiting the property in January 1740, Wybarne found it extremely difficult to gather any of the outstanding rent arrears. Moreover, he was threatened by the tenants that any attempt to enforce payment by a seizure of goods would result in many of his farms becoming untenanted. The animosity shown here by the tenants had arisen primarily from the previous steward's failure to visit and attend to important estate business. He collected the rents from Tasburgh's tenants, but little else seems to have been done in the way of estate management. This meant that for several years no maintenance to farmhouses, outbuildings, hedges and ditches had been carried out.[24] It was rare for farm tenants to accept the added financial burden of repair and maintenance work. For example, the steward of the Pembroke College estate at Saxtead knew that if no repairs were instigated after 'a great wind' in 1704 'the farmes will be turned into my hands'. It was not likely, therefore, that in a period of agricultural depression the tenantry at Flixton would be inclined to pay rent on time and faithfully keep their pasture and arable lands in good condition, when the landlord's workmen never appeared. A similar state of affairs seems to have existed on the Constable estate at

22 PRO, C112/181, instructions to Mrs Buck, 10 Aug. 1748.
23 ECAC, Box 20/N21.
24 SROL, 741/A4/2/31, 741/E1/5/110; SROI, HD148/5,7,8,10.

Everingham (Yorkshire) in the same period.[25] Not surprisingly Tasburgh's successor, John Wybarne, was reluctant to pay Mr Pullyn's outstanding salary of £60.[26] In addition, the estate's leasing agreements were clearly unsatisfactory. At least half of the tenants were on yearly 'at-will' agreements that only included covenants for maintenance and general repair work. The remaining tenants, on fixed terms of five, seven, fourteen or twenty-one years, had few more covenants in their leases than those with yearly agreements. There were no final year clauses specifying in what state the arable fields of the holding were to be left, and, perhaps more important, there were no restrictions on ploughing up old pasture lands. The consequences of these deficient contracts were that the property was 'beggared by plowing' and stripped of nearly all its tree stocks. The tenants-at-will seem to have managed their farms in a slovenly way, suggesting that a lack of tenurial security undermined the tenant's confidence in investing in any improvements, and that he preferred instead to opt for short-term gains.[27]

The disadvantages of absentee stewards were compounded further when they in turn employed agents and bailiffs to work on their behalf. It is certainly likely that many under-stewards enlisted in this period were of dubious worth. Just as the Leveson-Gower estate in Staffordshire was damaged in the 1670s and 1680s by leaving the administration of the property in the hands of local bailiffs, much the same seems to be the case on the Buck property at Cotton.[28] Four local men were employed in quick succession in this capacity between 1743 and 1750: John Rushbrook, Robert Graham, William Wright and Samuel Amys. There is good evidence that at least the first of these men actively colluded with the tenantry. In 1744, for instance, he helped sell hay and wood that had been stripped illegally by William Ward, the tenant of Cotton Hill Farm. He made little attempt to stop the widespread felling of trees and hedges across the estate; he also allowed neighbours to store corn in the farmhouse, which led to the cheese chamber floor being badly damaged. It would seem that the lessee's father bullied him into accepting every demand laid before him. There is no evidence of any fine payments being imposed for these misdemeanours, although they were clearly in breach of the covenants contained within the lease for the farm. Only at the end of his term was Ward evicted, having inflicted much damage in the preceding seven years.[29] In 1748 the steward acknowledged his mistake in hiring Rushbrook, by describing him as a 'wrong agent . . . who had suffered to be done many things he cannot justify'.[30] By this time, however, the damage had been done. The bailiffs employed were either weak or

25 P. Roebuck, ed., *Constable of Everingham Estate Correspondence, 1726–43*, Yorkshire Archaeological Society, Record Series 136 (1974), 16.

26 SROI, HD148/7,8,10; PCAC, Framlingham/W2.

27 SROL, 741/D3/1, 741/E1/5/110.

28 J. Wordie, *Estate Management in Eighteenth Century England: The Building of the Leveson-Gower Fortune*, London 1982, 18–19.

29 PRO, C112/181, observations upon the lease of W. Ward.

30 PRO, C112/181, instructions to Mrs Buck, 10 Aug. 1748. An earlier comment from this steward was more favourable to Rushbrook. He stated that Rushbrook was an 'honest man only a little hot, I am not infalible, nor I believe is he'.

easily corruptible, and, as they were the main contact with the landlord, the tenants probably believed Mr Buck to be of a similar character. Ultimately, his tenants lost their respect for him, and this is shown in a comment made by a tenant named Gleed, who rented a house in Cotton. He believed that Buck 'was not worth a half-penny'.[31]

The character of another of the local bailiffs at Cotton Hill suggests that he also would have been a poor choice as acting steward. Robert Graham was described in 1748 as a 'man of much passion and of strong resentments, as I have been told both poor and proud, I know he will drink when he can get it and is then apt to talk too fast so that I always spoke to him twice before I came to a resolution to follow his advice and directions'. Moreover, in 1750 Robert Stegwell, the tenant farmer at Cherrytree Farm, Bacton, was also performing some of the duties of the absent steward. He was instructed to keep a close eye on any dilapidations caused by the neighbouring Cotton Hill tenant, William Ward, in the final year of his tenure. It was perhaps inevitable that this measure created animosity between the two tenants. Stegwell adhered faithfully to his orders and on an October evening in 1750 noticed Ward's workmen taking wood off the property. Their response on being caught was verbally to abuse Stegwell. To quote, 'they called me a Creep Hedgely Rogue for seeing them'.[32]

It would seem that, in general, the absence of the steward could severely hinder the effective supervision of an estate. From her research into nineteenth-century estate management in East Yorkshire, Barbara English has concluded, however, that ignorance of farming practices was potentially even more damaging to the effectiveness of the steward than non-attendance. Non-resident agents, she maintains, 'coming only twice a year to the estates for rent days, could manage estates successfully as long as they were practical farmers'.[33] Unfortunately, as Edward Laurence noted in the 1720s, many English land agents were country attorneys with little or no farming knowledge.[34] Daniel Sayer and Joshua Nelson, whom we have already met, were attorneys at Harleston and Bungay, respectively. The steward for Cotton Hill Farm in the 1740s also had little idea of the established farming customs of the region. In 1743 he had to consult closely with Baron Pretyman of Bacton before being able to draw up a lease for the incoming tenant, William Ward. It is also very much open to question why he selected this man as a suitable candidate for the tenancy, since the Ward family seem to have had destructive intentions towards the farm from the outset.[35]

The consequences of leaving tenants to their own devices with little or no contact

31 PRO, C112/181.

32 PRO, C112/181. Though it is likely that they used the term 'creep hedgely' to denote the action of furtive surveillance, the phrase was also used in the eighteenth century to describe a prostitute.

33 English 'Patterns', 39.

34 E. Laurence, *The Duty of a Steward to his Lord*, 1971 reprint, 5.

35 PRO, C109/153 – various letters and C112/181 instructions to Mrs Buck on the 10 Aug. 1748.

with owner and steward, especially through periods of economic austerity, has already been indicated by the example of Cotton Hill Farm. Other instances that illustrate the deleterious impact of complete absenteeism include Abbots Hall Farm, Pettaugh and a holding at Haughley Green. On the former property in 1763 Lord Tollemache sent his steward to view the farm with an eye to purchasing it. The owner of the farm was an absentee, Mr Bennett of Witham, Essex. After inspecting the estate, the steward asked the tenant, Turner, if he could see his current lease; the tenant refused him permission, saying that he was under only one clause which bound him to do all repairs needed on the thatching and daubing of the house, and to maintain the hedges and stiles in the fields. From the surviving correspondence, it seems Tollemache's steward did not believe him. Luckily, the lease that the steward was not allowed to see survives in the Helmingham Hall archives. Within the document are numerous covenants concerning cropping and ploughing restrictions, tree lopping and end of term stipulations. It is clear that the tenant was concealing the truth from the prospective owner. It is also apparent that he had taken little notice of the lease, farming the estate the way he pleased. The steward's report suggests a high proportion of land was under the plough for a heavy clay farm of its size (approximately 170 acres) at that period. Nearly half of the estate was listed as arable, and the survey continues by lamenting that there was only one timber tree of any value left on the farm.[36]

Similarly, the farm at Haughley Green was left in an impoverished state by its tenant, Robert Hempson, and his under-tenant, the appropriately named Mr Mudd. Hempson was described in 1738 as neglecting the farm, having 'scarcely plowed, sowed or fedd the same' for several years, whereas Mudd had 'made away and converted' the livestock of the farm for his own use in 1735. The buildings and land of the farm were described in 1739 as in a 'ruinous, desolate condition' and because of this the owner, Thomas Best, was informed that no tenant would rent the property until it was put into proper repair. He was also told that to restore the farm to its former condition would take at least two years, and that until the work had been done the property would be in 'the Lyons Mouth'.[37]

(b) Resident Stewards

Estate management regimes on the five absentee properties and the two semi-resident 'home' estates that had a resident steward were certainly in a better state. It would seem, however, that the character and background of the agent employed differed between these two types of estate. For instance, whereas 'home' estates such as the North property at Glemham Hall usually employed a full-time professional land agent, secondary estates such as the Tollemache and Grimston examples engaged one of the more able tenant farmers on the estate in the role of part-time steward. From evidence to be found in the North and Tollemache archives there appears to

36 Helmingham Hall Archive (hereafter HHA), T/Hel/26/74, T/Hel/127/9/1.
37 RMSC, U480/C18 (Bundle 3); PRO, E134/11GEO2/EAST3.

have been little difference in the role of these agents as overseers of the tenantry. Both Daniel Wayth on the North estate and Thomas Brereton and, later, Peter Kersey on the Tollemache property seem to have been enlisting new tenants for farms, commissioning building and repair work, and drawing up effective lease agreements. Ploughing restrictions, cropping clauses and directives to lay down arable lands when ploughing up pasture fields were all permanent features of these leases. It would appear, moreover, that the full-time nature of Wayth's job enabled him to contribute more time to the running of Glemham Hall and its gardens, and to the management of any livestock that his master owned. He was also able to keep a keen eye on the local land market for any useful additions to the estate. From the archives it is clear that Wayth kept up a regular correspondence with North throughout the 1720s and 1730s.[38] Though the heyday of the resident agent on landed estates came in the nineteenth century, and their pre-1750 counterpart is often seen as being poorly trained, Wayth performed his duties with competence. He was certainly determined that all the tenants on the estate should abide by their lease covenants. For example, the tenant of Church Farm, Cransford, was forced by Wayth in 1725 to lay down Hungry Hill and Peartree Close with hay seed, as directed in a lease of three years earlier.[39] In comparison, he seems to have been a better choice for the post than other contemporary examples such as Earl Cowper's Hertfordshire steward or Sir Marmaduke Constable's agent at Everingham Hall, East Yorkshire.[40]

As suggested above, many of these positive comments can also be applied to the two stewards on the Tollemache estate. It is clear from documentary evidence that Peter Kersey was as determined as Daniel Wayth that tenants should comply with all their farming covenants. Between the mid-1750s and mid-1760s, for example, Kersey fined four tenants for various misdemeanours such as ploughing up grass borders around their arable fields, cutting down and selling timber, and, in one case, taking up the top soil from a pasture field. Nevertheless, the case of Thomas Brereton, a previous Helmingham steward, highlights one possible hazard of filling the post from the ranks of the tenantry. The tenant of the 85-acre Elm Farm in Helmingham, Brereton was one of the smaller farmers on the estate. Consequently, he would have been in charge of more substantial farmers than himself. It is perhaps not surprising, therefore, that the main dispute recorded in the archives between himself and another tenant was with William Moyse, farmer of the largest Helmingham farm – the 285-acre Bocking Hall. In 1719 Brereton confided in Tollemache that Moyse had little respect for his authority. Revealingly, Moyse was quoted at one point as saying that he refused 'to go to the foot [Brereton] when he could go to the head [Tollemache]'. It would seem that Moyse was also spreading rumours in order to poison opinion against Brereton. He circulated the news that Tollemache had cautioned Brereton for timber irregularities. More libellously he put about that Tollemache had called the steward 'a cheating son of whores'. In the end,

38 SROI, various correspondence in accession HA49.

39 SROI, HA49/C2/5/1–3.

40 Clay, 'Landlords and Estate Management', 243; Roebuck, 'Absentee Landownership', 2.

Brereton had the best of the dispute since in the following year Moyse was evicted from his farm. Whether this was a constructive decision or an act of revenge is open to question. Brereton admitted that Moyse had improved the farm by stubbing up unwanted bushes and trees and spreading manure where needed: yet there was also too much land under the plough.[41] What is obvious from this dispute is that, if landlords decided to appoint one of their tenants as steward, it was advisable to nominate the most senior and substantial individual from their ranks. The subsequent Tollemache steward, Peter Kersey of Framsden Hall, was certainly in this bracket, as was the Eames family of Rishangles Lodge on the Grimston property.[42]

Resident stewards were also found on the institutional estates in the region: these included the Crown farms at Brundish and the Pembroke College lands at Framlingham and Saxtead. The management system employed here, however, was subtly different. This involved a 'grand tenant' hiring the whole estate, paying the rent to the Crown or the College, and then sub-letting each farm to various local farmers. The duties of such men when supervising tenants were much the same as those discharged by the above-mentioned stewards. The 'grand tenants' at Brundish and Framlingham were usually local gentlemen farmers. Whatever their status, however, corruption was not unknown in their ranks. For example, three main accusations were levelled against Edward Alpe (both father and son), in the bundles of Pembroke College correspondence: first, that they allowed their sub-tenants to have too much land in tilth; secondly, that too many trees were felled under their direction; and lastly that Alpe senior falsified both his rent and repair accounts. However, the motives of Richard Porter of Framlingham who made these charges were questionable. He was the grand lessee whom Alpe succeeded, and he may therefore either have been seeking revenge for his removal or attempting to get his former job back. Though there is no way of confirming the accuracy of Porter's claims, his accusation that too much land was in tilth was noted by the Fellows of the college and dismissed. Their indifference stemmed from the fact that the amount of land illicitly in tilth was probably very small. For instance, the grand lease permitted 100 acres of arable, and when Alpe proposed new lease contracts in 1696 the amount in tillage was to be raised be a mere half dozen acres.[43]

The leasing agreements on these estates (known as grand leases) contained few if any farming covenants. Each document set out the yearly rent, the length of term (normally long, of between twenty-one and thirty-one years), and clauses about repairs and timber allowances. On the three estates above, only the Framlingham grand lease specified ploughing restrictions.[44] If more detailed farming covenants were agreed, then it was usually at the direction of the grand tenant when sub-letting

41 HHA, T/Hel/1/59 and 61, T/Hel/20/42.

42 Hertfordshire Record Office (hereafter HRO), X1.13.

43 Pembroke College Archive, Cambridge (hereafter PCAC), Framlingham/K3, notes for a speech to be made by T. Browne, Master of Pembroke College, to the inhabitants of Framlingham, dated 11 February 1695/6, and two letters from R. Porter to the Fellows of the College, 8 Oct. 1701 and 24 Aug. 1702.

44 PCAC, Framlingham/T2 and X1–X6.

took place. At St Edmund's Farm, Brundish, for example, the Crown's grand tenant, James Wyard Gooch, drew up a reasonably detailed lease in 1764.[45] The fellows of Pembroke College realised the potential defects of this system by the early years of the eighteenth century. In 1702, a surveyor's letter to the college commented that the grand tenant for Saxtead, Henry Smith, had 'unreasonably set back' the estate by allowing the arable lands to be cropped too often and taking down so many trees that there was not enough wood left even for the dairy copper. As a result of the latter depredations, firing had to be fetched from up to four miles away. Nevertheless, after one of the Fellows went to survey the estate and consulted the lease he concluded that the grand tenant had merely managed the estate in the way he was 'obliged' to by the lease covenants. He also admitted that the grand tenant had done more fencing and ditching work than was required. A subsequent grand lease in 1704 rectified these omissions.[46]

Once Pembroke College scrapped the grand lease system at Framlingham in 1696 and at Saxtead in 1722, both properties had farm leases drawn up that varied little from agreements made on private family estates.[47] The implementation of these contracts seems to have been fairly well monitored, though perhaps not always as closely as on some of those estates with resident stewards. For instance, there are subsequent examples of tenants having too much land under the plough. These included Adam Crosby of Little Lodge, Framlingham, who had roughly 40 acres ploughed in 1708 but was permitted a maximum of only 32, and Benjamin Luffingham of Great Lodge, Framlingham, who was allowed 120 acres of arable land in 1791 but actually had 127 acres under the plough. Nevertheless, Andrew Bedingfield, the previous tenant of Little Lodge, was fined £60 at the termination of his lease in 1702, because of a 'breach of articles' in his lease concerning 'overplowing and selling wood'.[48]

Finally, it is worth making a general cautionary point about the employment of resident stewards. In many respects the resident steward took on the mantle of surrogate landlord. He would have overseen the signing of leases, and the collection of rents, as well as keeping up a regular correspondence with his master. It was often the case that his homestead acted as the administrative and social centre of the estate, with annual festivities at harvest and Christmas taking place there. For example, the Grimstons gave the Eames family at Rishangles Lodge a yearly allowance in the seventeenth century for putting on dinners at these times for the tenants of the estate.[49] Problems, however, did occur when stewards overstepped their authority. If a landlord took little interest in farming matters, and lived many miles away, it is perhaps understandable that his steward would assume more authority than his position warranted. Occasionally, this provoked anger from the landlord, as was the case in 1820, when Lord Henniker's steward set new rent levels without consulting his

45 SROI, X1/4/3.2 (322).

46 PCAC, Framlingham/T2.

47 PCAC, Framlingham/K1, K3, Y1–5.

48 PCAC, Framlingham/K3; SROI, FEI/6/44, GB10/1/1.

49 SROI, P644/1; HRO, X1.13, X1.17.

master.[50] Similarly, in 1718 Lord Tollemache had to reprimand Thomas Brereton when he was informed that the steward had been embezzling timber from the estate. The relationship between steward and tenant was also adversely affected if the former misused his authority. Peter Kersey, for example, seems to have treated some of the Helmingham tenants heavy-handedly and taken too much pleasure from the detection of their misdemeanours. In a letter of 1768 he was keen to tell Lord Tollemache that after confronting the Garnham family at Paris Farm, Helmingham, over allegations of malpractice, he left them 'crying and swearing'.[51]

Conclusion

It is clear that a good resident steward was an essential requirement for the sound running of an absentee estate. Without an adequate level of inspection and control by the steward, misconduct on the tenant's part was likely to occur at some point. Not surprisingly, offences were more common in periods of economic austerity. Many of the examples cited here come from the difficult years of the 1730s and 1740s. On balance, the majority of resident stewards in the region seem to have been reasonably honest and competent at their job, except for succumbing to the occasional temptation to fell estate tree stocks. In Glamorgan, in the century after the Restoration, the quality of stewardship appears to have been extremely variable.[52] Not surprisingly, the eighteenth-century landowner was fearful of the unscrupulous or incompetent agent.

Considering the pivotal role stewards played in the supervision of rural properties, it is necessary in conclusion to evaluate briefly the extent to which the land agent promoted change in the pattern of farming. Unfortunately, documentary evidence from the region is inconclusive on this point. For example, it is not at all clear from estate correspondence requesting permission from the owner for changes in agricultural practice whether the steward was taking the lead or following the tenant. Certainly, as we have seen, the steward was often the most substantial tenant on the estate. Arthur Young was in little doubt that innovation was more likely to be initiated by the larger farmer. However, the examples given in his *General View* and Raynbird's *Agriculture of Suffolk* of celebrated tenant agriculturists, such as John Edwards of Poplar Farm, Ashbocking and Lionel Hayward of Stoke Ash Hall, do not concern men who were stewards on their respective estates.[53] In addition, evidence from the Helmingham Hall archives seems to suggest that the steward was not at the forefront when it came to promoting new agricultural techniques. When Lord Tollemache sought advice about the proposed changes requested by the incoming tenant, John Edwards, in 1774, he went to a professional land surveyor for guidance

50 SROI, S1/2/200 (Bundle 5).

51 HHA, T/Hel/1/166.

52 J. Martin, 'Estate Stewards and their Work in Glamorgan, 1660–1760: A Regional Study of Estate Management', *Journal of Glamorgan History* xxiii, 1979, 9–28.

53 Young, *General View of the Agriculture of Suffolk*, 33, 35, 47, 350–410; Raynbird, *On the Agriculture of Suffolk*, 115, 124, 129, 187.

rather than to his steward, Peter Kersey.[54] This is not surprising since one of the principal elements of the land agent's job was to protect the owner's property from unscrupulous tenants. Frequently, this resulted in management regimes which favoured the retention of long established farming practices, rather than the encouragement of new methods and techniques.

It would seem, therefore, that the impetus for agricultural change and improvement in the region came from the tenant farmer rather than the estate steward. The land agent, however, still had an important role to play in this process, primarily as a mediator between owner and occupier. Whether they were rent abatements in times of hardship before 1750 or the approval of financial support for new farming methods after this date, the tenant was more likely to achieve his objectives if there were good lines of communication between himself and his landlord. An attentive resident steward would normally have maintained these. In general terms, co-operation between owner and occupier was a central feature of any well-run estate. Its absence on a property, and specifically on the estates of total absentees discussed here, impeded the development of farming practice. Its presence, however, found across the region on semi-resident and well-run absentee estates alike, represents the steward's greatest contribution to agrarian change.

54 HHA, T/Hel/26/102 and 120.

Journal of a Tour through Suffolk, Norfolk, Lincolnshire and Yorkshire in the Summer of 1741

Richard G. Wilson[1]

Introduction

MY FIRST THOUGHTS about a contribution to this volume were to write an essay about the impressions Suffolk made on those travellers who journeyed through the county in the eighteenth century – Celia Fiennes, Daniel Defoe, William Gilpin, François de la Rochefoucauld, and especially the accounts of others less well known.[2] As journeys by the new turnpike roads became easier after the 1750s, sprung carriages more comfortable and the literature to guide them more plentiful, increasing numbers of the upper classes felt the urge to travel. They set forth each summer to appraise the regions of Britain, many of them articulating in highly personal terms their experiences and impressions in letters, diaries or journals.

Samuel Johnson approved of these exercises. He advised travellers to regulate their imaginations by reality, to see 'how things may be, to see them as they are'.[3] Travellers therefore wanted to become familiar with inns and roads, the state of towns and trade, to assess the impact of cathedrals, churches and public buildings, to imbibe spa waters, to enjoy an assembly and, above all, to view the country houses of the nation's ruling class. Visiting the latter to acquaint themselves with art, architecture and garden design became a key component of upper-class culture and

1 I am grateful to the Trustees of the British Library for permission to reproduce this Journal ('Itinerary of a Journey from Cambridge to Suffolk, Norfolk, Lincolnshire and Yorkshire', 1741. BL Add. MSS 38,488, fos 17b–49). In editing this journal I have received the most generous help from David Adshead, John Barney, Michael Begley, John Blatchly, Christine Clark, David Dymond, Andrew Moore, Pat Murrell and Merlin Waterson.

Editorial additions are all in square brackets; the author himself on occasion uses round ones. Abbreviations have been drawn out, minimal punctuation introduced, capital letters modernised, and paragraphs constructed.

2 Celia Fiennes, *The Journey of Celia Fiennes*, ed. C. Morris, London 1947; Daniel Defoe, *A Tour through England and Wales*, ed. G.D.H. Cole, 2 vols, London 1928; William Gilpin, *Observations in Several Parts of the Counties of Cambridge, Norfolk, Suffolk and Essex. Also on Several Parts of North Wales, 1769 and 1773*, London 1809; N. Scarfe, ed., *A Frenchman's Year in Suffolk*, SRS 30, 1988.

3 Quoted in I. Ousby, *The Englishman's England: Taste, Travel and the Rise of Tourism*, Cambridge 1990, 9.

behaviour. Sadly, Suffolk was never on the recognised routes of most eighteenth-century travellers. And, when it was, those who recorded their journeys half dismissed it in their haste to get to Norfolk to view the Palladian splendours of Holkham and Houghton, that brace of houses at the top of the list of any traveller with even the most perfunctory interest in architecture. When Charles Lyttleton, dean of Exeter and later bishop of Carlisle, set out from London in August 1758 on an East Anglian country house jaunt he wrote to his friend, the amateur architect Sanderson Miller, 'It surprised me a good deal to find that in so large a County as Suffolk and so near the Metropolis, not a single Gentleman's Seat that I saw or heard of, except the Duke of Grafton's at Euston, had been improved in the modern taste.' On the other hand he thought his correspondent must visit Norfolk, 'To a man of your taste no part of England is so well worth a visit at least none that I have ever seen . . . Lord Leicester's [Holkham] alone would pay you the trouble and expense of your journey.'[4]

Similarly, the earl of Oxford and the Honourable Philip Yorke only seriously viewed Euston in their journeys through Suffolk in the 1730s and 1750s respectively. Even there, Lord Oxford, contrary and brimful of Tory bile, could dismiss the house (but not the park) as 'very indifferent, the furniture old and bad, the pictures very poor and mean. I was extremely disappointed in every part.' Six years earlier, he had given Ickworth and Redgrave even shorter shrift.[5] Horace Walpole, the best known of all Georgian country house tourists, records no Suffolk houses in his 'Journals of Visits to Country Seats'; Mrs Lybbe Powys, just as tireless in her pursuit of them, mentioned none.[6] Indeed, she barely acknowledged the existence of the county as she swept through it in 1756 and 1781. Breckland she found depressing, Ipswich 'dreadful . . . a most melancholy place'.[7] And when the pursuit of the sublime and picturesque grew apace, especially with the virtual closure of the continent for two decades after 1793, Suffolk, as indeed did Norfolk, remained on few tourists' lists as they converged in their hordes on Derbyshire, the Lake District and the mountains of Scotland and Wales. When William Mavor compiled his six-volume pocket abridgement *The British Tour or Travellers Pocket Companion* (1798), a collection of all the better-known travel guides of the previous thirty years, Suffolk did not merit an entry.

It was in this search for Suffolk material that I came across, in the British Library, a tour made through Suffolk, Norfolk, Lincolnshire and Yorkshire in July and August 1741. Given its early date, before the general rush of tourist journals and travel guides, and its interest, I decided to edit it for a wider audience. It was not the

4 L. Dickins and M. Stanton, eds, *An Eighteenth-Century Correspondence: Being the Letters to Sanderson Miller, esq., of Radway*, London 1910, 397.

5 *HMCR, Portland* VI, 151, 170; J. Godber, ed., *The Marchioness Grey of Wrest Park*, Bedfordshire Historical Record Society 47, 1968, 125–63.

6 P. Toynbee, ed., *Horace Walpole's Journals of Visits to Country Seats, etc.*, Walpole Society 16, 1927–28.

7 E.J. Climenson, ed., *Passages from the Diaries of Mrs Philip Lybbe Powys of Hardwicke House, Oxon., AD 1756 to 1808*, London 1899, 2–3, 209.

easiest decision since Norman Scarfe is acknowledged to be the doyen of editors in this field. His lively translation of the tours of the young de la Rochefoucauld brothers and their tutor in the 1780s are brought wonderfully alive because he has bearded authorities to hone his discursive footnotes, ransacked libraries and museums for illustrations, and, not least, bringing his *Shell Guide* training to the task, travelled virtually every yard of the trio's journeys. My rendition of this brief journal is a tribute, however pale, to his skills and example.

The journal of a six weeks' tour through the four eastern counties, beginning in Cambridge and ending in York, is an anonymous compilation. It is located in the Liverpool papers deposited in around 1911 in the British Library. No clues to its authorship are given either in the text or the collection. About whether it was written by a member of the Jenkinson, Cope or Foljambe families (each connected with the two creations of the earldom of Liverpool in 1796 and 1905) it is idle to speculate. The only locational reference made beyond the record of the tour itself is to the Sussex downs. Since there are no foreign comparisons it is unlikely the author ever set foot on the Continent. Was he a fellow of a Cambridge college, since that is his point of departure and the journey made during the summer vacation? Certainly, he was a gentleman of education (albeit with somewhat careless Latin) who travelled by coach with at least one companion and who had easy access to a number of country houses en route.

Such journals as this seldom tell us what we most want to know. This is no exception. There is almost nothing on his mode of travel, virtually no mention of the inns in which he stayed. Nor is there little more on the state of the towns he visited and their trade and industry. What he does record reinforces accounts made by Celia Fiennes and Daniel Defoe: the half-mile long quay at Yarmouth, crowded with shipping, was one of the wonders of urban England; the fattening of geese at Beccles suggests almost a form of proto-factory rearing; employment in Bury St Edmunds (with its great medieval past still much in evidence) and Ipswich was tied to the Norwich worsted industry; Lincoln was deficient with regard to trade; the pre-eminence of York, except for the remarkable trio of buildings described here in some detail, was as Celia Fiennes had found forty years earlier, much exaggerated by Yorkshiremen. On the other hand, Leeds was bustling with its cloth industry and markets, its environs scattered with the comfortable villas of the town's leading merchants.

In 1741 England had enjoyed a generation of peace and almost a century of static population growth and gently accelerating prosperity. The sense of a country at peace and of great beauty emerges through the writer's pedestrian prose. All the forts he noted around the coast, utterly inadequate in themselves to withstand invasion, were in varying degrees of decay. The fields around Stowmarket were full of timber trees, mainly elm with some oaks. The river Orwell down to Harwich was bordered by 'fine hanging banks of corn or hanging woods, which with the water, fine houses, churches, and ships, compose as great a variety of pretty views as one can possibly expect to meet with'. Near Duncombe Park we audibly accompany the diarist as he describes how his conversation was 'perpetually disturbed by the purling and murmuring and sometimes clamorous noise' of the River Rye.

Agricultural improvement, spurred on by the export bounty on corn and innovations with turnips, is much in evidence. From the Lincolnshire heath crops of corn stretched as far as the eye could see. Good ale was plentiful. An abundance of wildlife proliferated. At Blickling the gardens were full of hares; on the road from Lincoln to Sleaford, 'the whole fenn abounded so much with wild-geese that we could have rode down at least an hundred in an hour'. In Scarborough he noted arrangements for the spending of this new won prosperity. There, as at other spas, this pursuit of leisure by increasingly prosperous members of the landed, trading and professional classes was being catered for with a commercialism of which he could not quite approve.

But it is the writer's interest in architecture and garden design that is the most evident feature of the journal. Even if he had never undertaken the Grand Tour, he seems to have imbibed some of the English architectural literature which began to pour forth after the 1720s. In his comments on the Great House at Ipswich, Yarmouth Town Hall, Holy Trinity church, Leeds, and the famous Assembly Rooms at York, the impact that Palladianism was making in the second quarter of the eighteenth century becomes clear. Cathedrals and churches are appraised with less knowledge (although he was clearly bowled over by the beauties of Lincoln cathedral). Here his opinions and interests mirror the accounts of other tourists in early Georgian England. It is not the wonders of Gothic and Elizabethan architecture that move him, but the excitement of Palladianism spreading its tentacles into the regions and best evaluated in the latest development of the country house. Therefore he visits Lady Bristol's recently completed town house in Bury (noting its rich interiors, fine tapestries and upholstery and the japanned cabinets she herself had lacquered), Houghton (Sir Robert Walpole's famed collection of pictures recorded in great detail), Castle Howard and Duncombe Park, the latter three houses on every tourist's route in the 1740s. Others, such as Little Glemham and the predecessor of the great Taylor and Wyatt house at Heveningham, were less well known. The gardens of Bramham Park and Studley Royal, as well as those of Houghton, Castle Howard and Duncombe Park and all in 'the modern taste of shady walks and vistos', alive with temples and statues, were again essential stops for any elite traveller wanting to acquaint himself with up-to-date, tip-top garden design. Others visited were on a smaller scale: the garden at Heveningham with its novel reed wall (had Mr Dashwood seen them in southern France or Italy?) or Ebberston, a fashionable, tiny villa almost engulfed by one of the most remarkable water gardens in England.

Of the writer himself we learn nothing beyond his interests. He is not without humour: rather heavy in his two comments about the celebrated hardness of Suffolk cheese; more percipient in his observations about the true-to-type Yorkshireman taking the waters at Scarborough, fretting and fuming 'all the while he is there' at the thought of dining upon chicken at home for three pence a piece while supping on them at the spa for half-a-crown. Even with its limitations, the journal deserves to be more widely known. It provides a good view of the four eastern counties of England. In its account of towns and of country houses and gardens, with its constant focus on the recent and novel, even in the constraints of its reactions and prose, it is entirely typical of the observations of the upper-class traveller in the middle years of George II's reign.

THE JOURNAL

Set out Monday the 13th July 1741 from Cambridge for Newmarket, country plain and full of corn with fenns on each side, till you come upon Newmarket Heath. Within a mile of Newmarket is the Devil's Ditch more for a boundary and defence to the East Saxon Kingdom. Newmarket consists of nothing but inns and here and there a hunting seat surrounded by hills east and west long ways.[8] We saw the Duke of Devonshire's house, nothing remarkable in it, but about four pictures of famous horses. Colonel Panton's, a convenient built house, one remarkable fine picture of a house in full proportion. One room was very handsomely furnished with Spittle fields damask. The great chairs had backs to lean the head against. Trade they have none, but an exceeding good corn market in samples every Tuesday. April and October, the race times are the times of their jubilee, the publicans clearing as much money in those two fortnights as in all the rest of the year.

Leaving Newmarket you travel over a plain for about four miles, after which you come to Kennet Inn, 'tis a little village from which the town of Kentford takes its name, which is just on t'other side of the brook, which brook has given the town the name of ford. Over the brook is a very high bridge for horses. The brook, upon suddain rains, being often impassable. On each side of the bridge is a wall built very compactly with flints which is now kept up at the charge of the parish and this is so old that the inhabitants have no reports as to the foundation of it. Just beyond this on the right hand is Barrow where there is an old uninhabited seat belonging at present to the Earl of Bristol.[9] The town derives its name from its situation among the woods. Between Kentford and Barrowbridge, about three miles, we met a shepherd who said he fed 300 sheep upon the waste there. Further on to the left is Risby village upon a rise, where lives Mr. Sparkes, a man of plentiful fortunes. From Kentford to Burry, an open country abounding with corn and here and there a fine grove.

At Burry, when opening an old monument in the chancel of the new church, about five years ago, was found a leaden coffin in the shape of a human body with this inscription, Mary Queen of France married to Charles Brandon, Duke of Suffolk. In the church a fine marble monument of Reynolds, Lord Chancellor; in the churchyard a stone with an inscription declaring that Mary Martin midwife brought into the world 2237 children. An hospital founded by Dr. Clopton for 12 decayed

8 John Kirby, *The Suffolk Traveller*, 2nd edn, 1764, 190: 'His Majesty hath a House here for his Residence during the Races, and there are many good modern Houses built by Noblemen and Gentlemen, who delight in Horse-Coursing, and sometimes condescend to countenance that Sport with their Prescence.' See also P. May, *The Changing Face of Newmarket, 1600–1760*, Newmarket 1984, 37–8.

9 Kirby, *Suffolk Traveller*, 217. 'The Ruins of their (the de Tybetots) seat a little South of the Church, bespeak it to have been a very noble structure.' The bridge was destroyed in the 1970s.

tradesmen with a salary of £300 a year. The wooden roof in the old church not so remarkable as we expected from the character given of it by Camden.[10]

In the Earl of Bristol's house small and neat ceilings fretted, and some very fine pictures chiefly of their own family. One room below pictures of the royal family, amongst the rest a very fine picture of Lady Jane Grey. In a closet a couch with fine tapestry, the story of the Prophet, the Lion and the Bees; another couch with the story of Sampson somewhat inferior to this. Lady Anne Harvey and Lady Isabella two beautiful pictures above stairs. A closet above full of small pictures very curious, a very exquisite enamel of Queen Caroline. Two originals of Sir Thomas More and Cardinal Wolsey upon copper. Some very curious cabinets in imitation of Japan, done by Lady Bristol. A bedchamber furnished with brocadillo resembling gold brocade on a green ground.[11]

After a very strict enquiry for St. Edmund's tomb mentioned by Camden, we could hear nothing of it; the only report that survives at present of St Edmund is that the Danes after murdering him, hacked his trunk all to pieces but left his head entire, which was afterwards found in a wood, guarded by a wolf, from whence the device of the crest of their town arms is at this day a king's head guarded by a wolf. The town is walled quite round, with five gothic gates at each of which are the ruins of a chapel.[12] The town itself is situated up a side hill with several shires [streets] cutting one another at right angles. The market house was formally a 'change, but is now turn'd into a large room for players, the bottom of it for cornfacters.[13] Two market

10 The writer's account of the two famous churches in a single churchyard at Bury St Edmunds is thoroughly confused. St Mary's possesses the celebrated roof and the remains of Mary, daughter of Henry VII and briefly Queen of France. St James (the cathedral church of the diocese of St Edmundsbury and Ipswich since 1914) contains the unsigned tomb of James Reynolds (1739), Lord Chief Baron of the Exchequer (not Lord Chancellor), MP for Bury, 1717–25, and a relation of the first Earl of Bristol. Mary's tomb had recently been opened in 1731.

Mary Martin had been buried, aged eighty-nine, in 1706. The number given here of her deliveries is confirmed in the burial register of St Mary's. Dr Clopton's Hospital (now the residence of the cathedral's Provost) was built in the late 1730s for the 'reception and maintenance' of twelve poor people, six men and six women of the age of sixty and above, chosen equally from both parishes.

11 The house (now the Manor House Museum) was built between 1736 and 1738 possibly to the designs of Sir James Burroughs (1694–1764), the Bury-born amateur architect, later Master of Gonville and Caius College, Cambridge. It was built for the first Earl of Bristol's second wife, one of Queen Caroline's Ladies of the Bedchamber. She had died two months before the visit recorded here. Although much is known about life at Ickworth from the Earl's letters, this tantalisingly brief glimpse of the recently fitted town house of the Bristols in Honey Hill is the only surviving account of the house besides those items of its contents mentioned in the Countess's will.

12 The five gates, East, West, North, South and Risby, were in a dangerous state by the early 1760s when they were demolished by order of the Corporation. At each there were the ruins of either medieval hospitals or chantries (see Warren's 1748 map of Bury St Edmunds).

13 The Market Cross survives in its second eighteenth-century remodelling by the Adam brothers in the 1770s. The account here records the conversion by the Corporation of its upper story into a theatre in 1734. The *Suffolk Mercury*, 9 Sept. 1734, records its 'repairing and altering for

days, Wednesday and Saterday well supplyed with fish from Ipswich and Leostoff [Lowestoft]. The chief manufacture is yarn for Norwich. The town is governed by 12 capital burgesses, 24 common council, the Alderman at the head. Two members of parliament chose by the Common Council and burgesses only. The Angel a good inn. Puffs: a direction was nailed upon a Suffolk cheese with four large nails for cart wheels, the cheese was so hard that it was with great difficulty they drove the nails through it, after which they clinched them on the other side, without fracturing the cheese in the least.[14] The Assembly House is very large and commodious consisting of two withdrawing rooms, and a ball room in one line; reckoned the finest Assembly in England.[15]

The ruins of the Abbey are exceeding venerable, a fine square Gothic gate, with portcullis, and the hinges remaining of the old gate. In the inside are six Coats of Arms, all three lyons en passant with this —— device over the top of the shield. The other is a Cross with five birds. I observed among the ruins of the old church that it had been divided into several small chappels; one of which is now a carpenter's shop, another a stable. The steeple of the Old Church remains entire, and serves as a steeple to what they now call the New Church [St James]. Over against the gate seem to be the ruins of an old house that probably might have been the palace of the abbot. The wall of the monastery takes in a piece of land of about six or seven acres; on t'other side the river, for fear of being cut off from water. And we shall find upon a strict enquiry that most of the monasterys in England lye low and near a river. It has been a matter of enquiry amongst the inhabitants to find out the reason why the churches were built upon lower ground than the town which breaks the custom that generally prevails in England, but the reason is very plain, the churches are built out of the ruins of the abbey, and to prevent the charge of carriage, were erected upon the spot, where all their materials lay in ruins.[16] In the walls are several Roman bricks about half an inch thick.

the Bury Company of Comedians (servants to his grace the Duke of Grafton) is now finished and made very commodious for the Reception of Quality and gentry: the said Players being to perform there at the ensuing Fair'.

14 Suffolk cheese had a poor reputation by the mid eighteenth century, largely because it contained a high proportion of skimmed milk, and was the butt of countless jokes. Cream from Suffolk dairies was principally used in butter production. Defoe noted that the county produced the best butter and the worst cheese in England. 'Dogs bark at it, pigs grunt at it, but neither of them can bite it.'

15 The Assembly House survived as the Atheneum, remodelled in 1789 and 1802–1804. Formerly a private house, it was first used for assemblies in Queen Anne's reign. The Earl of Oxford in 1732, 'took a view of their assembly room which is a very indifferent one, though much talked of' (*HMCR, Portland* VI, 150). Lord Oxford enjoyed pricking reputations.

16 Again the account of the ruins of the Abbey is telescoped. The 'ruins of the old church' is the west front of the Abbey Church; the 'steeple of the old church' is the Norman gate housing the bells of St James church; 'the palace of the abbott' was to the north of the abbey church and had been finally demolished in the 1720s; the churches of St Mary and St James had not been 'built out of the ruins of the abbey'. Norman in origin, they had been rebuilt in the early fifteenth and sixteenth centuries respectively. In the 1740s the abbey grounds belonged to Sir Jermyn

Puff: one Mr. Leeke, a parson near Stowmarket wanting a wheel to his wheelbarrow converted a tythe Cheese to that use, which without the assistance of fire only by dint of its own impenetrable hardness, bore the brunts of all weather and supported its charge with honour for seven years.

Witness apothecary

and landlord

The King's House at Newmarket is kept in repair and kept habitable by any person that the King pleases to put into it. The gentleman who lives in it at present is one Mr. Long who has a salary of £250 a year barely for living in it, without being at any expence.

Tuesday the 14th set out for Ipswich. As soon as we left Bury and crossed the River Lark (which is navigable within about a mile and half of Bury) we mounted a little hill, on the east side of Bury where we had a very fine prospect of the town and Sir J Davers's house & park.[17] We passed over a very fine country between Bury and Stow[market]. Through Woolpit the soil is all light, between a gravel and sand, produces fine turnips, tho' I think not so good corn as Cambridgeshire. There are some fine hop gardens by the road-side and they tell us many acres of hops about Mr Wollastons two miles and half from Stow[market].[18] The hedges were all full of timber trees chiefly elm and some few oaks. Stow[market], 14 miles from Bury. From Stow[market] we set out for Ipswich. The road bears to the left-hand, just after you come out of Stowmarket, which carries you to Needham a long village running east and west of very little account, but that the poor support themselves by spinning yarn for Norwich.[19] From Stow[market] to where you cross the river near Bramford you travel thro' enclosures: a fine hanging hill, all the way on the right, abounding with very fine corn of all sorts, a pretty many turnips, and some few hops. On the left side, you have a fine valley of no great breadth but seems to be very fine land, the river Orwell running thro' the middle of it to Ipswich. One mile from Ipswich down the river, on the right hand is Bone [Bourne] bridge, where a small creek runs up four or five miles. One mile lower on the left-hand side, as you go to Harwich is St John's Ness, where a 50 gun ship was building.[20] Almost opposite is St John's Ness, is Freston Tower, built to command a prospect down the river to Harwich. A little beyond Freston Hall is Woolvaston Hall, seat of Knox Ward Esq., where is a most beautiful park, the house upon a pretty eminence commanding the river to

Davers Bt of Rushbrooke Hall. His town house is now Abbey House (30 Angel Hill), altered in the nineteenth century.

17 Sir Jermyn Davers of Rushbrooke Hall, fourth Bart (*c.*1686–1743), MP for Bury St Edmunds, 1722–27 and for Suffolk, 1727–43.

18 William Wollaston (1693–1764), MP for Ipswich, 1733–41, of Great Finborough Hall, 'a fine seat in this parish which hath been greatly improved by him'. Kirby, *Suffolk Traveller*, 188.

19 Needham Market's reputation for poverty was well-established. Thomas Fuller, *Worthies of England*, 1662, 56, wrote, 'they are said to be in the high way to Needham who do hasten to poverty'.

20 See D. Defoe, *A Tour Through the Whole Island of Great Britain*, London 1927, I, 42–3.

Harwich.[21] Below this on the left-hand side is a pleasant seat belonging to Admiral Vernon, not so fine as Mr Brooks', situated a little below, four fine fronts, visto's, groves, and fine rows of trees.[22] Opposite to this is Pinmel, [Pin Mill], whither the king's ships used to send their boats to water. Opposite to this is Levington Creek, within sight of Harwich four miles from it. Near Harwich from the west comes in Maningtree river, navigable to Sudbury 30 miles. Harwich has been fortify'ed with a rampart and wet fossé. The southern side, sort of hornwork, the western a little irregular, flanked at one place, the northern and eastern fortyfied by the sea. The town of Harwich is a very bad one, entertainment not fit for gentlemen, bad wine, bad rum, water almost salt, impertinent innkeeper, and nothing curious but the goodness of its character. Over against it, to the east, is Langaard Fort, built of stone, mounts 21 guns, but is reckoned a fort of no manner of consequence.[23] The river down to Harwich is very fine, no fenns all the way, but fine hanging banks of corn or hanging woods, which with the water, fine houses, churches, and ships, compose as great a variety of pretty views as one can possibly expect to meet with. The situation of Ipswich is upon a bay of the river Orwell and is built in the shape of a half moon, all on one side of the river, upon an easy ascent. The buildings are nothing remarkable. There is a house built by Sir Robert Hitcham about 140 years ago with a great deal of Doric taste about it.[24] At the porch, facing the street, the freeze and the architrave are thrown into one large cyncase, and the hygliphs, metops and drops cut out upon it. The sides of the triglyps not parallel, but drawing nearer together till you come to the drops, which are too small. Instead of the gutters in the hyglip, a worm thrown out. I can't think there's any beauty in it, but it shows a very frantick taste in the architect. The area or court within side was very pretty in the Doric taste; the sides of the back-front were two very high turrets.

The Cross is I think a decagon (I forgot to count the angles when I was at it) built like a dome, supported by a Doric pillar at each angle; on the top is a clumsy cross, supporting the statue of Justice, in her left-hand a pair of scales, in her right a sword.[25] The Sheriff House is very large and commodious. An apothecary's shop

21 The ownership of Woolverstone according to the compilers of the second edition of Kirby, *Suffolk Traveller*, 1764, 71, had been in the Court of Chancery since 1720 when John Ward of Hackney, who held a mortgage on the property, claimed ownership. Knox Ward was Clarenceaux King of Arms. The present house was built in 1776 for William Berners to the designs of John Johnson.

22 Orwell Park and Broke Hall (the property of Philip Bowes Broke) both in the parish of Nacton and later extensively rebuilt. Admiral Vernon, a national hero after the capture of Porto Bello, was MP for Ipswich, 1741–57.

23 Langaard Fort (Felixstowe) was first built in 1540–45, rebuilt in 1624 and again in 1717–20.

24 This is Thomas Seckford's Great Place built in the 1560s. Sir Robert Hitcham of Framlingham briefly owned the house between 1631 and his death in 1636. For a full account see, J. Blatchly, 'Thomas Seckford's Great Place: a Lost Ipswich Tudor Town House', in C. Rawcliffe, R. Virgoe and R. Wilson, eds, *Counties and Communities: Essays in East Anglian History*, Norwich 1996, 203–12.

25 The octagonal Market Cross erected in 1628 was demolished in 1812.

remarkable for its largeness and the oddity of the building.[26] Their key [quay] is a pretty spacious one. They trade chiefly in large timber. The poor people spin for Norwich; they formerly made stuffs themselves, but have now lost that trade.

July the 16th we set out for Yoxford, passed over a heathy common to Woodbridge, which is a pretty situated town being upon a winding of the river Deben, which is navigable as far as Woodbridge for ships of 300 ton. The mouth of it is called Woodbridge haven, which is about four miles north-east of Langaard fort. They have a good corn market at Woodbridge, and one of the best inns I ever saw, the sign of the Crown. Leaving Woodbridge, we called to see Mr North's house, which is a very convenient house, fine proportioned rooms and very well furnished; the pictures not extraordinary, very few of the family, by which one would guess the family to have been of no great date.[27] Stands low, in the centre of a beautiful park; the stables very large at a convenient distance from the house. The place seems to want nothing that can make life agreeable, but 'tis reported, by the extravagance of a mistress, will soon want a master. As soon as we had left Mr North's, we passed by, on the left, about half a mile distance, Mr Rushe's house,[28] which made a very good appearance, but as they told us there was nothing worth seeing within side but the master, of whom we had great encomiums, we passed on to Yoxford where we saw an old house belonging to Sir Chas Blois, a minor.[29] Two or three very good rooms, and a great many very old pictures of the family. They let the gardens run to ruin, imagining that when Sir Charles comes of age, he'll pull down the old house and rebuild it upon higher ground.

17th of July dined with Mr Dashwood at Hevening[ham]. Just before we came there we passed by two good-looking houses, one belonging to Mr Wingfield, the other to Mr Scrivener.[30] Mr Dashwood's house is very well built and the offices are so good

26 There is a good account of the Ancient or Sparrow's House in N. Pevsner, *The Buildings of England: Suffolk*, 2nd edn, 1974, 301–2 and plate 56(a). He considers it 'more ornate and gayer than any other house of its date in England'. John Sparowe (1690–1762) was an apothecary, thirteen times Bailiff of Ipswich, and one of the Receivers-General of the Land Tax for Suffolk after 1729. See J. Blatchly, *Some Suffolk and Norfolk Ex-Libris*, The Bookplate Society 2000, 20–4.

27 Little Glemham Hall (*c.*1715–25) was rebuilt by Dudley North (MP for Thetford, 1710–22, and Orwell, 1722–30), who had purchased the estate from the Glemhams in 1708. He was a son of Sir Dudley North (Turkey merchant, economist and Lord Mayor of London) and a grandson of the 4th Lord North. His wife Catherine (d.1715) was daughter and co-heir of Elihu Yale, founder of the famous American university. Her marriage portion of £20,000 probably paid for the estate (it cost £15,620) and a remodelling of the house. In 1741 it was occupied by his son, also named Dudley.

28 John Rush had very recently bought the Benhall Lodge estate from Edmund Tyrell of Gipping, heir to the Dukes of Benhall, a family of baronets who died without male issue in 1732.

29 Sir Charles Blois, 2nd baronet of Cockfield Hall, Yoxford. The house was not pulled down, but the windows were sashed by Sir John Blois, the fifth baronet, in the 1770s and the interior modestly remodelled.

30 Charles Scrivener owned Sibton Abbey, built in 1610 by the Scriveners from the ruins of Sibton Abbey, the only Cistercian house in Suffolk. The property of Mr Wingfield is untraced.

that none of the family lodge in the great house.[31] The situation of it is upon a hanging hill, commanding more views, and more extensive ones, than are common in Suffolk. The park is about three miles round, out of which is taken about 20 or 30 acres for garden ground, visto's, shady walks, bowling greens etc. They have just erected a reed wall for fruit; a foot and a half from the ground, [upon a] brick wall and half brick thick; along the wall timber four inches thick; about every 18 feet, a post erected upon the wall four inches thick, six ft high; these posts have each supporters that stand slanting to them, with a cross beam and go a little way into the ground. Along the top of the posts, runs other timber four inches broad, two thick. The reeds are kept together by three slight pieces running parrallel to one another. These pieces are answered by three more, on the back-side, and so by screws are made always to keep the reeds close together when some of them begin to decay. This wall has two qualities which are thought to be of very good service to fruit. They are not so apt to scorch as a brick wall, and in hard rains these will take in the rain, while brick ones by reverberating of it cannot but bruise the fruit in its tender state either in blossom or in bud. Mr Dashwood showed us a model of a water cart which was to fill by the horses drawing into the water. The trunk or barrel was square, with a common valve at [the] bottom, a hole o'top to let the air out as the water came in; the trunk fix'd under the ecks[?] to the rods (which crossed the ecks at right angles and were projected about two feet behind) with iron hoops. Some fastening was also applied to the ecks. One objection to this scheme is the trunk hanging so low, but that instead of being fixed to the rods might be made to turn upon the ecks when full, and so ride on top as 'tis in other water barrels.

After leaving Mr Dashwood with regret, we passed thro a little market town called Halesworth, and went that night to Beccles, which is a large market town situated upon a bank which commands the level almost down as far as Norwich. A good beef market; the King's Head, a good inn. The steeple is built at the east end of the church by reason of the declivity of the ground on the west side. In the church is a good organ all of wood, made by a country fellow who is got to be a tolerable performer upon it. They breed abondance of geese here which fly about almost wild. The geese merchants come from London about harvest and buy them up. One merchant will drive up above 1500 geese in a flock. As soon as you are got over the levels, you mount a sandy common where is a prodigious large decoy called Fritton decoy. What I observed remarkable in it was the placing of the tunnels upon the plainest ground, when to all appearance there was the finest covers for them that could be.

On the 18th we reached Yarmouth, remarkable for one of the finest keys [quays] in Europe. It's above half a mile long, nearly streight, runs north and south, covered with shipping from one end to the other; a fine row of houses front it all the way at

31 Kirby, *Suffolk Traveller*, 1736 edn, noted of Heveningham Hall, 'from the Heveninghams it descended by Purchase to John Bence Esq, and now is the Lordship and Demesne of George Dashwood Esq who has his seat there'. Dashwood was High Sheriff of Suffolk in 1732. This house forms the core of the Robert Taylor and James Wyatt house of the late 1770s built for Sir Gerard Vanneck whose father had bought the estate in 1752.

about 20 yards distance from the river. There are two more streets which run parallel to this, the middle one narrow, the outer one next to the sea, a fine broad street, with an elegant chappel about the middle of it.[32] At the top a very spacious marketplace which is bounded at the north end by the old church [St Nicholas] which is a very large one, with a most melodious organ in it. 'Tis remarkable of the steeple that the spire stands some feet out of the perpendicular and has done so many years. The rows of buildings are cut about every 40 yards with small passages, just wide enough to admit the Yarmouth coaches which by having their wheels within their rods make it impractical to run against a post. Towards the upper end of the key [quay] is the town hall, the front of which is Doric, with ballustrades and a flat roofed portico. They have balustrades o'top for the sake of the prospect to the north, and [as] it was necessary to have an ornamental front they have run up four Corinthian pillars, whose entablature answers in all in its mouldings to the ballustrade in front; which may be reckoned a good contrivance in the architect, but the effect is not very wonderful.[33]

At the Haven's mouth they have been repairing a little brick fort which is towards the sea for the conveniency of mounting more cannon. [It] has two round bastions, towards the river two angular bastions, mounts about 18 or 20 guns, and seems pretty strong, but, as it is all built with brick, the first time any cannon plays upon it the splinters must necessarily make dreadful havock amongst the garrison. The harbour cannot but be very dangerous, I mean the coming in, if the wind does not set right in, for about a league out there's so many shoals, and in such variety of situations, that one would think it impossible for any memory to contain them all. Besides there is such a multiplicity of lighthouses that one would think the consequences of the confusion they must breed must be very near to terrible as those of darkness itsself.

We rode in the Yarmouth coaches to see Castre [Caister] light houses (about five miles from [the] ports mouth) which are built of very slight materials for the conveniency of moving them about, which is very often necessary by reason of the shifting of the sands. Yarmouth Road has one conveniency, that you may anchor in any part of it, but if a cable breaks in the night, a man has very little to do but to resign himself up to a plumb line and fortune. There are two light houses very conveniently placed to bring ships into Yarmouth harbour, so that if they escape the sands in the Road they are generally safe.

We left Yarmouth the 20th in the afternoon, passed by Castre Hall, a fine peice of the ruins of the ancient Castre mentioned by Cambden.[34] After which we crossed a

[32] St Georges' built to the designs of John Price and his son, also John, of Wandsworth. A chapel of ease to St Nicholas's, costing £5,861.

[33] The 'elegantly classical' Town Hall of 1715 was also built by John Price. It was replaced by the present town hall of J.B. Pease in 1878–82. N. Pevsner and B. Wilson, *The Buildings of England: Norfolk*, I, London 1997, 502.

[34] Caister Castle, West Caister, one of the most impressive late medieval castles in England, built by Sir John Fastolf between 1432 and 1443.

warren, passed over a bridge between two pretty lakes called Filby Broad. From thence we came to Ecle [Acle] Dam, passing the river Flegg, navigable up to Colson.[35] From Ecle to Norwich we passed over a country something like Cambridgeshire. The common people of Yarmouth are mostly tarrs, but of the most civilised sort; the gentry make a politer appearance than is common in sea port towns.

On Monday the 20th came to Norwich, situated upon the turn of a river; a very large city equal by computation to the city of London within the walls; is a county of itself; has its Sheriff, Bailiff and other officers, at the head of which is a Mayor, in the same manner as countys have. The buildings which have anything of grandeur in them are all Gothic. The cathedral is somewhat heavy within side, which may reasonable be excused because it was necessary as that prodigious lofty steeple stood in the middle of the church to give its supporters equal to its bulk, and had not the proportion of the other pillars been answerable to those which supported the steeple, the deformity in that case would have been worse than the heaviness of the building at present. The steeple and tower are very high and of a most elegant proportion. What they call the Castle is at present a prison, stands upon the loftiest ground in the city, and is a pretty near a cube with four round towers at each corner (not distinct from the building, nor higher at present), which are the staircases of the castle. Adjoining to the castle are the Sessions houses of the County of Norfolk.[36] The Assize house for the city is the town hall [Guildhall], the Crown barr at the top, the *nisi prius* at bottom. The Hall [St Andrews] its self is a very fine room, the roof supported by two rows of Gothic pillars and seems to have been a church of about the same date of St Peter's in Norwich, being very like it in all its proportions. There are seven or eight pictures in it, one of his present majesty, the rest of gentlemen that have done honour to the Mayoralty. In the cathedral is the tomb of Bishop Herbert the founder of it; the inscription of a much more modern date than the time of his interment, mentioning the other churches that he built but not the crime of simony, which Cambden mentions and for which he says, being under the censure of the Pope, he built these churches as an attonement. St Peter's Church is remarkable for being a very light building inside, has a fine organ, and has the honour to contain the venerable ruins of the learned Thomas Browne, author of *Religio Medici* and the *Vulgar Errors*, was born 1605, died 1682. Part of the inscription, *bonus literis, haud leviter imbutus scriptis per orbeir notissimus, vir picutissimus, integerrimus, doctissurimus. Posuit Conjux.* In this church is the monument of Judge Windham.[37]

35 Does he mean the River Bure navigable up to Coltishall?

36 See V. Morgan, 'The Elizabethan Shirehouse at Norwich', in Rawcliffe, Virgoe and Wilson, eds, *Counties and Communities*, 149–60, and for the castle, T.A. Heslop, *Norwich Castle Keep*, Norwich 1994.

37 The tombs mentioned in St Peter Mancroft are those of Judge Francis Windham (1592) and Sir Thomas Browne (1682) attributed to Jasper Latham. See Blomefield, *Norfolk*, iv, 184–221, for the full, correct transcription of Sir Thomas's monument see 193.

Down by the riverside at the west end of the town are publick gardens, which the inhabitants call Spring gardens. There is nothing very remarkable in them but that about the evening all the Beau Monde of the town resort there, ladies and gentlemen where they vouchsafe to admit even the clergymen, which are a numerous body in the city and not admitted to any other public assembly. The Assembly was furnished with a very fine appearance of ladies, and a great many of them beauties.[38] No want of gentlemen, but a strange want of regularity, the whole affair being conducted in a hurry with ill manners and hardly common decency. The gentry seem to keep up a little emulation in dress and figure, but good neighbourhood is at a low ebb with them. The common people are naturally riotous. As they are beneath the laws, they defy them, and keep such a garrison upon some parts of the town that constables and bailiffs never dare approach their lines. They manufacture crapes and stuffs 2000£s worth in a year; they used to return 7000£s in a year, but at present they have such a taste for idleness that industry and wealth have both given the slip.[39] Their river is navigable to Yarmouth.

Saturday the 25th left Norwich passed over a large warren came to Ailsham. Saw Lord Hobart's.[40] The house very old brick, with stone ornaments, Ionic upon Doric, the rooms generally speaking small. One very fine gallery furnished with pictures at full-length. A very bad picture of K.George, upon a very fine horse done by a different hand; a very good likeness of Mr Crawley. In the hall is a very good picture representing papers, inkhorns, books etc. hung upon strings – nailed to a deal panel. What they call the gardens is a piece of ground of about 30 acres, cut into vistos and shady walks, full of hares. Upon the highest part of the gardens fronting the house is a Doric temple, which has a very elegant effect. The house has been moated round. In the park is a very fine serpentine piece of water which is artificially made so that you can't see the end of it. You have a view of this piece of water from every part of

[38] The Assembly described here was held in Moore's Spring Gardens, first opened in 1739 (now the site of the Hotel Nelson), not Chapel Field House where winter assemblies were organised before its enlargement and alteration in 1754–55 to the present Assembly House. See T. Fawcett, 'The Norwich Pleasure Gardens', *NA* 35, 1970–72, 382–99.

[39] The traveller's figures are incomprehensible. The Norwich trade is estimated to have been worth perhaps as much as £1,000,000 annually in the 1740s although there were universal comments about the depressed state of the entire English wool textile industries in the 1730s. R.G. Wilson, 'The Supremacy of the Yorkshire Cloth Industry in the Eighteenth Century', in N.B. Harte and K.G. Ponting, eds, *Textile History and Economic History*, Manchester 1973, 230–5.

[40] Blickling Hall, one of the greatest Jacobean houses in England, was built between 1618 and 1629. It underwent major remodelling in the 1760s and 1770s under the direction of the Ivory brothers, Norwich masons and architects.

Of the three pictures mentioned: the still life is untraced; the full-length portrait of Mr Crawley (now removed to the Staircase Gallery) is by William Aikman; the equestrian portrait of George II (now in the Peter the Great Room) is by John Wooton and Charles Jervas. George Vertue records in 1732 that the latter painted the face only, 'the Horse etc. was much approved of, but the Kings not thought to be like, was much spoke against from thence'.

The gardens and lake in the form described here had been completed by the late 1720s. The Doric Temple (*c.*1730) was possibly designed by Matthew Brettingham.

the gardens and, if one may judge by the acclivitys all round, from every part of the park.

The road from Ailsham to Fakenham is exceeding pleasant, upon every little rise, you have a delicious prospect of the sea upon the right hand, and a fine enclosed country on the left. The road runs sometimes through enclosures, sometimes over cornfields, sometimes over commons. Sir Jacob Astley's is a fine situation, having an agreeable lawn before the house independent of the park, a prospect of the sea, and a plentiful country to look upon.[41] On Sunday the 29th [26th] we unfortunately and modestly passed by Ld. Townsends without seeing it.[42] At Rudham the men were all at stool ball in the afternoon.[43]

We lost our way in going from Ailsham to Sir Robert [Walpole]'s, but at last by the direction of one of his majesty's officers arrived safely at the inn, which is a very good one at Houghton Hall gate.[44] Next morning we walked up to the house, took a turn or two in the arcades, which is the whole length of the house vaulted with a double row of imposts, low pitch and serves for a support to the room upon the first floor. Had it been a little lower, it would have done for a cellar but the use that is made of it at present is to walk and sit in, in summer times. A little beyond this is a bed place and a marble bath. The staircase is mahogany and winding, in the middle are four Doric pillars, placed in a square, which, with their base, and entablature together, make a pedestal for a gladiator in brass, upon the same level as the first floor. This gladiator is the original from whence so many have since been taken, and are very common in grand gardens.

41 Melton Constable built by Sir Jacob Astley *c.*1664–1670.

42 Raynham Hall. The early seventeenth-century house had been recently remodelled in the late 1720s by William Kent and Thomas Ripley.

43 Stool ball, a primitive form of cricket, is usually associated with west country counties such as Wiltshire and Gloucestershire. It was clearly played over a much wider area. There are references to it being played at Castle Acre in 1615 and Saham Toney in 1596. See S. Amussen, *An Ordered Society*, Oxford 1988, 175.

44 It is the account given here of the pictures at Houghton, not of Colin Campbell's and William Kent's incredibly extravagant house built between 1722 and 1736 for the prime minister, Sir Robert Walpole, that is fascinating. The date of the visit, July 1741, seven months before Sir Robert's fall from office, is crucial. The description locates many of the best-known pictures, the most celebrated collection of its day, which Sir Robert had formed after 1718. It also comes two years before (the comment 'catalogues are so common' is puzzling) Horace Walpole's catalogue of the pictures at Houghton, the *Aedes Walpolianae*, compiled after some of the pictures had been rehung in the picture gallery formed at Houghton after 1742 when Sir Robert brought a selection of paintings formerly hanging in his Whitehall and Chelsea homes. Although earlier manuscript copies are known, the *Aedes Walpolianae* was not published until 1748, three years after Sir Robert's death. The writer's observations indicating a good eye, appear to be his own, although some of the facts and figures towards the end of the account of Houghton suggest comments provided by a guide, spoken or otherwise. For an excellent account of Houghton, its collections and sale of paintings to Catherine of Russia in 1779, see A. Moore, ed., *Houghton Hall, the Prime Minister, the Empress and the Heritage*, Norwich 1996, and Pevsner and Wilson, II, 428–36.

The pictures are collected with very great taste, and all good. Catalogues are so common that we shall take notice of those only which struck us most. In the common parlour are two very large pictures of a stag in one, and a boar in the other, overtaken by the dogs, some dead, some dying with their guts torn out, some fighting with all the expressions of anger that can be imagined. The whole executed in a most masterly manner by Abraham Hondius. What is remarkable in the Nativity of our Saviour is the reflection of his glory upon all the company, this by Carlo Chimiani. In the picture of the Eagle and Ganymede by Mic. Angelo, the complexedness of the posture is very remarkable: 'tis not easy to imagine how an eagle should carry a boy of 15 years old into the sky without hurting him, but the painter has hit upon the way. Ganymede folds his arms around the eagle's wings as near the body as possible. The eagle locks his legs with Ganymede so that the eagle seems to fly with pleasure and the posture of Ganymede looks easy. In the same room is a perspective piece, by Stenwich [Steenwyck], touch'd up with great elegance.

In Sir Robert's bedchamber is a fine picture of Sr. Wm. Chaloner by Vandike, and a sacred piece by Paul Rubens. In the Saloon, the Baptism of our Saviour, in the countenance and posture, the finest expression that can be imagined of humility, adoration and innocence by Albano. The taking up of St. Stephen after stoning, the easy posture of the corps, the concern of his friends, and the disposition of the 19 figures in one picture big as the life are inimitable, painter La Soeur. The Assumption of the Virgin Mary by Morellio [Murillo] has something very taking in it. The Cyclops forge, labour, strength, the swarthiness of their complexions and the fire are excellent, painter Luca Jordan [Jordano]. The Adoration of the Shepherds is an exquisite piece, the reflection of light is very remarkable in this, painter Morellio. Daedalus tying on Icarus's wings, by Le Brun: the resign'd gesture of Icarus is remarkable, but the face of Daedalus to want concern. The four markets, Fowl, Fish, Herbs and Fruit, the figures by Rubens, the fowl etc. by Snyder[s]: as they were done by the two most masterly hands that ever were in the world, and are such a composition of master pieces that the united pencils of all the painters in their present degeneracy must despair of imitating. The whole is rather larger than life. Upon the marble table lie in easy postures, two River Gods, Tiber and the Nile, in brass, two postures and features very fine about three feet long.

The ceiling of the saloon is painted with the story of Phaeton. Over the chimney piece is an elegant bust of Venus. There are two fine Corinthian doors and facing one another four prodigious sconces of silver embossed.

In the Green Velvit withdrawing room 12 pictures by Carlo Miratti [Maratti]. The Offering of the Wise Men, Zachariah and Elizabeth worshipping, and Galatea in the sea are very fine. Also Venus naked with Cupid pulling a thorn out of her foot. The tears running down her cheeks, and down her arms, her pouting cheeks, a little redness upon the part affected, and the industrious concern of Cupid, are all excellent. The Flight into Egypt, and the Crucifixion both by Morellio; in the last, the weight of the body seems to rest upon the nails thro' the feet; the arms extended not in a streight line, but bearing down wards from the hands; the whole expressing one of the most painful postures that the imagination can possibly form. In this room are several curious pieces more particularly a fruit piece and a flower piece on each side the chimney by Jan Van Huissum [Huysum] executed with inimitable softness and judgement, the strength of the colours to be equat'd by nothing but nature.

In the Green Velvit Bedchamber is a fine picture of Alexander adorning the tomb of Achilles by Nicholas Poussin: and a very pretty picture of a port and landscape by Griffier. The tapestry is very fine, the story of Venus and Vulcan: Cupids grinding arrows; Venus hanging upon Adonis's neck, Adonis catches Venus asleep; another Venus dallying with Adonis. The bed itself is very grand.

In the dressing-room is a fillagre chest of drawers and dressing plate. The tapestry is very fine, the pictures represent K. James the first and his queen, K. Charles the first and his queen; Christiaanus quartus Danii [King Christian IV of Denmark]. Over doors two pictures of dogs and partridge.

In the worked bed chamber, the Holy Family as large as the life by Nicholas Poussin. Tapestry: satyrs and nymphs dancing and dallying, Bacchus triumphing in a boat.

The Marble Parlour is a very neat room, on each side the chimney are two alcoves supported each by two Ionic pillars of very fine marble dug at Plymouth. Was this room ever so elegant, all its beauties would be disregarded and lost, being in company with the picture of the Prodigal Son, which abounds with so many excellencies that words will raise but a very flat idea of them. He's in profile kneeling, ragged shirt, ragged breeches, neither coat nor waistcoat, hair uncomb'd, begrimed, his complexion swarthy and sunburnt, his posture and expression suppliant, and his whole frame a melancholy composition of misery and penitence and despair. The painter of this glorious picture was Salvator Rosa. In this Parlour is a most beautiful picture of the Doctors consulting about the Immaculate Conception. You see reason and argument in their faces. Painter, Guido Reni. Over the chimney piece is a Roman sacrifice in basso releivo by Risbeck [Rysbrack].

The Hall is a very fine room, being a cube of 40 feet. It is all set round with fine busts, that are all antique, but one, which is a bust of Sr. Robt. by Riseback over the chimney piece. Over against the chimney piece is perhaps one of the most elegant pieces of statuary that ever was performed, being Lacoon and his two sons killed by serpents, all in brass. The expression of fear and pain in the two boys, of agony and concern in the father, the natural twistings of the serpents, the venom of their looks are so well executed, with such a masterly hand, and so surprisingly animated, that you looked upon the poor sufferers in brass with as much concern as if they were fellow creatures. In the hall too, are four large vases of alabaster from Italy, very highly finished and one smaller of bronze.

In the Yellow Dressing Room is a fine picture of Abraham bringing back Hagar to Sarah by Pietio Cortona, and on the left-hand side of the chimney piece, a picture of Barsheba bringing Abishag to David, all done with such inimitable softness of colours laid on with such justiness and nicety that it would be impossible with a microscope to distinguish the strokes of the pencil, and then the majestic gravity of

David, mixt with pleasure at seeing so charming a woman, the modesty of Abishag and the eagerness with which the old woman presents a beautiful young girl to the arms of a monarch, are all executed with such taste, and reason as must immortalize the name of Vanderwersse and set him upon a level with Rubens and Maratti.

In Hunting Hall a charming picture of Susanna and the Elders by Rubens, and a hunting piece by Wooton.

In the Corner Drawing Room a sweet picture of Ruben's wife drawn by himself, who was certainly the properest person to draw her as he must naturally be supposed to be the best acquainted with all her charms. Archbishop Laude a half length by Vandyck. Meleager and Atalanta a very grand chartoon, by P. Rubens.

In another room, the Battle of Constantine, with some family pictures. In another, Erasmus by Vandyke. Two rooms above furnished with good tapestry in antick posture. In another room Hero and Leander, and the Baptising the Black in very fine tapestry. There is one room where Sr. Wm Chaloner's picture is, very finely furnished with mahogany in the Ionic taste. The doors are all mahogony. There is a great many fine bedchambers above stairs, rather convenient than grand. They can make up at an hours warning 110 beds.

The front of the house to the gardens is Ionic, with a gallery and portico, a frontor with three statues upon the acroteria. The four corners of the house are four domes. The wings in which are the offices of all sorts are Ionic, the passages from the house to the wings Tuscan with a cloister. The garden is about 30 acres in the modern taste of shady walks and visto's, surrounded with a wall, the bottom of the wall of a level with the park paled round for fruit, the top of a level with the gardens. The park is about six miles round, feeds 1500 deer, is planted almost all round with woods. In the gardens and some of the woods are abondance of pheasants, my Lord Walpole who lives there the hunting season having contracted with a man to breed him 200 pheasants every year. Sir Robert has been at a great expence to cut away two hills, for a prospect into the country. The stables are very fine and spacious. Over the stables lodge the men servants. There is about eight acres of ground for the kitchen garden. The house was begun in 1722 and finished in 1735, being one of the compleatest buildings and most compleately furnished of any house in England.[45]

After leaving Sir Robts. we passed over a country something like the most even part of the downs in Sussex for about six miles, then about two miles over a sandy warren, thence to Lynn, marshy ground. We came to Lynn the 28th which is a tolerable good town situated near the mouth of the River Ouse. The marketplace is a very fine spacious one surrounded on all sides with very decent buildings. The cross itself is a

[45] The late geometric garden had been set out from Charles Bridgeman's plans in the 1720s and 1730s. Sir Robert's vast earth-moving schemes to open a vista to the east of the house were incomplete in 1741. See T.M. Williamson, 'The Planting of the Park', in Moore, *Houghton Hall*, 41–7.

The big quadrangular stables were built *c.*1733–35, probably by Thomas Ripley.

very elegant one, being a piece of regular architecture of 16 angles at bottom, the first story supported by 16 Ionic pillars, with a portico. The second story forms itself into an octagon four of whose sides are the larger, than the four others, and faced with frontons in the Corinthian order. In the smaller sides are niches for statues, in one of which is the statue of Justice having lost her balance, but retaining her sword. Over this is a sort of dome and then a quadrangular atick story for a bell; on the top a small cross. Behind this is a fish market, which with the two wings in Doric taste, form a semicircle. In the middle of the marketplace, stands a statue of K. William III in a loose robe somewhat injured by time, and standing in so publick a place, but beautiful even in its ruins.[46]

Toward the north end of the town is St Nicholas's Chapel which is supported without any charge to the town, by an estate left for that purpose. In the church-yard, are the following inscriptions:

Mary Fowle lies in the Dust
Till the resurrection of ye Just. March 8th 1700.

Our greatest Joys hath its succeeding sorrow,
To day we hugg what we must leave to morrow:
Willm. Hall.

But what can tears avail, or what relief
Can sad complaint expect; can weeping grief
Recall him from the gloomy shades of death
And warm his ashes with a second Breath?
Lament him not, his blessed state appears;
Now he's at rest, no subject for our tears.

Over against St Nicholas's church is a pretty regular fronted house belonging to Mr Allen a brewer.[47] The taste is Ionic, with an attic story. Quite at the north end of the town is an irregular bastion, without a breastwork where lie unmounted ten old six-pounders.[48] At the south end is what they call the Ball [Boal], from a sign that once hung there, where they now load timber. The water has left the woodwork above 30 feet in some places, so that their keys [quays] are a little inconvenient. They have a pretty good town-hall, and a good old church.[49] The walls of the town

46 Henry Bell's ambitious domed market cross, erected at a cost of £596 10s between 1707 and 1710, was the crowning glory of Lynn's famous Tuesday Market Place. It was demolished in 1831, the fish market and meat shambles six years earlier. The statue was of James II, not William III (Defoe made the same error).

47 Thomas Allen, member of a prominent Lynn merchant family, was, according to his water rate assessment, the largest brewer in the town.

48 The bastion was St Anne's Fort. The 'ten old six-pounders' (another account refers to them as twelve nine-pounders) dated back at least to the Civil War. They were replaced, after a petition from the Corporation, by ten eighteen-pounders installed in time to fire salutes on the death of Sir Robert Walpole in 1745.

49 St Margaret's church. The writer's visit was made five weeks before a tornado caused severe

are still remaining and so are the gates. The people are pretty rich, being chiefly wine and coal merchants.

We were civilly entertained by the Mayor as strangers and drank out of King John's cup which he made a present of to the corporation, and at the same time made them a present of his sword, which he took from his side as appears by the inscription. The mayor has a salary of £150 a year on purpose to buy sack, for the entertainment of strangers that come to see the cup. The mayor gives 500£ security for the cup during his mayoralty. The cup is of silver, gilt with gold in some places and enamelled in others; holds about half a pint. There is a cover to it; an irregular flat spheroidical ball between the foot and the cup, which ball turns round, as does the foot, which in the ceremony of drinking you turn one one way, the other the other way.[50]

After leaving Lynn, we passed over a wooden-bridge upon the Ouse at St. Germans and came to Wisbich. The road all the way being upon a dead flat; very hard clay and the finest road for a coach that ever was seen. Wisbich is a good pretty market town, with some good houses in it, situated upon a river, water salt and for want of a communication with the sea at low tides in summer, must be very disagreeable. They save their rain-water with a great deal of care, for besides that, they have no fresh water but what is sold them from the barges which come from Peterborough. The steeple is on the north side of the church, which is a large one and has a pretty organ in it.

From Wisbech on the 29th we set out for Boston, baited, where we met with a great rarity in so flat a country which was a spring of very fine water. Leaving Flete, we crossed Foss-dike without the least appearance of any danger. From Foss-dike to Boston which is a good pretty market corporation town with some good houses in it. The church is a very good one, a neat alter piece in the Corinthian taste; the tower is the highest and best proportioned that I ever saw, being 94 yards high.[51] We went to the top of it and tho it stands quite upon a flat by the river side, I believe it commands a prospect of at least 30 miles every way. The inns are tolerable, wine good, water in the springs almost salt. There is very little traffick through this town, being situated upon a by-road. All the people from the highest to the lowest are very

damage in Lynn. The steeple and south-west tower of St Margaret's collapsed into the nave. Together with the crossing, north and south transepts, it was rebuilt by Matthew Brettingham, 1742–46. Sir Robert Walpole persuaded George II to give £1,000 towards the church's restoration.

[50] The famous King John's cup (in fact *c.*1350) is now housed with King's Lynn civic regalia in the basement of the Guildhall in the Saturday Market Place. The mayor's security for the cup was £50, not £500. His annual expenses were £100 to cover some of his entertainments, including a grand Michaelmas mayoral feast, not £150 to purchase sack alone. N. Scarfe, *A Frenchman's Year in Suffolk*, SRS 30, 1988, 186–7 records the feast and ball of 1784 attended by François de la Rochefoucauld. See also Maximilien de Lazowski's account of Lynn, *ibid.*, 191–4.

[51] At 272 feet high, Boston Parish Church boasts the tallest parochial church steeple in England.

complasant to strangers, as they see them so seldom. In the church is this line at the bottom of an inscription:

Omnes sic ibant, sic imus ibitis ibunt.

On the 30th we set out for Lincoln. We passed over a fen ten miles long, which was now dry and a very good road. The whole fenn abounded so much with wild-geese that we could have rode down at least an hundred in an hour. We baited at Sleaford 14 long miles from Boston. Sleaford is a town of some repute, as lying in the London road from Lincoln. Leaving Sleaford we mounted a most charming heath, every hill afforded us a delightful prospect, while the valleys were alive with rabbits. This we passed over for about seven miles, and the next seven miles consisted of the same heath cultivated into the finest corn ground that ever was seen. We could see at some places corn for ten miles together. Before we reached Lincoln we left two pretty villages on the left hand. The cathedral of Lincoln and all the good houses are situated on the top of the hill, which commands the country round about, and is so very steep that carriages find great difficulty in mounting of it. The lower part of the town, beneath the hill, consists of one good street where live all the tradesmen of the town. Their river is navigable in winter only, or in case of large freshes, which is one reason why the town is deficient in regard to trade.

The cathedral is one of the most elegant Gothic buildings in the world. The west front will bear a long looking at and the strictest examination. The inside looses some of its grandeur by being too narrow for its height. There are very few monuments of note. Queen Eleanor's (where her bowels were buried, as is recorded in the books belonging to the church) is now taken up. There are some good inscriptions, amongst which the following will bear reading at least once. [The long Latin inscription to James Gardiner, 1734, is omitted.]

Provisions are cheap in Lincoln, their ale at four pence a quart as good as can be drank. At the west front of the cathedral I observed the capitals of some of the Gothic pillars, very nearly resembling those of the Corinthian order.

Leaving Lincoln, we travel'd for Doncaster. About two miles from Lincoln we passed by on the left hand, a charming village, called Burton situated on the side of the hill, with beautiful hanging woods on one of the side, and a fine valley on the other. After this we passed Littlebourough ferry, and dined at Bawtry. The country from the ferry, hilly, but plentiful; the road irregular, and not over good for a carriage. At Bawtry we got into the road from London to York, and found it good to Doncaster, but from thence to Tadcaster very uneven, the country all the way enclosed but not with very strong enclosures. All the way from Lynn to Bawtry, their wagons were very short, and drawn by four horses, two and two, the wheels like coach wheels. From Tadcaster to York, an even good road, upon the natural ground in summer and in winter a causeway with strong pavement of boulders, and these cause ways you have from town to town in several parts of Yorkshire. At Tadcaster is a very fine salmon fishery made in the middle of a rapid river [Wharfe] by a strong dam of timber and stone. From Tadcaster we afterwards went to Leeds; about two miles from Tadcaster, we passed along on the side of a very grand Roman cause-way for about two miles, after which we mounted a delicious common where we could see at one view almost all Yorkshire. Upon this common is the seat of Mr Fox, one of the pleasantest situations we have as yet seen in Yorkshire. Within the park-pale is a very large wood, cut out into visto's and green walks, with a fine dome in the centre. The turf of the park is as fine as that of the down in Sussex.[52]

Before we came to Leeds we observed that the road within two miles of it, look'd very much like the road about London. For the Leeds merchants are so polite that every one of them of any tolerable figure has a country house within two miles of the town.[53] The town itself is finely situated upon low ground, but upon the decline of the hill. It is reckon'd one of the greatest manufactures in England for cloth from 3s to 18s pr. yard. Their markets for cloths are Mondays and Saturdays, which are very remarkable for their largeness and dispatch of business. They have one very grand street running north and south, which is streight for a great way together, and above 30 yards wide. At the top of this street as a boundary stands the statue of Queen Anne in a nitch of the south face of the shambles, which is a piece of regular architecture and if I don't forget of the Corinthian order.[54] At right angles to this street runs another westwards, in which is a very pretty new church, the body of which, on the outside is very grand in the Doric style. The steeple above the building is rustic for about ten feet, then Ionic, and then Corinthian, without pedestals. Upon the top of the Corinthian all the four corners are four pilasters, or rather balustrades, supporting four neat urns, and in the middle a stone spire.[55] Higher up the grand street there runs out another very good street at right angles to the east, in which is the old church, which bears the character of a very fine one.[56]

The city of York is very far from coming up to the character which Yorkshiremen give of it: they cry it up as very little inferior to London in the grandeur of its streets, and the largeness of it. However, an impartial man must say, that it is not bigger than Norwich, and there is but one grand street in it which is before you come to the bridge from the south. What they have reason to boast of without fear of contradiction is their Minster, their Assembly House and their county Gaol, the cheapness of

52 Bramham Park, built by Lord Bingley in the 1700s, possessed one of the finest and largest gardens in the French manner of Louis XIV. The dome referred to must be the very recently completed Ionic rotunda (based upon Kent's Temple of Ancient Virtue at Stowe, *c.*1735) usually dated post-1745. See C. Hussey, *English Gardens and Landscapes 1700–1750*, London 1967, 70–7.

53 All visitors to Leeds, including Celia Fiennes and Daniel Defoe, noted the prosperity and the wealth of its merchants, many of whom owned villas in the pleasant villages to the north of the town.

54 The statue (1713) of Queen Anne by Samuel Carpenter of London (R. Gunnis, *Dictionary of British Sculptors, 1660–1851*, new edn, London n.d., 82), now in Leeds Art Gallery, formerly stood on the front of the Moot Hall in Briggate. The rear of its ground floor contained the butchers' shambles.

55 Holy Trinity, Boar Lane, built to the designs of William Halfpenny, 1721–27. It was built, principally by the town's merchants, to accommodate Leeds's growing population.

56 The medieval parish church of St Peter in Kirkgate was pulled down and replaced in the early Victorian period by one built to the designs of R.D. Chantrell.

their provisions, the goodness of their ale, the politeness of their inhabitants and neighbours, and the beauty of their women. Their Minster is prodigiously grand in all its parts, but falls far short of the neatness of Lincoln. The pillars within side that support the steeple, are four prodigious heaps of stone work'd out into regular Gothic pillars, very elegant. Amongst their curiosities I saw two silver cups gilt with gold, with the covers to them, which were taken off the breasts of corps that had been buried time out of mind. In one of the silver cups, when it was taken up, there was found a red liquor which they took to be the juice of the grape. The cups contained about two thirds of a pint, and were half a foot broad at the bottom, or foot. There was another cup of the same sort, taken up in some part of the church which was of pewter, and very justly supposed to have been buried there with somebody of inferior rank. The Chapter-house is a very fine room, and has a very curious wooden roof.

The next glory of York is their Assembly house. The [word missing] of it is semi circular, with composite pillars at bottom the next rank above is turn'd into arches, which by want of contrivance in the builder were made so weak that they were afterwards obliged to strengthen them with stone supporters within the arch. The Grand Room is 112 feet by 40, and about 45 in height. On each side a row of Corinthian pillars, very lofty and grand without their pedastalls, on the top of their entablature, over each Corinthian pillar, stands a pilaster composite, without pedastal, by it, with its entablature between these pillasters are the windows all around the room. At the top and bottom of the room are six pillars. If there is any fault in this room, tis that the pillars are rather too much crouded, and the height of the room too great in proportion to the width for there is at least 12 feet lost, by the bringing out of the lower pillars so far from the wall. Censures upon this building ought to be pass'd with very great caution in reverance to the name of Burlington. The room is illuminated with nine very large glass branches of wax candles. On the right hand side of the room is another fine room, which with a small Withdrawing Room, takes up the whole length of the great room. This room is used for dining in winter, and for concerts, which are in great perfection there. The left hand side is taken up by a room for the emolument of the ladies. At the coming into the house, you have a vestibulum, on the right hand of which is a coffee room, on the left a room furnish'd with eatables.[57]

The next piece of public grandeur is their prison, which is a fine piece of Doric architecture with two wings. The apartments of the debtors are very good and convenient. The felons are all put together in one large grand room on the right hand side; the ladies have an apartment separate from the men. Those that are under sentence are put into cells by themselves. They have a little court yard for the felons to walk in, and if a man behaves himself decently, and his crime is not very enormous, they suffer him to walk upon a green which is five or six acres and walled in. They have a porter at the gates, who constantly watches and lives there in his lodge, so that

[57] York's Assembly Rooms were built by public subscription to the designs of the Earl of Burlington in the early 1730s. See also note 66 below.

if you was not told you was going into a prison, you would imagine you was going into a noble man's palace.[58]

Their bridge is a fine one and as for any other buildings in York, I think there are none worth mentioning.

Leaving York, we passed over a little corn ground, chiefly rye, then a common, then more corn ground, and arrived at Boroughbridge, the 8th Augst. The bridge is a very fine one, the middle arch being near 20 yards over. West of the town stand three irregular pyramids of stone, the middle one of which is 25 feet high and about five feet thick and obtuse angled square at bottom, worn very much by the weather, especially the upper parts of them, which appear as if they had been fluted. One of the others is about three feet thick and seven feet broad. The three columns stand in a line N. E. and S. W. The country people call them the devil's arrows. Mr. Mason is very certain these are real stones, and tells you the quarry from whence they came, is near Knavesborough [Knaresborough]. They consist of three different strata, and upon digging around them they found the marks of the rod[?], which are certain testimonies that they were real stones.[59]

Next day we got to Rippon, which is famous for a good old minster; a fine market place and a spurr-maker. In the middle of the square stands an obelisk not much unlike the figure and is a great addition to the beauty of the square. In the church yard we met with two inscriptions not easily unriddled. Margaret Lupton died aged 74. She lived to be mother and grandmother to 150 children, and at the babtizing of her first grandchild the child had 10 grandfathers and grandmothers there present. *Hic Jacet Zacharias Jepson, cuius aetas fuit 49 perpacos tantum annos vixit.*

In the afternoon we went to see Mr. Aisleby's park, where we expected to see a place which nature and art had conspired to make a masterpiece of, as the place had the approbation and praise of every body that saw it.[60] We formed too great ideas of it, and upon that account were less surprized, for everything appeared to us to be rather neat than grand, and as the works were out of order, and under repair, we lost all the

58 The monumental Debtors' Prison (now the Castle Museum) was built in 1705, probably by William Wakefield in the manner of Nicholas Hawksmoor.

59 The Devil's Arrows situated south-west of the town. They consist of three large prehistoric monoliths, 16½ feet, 21 feet, and 22½ feet above ground and going down to the average depth of 5 feet. They average 18 feet in diameter. They are of the Middle Bronze Age period, ritual in purpose, and the millstone grit of which they are composed came from either Abbey Plain, Knaresborough, or Plumpton Rock, Harrogate. See N. Pevsner, *The Buildings of England: Yorkshire, the West Riding*, Harmondsworth 1959, 118.

60 The writer provides an early, detailed account of John Aislabie's creation, the most magnificent formal water-garden in England. Soon proclaimed 'the Wonder of the North', the gardens at Studley Royal (not the house) were in every genteel tourist's route through Yorkshire after 1730. Some of the buildings were added after Aislabie's death in 1742 and the ruins of Fountains Abbey and its grounds not incorporated until 1768. The writer was one of the few visitors who expressed a sense of disappointment, surprisingly commenting that 'the works were out of order and under repair'. See Hussey, *English Gardens*, 132–9, and *Fountains Abbey and Studley Royal*, The National Trust 1988.

beauty of the cascades and consequently good parts of the beauty of the place. We enter'd the park at a grand visto, which is a mile in length and takes in Rippon minster. About half way up in the right hand, stands the house which is rather like a keeper's lodge, than a house, tho' they tell you that what it wants in grandeur is very amply supplied in conveniency. The stables are very grand, and very large, built upon a square of 150 feet, room for 32 horses.

On the left hand side in a deep valley lie the gardens, something above a quarter of a mile from the house. At the entrance into them, on the outside on the left hand, is a pond of about seven acres and an half, into which falls the grand cascade, about 12 feet perpendicular, down five steps. On each side the cascade are two square buildings, and a ballustrade up to the gate. Just on the right hand side of the cascade is Lyons head, spouting water into a bason fixed in the wall from the brims of which falls a sheet of water. Streight from the cascade runs a canal 22 yds. broad, 404 long. At the top a sheet of water from another canal, which runs off in an obtuse angle to the left, at the top of which is a cascade, coming from a bridge of frost and rock work of three arches, two of which are fictitious, the middle one winds to the left and forms a cavern 30 yards long to the reservoir, which is about two acres, and when full, contains water enough to supply the cascades for eight hours. Over the cavern is a mount raised and planted with trees, on purpose to hinder a neighbouring gentleman from a prospect of the gardens, who deserves such usage for refusing to sell Mr. Aisleby about three acres of ground, which would have added much to the beauty of the place.

On the left hand side of the long canal, is a basin of about 104 yards in diameter, with a statue of Neptune in the middle. Above and below this basin are two ponds that are made on one side to humour the curve of the basin, on the other to humour the curve of the semicircular walk. At the side of each of these towards the canal stand two statues one of Bacchus, the other of a masculine Venus, head and thighs only feminine. In the middle of the circumference of the grand semicircle is a Doric temple dedicated to Jupiter: dimensions of the room abt. 20 by 16, fronting the door a prodigious large bust of Jupiter. On each side a bust in bronze, of some ancient phylosopher or orator. I took one for a Tully. On the top of a hill, which is very high in some places, craggy in others, planted with trees and cut into pretty walks, is an octagon room which commands a very agreeable prospect. Under this runs a cavern winding, which is high and broad enough for a chaize to pass, and is about 70 yards long. On the right hand side of which long canal is a semicirular pond on the side of which are three Bacchus's supporting a garland of flowers gilt with gold. Upon the hill on the right hand side is a rotunda supported by 8 Ionic pillars. On the right hand side of this rotundo is a banquetting room, with one alcove upon the right hand side, with a charming statue of Venus of Medici in brass. In another alcove, on the left, a tea table, dimensions of ye Room 20 feet by 30 with fret work upon the ceiling. Within a drawing room, with a Corinthian alcove and a yellow bed in it. Fronting this banqueting room is a pretty bowling green. On the right hand side of the little canal is a fine statue of Hercules and Antaeus.

Leaving Rippon we passed through Thirsk, a market town of some note, and about two miles from thence mounted Hambleton hills, which are the steepest I ever saw, and command a most extensive view of the North and East Riding of Yorkshire. On the side of the hill westward about half way up, is a pond of 10 acres, very deep, and very clear, well stored with pike, roach and perch and is visited by all curious gentlemen as a most remarkable piece of water, as it seldom overflows. 'Tis probable that it disembogues itself by some subterraneous passage. By its transparency one may judge that it is not in a perpetual stagnation.[61] From these hills we passed very near the course, which is incomparable good turf, and deserves the character it has of a very fine course.[62] From hence to Helmsly we passed through the most romantick valley that ever I set eyes on; rocks and precipices on each side, hanging woods, and meadows, where they bleach great quantities [of] linnen. They soak the linnen in lime water and afterwards beat out the lime with mills they have for that purpose. There's a small river in the vale, which every quarter of a mile falls down: a natural cascade. The bed of it consists of small stones, and the road lyes so near the river, that your conservation is perpetually disturbed by the purling and murmuring and sometimes clamorous noise of the water.

We reached Helmsly at night, 9th August with no small pleasure and the next day saw a seat belonging to Mr. Duncombe, which is by no means inferior to Mr. Aisleby's, but they both excell in different ways. The house is quite a palace. It was designed by Sir John Vanbrugh.[63] The outside is in very grand Doric taste, rather heavy. The hall is prodigious grand and in my opinion unexceptionally the finest room that ever I saw. The pillars are stone, Corinthian, fluted. Round the top are the heads of the ancients philosophers. A little below them the Caesars in profile. Below these, the statues of the heathen deities at full length. On each side of the hall is an excellent busto, one of Democritus, the other Heraclitus, the first much the finest. The dimensions of the room 60 feet by 40. Upon the ceiling in stucco is Apollo in glory. Out of the hall you are conducted into a long room with some good family portraits in it, and some fine marble work. The dimensions of this room is 90 ft. by 24. There are 5 other very fine rooms upon this floor, with wanton and gay represen-

61 Gormire Lake beneath Sutton Bank.

62 The training and racing of horses on the level ground at the top of the Hambledon Hills had been practised since at least the early seventeenth century. In the 1740s the Kings Plate of 100 guineas run on the Hambledon course was the centrepiece of its annual meeting.

63 The third volume of *Vitruvius Britannicus*, 1725, states that Duncombe Park was 'designed by William Wakefield Esqr., 1713', but H.M. Colvin, *A Biographical Dictionary of English Architects 1660–1840*, London 1954, 646, considers 'the influence of Vanbrugh is clearly apparent, and it is possible that he made plans whose execution was entrusted to Wakefield'. The house was largely destroyed by fire in 1879 and rebuilt after 1895. The writer's account of the Duncombe Terrace is sketchy, for the Ionic and Tuscan Temples at either end of the mile-long curving terrace above the River Rye had been completed around 1730. The famous Rievaulx terrace and temples, three miles away, were added by Thomas Duncombe's son, another Thomas, in the late 1750s. See N. Pevsner, *The Buildings of England: Yorkshire, the North Riding*, Harmondsworth 1966, 139–42, 307; Hussey, *English Gardens*, 140–6.

tations upon the ceilings in stucco, one remarkably so. Besides these rooms there are two very fine stair cases, one of mohogony.

From the house runs a Tuscan colonnade, in a segment of a circle to the stables, which are very fine and noble having room enough for 60 horses. On the other [side] of ye house are the offices which outwardly carry an aspect of grandeur. At the front of the house is a fine bowling green at least six acres. At the end of this upon the same level terras, upon the summit and the edge of a very steep hill which commands a prospect, and overlooks the kitchen garden (which is an octogon, calculated as I suppose, in that figure more for beauty than conveniency, as it must want a good portion of south wall) and a river, which is capable of being cut into all the artificial turns of Aislebys; and was it but somewhat improved, I think that terras of grass a quarter of a mile long, upon a regular curve, would excell anything that Aisleby can boast of. Likewise very extensive views at some places, and is fronted by a fine hill about half a mile on the other side. The house that Mr. Duncombe lived in before he built this, was patched up out of the ruins of the old abbey which has been a very grand one.[64] This house is now appropriated to the use of the poor.

Above 10 miles from Helmsly, road open, we passed thro' Pickering, a little market town, and about four miles from thence saw a little box, belonging to Mr. Thomson, Member for Scarborough. Before the door instead of a canal is a stream dribling and murmuring over a parcel of small stones. Directly behind the house are two small canals, with several little cascades: and just at the door, the whole width of the canal the water dribles down rock work and shell works about five feet. At the top of the canal are two statues one on each side, a shepherd smiling at a shepherdess. Above this canal upon a rise, is a pyramid of shell work with a Mercury on the top. On each side of this water are grass walks and two charming hanging woods cut into shady walks. Upon the front of the house towards the water is a grotto in rockwork with a looking glass in the middle, which has a very pretty effect. If I have not forgot the house is in the Tuscan taste. There is a very neat cold bath, the water of which is of a soft nature, whereas the water of the canals is of a petryfying nature and turns moss and all woody substances into stone. I took up a great deal of moss some of which was entirely petryfy'd, some of it only just crusted over. I intend, some leisure hour or so, to draw a sketch of this place, so shall forbear any further description of it.[65]

From hence we went to Brympton [Brompton], we passed over open corn ground for about three miles and then over a very barren heathy common to Scarborough, which must be allowed to be one of the finest situate towns in England. There is an exceeding steep hill which runs out to the east by north. On this are the ruins of a fine old castle. The hill round to sea-ward is guarded by an inaccessible rock, to the

64 Rievaulx Abbey.

65 The chief feature of Ebberston Hall, a delicious tiny Palladian villa on the edge of the North Yorkshire moors, built for William Thompson, MP, to the designs of Colin Campbell in 1718, was its water gardens. See Hussey, *English Gardens*, 65–9.

harbour ward, by a strong wall. Within the walls upon the top of the hill is a piece of ground above 20 acres, which is as fine a pasture as can possibly be. They have more than their share of grass in the dryest summers, which may be accounted for by the excessive heights of the place, by which it gains more than its share of dews and damps. On the top of this hill is a very fine spring of soft water, which is a very great rarity at Scarboro'. This spring never fails in the driest summers, but has been known to fail sometimes in a very wet one. The reason I conjecture to be this. About Scarbro' are a great many springs which springs often fail in dry summers. The reason why springs fail at all, is, because there is not a supply enough of water to keep open their channels. Only suppose these channels stopt up and the little dribling water which had not weight enough to keep open its own channel by some accident or other to find its way into the channel upon the hill, and this will be a substantial reason why it should abound with water in ye driest seasons. Why it should fail in wet seasons, if this be the case, is as easily accounted for. The springs all about, by great supplies of water, have their channels worn to such a bigness, that they can carry more water than is at all times supplied. Now let the water of the Spring upon the hill by some accident or other find its way into these channels and then the fact is accounted for. That tis possible for waters to change their subterranaous courses appears from springs failing at one place and breaking out at another and that this very spring is more liable to change its course than another, appears from a fact that is pretty well attested, and that is that it failed once upon firing the great guns upon the hill on a day of rejoicing and did not recover itself for some months.

At the foot of this hill lyes the Wapping of Scarbro upon the south side. At the end of the crag to the south runs out the stone pier which by means of one or two little piers more, makes a fine harbour, for shipping of five or six hundred ton burthens. This hill with that opposite to it, where the spar is, form a large bay near a mile over. About half way round this bay Lyes the town and runs up a great way westward where all the polite part of the town live or lodge. There are three very good streets in it; the long street, another crossing it at right angles, and another below called the Beast Market perpendicular to it. The diversions of the day at Scarboro' are like those of all other places, day after day, just alike. From seven o'clock in the morning they drink the waters, or wash in the sea; at eleven to a publick breakfast where you have pretty good music, and a breakfast for a shilling: and then to dancing till two o'clock, then to dinner, then to dressing, and between five and six to the ball room, where they dance and play at cards and roly poly till between ten and eleven, then to bed and the next morning they rise to act the same farce over again.[66]

[66] There is a delightful account, made by Sarah, Duchess of Marlborough, of taking the waters at Scarborough, almost a decade earlier, in July–August 1732. Typically, the spa was denounced as 'the worst that I ever saw in England', worse even than her recollections of Hanover. Her disapproval of Lord Burlington's unfinished Assembly Rooms at York, which she visited en route to Scarborough was equally hearty, 'it exceeds all the nonsense and madness that I ever saw of that kind, and that is saying a good deal'. G. Scott Thomson, ed., *Letters of a Grandmother 1732–1735*, London 1943, 41, 45–67.

The expences of the place are a five shillings subscription to each ball-room, five shillings to a bookseller, seven shilling and six pence to the spaw, and two shillings and six pence to the coffee house. Besides the subcription to the ball-room, every time you dance you pay a shilling to the musick. They have now quite lost a good custom of the gentlemen and ladies dining at an ordinary together, and besides that, the ordinaries are so crowded with gamesters and other shabroons [low fellows], that gentlemen are obliged to form themselves into parties of five or six in number and bespeak a dinner at the tavern at so much a head. The prices for everything are so extravagent as they are at London. a Yorkshire man frets and fumes all the while he is there. He dines upon chickens at home for three pence a piece, and sups upon them there for half a crown.

The poor people seem to be miserable lowe wretches. Their country everywhere within four or five miles of Scarborough is a barren heath, their houses are poor despicable cots, their soil so cold that their corn was green when we left the place. It was chiefly oats which the poor people live upon all winter. The better sort can sometimes afford to eat dryed scate [skate] of which they have a great plenty of at Scarbro. They catch their great quantities of soals and guernels, and codfish and herrings.

From Scarbro' the 16th we set out for York and after leaving the barren hills of Scarbro', we got into a very rich valley, which carried us to Malton, which is a tolerable good market town, and situated in one of the finest parts of Yorkshire. About four miles from Malton, we saw the gardens at Castle Howard. The house we were not permitted to see, because the late Ld. Morpeth then lay dead in it. The gardens are finely laid out upon a rising ground, which commands a pretty near prospect. Some of the walks are streight and some irregular, with statues, at every place where it was thought they would be any addition to the beauty of it. There's a Calliope upon a pretty pedestal of rock work, which is carved upon the side, with a great many rural views. By what they call the summer-house, there's some stone work which we all at first sight mistook for old pollard, which upon turning a cock Dribled water, which had a very pretty effect. There is a temple almost finished in imitation marble in shells which is done to such perfection that it may possibly deceive a very understanding eye. At the four corners of this temple without side are the four sybils.[67] Beyond the gardens upon a rising ground is a very fine piece of building in Doric taste, which they call a mausoleum and is designed for a church for the family.[68] In the gardens is a very neat fountain and a pretty room just beside

67 Vanbrugh's Temple of the Four Winds (1724–26). Its interior is dated 1739, but the writer suggests a completion date more than two years later.

68 Nicholas Hawksmoor's majestic mausoleum built, 1731–42, almost a mile from the house was never intended as a chapel for the family. Although the west wing of Sir John Vanbrugh's plan made provision for a chapel, it was not built, nor was Sir Thomas Robinson's west wing of the 1750s completed internally until the 1810s. The present chapel at Castle Howard, dating from the 1870s, replaced its early nineteenth-century predecessor.

it. The old trees are all leaded over, at the places which have begun to decay. On the right hand side of the gardens is a large piece of water, which when finished, will be a great ornament.[69]

Omitted in the acct. of Norwich, that all the stones of ye cathedral, the castle and the old church are remarkably small. There are some old buildings of flint, cut so exactly square that they joint as [word missing] as the smoothest bricks.

69 The South Lake.

Thomas Gainsborough as an Ipswich Musician, a Collector of Prints and a Caricaturist

Hugh Belsey

THOMAS GAINSBOROUGH moved to Ipswich in about 1752 after a four-year sojourn in his native Sudbury.[1] Recent research has shown that he visited Bath in 1758 before moving there permanently with his young family the following year.[2] Judging from the number of paintings that can be dated to the six years he worked in Ipswich, it was a period of great activity. Unfortunately there is little documentary material to support the pictorial evidence[3] and many of his early head-and-shoulder portraits, though distinctive likenesses, are repetitive in composition. With the exception of the late John Bensusan-Butt, few have attempted to examine the artist's Suffolk sitters in any detail.[4] Most other commentators have shied away from his early work, preferring to study his later paintings which made such an impact on visitors to public exhibitions in London. By publishing a couple of new acquisitions at Gainsborough's House, which with characteristic generosity Norman Scarfe has done so much to encourage, this article will examine Gainsborough's interest in music, caricature and printmaking, subjects that will interest cultural historians from many disciplines. Although there has been little comment about his early

I should like to thank Dr Brian Allen, David Alexander, Dr John Blatchly and Dr Susan Sloman for their help and encouragement, Judy Egerton for her constructive comments and the late John Bensusan-Butt for his amendments after reading an earlier draft of this article.

1 Gainsborough first moved to London in about 1740. He married Margaret Burr, an illegitimate daughter of Henry, 3rd Duke of Beaufort, there in 1746; and she gave birth to a daughter three months later. The child died in March 1747/8, and the painter's father, John, in November 1748: these two events appear to have prompted the couple's return to Sudbury. There Mrs Gainsborough gave birth to two daughters who were both baptised in the town.

2 M. Rosenthal, 'Testing the Water: Gainsborough in Bath in 1758', *Apollo* cxlii, September 1995, 49–54, and S.L. Sloman, 'Gainsborough in Bath in 1758–59', *Burlington Magazine* cxxxvii, August 1995, 509–12.

3 Only five of the 110 letters listed by Hayes date before 1760 (J. Hayes, *The Letters of Thomas Gainsborough*, New Haven and London 2001, 5–12, nos 1–5; hereafter Hayes 2001). In addition to the total number of letters, Hayes lists a further thirty-seven additional documents.

4 See J. Bensusan-Butt, *Gainsborough in his Twenties*, privately printed Colchester, 3rd edn 1993 (hereafter Bensusan-Butt 1993), and J. Hayes, 'Some Unknown Early Gainsborough Portraits', *Burlington Magazine* cvii, February 1965, 62–74, and his article in *The Painter's Eye*, exhibition catalogue, Gainsborough's House, Sudbury 1977, unpaginated.

paintings, Gainsborough's musicianship has proved, surprisingly, to be a subject of lively discussion.

The fencing master, Henry Angelo, tells us that Gainsborough 'could accompany a slow movement of the harpsichord, both on the fiddle and the flute, with taste and feeling';[5] and William Thomas Parke, the oboist, reports that Gainsborough was 'an excellent violin player'.[6] The best known commentator on Gainsborough's musical proficiency was his friend, William Jackson, who remarked on his ability to play the violin, viol da gamba, and harp, concluding, somewhat sourly, that 'he frittered away his musical talents; and though possessed of ear, taste, and genius, he never had application enough to learn his notes. He scorned to take the first step, the second was of course out of his reach; and the summit became unattainable.'[7] Such inconsistent reports make any intelligible appraisal of his abilities impossible. Perhaps Thomas Dodd's observation that he was 'marked with a capricious love for change in the instruments on which he practised' best reflects his enthusiasm and explains the attitude of his contemporaries.[8] From his own account of a concert in Ipswich, related to the actor, David Garrick, in a letter dated 27 July 1768, written some dozen years after the event, it is clear that his exuberance and wit must have contributed to the event as much as the music making itself:

> . . . you must know Sir whilst I lived at Ipswich, there was [a] benefit Concert in which a new Song was to be introduced, and I being steward, went to the honest Cabinet-maker who was our Singer instead of a better, and asked him if he could sing at sight, for that I had a new song with all the parts written out, yes Sir said he I can – upon which I order'd Mr. Giardini of Ipswich to begin the symphony and gave my Signal for the Attention of the Company; but behold a dead silence followed the symphony instead of the song; upon which I jumped up to the fellow: 'D—n ye Why don't you sing? did not you tell me you could sing at first sight? Yes, please your honor I did say I could sing at sight, but not first sight'.[9]

It is perhaps in this humour that the modern scholar should regard the lost painting, known only from written descriptions, of the *Musical Society at Ipswich*.[10] In this

5 H. Angelo, *Reminiscences of Henry Angelo . . .*, 2 vols, London 1830, I, 187–8.

6 W.T. Parke, *Musical Memoirs . . .*, 2 vols, London 1830, I, 335.

7 W. Jackson, *The Four Ages together with Essays on Various Subjects*, London 1798, 154.

8 BL Add. MS 33401, fo. 3.

9 Gainsborough's House, 1998.024 (Hayes 2001, 56–7, no. 34). Bensusan-Butt (1993, 49) identifies the singer as Josiah Harris (d.1783), an Ipswich cabinet-maker and auctioneer. For Felice de' Giardini and Gainsborough's portrait of him see L. Stainton, *Gainsborough and his Musical Friends*, exhibition catalogue, Kenwood, London 1977, no. 3 repr. (hereafter Stainton 1977), and E.K. Waterhouse, *Gainsborough*, London 1958, no. 311 (hereafter Waterhouse 1958).

10 This group has generally been described as the Ipswich Music Club, but it appears as the 'Musical Society at Ipswich' in the subscription lists of both Joseph Gibbs's publications, the *Eight Solos* of about 1746 and the *Six Quartettoes* of 1777 (see note 31 below). The Club also subscribed to John Hebden's *Six Concertos in Seven Parts*, London 1745, and William Hayes' *Six Cantatas Set to Musick*, London 1748 (F.J.G. Robinson and P.J. Wallis, *Book Subscription Lists: A Revised Guide*, Newcastle upon Tyne 1975, ref. 745HEB, 746GIB, 748HAY; hereafter Robinson and Wallis 1975. The *Guide* is augmented by a supplement of 1996). The Society may

light reexamining the evidence may show that the painting was more akin to the humour of the letters and caricature than to the posed conversation pieces generally associated with Gainsborough's early commissions in Suffolk.

On 19 June 1855 George Williams Fulcher, the Sudbury printer, local politician and poet, died 'very suddenly'.[11] In less than twelve months his son, Edmund Syer Fulcher, had assembled his father's notes and published them as the *Life of Thomas Gainsborough, R.A.* Excepting Philip Thicknesse's brief memoir of the artist 'written in one day'[12] – of which the younger Fulcher remarked 'we need not here say more, than that it deservedly enjoyed a fame of equal duration'[13] – Fulcher's *Life* is the earliest monograph on the artist. The elder Fulcher seems to have collected the material 'with diligence' over some time and the book itself, according to one critic, is 'animated with zeal'.[14] The publication was so popular that on 16 December 1856 E.S. Fulcher was preparing a preface to a fully revised second edition, including amendments and various additions.

In the book's rudimentary list of Gainsborough's work, Fulcher records a group portrait: 'The Members of the 'Musical Club' (Ipswich) 1 [foot] 3 [inches] by 1 [foot] 8 [inches] [in the collection of] J. G. Strutt Esq.'[15] Jacob George Strutt (1784–after 1856) was the second son of Benjamin Strutt who, as we will see below, described the painting in greater detail. It is worth quoting Ann Taylor's description of him:

have been disbanded after Gainsborough left Ipswich as it was not a subscriber to Joseph Eyre's *Eight Sonatas in Three Parts*, published in London in about 1765. The only professional musician in the group, Joseph Gibbs, did not subscribe to this publication although other members, John Mills, John Wood and Captain Abraham Clerke, did. I should like to thank Mrs Ruth Wallis of Project for Historical Biobibliography (PHIBB) for answering my repeated enquiries about subscription lists.

11 Death notice in *Bury and Norwich Post and Suffolk Herald*, 27 June 1855, 2. The same edition publishes a fulsome obituary. For his political and literary achievements see E.A. Goodwyn, *East Anglian Literature*, Ipswich 1982, 35–41, and for his publishing career see T. Copsey, *Book Distribution and Printing in Suffolk 1534–1850*, privately printed Ipswich 1994, 50–1.

12 P. Thicknesse, *Memoir of Thomas Gainsborough*, London 1788, 49.

13 G.W. Fulcher, *Life of Thomas Gainsborough R.A.*, ed. E.S. Fulcher, 1st edn, Sudbury 1856, iii (hereafter Fulcher 1856 i; the second edition is abbreviated hereafter Fulcher 1856 ii). It appears that Edmund Syer Fulcher took over the task of publishing the Gainsborough material immediately after his father's death. See T. Copsey, *Book Distribution and Printing in Suffolk 1534–1850*, privately printed Ipswich 1994, 73, 83 for the subsequent fortunes of the printing business.

14 A review by J. M[itford], 'Fulcher's Life of Gainsborough', *Gentleman's Magazine*, August 1856, 199 (hereafter *GM*). There is evidence that E.S. Fulcher attempted to add to his father's notes. In November 1855, requesting information about Gainsborough's activities in London after 1774 and asking for references to works for the brief catalogue, he was unhelpfully referred to Thicknesse's biography (*Notes and Queries*, 1st ser. xxi, no. 314, 3 November 1855, 347; 2nd ser. i, no. 10, 8 March 1856, 200; no. 14, 5 April 1856, 281). Hoping that a more specific question would yield fruit, he asked for the whereabouts of the full-length portrait of Carl Friedrich Abel (Waterhouse 1958, no. 1) with no success (*Notes and Queries*, 2nd ser. i, no. 14, 5 April 1856, 271).

15 Fulcher 1856 i, 225; Fulcher 1856 ii, 229.

> Mr Strutt himself is not easy to describe. What might be his occupation, or by what means he indulged his varied, peculiar, and sometimes expensive tastes, I never knew. He was an artist, musician, antiquary, poet, and author, an amateur in each. His fine grey head and dark penetrating eyes made his appearance singular and interesting, while a marked scowl and a taciturn austerity seemed intended to express a high disregard of society in all its forms of external elegance and conventional politeness . . . he was, I fully believe, naturally not only polite, but kind, so that . . . we soon felt at home and comfortable in his ornamental parlour . . .[16]

Some account of the same painting is given by John Constable in a letter to his mentor John Thomas Smith, dated 7 May 1797: 'in Ipswich they did not know his [Gainsborough's] value till they lost him. He belonged to something of a musical club in that town and painted some of their portraits in a picture of a choir; it is said to be very curious.'[17] In the text of his book, Fulcher quotes a letter from Benjamin Strutt which includes a fuller account of the painting:

> The picture of the members of the Musical Club . . . is still extant. 'Though very slight and unfinished,' remarks its possessor, Mr Strutt, 'it is exceedingly spirited, and is more interesting as it was composed from memory. Immediately in front of the spectator are the portraits of Gainsborough himself, and his friend Captain Clarke, who is leaning familiarly on the Painter's shoulder. The heads of both are tuned towards Wood, a dancing master, who is playing on the violin, accompanied on the violincello by one Mills. The latter figure is merely outlined, Gainsborough declaring that he 'could not recollect the expression of his phiz.' Gibbs, on the opposite side of a table which is standing in the centre, is sound asleep. There is a sly piece of satire in this, he being the only real musician in the party, and his sleeping would seem to indicate that the performance is not of first-rate quality. It is a candlelight scene, and by the condition of the table, some degree of conviviality appears to have prevailed. Gainsborough has his glass in his hand, that of Gibbs stands before him, as also does Clarke's, and one is overturned: a couple of lights are placed on each side of a music stand, before which are the two performers. The portrait of Gainsborough possesses much grace, and is very like that exhibited at the British Institute many years ago. He is dressed in a dark claret-colored coat; Clarke is in uniform; Wood, in blue; and Gibbs, in sober grey. When Gainsborough was leaving Ipswich, his friends paid a last visit to his studio, and expressed a wish to have some memorial of his pencil. The good-natured artist complied. One took one sketch; another, another; and finally that I have been describing came into my father's hands'.[18]

Surprisingly, the reference to the self-portrait relates to that presented in 1818 to the Royal Academy by the artist's daughter[19] and not to the unfinished portrait dated 1754 which is now at Houghton. The Academy's portrait had been shown at the British Institution in 1814, whereas the Houghton portrait was not shown until

16 *Memorials of Mrs Gilbert*, 2 vols, London 1876, I, 142–3. The late John Bensusan-Butt generously deposited notes about Strutt at Gainsborough's House.

17 *John Constable's Correspondence*, 6 vols, ed. R.B. Beckett, SRS 1962–68, ii, 11. The letter was first published by Fulcher 1856 i, 54.

18 Fulcher 1856 i and ii, 55–7.

19 Waterhouse 1958, no. 292, repr. pl. 208. The painting was also lent to the British Institution in 1854 and 1859.

1867 at the National Portraits Exhibition in South Kensington Museum.[20] The letter must therefore predate Strutt's death in 1827 and it would have been one of the earliest anecdotes recorded by the elder Fulcher. Judging from the reference in the catalogue list quoted above, the younger Fulcher was able to bring the information contained in the letter up to date and confirm that the painting had passed from father to son.[21]

Gainsborough's 'curious' painting of the Musical Society at Ipswich, described as 'very slight and unfinished', rests unhappily in the artist's oeuvre and seems to be unlike any other recorded painting by him.[22] Lindsay Stainton has suggested that it may have resembled the *Muilman Conversation Piece* or Sir Joshua Reynolds' smaller caricature groups,[23] but the wit and good-natured bawdiness of the subject brings the treatment closer to Hogarth's *Midnight Conversation*.[24] For the painting's precise composition the scholar must await the rediscovery of the canvas. Meanwhile it is worthwhile recording a little more about the sitters' biographies.

Presumably it was John Strutt from Coddenham near Ipswich, who later moved to Great Clacton on the Essex coast as a schoolmaster, who acquired the painting from Gainsborough at the artist's sale arranged immediately before he finally left Ipswich for Bath in October 1759. On 22 and 23 of that month he sold 'some PICTURES and original DRAWINGS . . . which, as he is desirous of leaving them amongst his friends will have the lowest prices set upon them'; and as Strutt has stated the oil sketch of the *Musical Club* was amongst those offered for sale.[25] Strutt may have acquired it as a memento for his wife, Mary Gibbs (*c.*1722–1817), a kinswoman of Joseph Gibbs (Plate 1), the distinguished composer and organist who appeared in the group.[26] In 1779 Strutt's son, Benjamin (1754–1827), an amateur

20 Waterhouse 1958, no. 290, pl. 8. The Houghton portrait was no. 533 in the 1867 exhibition.

21 The *Ipswich Journal* (7 April 1827; hereafter *IJ*) includes notice of an auction of Benjamin Strutt's effects which included one thousand volumes, musical scores, 'several paintings, Busts etc. etc'.

22 A long-case clock signed 'Moore Ipswich' in Christchurch Mansion, Ipswich has been erroneously associated with the Musical Society at Ipswich (A.L. Haggar and L.F. Miller, *Suffolk Clocks and Clockmakers*, privately printed Ramsgate 1974, 36, fig. 18b). It is decorated with two trimmed mezzotints, *Mirth and Friendship* and *Night Amusement*, which were published by Carrington Bowles in about 1770 (F.G. Stephens and M.D. George, *Catalogue of Political and Personal Satires . . . in the British Museum, to 1832*, 11 vols, London 1870–1954, nos 4505, 4506; hereafter *BM Satires*). The notion that the decoration is by Gainsborough and includes a portrait of Joseph Gibbs amongst the figures was first posed by R.H. Lingwood [pseudonym RAMBLER], 'Pribbles and Prabbles', *East Anglian Daily Times*, 30 June 1928.

23 Stainton 1977, no. 13.

24 The painting is known in many versions. The most accessible is that in the Yale Center for British Art, which is generally dated *c.*1732.

25 Notice of the sale, which is quoted by W.T. Whitley, *Gainsborough*, London 1915, 22, is given in the *IJ*, 20 October 1759. The only other painting that is linked to this sale is the *Artist's Daughters chasing a Butterfly* which was purchased by Revd Robert Hingeston, the headmaster of Ipswich School. The school was close to Gainsborough's house in Foundation Street and Hingeston sat to Gainsborough in *c.*1754 (Ipswich Museums and Galleries; Waterhouse 1958, no. 370).

26 A number of articles record his biography: R.H. Lingwood [pseudonym RAMBLER], *East*

artist and the author of the letter describing the group portrait, made a thumb nail etching after Gainsborough's portrait (Plate 2) and inserted it into his meticulously copied miniature manuscript of Gibbs's composition, *Eight Solos*.[27]

Gibbs was painted by Gainsborough in about 1756 (London, National Portrait Gallery)[28] standing before two large volumes inscribed with the name of his mentors, Arcangelo Corelli (1653–1713) and his pupil Francesco Geminiani (1687–1762). Both specialised in writing and performing violin sonatas – Geminiani was in London during the 1740s – and the sitter must have wished to make a connection between their work and his own. Another volume opened at a page headed 'SONATA' is placed conspicuously on a music stand with a quill standing in an inkwell beside it; and, although the notation does not match any of the *Eight Solos* which Strutt copied out thirty years later, the typography is the same.

Gibbs was born in Colchester in 1698, the son of a musician named John Gibbs and his wife Judith.[29] By 1727 he was performing in the town with his father and brother, and he may well have taken over the appointment of organist at St Peter's from his father. By 1733 he had begun to perform benefit concerts in Colchester which continued until at least 1750. Concurrently he was giving inaugural recitals on the new organs at Harwich (1734), Framlingham (1751) and Hadleigh (1754), but by 1745 he had moved from Colchester to Dedham where he is recorded performing between 1740 and 1759. There are notices of guest recitals in Eye (1747), Bungay (1747) and Sudbury (1748); and on 6 December 1763 he is mentioned playing continuo for a performance of the comic opera *Love in a Village*, written by Isaac Bickerstaffe with music by Thomas Arne, at the Ipswich Playhouse. The play had been 'acted last Season, seventy nights successively, at the Theatre Royal in Covent-Garden, and [is] now performing with general Applause'.[30]

In 1748 Gibbs moved from Dedham to become organist at the civic church of

Anglian Daily Times, 1 May and 30 June 1928; S. Bayliss, 'Joseph Gibbs', *The Strad* xlix, September 1938, 205–6; John Cooper: 'Eminently Distinguished', *East Anglian Magazine* xxxvii, June 1978, 414–15 (hereafter Cooper 1978 i); Joseph Cooper, 'Joseph Gibbs', *The Strad*, lxxxix, June 1978, 185–7, 185–7 (hereafter Cooper 1978 ii); Bensusan-Butt 1993, 54–6 listed most of the references to Gibbs given in this article.

27 SROI, f.s.787.154. Another copy, on Turkey Mill, Whatman paper with the identity of the engraver erased, belongs to David Alexander (Stainton 1977, no. 1). An inscription inside the back cover states that the transcription was 'begun 1773 and finished 15 September 1809'.

28 Waterhouse 1958, no. 313, pl. 28 and J. Kerslake, *National Portrait Gallery: Early Georgian Portraits*, 2 vols, London 1977, pl. 269. A second portrait belonged to the family of Charles Allix at Swaffham, Norfolk, until it was sold at Foster's on 6 December 1922 as lot 151 ('Gainsborough: Portrait of a Man'). It was identified as Gibbs by Allix in a note dated 19 October 1936 in the National Portrait Gallery archives (Kerslake, *ibid.*, 1977, 99). The absence of the books and quill in Strutt's engraving could be explained if he had based his design on this version of the portrait but, unfortunately, this cannot be verified as no photograph of the Allix painting is known to exist. Alternatively it could be based on the likeness in the missing group portrait.

29 Cooper 1978 i, 414 wrongly assumed Gibbs was born in Eye. He was corrected by Bensusan-Butt 1993, 54.

30 *IJ*, 3 December 1763 (quoted by Cooper 1978 ii, 187).

Plate 1. Portrait of Joseph Gibbs (1698–1788), by Thomas Gainsborough. *c.*1756. Oil on canvas, 60.7 by 50.2 cm. *National Portrait Gallery, London.*

Plate 2. Portrait of Joseph Gibbs (1698–1788), by Benjamin Strutt after Thomas Gainsborough. 1779. Etching, plate size 9.4 by 6.3 cm. *Suffolk Record Office, Ipswich.*

St Mary Tower (nowadays called St Mary-le-Tower) in Ipswich, a post he retained until his death. At Dedham he published *Eight Solos for a Violin with a Thorough Bass*, which have been praised for their Handelian lyricism, and in 1777 *Six Quartettoes for Two Violins a Tenor and Violoncello* appeared.[31] He is also named as the vendor of a volume of music *The Grove, or Rural Harmony*, by John Carr in about 1760.[32] Gibbs's wife, Mary, died in 1766 and is buried in All Saints', Colchester. He himself died at the advanced age of 89 on 12 December 1788 and an elaborate funeral was held six days later. An obituarist called him 'eminently distin-

[31] The copies are undated but a notice for the latter appears in the *IJ* on 19 July 1777. The subscribers list includes 'Mr Gainsborough 6 Sets' (SROI, q. S. 787); another copy, of the base part only, is in Cambridge University Library. A musical assessment of both publications is given by Cooper 1978 ii, 185 and S. Bezkorvany, 'The 8 Violin Sonatas of Joseph Gibbs', *The Strad* lxxxix, June 1978, 189–91.

[32] Between 1737 and 1760 Gibbs is mentioned as a subscriber to musical scores by Henry Carey, Michael Festing, and Alessandro Bezozzi (Robinson and Wallis 1975, ref. 737CAR, 744FES, 747FES, 759BEZ, 760CAR). Gibbs also subscribed to two travel books by John Green and Griffiths Hughes (Robinson and Wallis 1975, ref. 745GRE, 750HUG).

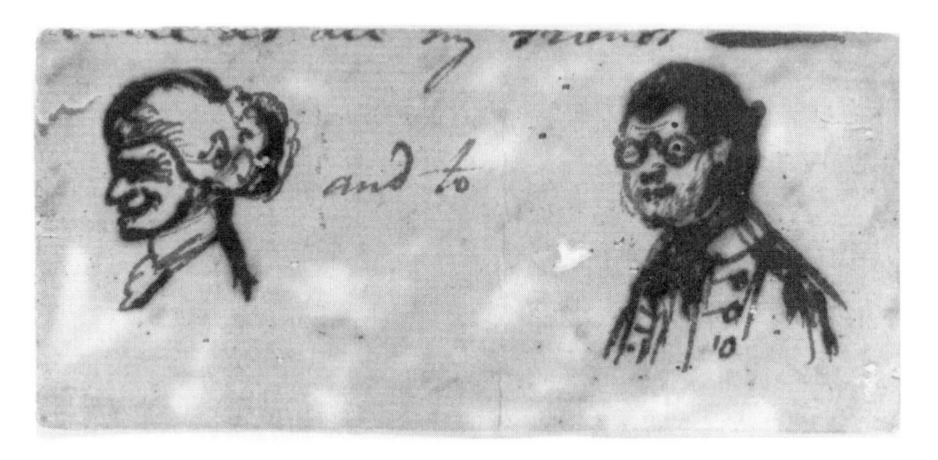

Plate 3. Fragment of a letter to James Hatley, by Thomas Gainsborough. *c.*1756. Pen and ink, 5 by 12 cm. *Gainsborough's House, Sudbury.*

guished, both as a composer and a performer. In private life the mildness, simplicity and integrity of his manners rendered him universally beloved and respected.'[33]

Other sitters in the lost painting of the Musical Society are also identifiable. The cellist was a cabinet maker named John Mills (*c.*1720–93). Two years before Mills's death a benefit concert was held at the Ipswich Assembly Rooms and his will included bequests of musical instruments, books, paintings and prints.[34] More is known of others in the group through a tiny fragment from a letter written by Gainsborough (Plate 3) to James Hatley. In the late eighteenth-century the fragment was cut from the letter and framed. Given that the script on the reverse side of the sheet runs at right angles to the two heads it seems likely that the sketches originally formed a witty pictographic postscript asking Mr Hatley to send greetings to '[two words partially missing] all my friends' Wood 'and to' Clerke by drawing caricature heads as a substitute for writing their names. The sheet is an example of the common parlour game occasionally commandeered by advertisers and generally won by those with a sense of the ridiculous and with some graphic facility.[35] Sadly the text on the reverse is too mutilated to make any sense.[36]

33 *GM* lviii, December 1788, 1130. An account of his elaborate funeral is given in both the *GM* and in *IJ*, 20 December 1788. The inscription formerly on his tomb in St Mary-le-Tower is cited by Cooper 1978 i, 414–15. Gibbs's posthumous sale on 21 March 1789 included two unidentified paintings by Gainsborough (*IJ*, 21 March 1789).

34 See *IJ*, 31 August and 7 September 1793, and Mills's will (SROI, IC/AA1/213/75).

35 Gainsborough's House 1994.070 (Hayes 2001, 7–8, no. 3 repr.). There are two other illustrations included in his letters. In a fragmentary letter, very similar to the scrap under discussion, dated Bath 28 July 1763, Gainsborough illustrates the point he is making in two landscape sketches (Hayes 2001, 16, no. 8 repr. and J. Hayes, *The Drawings of Thomas Gainsborough*, 2 vols, London 1970, nos 262, 263) and in another letter to Lord Mulgrave he explains the way to draw foliage with a number of scalloped pen strokes (Hayes 2001, 92, no. 55).

36 It reads as follows: '. . .t with regard. . . | . . . was agreed be. . . | . . .ke them away, . . . | . . .thing,

It is surprising that James Hatley (*c.*1721–87), the recipient of the letter, was not amongst the sitters in the Musical Society and remarkable that he never sat to Gainsborough. He was a respected resident of Ipswich who was described in a fulsome obituary in the *Gentleman's Magazine* as:

> descended from a very ancient family of that name in Bedfordshire. To a very fine natural understanding, highly cultivated by a very liberal education, he added a very thorough knowledge of the polite arts, with great gentleness and elegance of manners.[37]

His interests are endorsed by the publications he supported. He appears in subscribers' lists which include music by Henry Burgess, John Hebden, Joseph Gibbs, Giacobbe Cervetto, John Garth and Joseph Eyre, together with similar lists for books by Joshua Kirby, Nathaniel Ball and John Wright.[38] He married Mary, the elder daughter of Surgeon Alderman Philip Cornwallis of Harwich, who 'died after a lingering and painful illness' on 22 May 1796.[39] Both husband and wife are buried in the churchyard of St Nicholas's church, Ipswich.[40]

The identity of the recipient is given in a note which was fixed to the back of the frame when the tiny drawings were cut from the letter. The note, here transcribed, also identifies the sitters:

> These two Caricatures were done by Mr Gainsborough | scratched with his pen in a letter to James Hatley Esqr | – [Mr] Jack Wood – and to – Capt. Clarke – | Mr Wood was a dancing Master well known | in Suffolk, played ~~a good~~ an excellant second Fiddle, and was | a good musician; The above three Gentlemen | being all distractedly fond of music, Mr Wood | and family made one in all their musical meetings | [?and] constantly assisted at all their convivial | [par]ties – Capt Clarke was an Officer of great | merit, and respectability.[41]

A portrait (Plate 4), now in the Yale Center for British Art, was identified as 'Mr Wood the Violinist' when it appeared on the London art market in 1965.[42] The sitter wears a flamboyant wig like the caricature and, like the figure in the lost group

and the . . .| . . . opportunity of . . . | . . . that take the . . . | . . . I shall . . . | . . .strick is all I . . . | . . . & take a Rec. . . | . . . knows how . . .'.

37 *GM* lvii, August 1787, 742. His death is also recorded in *IJ* on 4 August 1787.

38 Robinson and Wallis 1975, ref. 740BUR, 749BUR, 745HEB (Hatley subscribed for three copies), 746GIB (he also subscribed to Gibbs's *Six Quartettos* of 1777), 750CER, 757GAR, 765EYR (where he is described 'Mr Hatley, of Ipswich'), 748KI, 754RAL and 765WRI respectively.

39 *IJ*, 28 May 1796. For more detail of the Hatley family see BL Davy MS 19134, fos 327–9.

40 The inscription is quoted in *GM* xcvi, June 1826, 503.

41 I am grateful to Christopher Hurst of the Hamilton Kerr Institute, University of Cambridge, for help in transcribing this text.

42 This portrait was sold anonymously by the Harbord family at Christie's on 2 April 1965 as lot 123 bt Sabin Galleries from whom it was purchased by Paul Mellon the following year. The identity of the sitter is established by an inscription on a label attached to the stretcher which read: 'Mr. Wood the Violinist, by Thomas Gainsborough'. Unfortunately the label was removed before it appeared at auction. I am grateful to the late Sidney Sabin for showing me his notes on the picture.

Plate 4. Portrait of John Wood (1718–83), by Thomas Gainsborough. *c.*1756. Oil on canvas, 76.2 by 63.5 cm. *Yale Center for British Art, New Haven, Paul Mellon Collection.*

portrait, he is dressed in blue. He is John Wood (1718–83), the son of Isaac Wood, a dancing master of Bury St Edmunds, and Hannah Bellamy. He married Harriet Hale at Little Saxham, near Bury St Edmunds, in 1737; and three years later he is described in the local newspaper as teaching dancing in Ipswich. He was one of the few dancing masters to be included in the subscription list of William Boyce's *Twelve Sonatas* of 1747 – 'Mr. John Wood of Ipswich, Dancing Master'[43] – and by 1750 he was advertising dancing classes at Dedham on Tuesdays, Colchester on Wednesdays, and Ipswich on Monday mornings and Thursdays.[44] By 1754 he had built a 'new Dancing-Room' in St Nicholas Street, Ipswich;[45] and in March 1757 Wood passed over his teaching commitments in Colchester to a John South and in Dedham to a Mr Aylmer[46] so that he could teach in Norwich 'in Hopes of advancing his Business':

> MR. WOOD from IPSWICH, has open'd his School to teach DANCING, in a commodious Room opposite St Simon's Church, where young Ladies and Gentlemen will be carefully taught, and punctually attended every Monday and Tuesday.[47]

After the death of his father late in the same year, the enterprising Wood took over his dancing classes in Bury St Edmunds. The advertisement in the *Ipswich Journal* of 31 December 1757 also announced that his wife returned 'thanks to Friends who have intrusted their children to her care, and also informing them that she continues her school with proper Assistants'. Their two careers now established, neither appears to have required further advertising, and the next press notice records Wood's death on 13 July 1783. In his will he left his music and instruments to his son Charles, who followed his father's profession and established his career at King's Lynn.[48]

The subject of the portrait on the right in the fragment of the Hatley letter is Captain Abraham Clerke (1718–72).[49] He was born in Norwich and inherited his father's interest in music.[50] He served an apprenticeship with an attorney Henry

[43] He may also have been the subscriber to Daniel Bellamy's *Miscellanies in Prose and Verse* published in 1740 (Robinson and Wallis 1975, ref. 740BEL, 747BOY).

[44] Advertisement in *IJ*, 23 March 1751. He advertises balls at Dedham, Ipswich and Colchester (*IJ*, 1 September, 20 October 1753 and 2 October 1756). References to Wood and Clerke mostly come from Bensusan-Butt 1993, 20–2, 30, 52–6.

[45] Peter Pelou, a 'Peruke-maker and Hair cutter', had taken the house adjoining Wood's new Dancing Room (*IJ*, 10 August 1754). After Wood's death the auction notice of his house in Queen Street, Ipswich, notes 'a large dancing-room' (*IJ*, 26 July 1783). Queen Street is the southern continuation of St Nicholas Street, so presumably both references refer to the same building.

[46] Notices from Mr South and Mr Alymer appear in *IJ*, 2 April 1757. The latter may be the 'M$^{r.}$ Rob$^{t.}$ Alymor' who subscribed to both Joseph Gibbs's *Eight Solos* of about 1746 and the *Six Quartettoes* of 1777.

[47] *The Norwich Mercury*, 16 April 1757. The advertisement is dated Norwich, 24 March.

[48] SROI, IC/AA1/203/65.

[49] The name is variously spelt Clarke, Clercke and Clerke.

[50] Citations in subscription lists to music scores by Michael Festing in 1730 and 1731 are pre-

Cocksedge of Thetford before joining the 7th Marines, where he rose to the rank of Captain. His company was disbanded in 1748 and he next appears thirteen years later as a lieutenant and adjutant in the Eastern Battalion of the Suffolk Militia, positions he appears to have retained until his death.[51] He died on 2 February 1772 when it was remarked that he was 'justly esteemed for his good sense and humanity'.[52]

The sketches from the letter to Mr Hatley provide rare evidence in his drawings for the *joie de vivre* which has so often been noted in Gainsborough's letters. The *Musical Society at Ipswich* may well be another example and, in this light, it is worth recalling that Gainsborough had a taste for amusing drawings and prints as he owned a pair of watercolours by the Suffolk-born amateur caricaturist Henry William Bunbury,[53] and a number of other satirical prints. Amazingly, Gainsborough's copies of some of these can be identified as they share the same provenance as the artist's much-altered studio cabinet which is now preserved in Gainsborough's House. Presumably they were tucked inside one of the drawers in the piece of furniture.

At his death Gainsborough left the porter at the Royal Academy, Charles Cranmer, his studio cabinet. Mr Cranmer's son, the artist Charles Cranmer, bequeathed it to his pupil, John Whitehead Walton, and it was sold at auction after his death.[54] A number of prints were also given by Walton to a Mrs Cleland of Stormont in Northern Ireland in 1882; and she mounted them, with others, in a large scrapbook.[55] Some time in the first half of the twentieth century they were

sumably those of his father who probably also subscribed to a volume of poems by Mary Masters in 1733 (Robinson and Wallis 1975, ref. 730FES, 731FES, 733MAS). The young Clerke may be identified as the subscriber to the anonymous anthology of poems published in Norwich in 1736 (Robinson and Wallis 1975, ref. 736 – P) and the legal text *Ordo Judiciorum* by Thomas Oughton published in 1738 where he is described as 'LLB, proctor' (Robinson and Wallis 1975, ref. 738OUG). Thereafter, between 1739 and 1745, Clerke subscribes to musical scores by Festing, Charles Avison and Henry Holcombe and he is also mentioned as subscribing in 1744 to Zachary Grey's *Hudibras in Three Parts* and Musgrave Heighington's *Six Select Odes of Anacreon* (Robinson and Wallis 1975, ref. 739FES, 740AVI, 744AVI, 744GRE, 744HEI, 745HOL).

51 *Army Lists (List of the Officers of the Several Regiments and Corps of Militia)*, 1761, 24.

52 Death notice in *IJ*, 8 February 1772. Afterwards Clerke's son, also Abraham, appears to have taken over his father's duties. His name continues in the Army Lists as adjutant of the East Suffolk Militia until his death on 2 October 1780 (*GM* l, 1780, 495).

53 The original watercolours are untraced but their ownership is recorded in the inscription on the stipple and line engravings published on 7 April 1788 as *The Storm* and *The Repose* by John Jones and J. Pettit and John Jones and T. Trotter respectively (Gainsborough's House, 1994.164 and 165). For Bunbury see *Henry William Bunbury 1750–1811*, exhibition catalogue, Gainsborough's House, Sudbury 1983.

54 His posthumous sale, Sotheby's 24 March 1897, lot 57 bt Glen. It then passed to William Hollins of Pleasley Vale at Mansfield who gave it to his brother-in-law, J. Blake Wirgman. He bequeathed it to his niece Lena Thevenard who sold it to the Victoria and Albert Museum in 1935. Ownership was transferred to Gainsborough's House Society in 1967 (1967.001). The desk is illustrated in J.N. Leonard, *The World of Gainsborough 1727–1788*, London 1969, 40.

55 The album bears the following inscription, 'These "Etchings" – Skits on the works of Wm Hogarth – formed part of a collection made by Thos Gainsborough R.A. and were left, by him,

Plate 5. An Antique Basso-Rilievo found in Pompeia, Benedetto Pastorini after Nathaniel Dance. 1778. Etching and aquatint, plate size 13.8 by 33.1 cm. *Gainsborough's House, Sudbury.*

purchased by a Mr Kirk of Shirley in Birmingham, whose daughter-in-law, Mrs Barbara Kirk, sold the album at Phillips Knowle in 1993.[56]

The prints in the album which may have belonged to Gainsborough include copies after old masters: Bartolozzi after Guercino *The Holy Family with an Angel* published in 1764,[57] Stephano Colbenschlag's print of Annibale Carracci's *Pieta* in the Capitoline in Naples,[58] two etchings by John Smith copied in 1770 from landscape etchings by Rembrandt,[59] and William Ryland's print of 1763 after Camillo Procaccini's drawing of the *Triumph of David*.[60] More interesting for the discussion in this paper is a small group of satirical prints. The album also includes a print by the amateur, Sampson Stawell, who was a pupil of John 'Baptiste' Malchair in Oxford.[61] The small print (the plate size measures only 10 by 17.6 cm), which

to his pupil, Charles Cranmer – With kindest regards from John W. Walton to Mrs. Cleland (of Stormont) 1882.'

56 24 November 1993, lot 274 bt David Temperley for Gainsborough's House Society (1993.100).

57 A. de Vesmi and A. Calabi, *Francesco Bartolozzi*, Milan 1928, 533, no. 2122. The print copies the drawing from the collection of Consul Smith in the Royal Collection which is now attributed to the School of Guercino (D. Mahon and N. Turner, *The Drawings of Guercino in the Collection of H. M. The Queen at Windsor Castle*, Cambridge 1989, 148, no. 451, pl. 340). It bears some similarity with the composition of Gainsborough's portrait of Lord Essex and John Clutterbuck of 1784–85 in the J. Paul Getty Museum, Malibu (B.B. Fredericksen, *Catalogue of the Paintings in the J. Paul Getty Museum*, Malibu 1972, no. 141).

58 D. Posner, *Annibale Carracci*, London 1971, 52, no. 119.

59 *Landscape with Trees, Farm Buildings and a Tower* (B 223) and *Landscape with Cottage and Large Tree* (B 225). The former is included in C. White, D. Alexander and E. D'Oench, *Rembrandt in Eighteenth-Century England*, Yale Center for British Art, New Haven, 1983, no. 150.

60 The drawing is in the British Museum (1853–10–8–4). See N.W. Neilson, *Camillo Procaccini: Paintings and Drawings*, New York and London 1979, 138–9, pl. 56. The print was included in C. Rogers, *A Collection of Prints in Imitations of Drawings . . .*, 2 vols, London 1778, i, 22.

61 Little is known of the artist. David Alexander has kindly brought to my attention the album of

shows a blind harpist in the centre randomly surrounded by five heads in profile, is signed twice, 'SS' in reverse on the upper left and 'SS ft.' bottom centre. On the back is a contemporary inscription in ink: 'Carit | Caricatures taken at the Music Room in Oxford, | A. D. 1763. by S. Stawel Esqr. – AB. of Ch: Ch: | NB. This was his first Attempt in Etching.' Stawell was born in about 1741, the son of Jonas Stawell of Kilbrittain, County Cork. He was admitted to Christ Church, Oxford, on 19 November and matriculated as a gentleman commoner three weeks later on 10 December 1760. He was tutored by one of the canons, Edward Smallwell, and he remained there until 1773. Two years later his younger brother, William, followed him to Oxford and Smallwell's tutelage.[62] Thereafter little is known of his artistic activity, and indeed it is hard to explain why Gainsborough bothered with one of his prints. Three other prints by Nathaniel Dance included in the album are more revealing.[63]

All three were published on 16 December 1778 and each was engraved by Benedetto Pastorini (active 1762–1806). Pastorini, who may have originated from Naples, was brought to London as a draughtsman and engraver by one of the Adam brothers for whom he had worked during the 1760s and 1770s. In the late 1770s he transferred his loyalty to Dance, whom he may have met in Rome during the latter's extended stay in the city between 1754 and 1765. In about 1783 Pastorini, whose professional reputation appears to have been considerable, worked as an assistant to Francesco Bartolozzi, and in 1803 he became a Governor of the Society of Engravers.[64] Each of the Pastorini prints is etched with aquatint added to provide modelling and, as Antony Griffiths has noted, they are amongst the earliest prints to use this medium in Britain.[65] The pair of prints represents contemporary figures shown as 'An Antique Basso-Rilievo found in Hadrians Villa' and 'An Antique Basso-Rilievo found in Pompeia'.[66] The latter (Plate 5), which records (according to the inscription) 'a Member of the BEEF EATERS COMPANY . . . making proposals of Marriage to an ATHENIAN VIRGIN' with the portly 'MASTER & WARDENS of that Company' attending, is taken from a drawing now at Stanford

amateur prints produced at Christ Church which includes examples of his work now in the Lewis Walpole Library at Farmington, Connecticut. See also Colin Harrison, *John Malchair of Oxford: Artist and Musician*, exhibition catalogue, Ashmolean Museum, Oxford 1998.

62 I am grateful to Judith Curthoys, Archivist, and Lucy Whitaker, formerly Assistant Curator, of Christ Church for this information.

63 A fourth print entitled *War*, published on 9 March 1783 (*BM Satires*, no. 6187), is described as being by James Gillray after Nathaniel Dance, but this ascription is unconvincing. I am grateful to Andrew Edmunds for helping me determine the status of several of the prints in the album.

64 I am grateful to David Alexander for providing biographical information about Pastorini.

65 A. Griffiths, 'Notes on Early Aquatint in England and France', *Print Quarterly* iv, 1987, 255–70 at p. 268, fig. 187 (hereafter Griffiths 1987).

66 Both prints are illustrated by M. Rosenthal, *The Art of Thomas Gainsborough*, New Haven and London 1999, 63, pl. 68 (hereafter Rosenthal 1999). A mock bass relief *al antica* is adopted again in the *White Sheet Frieze* of 1782 (London, Tate Gallery, see D. Goodreau, *Nathaniel Dance 1735–1811*, exhibition catalogue, Iveagh Bequest, Kenwood 1977, no. 46 repr.).

University Museum of Art.[67] Such jibes at pomposity and the uncritical devotion of his contemporaries to antiquity must have made the print especially attractive to Gainsborough. The third print, although political, has the same gentle wit and shows a pair of politicians beneath a map of New England dozing over the tedious reports published in the *London Gazette* as they await others which may prove to be more interesting in 'the Extraordinary Gazette'.[68]

Nathaniel Dance, like Gainsborough, quarrelled with the Royal Academy and refused to submit to the exhibition in 1773. Dance inherited a fortune three years later which encouraged him to reconsider his ambitions regarding the Academy. A neutral position made him an obvious mediator between the disillusioned Gainsborough and the institution. In the spring of 1777 Dance successfully persuaded Gainsborough to exhibit at the Academy's exhibitions again.[69] Freed from any need to earn a living, Dance was able to adopt the role of a dilettante, veering away from his interest in making oil paintings of classical subjects and moving towards drawing satirical sketches. The three prints under discussion were Dance's first efforts to bring this new style to a wider public. Of greater significance, for the purposes of this article, they form an enlightening parallel with Gainsborough's renewed interest in print making in the late 1770s.

Gainsborough regarded print making as a vehicle to indulge his fascination for new techniques and, during the late 1770s, he experimented with both soft-ground etching and aquatint. Experimenters with aquatint were not disposed to reveal the secret of the process, though it is interesting that the Reverend William Gilpin learnt the technique through the American amateur landscape painter, John Taylor. Taylor had been resident in Bath since 1762 and must have been known to Gainsborough, though, as yet, no prints by Taylor in aquatint or any other process have been identified.[70] Once examples of the medium had been shown at the Society of Artists exhibition in 1774 by Francis Xavier Vispré, and in the exhibition the following spring by Francis Jukes, Gainsborough's appetite was whetted for an understanding of the technique.[71] The process does not seem to have been as secret as the famous letter from the Honourable Charles Greville to Paul Sandby suggests but, it is at least a

67 L. Eitner, B.G. Fryberger, C.M. Osborne, *Stanford University Museum of Art: The Drawing Collection*, Seattle and London 1993, 325, no. 172.

68 The album also contains four prints published on 1 July 1783 of Irish topographical scenes after Francis Wheatley. Two of them are published by M. Webster, *Francis Wheatley*, New Haven and London 1970, E12, E13. Given the Irish provenance of the album, these prints were probably added to the group in the nineteenth century. A number of the early etchings by Sandby which satirise Hogarth's *Analysis of Beauty* reprinted on wove paper by Palser in the 1820s are also included and explain the inscription on the album (see note 55 above).

69 W.T. Whitley, *Gainsborough*, London 1915, 142.

70 In two letters dated 3 and 19 February 1781 Horace Walpole writes to Revd William Mason: 'Mr Gilpin tells me . . . that he would try aquatinta if he could learn the secret; I shall consult Sandby – nay, I believe it is no longer a secret' and 'Lord Harcourt has got me from Taylor at Bath the method of aquatinta, which I have sent to Mr Stonhewer this morning to transmit to him' (W.S. Lewis, ed., *Horace Walpole's Correspondence*, New Haven and London, 42 vols, 1937–80, xxix, 101, 112).

71 Griffiths 1987, 265–6.

Plate 6. Head of a Man, by Benjamin Green after Thomas Worlidge. 1775. Soft-ground etching, image size 18.3 by 14 cm. *British Museum, London.*

possibility that Gainsborough learnt it from the modest aquatints by Pastorini which he owned.[72] Another possibility is that he knew the rare caricature prints which were published by Philip de Loutherbourg as early as 1776, shortly before he sat to Gainsborough for the portrait that was shown at the Royal Academy in 1778.[73] On balance it seems unlikely that Paul Sandby, who had been using aquatint and exploiting its commercial potential for some time, would reveal the process to as talented an artist as Gainsborough. Though there may have been some contact, as

[72] Hayes assumed that Gainsborough learnt aquatint and soft-ground etching from Paul Sandby, whose earliest work in the medium was published in 1775 (J. Hayes, *Gainsborough as Printmaker*, London 1971, 11–15; hereafter Hayes 1971). Gainsborough recommends Sandby's talents as a topographer to Lord Hardwick in about 1764 (Hayes 2001, 30–1, no. 15); however, no other contact between the two artists is known and, consequently, Griffiths 1987, 264 is less inclined to make this connection.

[73] Griffiths 1987, 266–7. For the portrait see Waterhouse 1958, no. 456.

Plate 7. Milkmaid and Cows by a Cottage, by Thomas Gainsborough. *c.*1778. Soft-ground etching with aquatint, 20.5 x 27.5 cm. *Promised Gift of Dorothy Braude Edinburg to the Harry B. and Bessie K. Braude Memorial Collection in The Art Institute of Chicago.*

has been pointed out, Sandby's singular contribution to printmaking is the sugar-lift process, and this technical refinement only appears in the prints Gainsborough made in the mid 1780s, right at the end of his career.[74]

Unfortunately, the Sudbury album does not contain any examples of soft-ground etching. It is, however, worth speculating that Gainsborough would have known three prints by Benjamin Green (1739–98) made after drawings by Thomas Worlidge which, according to the inscription, belonged to Panton Betew (1722–99), the dealer who is known to have handled several of Gainsborough's early landscape paintings. Each print is dated 1775 (Plate 6).[75] When Gainsborough was still

74 Hayes 1971, no. 14.

75 I am grateful to Susan Sloman for bringing these prints to my attention and to David Tyler for sharing his work on Betew with me. The basic inscription, with slight variations, on each of the three prints is: 'TW | Thos Worledge | Benjn Green sculp | X^{ts} Hosp^{l} 1775 | The Original Drawing in the Collection of Mr. P. Betew | Printed for S. Hooper Ludgate Hill'. Two of them are in Peterborough Museum and Art Gallery (C. Dack, *Sketch of the Life of Thomas Worlidge, Etcher and Painter, with a Catalogue of his Works*, Peterborough 1907, 29), one of which is also in the British Museum (1925–6–27–4; Plate 6). The British Museum has another example (1925–6–27–3). The 'Six spirited heads in pencil' by Worlidge, which appeared amongst the

Plate 8. Peasant reading a tombstone, by Thomas Gainsborough, 1780. Soft-ground etching with aquatint, 29.6 x 39.3 cm. *Gainsborough's House, Sudbury.*

in Bath in the 1760s, Worlidge sold his large stock of prints through Mrs Wicksteed's toyshop in Orange Grove, an activity which was no doubt continued by his widow, Elizabeth (*née* Wicksteed), after his death in 1766, and Gainsborough may well have stayed in touch with her.[76] It is not known how Green learnt the process but, having seen examples of the technique, an etcher with an inquiring mind would not have required formal teaching to understand the nuances of using soft-ground etching. Green may have examined prints using the technique imported

items sold by Andrew Johnson from Betew's collection at Johnson's house in Hackney through Christie's on 5/6 December 1821 as lot 10, may have included the drawings from which these prints were taken. For Benjamin Green see J. Ball, *Catalogue of the 1951 Festival Exhibition of Pictures by the 18th-Century Halesowen Artists, James, Amos and Benjamin Green*, 41–6. Green contributed prints to Philip Morant's *History and Antiquities of the County of Essex*, London 1768, which, given Gainsborough's family connection with the area, may have been known to him. The British Museum has soft-ground etchings by Green of Arundel Church dated 1771 (1878–5–11–1233) and a pair of Battersea and Little Chelsea dated 1774 (1919–10–14–25 and 26). I am grateful to David Alexander for sharing his notes about the artist with me.

76 For Wicksteed's shop and Worlidge's sales see H. Belsey, 'Two Works by Gainsborough', *National Art Collections Fund Review*, 1992, 10, and S.L. Sloman, 'Artists' Picture Rooms in Eighteenth-Century Bath', *Bath History* vi, 1996, 134.

from Italy;[77] and, in turn, Gainsborough may have seen Green's work and experimented and refined the technique by himself.[78]

Gainsborough's urge to make prints seems to have lain dormant during his busy years in Bath.[79] Access to printing equipment must have been easier in London, and his experiments with the new techniques took place after his move there in 1774. Recently a print has come to light known through a single copy, which uses both aquatint and soft-ground etching. The image lacks the usual clarity we expect to see in Gainsborough's work and it suffers from being overworked. Its rarity confirms that the sheet must have been a proof and, by the quality, one must assume that it was amongst Gainsborough's first experiments using these new techniques (Plate 7).[80] Able to harness the media and, driven by a desire to popularise his work as a landscape painter, he produced three large prints in soft-ground etching over aquatint (Plate 8).[81] Each bears the inscription 'Publish'd as the act directs, Feby 1st 1780', but for some unknown reason Gainsborough's plans were aborted and all three plates remained unpublished.[82] Nevertheless, the Sudbury Album provides an insight into Gainsborough's exposure to the technical developments of printmaking, though it hardly explains his extraordinarily articulate use of the media.

Gainsborough's letters, tantalisingly few in number, have naturally been used as a key to his lively mind and subtle wit. The best portraits too show an empathetic humour between artist and sitter. These aspects of his complex character are rounded and amplified by the fragmentary letter to Hatley and the butt-end of a collection of prints once owned by the artist. The print collection also gives the modern print historian a further insight into Gainsborough's private interest in printmaking.

77 Some of Thomas Patch's work in soft-ground included in the group of *Twenty-Eight Caricatures* was produced as early as 1765, though the volume was only published in 1770 (F.J.B. Watson, 'The Life of Thomas Patch (1725–1782)', *Walpole Society* xxviii, 1939–40, 45, no. 58). It is known that copies were sent by Sir Horace Mann to Horace Walpole in August/September 1772 (PRO, Foreign Office papers 105/296, fos 38, 42). Few of them have been reproduced, but for a representative example see B. Ford, 'Sir Watkin Williams-Wynn: A Welsh Maecenas', *Apollo* xcix, June 1974, 435, pl. 1.

78 This suggestion was endorsed in a conversation with a practising printmaker, Caroline Wendling.

79 Hayes suggests that the experimental print of three cows which uses sugar-lift aquatint (Hayes 1971, no. 3) was produced in Bath. As this print uses, with little confidence, such a sophisticated technique, it is possible that it post-dates the three large prints of 1780, and was produced as a trial for the assured prints *Wooded Landscape with Riders* and *Wooded Landscape with Three Cattle in a Pool* (Hayes 1971, nos 14 and 15).

80 The print appeared in Christie's sale on 18 April 1995 and may have been seen by Fulcher (1856 ii, 28 note; see Hayes 1971, no. 22). The print copies a chalk drawing from the late 1770s which appeared in the same rooms on 14 June 1983, lot 44 bt Andrew Wyld (J. Hayes, 'Gainsborough Drawings: A Supplement to the Catalogue', *Master Drawings* xxi, 1983, 367–91 at 385, no. 935).

81 This print is fully published by H. Belsey, 'Two Prints by Gainsborough', *Gainsborough's House Society Annual Report 1989/90*, 42–4. For an explanation of the role of these prints in Gainsborough's career see Rosenthal 1999, 258–63.

82 Hayes 1971, 16–18, nos 9–11. Further impressions are recorded in H. Belsey, *Gainsborough the Printmaker*, exhibition catalogue, Peter Pears Gallery, Aldeburgh 1988, nos 17, 18 and 22.

Ipswich Museum Moralities in the 1840s and 1850s

Steven J. Plunkett

They favour learning whose actions are worthy of a learned pen.

George Herbert, coll.: Jacula Prudentum

IT IS A FACT often repeated, but one seldom fully appreciated, that the Museum established in Ipswich in 1846, and opened in December 1847, received the patronage and practical support of many of the most distinguished scientists of Great Britain.[1] The sixty lithographic Museum Portraits by Thomas Maguire, depicting many (but not all) of the Honorary Members and Vice-Presidents, were produced at the personal expense of George Ransome, FLS (l),[2] but are today known more as portrayals of eminent individuals than for the enlightened motives which surrounded their creation. Ransome, a townsman, was in many ways the prime mover in the Museum's formation. Excitement and acclaim surrounded the four Anniversary Meetings and the many public lectures, which reached their high point in the visit of the British Association for the Advancement of Science to Ipswich in 1851. They were also owing to the energetic involvement of Professor J.S. Henslow (1796–1861) (l) (Plate 1), who assisted and advised from the beginning, delivered the Museum's inaugural lecture, and in 1850 became its President.[3] Although these

Acknowledgements. I wish to thank Dr Adrian Desmond and Dr John Blatchly for having read and commented helpfully on earlier drafts of this paper, Paul Fincham for access to notes, and Robert Markham for various references. The conclusions and errors are my own. Much of the archival research was undertaken while the author was employed at Ipswich Museum, and has since been assisted by Lisa Harris, Martin Sanford and David L. Jones. I am grateful to Sally Dummer of Ipswich Borough Council Museums and Galleries for permission to use images in their possession.

1 Essays on the early history of the Ipswich Museum (hereafter: IM) are contained in J.E. Taylor, *A Guide to the Ipswich Museum*, Ipswich 1871; P. Fincham, 'The Old Ipswich Museum – An Essay in Early Victorian Culture', *East Anglian Magazine*, Apr. 1960; R.A.D. Markham, *A Rhino in High Street*, Ipswich 1990 (hereafter: *Markham*). A detailed study of the pre-1861 collections, sources and donors is much needed. Many details are listed in monthly press notices of the time. Inventories of displayed specimens (case by case) and of books, as handed over in 1853, exist (IM Archives) but remain unpublished.

2 T.H. Maguire, *Portraits of the Hon. Members of the Ipswich Museum*, Ipswich 1847–52. In this article (l) denotes a lithographed Hon. Member of the Museum, and (u) an unlithographed one. By no means all are mentioned.

3 Standard lives of Henslow are L. Jenyns, *Memoir of the Revd John Stevens Henslow, M.A., F.L.S., F.G.S., F.C.P.S.*, London 1862, and J. Russell-Gebbett, *Henslow of Hitcham: Botanist, Educa-*

national expectations and celebrity performances were attenuated by the financial collapse of the Museum in January 1853 and its adoption soon afterwards by the Town of Ipswich (sanctioned by public referendum) under the provisions of the 'Beetle Act',[4] Henslow remained closely involved in a curatorial way until his death, and maintained his original educational objective, which was nothing less than the moral, intellectual and spiritual empowerment of ordinary people.

There could hardly have been a more portentous hour in the history of the modern understanding of our natural environment, and our place in it, nor more suggestive auspices than those represented by Henslow in his relation to the wider scientific establishment, than the two decades which directly preceded the publication of Darwin's theory of Natural Selection in 1859,[5] and the social, theological and scientific ramifications of that synthesis of theories, which still continues to be explored.[6] In an age of revolutions, the decades either side of 1800, the unlocking of geological time had been advanced by the descriptions of stratigraphy (based on fossil fauna) given by William Smith (1769–1839) the canal engineer, the theory of the continually self-renewing nature of the earth's surface configuration by James Hutton (1726–1797), and the correlation of taxonomic evidences of extant and prehistoric animals by the brilliant comparative anatomist, Baron Cuvier (1769–1832). Although not an evolutionist, Cuvier recognised that the anatomies of extinct life forms were to be interpreted as relating to those of living ones, and that there were multiple ramifying developments from past forms, not all assembled on the same ladder of development. As expedition and exploration increasingly left little room on the planet for the presumed survival in remote places of living descendants of the fossil monsters, the fact of mass extinctions came to be accepted, and was reconciled with Christian theology (in one school of thought) by the theory of Catastrophism: ours was the last in a long series of finite creations which had ended in deluge or cataclysm. Against this view, the Uniformitarian theories (leading from Hutton) proposed a single continuous development of life on the planet over immense periods, and according to some this involved the transmutation of species. Others reconciled this with a concept of progressive evolution with man as the highest type. In these concepts Charles Darwin (l) was most influenced by the theories of his grandfather Erasmus Darwin, by those of Jean-Baptiste Lamarck (1744–1829) – to which he was introduced by his Edinburgh professor, Robert Grant (l), at the age of 16 – and by the great uniformitarian geologist, Sir Charles Lyell (l), whose *Principles of Geology*[7] Darwin first read aboard the *Beagle*.

tionalist and Clergyman, Lavenham 1977. See also N. Barlow, ed., *Darwin and Henslow: The Growth of an Idea, Letters 1831–1860*, London 1967 (hereafter: *Darwin and Henslow*); G. Henslow, 'Reminiscences of a Scientific Suffolk Clergyman', 8 parts, *Eastern Counties Magazine* i and ii, 1900–1902 (hereafter: *Reminiscences*); S.M. Walters and E.A. Stow, *Darwin's Mentor*, Cambridge 2001.

4 *Markham*, 13–14.

5 C. Darwin, *On the Origin of Species by Means of Natural Selection*, London 1859.

6 A useful modern synoptic study is P. Bowler, *Evolution: The History of an Idea*, London 1984.

7 C. Lyell, *Principles of Geology*, 3 vols, London 1830–33.

The years surrounding the foundation of the Ipswich Museum were also an age of revolutions: in the British Isles, the potato famine and the Chartist movement, and the shadow of European revolutions of 1848, were counterposed by expressions of Empire such as Selwyn's mission to New Zealand, the Great Exhibition, the Crimean and Indian Wars. Against urban expansion, industrial change, railway communications and educational Institutes for working men, academic deliberations upon questions of extinct creatures and geological succession might seem a quaint superfluity. In December 1848, at the Museum members' meeting, Edwin Sidney (l) (Plate 5) remarked that 'they were assembled there, in the midst of all the changes and convulsions of nations, in peace and security, to carry on all their projects for the amelioration of the human race. (Applause.)'[8] The moral, scientific and political questions were deeply interwoven. Like Smith's canals, the building of the Ipswich railway revealed to townspeople the remarkable fact that Stoke Hill, far from being the dull heap of earth they had always assumed it was, contained very large numbers of elephants's teeth of great antiquity. In the same decade, Henslow had recognised the agricultural value of phosphatic fossils in the basement layers of the Suffolk Crags,[9] so laying the basis of one of the largest and most beneficial industries working through Ipswich docks during the later nineteenth century, and simultaneously improving both the crop-yield of Suffolk farmland, and the cabinets of collectors of the mollusca of the lower Pleistocene.

Some Contributory Energies

The Suffolk Crag, a formation unique to the south-eastern coastal area of Suffolk, aroused the greatest interest because, in the changing horizons of its fossil mollusca and mammalia, it shows increasing proportions of living as opposed to extinct species, and also contains species now living only in other areas of the world, from the warm but cooling seas which overlay this part of the land in the two million years or so which preceded the great Ice Age;[10] it therefore forms a bridge between living natural systems and extinct ones, a point of exceptional interest to the scientific preoccupations of the early nineteenth century.[11] Edward Charlesworth (u), of Burstall Hall near Ipswich, first described the subdivision between the Coralline and Red Crags in 1835,[12] and before 1844 curated the Ipswich Literary Institute's Museum,

8 *Suffolk Chronicle* (hereafter: *SC*), 16 Dec 1848.

9 *Reminiscences*, i, 22–30.

10 The glacial theory was being developed by Louis Agassiz during the 1840s, and cleared the way for the abandonment of both progressionism and its antithetic stance, Lyell's uniformitarian non-progressionism.

11 Study of the Crags ('with the help of museums and collections') led even the geologist Hugh Miller, formerly a six-day creationist, to change his opinions; cf. H. Miller, *The Testimony of the Rocks*, Edinburgh 1857, ix–xii.

12 E. Charlesworth, 'Observations on the Crag-Formation and its Organic Remains: with a View to Establish a Division of the Tertiary Strata Overlying the London Clay in Suffolk', *Philosophical Magazine* Ser. 3, vii, Aug. 1835, 81–94; E. Charlesworth, 'On the Crag of Suffolk, and

after which he moved to the York Museum.[13] Researches into the Crag mollusca were continued authoritatively by Searles Valentine Wood (u), father and son, of Melton and Hasketon near Woodbridge, their monographs appearing as the very first volumes of the Palaeontographical Society publications in 1848.[14] Their involvement with the Museum was only slight because geological debates were at that time more focused at Norwich. As with Dr Edwin Lankester (l)[15] (also of Melton), pupil of Lindley's and Grant's, the Museum sought both to honour, and to be honoured by, the affiliation of eminent scientists with local connections; and so they got Professors Lindley (l) and Grant as well. Many Honorary Members, like Audubon (u), probably never saw the Museum. Others, like Sir R.H. Schomberg (u)[16] the America explorer-surveyor, did not attend but gave valuable specimens to the collections.

The first Curator, 1847–50, Dr William Barnard Clarke (1807–1894), prepared most of the original exhibits before the opening, and obtained several large dead creatures from Wombwell's travelling menagerie. Clarke was not merely a suitable local man, but a gifted if eccentric polymath.[17] His father was a Senior Portman of Ipswich, and Bailiff in 1820, and a cup-bearer to George III; his mother was 'Pretty Miss Conder', daughter of Thomas Conder the leather-cutter, of the same family of which James was the author of a celebrated study of Trade Tokens.[18] William jun. obtained an MD at Edinburgh, but turned to architecture, restoring the Eleanor Cross at Waltham (Herts), and became President of the Architects' Institute in London. During the 1830s he made an illustrated study in MS of the fossil mollusca of the Crag.[19] He had assisted in the arrangement of the Ipswich Mechanics' Institute[20] Museum in 1836, and corresponded with an Italian conference on Etruscan antiquities during the 1840s.[21] In 1849 he conducted dredging expeditions for

on the Fallacies Connected with the Method Now Usually Employed for Ascertaining the Relative Age of Tertiary Deposits', *ibid.* Ser. 3, viii, pp. 529ff. I am grateful to Robert Markham for these sources.

13 Charlesworth had two literary sisters, and was brother-in-law to Edward Byles Cowell, Cambridge Sanscrit Professor, who with Elizabeth Charlesworth gave Fitzgerald the inspiration for his *Rubáiyát.*

14 S.V. Wood, *A Monograph of the Crag Mollusca, I: Univalves,* Paleontographical Society 1848.

15 Lankester's life and work is admirably told by M.P. English, *Victorian Values: The Life and Times of Dr Edwin Lankester M.D., F.R.S.,* Bristol 1990 (hereafter: English). He was lithographed twice.

16 Audubon's, Schomberg's and Charlesworth's Honorary Memberships were among those announced in *IJ* (hereafter: *IJ*), 20 May 1848.

17 Clive Cheeseman (British Museum) has kindly shared his findings on Dr Clarke.

18 Rambler (ps. H.R. Lingwood), 'William Barnard Clarke', *East Anglian Daily Times,* 13 Jan. 1934.

19 IM Archives. He is not to be confused with Revd Dr William Branwhite Clarke of East Bergholt, Tom Churchyard's school-fellow, who also studied the Crags, for whom see E. Grainger, *The Remarkable Reverend Clarke: The Life and Times of the Father of Australian Geology,* Oxford 1982.

20 See E.H. Hanson, *An Historical Essay of the Ipswich Institute 1925–1987, with a reprint of 'The Ipswich Institute 1824–1924' by Herbert Walker,* Ipswich 1989.

21 He addressed the Ipswich Philosophical Society on the subject of 'Sponge and Flint' in

the new Museum on the Orwell; aboard, he met an old sailor called Nunn, who had spent years with the whale and seal fisheries on the Isle of Desolation – Kerguelen Land – in far southern latitudes. Clarke took down his story and published it as a book in 1850, supported by subscription of many people connected with the Museum.[22] In 1865, he appears in Freiburg as a translator of Goethe's *Faust*.[23] His brother Dr Edward Clarke (who emigrated to Australia), another medical practitioner, had some skills as an illustrator, and his sister married Dr Henry Pilkington Drummond, who was active in the work of the Mechanics' Institute.

Charlesworth, Clarke and others associated with the Museum belonged to a select circle of intellectual men who formed themselves in 1842 into the Ipswich Philosophical Society. One member was required to deliver a serious scientific paper at each of its meetings, which was then discussed, and written by the speaker in full, with diagrams, in the minute-books, as if for publication.[24] No doubt members of such a Society also felt social and political benefits. Mainly Dissenters and Liberals,[25] they included representatives of the Alexander and Ransome families, interested in improving the social, as well as spiritual, welfare of the working population, several being large employers. Among them, W.S. Fitch,[26] W.H. Alexander, George Ransome, Garrett Garrett,[27] William Dillwyn Sims,[28] and Dr W.H.B. Webster (as well as Clarke) all became active officers of the 1847 Museum, and others of their group assisted Museum work in various ways.[29] Others, including Richard Dykes Alexander, aldermen or mayors, were involved in the committee management of the Museum for the town after 1853. The libraries were housed together, and the Philosophical Society fell dormant in 1855. Thus the social, political and intellectual aspirations of a particular class came to be absorbed, and were corporately and publicly disseminated through the Borough. Theirs, however, were not the only values so to be assimilated within the new institution.

In Cambridge, as Professor of Botany, Henslow had admitted Darwin (already a

October 1848. See also W.B. Clarke, 'On the Vital Principle in Animals and Vegetables', M.D. Diss, Univ. Edinburgh 1834; W.B. Clarke, *The Guide to Hayling*, n.p. 1836; W.B. Clarke, 'Sketch of the Flora of the Neighbourhood of Ipswich', *Magazine of Natural History*, 1840.

22 W.B. Clarke, *Narrative of the Wreck of the 'Favorite' on the Island of Desolation*, London 1850. Cf. *Darwin and Henslow*, 172, Letter 78, 17 Nov. 1854.

23 W.B. Clarke, *A Translation of Goethe's Faust*, Freiburg 1865.

24 Ipswich Philosophical Society, Minutes.

25 The relations between the Dissenting supporters of provincial Institutes and the Oxbridge and London scientists are excellently considered by I. Inkster and J. Morrell, *Metropolis and Province*, London 1983.

26 A.H. Denney, 'William Stevenson Fitch, 1792–1859', *PSIA* xxviii.2, 1959, 109–35; J.I. Freeman, *William Stevenson Fitch: Antiquary & Thief*, London 1997.

27 Garrett Garrett (1808–1890), naturalist, nephew of Richard Garrett (1755–1839) who started the Leiston works in 1778. He worked for years with Henslow and afterwards with Taylor, especially on the entomological collections of the Museum (IM Minutes and Archives).

28 The character of Sims, a Chartist Quaker involved with Ransome's foundry, is given elegantly by R. Gowing, *Public Men of Ipswich and East Suffolk*, Ipswich and London 1875.

29 IM Minutes, I (1846–53).

trained naturalist under Grant's teaching) to his immediate circle.[30] Both Henslow and his brother-in-law, the Bath geologist Leonard Jenyns, contemplated going aboard the *Beagle* as naturalist in the voyage of 1831–36,[31] but for various reasons made way for Darwin, thereby providing experiences which led to the synthesis of his great work. Naval surveys and explorations loom significantly behind early Museum developments at Ipswich. The little-documented collections of the Literary Institute, afterwards absorbed into the New Museum, included South Seas material which came to them from Admiral Benjamin William Page of Ipswich (d.1845), a very widely travelled naval officer.[32] Dr Edward Stanley (l), bishop of Norwich, Museum Patron 1847–9, combined in one person a senior figure of the Royal and Linnean Societies and of the Archaeological Institute, and nautical connections; these were expressed in his gift of a stuffed frigate bird.[33] His son Captain Owen Stanley (a celebrated Arctic and Indo-China surveyor) on his last survey, to the Torres Strait, took the young Thomas Huxley as junior surgeon aboard the *Rattlesnake*,[34] who returned just in time to make his first appearance before the British Association at Ipswich in 1851. Ray Lankester[35] often recalled that Huxley had carried him, aged four, across the beach at Felixstowe on that occasion.[36] The younger Hooker (l), grandson of Dawson Turner, and son of Kew Gardens Director (and Ipswich Museum Vice-President) Sir William J. Hooker (l) (of Halesworth), had botanised in the Antarctic aboard the *Erebus* in a voyage which ended in 1843,[37] and around 1851 became Henslow's son-in-law. Edward Clodd when *he* was four had seen the *Erebus* and *Terror* anchored at Aldeburgh, as Franklin launched his doomed search for the North-West Passage in 1845.[38]

The founding President of the Museum, the Revd William Kirby, FRS, FLS (1759–1850) (l), Rector of Barham,[39] was a considerable and eminent scientist. His publications[40] include an important early work on English bees, a study of animal

30 Henslow's Botanic Gardens at Cambridge began to be planted during Ipswich Museum's first year.

31 A. Desmond and J. Moore, *Darwin*, London 1991. I am very grateful to Dr Adrian Desmond for having read and commented upon an earlier draft of this paper.

32 Page, who conducted naval convoys between Calcutta and Canton, may not have collected the specimens, but they reflect an earlier phase of maritime exploration and acquisition; he may have had contact with one Jack Hatley in Ipswich, who sailed with Cook (pers. comm. D.L. Jones, IM).

33 Cf. unsourced cutting, G. Ransome Scrapbook I (IM Archives), 19 Dec. 1847. Some early unregistered specimens were identified for the author's 1997 Exhibition *Marvels of 1847* (hereafter: *Marvels*).

34 A. Desmond, *Huxley: From Devil's Disciple to Evolution's High Priest*, Harmondsworth 1998 (hereafter: Desmond), 53–153.

35 Sir E. Ray Lankester was President of Ipswich Museum, 1901–29.

36 English, 56.

37 Desmond, 36.

38 E. Clodd, *Memories*, London 1926, 1.

39 For his life, see J. Freeman, *Life of the Revd William Kirby, M.A., F.R.S., F.L.S., etc., Rector of Barham*, London 1852.

40 W. Kirby, *Monographia Apium Angliae*, 2 vols, Ipswich 1802. W. Kirby and W. Spence, *An*

behaviour and instinct, and a four-volume *Introduction to Entomology* with William Spence (l) of London,[41] which mostly fell on Kirby owing to Spence's illness. Kirby attended the opening night, but was too frail to say more than a few words.[42] The Museum acquired a herbarium given, but not made by him, containing many specimens collected before 1800.[43] Accepting the Presidency in 1850, Henslow remarked that he, as a schoolboy, had developed his first interests in natural history through the works and personal encouragement of Kirby, and had 'looked up to him as the father of anything I knew upon the subject'. Moreover, in 1825 Kirby (aged sixty-six) had kindly written to him to say he would waive his own ambitions, when Henslow applied for the botanical chair at Cambridge.[44] The two had discussed and agreed the principles upon which the Museum should be run, so that Henslow's work may in part be seen as fulfilling Kirby's intentions. William Spence was a Museum Vice-President, as was William Yarrell (l),[45] and both attended early meetings. So too were Dr Buckland, Professors Sedgwick, Owen and Forbes, Sir Charles Lyell, George Biddell Airy, Revd Edwin Sidney (all (l)), and Professor Whewell (u), of all of whom more anon.[46] Henslow was, doubtless, the man who drew these powers together for Ipswich.

Lecturers, Donors and Patrons

Until 1851, the annual Anniversary Meetings, held in December, were the great occasions upon which many of the Honorary Members made an appearance. The first was the opening itself, in 1847, and was so taken up with speeches regarding the Museum's future that no scientific lecture was held. The course of six lectures given by George Biddell Airy (Plate 4), the Astronomer Royal, in March 1848, was the first grand offering.[47] These were immediately published as a book, which ran to

Introduction to Entomology, 4 vols, London 1815, 1817, 1826, 1826. W. Kirby, *On the History, Habits and Instincts of Animals*, Bridgewater Treatises VII, 2 vols, 2nd edn, London 1835.

41 William Spence, FRS, FLS, was a Vice-President of the Entomological Society.

42 *IJ* and *SC*, 18 Dec. 1847. See also *SC*, 22 Feb. 1865.

43 Kirby presented this to the Literary Institute Museum, and IM purchased it in 1851 (IM Minutes, I, 105–10). Another, made by Henslow with the help of Hitcham children, is also preserved, and there are several others. See F.W. Simpson, *Simpson's Flora of Suffolk*, Ipswich 1982, 45–6.

44 *IJ* and *SC*, 28 Dec. 1850.

45 Yarrell, Vice-President of the Linnean and Zoological Societies, was author of engraved studies in the Thomas Bewick style: W. Yarrell, *History of British Fishes*, London 1835–36, and W. Yarrell, *History of British Birds*, London 1839–43. Original inscribed copies are in the Museum's Library.

46 There were several other Vice-Presidents, variously (l) and (u), whose involvement with the Museum is less well understood.

47 A pair of large globes, astronomical and terrestrial, were loaned for Airy's lectures by Malby of London, and afterwards purchased through W.S. Fitch (IM Minutes I, March to April 1848). Heaven and earth were moved, cleaned and repaired for *Marvels*. An early plan for an Ipswich observatory was dropped when George Tomline offered members the use of his, at Orwell Park.

four editions within the year.[48] Museum Natural History education thus began in Ipswich with a full exposition of the accepted mechanistic cosmogony afforded by Natural Philosophy. There were four grand Anniversary Lectures, and they were given by Professors Adam Sedgwick (1848), Richard Owen (1849), Edward Forbes (1850), and Sir Charles Lyell (1851) (Plate 3). These men were scientific giants of their time. The Anniversary Meetings were held on the day after the lectures, followed by a dinner, and closed with a large soirée at the Museum at which other Honorary Members, such as John Gould (Plate 4) the ornithologist (l),[49] Lovell Reeve the conchologist and publisher (l), and James Scott Bowerbank (Plate 4), a leading palaeo-botanist and sponge expert (l), assisted with public demonstrations. Several gave Museum lectures during the year, most notably Henslow himself,[50] Revd Edwin Sidney,[51] John Brown of Stanway (u),[52] Professor David Ansted (l),[53] Dr William Carpenter (l),[54] Arthur Henfrey (u),[55] Dr Lyon Playfair (l),[56] and Professor Edwin Lankester;[57] these were supplemented with shorter lectures by Dr W.B. Clarke (Curator) and George Ransome (Secretary). These survive as substantial, sometimes verbatim, press reports, but have never otherwise been published. There are also accounts of many votes of thanks, after-dinner speeches and statements at business meetings, which, full of religious sentiment and grandiose expectations, reveal their vision of how the Museum might improve the spiritual and cultural wel-

48 G.B. Airy, *Six Lectures on Astronomy*, London and Ipswich 1848 (hereafter: Airy).

49 Gould's 5-volume *Birds of Europe* (*Marvels*), with many illustrations by Edward Lear, was purchased new by the Museum by subscription for £78 (*IJ*, 15 Apr. 1848). It was rescued at the eleventh hour from an auction actually in progress, after transfers following Local Government Review of 1974 (pers. comm. Howard Mendel). Gould was a frequent visitor and demonstrator at the early meetings, and presented substantial collections of stuffed exotic birds (*IJ*, 15 Apr. 1848).

50 The references given to press reports of lectures in this and the following footnotes are to substantive transcripts of the lectures, and represent the entire 1848–53 series apart from those referenced elsewhere in this paper. Henslow: Introductory address (*SC*, 11 Mar. 1848); on 'Botany' (*IJ*, 2 Dec. 1848); on 'Geology', two (*SC*, 17 Nov. 1849, and Nov. 1850); on 'Typical Arrangements', and on 'the Tertiary System' (*IJ*, 15 Nov. 1851).

51 Lectures: on 'the Galvanic Battery', two (*SC*, 10 Mar. 1849); on 'Chemistry of Carbon' (delivered 13 Mar. 1850); on 'Nitrogen' (*SC*, 29 Mar. 1851).

52 Lecture: on 'the Mammalian Fossils of Norfolk, Suffolk and Essex' (*IJ* and *SC*, 19 May 1849, *Ipswich Express*, 22 May 1849).

53 David Ansted, FRS, FGS, was professor of Geology, King's College, London. Lectures: on 'the Geology of Stone and Iron' (*IJ*, 2 June 1849); on 'Coal', four (*IJ* and *SC*, 19 and 26 Jan. 1850, *Ipswich Express*, 22 Jan. 1850); on 'the Inlaid and Ornamental Stonework exhibited in the Crystal Palace' (*IJ* and *SC*, 8 Nov. 1851).

54 William Carpenter, MD, FRS, FGS. Lectures: on 'the Instinct and Reasoning Powers of Animals', two (*Ipswich Express*, 22 May 1849; *SC*, 26 May 1849).

55 Henfrey had formerly been botanist to the UK Geological Survey, and was Lecturer in Botany at St George's Hospital. Lecture: on 'the Natural History of Flowerless Plants' (Nov. 1850).

56 Playfair was Chemist to the Museum of Practical Geology, Jermyn Street. Lecture: on 'the Food of Man, under Different Circumstances of Age, Condition and Employment' (*SC*, 29 Mar. 1851).

57 Edwin Lankester was at this time professor of Natural History at New College, London. Lecture: on 'the Uses of Plants to Man' (*SC* and *IJ*, 27 Sept. 1851).

fare of the working people, by freely offering a modern understanding of Natural History and Natural Philosophy in illustration of the Higher Purpose.

This is illustrated most notoriously, because unwittingly, by the comments of Dr William Buckland (Plate 4), Oxford Professor of Geology and dean of Westminster, at the Museum's opening, when he spoke to the effect that poor people in a hungry winter could now learn the folly of social unrest by studying, at a Museum, the hibernatory habits of lower animals, and tucking themselves all up in bed for a season so as to reduce outgoings on food and heating.[58] Others were more humane. Buckland was the – somewhat eccentric – veteran of famous excavations in early cave deposits, the hyaena cave at Kirkdale[59] and Kent's Cavern near Torquay. Excavations on the latter site by Father McEnery showed flint implements and bones of extinct animals sealed together in red cave earth. McEnery was open to evidence for the greater antiquity of Man, but his views remained unpublished,[60] unlike Buckland's, who explained the problem otherwise; some of McEnery's specimens were in the early Museum,[61] presented by William Long (u) of Hurts Hall (Saxmundham). The Abbeville palaeolithic discoveries[62] were not as yet widely known or recognised as such in England: William Whincopp, Woodbridge wine-merchant and antiquary, supplied flint implements from Suffolk to Dr Buckland himself during the 1840s, but never thought any were more than a few thousand years old.[63] Long was for philanthropy; at the Museum opening, he referred to the help which his family, in the person of Dudley North, had given to the poet Crabbe in his youth. The reforming, Quakerly, aspect of the Museum's political constitution was embodied in Hayden's painting of Thomas Clarkson addressing the Anti-Slavery Convention, which hung at the top of the stairs in the Museum near the entrance to the hall, borrowed for the purpose from the Anti-Slavery Society and not returned for many years, despite repeated requests.

As scientific inquiry seemed to threaten the moral foundations of philanthropy, scientists brought their highest affirmations of the natural world as the perfectly organised expression of the will of God. Sedgwick, in his 1848 lecture at Ipswich, devoted several minutes to the question, and concluded:

58 *IJ* and *SC*, 18 Dec. 1847.

59 W. Buckland, *Reliquiae Diluvianae*, London 1823. Both Buckland and Lyell had given their firm approval to Edward Charlesworth's analysis of the Crag in 1835–36.

60 Their (posthumous) publication was delayed until the French palaeolithic discoveries attracted the interest of British prehistorians. E. Vivian, ed., *Cavern Researches by the Rev. Mr McEnery*, London 1859.

61 *IJ*, 24 July 1847; *Marvels*.

62 The Abbeville discoveries of 1841–44 were described by Boucher de Perthes, *Antiquités Celtiques et Antédiluviennes*, Paris 1847, but little notice was taken of them in England until after the publication of a second volume in 1857, and the comparable work of Dr Rigollot, *Mémoire sur des instruments en silex trouvés à St Acheul près d'Amiens*, Amiens 1855. These findings were exactly contemporary with Henslow's tenure at Ipswich.

63 W. Whincopp, *Important Discoveries which have Led to the Elucidation of the Deposit of Flint Implements in France and England*, Woodbridge 1865.

> let us believe that these two kinds of truth embodied in physical history and in revealed religion, so far from being conflicting, are entirely in unison and harmony, if we investigate the one, and read the other, in a right spirit.[64]

These were no empty words. Hence Bishop Stanley's patronage was so important. After his death, Sedgwick (a close friend) wept publicly as he unveiled Stanley's portait at the Museum in December 1849:

> His utterance became half-choked, and his feelings found vent in tears honourable to the clergyman of the Church of England, as well as honourable to his heart, as a *man*. The scene altogether was exciting and solemn. It was one of those that stamps the heart with an impress which the hard-rubbing of the world can never efface. It was not before several minutes had elapsed that Professor Sedgwick was enabled to proceed, when he delivered a long speech . . .[65]

In other addresses, however, he appears as quite a humorist.

The Anniversary Lecturers (and What They Said)

Adam Sedgwick,[66] by 1848 already for some thirty years professor of Geology at Cambridge with responsibilities for the Woodwardian Museum, was closely connected with early Museum developments at Norwich. In 1856 he preempted the Suffolk Institute in obtaining Revd Thomas Image's Crag fossil collection for Cambridge,[67] just as on another occasion he whisked a whole dinosaur from Whitby from under the noses of their local Institute. He was with Henslow and Whewell when John Gage and Lord Maynard opened the Bartlow Hills,[68] and again with Henslow at the opening of the Rougham tumuli in 1843–44.[69] He and Henslow were great friends, and both had encouraged the young Darwin. At his 1848 lecture[70] he spoke (at Edwin Sidney's suggestion) on the fossil giant sloths and armadillos of South America (which had so stimulated Darwin when he found them) and their diminutive living counterparts. By studying the fossil remains, he showed that the extinct varieties had been fully in harmony with their environment, though this had been doubted by even the most convinced 'harmonists'. But, he went on, some would have us believe that the living animals are the degenerate progeny of those giants, and that species transmutated as between monkeys and men, because their progenitors are not found in the older rocks. 'And all for what? To support the beg-

64 *IJ*, 15 Dec. 1848.
65 *IJ*, 15 Dec. 1849.
66 J.W. Clark and T. McK. Hughes, *The Life and Letters of the Reverend Adam Sedgwick*, 2 vols, Cambridge 1890.
67 'Quarterly Meeting, Norton, April 24, 1856', *PSIA* ii, 1859, 220.
68 T. McK. Hughes, 'Papers read at a joint meeting of the Essex Archaeological and Cambridge Antiquarian Society, May 24 1889', *Cambridge Chronicle*, 31 May and 7 June 1889.
69 C. Babington, 'Roman Antiquities Found at Rougham in 1843 and 1844 (with accounts by Rev. Prof. J.S. Henslow)', *PSIA* iv.5, 1872, 257–81.
70 *IJ*, 15 Dec. 1848.

garly doctrines of materialism.' He accused the author of *Vestiges of Creation*[71] of the falsest philosophy, and of having no apprehension of the sanctity of truth. Yet at the Anniversary Meeting the next day he amused everyone with stories and, holding up the example of the excellent Mr Edward Charlesworth ('with whose name they were familiar in that town – [Applause]'), now doing so well in York, he exhorted them to found in Ipswich a class 'for instruction in geology' and the investigation of local geology. Bowerbank followed with a motion to found classes for the study of zoology, particularly of the county, and Captain Smyth (u) proposed similar classes for astronomy and mathematics. It was a significant moment in the educational history of the town.

During 1849 the geologist Professor John Phillips (l) came to Ipswich on behalf of the British Association, and met J. Allen Ransome (l), Charles Gower, and W.H. Alexander to discuss the possibility of a future meeting at Ipswich. That winter's lecturer, Richard Owen (Hunterian Professor of the Royal College of Surgeons, and Vice-President of the Royal Society), the foremost comparative anatomist, embodied scientific authority and moral safety. He considered the development of the Gigantic Birds of New Zealand, into which he had been researching since 1839. How was it, he asked, that these giant creatures which could neither fly nor swim should appear related, sometimes very closely, to others of their order living in lands separated from them by impassable distances of sea? The distribution of all types of creatures, in their various orders, did not substantiate the theory that they had been dispersing from some 'singular Asiatic centre' over a period of only a few thousand years. Owen ran out of time at his lecture, and did not offer many answers.[72] However, he presented a large collection of casts of fossil bones of extinct flightless birds, great leg-bones a foot long, so that his question should continue to be contemplated; on last inspection, the Museum had them still.[73] There is also a set of giant antlers, found in Essex, which were among those described by Owen, and which have been on display almost continually for 152 years.[74] These were presented by John Brown of Stanway, Essex (1780–1859), an interesting early geologist who began life as a journeyman stonemason and amassed wealth by industry.[75]

71 (R. Chambers), *The Vestiges of the Natural History of Creation*, London 1844.

72 *IJ*, 15 Dec. 1849.

73 *IJ*, 5 May 1849; *Marvels*.

74 *IJ*, 6 Jan. 1849. Cf. J. Brown, 'Discovery of a Large Pair of Fossil Horns in Essex (Clacton)', *Magazine of Natural History* (2) ii, 1838, 163; R. Owen, *A History of British Fossil Mammals and Birds*, London 1846, 466.

75 A.P. Wire, 'Essex Worthies, I: Memoir of the late John Brown, F.G.S., of Stanway', *Essex Naturalist* iv, 1890, 158–68. Brown was active at the Museum, on familiar terms with Henslow and Owen, and assisted Prestwich at Hoxne in 1859; attending Sedgwick's soirée, he was described as 'a little man in a brown coat and a brown wig, with a singular countenance, an enthusiast in Geology, and like all enthusiasts, somewhat peculiar in his manners. He might be seen, after having received a piece of information from Professor Sedgwick upon some point about which his own investigations had not entirely satisfied him, rubbing his hands with great glee, and heard exclaiming to himself "it's very extraordinary; I thought it was so" ' (*SC*, 16 Dec. 1848).

Edward Forbes, professor of Botany at King's College, London,[76] with a post at the Geological Survey, spoke in December 1850. An expert in jellyfish and starfish, whose own early Survey had been conducted in the Aegean, he had lately conducted a dredging survey around the seas of Britain from Portland to Cornwall, and from Cornwall to the Shetlands. Late in 1850 he was encouraging Huxley (fresh off the *Rattlesnake*), reading and having published his first papers, and (at Clunn's Hotel, in the Strand) introducing him to senior geologists such as Sir Roderick Murchison (l), Sir Henry de la Beche (Director of the U.K. Geological Survey (l)) and Sir Charles Lyell. The dynamic Forbes was greatly admired by Darwin, and he was 'a paradox, a bon viveur who straddled the divides'[77] between Anglican belief and the dubieties of scientific interpretation. His subject at Ipswich (Corn Exchange) was the 'Distribution of Organized Beings in the European Seas', and he described the different sea provinces, each with its own economy of plant and animal life, its own species, and within each the different zones according to depths and currents. He contrasted them with the systems represented in the underlying rocks. He concluded roundly that this divine prevision and preparation had been fashioned through successive epochs, so that mankind should derive both the bodily and intellectual sustenance necessary to stimulate both his exertions and his ambitions. The next day, visiting Honorary Members such as Edwin Lankester, Richard Taylor (an early Crag geologist of Norwich (l)), Nathaniel Wallich (student of Asiatic botany (l)), and Lovell Reeve made speeches referring to the success of the Museum; Reeve mentioned his chance meeting with Henslow at the Cambridge British Association meeting twenty years previously, and how this had inspired his first interests in the pursuit of science.[78]

Forbes's lecture was also the occasion which prompted the resignation of the Curator, Dr Clarke. He found the behaviour of certain lewd people among the free admissions on Museum open nights repulsive, and, embittered by the Committee's refusal to act on his complaints, finally snapped when, arriving at the Anniversary Lecture, he and his wife were forcibly excluded from the lecture hall by the doorman (who did not recognise them), possibly with the deliberate connivance of a Committee member. Henslow, appointed President the next day, accepted his resignation and refused to become involved.[79] In public correspondence, Clarke accused an unnamed member of 'gross cowardice, base duplicity and prevarication', and regretted that Henslow 'should have so completely lent himself in these nefarious proceedings'.[80] Clarke's assistant, William Bilson, left at much the same time,[81] and in his place Thomas Baker worked closely with Henslow and the curators, and was still in

76 See G. Wilson and A. Geikie, *A Memoir of Edward Forbes*, Edinburgh 1861.

77 *Desmond*, 152–4.

78 *IJ* and *SC*, 28 Dec. 1850.

79 He wrote to Clarke, 'They who in quarrels interpose, must often wipe a bloody nose' (Letter in IM Minutes I).

80 *SC*, 18 Jan. 1851.

81 Bilson appears to have set up as a taxidermist in Bury St Edmunds, and sent ornithological notes to the *Quarterly Journal* of the Suffolk Institute in 1869.

post at Dr Taylor's resignation in 1893. After Clarke's resignation ('leaving *anguis in gramine* to his own conscience'), David Wooster was appointed, and was unanimously re-appointed after the takeover of 1853; but upon learning he must also act as Secretary to the Museum Committee, he resigned the same day, pleading 'nervous irritability',[82] and became attached to the Trevelyans at Wallington.

Sir Roderick Murchison, the soldierly author of *Siluria* (an authoritative study of early Palaeozoic formations), helped to bring the British Association Congress to Ipswich, having been acquainted with the town since he was stationed in the Anglesey Road barracks many years before. There can never have been more of the Honorary Members together at Ipswich than during those several days in the middle of 1851.[83] The Museum Visitors' Book for that occasion is filled with the signatures of the scientific great and good, beginning with that of HRH Prince Albert (l), who had already agreed to become the Museum's Patron; it was a great recruiting opportunity for Henslow, who, in front of the new 'Lion's Den' diorama given by Lord Frederick Hervey (marquess of Bristol (l)), publicly presented the Prince Consort with a bound copy of the Maguire portraits.[84] Opening the Congress, Sir David Brewster, the outgoing President, gave way to George B. Airy, then perhaps the most senior scientist with personal Ipswich connections. Commencing his 1848 lectures, he recalled that the first object of astronomical interest that he was ever shown was Saturn, by the elder Mr Ransome, through a telescope made by his own hands; and, referring to the vital work of the instrument makers, he noted that the latest instrument erected at Greenwich was manufactured in Ipswich.[85] What was spoken and done in the Sections, it would be interesting to explore; more unknowable are the informal exchanges between the learned, the dinner gatherings where ideas are set in motion long before they coalesce. 'Wise men shall exchange riddles', wrote an Anglo-Saxon, and no doubt they did on their excursions to Orford, Bawdsey and Felixstowe, Colchester, Harwich and Bury, and on their perambulations at Shrubland Park, which was thrown open.[86]

1851 closed with what was to prove the last of the Anniversary Meetings. The speaker was Sir Charles Lyell, the pre-eminent geologist and stratigrapher whose *Principles of Geology* had become a standard text through several editions since it was published twenty years previously. Lyell, a relation by marriage of Sir Charles Bunbury, was a cultured man, trained as a lawyer, who made geology his vocation and lived by private means. His rather individual non-progressionism, a view of progress which he felt later to have assisted the arguments of Darwin (to which he became largely accommodated), was then much to the fore in his Anniversary

82 IM Minutes II (1853–71), 16 June 1853.

83 *Ipswich Express*, 8 July 1851; *Illustrated London News*, 12 July 1851, 48ff. The early history of the Association's meetings is told by J. Morrell and A. Thackray, *Gentlemen of Science*, Oxford 1981.

84 The actual volume, it appears, came into the hands of the Brassey family. It was offered to Ipswich Museum during the mid-1990s by a bookseller for several thousand pounds, but was declined.

85 Airy, 2–3.

86 *Ipswich Express*, 8 July 1851.

Address to the Geological Society of London.[87] At Ipswich he lectured on the White Chalk formation, showing it to be a marine deposit laid down over a vast period.[88] Progressionists, he declared, pointed to the absence of higher types in the earlier rocks of the thirty different palaeontological ages which geological science had described – but upon negative evidence only. With new research, reptiles were being found in early formations: Forbes's dredging survey had shown that the marine deposits around the coast of Britain, apart from a little modern refuse near estuaries, gave no indication that Man was native to the island even today – why, therefore, should one expect evidence of higher types such as mammalia in the fossil marine deposits? We must keep searching.[89] Lyell was resisting a theory of transmutations which might ultimately allow atheist forces in society to exploit their brethren in the name of scientific amorality.

Henslow's Evolving Objectives

Henslow, closing the 1851 Lecture, remarked that Lyell had brought forward 'debateable ground'. His long encouragement of his prodigal, Darwin, shows Henslow a believer in the sanctity of scientific truth, however dangerous. In discussions with Owen and perhaps with Kirby, Henslow resolved on a new model arrangement for Ipswich Museum, with a selective central display representing an archetype classification, to which other exhibits could be related. Henslow said at Ipswich in December 1850 that 'Professor Owen fully agreed in the importance of there being a new plan adopted to which might be given a new name – a "typical" arrangement of certain portions of the Museum. (Hear hear).' Henslow suggested 'they should take a certain number, as far as possible, of common objects – that these should be grouped so as to illustrate the main groups of which the animal, vegetable, and mineral kingdoms are composed. (Applause.) It was thought desirable by Professor Owen that this system should be adopted in all country museums', Henslow went on '. . . we should suggest to all similar institutions in England the adoption of the arrangement, which should be permanent, without any shifting whatever; being devoted solely to one side alone of each Museum. It would thus be found extremely convenient for the study of objects, while reference could be easily made to the types, in correspondence carried on by members with other students at a distance. (Applause).' Further, 'this typical arrangement should be made the constant object of short lectures', weekly, 'to be carried on quite independently of the lectures usually given (Hear, hear)'. And furthermore, 'that from 300 to 500 of the householders amongst the working classes, have each 2 or 3 tickets given to them for free distribution to enable their friends to give their attendance; thus they would be

[87] C. Lyell, 'Anniversary Address of the President', *Quarterly Journal of the Geological Society of London* vii, pp. xxxii–lxxi.

[88] Lyell gave to IM specimens of modern rain-drop impressions from Nova Scotia, collected for a comparative study showing uniformity of ancient and modern climatic conditions (*Marvels*).

[89] *SC* (?), 20 Dec. 1851 (unsourced cutting in G. Ransome's scrapbook (IM)).

responsible to each other for good behaviour – not that any thing contrary to this had as yet taken place[90] – and for their mutual instruction in matters even beyond what the Museum could afford. (Applause)'.[91] This was evidently a very popular suggestion, and Henslow set out to implement his plan.

So rapid was the influx of new information, however, that the Typical Series had to be updated: the after-dinner speech became by 1855 a learned address before the British Association. Henslow's ultimately Platonic and Aristotelian system was to be overturned by Darwin's explanations of the mechanism of evolution, and the Creative Source dislodged from the continuous tutelary present to a single and invisibly remote past event. If the argument was about Adam and Eve, it was also about the primary Christian allegory giving authority for the existence of morality. After Sedgwick's 1848 lecture, Henslow had spoken at the soirée of 'the necessity of the minute and accurate investigation of certain prevalent opinions which science could not accept without stricter proof of their scientific truth'. Now, knowing the old order to be changing, he made Ipswich Museum a last monument to it, where the new should be better observed as it arrived. A rector beyond the need of further academic ambition, he was strongly pastoral, teaching his villagers a love of natural history and its moral, economic and industrial benefits. That is why his Horticultural Shows with temporary museums, his herborisations with children, his village excursions to Harwich or to Ipswich Museum, and his lecturing on industrial applications to Institutes in Suffolk became the focus of his educational activities there after 1853. He would show them the tongues in trees, the books in the running brooks, the sermons in stones, and the good in every thing. And *that* is why it was so poisonous of someone to say to his son, the scientist Revd George Henslow, that 'the people of Hitcham never knew what Christianity was until your father died'.[92]

The Bury and West Suffolk Institute of Archaeology and Natural History, which possessed a Museum, voted to become an Institute for all of Suffolk in March 1853. This was almost certainly arranged between Lord Arthur Hervey (President) and Professor Henslow (Vice-President), in case the Ipswich Museum should actually fail, as was anticipated in January 1853; significant collections, and some Ipswich subscriptions, might thus have been salvaged.[93] In the event, the people of Ipswich voted overwhelmingly to keep their Museum and to pay for it themselves, because they had seen and heard from the highest quarters (the Prince Consort) what an ornament it was to the town, and though they might not fully understand its purpose, they were not going to have Ipswich lose face by letting such an admired project fail through not caring about it. Henslow, with a new Curator, George Knights (his fascinating correspondence with whom is largely preserved),[94] embarked on a new phase of work, offering the Museum five lectures a year, at least

90 This disavowal is a reference to the dispute with Dr Clarke, then at its height.

91 *IJ* and *SC*, 28 Dec. 1850.

92 *Reminiscences*, ii, 354, note.

93 S.J. Plunkett, 'The Suffolk Institute of Archaeology 1848–1998: Its Life, Times and Members', *PSIA* xxxix, 1998, 165–206, at p. 171.

94 Henslow's Letters, IM Archives.

two of which he would 'swap' with Lord Arthur Hervey and Revd Edwin Sidney, or with Dr Rigaud (I) of Ipswich School (where he sometimes lodged), so that the same lectures could be recycled before different audiences. Muddles over the dates booked and promises made often imposed much overwork on Henslow, who still had Cambridge examining to do; but the plan enriched the adult education provided by the Mechanics' Institute. The involvement of Revd Edwin Sidney of the Sudbury Institute, a Vice-President most active in the Museum from the beginning, was paramount.[95]

Darwin wrote of Henslow, that 'he talked on all subjects, including his deep sense of religion, and was entirely open'. His son-in-law Joseph Hooker called him 'a man who, with strong enough religious convictions of his own, had the biggest charity for every heresy so long as it was conscientiously entertained'.[96] Henslow's abundant humanity, his tireless balancing of demands upon his time and energy, his kindness and firmness, appear clearly in his unpublished Museum correspondence. Enough that in 1859 he witnessed the publication of those views which he had for many years heard openly and honestly from his celebrated pupil, though he was not ready to accept them. How then did Henslow feel, taking the chair at the 1860 Oxford B.A. meeting, in the new Natural History Museum there? Before his very eyes, Bishop Wilberforce, strongly prompted by Owen, denounced the 'casual' Darwinian theory. To the cat-calls of undergraduates, Huxley (becoming Darwin's spokesman) and J.D. Hooker in their turn denounced the bishop for the slightness and unworthiness of his sarcasm, Lady Brewster fainted, and poor Captain Fitzroy of the *Beagle* stood waving a bible and shouting, over an uproar, that only here was the truth.[97] Henslow's dear friend Sedgwick was not only strongly, but bitterly, opposed to his student's theory; Sedgwick's tears at the Museum remind us of his passionate sincerity, rather than of his academic intransigence. But so many said, and remembered, of Henslow, that his speaking in natural science was most clear and informative and beautiful (long before that was said of Huxley, or of Ray Lankester, or of our own Dr J.E. Taylor by Lankester), and loved his great charity, that what Henslow could tolerate, others might hesitate to disclaim.

Henslow's devout advocacy of popular scientific teaching helped to build the process of 'diffusion' which was afterwards taken over by Huxley and the Rationalists, and used to promote their own new formulations both of science and of morality. They were among the precursors of Lord Reith, H.G. Wells (Huxley's student) and the British Broadcasting Corporation, but some were still sufficiently true scientists also to be true moralists. In 1859–61 Prestwich and Evans were making known the similarity between the Abbeville flint implements and those from Hoxne, and their tremendous implications for the age of mankind,[98] even before Lyell's *Antiq-*

95 Sidney was author of a *History of Methodism*, and nephew of the celebrated preacher Rowland Hill.

96 Quoted in *Darwin and Henslow*, 18–19.

97 Desmond, 277–81.

98 J. Prestwich, 'On the Occurrence of Flint Implements, Associated with the Remains of Animals of Extinct Species in Beds of a Late Geological Period', *Philosophical Transactions* ii, 1860, 277–317.

uity of Man appeared in 1863. Henslow, in probably his last public lecture in Ipswich, in February 1861, spoke to a 'large and delighted' audience on 'Stone Implements of the Historic and Pre-historic Periods' Apparently he had inspected the French sites in 1860, and had brought back implements which he now exhibited. He declared that geologists had no longer any doubt that they belonged to a period antecedent to the last geological changes that had given the present configuration to the surface of the earth. Referring to John Frere's expression, 'beyond the present world', he supposed Frere meant before the time when the present configuration was given to the earth's surface, and not that the implements were pre-Adamite.[99] He concluded that they must be 'cautious in deducing inferences adverse to hitherto prevalent notions regarding the chronology of the human race', and expressed his own conviction that, 'should it be found necessary to extend our received chronology, such an alteration will never militate against the idea that the Scriptures are the inspired Word of God'.[100] Henslow would not have been one to 'go the entire orang', to use Lyell's expression.

A Contract to be Honoured

Edwin Sidney, always dependable for a fine thought, said in 1851 that the rewards for the Museum's endeavours would be, the better they worked, that 'peace, prosperity and order, and mutual respect and kindness, would be interwoven in a golden thread of light through every bond and link of the social system'.[101] The Museum tangibly cemented social bonds, providing different benefits to different groups: it brought public exegesis for the scientists, patronage for the titled, improved agricultural practice for the landed, social conscience for the industrial employer, self-training for the engineer, political capital for its promoters, professional status for the officers, learning in depth for the curious, and an alternative to the public house for the labourer. Social needs converged there, because that was where the community's material and social relations were publicly justified, through science, religion and patrimony. When the Darwinian theory appeared in Victorian museums, it alighted precisely where these relations were actively and cognitively convened.

Darwin's old teachers made of Ipswich Museum a great experiment. They chose an urban centre in the heart of the Crag lands (where the extinct to modern succession was uniquely evidenced), where there existed some deeply philanthropic traditions among the informed classes, excellence of technological industry and agricultural application, and a working class susceptible to the diffusion of scientific knowledge. The success of their experiment in a changing world can be traced clearly through to the 1930s, and was substantially promoted by Dr Taylor, Curator

99 J. Frere, 'Account of Flint Weapons Discovered at Hoxne in Suffolk', *Archaeologia* xiii, 1800, 204. In fact, Frere might well have meant they were pre-Adamite. It was Henslow who now had to suppose that they were not.

100 *SC*, 16 Feb. 1861.

101 *SC* (?), 20 Dec. 1851 (unsourced cutting in G. Ransome's scrapbook (IM)).

1872–93. They helped to create the manners and social occupations of several generations of Suffolk people. Huxley the agnostic, and on his back the atheists and socialists, undertook a world-historic commitment to the continuation and growth of the diffusion of natural knowledge, so that the populace could discover 'the necessity . . . of cherishing the noblest and most human of man's emotions, by worship "for the most part of the silent sort" at the altar of the Unknown and Unknowable', when they overthrew 'authority as the soundest basis of belief', because 'the man of science has learned to believe in justification, not by faith, but by verification'.[102] Has this contract with the world, this commitment to the moral welfare of its people, been honoured?

We have forgotten the religion, and the social order hammers at our doors; science marches ahead of its moral implications. What was fascinating to many of the Victorian working classes, who repeatedly sat through two-hour lectures and read detailed scientific accounts, would try the patience of their modern equivalents. The Institutes had truly elevated intellectual life: the clergyman scientists tended the needs of common people, not only in their own but also in the forthcoming generations, empowering them to participate in the moral, as well as the scientific and social, debates of the day. Are we doing so today? Have we ever intended to surrender our community's cultural property to politicians, to be tossed mockingly from hand to hand around their envious court? For it is not only *what* we learnt about the natural kingdom and our place in it, but also *how* and *why* we learnt it, that is part of the special inheritance that is Ipswich Museum, its collections and archives; and there are forces abroad that no longer wish us to think for ourselves in such a way. Theirs is the penalty of Adam: 'And all for what? To support the beggarly doctrines of materialism.'

[102] T.H. Huxley, 'On the Advisableness of Improving Natural Knowledge: A Lay Sermon, Delivered . . . January 7, 1866', *Lectures and Lay Sermons*, Everyman: London 1910, 41–54, at pp. 52–3.

Plate 1. Revd Professor John Stevens Henslow, President of Ipswich Museum 1850–1861. Photographic Portrait by Maull of London, 1850s. *Courtesy of Ipswich Borough Council Museums and Galleries.*

Plate 2. Ipswich Museum interior during the 1850s: (above) View from the balcony looking towards the entrance; (below) View from the entrance. *Courtesy of Ipswich Borough Council Museums and Galleries.*

(c) (d)

Plate 3. The four Anniversary lecturers: (a) Revd Professor Adam Sedgwick (1848); (b) Professor Richard Owen (1849); (c) Professor Edward Forbes (1850); (d) Sir Charles Lyell (1851). Lithographs by T. Maguire. *Courtesy of Ipswich Borough Council Museums and Galleries.*

(a) (b) (c) (d)

Plate 4. Four active contributors: (a) Very Revd Dr William Buckland; (b) George Biddell Airy; (c) James Scott Bowerbank; (d) John Gould. Lithographs by T. Maguire. *Courtesy of Ipswich Borough Council Museums and Galleries.*

Plate 5. Revd Edwin Sidney. Lithograph by T. Maguire. *Courtesy of Ipswich Borough Council Museums and Galleries.*

John Cordy Jeaffreson (1831–1901) and the Ipswich Borough Records

Geoffrey Martin

THE MUNICIPAL RECORDS of Ipswich are as full and as justly celebrated as those of any historic English borough, and rather more than most. They range over eight centuries, and include the text of one of the earliest borough custumals in England, known as the Black or Ipswich Domesday, with its origins in the traditions of the Anglian settlement. In 2000 they were the subject of a detailed catalogue published to commemorate the eight-hundredth anniversary of King John's grant of the borough's first charter, in May 1200.[1] The catalogue, to the costs of which both the borough and the county council, together with the British Library, contributed, was an appropriate marker of the event. It was also the forty-third volume published by the Suffolk Records Society, itself one of many felicitous enterprises for which the county and region are indebted to Norman Scarfe, that redoubtable Suffolk man.

The borough records are now housed in the Suffolk Record Office in Gatacre Road, some way beyond the ramparts of the medieval town, but comfortably within its liberties, which in the middle ages made up the half-hundred of Ipswich. The core of the building, including the present reading room and library, is the premises of the former Bramford Road council school. It is the latest, and certainly the best appointed, of a series of lodgings which the records of Ipswich have occupied over eight centuries.[2]

We know rather more about the origins of those records than we know of many others, and indeed have an account of them which is unique in its detail. We know less about the places in which they were kept in their earliest days, though in the circumstances it is remarkable enough that there should be anything recorded about the matter at all. One fact that does emerge is that they were not always kept as carefully as they might have been, but the fluster that occurs when things go wrong is often more informative than the smooth course of an established routine.[3] That they survived the hazards of existence for so long before they reached their present haven is a matter of good fortune, with some timely assistance from individuals. One to

1 See D. Allen, *Ipswich Borough Archives: A Catalogue*, SRS XLIII, 2000, xi.

2 On the history of the record office, and the more recent peregrinations of the borough records, see D. Charman, 'The Ipswich and East Suffolk Record Office' *Archives* iv, 1959–60, 18–28.

3 Not a precept for daily life, but a constant consolation to the historian.

whom Ipswich is particularly indebted is another Suffolk man, John Cordy Jeaffreson.

The foundation of the surviving borough archive was King John's charter. There may well have been some written records in the town before 1200, but if there were we have no example of them.[4] The royal charter conferred both privileges and responsibilities on the burgesses, and established an imposing point of reference. It also induced a strong sense of occasion. It was sealed at Orival (Seine- Maritime), on the great bend of the river above Rouen, on 25 May 1200, and was in Ipswich by the end of June. It was formally displayed there on 29 June, and although the public ceremonies in which it figured would have taken a little time to prepare it had probably arrived not long before.

The burgesses had been negotiating for a charter for several years, and as we see the middle ages largely in the terms of their own iconography it is natural to think of the petitioners in anxious and grateful attendance on the king. In fact the negotiations were over, and the bills paid.[5] John's chancery was a busy office, and his clerks went about their tasks with no more emotion, though no doubt more occasional apprehension, than a modern bank teller receiving a cheque. The sealed charter most probably went into a bag with the other documents of the day, and made its way across the Channel and to Ipswich by the network of messengers on which the royal administration depended.[6]

Its reception in the town was another matter. The townsmen convened a celebrated series of meetings from 29 June to 12 October 1200, four in the churchyard and one in the church of St Mary Tower, at which the charter was shown and read, and a constitution devised for the new borough. The first assembly elected two bailiffs as chief magistrates and two others to act with them as coroners, and then agreed to have a sworn council of twelve chief portmen, who were appointed before the whole community at the second meeting on 1 July.[7] The charter licensed a gild merchant, and in due course the burgessses appointed an alderman, or master, to conduct it. In doing so they were most probably legitimizing and perpetuating the

[4] In 1086 the royal demesne was in the sheriff's hands, and Ipswich with it. There is therefore no trace in Domesday Book, as there is at Colchester, of a rental or annotated list of the burgesses at that date. The townsmen's negotiations with Richard I and John are recorded only in the royal archives, but they may have had memoranda of their own. See further *Ipswich Borough Archives*, 18–19, and below, n. 5.

[5] The negotiations were in progress by 1196: see *The Chancellor's Roll for the Eighth Year of Richard I*, ed. D.M. Stenton, Pipe Roll Society XLV, 1930, 125.

[6] See M. Hill, *The King's Messengers*, London 1961, 12–13. Six documents were sealed at Orival on 25 and 26 May 1200. The court had been at Les Andelys (Eure) a few days earlier: *Rotuli chartarum in Turri Londinensi asservati*, ed. T.D. Hardy, vol. 1 pt 1, *1199–1216*, London, Record Commissioners, 1837, 65, 96.

[7] Bailiffs were often replaced later in the middle ages by a mayor, but Ipswich kept them until 1836. Coroners were literally keepers of the pleas of the crown, their business not to try such actions, but to discover and reserve them for the royal judges. The modern coroner has only the vestiges of that power, being concerned with the circumstances of sudden death and the fact of treasure trove. On the sworn council, and the proceedings as a whole, see further *Ipswich Borough Archives*, xix–xxi, and the references there.

body which had negotiated with the king to secure the liberties which they were now savouring, but the formal recognition of the gild now took second place to the affairs of the borough.[8] In the mean time at a third meeting the officers had ordered the making of a common seal, which was displayed at the last meeting, in October, when the alderman was eventually elected. The seal depicted a ship and a stylized view of the town. The proceedings throughout were eloquent and highly interesting, and the survival of their story is extraordinary. Fortunately the townsmen's sense of occasion had extended to a written record.

The third meeting, on 13 July, was attended only by the officers, who made a series of ordinances. They made arrangements for the regular collection of the king's dues, and decreed, besides the making of the seal and the appointment of the alderman, the appointment of town serjeants to carry out the magistrates' orders, and the formal communication of the charter to the county courts of Suffolk and Norfolk. They also ordered that to trade freely in the borough a merchant would have to contribute to its common taxes, scot and lot, a provision that has to be read against the subsequent regulations of the gild.

At the fourth meeting, on 10 September, the whole community assembled to hear the officers' ordinances read. That is the first reference to a written document other than the charter itself, but it shows that at least some of, and probably all, the proceedings since the charter arrived had been minuted. At the end of the fifth meeting the whole assembly decreed that the laws and free customs of the town should be inscribed in a roll to be called the Domesday, and that the roll should be delivered for safe keeping to the bailiffs. Evidently the laws had reposed until that time in the townsmen's minds, though we need not suppose on that account that they lacked precision. The assembly went on to order that the statutes of the gild should also be recorded on a roll, as was the practice elsewhere in cities and boroughs which had such gilds. In that respect, as probably in others, they were notably well up-to-date.[9]

Besides those two rolls, however, there was another: the account of the proceedings itself. It was clearly not part of either the Domesday or the gild roll, but was given a separate and distinctive heading, as 'The manner and form of choosing the bailiffs and coroners in Ipswich in accordance with the charter of the lord King John'.[10] It shows that the bailiffs who were elected at the first meeting were

8 See G.H. Martin, 'The Medieval and Early Modern Borough', in *Ipswich from the First to the Third Millennium*, ed. R. Malster and N. Salmon, Ipswich 2001, 7–17.

9 Rolls of admissions to gilds merchant are the earliest administrative records that we have from boroughs in the British Isles. Only the rolls of Dublin and Leicester, which both survive in their original form, are older than the first entries recorded at Ipswich. See further *The Dublin Guild Merchant Roll, c.1190–1265*, ed. P. Connolly and G.H. Martin, Dublin 1992, x–xx.

10 The account survives only in the borough custumal, where it is said to be copied from 'the roll made in Ipswich in the second year of the reign of King John . . . which begins thus: In the roll of the manner and form [etc.]'. That wording might suggest that the older roll was itself a transcript, perhaps of the original minutes and notes. 'Manner and form (*modus et forma*)' is a stately phrase, and a reminder that we do not know much about the early civic clerks' background and experience.

re-elected at the fourth, on 10 September. That established the practice of electing or confirming the officers who had to answer to the king for the town's fee-farm, or annual dues, in time for the Michaelmas audit of the royal exchequer. The meeting then elected executive officers in accordance with the ordinances of 13 July, but other business had to be held over to the last assembly. There the townsmen duly admired the seal, elected the alderman, gave the portmen the use of the meadow which now lies under Portman Road, and provided for the safe custody of the gild roll and the roll to be called the Domesday.

That was an exceptionally promising start. The subsequent history of the records, though full of interest, is not all as happy. The custumal was compiled, the gild kept its register of admissions, and the borough court also enrolled its transactions. Then in 1272 the common clerk, John Black or le Blake, absconded with a number of court rolls and the roll called Domesday. It seems that all that he left behind him were two rolls of the portmanmote, the gild roll, and some loose membranes, including the roll of 1200. It took the town twenty years to repair the loss, but the free customs were eventually recalled and restated. They included some reprehension of false entries in the records made by fraudulent clerks, which was clearly a lock for the stable door, but they had many other features suggesting that they represented a serious effort to reconstruct the original. That would have been a task less formidable to minds still charged with oral tradition than to those sapped first by literacy and more recently by television. When it was done, the custumal was copied and recopied over the next two-and-a-half centuries, partly from a natural concern with security, and partly to keep pace with the times.[11]

Despite some turmoil in the 1280s, when the borough was taken into the king's hands for six years,[12] the late thirteenth and early fourteenth centuries saw a rapid development of the borough's administration, chiefly expressed in the elaboration of its courts and their records. There was then a reaction in the 1320s against the monopoly of power by a small group in the town. It produced a new copy of the custumal, new financial officers, called chamberlains and clavigers, and a duplication of records to keep a tighter hand on fees and other income. The survival of some of those duplicates shows that the reforms had at least one lasting effect, but there is another eloquent comment on the proliferation of records in an inventory which was made in or shortly after 1333.[13]

The inventory shows that the rolls of the great and petty courts, into which the portmanmote had developed, were distributed between two chests, and it provides notes on some of their contents as a finding aid. Together with the recensions of the custumal and the material added to them it measures the distance the administration had come from the meetings in and about St Mary Tower.

The record chests, like the courts themselves, were housed in the town hall, vari-

[11] See G.H. Martin, 'The Diplomatic of Borough Custumals', *La diplomatique urbaine en Europe au moyen âge*, ed. W. Prevenier and T. de Hemptinne, Leuven/Apeldoorn 2000, 307–20.

[12] Edward I formally restored and confirmed the liberties in the summer of 1291: *CChR, 1257–1300*, 402–3.

[13] Now SROI, C/7/1/1. See also below, n. 48.

ously called the moot hall, the hall of pleas, and the toll house, which stood on the Cornhill, and was in part the former church of St Mildred. St Mary Tower is distinguished today as the civic church. Its churchyard may have been a traditional place of assembly, or it may have been used in 1200 simply because the church was large enough to shelter a large company. On the other hand St Mildred's had a suggestive pre-Conquest dedication, and its position in the principal market place, the Cornhill, suggests that it was an ancient and probably the original focus of civic affairs. It so remained, and the records in it, until the nineteenth century.

In 1521 Richard Percyvale (*c.*1480–1529) compiled the last recension of the Domesday, with the aid of the town clerk, Robert Bray. Percyvale, one of the chief portmen since 1511, was a bailiff three times between 1513 and 1525. His Domesday is a great folio coucher, a solemn compilation of the customs, charters, oaths, and ordinances of the medieval borough, together with what historical material he could gather. Its text was extended over the following decades, and it was used until the early nineteenth century for making proclamations and on other formal occasions, but it in fact marks off the medieval from the modern town. Administrative practices and forms changed, Latin fell out of use, and the medieval records became little more than curiosities and an occasional quarry for precedents. There were still, however, innovations which continued the archival experiments of the earlier borough, including registers of poor-relief administered, and a census of the poor and their needs, arranged schematically parish by parish, made in the autumn of 1597.[14]

In the seventeenth century Nathaniel Bacon (1593–1660), the parliamentarian recorder of Ipswich, compiled a survey of the borough's history called 'The Annalls of Ipswiche' which showed a wide knowledge of the records.[15] Bacon was an active politician in the eastern counties, a member of the parliamentary Association there, and an MP for the borough. He was also the author of a constitutional history of England which displayed an historical curiosity and shrewdness similar to that in his Annalls.[16] He had no close successor as an historian in Ipswich, but in 1696 the clavigers compiled an inventory of the borough records in their care. It was a competent house-keeping exercise, disappointing now because it takes no account of the medieval court rolls, but it does show that John's charter was then still in safe keeping.[17]

The omission of the court rolls from the inventory underlines the remoteness of the medieval system, and the absence too by the end of the seventeenth century of

14 For Percyvale's Domesday, SROI, C/4/1/4, see *Ipswich Borough Archives*, 414–15, 418–21. For the census of the poor, SROI, C/3/4/1/4–7, see the text and commentary in J. Webb, *Poor Relief in Elizabethan Ipswich*, SRS IX, 1966, 75–95, 119–40.

15 It remained in manuscript until 1884, when it was published without apparatus: *Annalls of Ipswiche by Nathaniell Bacon*, ed. W.H. Richardson, Ipswich 1884.

16 *An Historical Discovery of the Uniformity of the Government of England: The First Part from the First Times to the Reign of Edward III*, London 1647, and *Continuation . . . until the End of the Reign of Queen Elizabeth*, 1651. A fifth edition was published in 1760.

17 SROI, C/4/7/1/2. The charters of John, Henry III, Edward I, and Edward II were kept together in a black box: *Ipswich Borough Archives*, 1.

Nathaniel Bacon's lawyerly antiquarianism. There was, however, more than the antiquarian spirit lacking in the town. Until the nineteenth century there were no new manufactures to supplement or replace the declining cloth industry in East Anglia, nor to stimulate its shipping as the Atlantic trade was developing the west coast ports. The most obtrusive of the absentees were perhaps the non-resident freemen of the borough, who were mustered for treats at parliamentary elections. As in many other towns the corporation itself, torn between factions, functioned for much of the time like a declining private club. An improvement commission established by statute in 1793 was resisted by the corporation as likely to diminish the authority which the corporators had no will to use. Torpor is, however, generally not harmful to archives. There was no prospect of reform, and with it any prospect of bureaucratic activity in the boroughs, until the parliamentary franchise was reformed.[18]

Parliamentary reform hung fire, through bad years and good, until 1832. Then a Whiggish commission brimming with reformative intent descended on the boroughs in 1833, and the Municipal Corporations Act of 1836 imposed a uniform constitution on the survivors. Ipswich lost its bailiffs but gained a mayor. However, the original hopes of the reformers were largely disappointed, because as the old corporations had been seen to spend much of their income on wine for the few and bread and circuses for the many, their successors judged it safer and more seemly to spend theirs on nothing at all.[19]

Just before the turmoil of reform Ipswich suffered an unintended loss by the loan of two copies of its custumal to Sir Francis Palgrave (1788–1861). Both sides to the transaction acted with the best of intentions. The borough wanted an expert opinion on an imposing but unintelligible possession. Palgrave was an established barrister and historical writer, with a particular interest in Anglo-Norman texts. As he was also the son-in-law of Dawson Turner, the savant and antiquary of Great Yarmouth, his qualifications were unexceptionable, and they were soon greatly enhanced. Practice in peerage cases and close study had given him unrivalled archival knowledge. Knighted in 1832, he was not only appointed a member of the municipal corporations commission but in 1838 became the first deputy keeper of the public records, and the deviser of the Public Record Office in Chancery Lane.[20] He gave the town clavigers a receipt for the volumes, but kept them both until his death in 1861, when his executors sold them to the British Museum.[21]

18 On the eighteenth-century corporation, see further R. Malster, *A History of Ipswich*, Chichester 2000, 134–9.

19 For the commission's reports, see below, n. 47. See also G.H. Martin, 'Introduction', *The History of the Boroughs and Municipal Corporations of the United Kingdom by H.A. Merewether and A.J. Stephens*, Brighton 1972, first published 1835, v–xiv; and below, n. 35.

20 Historical scholarship owes a permanent debt to Palgrave, an instinctive archivist without professional precedents to guide him. Not the least of his services was to insist upon the preservation, under long closure, of the detailed returns of the decennial census from 1842 onwards. See further G.H. Martin, 'Sir Francis Palgrave', *New DNB*, Oxford forthcoming.

21 See Palgrave's receipt, SROI, C/4/7/1/7, dated 13 Oct. 1832. The two texts, now BL MSS Add. 25,012 and 25,011, were subsequently chosen to be printed in *The Black Book of the Admiralty*, ed. T. Twiss, RS LV, 1871–76, ii, 1–207. See also below, n. 52.

It was an unfortunate overture to the age of historical enlightment in Ipswich, and worse was to follow. In the middle decades of the century the most dedicated consulter of the archives was William Stevenson Fitch (1792–1859).[22] Fitch, Ipswich born and educated, took over his father's business as a druggist in 1815, and in 1837 became postmaster of the town. In the mean time he acquired considerable antiquarian knowledge, and turned it to account by pillaging the collections in which he was allowed to work. His tastes were in a sense conventional but shrewd. He preferred seals and autographs to administrative records, and covered his tracks well enough to arrange a sale of his winnings in his own lifetime, which still left the materials for two more after his death.[23]

Fitch's depredations at Ipswich were probably aided by the haphazard state of the archives, though he may have left further disorder behind.[24] The discovery after Palgrave's death that the custumal had been irretrievably lost roused indignation, which was aggravated by some unfeeling reference to the episode at a meeting of the British Archaeological Association in the town in 1864.[25] Nothing could be done to recover the volumes from the national collection, and it does not seem to have occurred to anyone to see what else there might be in the strong room to be cherished. Help, home-bred in Suffolk, was on its way in the person of John Cordy Jeaffreson, but did not arrive in Ipswich until 1880.

Jeaffreson was born in Framlingham in 1831.[26] His father was William Jeaffreson (1790–1865), a well-known surgeon, and his mother Caroline, née Edwards (1795–1863). John was the Jeaffresons' second son, and they also had seven daughters. He was named after his mother's uncle, John Cordy (1762–1828) of Woodbridge, a dealer and landowner who had made a substantial fortune from surplus supplies at the end of the Napoleonic wars. After attending schools at Woodbridge and Botesdale Jeaffreson was apprenticed to his father in 1845, but three years later a serious illness moved him to give up medicine and go to university with the intention of taking orders. He graduated BA from Pembroke College, Oxford, in 1852, but by that time he had also renounced the idea of entering the church. He now resolved to write for a living, and to seek pupils as a private tutor until he could establish himself. He joined his friend Henry Kingsley (1830–76) and others from Oxford in London, and in 1854 published *Crewe Rise*, the first of nearly a dozen three-volume novels which he wrote over the next thirty years. From 1856 he contributed regularly to the *Athenæum*, and was able to give up teaching. He entered Lincoln's Inn that same year, and was called to the bar in 1859, but he

22 See J.I. Freeman, *The Postmaster of Ipswich: William Stevenson Fitch, Antiquary and Thief*, London 1997.

23 The sales were held in 1855 and 1859: Freeman, *The Postmaster of Ipswich*, 127–33. Fitch was probably responsible for the disappearance of much of the town's early modern correspondence, some of which has since been recovered: *Ipswich Borough Archives*, 571–603.

24 See below, p. 346 and n.

25 See below, p. 348.

26 The details of Jeaffreson's life which follow are principally taken from his autobiography, *A Book of Recollections*, 2 vols, London 1894. See also G.H. Martin, 'John Cordy Jeaffreson', *New DNB*, Oxford forthcoming.

did not practise, and regarded the Inn rather as one of his clubs. He was attracted to historical and literary studies, and in 1858 published *Novels and Novelists from Elizabeth to Victoria*. It led him on to a more lucrative formula, which he first used in *A Book about Doctors* (1860), an essay in anecdotal social history. *A Book about Lawyers* followed in 1866, and then *A Book about the Clergy* (1870), *Brides and Bridals* (1872), and *A Book about the Table* (1875).

In 1860 Jeaffreson married Arabella Ellen, daughter of William Eccleston, FRCS (d.1847). They had a daughter, Caroline, who died in 1909. After their marriage the Jeaffresons lived in Heathcote Street, Mecklenburg Square, but in 1866 they moved to 43 Springfield Road, St John's Wood, then redolent 'of the wild flowers and the new-mown hay of the Hampstead meadows'. Arabella's pleasure in her garden and the fresh air of Maida Vale soon reconciled her husband to his removal from the enticements of Bloomsbury, 'a quarter of London so conveniently near the Inns of Court, the newspaper offices, the theatres, and the British Museum'. They subsequently moved to Carlton Road, and later to Portsdown Mansions, in Maida Vale.

Happy in his family life, Jeaffreson was an ebullient man, well intentioned, benignly curious, and determinedly good-humoured. He had a large circle of friends and an immense range of acquaintance. They are not readily to be distinguished, for he was uncommonly gregarious, but they included John Leech and Charles Keene, and he was variously on close terms as a young man with Sir George Jessel, who was Master of the Rolls from 1873 to 1883, and later with William Makepeace Thackeray. About the time of his marriage, he met Thomas Duffus Hardy, and the friendship that grew up between them lasted for the rest of Hardy's life, and in a sense of Jeaffreson's too.

In 1861 Hardy became Deputy Keeper of the Public Records, in succession to Sir Francis Palgrave. The two had been at odds for many years. They were both deeply learned, but wholly different in temperament, Palgrave fastidious and hypersensitive, Hardy robustly sociable, but beset by a mistaken belief that he had been deprived of the deputy keepership in 1838 by some machination of Palgrave's.[27] Jeaffreson accepted and later published the story, though the truth was that Palgrave had been in all ways the more experienced and better candidate.

Hardy lacked some of Palgrave's instinctive skills as an archivist, but he was strongly committed to scholarship and the dissemination of historical material. He played a large part in establishing the Rolls Series, an enterprise funded by the Treasury and directed by the Master of the Rolls, for the publication of chronicles and other medieval sources. In 1869 he similarly furthered the Royal Commission on Historical Manuscripts (1869), now known as the Historical Manuscripts Commission, or HMC, to promote the listing and publication of records other than public records. Hardy himself became a commissioner, and took a close interest in the work, which was managed under his direction from the Public Record Office.

The Commission began with an establishment of two inspectors, but it was

[27] See further G.H. Martin, 'Sir Thomas Duffus Hardy', *New DNB*, Oxford forthcoming.

obvious even in its first year that more would be needed, and another two were recruited, for work in Scotland and Ireland. All were experienced antiquaries or archivists, so far as those categories were then to be distinguished, and the Irish inspector was Sir John Thomas Gilbert, the first secretary of the Public Record Office in Dublin.

In 1871 Hardy surprised Jeaffreson by suggesting that he too should become one of the Commission's inspectors.[28] He had studied Jeaffreson's books and believed that he had the qualities that the work demanded. To Jeaffreson's immediate objection that he knew nothing of palaeography and the nature of archives Hardy answered that he would teach him all that he needed to make a beginning, being confident that experience would do the rest. He spoke both authoritatively and persuasively. Jeaffreson began a course of study and transcribing in Chancery Lane under Hardy's supervision, and two years later, in May 1874, Hardy pronounced him qualified, and set him to inspect and report upon the family manuscripts belonging to Edmund Field, the chaplain of Lancing College. The trial was a success, and Jeaffreson moved on to the parish records of Mendlesham, Suffolk, and the manuscripts of Miss Conway Griffith of Carreglwyd, Anglesey. His reports on those collections appeared in the appendix to the fifth report of the commissioners, published in 1876. Twenty-six others followed over the next decade.[29] Hardy evidently had an astute idea of Jeaffreson's capacity and potentiality when he recruited him. The learned conception of what was historically significant was broadening as the wealth of the public records in Chancery Lane was revealed in the deputy keeper's annual reports, and in consequence of the work of the Commission itself. Jeaffreson's own interests in what came to be known as social history accorded well enough with those changes, and that he was a natural publicist, in constant search of an audience, was not at all a disqualification. It was obvious that he had some critical acumen and was energetic and industrious. It was not less important that he also had some address, and an affability that seems to have been universally reassuring. There were always private owners whose apprehensions needed to be soothed, and corporate bodies too have their anxieties and suspicions.

At the end of 1876 Jeaffreson was eager to begin work on the manuscripts of the Royal Institution, but he was restrained by the assistant secretary of the commission, James Joel Cartwright, who explained he had no funds to hand, and that things would remain tight until the end of the financial year.[30] Subsequently, however, Jeaffreson was sent to survey a number of private collections, including those of the

28 See *A Book of Recollections* ii, 37.

29 They are all listed, but without the volume numbers, in *A Book of Recollections* ii, 91–3. The HMC reports run from the 5th (C.1432 and 1432–i of 1876) to Appendix III of the 11th (C.5060–ii of 1887).

30 *Semper eadem.* Jeaffreson's work as an inspector, with some occasional personal sidelights, is recorded in his correspondence with Cartwright: PRO, HMC 1/167. The papers in the file are unnumbered, and not all the letters are dated, but they fall into a coherent sequence. Cartwright was assistant secretary of the Commission from 1875 to 1894, and then secretary until his death in 1903. He was also secretary of the PRO from 1887 until 1903: J.D. Cantwell, *The Public Record Office, 1838–1958*, London 1991, 570.

earl of Portsmouth at Farleigh Wallop and of William More Molyneux, of Losely Place, Surrey, and in July 1877 he informed Cartwright that he would be staying with Lt-Col. G.H.A. Forbes at Dursley on a sweep through the west country.[31] In the autumn of that year he was excising some passages from the Molyneux report which he thought might have ruffled the family's sensitivities.[32] In 1878 he returned some manuscripts to Lord Portsmouth, which he may have borrowed for his own work rather than for the Commission's, and corrected the proofs of his report on the Somerset county records.[33] His surveys of that collection and the Molyneux papers appeared together in the Commissioners' seventh report, published in 1879.

In September 1878 Jeaffreson began work on the records of the city of Chester and its civic companies.[34] Chester's was the first municipal archive that he examined, the English boroughs having largely been left to Henry Thomas Riley (1816–78), one of the original two inspectors, who died that year. After a visit to Yorkshire in the winter Jeaffreson spent some time in London, in the course of which he began to address Cartwright, whose earlier style had been a little stately, as 'Dear Cartwright' rather than 'Mr Cartwright', and soon after regularly signed himself 'Ever yours cordially'. It was not only the owners and custodians of manuscripts who softened under Jeaffreson's untiring bonhomie.

Jeaffreson's report on Chester was published, together with that on Lord Portsmouth's papers, in the Commission's eighth report (1881). They were accompanied there by two others on the civic records of Leicester and Pontefract. At Leicester the city records had been rescued from neglect and decay in the middle of the century by the work of local antiquaries, and in the 1870s a strong-room was prepared for them in the new town hall. The council sought Hardy's advice on their care, and Hardy despatched Jeaffreson, who rounded off his work with a guide to the records published in 1878 at the corporation's expense.[35] The next year, 1879, found Jeaffreson travelling in Devon, to report on the records of Plymouth and Barnstaple. Work at Plymouth was delayed by the town clerk's absorption in parliamentary business in the spring, but by July Jeaffreson was installed in 'comfortable lodgings' on the Hoe, and at Barnstaple he was able to work in a private library with a handsome view of the sea from its windows.[36] He relished the view, but it manifestly did not distract him from his business; he could take both the

31 PRO, HMC 1/167, undated, but marked July 1877.

32 PRO, HMC 1/167, 22 Sept. 1877.

33 PRO, HMC 1/167, 11 April and 15 July 1878.

34 PRO, HMC 1/167, 6 June 1878; and see *A Book of Recollections* ii, 133–9.

35 On the building of the new town hall, and the modest operations of the reformed corporation in Leicester down to that time, see J. Simmons, 'Mid-Victorian Leicester', *Transactions of the Leicestershire Archaeological and Historical Society* xli, 1965–66, 41–56, at 45–7. On the records, see J.C. Jeaffreson, *An Index to the Ancient Manuscripts of the Borough of Leicester, with a Key to some of their Various Styles of Writing*, Westminster 1878. Jeaffreson's advice to would-be students of the MSS (pp. 4–7) shows that he had readily come to Hardy's way of thinking: 'The difficulties and perplexities of medieval calligraphy disappear quickly before a resolute purpose of mastering them.' See also below, n. 42.

36 PRO, HMC 1/167, 9 May and 12 Sept.1879, and HMC *9th Report*, 1883, 204.

exigencies and the occasional amenities of his work in his stride, and his professional and his social skills went very harmoniously together.

In the spring of 1880, between visits to Stratford-upon-Avon and Yorkshire, and with his accounts all rendered, Jeaffreson referred to the prospect of a visit to the eastern counties in the autumn. 'The notion . . . grows pleasantly in my imagination. I should like to do Ipswich, Beccles, and Yarmouth, all on one line of railway', a reflection perhaps more reassuring then than it might be now. 'I have long had reason to think that Yarmouth and Ipswich would yield some important information respecting maritime exploration in Tudor times.'[37] By June he was contemplating 'running about in the service of HM's commissioners . . . I shall be delighted to go to Yorkshire, Cambridgeshire, or anywhere else' in so pleasant a season, but he added 'I have already pulled a string at Ipswich, and will let you know in due course if any good results from my action.'[38]

The Ipswich string was attached to Charles Cheston, 'a powerful City solicitor who married a daughter of Mr Packard, whilom mayor and still a chief power of Ipswich'. Jeaffreson already knew the town clerk, John Orford, as 'a good fellow', and he hoped that a letter which he had sent to Cheston to pass on to Edward Packard, JP, DL, would 'conciliate his father-in-law who as a strong Conservative has a wholesome suspicion of mere busybodies prying into the secrets of muniment rooms'.[39] The ground could hardly have been better prepared.

Jeaffreson was at work in Ipswich by June.[40] He visited Wisbech in July, but spent September and October in Ipswich, where his wife and daughter joined him. He wrote during that time in good spirits to Cartwright, saying 'I am wearing white waistcoats and feeling only thirty years old.' He had by then finished his official work, but proposed to stay on at the corporation's request to put the records in order. 'In respect to confusion', he observed mildly, 'they had surpassed any collection of writing it had been my duty to examine.'[41]

It is difficult now to appreciate the state in which the commission's inspectors and other inquirers in the nineteenth century commonly found local records. Responsibility for the muniments in boroughs was vested traditionally with particular officers – in Ipswich with the clavigers, since the early fourteenth century

37 PRO, HMC 1/167, [23] May 1880.

38 PRO, HMC 1/167, [June 1880].

39 PRO, HMC 1/167, 23 June 1880. Packard's suspicions were widely shared. See, e.g., I.G. Doolittle, *The City of London and its Livery Companies*, Dorchester 1982, 95–6: 'most companies complied [with the requests of the Royal Commission of 1880–84] though usually, on legal advice, they protested against the enquiries as an illegal infringement on chartered privileges and declined to reveal their title to [what they deemed] private corporate property'.

40 *East Anglian Daily Times*, 12 June 1880.

41 PRO, HMC 1/167. JCJ to JJC: an undated letter addressed from Salisbury House, Anglesey Road, Ipswich, probably written early in September 1880. Jeaffreson had spoken in June of a kinsman in Ipswich with whom he implied he might stay (23 June, above, n. 38), but Salisbury House was a boarding house kept by Mrs Sarah Last (*White's Directory of Suffolk*, 1870, and *Census* 1881), and Mr Geoffrey Cordy, of Felixstowe, a remote but benign and well informed kinsman of JCJ's, tells me that he knows of no connection between the Jeaffresons and the Lasts.

– and it sat lightly enough upon them. The idea of security rarely extended beyond seclusion: it was enough that the records should be kept from prying eyes, and if the price of their isolation was decay there were few to care.[42] There was little general sense of records having an historical value. Charters might be seen as witnessing authority, and were often kept with more care than other documents, but the governing charter was likely by definition to be late, and medieval seals, especially the great seal, were notoriously tempting to collectors.[43] The medieval and early modern administrative records were largely unintelligible, and had little obvious relation to later practice. Where they aroused the interest of antiquaries they were in danger of being removed and dispersed.

Archival science was still in the making, and that only in national institutions. In the city of London, where there was a strong tradition of concern for the care of the records, their custody was firmly vested in the town clerk, and it took some decades to persuade him at last in 1876 to appoint a deputy keeper, when the learned Reginald Sharpe became clerk of the records. It was a precedent that other municipalities were slow to follow.[44]

When Jeaffreson arrived in Ipswich he found the muniments comparatively well housed, but in a remarkable state of disorder. They had then been stored for many centuries on the same site, in the town hall on the Cornhill. The town hall had grown out of and around St Mildred's church by accretion. It was modernized, which is to say that it was given a classical shell, in instalments between 1818 and 1841, and then entirely rebuilt, in an Italianate style with French features, or arguably *vice versa*, in 1867. Removal from one repository to another is ordinarily a perilous business for archives, both from the danger of inadvertent losses and from the temptation to spare further effort by throwing things away. The Ipswich records may have incurred some such attrition, but they had also suffered from Fitch's systematic pilfering and more casual antiquarian rifling.[45] Jeaffreson was inclined to think that Fitch, or some earlier intruder, had deliberately shuffled and re-tied rolls and bundles of papers to cover his tracks.[46] Jeaffreson had a critical eye and a good deal of experience, but as he said long neglect and well-meaning incompetence

[42] As at Leicester: 'The chamberlains' accounts, now collected into 38 volumes, were at the time [1836] lying in a confused mass, mixed with other papers, in a corner of the muniment room, a prey to rats, and saturated with water caused by the overflowings of a water-butt filtrating through the porous stone wall of the building': Jeaffreson, *An Index to the Ancient Manuscripts of Leicester*, p. [iii], quoting William Kelly (1864). The room was at least ventilated: there was a grated window looking on to St Martin's churchyard.

[43] Ipswich lost John's charter either to Fitch or to some earlier predator, between 1696 and 1880. See *Ipswich Borough Archives*, 1, and above, n. 17.

[44] See P.E. Jones and R. Smith, *A Guide to the Records in the Corporation of London Record Office and the Guildhall Library Muniment Room*, London 1951, 13–14; and B. Masters, 'Local Archivist 1876–1914: Dr Reginald R. Sharpe', *Journal of the Society of Archivists* v, 1974–77, 275–82.

[45] See *Ipswich Borough Archives*, 571.

[46] 'The disorder differed in a remarkable manner from the confusion into which MSS are apt to fall through the inadvertence or negligence of unmethodical searchers . . . the curious mis-arrangement may have been the work of an incompetent meddler, or the work of a person who

could have produced some of the same results. Not a man lightly to be deterred, he began work on a formidable mass of material with very little to guide him.

He accomplished his task in a remarkably short time, though he continued to think about Ipswich amongst his further labours, and his report was not published until 1883. It seems that most of his work was done, and well done, in some eight to ten weeks. The Commission wanted a report on the muniments as a whole, with some judgment on their historical value and an indication of their scope. A holding accumulated over six centuries, even if it were in good order, presented an adequate challenge, and at Ipswich the constituents of the heap had to be identified and arranged before anything else could be done. By all accounts, Jeaffreson seems to have enjoyed himself.

There were at the time few guides to early, or for that matter to later, municipal history. The reports of the municipal corporations commission contained an undigested mass of material which would be valuable for purposes of comparison but would require much application to master.[47] Jeaffreson and his colleagues had no time for such research, and few other extraneous sources of information. They were compelled instead to rely upon the archives themselves. Jeaffreson made his own way so successfully that the extracts in his reports were used and cited by later commentators such as Charles Gross and James Tait, who readily appreciated their cogency and reliability.

Jeaffreson distinguished five categories of documents: rolls, royal charters and letters patent, municipal and private deeds, books, and a sump which he called miscellaneous writings, a term which conscientious professionals would wish to avoid but which extremity may make irresistible.[48] Modern practice seeks to classify archives by their administrative provenance and function, but Jeaffreson's scheme was entirely defensible, both in respect of the conditions in which he had to work, and also considering its practical results. His instinctive emphasis on the court rolls was sound. In medieval Ipswich, as in other towns, administrative business was conducted in the courts, and proceedings of all kinds were literally enrolled until the later middle ages, and in some instances beyond. The rolls of the portmanmote gave rise to other series in which particular kinds of business were distinguished, and the establishment of a separate record on one occasion at least created a new court.[49] Within his broad categories Jeaffreson distinguished the nature of the different series with great care. He defined and described them, and made judicious and often quite

at some remote time deliberately added to the confusion of the MSS . . .' HMC *9th Report*, 261–2.

47 *Reports of the Commissioners Appointed to Inquire into the Municipal Corporations of England and Wales*, 7 vols, House of Commons Sessional Papers (hereafter SP): 1835, 116, vols xxiii–xxvi (284 boroughs); 1837, SP 239, vol. xxv (London, Southwark, and London companies); 1837–38, SP 686, vol. xxxv (14 boroughs, of which 11 in Wales); 1839, SP 402, vol. xviii (index).

48 There was a sub-category called 'Curious and Choice', in which the most interesting item was the fourteeenth-century inventory, C/4/7/1/1: see above, p. 338. It is extremely abraded, and seems to have been the only document that Jeaffreson was unable to read.

49 The petty court of recognizances: see *Ipswich Borough Archives*, 42 and 73.

substantial extracts from them. His report even now provides a succinct and informative conspectus of the borough's historic evidences.

Thomas Wolsey is the most famous native of Ipswich, and in traditional terms the town's principal reference to national history. Besides looking to them to yield evidence of Tudor maritime enterprise, Jeaffreson had naturally expected the Ipswich records to illuminate Wolsey's family and career, and he was surprised and mildly suspicious to find that it did not. He was, however, amply compensated by what he did uncover in 'one of the most comprehensive and, on the whole, one of the most entertaining collections of archives in the possession of our provincial municipalities'.[50] It was a just assessment, which rested upon both acute observation and a good deal of simple physical labour.

Jeaffreson rounded off his work in the town hall, as he was always willing to do, by proposing and supervising a scheme for housing and arranging the records in the newly fitted strong room.[51] His work for the Commission was more exacting. Besides surveying the records, which in Ipswich had involved an uncommonly close sifting and inspection of the entire contents of the muniment room, he had to prepare and edit extracts from them which would not so much illustrate their nature, though they do that admirably well, as demonstrate their general historical importance. His success, over forty closely printed folio pages, in double columns, in the Commission's ninth report obviously owes something to his previous experience in Chester, Leicester, Pontefract, Barnstaple, and Plymouth. It is the more remarkable when we remember that he was at the same time not only editing some of those surveys but was also working intensively on the records of Great Yarmouth (a fine collection which has many affinities with the material at Ipswich), Wisbech, and the West and North Ridings of Yorkshire.

The discovery which pleased Jeaffreson most was that Ipswich still possessed two copies of its custumal, which were intrinsically of greater interest than the two which had been recently and so painfully lost to the British Museum. By his account 'an indiscreetly jocose orator' at the twenty-first annual meeting of the British Archaeological Association, an important historical assembly held at Ipswich in 1864, had rallied the townsmen over the loss of the celebrated *Liber niger* of Ipswich, and had told them that they had forfeited a national treasure. Jeaffreson was himself a joyful raconteur, and liked to add a little colour to his stories. The official text of Edward Levien's paper 'On manuscript collections relating to Suffolk in the British Museum' is altogether more austere, but any reference to the Domesday would be painful and, like Hansard, the Association's *Journal* might seek to do justice to the occasion without descending to the merely literal.[52] At all events, it pleased Jeaffreson to be able to reassure the burgesses that what they held was fully as valuable and consequential as what had been reft from them, and he did so, both in

50 HMC *9th Report* (C.3773 of 1883), p. xiii.

51 The town council accepted his recommendations with thanks on 9 Nov. 1880: SROI, DA8/151/10. It paid him £75 12s for his work (3 guineas a day for twenty-four days), and a further £19 5s to two assistants. See also above, n. 41.

52 *Journal of the British Archaeological Association* xxi, 1865, 5–21.

his published report and in the valedictory lecture which he gave in the town, as he liked to do on such occasions. The lecture, first announced as a lecturette, presumably as less daunting, had to be postponed from November 1880 upon the death of Alderman G.C.E. Bacon, but Jeaffreson eventually gave it on 27 June 1881.[53]

After his East Anglian season in 1880–81 Jeaffreson went on to report on other collections, official and private, including the records of Eye, King's Lynn, and Southampton. He also gave cogent advice and strenuous assistance to the record committee of the Middlesex bench, who sought his aid in 1883.[54] He published his autobiography in 1894, but then retired, disabled by illness in his later years, and died in 1901. By that time Vincent Burroughs Redstone (1853–1941), teaching at Woodbridge, had taken up Suffolk history, and was about to turn to Ipswich, which engaged his attention for almost forty years. Redstone's daughter Lilian (1885–1955), who joined the Victoria County History in 1904 fresh from 'happy school holidays' spent in the Public Record Office, worked on Ipswich with him, and later became archivist to Ipswich corporation, and the first archivist of both the East and West Suffolk record offices.[55]

Jeaffreson's reports to the HMC, and particularly his report on Ipswich, were a contribution to both national and local history. He sensed something in the Ipswich records which went beyond the conventional historical patterns, a continuous tradition expressed in an administrative process, and revealing a rich lode of social comment. His impress on the records survives in the vellum labels which he made out in neat copperplate, but also in the coherent and accessible order in which he left them to his successors as archivists and historians. He has his own assured place in the history of Ipswich and, in a wider context, of the English borough.

53 *East Anglian Daily Times*, 28 June 1881.

54 His work is described by E.D. Mercer in 'The Middlesex County Record Office', *Archives* vi, 1963–64, 30–9, who observes justly: 'Middlesex, in common with a number of other counties, is considerably indebted [to Jeafffreson] for his vigorous and basically sound treatment of its records.'

55 See above, n. 2, and Norman Scarfe's memoir of the Redstones in the SRS's first volume: *Suffolk Farming in the Nineteenth Century*, ed. I.J. Thirsk and J. Imray, 1958, 7–13.

The Caen Controversy

Michael Howard

EARLY ON the morning of 6 June 1944 the greatest armada mankind had ever put together landed on the coast of Normandy.

Four years earlier the British had been chased off the mainland of Europe and had since watched helplessly as Hitler consolidated his empire between the Channel and the Vistula and then extended it eastward towards the Caucasus. They had been able to hold their own in North Africa against Germany's ally Italy, but saw no prospect of re-entering the Continent unless the Third Reich collapsed as a result of British bombing, blockade and subversion; a pretty remote possibility. Only with the entry of the United States into the war in December 1941 did such a re-entry become possible, and the Americans had both the resources and the determination to carry it out. The British, who had a livelier sense of the difficulties involved and the professional expertise of their adversaries, insisted on delaying the operation until the odds were overwhelmingly favourable. By 1944 this had been achieved. Two thirds of the German armed forces were now pinned down fighting a losing battle on the Russian front. 'The Battle of the Atlantic' against German U-boats had been won, making it possible for American troops to pour uninterruptedly into the British Isles. The German Air Force had been bled almost to death defending its cities against Allied bombers, and Allied aircraft commanded the skies over north-west France. Operation OVERLORD was the climax towards which the entire allied war effort had been building since 1941.

The Allied forces landed on the French coast between the Seine estuary and the Cotentin peninsula. In the west the First US Army landed on either side of the Vire estuary, with the task of cutting off the Cotentin peninsula and capturing the port of Cherbourg. The British Second Army landed further east, between Arromanches and the mouth of the Orne at Ouistreham. On the extreme left of the British Army was the Third Division, whose white triangle arm flash indicated the spearhead role it would play in the invasion. Landing with the first wave was a young gunner officer who was later to write the history of the Division[1] and so lay the foundations of a notable career as a professional historian: Lieutenant Norman Scarfe, R.A.

The task of the Third Division was to sweep down the left bank of the Orne – the bridges over the river having been seized during the night by 6th Airborne Division

1 N. Scarfe, *Assault Division: The History of the Third Division*, London 1947.

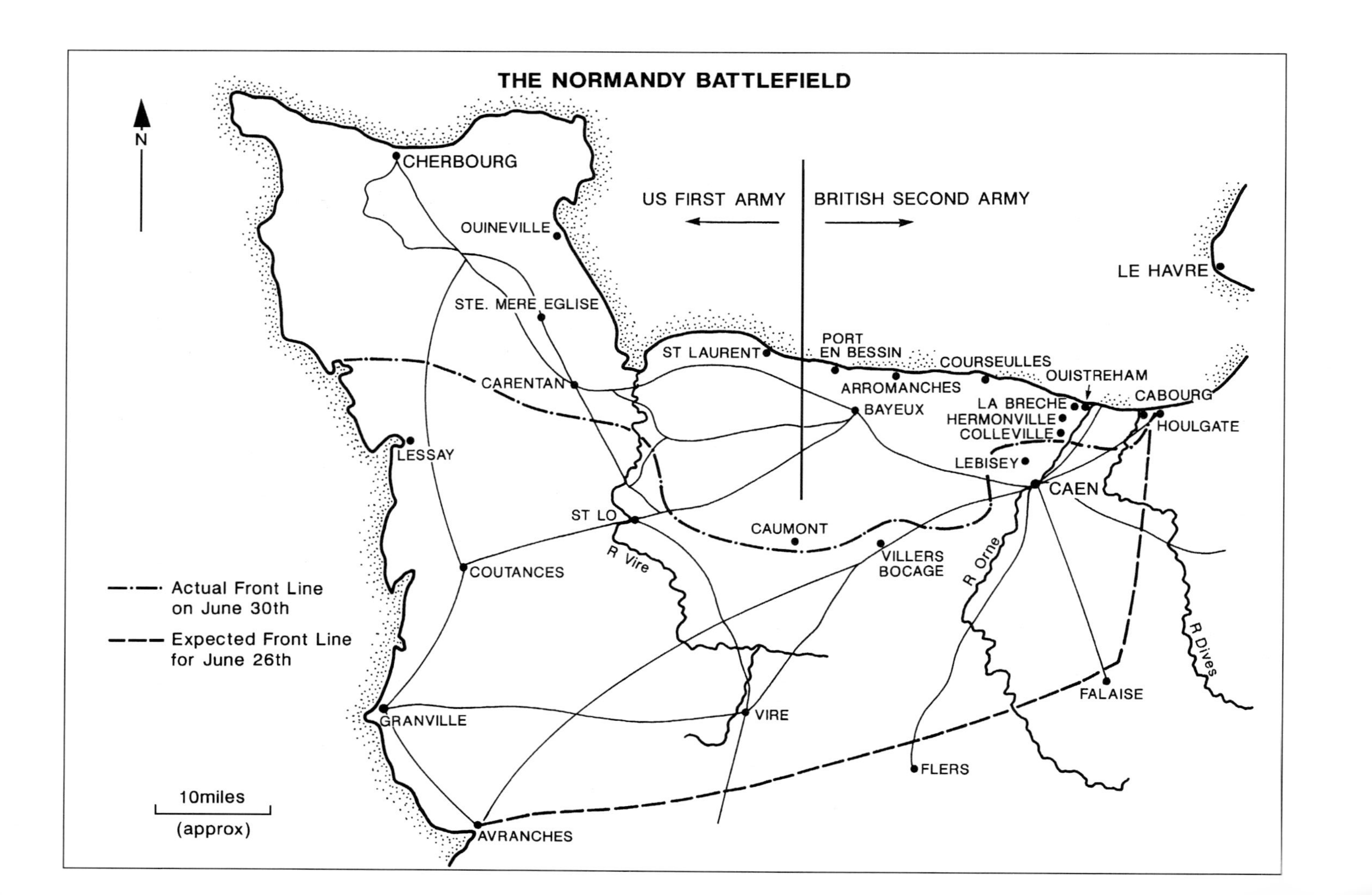
THE NORMANDY BATTLEFIELD
N
US FIRST ARMY
BRITISH SECOND ARMY
CHERBOURG
OUINEVILLE
STE. MERE EGLISE
CARENTAN
LESSAY
ST LAURENT
PORT
EN BESSIN
ARROMANCHES
COURSEULLES
OUISTREHAM
CABOURG
HOULGATE
LE HAVRE
LA BRECHE
HERMONVILLE
COLLEVILLE
LEBISEY
BAYEUX
CAEN
ST LO
R Vire
CAUMONT
VILLERS
BOCAGE
R Orne
R Dives
COUTANCES
FALAISE
GRANVILLE
VIRE
FLERS
AVRANCHES
Actual Front Line
on June 30th
Expected Front Line
for June 26th
10miles
(approx)

– and capture the city of Caen, some ten miles inland. Opposition was expected mainly from one static German infantry division, the 716th, although there were reports that a formidable armoured division, 21st Panzer, had recently moved into the area and that a second, 12th Panzer, was within reach. Nobody in the Division doubted its ability to reach its objective and so make possible a further advance to the south. Nor, evidently, did the commander of the Allied Land Forces who had set them their task, General Sir Bernard Montgomery. Nor did the Supreme Allied Commander, General Dwight Eisenhower, or anyone else at his vast and complex Headquarters. Everyone assumed that if only the difficulties of the landing itself could be overcome, everything else would go according to plan.

The landings did succeed, but everything did not then go according to plan. Caen was not taken on the evening of 6 June or even the following morning. It did not fall until nearly five weeks later. The consequences of this delay were to set on foot a controversy, first among allied commanders and then among military historians, that has not yet entirely died down.

Three questions have to be answered. First, why did Third Division fail to take Caen as planned? Second, why was the failure to take it regarded with such concern by the Supreme Allied Command? And finally, did the failure to capture the city seriously affect the course of the campaign?

Everyone realised that the landings themselves would present huge problems. The Germans knew that the Allies were coming, even though they could not be sure exactly where or when. They also knew from experience that once the Allied armies had landed, their enormous aerial superiority would make it virtually impossible to get them out again. The invasion therefore had to be smashed at once, if possible on the beaches themselves. This called both for strong fortifications on the spot, and for an immediate counter-attack by powerful armoured forces at the point of landing. The trouble was that the German High Command could not be sure exactly where, between the tip of the Cotentin peninsula and the Belgian frontier, the allies intended to land. So the Army Group Commander, General Erwin Rommel, wanted to keep his armoured reserves as far forward as possible to smash the landings on the beaches. But his superior officer, General von Rundstedt, wanted to hold them back until he knew exactly where they could best be used. And behind von Rundstedt – a long way behind – was the Commander-in-Chief of the Armed Forces, Adolf Hitler, whose mistrust of his generals made him insist on micro-managing the movement of every unit on every front.

The Allied High Command knew very well that the outcome of the campaign would depend on their ability not only to get ashore, but to build up their forces in the first few vital days faster than the Germans could build up theirs. Their entire planning for the past eighteen months had been directed to this end. The campaign in the Mediterranean had been prolonged to contain as many German forces in that theatre for as long as possible. The Royal Air Force had concentrated for weeks on smashing German rail communications in north-west France, ably assisted by the sabotage operations of the French Resistance. Perhaps most important of all, skilful deception measures had successfully persuaded the Germans that, even if landings did take place in Normandy, these would be only preliminary to the main attack which would be mounted by a non-existent First US Army Group across the Straits of Dover against the Pas de Calais.

All this helps to explain why the Allied forces, and the Third Division in particular, were not attacked and crushed by strong German armoured units within a few hours of their landing. But they still had to overcome the defences on the beaches themselves. They knew what to expect in every detail: the depth of the water, the gradient and consistency of the beaches, the nature of the artificial obstacles both underwater and on the beaches themselves, the location of the barbed-wire entanglements and minefields and the concrete emplacements from which machine-gun fire covered every yard of the shore. They had indeed rehearsed their landings so often, and against so exactly similar a stretch of coast, that when they saw their objective at dawn on 6 June, after a twenty-hour crossing in landing-craft buffeted by the waves and winds of a storm so violent that the entire enterprise had almost been postponed, the thought crossed their minds that this was yet another exercise, if one more realistic than its predecessors.

Thanks to first-rate intelligence, careful planning, excellent training and the resourcefulness and courage of all concerned, the initial landings succeeded so well that the leading infantry units were able to disembark and seize their first objective, the village of Hermonville a mile or so inland, by10 a.m. Then problems multiplied. The storm had caused high tides that left the beach a bare thirty feet wide instead of the anticipated thirty yards. As the supporting troops came ashore confusion mounted. Norman Scarfe describes how his own guns were landed in the surf and had to open fire in several feet of water while further craft deposited men and vehicles all around them. They remained there in action for five hours before they could move inland.[2] Soft sand restricted the exit-routes from the beaches. Minefields caused further delays. The Germans began to shell the beaches heavily and accurately. The tanks due to assist the infantry advance were held up for hours, so the infantry had to attack the strong-points further inland on their own. One of these, the heavily protected headquarters of the German coastal defence forces, held out all day. German armoured units arrived in time to launch a counter-attack during the afternoon, but it was successfully repelled. By nightfall the leading elements of the Division were still three miles short of Caen. When they tried to resume the advance the following morning, units of 12th Panzer Division had arrived. The German attacks were broken up by artillery fire, but their infantry stood firm against all British attempts to advance. The positions reached by Third Division on 7 June were to remain the British front line for another four weeks.

The failure to capture Caen as expected was to bring down heavy criticism on the division and its commanders; notably from the distinguished military correspondent and historian Chester Wilmot, whose book *The Struggle for Europe*[3] was to remain for years the most authoritative account of the entire campaign. Wilmot attributed that failure to two causes: partly a lack of 'drive' on the part of the leading

2 *Ibid.*, 77.
3 C. Wilmot, *The Struggle for Europe*, London 1952.

battalions once they had overcome the difficulties of the initial landings, and partly shortcomings in their training for which the senior officers in the Division – 'ponderous' and defensive-minded – should take the blame.[4] This view was strongly contested by a historian of a later generation, Carlo d'Este, whose book *Decision in Normandy*[5] was based on a far wider range of sources, and who laid the blame rather on the British High Command as a whole, for not devoting as much attention to plans for exploiting the beachhead as they did to establishing it.

A careful study of Scarfe's own history, together with some operational experience of his own, has led the present writer to reject Wilmot's criticisms. Later in the campaign certain British units certainly became, in the parlance of the time, distinctly 'sticky', but on that first day of operations Third Division was clearly full of the enthusiasm that normally characterises well-trained troops in action for the first time, as distinct from the cautious wariness that can develop all too quickly when prolonged action has blunted their finely-honed edge. It is indeed hard to see how the division could have done more or advanced faster than they did. The task they had been set, an opposed landing after a rough all-night channel crossing followed by an advance against stiff opposition to seize a city ten miles inland, was a very tough one indeed; but previous experience, not least at Anzio only five months earlier, had shown the importance of deep and immediate penetration if the beach-head was to be successfully held and reinforced. Had the landings themselves gone exactly according to plan and enemy opposition thereafter been negligible, all might have been well. But in war nothing ever does go according to plan, and enemy opposition – especially the opposition of the *Wehrmacht* in the Second World War – is seldom negligible. If the German 716th Division had been the only enemy unit to be dealt with the task might still have been feasible, but 21st Panzer Division was known to be in the area and units of 12th Panzer not far away. To allot Caen as the *aspirational* objective for Third Division was entirely legitimate: for planning purposes, nothing short of that would have made very much sense. But to make its capture on the first day of operations the linch-pin of Allied strategy was quite unrealistic unless far greater resources had be allotted to the task than those of a single infantry division; and more resources could not possibly have been funnelled through the bottle-neck of the beach-head in the time available.

Why then was Caen regarded as so important; and why was the failure to capture it later seen as such a disaster?

We must now look at Montgomery's strategy for the Normandy campaign as a whole. Since this has itself been a matter of continuing controversy, it seems reasonable to start with the presentation he made to the assembled Anglo-American High Command at St Paul's School in London on 7 April 1944.[6] First he outlined the task of the Americans, which was, as already described, to cut off the Cotentin peninsula, capture Cherbourg and then advance west into Brittany. The British were, in his

4 *Ibid.*, 278–9.

5 C. D'Este, *Decision in Normandy*, London 1983.

6 The fullest account is in N. Hamilton, *Monty, Master of the Battlefield, 1942–44*, London 1983, 559.

own words, 'to assault to the west of the R.Orne and to develop operations to the south and south-east, in order to secure airfield sites and protect the eastern flank of the First US Army while the latter is capturing Cherbourg. In its subsequent operations the Army will pivot on its left [CAEN] and offer a strong front against enemy movement towards the lodgement area from the east.' By D + 20 the armies should have reached a line some fifteen miles south of Caen, from Avranches on the west coast of the Cotentin peninsula, through Falaise to Cabourg on the channel coast east of the Orne; and, continued Montgomery, 'we will fight continuously till we get it'. Further, in order to disrupt enemy plans and retain the initiative, mobile armoured units should be ready to penetrate inland even beyond these limits so as to create the maximum confusion in the enemy rear.

The intention was clear, and so was the reasoning that lay behind it. The objective was not so much Caen itself as the area further south, beyond the Orne. Unless that space was gained, the Allies would be bottled up in a narrow bridgehead, much of it vulnerable to artillery fire and all of it to air attack. British forces could not then be adequately deployed as a shield for the Americans; and – most important in the eyes of senior air force officers – until the airfields south of Caen had been captured, Allied air forces would remain based in England, with a continuing restriction on their operational capacity.

So in the aftermath of D-Day the Second British Army still had a long way to go. Since Caen had not fallen to Third Division, Montgomery tried to launch a further assault before the Germans could consolidate its defences. He did not as yet have the strength to mount a frontal attack ('I have decided not to have a lot of casualties by butting up against the place', he wrote on 8 June[7]) so he left Third Division where it was and planned to envelop the city from east and west while dropping an airborne division to the south. But the RAF commander vetoed the drop ('gutless bugger' commented Montgomery),[8] a German counter-attack disorganised the British plans on the left flank, while a humiliating rebuff to 7th Armoured Division at Villers-Bocage on 13 June destroyed the opportunities on the right. By 16 June, ten days after the landings, the Germans had made Caen invulnerable to anything but a set-piece attack on a scale that the British did not as yet have the forces to mount.

Montgomery therefore changed his plans. His intention now became, according to his memoirs,[9] 'so to stage and conduct operations that we drew the main enemy strength on to the front of the Second British Army on our eastern flank, in order that we might the more easily gain territory in the west and make the ultimate break-out on that flank . . . On the eastern flank, in the Caen sector, the acquisition of ground was not so pressing; the need there was by hard fighting to make the enemy commit his reserves, so that the American forces would meet less opposition in their advances to gain the territory that was vital on the west.' The Germans were anyhow likely to fight hard to retain Caen. It was a major communications centre, and not only did the bulk of German reserves have to be brought from north of the

7 D'Este, 160.

8 *Ibid.*, 162.

9 *The Memoirs of Field-Marshal the Viscount Montgomery of Alamein*, London 1958, 254.

Seine, but a break-out from Caen south-east down the Seine valley to Paris – perhaps in combination with the expected thrust from the Pas de Calais – seemed to the Germans the most probable Allied strategy. Caen was thus essential to the Germans both for offensive and defensive purposes, and Montgomery intended to bleed them to death there.

Montgomery's strategy was both skilful and sagacious. The trouble was that nobody understood it. Although he always maintained that he was simply implementing a 'master plan' that had been lucidly explained and generally agreed from the beginning, this was not what Montgomery had led his allies – or indeed his superiors – to expect. He had always made clear his intention of using the Second British Army as a 'shield' to protect the American operations to capture Cherbourg, but it was generally assumed that this shield would be pushed very much further to the south; that it would gain space for the construction of forward airfields; and that in general the operations conducted in the British sector would be as mobile and offensive as those in the American. As it was, for a full six weeks after D-day the British Army was immobilised before Caen while the Americans, struggling forward first towards Cherbourg (which fell on 1 July) and then through the thick *bocage* country to cut off the Cotentin peninsula, seemed to be doing all the fighting. So at least it appeared to the Americans, and particularly the American press. The British air chiefs were equally unhappy because they had not received their promised airfields; not that this seems to have affected their capacity to maintain unchallenged air superiority over the battlefield and beyond. More important, lack of space seriously constricted the rate of build-up of Allied forces in the bridgehead; but most serious of all, the first V1 'flying bombs' were beginning to fall on Southern England. It rapidly became clear that there was no defence against these novel and sinister weapons, and that the only protection lay in capturing their launching-sites in the Calais region as quickly as possible. Not only General Eisenhower but the Prime Minister and the entire press of both Britain and the United States began to press Montgomery to take immediate and spectacular action.

The British were certainly not sitting on their hands in front of Caen. To secure even defensible positions, as well as to draw in the German reserves as intended, they had been launching a series of limited attacks. These involved tough fighting, and the ground conquered was measurable only in yards. Memories of the Western Front in the First World War began to cast ugly shadows. Caen itself was entered, after a heavy air bombardment, on 8 July, but the Germans still held the high ground on the right bank of the Orne, blocking all further advance. Montgomery tried to break the deadlock with a major armoured attack launched with massive air support, Operation GOODWOOD, on 17 and 18 July, but failed to shake the German defences. Indeed, since Montgomery had rashly suggested at a press-conference that the initial success would lead to a breakthrough, he only made matters worse. When the real breakthrough did come a week later it was at the other end of the front. The First US Army smashed through the last German defences and cleared the way for the encirclement of the German forces and General George S. Patton's spectacular sweep through France. The contrast with the British performance appeared painful. Although Montgomery remained popular enough with the

British public and the troops under his command, he never regained the confidence of his American allies, and thereafter his relations with General Eisenhower would go from bad to worse.

Montgomery's failure was one not so much of strategy as of public relations – a dimension of warfare of increasing importance throughout the twentieth century. His initial plan had failed – as indeed his initial plan for the Battle of el Alamein had failed – but he refused to admit it. In fact, as at el Alamein, he brilliantly adjusted to the new circumstances, and made the best of a bad job. Certainly Norman Scarfe's Division did not achieve all that was asked of it, but the question may legitimately be asked: 'What if it had?' It was easy enough to allocate Caen as the divisional objective; but Caen was a substantial town with sprawling suburbs, overlooked by high ground to the south. By the time Third Division had established itself ashore it had available, for the capture and occupation of Caen, only the depleted elements of two Brigades – 185th and 9th. These troops, after spending a night in their landing-craft and a day fighting their way inland, were required, as darkness was falling, not just to 'take' the city of Caen, now defended by the formidable 21st Panzer Division, but to establish themselves on the high ground beyond it, ready to beat off the counter-attack that 12th SS Panzer Division was preparing to launch at dawn next day. Even if they had been able to fight their way – or even, in the darkness, *find* their way – through Caen, the strong likelihood is that next morning they would have been not only defeated but cut off and destroyed; and then farewell to any hopes of further advance to the south. By halting north of the city Third Division secured the essential objective of establishing a firm defensive position protecting the Allied left flank until enough troops had been landed to make possible a further advance. Until that was done, any hope of advancing south of the Orne and establishing forward airfields – let alone unleashing mobile units to create confusion in the enemy's rear – were mere pipe dreams.

Norman Scarfe admitted that his division 'felt pretty disappointed and frustrated NOT to have got into Caen as planned on D-Day',[10] but in retrospect he agreed that 'to have taken, according to plan, a bridgehead across the Orne in Caen would have needed, in the existing circumstances, some sort of miracle'.[11] Even if that bridgehead had been secured, it would have taken another miracle for British forces to have been built up fast enough to expand it to the south to the extent visualised by Montgomery in his original plan, especially since storms were to wreck one of the artificial harbours on which the Allied forces depended until Cherbourg could be brought into use. The important thing was to seize and hold a hard shoulder *at* Caen, and, in military parlance, 'deny' it to the enemy. This could be done quite as effectively and a great deal more economically by digging in to the north of the city rather than to the south of it. The whole subsequent controversy might have been avoided if Montgomery had been rather more honest; or if more people had read Norman Scarfe's first published work.

[10] Letter quoted in D'Este, 111.
[11] *Ibid.*, 141.

Select Bibliography of the Writings of Norman Scarfe

compiled by John Blatchly

Books

Assault Division: A History of the 3rd Division from the Invasion of Normandy to the Surrender of Germany, London 1947
Letters from the Peninsula: The Freer Family Correspondence, 1807–1814, Leicester 1953
Suffolk: A Shell Guide, London 1960; 4th edn retitled *The Suffolk Guide*, Bury St Edmunds 1988
Essex: A Shell Guide, London 1968
The Suffolk Landscape, London 1972; revised edn, Bury St Edmunds 1987
Cambridgeshire: A Shell Guide, London 1983
Suffolk in the Middle Ages: Studies in Places and Place-Names, the Sutton Hoo Ship-Burial, Saints, Mummies and Crosses, Domesday Book and Chronicles of Bury Abbey, Woodbridge 1986
A Frenchman's Year in Suffolk: French Impressions of Suffolk Life in 1784, SRS XXX, Woodbridge 1988
In Praise of Suffolk: An Anthology, Bury St Edmunds 1988
Innocent Espionage: The La Rochefoucauld Brothers' Tour of England in 1785, Woodbridge 1995
To the Highlands in 1786: The Inquisitive Journey of a Young French Aristocrat, Woodbridge 2001

Pamphlets, Booklets and Major Articles

'Sir John Hayward, an Elizabethan Historian', *PSIA* xxv, 1949, 79–97
The Growth of Aldeburgh, Felixstowe 1951
'Whitney and Reed: Two Regency Estate Agents', *PSIA* xxviii, 1959, 185–96
Bury St Edmunds Official Guide, historical sections, Bury St Edmunds 1964
'Shakespeare, Stratford-upon-Avon and Warwickshire', in *Shakespeare: A Celebration*, ed. T.J.B. Spencer, Harmondsworth 1964, 15–29
'Markets and Fairs in Medieval Suffolk', *SR* iii 1, 1965, 4–11
'Markets and Fairs in Seventeenth-Century Suffolk', *SR* iii 2, 1965, 11–15

Norman England, London 1968
'The Body of St Edmund: An Essay in Necrobiography', *PSIA* xxxi, 1969, 303–17
'Notes on the Historical Record of Dunwich's Defences', *PSIA* xxxii, 1972, 34–7
'The Bury St Edmunds Cross', *PSIA* xxxiii, 1973, 75–85
'John Constable's Biographer, R.B. Beckett: An Editorial Appreciation and Personal Tribute', SRS XVIII, 1975, xiii–xix
'John Ives, FRS, FSA, Suffolk Herald Extraordinary', *PSIA* xxxiii, 1975, 299–309
Suffolk Churches: A Pocket Guide (with others), Suffolk Historic Churches Trust, Woodbridge 1976
A Monk Named Jocelin, Edinburgh 1976; revised as *Jocelin of Brakelond*, Leominster 1997
'The Place-Name Icklingham: A Preliminary Enquiry' (with E.A. Martin), *East Anglian Archaeology* iii, 1976, 127–34
Snape Maltings Concert Hall: A Brief History and Guide, Aldeburgh 1977
Notes on Aldeburgh Buildings, Aldeburgh Society 1978
Erasmus the Wise and his Friends, Edinburgh 1979
'Raedwald's Queen and the Sutton Hoo Coins', *PSIA* xxxiv, 1980, 251–4
The Superior Seaside ii: A Tour of Aldeburgh, Thorpeness and Aldringham, The Victorian Society, 11 September 1982, Aldeburgh
'Iken, St Botolph and the Coming of East Anglian Christianity' (with S. West and R. Cramp), *PSIA* xxxv, 1984, 279–302
'The Decay of Inclination: Correspondence in 1764 between the 3rd Duke of Grafton and his First Duchess', in *Domestic Warfare: A Festschrift for Sir Michael Howard*, ed. M. James, Eastbury 1987, 59–72
Hintlesham Hall: The House and its Associations, Hintlesham 1988
'Patterns of Suffolk Building', in *Suffolk for Ever*, ed. C. Jennings, Bury St Edmunds 1989, 55–74
'Edgar's Farmhouse, Combs, Suffolk', in *Counties and Communities: Essays in East Anglian History presented to Hassell Smith*, ed. C. Rawcliffe *et al.*, Norwich 1996, 57–68
'Jocelin of Brakelond's Identity: A Review of the Evidence', *PSIA* xxxix, 1997, 1–5
'Domesday Churches', 'Medieval and Later Markets', 'Medieval and Later Fairs', in *An Historical Atlas of Suffolk*, 3rd revised edn, ed. D. Dymond and E. Martin, Bury St Edmunds 1999, 52–3, 76–9
'Beware of the Trains: Reflections and a Few Footnotes on the Railways in Suffolk', in *The Impact of the Railway on Society in Britain: Essays in Honour of Jack Simmons*, ed. A.K.B. Evans and J.V. Gough, Aldershot 2002

Norman Scarfe has also written numerous short articles, notes, obituaries and reviews in *Country Life*, *PSIA*, *SR* and in various national newspapers, and has made regular contributions to the Aldeburgh Festival Programme Books and (on many Suffolk churches) to the 'Music in Country Churches' concert programmes.